Cr

Is There Progress in Economics?

Is There Progress in Economics?

Knowledge, Truth and the History of
Economic Thought

Edited by

Stephan Boehm

Associate Professor of Economics, University of Graz, Austria

Christian Gehrke

Associate Professor of Economics, University of Graz, Austria

Heinz D. Kurz

Professor of Economics, University of Graz, Austria

Richard Sturn

Associate Professor of Economics, University of Graz, Austria

Edward Elgar
Cheltenham, UK • Northampton, MA, USA

© Stephan Boehm, Christian Gehrke, Heinz D. Kurz, Richard Sturn 2002
Chapter 10 © Philippe Mongin, 2002

Published by
Edward Elgar Publishing Limited
Glensanda House
Montpellier Parade
Cheltenham
Glos GL50 1UA
UK

Edward Elgar Publishing, Inc.
136 West Street
Suite 202
Northampton
Massachusetts 01060
USA

A catalogue record for this book
is available from the British Library

Library of Congress Cataloguing in Publication Data

Is there progress in economics?: knowledge, truth and the history of economic
thought/Stephen Boehm . . . [et al.].
    p.cm.
    Includes bibliographical references and index.
    1. Economics—History. 2. Progress—History. I. Boehm, Stephan.

HB75.1753 2002
330′.09—dc21   2001054305

ISBN 1 84064 683 7

Typeset by Cambrian Typesetters, Frimley, Surrey
Printed and bound in Great Britain by MPG Books Ltd, Bodmin, Cornwall

Contents

Figures and tables

FIGURES

TABLES

Contributors

Roger E. Backhouse
Professor of the History and Philosophy of Economics at the University of
Birmingham, UK

Jack Birner
Professor of Economics and the Philosophy of the Social Sciences at the
University of Trento, Italy

Mark Blaug
Visiting Professor at the University of Amsterdam and at Erasmus University
Rotterdam, The Netherlands

Sergio Cremaschi
Associate Professor of Moral Philosophy at the Amedeo Avogadro University
at Vercelli, Italy

Manuel Fernández López
Professor of Economics at the University of Buenos Aires, Argentina

Pierangelo Garegnani
Professor of Economics at the University of Rome III, Italy

Sandye Gloria-Palermo
Assistant Professor at the University Jean Monnet at Saint-Etienne, France

Augusto Graziani
Professor of Economics at the University of Rome La Sapienza, Italy

Klaus Hamberger
Assistant Professor of Economics at the Vienna University of Economics and
Business Administration, Austria

Hansjörg Klausinger
Associate Professor at the Vienna University of Economics and Business
Administration, Austria

Heinz D. Kurz
Professor of Economics at the University of Graz, Austria

Maurice Lagueux
Professor of International Economics and Philosophy at the University of Montreal, Canada

Uskali Mäki
Professor of Philosophy of Science at the Erasmus University of Rotterdam, The Netherlands

Andrea Maneschi
Professor of Economics at the Vanderbilt University in Nashville, USA

Stephen J. Meardon
Assistant Professor of Economics at Williams College, Williamstown, MA, USA

Philippe Mongin
Senior Research Professor at the University of Cergy-Pontoise, France

Sergio Parrinello
Professor of Economics at the University of Rome La Sapienza, Italy

Luigi Pasinetti
Professor of Economics at the Catholic University of Milan, Italy

Fabio Ravagnani
Assistant Professor of Economics, at the University of Rome La Sapienza, Italy

Neri Salvadori
Professor of Economics at the University of Pisa, Italy

Erich W. Streissler
Professor of Economics, Econometrics and Economic History at the University of Vienna, Austria

Hans-Michael Trautwein
Professor of International Economics at the Carl von Ossietzky University of Oldenburg, Germany

Richard van den Berg
Assistant Professor of Economics at Kingston University Business School, Kingston-upon-Thames, UK

Donald Winch
Research Professor at the Graduate Research Centre in the Humanities at the University of Sussex, UK

NA

Foreword

The University of Graz is the venue where arguably one of the greatest historians of economic thought, Joseph Alois Schumpeter, taught at the beginning of last century. Therefore it immediately suggested itself as the place to hold the 2000 conference of the European Society for the History of Economic Thought (ESHET). At the beginning of a new millennium, it was natural to devote the thematic part of the conference to the question, 'Is there progress in economics?'

We take the opportunity of the publication of the conference proceedings to express our gratitude to the institutions and people who have been of great help in getting this conference off the ground and in completing the present volume in a relatively short time. Generous financial support was received from the Austrian Ministry of Science, the Government of Styria, the City of Graz, the University of Graz, the Styrian Chamber of Labour, the Styrian Chamber of Trade and the Styrian Confederation of Industry. The enterprise was supported by the Rector of the University of Graz, Professor Lothar Zechlin, the Dean of the Faculty of Social and Economic Studies, Professor Lutz Beinsen, and members of the Departments of Economics, Public Economics and Economic and Social History. Clemens Keil and his aides and members of the secretariat of the Department of Economics, in particular Elisabeth Colantonio and Anita Pauritsch, played an important role in organizational, logistic and other matters. We would like to thank the officers of ESHET and especially the members of the Scientific Committee of the Graz conference, Lars Magnusson, Bertram Schefold, Ian Steedman and Gianni Vaggi, for their smooth collaboration over the months during which the conference was prepared, and the Executive Committee of ESHET for entrusting us with the task of editing the proceedings. We are grateful to all the scholars involved in reviewing the papers contained in this volume and to the papers' authors for the efficient manner in which they have both responded to the referees' criticisms and suggestions and respected the deadlines imposed on them. It was a pleasure to collaborate with them. Last but not least, we would like to thank Astrid Wlach for preparing the final typescript and Bob Pickens from the publisher for swiftly arranging its publication.

Stephan Boehm, Christian Gehrke, Heinz D. Kurz and Richard Sturn

Graz, January 2001

Bk Title:

Introduction N IA

Stephan Boehm, Christian Gehrke, Heinz D. Kurz and Richard Sturn

PROGRESS AND CRITIQUE

'Systematic progress in philosophy is nothing but remembering what oneself has said.' Many economists will find this statement by the German philosopher Hegel puzzling at best. If applied to economics, it is likely to be deemed abstruse rather than useful. Yet some reflection shows that this statement casts some light on the situation of historians of economic thought. Discussing and scrutinizing systems of knowledge, theories or particular models in terms of progress is inevitably linked to some idea of critique, that is, to the ability to give some account of the scope of intellectual achievements promoted by these models, theories or systems of knowledge.

Hegel's statement invokes a broad idea of critique not necessarily attached to an evaluative stance. Such an open concept of critique is useful for understanding radical differences between different styles in the history of ideas and may summarize the common ground between quite different approaches to the latter. For instance, it encompasses rational reconstruction as the attempt to clarify the truth of conjectures and the scope of explanatory sketches by means of analytical models. This may be thought of as a positive aspect of critique leading to progress in knowing what exactly can be stated as positive results and what remains a more or less plausible conjecture. This positive critique is essential for a diagnosis of success or failure in terms of a given theory's own explanatory or normative purposes. Hence it is crucial for assessing whether in some historical period progress occurred in the sense of unfolding the potential of a particular theory, or whether some theorist was a precursor of a certain theoretical development (whether or not (s)he played a role in triggering this development). Put in a more general way, critique is crucial for the idea of progress *within* certain intellectual traditions or within particular theoretical discourses. As John Chipman once put it, 'What makes the history of economic thought interesting is the study of how truth comes out of controversy'.

The general idea of critique also entails negative dimensions making clear what *cannot be said* relying solely on the models, theories and systems of knowledge. This type of critique helps us to discriminate between different types of failure. Does a theory fail because of internal reasons, that is, the inconsistency of its assumptions or axioms? Or does it fail because of some external reason, because aspects are systematically neglected by this particular theory, or else because these aspects are just incidentally left out, or ruled out, by some capricious set of assumptions? Negative critique sometimes has the potential to develop new horizons: the negative style of critique is often linked to arguments which show, or purport to show, why it would be interesting to be able to say something precisely on those matters which are beyond the scope of the theory under consideration in its present state. Philippe Mongin's account of the development of *normative economics* comes close to the conception of a dialectics of progress along the lines just sketched, where some qualified diagnosis of failure (such as Arrow's impossibility theorem) is the crucial starting point for new theoretical developments.

Perhaps the style of positive critique is most promising with respect to the set of particular models which operate against a common background of assumptions and definitions and a common pre-analytic vision. With respect to such theoretical contexts, it may make sense to say that a new theory is better than an old one if and only if it explains everything which was explained by the old one and something more. Limiting oneself to positive critique is problematic with regard to whole systems of knowledge, for example with respect to epistemic systems as understood by the French philosopher Michel Foucault. It is impossible when different systems of knowledge are related to each other in a way which, in the tradition of Isaiah Berlin, could be called 'irreducibly pluralistic'. Pluralism of this kind may make the very idea of theoretical progress obsolete, much in the same way as it arguably fails to make sense to ask whether Goethe is superior to Shakespeare or whether Shakespeare is superior to Homer.

At first sight, the question 'Is there progress in economics?' seems to be challenging *only if* progress, in one sense or another, is understood as an evaluative concept. For if 'progress' is just a synonym for any kind of change, if it lacks any connotation of improvement or development, the answer seems to be trivial. Something is always changing, if only the number of active professional economists or of university departments and journals in economics.

Klaus Hamberger's paper shows that the diagnosis of progress does not become trivial even if its evaluative meaning is set aside. There may be disagreement regarding the assessment of when, how and why a shift of epistemic ground occurs. Hence it *may* make sense to approach the question of change *without* the evaluative stance invoked by the word 'progress', provided the author focuses on the relevant aspects of change. A non-evaluative notion of 'progress' may thus be found suitable for the history of systems of knowledge. Taking this insight on board, it becomes almost inevitable to ask the question which Donald Winch has chosen as the title of his chapter: 'Does progress matter?' Perhaps it does *not* matter because it would make sense only if used in a weak, non-evaluative sense. It may well be the case that the more demanding, evaluative conception of progress rather than the more trivial one renders the question 'Is there progress in economics?' meaningless. In this more demanding interpretation, an answer to the question presupposes at least some common epistemic ground. If economics is taken seriously as a practical subject, it must even presuppose common ethical ground. But is this requirement not something that should be avoided, given the degree of heterogeneity of the different schools of economic thought and the heterogeneity of moral credos? Some believe these days that it should be avoided at all costs. Yet to push this point too far carries with it the risk of being self-defeating, at least if one sticks to the idea that historians of economic thought are in the business of putting forward true propositions concerning systems of knowledge. This seems to imply that there *is* some minimal common ground because otherwise there is no basis for settling such truth-claims.

There is another reason for rejecting sweeping dismissive attitudes with respect to evaluative interpretations of progress in economics. Of course, many problems with evaluative conceptions of progress do not emerge in theoretical contexts, which are clearly limited in one way or another. Several chapters in this volume devoted to developments in particular fields, such as monetary economics or trade theory, or particular currents of thought, such as Austrian economics, or particular analytical issues within a certain framework, such as modern classical economics, provide ample evidence of the usefulness of a more demanding conception of progress in the history of ideas. Mongin's short history of normative economics shows how productive positive and negative critique *from within* may be. Mark Blaug's contribution is a vivid example that even the problems linked to the heterogeneity of explanatory purposes and analytical frameworks across different strands and styles of thought can be coped with. Blaug's critique of Walrasian general equilibrium theory shows that meaningful evaluative critique need not be from within but may get its momentum from a confrontation with problems which are not internal problems of the theory. Finally, Sergio Cremaschi studies the role of metaphors in Smith's *Wealth*. He rejects the post-modernist view that the use of rhetorical devices *ipso facto* proves that there is no truth and theoretical progress in economics. On the contrary, it was not least Smith's judicious choice of new metaphors which allowed him to widen the scope of economic explanation.

SOME METHODOLOGICAL ISSUES

If it were not for its teleological, linear overtones one might be tempted to use *progression* for 'progress' in the aforementioned evaluative sense. Indeed, in order for 'progress' to make any evaluative sense, there has to be some sort of progression, an accumulation of knowledge handed down from generation to generation rather than the perennial replacement of those who had in turn replaced their progenitors. It is in this loose sense that progress in economics is closer to the sciences than to the arts or humanities. It may be instructive to consider the starkly different situation in philosophy in order to dispel any lingering doubts about the status of economics. The history of philosophical thought may be said to exhibit strong discontinuities, that is to say, progress in philosophy seems to consider itself as a complete break with the past, as a new beginning or clean slate, involving a repudiation, even negation, of the past, including all the numerous earlier new beginnings which at the time had also been held to provide the subject with secure foundation for years to come. It seems to be a mark of the really great philosopher to claim that *everything* that had gone on before rested on a fundamental mistake and had therefore to be rejected *in toto*. And this is one way to keep the past alive: by the need of those who wish to place the subject on a new footing to disassociate themselves from their progenitors by some monumental destruction exercise. Thus conceived, the history of philosophy emerges as nothing but a succession of bold visionaries helping us to liberate ourselves from the nightmares of the past. So instead of something being passed on from one generation of scholars to another, an accumulated body of knowledge, there is a continual replacement of those who had in turn replaced their forerunners. Previous stages in the history of the subject are not stages of discovery of what we now know, nor is the present a stage of discovery of what will eventually be known. There is no systematic cognitive development; what went before is rather like a bad dream from which we are liberated by the arrival on the scene of the great figures.

Consider the situation in economics. Notwithstanding faint echoes of progress being aided by the current generation of incumbents passing away, can anybody seriously claim that any of the revolutionary economists who are usually admitted to the pantheon of the history of the field, be it Smith, Marx or Keynes, made their respective contributions by jettisoning everything that had gone on before? To pose the question is to answer it.

That 'progress' in economics is an essentially contested concept on which there is bound to be widespread disagreement emerges as a common thread uniting the chapters assembled in this volume. Roger E. Backhouse refers to progress as being 'a very complex phenomenon'. (The 'complexities of a contestable concept' also figure in Uskali Mäki's contribution.) Backhouse points to a distinction that he has made in earlier work between *theoretical* and *empirical* progress. Blaug takes over the distinction and applies it to contemporary economics, and concludes that contemporary economics clearly exhibits theoretical progress, while it is found lacking with respect to empirical progress. Historical analysis is necessary to ascertain what conceptions of progress could be used to analyse past economists' work without imposing on them criteria that they would not have understood. Judgements about progress might have to be local, restricted to limited periods of history; they are not meant to be absolute, but this would be good enough for most purposes. The distinction between *local* as opposed to *overall*, *global* progress seems to be highly pertinent in economics.

Another dimension along which progress can be delineated relates to the unification and expansion of its domain. Uskali Mäki, in particular, raises the issue of economics imperialism and scientific advance. He notes several of the ways in which economics imperialism might be construed (i) as progress by conquest, and (ii) as conducive to generate progress. Luigi Pasinetti, on the other hand, points out that a commonly recognized process does not exist in economics whereby scientific progress can unambiguously be ascertained. Owing to the particular characteristics of economics, scientific advance may frequently be described by the co-existence of competing – and sometimes complementary – research traditions, or 'paradigms'. Co-existence should be seen as a sign of vitality rather than of immaturity; and discussions across paradigm boundaries should be encouraged rather than suppressed.

Jack Birner points to the discovery that what was thought to be the truth is neither the whole truth nor nothing but the truth as an important engine of progress in science. This mechanism, christened 'the correspondence principle' by Karl Popper, says that science advances by replacing a theory that was believed to be complete and true by incorporating it into another theory, which explains why the previous theory was incomplete and wrong, why those who held it thought it to be true, and in addition explains phenomena the previous theory did not explain. This mechanism has been further analysed by Wladislaw Krajewski, Noretta Koertge and Heinz Post, who called it 'conservative induction'. Birner contends that the twentieth century has seen several episodes in which economists made use of the correspondence principle, probably unaware of this philosophical literature.

Erich Streissler's provocative contribution, culminating in the sweeping claim that as far as economic content is concerned, '[t]here has been little which is new in macroeconomics since the early heyday of our science in the eighteenth century', is bound to raise some eyebrows. What is particularly noteworthy here is that Streissler's striking thesis amounts to some kind of 'reverse whiggism', or 'anti-whiggism', in sharp contrast to the prevalent (among non-historians) condescending Whig interpretation of the history of economic thought ('Whig fallacy', 'presentism'). It is the chief characteristic of the latter view that it reads history backwards, interpreting and evaluating the achievements of the past in terms of the prevalent standards, criteria and questions of the present.

THE PROBLEM OF PROGRESS IN SELECTED FIELDS OF ANALYSIS

Whether progress or regress has occurred in certain sub-fields of economics is investigated in a number of contributions focusing attention on four different fields: normative economics, monetary economics, trade and location theory, and modern classical economics. In addition, there is a set of individual contributions, each of which discusses progressive (or regressive) elements in the historical development of different currents of thought, ranging from conceptualizations of the circular flow in physiocratic and post-physiocratic writers to the parallel treatment of information costs, deliberation costs and transaction costs in modern microeconomic theory.

Two papers are concerned with developments in monetary economics. Hans-Michael Trautwein provides an assessment of the credit theory of Carl Knies, which has not received much attention outside the German-speaking countries. He argues that a close examination of Knies' failure to integrate money and credit into the framework of value theory is instructive in exposing the fundamental difficulties of modern attempts to integrate intrinsically useless money into the framework of general equilibrium theory. Augusto Graziani's paper on 'New lines of research in monetary economics' emphasizes that while in Irving Fisher money performs essentially the role of a means of payment, in John Maynard Keynes the emphasis is on money as a stock of wealth. According to Graziani, the Keynesian concept has several analytical advantages; nevertheless the Fisherian concept has seen a revival in more recent times. Moreover, Graziani argues that limiting the analysis to positions of full equilibrium neglects important features of a monetary economy. As a promising new line of development, he then turns to more recent contributions of the so-called 'circulation approach' to the theory of money, in which money is contemplated both in its role as a flow (means of circulation) and a stock (money balances as a stock of wealth).

Four papers take up the theme of trade and location theory. Andrea Maneschi examines what is known as 'new trade theory', which was developed over the past two decades. He asks what the novelties of this paradigm are relative to conventional Heckscher–Ohlin–Samuelson trade theory. His answer is that there was indeed progress, but much less than some of the practitioners of the new paradigm maintain, because many of the findings had been anticipated by authors such as Bertil Ohlin. Sergio Parrinello focuses attention on the institutional factor in the theories of international trade, old and new. He argues that the new trade theory has the merit of dealing explicitly with this factor, but that the way it does so is problematic: the institutional factor cannot be reduced to the single notion of a public good. He then turns to the question of how the old trade theories could incorporate that factor; special emphasis is placed on the non-Walrasian approach. Stephen J. Meardon deals with an offspring of new trade theory, the 'new economic geography', and scrutinizes Paul Krugman's claim that the new economic geography is able to capture long-known ideas which previously fell flat because they could not be expressed in terms of a mathematical general equilibrium model. Meardon argues that, alas! Krugman's criteria of progress are self-referential and his assessment therefore unconvincing. However, in terms of the explicit criteria of progress put forward by scholars such as Ohlin, Lösch and Myrdal, the new economic geography represents qualified progress. Manuel Fernández López presents two cases of independent discoveries or anticipations of important doctrines or analytical tools: one concerns spatial economics, where Johann Heinrich von Thünen has been said to be the 'founding God' (Samuelson); the other concerns linear programming, which is closely associated with the name of George Dantzig. López attempts to establish the fact that the two were anticipated in important respects by two Spanish scholars: Thünen by the engineer Pedro Antonio Cerviño (1757–1816); and Dantzig by José Barral-Souto (1903–76).

Richard van den Berg surveys contemporary responses to François Quesnay's *Tableau économique*. He shows that its usefulness as an analytical tool was not appreciated for a considerable time and that it took several generations of economists before further refinements and new applications were forthcoming. Sandye Gloria-Palermo attempts to identify, at the level of methodological and conceptual considerations, progressive and regressive elements in the development of Austrian economics from Carl Menger's original contribution to those of modern Austrians. Hansjörg Klausinger tells the story of the development of a consistent general equilibrium framework for stock-flow analysis in the IS–LM model as an example of progress in macroeconomics and then shows that the insights gained from this formulation seem to have been lost again. He illustrates his thesis by referring to three examples of 'regress': the confusion over the meaning of the flow equilibrium condition of the market for bonds; the interpretation of the liquidity trap; and the validity of Poole's rule. Maurice Lagueux argues that the extension of the notions of information costs, deliberation costs and transaction costs to non-market domains is bound to make the concept of rational choice vacuous.

The papers by Fabio Ravagnani, Heinz D. Kurz and Neri Salvadori, and Pierangelo Garegnani deal with the meaning and scope of the long-period method as it was developed by classical economists from Adam Smith to Ricardo and revived by Piero Sraffa. Ravagnani argues that the normal prices determined in a classical framework of the analysis are not limited to economies characterized by stationary or quasi-stationary conditions. Such prices may on the contrary be considered as useful theoretical approximations of observable magnitudes even outside such conditions. In their comment,

Kurz and Salvadori stress that the long-period method is an indispensable tool of analysis, but that certain important aspects of real economic systems require this tool to be complemented by others in order to achieve a better understanding of the problems at hand. Garegnani recalls the fact that the abandonment of the long-period method by marginalist authors was motivated, first and foremost, not by an attempt to render the theory more 'realistic', but by the difficulties the long-period demand-and-supply theory encountered because of its deficient concept of capital. He contends that a formalised dynamic *theory* is in conflict with the premises of classical theory; this does not preclude, however, the formulation of dynamic economic *models* which help to explore the implications of special assumptions.

A FINAL WORD

The 'Whig interpretation' focuses attention on those lines of development in the past – to the exlusion of all others – which culminate, or seem to culminate, in present arrangements. Therefore, it is by definition that historians of economic thought are 'anti-Whiggish'. It is testimony to the seriousness of the contributions to this volume that estimations on the price of progress, musings on 'the world we have lost' or revelling in the pastness of the past have not been on the agenda. What may be recorded, though, as one of the overriding impressions emerging from the present volume is the relevance, indeed the indispensability, of the history of economic thought for contemporary cases of theory evaluation. The views documented here are a striking antidote to the notion that the historical origin and development of a doctrine or research tradition are irrelevant to its rational acceptability.

PART I

Progress: A Contested Concept?

1. Does progress matter?

Donald Winch

My question gestures towards the organizing theme of this conference, but a more appropriate one, as I hope to show, would be Voltaire's conclusion in *Candide*. I shall mention progress now and then, but I feel more comfortable with something less grandiose, a miniature painting rather than the kind of broad philosophical landscape that anything connected with progress in the eighteenth- or nineteenth-century sense, or modernization in mid-twentieth century mode, suggests or requires. My miniature begins with the following quotation from John Stuart Mill's correspondence.

> '*A History of Political Economy* is not a kind of book much wanted on its own account, but it would afford an opportunity for interesting discussions of all the contested points, and for placing them in the strong light which results from the comparison of conflicting opinions and from a study of their origins and filiation. Though, therefore, it is a work I should hardly suggest to anyone, yet if any competent political economist with a talent for philosophical controversy feels spontaneously prompted to undertake it, the result is likely to be useful and interesting to those who care for the subject.' (Mill, 1972, XV: 907)

Judging from this response to an inquiry from his disciple, Henry Fawcett, who had just had the good fortune to be elected to the Chair of Political Economy at Cambridge at the tender age of thirty, it does not sound as though Mill was enthusiastic about our branch of historical scholarship. Fawcett would have been even more discouraged if he had read Jean-Baptiste Say's sweeping dismissal of the history of economic thought a generation or so earlier.[1] Fawcett had recently published a Millian textbook, his *Manual of Political Economy*. It was his chief qualification for the Cambridge Chair, and the fact that he had written it helped to overcome doubts connected with his physical disability, blindness. He was giving some early thought to his next project, casting around for the kind of book he might write now that he was a professor and was therefore expected to give lectures and write books based upon them. Given the lukewarm advice he received from the most important member of his personal pantheon, it is hardly surprising that Fawcett abandoned the idea, though in vulgar market terms he might have found a niche; there were not many textbooks on the subject in English at the time.[2] Mill said that a history of political economy was not 'much wanted on its own account', and while it might allow a 'competent economist with a talent for philosophical controversy' to write something useful, he seems to be condemning the idea by implying that it would chiefly be interesting to those who already find such things interesting. It would neither advance the science nor make new converts. Nor did it have the characteristics Mill felt were essential in his own work on political economy: it would not eliminate misunderstanding of the abstract science (as he hoped he had done for Ricardo), and it would not bring enlightenment on questions of 'social philosophy' to a wider public. That surely is the response we should expect from any active contributor to what Léon Walras would later over-scrupulously divide, in the French manner, between *économie pure, économie appliqué* and *économie sociale*. Each of these activities was considered to be progressive in different ways. If their devotees did not believe this to be the case, why were they undertaking them? For reasons of fame or fashion? It would have defied logic for Mill, or any serious economist later, to say that he wanted to contribute to the *history* of economic thought. It would have been both immodest and over-modest at the same time.

Nevertheless, read in today's light, Mill concedes some things that make the idea seem attractive: it would 'afford an opportunity for interesting discussions of all the contested points, and for placing them in the strong light which results from the comparison of conflicting opinions and from a study of their origins and filiation'. What is wrong with that, especially as a device for teaching budding economists? Isn't that what successive generations of authors of general histories of economic thought have tried to do? Since 1863 many have felt 'spontaneously prompted to undertake' this task, making it that 'irrepressible activity' about which Mark Blaug (1991: Introduction), the author of one of our generation's most accomplished textbooks, has written so persuasively.

I have begun with a banal snippet of correspondence because, along with the heavy volumes we study, it is typical of the scraps of evidence many of us collect in order to write our own books and articles on the history of past economic thinking. We do so, however, in an intellectual climate and in academic settings that bear only a distant relationship to the one in which the letter was originally written. Mill made speeches, but did not have a university degree, let alone aspire to be a professor. Fawcett was the last of the non-professional breed to occupy the Cambridge Chair: his successor, Alfred Marshall, as his pupil John Maynard Keynes told us, with a little Anglocentric exaggeration, was 'the first great economist *pur sang* there ever was' (Keynes, 1972, X: 222). Biographically, my trivial piece of evidence says something about Mill, his relationship to Fawcett, and the duties attached to public and academic life in Victorian England. With a little more elaboration it can be made to say something about the shifting role, over time and place, that histories of economic thought have played in the history of economics as an organized discipline within university systems across Europe and North America – systems that differ in their origins and their cultural location within their respective societies. We can employ the evidence, then, either as a small piece of discarded marble to be used in a mosaic devoted to historiography, thereby moving upwards in level towards one form of meta-history, or as part of an inquiry into the comparative history of university systems.

It can also be made to serve as profoundly ironic commentary on some developments that were not and could not be known to either party when Mill wrote his letter. For example, earlier in the same year Karl Marx had finished what he called the 'historico-critical' side of his task, later published as *Theories of Surplus Value*, still perhaps the most ambitious work of its kind. For Marx, such an exercise in clearing the ground was an essential prologue to *Das Kapital*, the work that began to appear five years later. Among his near-contemporary predecessors only Ricardo emerges relatively unscathed from Marx's account. Contrasted with Ricardo's ruthless 'scientific honesty', Mill was assigned to the category of 'vulgar' disciple or 'shallow syncretist', too much of a competitor for Ricardo's mantle, perhaps, to be treated fairly. Mill was to remain unaware of the Marxian challenge to his political economy, though he did know something about the ideas of the revolutionary circle in which Marx lived. Nor could Mill know that for the succeeding generation of economists the study of 'origins and filiation' was going to become a major weapon, newly forged by critics of what became known as 'classical' political economy, in their attack on the intellectual credentials of the orthodox English version of the science and the kinds of policies with which those credentials had become associated. Even those who stood by the existing deductive dispensation, Jevons and Marshall, found themselves heavily engaged in writing new genealogies for their own enterprises. Mill was to be regarded in these revisionist histories as the last major figure in the 'classical' mould, with Fawcett revealing, as eager acolytes often do, how barren and dogmatic the creed had become.[3]

In Britain alone, where 'classical' authors could claim their most conspicuous successes in both theory and policy, one of the first of the new histories to be published was Arnold Toynbee's lectures on *The Industrial Revolution of the Eighteenth Century in England*, the work that was once thought, mistakenly, to have coined the term in its title. Although these lectures can be regarded as a pioneering contribution to the economic history of industrial society, Toynbee combined this with a history of political economy, as represented by the four canonical figures, Smith, Malthus, Ricardo and Mill, each standing for a specific stage in the development of the British economy. Toynbee's story was a tale of unconscious betrayal, with Ricardo being cast as the villain of the piece, and Mill as the person who had done a great deal to repair the damage, but might have done more to restore the authority of the science in the public mind by renouncing the abstract and unempirical habits of his Ricardian upbringing. Notice, in passing, that it was the public rather than the academic mind that concerned Toynbee: he too was not a conventional academic in the mould later created in Britain by Marshall and his pupils. Toynbee's new story, with its progressive and hence relativistic message (what was good enough for an earlier generation was not good enough to meet the higher moral expectations of the third quarter of the nineteenth century), was designed to serve as a critique of the inhumane aspects of industrial society and of the role played by Ricardo's methods and conclusions in appearing to justify them.

Toynbee's fascination with Ricardo, then, mirrors that of Marx, though with one major difference: that Ricardo had supplied Marx with a theory of value which could be used to attack existing society was one of Toynbee's most important criticisms of Ricardo. He had been 'at once the great prop of the middle classes, and their most terrible menace'; he had done more than 'any other author to justify in the eyes of men the existing state of society'; and he had given rise to 'two great text-books of Socialism', *Das Kapital* and Henry George's *Progress and Poverty* (Toynbee, 1923: 109). Yet from a longer historical perspective we can see that Toynbee and Marx were united in advancing different versions of an economic history of economic thought of a kind that has often been attempted since. In making Ricardo the focal point of their historico-critical studies, they set another pattern that was to be followed by Keynes when examining the outcome of the Malthus–Ricardo disputes in the interwar period; and later by Piero Sraffa and his followers, particularly in parts of Cambridge and Italy.

Toynbee's book served as inspiration for many social reformers after his premature death in 1883 (Coleman, 1987: 59–62). He had a constructive purpose in mind when seeking to reformulate political economy, but his message chimed with other, more destructive voices during this period, notably those of Thomas Carlyle and John Ruskin. A more typical textbook product was written by John Kells Ingram a few years later. Ingram was the spokesman for Auguste Comte's view that political economy should be relegated to a branch of sociology and pursued along lines pioneered by the German historical economists and their Anglo-Irish equivalents. Ingram's campaign began with an attack on the methodology of political economy in 1878 and was completed ten years later by his *History of Political Economy* where he pronounced a requiem over a dead or dying science, coupled with a welcome to all that seemed most promising in the work of its foreign and domestic critics (Ingram, 1885). Among the latter, and prominent in Ingram's own pantheon, was Thomas Cliffe Leslie, a more original fellow-Irishman. In the 1860s and 1870s, Leslie had conducted his campaign against the orthodox school by means of a series of historical and philosophical essays that made a serious attempt to differentiate between the methodologies employed by Smith (mostly good, some bad), Ricardo (all bad) and Mill (mostly good, but still insufficiently emancipated). One of these essays was later to be acknowledged by Henry Sidgwick, alongside Mill's recantation of the wage fund in 1869, as marking the end of the 'halcyon days' of 'classical' political economy (Leslie, 1888; Sidgwick, 1887).

In their very different ways, then, Marx, Toynbee, Ingram and Leslie were deeply engaged by what Mill had damned with faint praise. They had all constructed *causal* accounts of the history of political economy that were intended to be both explanatory and critical, hoping thereby to undermine orthodoxy and point the way towards new scientific and social Jerusalems. Only Marx, it could be argued, was successful in this respect, though the emergence of economic history as a distinct branch of academic study was another byproduct in Britain. By comparison with such ambitious causal/critical versions of history, the story I have just sketched is merely that: a story, a narrative of persons, ideas and events that can be connected, not implausibly, with what in itself was a minor episode. The narrative has expanded into an international debate involving the Marxist critique of 'vulgar' political economy and the *Methodenstreit*, both of them full of significance for one of the major revolutions that occurred in the history of economics during the nineteenth and early twentieth centuries.

With sufficient time and more skill, I could also connect the story with various ideas of progress. I could argue that it reveals something significant about the way in which a confident, though not in Mill's case, an entirely complacent form of orthodoxy proved more indifferent to the past because it believed that intellectual progress had been achieved, and that social progress had been furthered by application of the conclusions of the science to policy, with many desirable objectives still to be attained. Thus when Mill outlined his hopes for the future in his *Principles* and in his *Autobiography*, it was to express his hopes for a zero-growth end-state to the history of economic progress. 'The social problem of the future', he said, would be 'how to unite the greatest individual liberty of action, with a common ownership in the raw material of the globe, and an equal participation of all in the benefits of combined labour' (Mill, 1981: I: 239). At best these beliefs supported a history that was mainly concerned with the victory of truth over error, a teleological or Whig history that was not inevitabilist, but profoundly presentist, even futurist, in its priorities. We are all familiar with the presentist version of this kind of history because until recently it was the dominant form of historiography, within the English-speaking world at least. It has been blessed by some distinguished practitioners who combined their expertise as original economic thinkers with an interest in history: Joseph Schumpeter, George Stigler and Paul Samuelson come readily to mind.

On the other side there was a heterogeneous grouping, no less committed to scientific and social progress, though along different lines. For them history was a weapon serving equally presentist/futurist purposes, stressing the errors that still needed to be overcome. It could be a Comtean story of the triumph of 'positive' methods over 'metaphysical' ones; a victory for 'scientific social-ism' over utopian alternatives and vulgar apologetics; and finally, and most influentially perhaps during the last quarter of the nineteenth century, a view that took confidence from a combination of the infinitesimal calculus with the evolutionary perspectives associated with Charles Darwin and Herbert Spencer: Marshall's position (Collini et al., 1983: 309–37). Although these two alternatives start from different premises and assign different values to history, they agree *au fond* in their historiography.

The episode I have used for illustration has been recounted many times and with more finesse than is suggested above. From this point on I shall concen-trate on our present practices as historians, calling on my own experience in doing so. Let me dispose of the most embarrassingly self-referential part at once by connecting myself with the exchange between Mill and Fawcett. Almost exactly one hundred years later, in 1962, I delivered what a fellow historian of economics described over-dramatically as a 'traumatic paper' enti-tled 'What price the history of economic thought?' (Corry in Blaug, 1991: 125; and Winch, 1962). The answer I gave to this vulgarly worded question was that since the history of economics was becoming about as relevant to the education of economists as the history of physics was to modern physicists, we needed a new rationale for continuing to study the history of economics. I reviewed in sceptical fashion the existing forms of justification, still over-whelmingly 'Whiggish' in orientation, and suggested other priorities, other historiographic models, particularly those derived from the history of science, where Whig history had disappeared.

Although the article expresses (badly and baldly) my opinions at that time, and still to a large extent today, it illustrates another generalization: historio-graphic pronouncements are chiefly attractive to the young or to the very old. For the young it is an inquiry into what one's elders have left for one to do, where they may have failed, and where new work should begin. For the old it is a Nestor-like activity based on memories and personal experience, recounted with more or less modesty, on what has been achieved and why. You rarely hear that it has all been a terrible mistake. Having indulged in this activ-ity when young – when I had been teaching for only three years, and had completed just one piece of historical research, my doctorate – I find the role of Nestor problematic. Nestor, you will recall, has the unpleasant habit of boring the younger soldiers with tales of the more heroic figures in whose giant shadows they live. I have known some heroes: Jacob Viner, my doctoral supervisor, occupied that role in 1962, and I was later given an opportunity to pay my personal and public dues to him (Winch, 1981, 1983).

But there are two reasons for evading Nestor's fate. The first is a practical, bread-and-butter one. The nearer one gets to retirement, the less appreciative one becomes towards the circumstances in which research is conducted: the departmental teaching realities, the pressures to publish, the need to justify applications for funds and the role of conferences. Having survived these pressures, it is easy to forget that others still have to survive them. The second reason is more personal. Acting on my conclusions in 1962, I decided that the best way of preserving my own interests was to forsake the imperatives attached to being a historian writing for fellow economists, to being an economist *manqué*. I chose to follow the career of an intellectual historian rather than as an historian of economic thought *tout court*. That may not be an available or a welcome solution for many people here, but it should be borne in mind as the background to the rest of this talk. Another fact is relevant: partly for reasons of history and my patchy command of other languages, I have mostly made my living in an Anglo-American academic world, where the 'new rigorism' in the social sciences (Schorske, 1997) has been most influential and where utilitarian pressures of one kind or another have increasingly been dominant. These influences may be less in evidence on the continent of Europe during the same period, with different consequences for the pursuit of scholarship in our field.

The situation I described in 1962, with a good deal of help from Viner's attitude towards his own historical pursuits, has in some respects become an accepted reality. Historians of economic thought can no longer complain about the increasing unwillingness of the regular economic journals to publish in our field, with editors acting as Say or Mill might have done in assigning historical work to the third or fourth rank. An index based on the number of such articles that have appeared in the main economics journals over the century that has passed since 1890 would, I predict, show a decline from around a maximum of quarter of the contents to near zero. Although we may not have attained the prestige and autonomous status afforded to historians of the natural sciences, the social economics of university expansion and publishing have made it possible for us to mount our own journals, beginning with *History of Political Economy* and now followed by *The European Journal of the History of Economic Thought* and a large number of other national newsletters and journals. Japan, in particular, and for special cultural and historical reasons, has become a major centre for the study of all aspects of Western and Japanese economic thought.

In other respects, however, little has changed. I suspect that the overwhelming majority of those here today continue to be employed in economics departments. This encourges us to think that we still cultivate a sub-discipline within economics, akin to other sub-disciplines, and enjoying varying degrees of tolerance from the members of the 'core' discipline – if such a 'core' can still be said to exist in the ever-increasing refinement in the division of labour within economics. If this is the case, you will be used to overhearing remarks about antiquarianism (some of them justifiable), with papers on the subject receiving that most dismissive of welcomes, 'so what'. Assuming that there are as many brilliant and mediocre pieces of historical research as there are original and uninspired research activities in economics, I would still not wish the historical ones to be judged by the unhistorical priorities of economists.

Having partially cast aside our auxiliary role as handmaiden to economics, as keeper of the professional museum or memory bank, to be rolled out chiefly for centenary performances, what other justification for our occupation is available beyond that of tradition and the inertia that often accompanies it? The causal/critical approaches mentioned earlier are still available, but I suspect that the number of firm adherents they command has fallen drastically. What will be the twenty-first century equivalents of those grand nineteenth-century meta-historical narratives of progress constructed by Comte, Marx and the social Darwinists? We have even had our Freudian episodes and some remarkable attempts at psycho-biography, especially when dealing with the more flamboyant sex lives of some leading economists. Keynes has been given this treatment by some of his biographers, and there have been gestures in the same direction when dealing with the far less promising case of Adam Smith.[4] None of these seem to have left a permanent mark on how we interpret the writings of economists; they are chiefly attempts to colonize economics by applying a theory developed in and for another domain.

During the 1960s and 1970s, in the Anglo-American world at least, the philosophy-of-science perspectives supplied by the dispute over Popperian, Lakatosian and Kuhnian models of how 'normal' science does or does not progress, served a useful meta-historical purpose.[5] For Kuhnians the model provided a terminology for discussing revolutions within mature or immature scientific communities, leading to some interesting work on the historical sociology of our particular knowledge community.[6] There are also interesting studies which I associate with the name of Philip Mirowski (1994) on the role played in economics by images or metaphors derived from the natural sciences, physics in particular. Mark Blaug proudly continues to fly the Lakatosian flag, pursuing the idea that we should be concerned with whether the economic theories whose history we write are true or not when judged by their testability in principle as well as their actual capacity to survive tests.[7] In pursuing the latter goal he has subjected past economic theories to the tests supplied by economic history (Blaug, 1980, 1986).

As a minor Popperian (I attended his classes as an undergraduate at the London School of Economics) – though having also been intrigued by Kuhn

– I accept that there can be no golden rule or iron prohibition as to where we should look for our initial hypotheses when interpreting the past. Indeed, the closer we get to the present, the more I would expect modern economics to supply some of those hypotheses. I would add the important proviso, however, that if we employ the shifting (I doubt if they are all progressive) categories of modern theory, or expectations derived from a modern philosophy of science, we should be prepared, first, to accept the possibility that the historical evidence may yield only partial confirmation, sometimes a null hypothesis. Secondly, we should acknowledge that our historical protagonists may have been operating according to philosophies of science, and related styles of persuasion or standards of proof, that are not our own. Since Mark Blaug (1999) has increasingly expressed his preference for historical as opposed to rational reconstructions of the past, I am sure he would accept these points, while still wishing to discriminate between true and false theories.

One of the tasks historians of economics can perform – a task that might help to keep open lines of communication with economists – is to act as a policeman patrolling the boundary between rational and historical reconstructions, showing where one is masquerading as the other. In my own experience, however, economists are incorrigible recidivists. Dialogue with them and others who have formed a view on the significance a past economist has to their own identities is usually one-sided: we listen to them, but they do not return the compliment. Samuelson may yield a little to those who question the historical accuracy of his 'canonical' model of classical growth theory (Blaug, 1991: Samuelson's response to Kurdas, 1988; see also Winch, 1997), but – and here I speak from personal experience – you will not change the view of Smith that has been formed by economists and ideologues attached to the Adam Smith Institute, the Institute for Economic Affairs, or the Mont Pélèrin Society. Anachronistic readings may not be the only sin we should avoid as historians, but unless we pay it due regard there will always be some doubt as to whether we are actually engaged in writing history at all.

Let me give a simple illustration that reverts to my opening story. Mill's statement that 'there is nothing in the laws of value which remains for the present or any future writer to clear up' (Mill, 1965, III: 456) acted as a red rag to Jevons. It was a symbol of everything wrong about being subject to the authority of an older man defending a corrupt *ancien regime*. Marshall reacted with less revolutionary fervour, but he reacted nonetheless. If our chief concern is with Mill, it may be legitimate to ask such counter-factual questions as how would Mill have rewritten his fundamental propositions on value and capital if he, like us, had been able to read Walras, Menger or Marshall? That is one of the benefits we derive from hindsight. But it should be a self-conscious benefit rather than a source of unquestioning omniscience, the chief fault of unexamined teleological assumptions based on the idea of progress.

What has to be assumed when asking such questions? How can their relevance to the interpretation of Mill, as opposed to the pioneering marginalists, be demonstrated? I remain more impressed by a piece of partially counterfactual research conducted on this issue by Neil de Marchi (1972), who considered the evidence relating to Mill's actual and likely grounds for rejecting what an early marginalist like Jevons had on offer. This has recently been supplemented by Jeffrey Lipkes (1999), who has expanded the study to include Mill's late friends and disciples: why did John Elliot Cairnes and Fawcett resist Mill's recantation of the wage fund theory, while William Thornton and Cliffe Leslie applauded it? Why did all four figures resist the Jevonian challenge? Nor is it surprising that in pursuing his answers Lipkes, in common with de Marchi, has had to go well beyond the normal boundaries of the history of economics to include biography, methodological preferences, politics, and religion.

The result of such research is genuinely historical. It makes use of but is not a prisoner of hindsight. In this respect it contrasts with the rational reconstructions advanced by those who, following Schumpeter (1954: 603–4; Blaug, 1958: Ch. 9), see Mill as almost necessarily trapped in some 'half-way house' between the imperatives of 'classical' or 'neoclassical' economics. It should be the task of historians to point out that both of these categories are retrospective creations, even reified entities. An explanation of what happened can make use of such categories, but should not substitute them for those that claim to be dealing with the historical reality faced by our protagonists.

Counter-factual inquiries can be useful in reconstructing the lineaments and consequences of debates that have common sources, but range over different generations of contributors. How might Smith or Malthus have responded to a later development, whether criticizing or claiming to be derived from their positions (Winch, 1997)? Seeking the kind of evidence that would lend plausibility to our answers, discarding the merely fanciful, acknowledging where the evidence does not allow a firm conclusion – all these are a legitimate challenge to our capacity for disciplined historical imagination. By accepting the possibility of different outcomes we furnish ourselves with another way of avoiding omniscience: we open historical issues rather than foreclose on them.

The range of meta-historical theories that can be applied to past linguistic performances has greatly expanded in recent decades as part of that broad movement known as the 'linguistic turn'. As German-speaking readers will know better than I do, one example of this can be found in the enterprise known as *Begriffsgeschichte*, the history of social, legal, political and economic concepts. It departs from earlier German models summarized by such terms as *Geistesgeschichte* and *Ideengeschichte*, and clearly supports wide-ranging and precise scholarly work. It also has ambitious philosophical and sociological underpinnings connecting diachronic usage with the theme of progress in a way that goes beyond mere word coinage and change of usage. It is part of a larger philosophical or political inquiry into the meaning of modernity or *Neuzeit*, the crucial period, or *Sattelzeit*, being the century that followed after 1750.

As befits the home of modern historicism, Germany and the history of modern Germany has also been the site of an *Historikerstreit* that attempts to come to terms with the idea of a German *Sonderweg* centring on the meaning of the Holocaust to our understanding of the German past and present. It has bequeathed to us – even those who have difficulty in stringing together a proper sentence in German – a marvellous word expressing a complex idea: *Vergangenheitsbewältigung*, coming to terms with or overcoming the past (Maier, 1988; Blackbourn and Eley, 1984). Unlike Marx, who felt this need acutely, I can see no equivalent in our more humble branch of history. Yet as historians it behoves us to be aware of the nature of the debate, particularly when mounting comparative exercises involving national cultures and the role played by intellectual developments within them.[8]

Begriffsgeschichte has sometimes been paired or contrasted with an approach to the study of texts within historical contexts that can be most readily identified with the work of two leading intellectual historians, John Pocock (1985) and Quentin Skinner (Tully, 1988), who have also done most to expound the philosophical foundations of their practice as historians of political thought. Here the emphasis is not so much on individual concepts as on the intentional deployment by authors – whether acting conventionally or innovatively – of the resources embedded in the political and moral languages available to them. Recovering those intentions requires a study of what it was possible to do with these contemporary linguistic resources by asking what kinds of principles, actions or behaviour were being enjoined or endorsed, what it made sense to argue in a specific historical context. As with *Begriffsgeschichte*, some of the best results of this approach can be found in work on political and legal thinkers, though in this case for the pre-1800 period: from Machiavelli to Hobbes and Locke, and on to Gibbon and Burke. When working on Smith, seen against his particular eighteenth-century and Scottish background, I found, and continue to find, this approach both liberating and inspiriting (Winch, 1978).

For the reasons mentioned earlier, however, there may be more resistance, or a different kind of resistance, to the resulting interpretations. For economists and those historians of economic thought who take their cue from modern economics this often takes the form of simple bemusement: how could any such historical interpretation be of interest to what economists now consider to be their main task? The 'so what' response, delivered with more or less politeness. From political theorists, philosophers and historians of political thought the reaction has been different. Those who have a good deal invested in the canonical status of a figure, where the chosen figure represents a significant way of speaking to the modern condition, are disconcerted by being told that the figure is not saying what they have always thought he was saying, or could, with sufficient ventriloqual skill, be made to say. Arguments of this kind reflect the longer and closer relationship that exists between modern practitioners of political science and those figures who have had canonical status thrust upon them over the decades in which it has been accepted pedagogic practice to teach the history of philosophy or political thought as an integral part of teaching philosophy or politics as academic pursuits. Economists ceased to do this in some national and academic settings a long time ago, perhaps at the beginning of the twentieth century. There were still vestiges of this in Scotland in the 1960s: hence in part my juvenile revolt – a revolt that may or may not have been traumatic to historians, but received such a lacklustre response from economists that it showed how few confident defenders of the status quo there were. Political scientists in the Anglo-American mould broke away from what they saw as the tyranny of the past in the 1950s, and provoked a counter-reaction as a result.[9]

No hurried *tour d'horizon* would be complete without brief mention of those movements within the general current of thought known as post-modernism: the various theories or techniques employed in textual decon-struction and the analysis of discursive formations, with their rhetorical properties being given special status. Expressed briefly, but not I hope disre-spectfully, it is a form of linguistic turn with a rhetorical twist. The economic historian D.N. McCloskey (1994) has attempted to show why economics is a form of rhetoric.[10] Adam Smith began his own career with lectures on rhetoric and *belles lettres*, but it is his canonical status as the author of two richly complex works, the *Wealth of Nations* and the *Theory of Moral Sentiments*, that has made him attractive to those who employ these types of discourse analysis (Brown, 1994; Copley and Sutherland, 1996). Understandably, it has often been scholars with a background in literary theory, with support from feminists and those interested in the way language can be used to marginalize other groups, who have been prominent in making these applications: hence too their claim to be making inter- or cross-disciplinary 'interventions'.

The main area of friction between studies based on linguistic turn and those devoted to rhetorical twist centres on the issue of authorial intention: what the 'turners' find a necessary challenge, the 'twisters' regard as being at best deeply problematic or, as they say, 'untheorized'. When speaking more frankly, they think it illusory. For them textual peculiarity replaces historical specificity, giving a new meaning to 'meaning', one that arises directly from the process of intertextual reading rather than from authorship exercised within particular historical settings. As I have already revealed, this would not be my natural approach if I had to make a choice of meta-historical rationales.

But on Popperian grounds of the absence of prior golden rules and iron prohibitions, I would try to keep an open mind and seek proof of the pudding in the historical eating – as long as history genuinely is a shared concern. But if the number of possible 'readings' is unlimited, and there are no independent criteria according to which we can justify the notion of what constitutes a good, bad or indifferent reading, then I suspect we cannot sustain cross-meta-historical dialogue. The idea of progress may have become more problematic, but my own notions of truth-telling remain naïvely non-post-modern.[11]

Each of us at some point in our careers has to make a choice between the kinds of second-order approaches I have been sketching, plus many more that are beyond my ken. Some people – those with a natural philosophical bent or a desire to join the latest game – may be able to hop from one to the other with ease. Having found, or rather fallen into, a position that seems to suit me best, I do not feel inclined to shift my stance at this late stage in my own personal game. Nor do I wish to proselytize for my personal preferences. In case that sounds complacent, or an attempt to be all things to all men and women, let me end by giving a few reasons why I am now content with narratives as opposed to explanations – narratives that license, where possible, what the anthropologist Clifford Geertz (1973) has called 'thick descriptions'.

I am fond of an activity that appears quite frequently in the work of the rhetorical 'twisters': dialogue or conversation. In my case, however, it derives from a pre-post-modern interest in reconstructing past arguments or debates. It has been fortified by what I have learned from two friends, ex-colleagues, and collaborators, John Burrow and Stefan Collini, both being intellectual historians. Burrow (1987) has neatly characterized intellectual history as 'eavesdropping on the conversations of the past'. Conversations do not have to be friendly, but they do allow degrees of freedom often denied by the more common practice of seeing our historical protagonists as locked in dualistic debates: between historicism and deductivism, between classical and neoclassical imperatives and so on. Conversations allow the participants to change their positions and even to occupy different positions at different times. After all, it is to be hoped that we sometimes change our minds as a result of what others say to us. When addressing their readers in books, especially textbooks, past economists naturally adopted didactic postures. But when formulating their positions, especially if they felt they had something new to say, they were more often engaged in conversation with their chosen predecessors and contemporaries, as well as their earlier selves. As historians we are joining these conversations when they may have been going on for some time, trying to figure out what is being said to whom and for what purpose. The conversation may be part of some larger 'discursive formation', but understanding the ordinary conventions that continue to govern our own conversations seems adequate for most purposes.

This reveals my assumption, denied by 'twisters', that while establishing the intentions of past authors may require me to acquire a new language, those intentions are not entirely beyond my comprehension. Moreover, in learning 'their' language I do not lose my capacity to speak the one I use with my contemporaries. I notice too that when 'twisters' dismiss authorial intention at the outset, it often comes in again by the back door, frequently carrying something looking suspiciously like an ideology or an intention. I find it more interesting to join these conversations, with the option of making my own contribution, than engage in what often seem like exchanges between modern academics united more by their interest in a theory of literary or linguistic communication than by their concern with the historical object under examination. The method has become the message, creating a barrier between the reader and the object of inquiry, a past conversation that is of interest to us for reasons that can be defended.

As with all methods, even those that are merely rules of thumb, there are risks of becoming one-eyed. One of these can be described as a Rankean form of nominalism, revelling in the pastness of the past and thereby failing to address the legitimate questions that a modern audience might wish to ask. I am sure this risk exists, but not if one is aware of the danger. Thus a common criticism of intellectual histories that pay so much attention to historical context is that they imprison authors within that context, thereby severing them from their future. It has even been caricatured recently (and dare I say, nervously) from a Whig perspective as the belief that 'the researcher must pretend to lack knowledge of the future' (Hollander, 1997: xiv). That of course would be both impossible and absurd. All that is being counselled is that one should not frame one's questions or write as though one's historical protagonists were equipped with *our* knowledge of the future. Reverting to my tiny stock of German once more, while *sein* must not be confused with *werden* in the kind of study I have in mind, it could be the best basis on which to consider the *Wirkungsgeschichte* of an author or theory, one that brings us closer to *Begriffsgeschichte*. Listening closely to conversations has always been a good way of noticing the entry of new themes, new tones of voice, of tracing discontinuities as well as continuities.

Past conversations, even among single-minded economists, do not always stick to the points that we, with hindsight, believe to have been the essential ones. Schumpeter (1954: Chapter 3) made some strong recommendations to the historian of economic analysis to ensure that he was not distracted by such extraneous matters as philosophy, politics or religion. Fortunately, he was unable to stick to this kind of puritanism; he allowed a large number of these discordant elements to be reintroduced as 'economic sociology'. I do not see why past economic thinking should have a modern professional economists' straitjacket imposed upon it. Fashions, even in straitjackets, change, and we stand to lose the capacity to allow past conversations to teach us something that is not already part of the corpus of economic knowledge.

This brings me to the final part of this sermon. The kind of intellectual history I have in mind is inherently interdisciplinary – or rather, since that word has acquired a tendency to be self-certifying, even self-congratulatory – it requires one to be catholic in one's tastes. The puritanism of much writing in the history of economics has led to narrowness and airlessness. We often seem to be copying those periods in the writing of ecclesiastical history when only those in holy orders were licensed to write such history. Shifting images to an activity I know better, instead of working in a walled garden marked the History of Economic Thought, with a sign on the door warning all those not trained in economics to stay away, why don't we knock down one or two of the walls and swap a few plants with fellow historians working in the neighbouring gardens? We might even succeed in growing a few strong hybrids. We are still behaving as though we had to produce flowers for the economists' dinner table, ignoring the opportunities to show more appreciative audiences how fertile our garden has been. No wonder they have taken to growing inferior versions of our flowers in their gardens. That is professional loyalty speaking: I would also have to admit that they are often growing superior versions as well, and not just when judged by the brightness of the colours.

At the end of all the painful adventures that Voltaire made Candide undergo, one of them consisting of being forced to listen to inconclusive metaphysical (meta-historical?) speculations, he concludes as I wish to conclude: '*Il faut cultiver notre jardin*'. The emphasis should fall on *notre* in relation to economists, but it should not prevent us from joining other intellectual historians cultivating adjacent historical plots of land.

POSTSCRIPT

Having posed a slightly irreverent question in my title, I now feel obliged to give a brief answer to it. Progress matters to us as historians because it mattered to many, perhaps most of those about whom we write. Indeed, many of them during the nineteenth century would have preferred to speak of Progress with a capital P. Like us, in varying degrees, they believed they were advancing knowledge, directly or indirectly, adding to the capacity to improve the world in some way. As historians of their activities we are free to uphold or dispute their claims to have succeeded in these enterprises, employing whatever criteria for success or failure we regard as defensible. But historians, more than most other people, should be aware of the pitfalls involved in making such judgements. Our freedom to indulge this propensity does not amount to an obligation. Indeed, the histories we write may be more interesting if we do not make progress our leitmotif. In that sense progress does not matter as much to us as it may have done to our historical protagonists.

NOTES

1. Say (1837: 564) had asked: 'Que pourrions-nous gagner à recueillir des opinions absurdes, des doctrines décriées et qui meritent de l'être? Il serait à la fois inutile et fastidieux'.
2. J.R. McCulloch had acted as bibliophile and historian to an earlier generation of English readers; see McCulloch (1825, 1845). See also O'Brien (1970: 80–83). For another example of the existing literature in English, see Twiss (1847). Before 1863, France and Italy were better served by histories written by Pecchio, Blanqui, Villeneuve-Bargemont, the Daire and Custodi collections, and the Coquelin and Guillaumin dictionary. For an even earlier body of literature disputing the national origins of political economy, see Winch (1994).
3. For a modern assessment of Fawcett's career, see Deane (1989) and Winch (1989).
4. My favourite example appeared in a review of Ross (1994). The reviewer in the *History of Political Economy* (1997: 171) pointed out that sodomy in the eighteenth century was subject to capital punishment and added the following syllogism: 'Given the legal, moral, and social climate regarding gays; Smith's extreme discretion; and other hints in his life, the theory that Smith was indeed gay merits serious consideration, perhaps even investigation'. On the basis of this deductive chain, and leaving aside the 'hints in his life' that the reviewer does not reveal, it would be equally cogent to suspect Smith of being a cattle rustler.
5. The Kuhn-related literature is too large to document here. For the influence of Popper, see de Marchi (1988).
6. A.W. Coats (1993) pioneered this approach.
7. Terence Hutchison has pursued a similar agenda via the idea that revolutions entail losses as well as gains; see Hutchison (1978, 1988).
8. For a recent penetrating insight into such matters that lays a foundation for the kind of comparative treatment of university systems mentioned earlier, see Ringer (1992).
9. For some reflections on this topic that are genuinely comparative, between nations and disciplines, see Collini (2000).
10. Those who now apply the idea to historical texts in economics are more likely to derive inspiration from Michel Foucault, Roland Barthes, Jacques Derrida, Mikhail Bakhtin and Richard Rorty.
11. For some remarks on this problem from a point of view with which I sympathize, see Ringer (1992: 314–23).

REFERENCES

Blackbourn, D. and G.O. Eley (1984), *The Peculiarities of German History: Bourgeois Society and Politics in Ninteenth-century Germany*, Oxford: Oxford University Press.

Blaug, M. (1958), *Ricardian Economics*, New Haven: Yale University Press.

Blaug, M. (1980), *The Methodology of Economics; Or How Economists Explain*, Cambridge: Cambridge University Press.

Blaug, M. (1986), *Economic History and the History of Economics*, Brighton: Harvester Press.

Blaug, M. (1991), *The Historiography of Economics*, Aldershot: Edward Elgar.

Blaug, M. (1999) 'Misunderstanding classical economics: the Sraffian interpretation of the surplus approach', *History of Political Economy*, 31: 213–36.

Brown, V. (1994), *Adam Smith's Discourse; Canonicity, Commerce and Conscience*, London: Routledge.

Burrow, J.W. (1987), 'The history of ideas in theory and practice', The John Coffin Memorial Lecture.

Coats, A.W. (1993), *The Sociology and Professionalization of Economics; British and American Economic Essays*, London: Routledge.

Coleman, D.C. (1987), *History and the Economic Past*, Oxford: Oxford University Press.

Collini, S., D. Winch and J. Burrow (1983), *That Noble Science of Politics: A Study in Nineteenth-century Intellectual History*, Cambridge: Cambridge University Press.

Collini, S. (2000), 'Disciplines, canons, and publics: the history of "the history of political thought" in comparative perspective', in D. Castiglione and I. Hampsher-Monk (eds), *The History of Political Thought in National Context*, Cambridge: Cambridge University Press.

Copley, S and K. Sutherland (eds) (1995), *Adam Smith's Wealth of Nations: New Interdisciplinary Essays*, Manchester: Manchester University Press.

de Marchi, N. (1972), 'Mill and Cairnes and the emergence of marginalism in England', *History of Political Economy*, 4: 344–63.

de Marchi, N. (ed.) (1988), *The Popperian Legacy in Economics*, Cambridge: Cambridge University Press.

Deane, P. (1989), 'Henry Fawcett: The Plain Man's Political Economist', in L. Goldman (ed.), *The Blind Victorian; Henry Fawcett and British Liberalism*, Cambridge: Cambridge University Press: 93–110.

Geertz, C. (1973), *The Interpretation of Cultures*, New York: Basic Books.

Hollander, S. (1997), *The Economics of Thomas Robert Malthus*, Toronto: Toronto University Press.

Hutchison, T. (1978), *On Revolutions and Progress in Economic Knowledge*, Cambridge: Cambridge University Press.

Hutchison, T. (1988), *Before Adam Smith*, London: Blackwell.

Ingram, J.K. (1878), 'The present position and prospects of political economy, a presidential address to the British Association for the Advancement of Science', in R.L. Smyth (ed.), *Essays in Economic Method*, New York: McGraw Hill: 41–72.

Ingram, J.K. (1885), *A History of Political Economy*, London.

Keynes, J.M. (1972), 'Alfred Marshall' in *Essays in Biography* as reprinted in *The Collected Writings of John Maynard Keynes*, X: 161–321.

Kurdas, C. (1988), 'The Whig historian on Adam Smith: Paul Samuelson's canonical classical model', in M. Blaug (ed.) (1991): 181–208.

Leslie, T.E.C. (1888), *Essays in Political Economy*, edited by J.K. Ingram and C.F. Bastable, London.

Lipkes, J. (1999), *Politics, Religion and Classical Political Economy in Britain: John Stuart Mill and His Followers*, London: Macmillan.

Maier, C.S. (1988), *The Unmasterable Past: History, Holocaust, and German National Identity*, Cambridge: Harvard University Press.

McCloskey, D.N. (1994), *Knowledge and Persuasion in Economics*, Cambridge: Cambridge University Press.

McCulloch, J.R. (1825), *Discourse on the Rise, Progress, Peculiar Objects and Importance of Political Economy*, London.

McCulloch, J.R. (1845), *Literature of Political Economy*, London.

Mill, John Stuart (1965–91), *The Collected Works of John Stuart Mill*, Toronto: Toronto University Press.

Mirowski, P. (1994), *Natural Images in Economic Thought*, Cambridge: Cambridge University Press.

O'Brien, D.P. (1970), *J.R. McCulloch: A Study in Classical Economics*, London: Allen & Unwin.

Pocock, J.G.A. (1985), *Virtue, Commerce, and History*, Cambridge: Cambridge University Press.

Ringer, F. (1992), *Fields of Knowledge: French Academic Culture in Comparative Perspective, 1890–1920*, Cambridge: Cambridge University Press..

Ross, I.S. (1994), *The Life of Adam Smith*, Oxford: Oxford University Press.

Say, Jean-Baptiste (1837), *Cours Complet d'Économie Politique Pratique*, 3rd edition, Brussels.

Schorske, C. (1997), 'The new rigorism in the social sciences, 1940–1960', *Daedalus*, 126: 289–308.

Schumpeter, J.A. (1954), *History of Economic Analysis*, London: Allen & Unwin.

Sidgwick, H. (1887), *Principles of Political Economy*, 2nd edition, London.

Toynbee, A. (1923), *The Industrial Revolution of the Eighteenth Century in England*, London, originally published in 1884.

Twiss, T. (1847), *A View of the Progress of Political Economy in Europe since the Sixteenth Century*, London.

Tully, J. (ed.) (1988), *Meaning and Context; Quentin Skinner and his Critics*, Cambridge: Polity Press.

Winch, D. (1962), 'What Price the History of Economic Thought?', *Scottish Journal of Political Economy*, 9: 193–204.

Winch, D. (1978), *Adam Smith's Politics; An Essay in Historiographic Revision*, Cambridge: Cambridge University Press.

Winch, D. (1981), 'Jacob Viner', *The American Scholar*, 50: 519–25.

Winch, D. (1983), 'Jacob Viner as intellectual historian', in W.J. Samuels (ed.), *The Craft of the Historian of Economic Thought*, Connecticut: JAI Press: 1–17.

Winch, D. (1989), 'The plain man's political economist: a discussion', in L. Goldman (ed.), *The Blind Victorian; Henry Fawcett and British Liberalism*, Cambridge: Cambridge University Press: 111–19.

Winch, D. (1994), 'Nationalism and cosmopolitanism in the early histories of political economy', in M. Albertone and A. Masoero (eds), *Political Economy and National Realities*, Turin: Fondazione Luigi Einaudi: 91–105.

Winch, D. (1996), *Riches and Poverty: An Intellectual History of Political Economy in Britain, 1750–1834*, Cambridge: Cambridge University Press.

Winch, D. (1997), 'Adam Smith's problems and ours', *Scottish Journal of Political Economy*, 44: 384–402.

2. Is there really progress in economics?

Mark Blaug*

The notion of what is progress or growth or knowledge in the history of a subject arises naturally in hard sciences like physics, chemistry and biology, and by posing the question with reference to economics, we seem to be claiming that a social science like economics is not unlike a natural science. After all, the concept of progress does not apply to literature, music and the visual arts. There is no sense in which James Joyce is better than Geoffrey Chaucer or Bartok an improvement on Beethoven; they may be technically more proficient but, from an aesthetic standpoint, they are neither better nor worse but simply different. So, my first claim is that it is perfectly legitimate to raise the question of whether there has been progress in economics; economics is a soft science, indeed a very soft science, but it is a science and not just a peculiar sort of literature. Donald Winch's chapter bears the intriguing title, 'Does progress matter?'. Yes, I assert, it does matter because as economists we are ultimately in the business of understanding how the economy works in the same way that a physicist or biologist is engaged in understanding how nature works. How naïve, some of you, drunk on a post-modernist wine, will say: economics is an art, not a science; not *some* economics is an art, which I also believe, but all of it is nothing more than art, a balm for politicians, a secular religion for the powers that be, a type of poetry written in awful prose, etcetera, etcetera. I deny all that and claim moreover that every economist appraising developments in economics, even when he or she is denying its scientific claims, inadvertently ends up either praising or deploring the amount of progress in the subject. In other words, we always react as if it matters whether there has been progress in economics. Schumpeter (1954: 7) once defined a 'science' as 'any kind of knowledge that has been the object of conscious efforts to improve it'. My second modest claim is that economics is a science if only because economists have always struggled to improve their subject.

TYPES OF PROGRESS

Economics, as far back as the seventeenth, perhaps even the sixteenth, centuryhas been characterized by progress, but progress in what sense? To come to grips with that question we must make some distinctions. Most of us invited to defend the thesis that there has been progress in economics invariably seize on some technical concept, like the elasticity of demand or the concavity of production functions or the beta coefficient in portfolio theory, to demonstrate that there has obviously been progress in analytical techniques. Alternatively, they point to some of the bright new ideas, such as asymmetric information or transaction costs or the natural rate of unemployment, that have illuminated old problems, providing deeper insights than were available to economists in days gone by. I shall bundle both of these interpretations of progress together under the heading of 'theoretical progress', meaning the refinement of tools, the sharpening of distinctions, the honing of definitions, in short, greater clarity of the language we employ to talk about economic phenomena. In addition, theoretical progress may consist of expanding the domain of our theories or formulating them with greater precision and rigour (Backhouse, 1997: Ch. 8). In that sense, theoretical progress is just as applicable to normative as to positive economics – and perhaps more so. We might include in 'theoretical progress' what is better called 'statistical progress' in econometrics, as for example the use of cointegration techniques in time series analysis. This is the easy part of the argument because to deny that there has been progress in economics, in the two senses just defined, is to convict oneself of ignorance.

The hard part of the argument is to claim not just 'theoretical progress', not just 'statistical progress', but 'empirical progress', that is, a more substantive understanding of economic forces than previous economists had achieved (Blaug, 1994). That definition sounds very well but how would one *know* that one had actually achieved empirical progress? There is, I think, only one clear-cut answer to that question: empirical progress is characterized by a greater capacity accurately to predict the outcomes of economic action and, hence, to control these outcomes at least to some extent. Now I do not mean this to be taken literally as repeating the good old symmetry thesis of logical positivism, which is that to explain events that have occurred is logically equivalent to predicting them before they have occurred; in a nutshell, without the ability to make at least conditional predictions of the if–then variety, explanations are just ex post rationalizations (Blaug, 1992: 7–10). But the old logical positivists nevertheless put their fingers on an important truth: without predictability, scientific explanations have to be judged on such vague criteria as plausibility, consonance with background knowledge, conformity with easily ascertainable facts and the like. As we all know, economics lacks controlled laboratory experiments, and experimental economics, it is argued, fails to match its experiments with the realities of the market place (more of this anon). Even econometrics, some have said, can estimate economic relationships but can never test the validity of economic hypotheses if only because the data it relies on to carry out these tests were not collected in appropriate circumstances

(Backhouse, 1997: Ch. 12; Keuzenkamp, 2000). In other words, making predictions in economics is at best very difficult and, at worst, impossible. If that is so, however, it amounts to the denial, not just of empirical progress in economics, but of the meaningfulness of the very question of empirical progress. We just do not *know* if we understand how an economy works any better than did Adam Smith. When a post-modernist like McCloskey (1985: 174–5) tells us that 'the main achievement of economics is not the prediction and control assigned to it by modernist social engineering, but the making sense of economic experience', she has abandoned the troublesome concept of empirical progress and slipped into the much more comfortable concept of 'theoretical progress'. Does one make 'sense' of economic experience by inventing new labels for old ideas? Is this not just a little too easy, a little too permissive?

EMPIRICAL REGRESS

My last claim was that the very question of progress in economics is a meaningful one. My third claim is that there has been both theoretical and empirical progress in economics but the empirical progress has by no means been overwhelming nor uniform in all aspects of the subject. (From this point on, almost everything I have to say will be displeasing to someone or other, so give me a moment to put on my bullet-proof vest!) In some areas, I believe that we have actually gone backwards and regressed in our empirical understanding. The principal area in which we have regressed is nothing less than that of competition and market processes, which might be fairly said to be at the very heart of economics ever since Adam Smith. Let me explain. Throughout the development of economics as far back as Adam Smith, and even William Petty, there have always been two very different notions of what is meant by competition: competition as an end-state of rest in the rivalry between buyers and sellers, and competition as a protracted process of rivalry that may or may not terminate in any end-state. In the end-state conception of competition, the focus of attention is on the nature of the equilibrium state in which the contest between transactors is finally resolved: if there is recognition of change at all, it is change in the sense of a new stationary equilibrium of endogenous variables defined in terms of a different set of exogenous variables, but comparative statics is still an end-state conception of competition. However, in the process conception of competition, it is not the existence of equilibrium that is in the foreground of analysis but rather the stability of that equilibrium state: how do markets adjust when one equilibrium is displaced by another and at what speed will these markets converge to a new equilibrium?

But surely, it will be said, all theories of competition do both? Surely, existence and stability are tied up together and to address one is to address the other? By no means, however, because for centuries competition meant an active process of jockeying for advantage, tending towards, but never actually culminating in, a perfectly coordinated end-state. Only in 1838, in Cournot's *Mathematical Principles of the Theory of Wealth* was the process conception of competition actually displaced by the end-state conception of market-clearing equilibrium. At first this did not succeed in wiping the state entirely clean of an interest in competitive process – it remained alive and to the fore in Marshall's treatment of 'free competition' – but in the 1930s the Imperfect Competition Revolution and the Hicks–Samuelson rehabilitation of general equilibrium theory succeeded in enthroning the end-state conception of competition, and enthroning it so decisively that the process view of competition was virtually forgotten (Blaug, 1997). The process view of competition has to do with what happens out of equilibrium, but by the 1930s the very phenomenon of disequilibrium had virtually disappeared from economics (de Vroey, 1999). How that happened is part and parcel of the extraordinary conquest of Walras over Marshall, first in the 1930s and then triumphantly in the 1950s, with the publication of the famous paper by Arrow and Debreu providing a new rigorous proof of the existence of general equilibrium in a decentralized economy.

WALRASIAN GE THEORY

Let us go back for a moment to Walras, who was virtually the first to drive disequilibrium out of serious economics. Walras's genius lay not so much in seizing on multi-market equilibrium as a central problem for economic theory as in hitting on the algebra of simultaneous equations as the appropriate metaphor for tackling that problem. Just as partial equilibrium means solving a single demand and supply equation for one equilibrium price and one equilibrium quantity, so, Walras claimed, general equilibrium means solving a large set of n demand and supply equations for n prices and quantities. In the use of that somewhat forced metaphor is embodied all the strengths but also all the weaknesses of Walrasian general equilibrium (GE) theory.

Firstly, it caused Walras, as well as those who came after him, to forget that actual prices in the real world are not determined simultaneously but rather sequentially, not just from factor markets to product markets, but in all markets from inputs to outputs, so that a final equilibrium synchronization of prices is at best an exception rather than a rule. Secondly, it led Walras to demonstrate the existence of general equilibrium in ways that were exactly analogous to a mathematical solution of a system of n simultaneous equations in *n* independent variables: he wrote down a set of perfectly general demand and supply equations on the assumption of perfect competition, perfect factor mobility and perfect price flexibility and then showed that he had just enough known equations to solve for the unknown prices and quantities. This was all there was to his so-called existence proofs for general equilibrium. But Walras did much more than prove existence. He briefly discussed the question of whether the equilibrium price sector was unique and then entered into a lengthy explanation of how competition establishes an equilibrium in practice, namely by price adjustments in response to the appearance of excess demand and supply, a process which he quite rightly labelled *tâtonnement*, a groping by trial and error on the part of independently acting buyers and sellers.

Since equilibrium trading at other than market-clearing prices alters the distribution of goods among buyers and sellers before equilibrium is reached, there is little reason to believe that a final equilibrium will always emerge in a real-world competitive process; to prove rigorously that it does calls for a little more than counting equations and unknowns. Walras hankered after a realistic description of the temporal sequence by which actual markets reach a final equilibrium solution but slowly realized in successive editions of his *Elements of Pure Economics* that the more cogently he described the *tâtonnement* process, the more suspect became his existence proof. And so, as Donald Walker has shown in his brilliant study, *Walras's Market Models* (1996), Walras gradually abandoned his aim of descriptive realism, got rid of disequilibrium transactions at what he revealingly called 'false trading', and settled for what later GE theorists describe as the concept of a fictional auctioneer, announcing purely notional prices until a final equilibrium price is discovered. In the fourth and last edition of Walras's *Elements*, therefore, we have a perfect example of the end-state conception of competition, displaying the curious trade-off that seems to prevail between existence proofs and stability proofs in GE theory.

That brings us to the Arrow–Debreu paper, which is still further evidence of that trade-off. As everyone knows, Arrow and Debreu tackled the problem that had defeated Walras: they provided a rigorous proof of the existence of multi-market equilibrium. Their proof, however, required some assumptions that clearly violated economic reality, for example that there are forward markets for every commodity and for all conceivable contingencies in all future periods and yet that no one holds money for more than one period. Even so, they did not manage to prove that such a general equilibrium is either locally or globally stable in the sense that it is actually attained from whatever position we start from; even to this date, such a proof has never been provided by any GE theorist (Ingrao and Israel, 1990).

This 1954 paper by Arrow and Debreu soon became a model of what economists ought to aim for as social scientists – and it has remained such a model ever since. Few readers realized, however, that Arrow and Debreu had quietly abandoned the vision that had originally motivated Walras. For Walras, GE theory was intended to be an abstract, but nevertheless realistic, description of the functioning of a capitalist economy and he never entirely lost sight of that even in the last edition of the *Elements*. By the time we get to Arrow and Debreu, however, GE theory has ceased to make any descriptive claim about actual economic systems and has become a purely formal apparatus about a virtual economy; it has become a perfect example of what Ronald Coase has called 'blackboard economics': a model that can be written down on blackboards using economic terms like 'prices', 'quantities' and 'factors of production', but which nevertheless is blatantly and even scandalously unrepresentative of any recognizable economic system.[1]

To make things worse, the Arrow–Debreu model was rapidly augmented by the so-called fundamental theorems of welfare economics, namely that every perfectly competitive economy in a state of general equilibrium is Pareto-optimal and, moreover, that any Pareto-optimal allocation of resources can be attained by means of perfectly competitive equilibrium once we make an appropriate redistribution of initial endowments. This is said to nail down precisely what Adam Smith perceived only dimly two hundred years ago with his simile of the 'invisible hand' of competition.

Alas, what a historical travesty is here! What Adam Smith meant is what the man in the street means when he applauds the competitive process (Machovec, 1995). A competitive economy tends to produce the kinds of goods people want at the lowest possible prices because it encourages entrepreneurship and technical dynamism through a relentless struggle for advantage, a struggle that is not confined to price competition but includes non-price variables such as new goods, better old goods, better-serviced goods and more quickly delivered goods. In other words, for Adam Smith, David Ricardo, John Stuart Mill and the man in the street, competition is a type of behaviour on the part of businessmen, and not a market structure like 'perfect competition' according to which business firms are purely passive 'price takers' rather than active 'price makers'. This is what Richard Lipsey (1997) calls the 'informal defence' of competition in contrast to the 'formal defence' enshrined in proofs of the fundamental theorems of welfare economics. It is exactly the same contrast that Hayek and Schumpeter (Schumpeter 1942: 106–10) drew over 50 years ago between 'dynamic efficiency' that encourages the innovative process and 'static efficiency' that excludes it.[2]

Perfect competition never did exist and never could exist because even when firms are small, they do not just take the price as given but strive to make the price. All the current textbooks say as much, but then they immediately go on to say that the cloud-cuckoo land of perfect competition is the benchmark against which economists can say something significant about real-world competition in the same way that a frictionless plane in physics tells a physicist how fast a ball will travel along an actual inclined plane. But how can an idealized state of perfection be a benchmark when we are never told how to measure the gap between it and real-world competition? It is implied that all real-world competition is 'approximately' like perfect competition but the degree of the approximation is never specified, even vaguely.[3] Besides, there is a well-known Lipsey–Lancaster theorem which says that when an economy is not in a first-best optimum, say because of taxes or tariffs, there is no way of distinguishing a third-best from a second-best situation and no way of telling whether a given change takes us nearer or further away from the first-best optimum. This theorem is widely acknowledged in all the textbooks and yet this has done nothing to displace the notion that perfect competition is an ideal that somehow casts light on the admittedly imperfect competition all around us.[4]

Perfect competition is an utterly misleading concept, not least because it directs attention to what equilibrium looks like when we get to it, whereas the real problem is that of understanding the process of getting to it. In short, competition is a disequilibrium phenomenon, and yet general equilibrium *à la* Arrow and Debreu, the existence problem, the fundamental theorems of welfare economics, perfect competition and the like all foster concern with the end-state of competition at the expense of thinking about competition as a dynamic process (Kasper and Streit: 1999, Ch. 8).

So why do modern economists spend so much time teaching their students the model of perfect competition, while denigrating discussion of actual competition in courses on industrial organization as 'mere description'? It is because the model of perfect competition allows one to make unambiguous comparative static predictions about prices and quantities; one may only be able to say a little, but what one says is precisely said. On the other hand, when it comes to imperfect competition, what one says covers the waterfront of business behaviour but always has to be accompanied by exceptions and qualifications. A modern economist would rather say little precisely than much imprecisely, irrespective of the relative significance of what is being said, and he or she has learned this methodological standard sitting at the feet of Arrow and Debreu (Rosen, 1997). If there is such a thing as 'original sin' in economic methodology, it is worship of the idol of mathematical rigour, more or less invented by Arrow and Debreu (1954) and then canonized by Debreu (1959) in his Theory of Value five years later, probably the most arid and pointless book in the entire literature of economics. Even Sraffa's *Production of Commodities by Means of Commodities* (1960), emanating from a totally different intellectual quarter, is quite clearly a species of the same genus: Sraffa does not waste a word on telling us how markets actually reach equilibrium and, by page 5, he is already counting equations and unknowns to establish the determinacy of long-run equilibrium prices. Of course, Sraffa showed a preference for Walras over Marshall, for general equilibrium over partial equilibrium theory, throughout his entire career.

The result of all this is that we now understand almost less of how actual markets work than did Adam Smith or even Léon Walras. We have forgotten that markets require market-makers, that functioning markets require middlemen willing to hold inventories, that markets need to be organized, and that property rights need to be defined and enforced if markets are to get started at all.[5] We have even forgotten that labour markets and customer commodity markets adjust as often in terms of quantities as in prices, something that Alfred Marshall knew very well but Walras consistently ignored. So well have we forgotten that fact that a whole branch of economics sprang up in the 1970s to provide 'microfoundations' for Keynesian macroeconomics, that is, some new explanation for the well-known fact that a decline in aggregate demand causes, not falling real wages at the same level of employment, as we might expect on the basis of received Walrasian theory, but rather unemployment at the same real wage.[6]

No wonder that we have been worse than useless as a profession in advising governments in Eastern Europe on how to handle the transition from a command economy to a market economy (Murrell, 1991). This is the awful legacy of general equilibrium theory and the prestige accorded to analysis of end-state competition. The failure of communist economies has nothing to do with the failure to achieve Arrow–Debreu optimality and everything to do with the failure to grasp Adam Smith's qualitative understanding of market processes, which has only been kept alive by neo-Austrian economists (see Boettke and Prychitko, 1994). If this is not empirical regress, what is?

GAME THEORY

But surely this is old hat? Nobody bothers much these days with general equilibrium and perfect competition; the only game in town is game theory.

Game theory is made to order for modern economists: it assumes rational players seeking to maximize their own pay-offs while taking due account of the same motivation on the part of their rivals. But game theory has turned out to be an even more seductive technique for economists than GE theory, encouraging the persistent tendency of modern economists to look away from the world and to engage instead in arm-chair deductive theorizing. Game theory is most powerful in dealing with one-shot cooperative games in which pay-offs can be expressed in money or any other one-dimensional variable. But economic behaviour is typically a repeated non-cooperative game with a complex informational structure in which outcomes are not always measurable in one-dimensional terms. It is well known that repeated games typically exhibit an infinity of equilibria and game theory itself gives no reason why the players will prefer one equilibrium rather than another. In consequence, game theory does not provide definite predictions of behaviour in repeated-game situations, that is, in the sort of situations with which economists have traditionally been concerned, such as buying and selling in highly contestable markets.

Much, if not most, game theory is prescriptive, concerned with how rational players *should* make decisions, and characteristically enough, very little experimental work has been carried out to develop a realistic description of how people actually make decisions in situations of strategic interactions (Gibbons, 1997). Like traditional economic theory, game theory has been exclusively concerned with what Herbert Simon calls 'substantive' rationality and rarely with 'procedural' rationality, that is, with what players do when they are perfectly informed about all available alternatives, have unbounded calculating abilities and have nothing to learn from experience, and not with the social norms and rules of thumb they are forced to adopt in the face of imperfect information and limited cognitive abilities. And just as GE theory solved the stability-of-equilibrium question by ruling out disequilibrium trading, game theory likewise adopted a static approach to the equilibrium outcomes of games by simply ignoring the adjustment process by which equilibrium is achieved; even sequential decision-making, which allows one player to learn what to do from the previous move of the other player, is frequently eliminated in favour of simultaneous decision-making. If anything, game theory has in recent years witnessed increasing conceptual proliferation, drawing it even further away from a positive descriptive account of interactive decisions.[7] Indeed, for all its undoubted abstract intellectual appeal, game theory has fed the economist's addiction to formal modelling regardless of its practical relevance. In the field of industrial organization, which has been more systematically colonized by game theory than any other branch of economics, its principal effect has been to put old wine into new bottles: it is difficult, nay, impossible, to think of a single novel observation that has come out of the 'new' industrial organization infused by game theory that was not already part and parcel of the 'old' industrial organization based as it was on the so-called 'structure–conduct–performance approach' to business behaviour.[8]

The main contribution of game theory has been rather different. It has taught us better to appreciate the infinite subtleties of so-called 'rationality', reminding us that the standard economist's account of rational behaviour is woefully inadequate in spelling out the implicit informational structure and learning processes on which equilibrium outcomes in markets do in fact depend. *Homo ludens* has turned out not to be quite like *homo economicus*. This is theoretical progress but it is not yet empirical progress in helping us to predict how the price system actually works.

What runs through all this is the licence that Friedman's 'methodology of positive economics' gave economists to make any and all unrealistic assumptions, provided only that their theories yielded verifiable implications. But even if one grants for the sake of argument that assumptions do not need to be descriptively accurate, Friedman failed to insist that they do need to be robust, that is, capable of being relaxed without fatal damage to the model they underpin. In consequence, the assumptions that economists typically make are reminiscent of the oldest anti-economist joke of them all: 'let us assume that we have a tin-opener' says the castaway economist on a desert island. Think of the following typical assumptions: perfectly infallible, utterly omniscient, infinitely long-lived identical consumers; zero transaction costs; complete markets for all time-stated claims for all conceivable contingent events; no trading of any kind at disequilibrium prices; infinitely rapid velocities of prices and quantities; no radical, incalculable uncertainty in real time but only probabilistically calculable risk in logical time; only linearly homogeneous production functions; no technical progress requiring embodied capital investment and so on. All these are not just unrealistic but also singularly unrobust assumptions, and yet they figure critically in leading economic theories – remove them and hardly a single neoclassical theorem is left standing!

THINKING POSITIVELY

These negative thoughts are uppermost in my mind every week on Tuesday, Thursday and Saturday, but on Monday, Wednesday and Friday I draw heart from the new work on experimental economics in the last ten to fifteen years that is beginning at long last to break the stranglehold of rational choice theory, particularly in its expected utility version. In a wide variety of experimental situations, economic agents have been shown to overweight out-of-pocket costs, to give full weight to sunk costs, to forego choices that might entail regret, to endow possessions with more than their market value, to precommit their choices, to act as if their time preference rates varied inversely and non-linearly with the length of time to be waited, to overreact to new information in forming expectations, to value the fairness of outcomes as relevant to the choices they make, in short, to behave again and again in clear violation of expected utility theory or indeed any generally agreed upon version of rationality (Hey, 1991; Loomes, 1991; Thaler, 1994; Loewenstein, 1999). Experimental economists have been stridently attacked for the artificial setting in which so many psychological experiments have been conducted – student subjects, small monetary incentives, lack of repeated experiments to permit learning and so on – but experimentalists have attempted to defuse these criticisms by designing new experiments to meet every objection that theorists have raised (Ball, 1998; Starmer, 1999; Tammi, 1999). Experimental economics shows every sign of being an empirically progressive research programme that has finally begun to study economic behaviour, not as it should be, but as it actually is.

For those who believe that no theory in economics is ever abandoned because of adverse empirical evidence, behold the almost-dead expected utility theory of Neumann–Morgenstern fame and, even more strikingly, the rapid demise in recent years of the efficient market hypothesis in organized security markets, which really ought to be ideal markets for displaying rational behaviour: stock markets are too volatile, react too violently to past price changes, do not vary purely randomly and hence are not exclusively populated by perfectly rational agents (Lo, 1997; Schwartz, 1998). After a century of disparaging every attempt to bring economics and psychology closer together (Rabin, 1998; Bowles, 1998), we may now be on the brink of a new era of establishing economics as a genuine behavioural science (Simon, 1997).[9]

MACROECONOMICS, NEW AND OLD

As I said, that is what I think on Monday, Wednesday and Friday. But then Saturday comes round and I start thinking of what has happened to macroeconomics. So far, after all, we have only touched on microeconomics but, as everybody knows, if we want to study the type of economics that is intimately concerned with policy questions we should be looking at macroeconomics. Unfortunately, macroeconomics in recent years has fallen prey to empty formalism in which the principal goal of theorizing seems to be analytical elegance and not a better grasp of practical problems and hence greater control of economic events. Classic monetarism of the Friedmanite variety more or less died out in the 1980s, largely as a result of financial deregulation, and was superseded by the new classical macroeconomics with its concept of 'rational expectations'. This came in two different versions, which served to disseminate the new doctrine to different audiences. The weak version of rational expectations simply asserts that rational economic agents always take full advantage of profit opportunities, thus forming price expectations on the basis of all available information. This has all the appearance of a reasonable assumption, but it tacitly implies continuous market-clearing, ruling out the very disequilibrium phenomena that macroeconomics was created to explain. The strong version of rational expectations, however, asserts even more controversially that the subjective expectations held by economic agents are the same as the mathematical expectations of the endogenous variables in the best probability model of the economy. What we have here is the traditional assumption of perfect information all over again, but allowing for the fact that uncertainty makes it impossible to predict each future event perfectly; however, we do have perfect foresight on average so that the mean expected error of rationally expected forecasts is always zero (Arrow, 1986: 210–12). With perfect stochastic foresight and competitive markets that clear continuously, even business cycles must be viewed as the unavoidable forecasting errors of rational economic agents in the face of exogenous shocks.

To say that this is an unrealistic assumption is to state the obvious. Were it so, it would follow that monetary and fiscal policies can only influence real variables such as output and employment momentarily because as soon as these policies are announced, they will be incorporated into price expectations by individuals, more or less instantaneously. This is the so-called 'policy-ineffectiveness' hypothesis, the principal anti-Keynesian conclusion of the new classical macroeconomics. If expectations were indeed rational in this strong sense, it would imply that the growth path of real output or employment is not correlated with *systematic* changes in the money supply, the size of budgetary deficits, the rate of interest, the exchange rate or policy pronouncements about any of these variables, because if they were so correlated, private agents would have incorporated these correlations into their pricing forecasts, in which case they would have appeared as purely nominal adjustments to wages and prices. But the evidence that output and employment are capable of being influenced by monetary and fiscal policy, that there is indeed a short-run trade-off between inflation and unemployment, is so overwhelming that even the leading spokesmen for the new classical macroeconomics, Robert Lucas and Thomas Sargent, seem to have retreated from the strong version of the doctrine of rational expectations (Blaug, 1992: 201–4).

The new classical macroeconomics has been increasingly supplanted by real business cycle theory. The notion that there is no short-run Phillips curve, that the long-run Phillips curve is vertical at 'the natural rate of unemployment', which is now a standard feature of non-Keynesian macroeconomics, suggests that business cycles can only be caused by random shocks to the economic system. Lucas and Sargent used to argue for monetary demand-side shocks but these have now given way in real business cycle theory to the idea of supply-side shocks in the form of random changes in technology. Real business cycle theory is, like new classical macroeconomics, an equilibrium explanation of the business cycle (which would at one time have been considered an oxymoron): agents are relentless maximizers and form expectations rationally; markets clear continuously; even momentary disequilibria are ruled out as methodologically inadmissible; and changes in technology or new marketing practices are purely random and hence are unpredictable. Mindful of the poor empirical track record of rational expectations, real business cycle theorists, such as Edward Prescott and Finn Kydland, have adopted a new method for confirming their theories. Instead of providing models that are capable of being tested by standard econometric methods, they subject them to 'calibration', that is, they quantify the parameters of a model on the basis of casual empiricism or a variety of unrelated econometric studies so chosen as to guarantee that the model mimics some particular feature of the historical data. The claim of real business cycle theorists is that their models do indeed track the important time series fairly closely and even depict widely accepted 'stylized facts' about the business cycle.

However, the hurdles that these models are expected to jump are not very high (Pack, 1994; Hoover, 1995). It remains doubtful whether supply-side shocks are large enough and, in particular, frequent enough to generate the observed cyclical fluctuations of output and prices; and of course it has to be the cyclical fluctuations of actual total output. Real business cycle theory has abandoned the century-old tradition of analysing business cycles as a series of short-term output fluctuations around a smoothly growing trend level. Assuming as it does that all markets clear instantaneously, it is driven to explain the cycle, not as the short-run fluctuations of a detrended time series, but as fluctuations in potential output itself due to shocks in technology. The no doubt ingenious story that real business cycle theorists tell is more convincing for booms than for slumps and, indeed, they have not so far provided a convincing account of why economies turn down not just occasionally but periodically. Real business cycle theorists remind one of what Dr Johnson said of a dog walking on its hind legs: 'It is not done well; but you are surprised to find it done at all'.

Note that nothing has really changed between Lucas–Sargent and Prescott–Kydland: any unemployment we observe is still voluntary unemployment because the labour market, like all other markets, is said to be always in equilibrium. Money is 'neutral' or, alternatively expressed, there is always a long-run vertical Phillips curve, and business cycles would never occur were it not for the fact that there are unpredictable shocks of one kind or another which, for a while, surprise us until we adjust to them. In Friedman's monetarism of the 1970s there was a negatively sloped short-run Phillips curve, so that stabilization policies did have real effect, even though they did not last beyond two to five years (Friedman's own estimates), but by the time we reach Prescott and Kydland even this thin reed has been broken.

It is amazing how thoroughly the idea of a 'natural rate of unemployment', that is, of a vertical Phillips curve, has caught on in modern macroeconomics, infecting even avowedly neo-Keynesian writers. Now, there is no denying that there is some rate of unemployment below which demand pressures on resources will cause prices to rise, so that there is something to the idea of an equilibrium rate of unemployment, a lower limit to the onset of inflation. But to draw it as a line instead of a thick band is a mistake, because we have no firm idea whether it is a 3–4 per cent or a 6–7 per cent unemployment rate and no warrant for believing that it is a well-defined, stable level of unemployment, capable of serving as a bedrock for anti-inflationary policies. Moreover, statistical estimates of the natural rate of unemployment on both sides of the Atlantic have shown that it trails behind past rates of unemployment, rising and falling as they do. In the now fashionable language of physics, the natural rate exhibits 'hysteresis': its level depends on the path taken to reach it because the longer unemployment lasts, the greater is the proportion of the unemployed who have become unemployable (Cross, 1995: Chs 2, 3). In short, the so-called natural rate of unemployment is an unstable range of rates as wide as 3–4 percentage points apart and it is subject to a steady rightward drift. How did such a vaguely specified idea ever come to be regarded as an article of faith?

What is really worrying about all the recent developments in anti-Keynesian macroeconomics is not so much the unpalatable implication of policy-effectiveness but rather the abandonment of anything like empirical testing of macroeconomic models. The tendency now is to resort to ever more esoteric techniques in the attempt to produce models that have no ambition other than to replicate actual time series. 'Calibration' as a method of choosing between macroeconomic theories is, to put it mildly, something of a fraud because it simply cannot fail to confirm just about every model. While complaints of the inconclusiveness of econometric testing abound in the literature (Summers, 1991; Ryan and Mullineux, 1997), the calibration methodology lacks even the discipline imposed by traditional econometric methods. Even the new 'endogenous growth theory', while ostensibly concerned to explain the failure of country growth rates to converge over time as predicted in the old exogenous growth theory of Solow, has virtually abandoned the goal of empirical verisimilitude, preferring instead to lean, and to lean heavily, on the plausibility of the notion that the interfirm externalities of R&D somehow account for the self-sustaining character of economic growth.[10]

All in all, I see a lot of analytical refinements in recent macroeconomics but very little sign of empirical progress, of a genuine growth of knowledge about business cycles, about policies designed to dampen the amplitude of cycles, about the causes of economic growth and the factors that bring about convergence in the growth rates of different countries – and I think that I know why.

THE DISEASE OF FORMALISM

For over fifty years, more or less since the end of World War II, economics has been in the grip of a disease that I call 'formalism' (Blaug, 1999), by which I mean giving absolute priority to the form of economic theories rather than their content. Open the pages of any of the leading journals, such as the

American Economic Review, the *Journal of Political Economy* or *Econometrica*, and we immediately encounter symptoms of that disease: every paper, irrespective of its subject matter, is set out in the form of a mathematical model whose solution is said to involve some quantitative or qualitative implications which then may be verified by means of published data. As such, this is unobjectionable, but what is objectionable is, first of all, that lavish care is devoted to the mathematical formulation of the model and very little care to the verification or testing of the model's implications – the theory to evidence ratio in these papers is typically very high – and secondly, that any problem that cannot be modelled mathematically is brushed aside as irrelevant or banished from economics proper. As a result, economics as a discipline has become increasingly directed towards solving intellectual puzzles that economists have themselves invented instead of addressing problems encountered in the real world; the possible existence of multi-market equilibrium is a perfect example of the former and the effect of minimum wage law on employment patterns (Freeman, 1997) is a perfect example of the latter.

Let me offer just one more striking example of formalism in modern economics, namely the so-called 'new economic geography'. Its leading advocate, Paul Krugman (1991, 1994, 1996), makes great play of the extent to which mathematical models incorporating the concepts of imperfect competition and increasing returns to scale have breathed new life into the old, defunct spatial economics of Thünen, Weber, Christaller and Lösch. His technique is to write down non-linear general equilibrium equations expressing various pull and push aspects of local advantage and then solving them by using Fourier expansions; different locational outcomes are then simulated by altering the key parameters in the equations. But apart from oblique references to illustrative cases, such as Silicon Valley or the Cambridge area in Massachusetts, Krugman provides no empirical applications of the new approach and it is difficult to see how the new economic geography illuminates the locational aspects of economic activity any better than the old economic geography. What we have here is a paradigm instance of considerable theoretical progress with little if any empirical progress (Martin, 1999: 80–82).

Economic hypotheses can be judged by their logical coherence, their generality, their fecundity, their explanatory power and, ultimately, their ability to predict. Why are economists concerned with predictability? Because it is the ultimate test of whether our theories are true and really capture the workings of the economic system independently of our wishes. That is not to say that we should instantly discard hypotheses that have not yet yielded empirically falsifiable implications, but simply that theories, such as GE theory, that are untestable even in principle should be regarded with deep suspicion. At the same time, economists have been unduly narrow in testing the falsifiable implications of theories in the sense that this is invariably taken to mean some statistical or econometric test. But what Friedman calls the 'natural experiments' of history are just as much a test of predictable patterns and trends in economic events as is regression analysis, the more so as the low power of available econometric techniques do not permit unambiguous interpretations of test results. Economists are loath to examine their assumptions by the use of survey techniques, by simply asking agents what they believe or what they do, because Friedman's methodology gave economists the false impression that nothing can ever be learned by such means (Hausman, 1987; but see Blinder, 1991). Perhaps the real trouble is our age-old belief, going back to Ricardo, that economics is essentially a deductive science, in which we infer economic behaviour on the basis of some assumptions about motivations and some stylized facts about prevailing institutions, suppressing even the temptation to ask whether these are descriptively realistic motivational assumptions and accurately chosen institutional facts. It is high time economists re-examined their longstanding antipathy to induction, to fact-grubbing, to the gathering of data before and not after we sit down to theorize. Yes, I know as a student of Popper that simple-minded induction is impossible, but there is much to be said in favour of Kaldor's (1972, 1989) insistence on starting with 'stylized facts' and inferring an economic model to account for these facts, whose assumptions and implications are then in turn subjected to further corroboration.

In a symposium on American academic culture, Solow (1997) noted that 'many observers in the other social sciences and in the wide, wide world, perceive that economics has become formalistic, abstract, negligent of the real world. The truth is, I think, that economics has become technical, which is quite different'. Yes, it *is* different, but what characterizes 'formalism' is that technicalities are prized as ends in themselves, so that the theories which do not lend themselves to technical treatment are set aside and with them the problems they address. Formalism is the *worship* of technique and that is what is wrong with it.

To be sure, formalism, particularly mathematical formalism, brings clarity and rigor to arguments but such merits are almost always purchased at a price. To be dedicated to formal modelling at whatever cost is to close the door on the analysis of certain problems that so far have not lent themselves, and may never lend themselves, to rigorous mathematical treatment, as for example technical progress, entrepreneurship and the long-term evolution of economic systems. If we are to come to grips with such problems, we may have to settle for a looser, fuzzier style of analysis than that afforded by mathematical modelling. Among the most hopeful, and I believe most fruitful, developments in economics is the recent growth of evolutionary economics in books like *An Evolutionary Theory of Economic Change* by Richard Nelson and Sidney

Winter (1982), *Exploring the Black Box* by Nathan Rosenberg (1994) and *Technical Change and Economic Theory* by Giovanni Dosi and others (1988).[11] The two primary intellectual progenitors of this evolutionary approach to the study of economic institutions and organizations are Herbert Simon and Joseph Schumpeter, as Nelson and Winter are the first to acknowledge, and 'bounded rationality' and 'innovations' are clearly the two leitmotifs of the recent flowering of evolutionary economics. The style of all these works is less mathematically rigorous, less enamoured of precise results, less inclined to thought-experiments employing logical deduction than we are accustomed to from reading mainstream economic literature. But they more than make up for that by their continuous reference to real-world issues and their continuous attention to empirical evidence to validate their findings.

NOTES

*   An earlier version of this paper, entitled 'The Disease of Formalism in Economics', appeared in *Lectiones Jenenses*, Max Planck Institut zur Erforschung von Wirtschaftssystemen, Jena, Germany, 1998.
1.   As Clower (1995a: 317) has argued, Arrow–Debreu GE theory is not really economics, but is just set-theoretic logic: 'In every branch of physical science, "equilibrium" refers to a "balance of forces", such as might be associated with an olive resting at the bottom of a cone-shaped martini glass; and the word misleadingly conjures up analogous images when it is used by economic theorists. Strictly speaking, however, the "equilibrium" that neo-Walrasian theory shows to exist are more correctly called *solutions* to a system of implicitly-defined algebraic equations, so understood, the important achievements of neo-walrasian general equilibrium theory lose much of their apparent lustre'. Walrasian GE theory has no empirical content, but computable GE models are capable of providing numerical solutions to specific questions, such as the effect of a given change to the tax system (see, for example, Shoven and Whalley, 1992). However, it is an open question as to whether the costly construction of such elaborate computable GE models actually gives a more accurate answer than much simpler partial equilibrium models; in any case, no systematic comparisons along these lines has so far been carried out.
2.   It is ironic that Michael Porter's best-selling *Competitive Strategy* (1980) brought back the old classical concept of competition, not as a market structure, but as a strategy of rivalry. It took a book aimed at managers to bring back the process conception of competition and to remind us that this is how businessmen have always thought of competition.
3.   Hahn (1994: 252) produces the misleading defence, 'I do hold the view that if one formerly keeps in mind that one is a good many stages removed from actual economies, the perfect competition hypothesis has been fruitful in answering *the purely intellectual* question – can an economy in which all decisions are taken by self-regarding agents be orderly with no greater array of information signals than prices?' (my italics). To which, of course, the answer is 'no', even posed as a purely intellectual question.
4.   In that respect it differs from the Coase theorem, another abstract mathematical theorem, which can however be converted into an operational tendency statement. The proposition that all parties to a transaction that generates externalities will enter into Pareto-superior voluntary agreements holds only if the transaction costs of negotiating, specifying and monitoring the enforcement of contracts are zero. But since Coase himself insists that transaction costs never can be zero in the real world, it appears that the Coase theorem, like the concept of perfect competition, lacks real-world applicability. But transaction costs can be quantified, and when transaction costs are positive but small, parties will bargain to efficient

results; it is in this guise that the Coase theorem has proliferated through law and economics (Medema, 1999).

5. I am only echoing what has been said so much better by Robert Clower (1995a, 1995b). Walker (1999: 438) has rightly observed, 'We should not continue to accept economic models as logically valid if the results that they are alleged to have are not generated by institutions, procedures, technologies, rules, and other structural and behavioural under-pinnings in the model'. Walras ignored this methodological dictum in his later work and so do most modern GE theorists.

6. See Howitt (1997) for the crippling influence of general equilibrium theory on the development of Keynesian economics.

7. Even Ariel Rubinstein (1995), in a tribute to John Nash, 'the master of economic modelling', denies that the Nash bargaining solution, the standard game-theoretic tool in modelling non-cooperative interactions among transactors, is a good predictor of bargaining in real markets. And he adds insult to injury by claiming that all economists employing game theory know this perfectly well.

8. A comparison between an old-style text like Scherer and Ross (1990) and a new-style text like Tirole (1988) says it all: there is nothing of substance in the latter that is not also in the former and indeed there is much less substance in the latter than in the former. For a similar judgement, see Fisher (1989). On a more positive note, there is the beginning of a literature on the design of special markets, such as the college admission problem and auctions of the radio spectrum, using game theory (Roth, 1999).

9. Apropos of our distinction between the end-state and process conception of competition, consider how one prominent experimental economist describes the future agenda of experimental economics: 'We should shift the focus away from comparative statics analysis based on assumptions that some equilibrium exists and that (somehow) movements in the direction of that equilibrium will occur, and look instead at the process of reaction and adjustment in a world that can never really be expected to attain equilibrium. Moreover, it is suggested that less emphasis should be given to optimal strategies which, as experiments show, are difficult enough for agents to generate even under highly favourable conditions, and that more attention should be given to the heuristics, rules of thumb and approximations which agents fall back on to deal with the environment and the problems presented to them' (Loomes, 1991: 610).

10. As Solow (1991: 412) has trenchantly remarked; 'If the goal of growth theory is the elaboration of a complete preferred model ready for formal econometric application to observed time series, as many economists seem to believe, then the new growth theory falls well short. One is struck by the proliferation of special assumptions about technology, about the nature of research activity, about the formation and use of human capital, about market structure, about family structure, and about intertemporal preferences. Most of these particular assumptions have been chosen for convenience, because they make difficult analytic problems more transparent. There is no reason to assume that they are descriptively valid, or that their implications have significant robustness against equally plausible variations in assumptions'.

11. See also Hodgson (1985, 1993), Vromen (1995), Lydall (1998) and the symposium on technical change in *Economic Journal*, 107, September 1997.

REFERENCES

Arrow, K.J. (1986), 'Rationality of self and others in an economic system', in R.M. Hogarth and M.W. Reder (eds), *Rational Choice*, Chicago: University of Chicago Press.

Arrow, K.J. and G. Debreu (1954), 'Existence of an equilibrium for a competitive economy', *Econometrica*, 22(3), July: 265–90.

Backhouse, R.E. (1997), *Truth and Progress in Economic Knowledge*, Cheltenham: Edward Elgar.

Ball, S.B. (1998), 'Research, technology and practice in experimental economics: a progress report and review', *Southern Economic Journal*, 64(3): 772–9.

Blaug, M. (1992), *The Methodology of Economics*, 2nd edition, Cambridge: Cambridge University Press.

Blaug, M. (1994), 'Why I am not a constructivist: confessions of an unrepentant Popperian', in R.E. Backhouse (ed.), *New Directions in Economic Method*, London: Routledge.

Blaug, M. (1997), 'Competition as an end-state and competition as a process', in B.C. Eaton and R.G. Harris (eds), *Trade, Technology and Economics*, Cheltenham: Edward Elgar.

Blaug, M. (1999), 'The disease of formalism, or what happened to neoclassical economics after the war', in R. Backhouse and J. Creedy (eds), *From Classical Economics to the Theory of the Firm*, Cheltenham: Edward Elgar: 257–80.

Blinder, A.S. (1991), 'Why are prices sticky? Preliminary results from an interview study', *American Economic Review*, 81(2), May: 80–96.

Boettke, P.J. and D.L. Prychetko (1994), *The Market Process: Essays in Contemporary Austrian Economics*, Cheltenham: Edward Elgar.

Bowles, S. (1998), 'Endogenous preferences: the cultural consequences of markets and other economic institutions', *Journal of Economic Literature*, 36(1), March: 75–111.

Clower, R.W. (1995a), 'Axiomatics in economics', *Southern Economic Journal*, 62(2), October: 307–19.

Clower, R.W. (1995b), 'Economics as an inductive science', in R.W. Clower, *Economic Doctrines and Method: Selected Papers of R.W. Clower*, Cheltenham: Edward Elgar.

Cross, R. (ed.) (1995), *The Natural Rate of Unemployment: Reflections on 25 Years of the Hypothesis*, Cambridge: Cambridge University Press.

Debreu, G. (1959), *Theory of Value. An Axiomatic Analysis and the Theory of Markets*, Cheltenham: Edward Elgar.

de Vroey, M. (1999), 'Equilibrium and disequilibrium in economic theory', *Economics and Philosophy*, 15(2), October: 161–85.

Fisher, F. (1989), 'Games economists play: a noncooperative view', *Rand Journal of Economics*, 20(1), Spring: 113–24.

Freeman, R.B. (1997), 'In honor of David Card: winner of the John Bates Clark model', *Journal of Economic Perspectives*, 11(2), Spring: 161–78.

Gibbons, R. (1997), 'An introduction to applicable game theory', *Journal of Economic Perspectives*, 7(4), Fall: 127–49.

Hahn, F. (1994), 'An intellectual retrospect', *Banco Nazionale Lavoro Quarterly Review*, 190, September: 245–58.

Hausman, D. (1987), 'Theory appraisal in neoclassical economics', *Journal of Economic Methodology*, 4(2), December: 289–96.

Hey, J.D. (1991), 'Uncertainty in economics', in D. Greenaway, M. Bleaney and I. Stewart (eds), *Companion to Contemporary Economics*, London: Routledge: 252–73.

Hodgson, G.M. (1985), *Economics and Institutions: A Manifesto for a Modern Institutional Economics*, Cambridge, UK: Polity Press.

Hodgson, G.M. (1993), *Economics and Evolution: Bringing Life Back into Economics*, Cambridge, UK: Polity Press.

Hoover, K.D. (1995), 'Facts and artifacts: calibration and the empirical assessment of real business-cycle models', *Oxford Economic Papers*, 47(1): 24–44.

Howitt, P. (1997), 'Expectations and uncertainty in contemporary Keynesian models', in G.C. Harcourt and P.A. Riach (eds), *Second Edition of the General Theory*, Volume I, London: Routledge: 238–60.

Ingrao, B. and G. Israel (1990), *The Invisible Hand: Economic Equilibrium in the History of Science*, Cambridge, MA: MIT Press.

Kaldor, N. (1972), 'The irrelevance of equilibrium economics', *Economic Journal*, 82(4): 1237–55.

Kaldor, N. (1989), *Economics without Equilibrium*, Cardiff: University College Cardiff Press.

Kasper, W. and M.E. Streit (1999), *Institutional Economics, Social Order and Public Policy*, Cheltenham: Edward Elgar.

Keuzenkamp, H.A. (2000), *Probability, Econometrics and Truth: A Treatise on the Foundation of Economic Inference*, Cambridge: Cambridge University Press.

Krugman, P. (1991), *Geography and Trade*, Cambridge, MA: MIT Press.

Krugman, P. (1994), *Peddling Prosperity*, New York: W.W. Norton.

Krugman, P. (1996), *The Self-organizing Economy*, Oxford: Basil Blackwell.

Lipsey, R.G. (1997), 'Can the market economy survive?', in *Micro-economics, Growth and Political Economy: Essays by Richard G. Lipsey*, Vol. I. Cheltenham: Edward Elgar: 367–401.

Lo, A.W. (1997), 'Introduction', *Market Efficiency: Stock Market Behaviour in Theory and Practice*, Vol. 1, Cheltenham: Edward Elgar.

Loewenstein, G. (1999), 'Because it is there: the challenge of mountaineering . . . for utility theory', *Kyklos*, 52, 3: 315–44.

Loomes, G. (1991), 'Experimental methods in economics', in D. Greenaway, M. Bleaney and I. Stewart (eds), *Companion to Contemporary Economics*, London: Routledge: 593–613.

Lydall, H.F. (1998), *A Critique of Orthodox Economics: An Alternative Model*, London: Macmillan.

Machovec, F.M. (1995), *Perfect Competition and the Transformation of Economics*, London: Routledge.

Martin, R. (1999), 'The new "Geographical Turn" in economics: some critical reflections', *Cambridge Journal of Economics*, 23: 65–91.

Mayer, T. (1999), 'The domain of hypotheses and the realism of assumptions', *Journal of Economic Methodology*, 6(3), 319–30.

McCloskey, D.N. (1985), *The Rhetoric of Economics*, Madison, WI: University of Wisconsin Press.

Medema, S.G. (1999), 'Legal fiction: the place of the Coase theorem in law and economics', *Economics and Philosophy*, 15(2), October: 209–33.

Murrell, P. (1991), 'Can neoclassical economics underpin the reform of centrally planned economies?', *Journal of Economic Perspectives*, 2(4), Fall: 159–64.

Pack, H. (1994), 'Endogenous growth theory: intellectual appeal and empirical shortcomings', *Journal of Economic Perspectives*, 9(1), Winter: 55–72.

Porter, M.E. (1980), *Competitive Strategy*, New York: The Free Press.

Rabin, M. (1998), 'Psychology and economics', *Journal of Economic Literature*, 36(1), March: 11–46.

Rosen, S. (1997), 'Austrian and neoclassical economics: any gain from trade?', *Journal of Economic Perspectives*, 11(4), Fall: 139–52.

Roth, A.E. (1999), 'The redesign of the matching market for American physicians:

some engineering aspects of economic design', *American Economic Review*, 89(4), September: 748–80.

Rubinstein, A. (1995), 'John Nash: the master of economic modelling', *Scandinavian Journal of Economics*, 97(1): 9–13.

Ryan, C. and A.W. Mullineux (1997), 'The ups and downs of modern business cycle theory', in B. Snowdon and H.R. Vane (eds), *Reflections on the Development of Modern Macroeconomics*, Cheltenham: Edward Elgar: 128–57.

Scherer, F.M., and D. Ross (1990), *Industrial Market Structure and Economic Performance*, 3rd edition, Boston: Houghton Mifflin.

Schumpeter, J.A. (1942), *Capitalism, Socialism and Democracy*, 2nd edition, New York: Harper.

Schumpeter, J.A. (1954), *The History of Economic Analysis*, Oxford: Oxford University Press.

Schwartz, H. (1998), *Rationality Gone Awry? Decision-making Inconsistent with Economic and Financial Theory*, Westport, CO: Praeger.

Shoven, J.B. and J. Whalley (1992), *Applying General Equilibrium*, Cambridge, Cambridge University Press.

Simon, H. (1997), *An Empirically based Microeconomics*, New York: Cambridge University Press.

Solow, R.M. (1997), 'Growth theory', in D. Greenaway, M. Bleaney and I. Stewart (eds), *Companion to Contemporary Economic Thought*, London: Routledge: 393–415.

Solow, R.M. (1997), 'How did economics get that way and what way did it get?', *Daedalus*, Winter: 39–57.

Sraffa, P. (1960), *Production of Commodities by Means of Commodities*, Cambridge: Cambridge University Press.

Starmer, C. (1999), 'Experiments in economics: should we trust the dismal scientists in white coats', *Journal of Economic Methodology*, 6(1): 1–30.

Summers, L.H. (1991), 'The scientific illusion in empirical macroeconomics', *Scandinavian Journal of Economics*, 93(2): 129–48.

Tammi, T. (1999), 'Incentives and preference reversals: escape moves and community experimental economics', *Journal of Economic Methodology*, 6(3): 351–80.

Thaler, R.H. (1994), *Quasi Rational Economics*, New York: Russell Sage Foundation.

Tirole, J. (1988), *The Theory of Industrial Organisation*, Cambridge, MA: MIT Press.

Vromen, J.J. (1995), *Economic Evolution: An Enquiry into the Foundations of the New Institutional Economics*, London: Routledge.

Walker, D.A. (1996), *Walras's Market Models*, Cambridge: Cambridge University Press.

Walker, D.A. (1999), 'Some comments on Léon Walras's health and productivity', *Journal of the History of Economic Thought*, 21(4): 437–48.

PART II

Progress in the History of Ideas:
Alternative Approaches

3. On applying Foucauldian methods to the history of economic thought

Klaus Hamberger*

INTRODUCTION

Despite the crucial position of economics in Michel Foucault's major work, *The Order of Things* (*Les Mots et les Choses*, 1966), his achievements as an historian and philosopher of science have largely been neglected by historians of economic thought. As compared with the reception of Foucauldian ideas by political science, sociology, medicine and so on, Foucault's impact on economics is still negligible; and after all, Foucault himself left behind the subject of economics when he passed from the field of epistemology into the arena of political philosophy (thereby also dissolving his last bonds to structuralism). Unfortunately, the scientific community willingly joined him in dropping his earlier issues, and thus a whole treasure of questions sank back into the dark before they could prove their methodological power and philosophical fertility. This was a missed opportunity not only for the history of economic thought but also for the general philosophy of science, which has seldom or never endeavoured to treat the 'young' and still 'impure' science of economics not only as a legitimate object of, but even as a model for, epistemological work.

The history of economic thought still comprises an extraordinary variety of instruments, styles and genres. We find rational reconstructions as well as sociological investigations, biographical anecdotes and literary statistics, criticisms of ideology and metaphysics of history. This methodological variety, which sometimes might seem close to a complete lack of method, may partly be due to the fact that, on the one hand, the history of economic thought is for the most part still done not by historians but by economists, who naturally tend to take their own work as a point of reference, while on the other hand, economics has always been so closely connected with real economic development that it might seem futile to treat it through purely cognitive means.

This profound ambiguity between the 'internal' and the 'external' treatment of the history of economic ideas represents a typical example of that general antinomy in the history of ideas to which Foucauldian 'archeology' attempted a new solution. For the empirical treatment of intellectual systems there seem to be only two alternatives – either to allow purely cognitive attributes (such as consistency, generality and robustness) to unfold themselves in historical time, or to regard scientific discourse as a mirror of general political, social or cultural developments. So the central antinomy of the history of thought apparently leaves only the alternatives either to start with its objects (so that it becomes simply the retrospective appendix of the respective science), or to start with its subjects (so that it becomes a sub-discipline of social history or biography). In neither case, however, does it deal with *thought* itself.

If, thus, a 'historical epistemology' is possible which is reduced neither to historical analysis aided by epistemological reflection, nor to epistemological reflection somehow furnished with historic material – nor (what is probably the greatest peril) to a hybrid mixture of epistemology and history – this first of all means to conceive thought, to conceive the *globus intellectualis*, as a genuine object in its own right.[1] That does not imply that the empirical structures of knowledge have nothing to do with the patterns of culture and society or with the laws of discursive logic; but in order to be compared or contrasted with these quite different symbolic orders, the epistemic systems must first be acknowledged as a separate and autonomous object of analysis. Just as constructional styles in architecture cannot simply be 'derived' from the elementary laws of statics nor from the various functions of the building, the genuine structure of thought is neither the transparent revelation of the logical nature of scientific problems nor the superficial veil of hidden interests. Thus, while 'abstracting' from the author, the oevre, the institutional background and so forth, the empirical science of thought at the same time has to develop its own categories, its own principles, and thus to constitute its own system of objectivity.

In this chapter, I attempt a critical reassessment of this approach as applied to the history of economic thought. In doing so, I shall take a somewhat 'structuralist' point of view, relating the concept of *episteme* closely to the method of structural comparison and the idea of epistemological transformations. Against this background, I shall test the Foucauldian method both by examining its actual results (as presented in *Les Mots et les Choses*) and by confronting them with what it could yield if applied to the study of that historical shift which, despite the prominence attached to it by all conventional histories of economic thought, has been almost entirely left in the dark by Foucault: namely the so-called 'marginal revolution' of the 1870s. It has always seemed puzzling that Foucault did not even downplay, but simply disregarded, this notorious 'event'; and in a way, this disregard could even be interpreted as a kind of scientific 'repression' (in the psychoanalytic sense of the word). In fact, a thorough 'Foucauldian' analysis of the Jevonian turn would ultimately lead to a fundamental challenge of Foucault 's account of the

Ricardian transformation: once having raised the dichotomy of 'labour' and 'utility' to the level of an 'epistemological break', Foucault of course would not have been able to describe the 'marginal revolution' as a mere inversion of terms within an unchanged 'epistemic' structure.

The purpose of this paper is therefore not only to address a remarkable gap in Foucault's treatment of economics, but also to point at an important correction which seems to me crucial for any useful application of Foucauldian methods to our science, namely that the labour–utility dichotomy, just like all other dichotomies of contents of thought (as distinguished from modes of thought), can be grasped in its proper value only if we conceive of it as an opposition *within*, and not *between*, epistemic formations. In a way, this ahistorical revaluation of an entirely modern dichotomy seems closely connected with Foucault's belief in a unique 'anthropological' turn of science at the beginning of the nineteenth century. Being the result of an overt deviation from his own methodological principles, however, it paradoxically just reinforces the importance of Foucault's original approach.

OUTLINES OF FOUCAULDIAN METHODOLOGY

Foucault has repeatedly compared his work with the structural analysis of myth as it had been elaborated by Dumézil and Lévi-Strauss.[2] Against this background, his own 'archeological' study of science and ideas could be interpreted as just another ambitious attempt towards a comparative anatomy of symbolic systems.[3] In fact, the system-character of the respective field of positivity acts as the main regulative idea for both kinds of projects, if we define the relevant concept of 'system' by two decisive features emphasized by both Lévi-Strauss and Foucault: first, that no element can be changed without changing all the others; and second, that every system can be transformed into a number of other systems by a group of transformations, which in turn allows one to isolate some invariant structure relative to the whole group.[4]

Methodologically, this approach implies a particular stress on comparative analysis, provided that 'comparison' is not understood as a search for some common features or casual analogies, but as a reciprocal transformation of entire systems, where ideally every element of the one side is substituted for an element of the other side (leaving a certain pattern of relations invariant), and which, most important, must be identically applicable in a meaningful way to all other systems of a given totality. This *transformational* point of view also prevents us from sticking to the progressive development of any isolated feature (for example, the explanation of value) separated from the corresponding transformations of those other parts of the system which happen to fall outside our momentary interest. Conversely, the same point of view directs our attention to those long-term structures which may reveal fundamental correspondences between the most distant and different scientific positions, and even more fundamental differences between apparently similar traditions or schools.

In this respect, the historian's outlook would appear as the precise analogon of the ethnographer's point of view, and the history of scientific discourse would, in the same way as the comparative study of myth, start by recognizing methodologically the radical 'foreignness' of its object with respect to the researcher's own cultural or scientific system. Just as Lévi-Strauss claimed to study myth in its own right, without reducing it to any pre-scientific mode of explaining nature, Foucault calls for accepting past sciences as complete and connected systems in their own time, instead of reducing them to the dispersed, pristine beginnings of our present sciences (a claim of particular import for the history of economic thought).[5]

So far, Foucault's methodology is in fundamental agreement with traditional structuralist premises.[6] His genuine innovation with respect to this background is the thesis of *discontinuity* and his corresponding adoption of the Bachelardian concept of 'epistemological breaks'. For Foucault, the totality of transformations that can be defined on the set of intellectual systems falls into two radically different classes: on the one hand, those transformations which underly the synchronic comparison of discourses across authors, schools and disciplines, leaving precisely those structural features invariant which constitute an *episteme*; on the other hand, those 'epistemological breaks' which involve a complete reorganization not so much of the elements, but of the basic structure itself, and give to the history of thought the characteristic shape of a discontinuous succession of relatively stable, immobile and durable formations. As is well known, Foucault has distinguished three such formations: the Renaissance, the so-called 'classical' age,[7] and modernity (beginning with the nineteenth century). With respect to economics, the last 'epistemological break', according to Foucault, would run between Turgot and Ricardo (with the work of Smith playing a transitional role).

Of course, the epistemic 'affiliation' of any particular piece of discourse cannot be assessed by checking off a list of selected 'characteristics'. This follows almost trivially from the very nature of the transformation method (which is just another name for the method of structural analysis): there is simply no 'characteristic' which could not be changed without altering the basic structure, provided that all the other elements of this structure are also changed in a systematic manner. As Foucault has repeatedly stressed, the *episteme* is something entirely different from any 'spirit of the age' which could be characterized by a sample of leading ideas, scientific ideals or methodological habits. The *episteme* does not denote a number of common traces abstracted (more or less arbitrarily) from the various systems of thought; it rather denotes their immanent 'principle of order',[8] determining both the formal architecture of a given system and the peculiar kind of synthesis which holds the whole edifice together.

Roughly speaking, Foucault describes the successive types of structure respectively as a network of 'similitudes' (for the Renaissance), a table of identities and differences (for the classical age), and finally as a field of organized wholes (for the nineteenth century). Each structural type involves a separate principle for the selection of the basic elements of the structure (viz. the signs of hidden affinities, the primary elements of the natural combinatoric, or the constituent relations of organized systems). In the Renaissance, each significant similarity is revealed by another similarity (so that the knowledge of the universe is just the limit of an infinite series of references); classical thought attempts to deduce the criteria of distinction from the very nature of things (so that the progress of knowledge consists in the reconstruction of their natural order at the level of representations); and for modern thought, the comparison of structures is guided by the assessment of their original functions (which typically consist in the maintenance of some essentially finite process). In a nutshell, we thus have three successive *modes of construction* (iteration of similarity patterns, combination of primary elements, transformation of organic structures) and three corresponding *types of relation* (reference, representation, function).[9] As it is quite useless to talk about these structural patterns at the abstract level, we shall instead directly proceed to investigate their particular import in the field of economic thought. In doing so, we should however keep in mind that the above-mentioned patterns were not abstracted from the isolated corpus of economic texts, but generated by the comparative analysis of three different scientific fields (those which should eventually turn into modern economics, linguistics and biology). The first two parts of the following section are chiefly a summary of Foucault's results.

ARCHEOLOGY IN THE FIELD OF ECONOMICS

Money and Value in Renaissance Thought

Up to the sixteenth century, quantitative relations (such as value) had been conceived as a special (and indeed the most important) sort of 'similitude'. Proportions were just another kind of analogy, and nothing could reveal a hidden sympathy more purely to men's eyes than numeric equality. The deep analogy between the manifold desires growing in the hearts of men and the precious metals growing in the depths of the earth, as manifestly revealed in man's unsurpassable desire for gold and silver, in turn pointed to a precise numerical correspondence between all the hidden pieces of gold and the entirety of future wants, and this correspondence served as a rationale for the actual process of exchange.[10] This process of course was inseparable from the totality of physiological, psychological and physical processes that made up the cosmos of experience: the relationship between human desires and precious metals had its counterpart in the relationship between the products of nature and the stars of the sky; economic exchange itself was opposed to the astral influences (the paradigm of all causation) just as inside and depth was opposed to surface and height, as desire was opposed to knowledge, as Saturn was opposed to the sun. The relations between money, wants and commodities were conceived of as integral parts of a complex system of references and signatures. To understand an economic process did not mean to explain it, but to *read* it correctly: just like the physicians or the astrologists, the merchants too were primarily seers within their limited field of vision.[11]

The Classical 'Analysis of Riches'

In the seventeenth and eighteenth centuries, this art of infinite translation was replaced as a ruling principle by the new technique of analysing each complex phenomenon according to its primary elements. Just as the numerous classification systems of 'natural history' sought to reduce the vast diversity of the animal, vegetable and mineral kingdoms to combinations of a few elementary qualities, the classical 'analysis of riches' endeavoured to resolve the exchangable values of all commodities into their elementary arithmetic components. This procedure presupposed the representation of all values by some universal standard (such as money) – meaning not only an intellectual process, but the real act of exchange. Thus represented, things turned into values, and at the same time ceased to be riches in the genuine sense of a physical surplus disposable to satisfy the want of some other person, or, so to speak, the 'surplus' of this other person's mental representation over what is actually present.[12] The act of exchange was conceived precisely as the passage from presentation to representation – but since this passage had to be mediated by money (a thing exluded from the common realm of riches in order to represent them all), the table of relative values could always be regarded from two sides, being composed either of products of nature or of objects of desire. As a result, the classical 'analysis of riches' exhibits two independent but complementary modes of construction (quite similar to the alternative modes of classification by structure or by function in classical natural history, where the representational role of the currency was accomplished by the nomenclature).

One of the most challenging features of this reconstruction of a coherent 'analysis of riches' at the bottom of all the dispersed discourses on money, interest, trade and so on up to the end of the eighteenth century, is that it renders each of the three main 'traditions' conventionally isolated for that time span – mercantilism, utilitarianism and physiocracy – conceivable as separate aspects of one integrated system. First, the 'mercantilistic' discourse concentrates on the representational role of money. As it is only the view to exchange which turns mere surplus into wealth, any improvement or deterioration in the medium of exchange will necessarily affect the scale of manufacture, the division of labour and the progress of the arts – hence the famous economic controversies as to whether the representational power of money could be enhanced by expanding its quantity or rather would suffer from the slightest alteration of the standard; whether the function of representation was best accomplished by the precious metals or rather by paper credit; whether the specie flow should be adjusted to, or rather was regulated by, the various cycles of agriculture, population and foreign trade, and so on. In all these discussions, the circulating medium of exchange is addressed in the same role as the general medium of discourse in the contemporary debates on natural language: what is at stake is the internal cohesion and regularity of the system of representations, which manifests itself both in the cognition of nature and in the wealth of nations.[13]

From the same point of view, the two seemingly contrary systems of the 'utilitarians' and the 'physiocrats', respectively, can be regarded as two complementary modes of constructing a 'table' of values. As Foucault insinuates, they could almost be conceived of as two separate disciplines, just as the contemporary study of language ('general grammar') fell into the analysis of sentences (which meant to *relate* nouns to the verb) and the analysis of names (which meant to *resolve* nouns into their primitive roots).[14] Probably the analogy can even be expanded if we take into account that the utilitarian analysis of value *relates* it to the subjective need of the individual, whereas physiocratic analysis *resolves* it into its elementary components (such as wages, transport costs and so on, and finally rent as a residual). Each type of analysis presupposes the opposite relationship between the origin of value and the process of exchange: The utilitarian analysis of *relations* puts the pattern of values at the bottom of the actual process of exchange, which only adjusts the distribution of riches to the distribution of wants and thus *generates* a real surplus value to be divided between both parties.[15] By way of contrast, the physiocratic analysis of *components* calculates value itself as the cumulative result of a series of partial exchanges (of the product of nature for the services of labour, transport and so on), so that only the remaining part of the original product which *escapes* the exchange process constitutes a real surplus, whereas exchange itself by definition is incapable of yielding a gain.[16]

Against this background, we can now proceed to reassess Foucault's portrayal of the epistemological transformation associated with the emergence of political economy at the beginning of the nineteenth century.

The Ricardian Break

Any assessment of the Ricardian turn will depend crucially on the interpretation of Ricardo's fundamental theorem that value depends on the quantity of labour required for the production of the respective commodity, and *not* on the quantity of commodities given in exchange for that labour.[17] As the positive part of this assertion indicates, the characteristic of a commodity (at least as an object of economic analysis) is no longer that it can be exchanged (via the mediation of money), but that it has to be produced. Labour, instead of money, has taken the role of establishing the belonging of goods to the system of commodities. This, however, does not imply that labour has equally taken the role of a common measure – rather, the problem of finding an invariant measure of value has ceased to coincide with the problem of founding the system of relative values. Whether or not labour might be designated that special commodity which is separated from all the others in order to represent them – as long as it is taken as a commodity, it remains subject to just the same laws as any other element of the system; and this means in the first instance that it cannot itself determine the relations between these elements.

The latter point already indicates the decisive change: it is not the *element* which has to be excluded from the system in order to found its unity, but the *relation* which it maintains with all the elements of the system (including itself). Labour determines the value of commodities by *producing* them, not by *exchanging* for them; it regulates exchange without mediating it; it is the common *source* of values and not their common *sign*. And this again cannot mean that one of the various components of value should rise to the rank of a 'determinant' factor (as the negative part of the opening theorem makes clear): a common rise in wages would not result in a common rise in prices, but simply in a fall of profits. Contrary to its role in Adam Smith's system, labour within the Ricardian context acts neither as a measure nor as a component of value, but as its direct correlative (which Marx will even call its 'substance'). For the first time, the relation of production is thus clearly separated from the relation of exchange. Throughout the eighteenth century (including Turgot and Smith), labour had been just another sort of expense.[18] With Ricardo, the reduction of values to the natural values of the primary factors is replaced by tracing them back to the physical quantities of labour inputs, which are not meant to be measured by wages, but to be measures of production – of that entirely new economic relation which at once transcends, precedes and structures the circular process of exchange.[19]

Taken by itself, this is of course not a peculiarly Foucauldian insight.[20] The important point is whether this single (albeit momentous) modification can be regarded as an instance of a more fundamental structural break. That means, first, whether the transformation of labour from a *component* into a *source* of value (and the corresponding replacement of the *measure* of value as keystone of the system) can serve as a paradigm for a change in the type of that fundamental relation which ties the whole system together. In our short sketch of the 'epistemological breaks', we have specified this change for the early nineteenth century as a turn from the representational to the functional type. Now Foucault has never left any doubt that he regarded Ricardo's 'labour' as a perfect analogon of Cuvier's 'life'; and his whole concept of 'finiteness' rests not for the least part on the alleged analogy of these two versions of man's struggle against death. However, contrary to his minute analysis of Cuvier's turn from classical taxinomy (based on the combination of elementary characteristics) to the new paradigm of 'organization' (based on the isomorphy of entire structures), Foucault does not indicate any corresponding change in the mode of theoretical construction which, by analogy, should turn the analysis of value *components* into a comparison of the inner *structures* of values. Now such a shift indeed *can* be traced in Ricardo, and the overt analogies to Cuvier's concept of organization even become explicit as soon as we proceed to Marx – all the more astonishing it is that Foucault does not say a word about the undisputed master concept of nineteenth-century economics: capital.

After all, Ricardo has not merely grounded the system of values in a corresponding system of labour quantities. These quantities are essentially dated, so that the value of each finished product exhibits a temporal deep structure which also governs its different reactions to changes in wages or profit rates. Thus the production relation determines not so much the relative values of commodities, but rather the internal value architecture of capital. Precisely Ricardo's (as it seemed to him) minor 'modification' of the law of value by the difference in the degree of durability of capital indicates the fundamental change which has involved the very object of economic inquiry: what economics deals with is no longer the characteristic 'table' underlying the circulation of commodities within and between nations, but the mutual communication of historically grown commodity systems, some of them old and archaic, others young and highly differentiated, but each of them enlivened by the ongoing activity of labour. It was left to Marx to emphasize the manifold similarities between real living organisms and those structured value totalities (which he bluntly regarded as 'monsters').[21] Now should we regard this additional evidence as giving support to Foucault's interpretation that economics has found its new principle, off the 'play of representations', in 'that perilous region where life is confronted with death', and that it thus ultimately refers to 'that order of rather ambiguous considerations which may be called anthropological'?[22]

THE 'ANTHROPOLOGICAL' CONSTITUTION OF MODERN ECONOMICS

Let us first note that Foucault substantiates this thesis by emphasizing the 'perpetual and fundamental situation of scarcity'[23] which he finds expressed in the laws of diminishing agricultural returns and accelerating population growth. As is well known, the combination of these laws is crucial for Ricardo's assumption of constant real wages, increasing labour costs and the corresponding fall in the profit rate. But already the extremely long-run perspective of these considerations makes it perfectly clear that the true *homo oeconomicus* thus portrayed appears not as a human being haunted by the constant 'imminence of death',[24] but as a mere agent of capital who struggles not so much for life but for accumulation. As Marx has emphasized (not least by the twofold use he makes of the biological term 'metabolism'),[25] the principle which governs the historical development of capital structures is not the labour process, but precisely its reverse: the exploitation process, which, contrary to the former, is definitely not a 'nature-imposed condition of human existence'.[26] The economic counterpart of the biological individual is not labouring *man*, but the (private or national) *capital* which constantly adjusts its 'organic' structure to its changing economic, technological and geographical conditions of existence – precisely this analogy eventually accounts for the exhaustive use of biological metaphors in nineteenth-century economics.[27]

So the dismal picture of human life as a continuous struggle against starving, dominant as it may be, does not give evidence of any fundamental change in the structure of economic theory itself. But after all, that structural transformation of economics, biology and linguistics which Foucault characterized as an 'anthropologization' of these sciences has virtually nothing to do with the attention paid to 'man' as an *empirical* object of investigation – on the contrary, at the turn of the nineteenth century man definitely ceases to count for more than a particular animal, a particular factor of production, or a particular medium of communication. If the emergence of the new *episteme* entails the 'appearance of man' in the pivot of sciences which hitherto had done well without any peculiar reference to human nature, this is not because any special role is assigned to human labour, human life and human language, but because labour, life and language come to be acknowledged as conditions and constraints of human *thought*.

Until the end of the eighteenth century, the object of the sciences thus involved had formed part of the general problem to reconstruct a natural *order* (of species, of riches, of names). These orders were basically taxonomies, and as such rested crucially on a representational theory of discourse.[28] With the nineteenth century, precisely the realm of representations, which the sciences had hitherto conceived of as a fundamental logical domain (just as the realm of numbers) independent of any empirical consciousness, now came to be regarded as a mere supplementary subsystem (and representation itself as only a partial function) of a finite organism, while at the same time the dominant functions of this organism – production, subsistence, expression – appeared as the true organizing principles at the root of the preceding classical 'orders'. The 'anthropological' turn thus refers not so much to a finite *being*, but first of all to a limited *consciousness*, as it appears determined by its empirical conditions of existence. Put in Foucault's own formula, man is constituted as 'the one who lives, labours and speaks, at the same time *knows* life, labour and language, and finally becomes *known* himself to that degree as he lives, labours and speaks'.[29]

With this 'empirico-transcendental reduplication',[30] the system of representations loses its foundational role for the structure of possible knowledge, and turns itself into a mere superstructure of one of the basic systems. It is precisely this functional heteronomy of thought which characterizes its 'anthropological' turn: while it would be a useless attempt to isolate 'man' within the basic systems themselves, it is the system of thought which, *in the service* of life, production and expression, takes the peculiar shape of psychic processes, of legal and moral ideas, of mythical and literary creations, in short, of all the genuine products of the 'human mind'. Actually, this way of reshaping the humanities in 'functional' terms is just the corollary of subjecting them to a 'structural' analysis as it had been propagated throughout the nineteenth century.[31] Contrary to these traditions, however, Foucault entirely neglects the issue of an *autonomous* symbolic function[32] (other than representation). So it still remains to determine the criterion which qualifies precisely the structures of life, labour and language to engage the symbolic faculties in order to represent themselves as those fundamental modes of 'finiteness' which constitute the *condition humaine*. This question also brings us back to the evaluation of an alleged 'anthropological turn' in economics.

There seem to be two possible answers. First, all three structures exhibit some formal characteristics of 'organic' systems as they were conceived in the nineteenth century, such as the primacy of the whole over its parts, the metabolic exchange with the spatial environment, or the temporal rhythm of development, growth and decay (accordingly, both language and capital have been almost habitually hypostatized as 'living organisms' throughout the century). Each of these characteristics reveals an aspect of empirical 'finiteness', and it is primarily *this* sort of 'finiteness' which Foucault seeks to uncover at the root of nineteenth-century theories of economic development. However, he does not content himself with a mere formal analogy, and instead sticks to interpreting the finiteness of the economy as a kind of secret 'prolongation' of the *natural* finiteness of man.[33] As compared with his quite contrary remarks on the purely immanent historicity of language, this attempt to reduce the economic process almost to a mere supplement of physical metabolism might appear rather odd. In fact, there is a fundamental ambiguity in Foucault's notion of finiteness with respect to the physical and economic condition of 'man'. His *homo oeconomicus* remains a split personage, being at the same time a psychological type (as far as the survival of the biological individual is at stake) and a sociological instance (as far as the development of the economy is concerned). In a sense, this ambiguity is just another manifestation of the two-sided nature of the production process and the double meaning of the labour category; and as such, it would not have caused any problems, unless Foucault had made labour the pivot of his analysis, thereby – contrary to his own methodological maxims – retracing the career of a single category instead of reducing its apparent displacements to a reorganization of the whole categorical framework.

The second rationale for the Foucauldian triad of life, labour and language refers, albeit in a more implicit manner, to the 'transcendental' meaning which the notion of 'finiteness' assumes if we relate it no longer to any limitations of space and time, but to the limitations of possible knowledge. As Foucault points out, none of the various aspects of empirical finiteness – not the scarcity of resources, nor the opacity of words, nor even the mortality of the body – bears the necessity of eternal truths; each of them could be ultimately belied by an 'infinite understanding'.[34] However, the very fact that human understanding is not infinite (viz. eternal, intuitive and creative),[35] but bounded by the forms of sensuality, discourse, and imagination, again points to the triad of conditions of existence: due to the temporal and spatial location of the body, the discursive mode of language and the imaginary representation of the absent objects of desire,[36] we find the objects of biology, linguistics and economics mirrored by the conditions of knowledge themselves. This mutual reflection of transcendental and empirical structures belongs without doubt to the most obscure (though perhaps also most revealing) parts of Foucault's work, and we won't explore it further. There is just one detail which should, however, be noted, namely the fact that economics suddenly seems no longer tied to *production*, but is bluntly addressed as the domain of *desire*. Could it be that the 'empirico-transcendental' dichotomy itself is the key to Foucault's unequal treatment of the categories of 'labour' and 'utility'?

THE PLACE OF UTILITY

The modern dichotomy between labour and utility had no precedent before the dawn of the nineteenth century. True, both concepts had already played a major role in the earlier value theories, but they were neither symmetric nor opposed to each other; they had never served as banners in any controversy;

they were equally present in the works of such systematic thinkers as Turgot or Cantillon; in short, they were far from labelling that fundamental divide which today has rendered the separation of the 'ancients' from the 'moderns' such an easy matter. Throughout the eighteenth century, both use and cost value (the latter including labour as just one of its elementary components) had been conceived of in an almost exclusive connection with exchange. The difference in the use values of the *same* commodity (when put into different *relations*) provided the *motive* for exchange, while the equivalence of the cost values of *different* commodities (when resolved into the same *components*) supplied the *rule* for it; moreover, both the relation to the final need and the composition of the original expenses were considered as modes of exchange.[37]

As Foucault has pointed out, it is this typical levelling of production, consumption and exchange relationships 'in the transparent element of representation'[38] which foils any continuous mapping from Galiani and Quesnay to Jevons and Ricardo,[39] and which still lies at the bottom of Smith's notorious 'confusion' of embodied and commanded labour.[40] In fact, there simply was no 'embodied' form of labour for Smith to 'confound' with the only possible form which labour could assume at the surface of exchange: that of a commodity commanded by, and itself commanding, other commodities, that is, either that of a representable component of value (like corn) or that of a representing measure of value (like gold). Only in the 'early states of society', when labour was the only component (and therefore the sole determinant) of value, did its cost and its price character coincide, so that even the quantitative distinction between working and buying ultimately vanished.[41] All of this reasoning exhibits clearly the structure of eighteenth-century thought; and insofar as Smith does not even attempt to reduce the diverse components of value to an elementary standard, and renounces the search for a general 'par' between labour and land in favour of the well-known 'trinity formula' of value, he might even appear more remote from Ricardo than Cantillon or Petty. However, precisely this omitted reduction of labour to food (and its consequent recognition as a primary component of value) seems sufficient for Foucault to state Smith's 'essential detachment' (*décrochage essentiel*) from any of his predecessors.[42]

It is not easy to grasp the fundamental difference which Foucault claims to exist between labour and food as primary elements of value. Once production and exchange are regarded as similar forms of substitution, it should not matter whether food is reduced to labour or vice versa. According to Smith, money saves toil just as toil saves money,[43] which is far from asserting the 'radical heterogeneity'[44] of labour. Nor does Smith's argument for the choice of labour as a measure of value really involve its radical separation from the inclinations and appetites of men;[45] rather, labour itself is established as the immediate object of aversion and a direct source of negative utility.[46] In short,

Smith's value theory contains no indication of any fundamental break, unless we regard the shift of stress from food to labour *by itself* as an accepted 'symptom' of such a transformation. But this is precisely the case with Foucault: his whole interpretation of Smith rests on the supposition that labour as such refers to the finiteness, temporality and mortality of man, whereas food (and more generally the objects of desire) as such belong to the sphere of representations.[47] In this way, the reorganization of entire conceptual structures is boiled down to the turnover of single concepts, and the epistemological break between the classical 'analysis of riches' and modern political economy appears 'symbolized', as it were, by the headway of labour into the centre of economics, and the corresponding withdrawal of the wants to the subordinate sphere of psychology.[48] However, as Foucault remarks in a casual aside, this psychological exile of the wants is precisely the place where the marginalists should eventually discover their central notion of utility.[49]

Now, such a construction is not only historically belied, but also fundamentally inconsistent – unless, of course, we are ready to interpret the 'marginal revolution' as a straightforward rescission of the Ricardian break, and perhaps even as an early instance of that 'reappearance of the sign' (closely connected with a revival of mathematical thought) at the beginning of the twentieth century, which Foucault has read alternatively as a 'superposition' of classical age and modernity, or as a preliminary symptom of the foretold 'disappearance of man'.[50] Notwithstanding the sporadic attempts of a 'post-modern' reading of Jevons, it is quite obvious that no serious examination of the marginalist turn could have corroborated this kind of mysticism. Rather, it would have rendered manifest the basic error at the root of Foucault's profound misinterpretation of nineteenth-century economics, namely the attempt to project a structural break into a dichotomy of ideas (which in turn had to be deemed invariant across history). Yet, as I want to emphasize in my concluding remarks, such errors are less due to a failure of 'Foucauldian' methods than to a certain lack of rigour in applying them.

CONCLUDING REMARKS

A consequent pursuit of Foucault's own methodological maxims need not confine itself within the borders plotted by keywords such as 'labour', 'history' or 'man'. Once the comparative analysis of systems of thought consequently abstains from looking for easily visible 'characteristics' of this or that *episteme*, it equally admits of establishing structural equivalences between, say, the time structure of capital and the 'timeless' structure of market prices, or between the labour embodied in its products and the utility produced by their disembodiment[51] (isomorphies like these may then also shed new light on numerous historical statements such as, for example, Wicksteed's assimilation of *production* and *satisfaction*,[52] or Torrens' contrasting of *capital* with the *market*).[53]

None of these traces, and probably not even the main axes of nineteenth-century economic thought, would ever become visible if we stuck dogmatically to petrified Foucauldian theses concerning, for example, the indispensable role of labour in modern political economy, the fundamental historicity of nineteenth-century thought, or the incompatibility between the order of man and the order of signs. Perhaps we will even have to give up the concept of epistemological breaks and retain only the more general notion of transformations. Yet such an analysis will remain 'Foucauldian' in the sense that it proceeds from the same central idea that guided the project of *Les Mots et les Choses*: that scientific thought is neither a mere aggregate of ideas nor a neutral mechanism for solving problems, but a genuine symbolic form, an *architecture* which 'consists' of ideas as much as a building 'consists' of walls, and which 'applies' the principles of logical reasoning as much as construction 'applies' the law of gravity.

Of course, any of the simultaneous specifications and generalizations of Foucault's methods required for the extension of their domain of application also point at the peculiar limitations and missing theoretical foundations of his basic methodological concepts. Why, for instance, should we divide the whole group of transformations into fundamental 'breaks' and superficial 'retouches'? Why should the divide separating Smith and Ricardo from Jevons be less or more 'deep' than the divide separating Ricardo and Jevons from Smith? Why should all 'epistemological' transformations be diachronic? And if so, is there any 'law of progress' which may account for their peculiar sequence? Foucault has been extremely tacit on these properly theoretical questions. But after all, these are the constitutive problems of a new empirical science, which could not have been raised at all without the acknowledgment of scientific thought as an autonomous object of study. Foucault's main achievement lies probably not so much in the introduction of new methods into the history of ideas, but in his attempt to transform it from a mere record office of current disciplines into a genuine science of the structures and transformations of scientific thought. For everyone who searches more in the past than the traces of the present, the epistemological work of Michel Foucault will remain an invaluable source.

NOTES

*   I wish to thank Annie Cot, Erich Streissler and Michael Zouboulakis for helpful comments and discussions.
1. Foucault has characterized this object by the term 'archive' in order to emphasize that 'so many things, said by so many men, for so long, have not emerged in accordance with the

same laws of thought, or the same set of circumstances, . . . but . . . by virtue of a whole set of relations that are peculiar to the discursive level' (Foucault [1969] 1993: 129).

2. Cf. for example Foucault (1966c: 514). The model function of Dumézil's studies goes back to the days of *Madness and Civilization*. Cf. for example the (French) preface to *Folie et Déraison*, 1961: x., or the interview in *Le Monde* of 22 July 1961: 'Like Dumézil has done it with the myths, I have attempted to discover structured norms of experience, the scheme of which can – modified – be found again on different levels' (quoted in Dosse, [1991] 1996, 1: 228).

3. '. . . c'est que l'on recherche essentiellement, ce sont les formes, le système, c'èst-à-dire que l'on essaie de faire ressortir les corrélations logiques qui peuvent exister entre un grand nombre d'éléments appartenant à une langue, à une idéologie (comme dans les analyses d'Althusser), à une société (comme chez Lévi-Strauss) ou à different champs de connaissance; ce à quoi j'ai moi-même travaillé. On pourrait en gros décrire le structuralisme comme la recherche de structures logiques partout où il a pu s'en produire' (Foucault, 1968: 652).

4. See Lévi-Strauss ([1952] 1978: 279); cf. also Foucault (1966c: 514). This concept of structure has been adopted from linguistics (Jakobson) and biology (Cuvier), and is closely oriented to the mathematical transformation concept first employed in the group-theoretic reconstruction of geometry (Klein).

5. 'Il faut donc éviter une lecture rétrospective qui ne prêterait à l'analyse classique des richesses que l'unité ultérieure d'une économie politique en train de se constituer en tâtons. . . . En fait, les concepts de monnaie, de prix, de valeur, de circulation, de marché, n'ont été pensés, au XVIIᵉ et au XVIIᵉ siècle, à partir d'un futur qui les attendait dans l'ombre, mais bien sur le sol d'une disposition épistémologique rigoureuse et générale' (Foucault, 1966a: 177–9). Actually, the assessment of the 'marginal revolution' is perhaps the most appropriate example to illustrate the difference between the two approaches. While historians of ideas have laboured much over the question of why and how the same discovery could have taken place independently at three different places, everyone who endeavours a 'morphological' comparison of the complete theoretical systems, or even only of the complete value theories, of Jevons, Menger and Walras, respectively, simply cannot understand how one could ever get the idea to group these three heterogeneous authors together just because they agree on *one* single item, to which, moreover, each of them attached a quite different meaning and importance.

6. Both the assumption of long-term structures underlying historical processes and the application of structural methods to the realm of diachrony and singularity had already been advocated by the *École des Annales* and emphasized also by Lévi-Strauss (cf. for instance Lévi-Strauss, [1960] 1976: 16).

7. There is a certain ambiguity in the term 'classical', which Foucault uses for the seventeenth and eighteenth centuries (the French *âge classique*), whereas in the history of economic thought it usually denotes the English tradition of 'political economy' of the nineteenth century.

8. See Wahl ([1968] 1981: 327).

9. For a more detailed comparative survey of the various *epistemes*, see Wahl ([1968] 1981). We shall not address here the question of the logical rationale for the peculiar sequence and the mutual correspondence of constructional types and basic relations. I have treated this problem in a separate paper, ' "Archeology of Knowledge" and "Morphology of Mind" ' (presented at the 3rd HOPOS conference in Vienna, June 2000).

10. See Foucault (1966a: 184 ff.) (referring to Davanzati's *Lezione delle Monnete* of 1582).

11. See Foucault (1966a: 185).

12. See Foucault (1966a: 204 f).

13. This does not of course mean that eighteenth-century economics had reduced wealth, value or capital to money – on the contrary, almost every author explicitly emphasizes the contrary assertion. But just because money cannot be deemed the essence of wealth, it can serve as its universal representation, and just because it contributes nothing to the creation of values, it is apt to circulate them: 'All commodities represent money, and money represents them all', says Turgot ([1766] 1903: 68). Both Turgot and Cantillon – two typical 'forerunners' of

nineteenth-century capital and value theory – conceive of the process of distribution of the produce of earth (which alone constitutes wealth!) essentially as 'circulation of money' (cf. Turgot, [1766] 1903: 51; Cantillon, [1755] 1931: 81).

14. See Foucault (1966a: 204).
15. See Foucault (1966a: 210).
16. See Foucault (1966a: 206 ff).
17. See Ricardo ([1817] 1970: 11).
18. 'Independent of any contract, earth pays him [the peasant] immediately the price of his labour' (Turgot, [1766] 1903: § 7); 'What is bought with money or with goods is purchased by labour as much as what we acquire by the toil of our own body. That money or those goods indeed save us this toil. . . . Labour was the first price, the original purchase-money that was paid for all things' (Smith, [1776] 1976: 47 ff).
19. See Foucault (1966a: 266 and *passim*): 'La valeur a cessé d'être un signe, elle est devenue un produit'.
20. See for instance Dobb (1973: 38 ff).
21. Take, for example, his concept of the 'organic composition' of capital (Marx, 1864: 640) and the conception of the commodity form as its 'cell form' (cf. Marx, 1864: 11), a metaphor which Engels (1973: 68) later transferred to the sociological domain. In a way, Marx's characterization of the capital 'monster' as 'dead labour' which constantly swallows and transforms 'living labour' (Marx, 1864: 209; cf. also Engels, 1973: 446) could even be regarded as a straightforward inversion of Cuvier's portrayal of living bodies as successively transforming and temporarily animating dead substances (Cuvier, *Leçons d'Anatomie Comparée*, tom I (1800: 5), quoted in Foucault, 1966a: 290). Both Marx and Engels were well acquainted with the work of Cuvier and appreciated especially his achievements in paleontology (cf. Marx's letter to Engels, 25 March 1868, in Marx and Engels, 1985: 224; Engels, 1925: 457). On Marx's employment of cell theory, refer also to Freudenthal (1997: 190 ff).
22. 'Ce n'est plus dans les jeux de la représentation que l'économie trouve son principe, mais du côté de cette région périlleuse où la vie s'affronte à la mort. Elle renvoie donc à cet ordre de considérations assez ambiguës qu'on peut appeler anthropologiques' (Foucault, 1966a: 269).
23. 'Une perpétuelle et fondamentale situation de rareté' (Foucault, 1966a: 269).
24. 'L'homo oeconomicus, . . . c'est celui qui passe, et use, et perd sa vie à échapper à l'imminence de la mort' (Foucault, 1966a: 269).
25. Marx (1859: 37; 1864: 192 ff).
26. Marx (1864: 198).
27. Darwin's theory of evolution has been quoted as a model for history both by Marx (1864: 292, fn. 89) and Engels (in his famous eloge at Marx's funeral; Engels, 1883: 335). The affinities between economics and biology are more obvious for the German historical school. Both traditions have in a way adopted (more or less explicitly) Cuvier as a paradigm, albeit with different accents: while Engels (1973: 37–8) employed the example of paleontology for reconstructing ancient societies, Roscher (1922: 77) accentuated a comparative anatomy of economies.
28. See Foucault (1966b: 501).
29. '. . . l'homme s'est constitué, un homme qui est aussi bien celui qui vit, qui parle et qui travaille, que celui qui connaît la vie, le langage et le travail, que celui enfin qui peut être connu dans la mesure où il vit, parle et travaille' (Foucault, 1966b: 501, my italics).
30. See for example, Foucault (1966a: 329).
31. Most explicitly perhaps by Marx and Engels; cf. Engels (1973: 37 ff).
32. The notion of 'function' was introduced into the theory of knowledge by Kant at the end of the eighteenth century. Before that, Leibniz had detached the notion of function from its original physiological context and established it as a mathematical concept (cf. Schulthess, 1981: 219 ff).
33. 'Il n'y a histoire (travail, production, accumulation, et croissance des coûts réels) que dans la mesure où l'homme comme être naturel est fini: finitude qui se prolonge bien au-delà des limites primitives de l'espèce et des besoins immédiats du corps, mais qui ne cesse

d'accompagner, au moins de sourdine, tout le développement des civilisations' (Foucault, 1966a: 271).
34. See Foucault (1966a: 325).
35. See Kant (edition B: 72, 135).
36. See Foucault (1966a: 325 and *passim*).
37. Thus, for example, it was possible for Cantillon to proceed in a straight line from the corn *yielded* by a piece of land to the labour *feeded* by the corn, the wool *furnished* by the labour, the corn *traded* for the wool and so on (cf. Cantillon, [1755] 1931: 27 and *passim*).
38. See Foucault (1966a: 265).
39. See Foucault (1966a: 204, 269).
40. See Foucault (1966a: 265).
41. See Smith ([1776] 1976: 65).
42. See Foucault (1966a: 327 and *passim*).
43. See Smith ([1776] 1976: 47 ff).
44. See Foucault (1966a: 237).
45. See Foucault (1966a: 236).
46. See Smith ([1776] 1976: 50).
47. See Foucault (1966a: 237 f). In this sense, Amariglio's statement that 'the contradiction in Smith's work bespeaks Smith's straddling of two *epistemes*: the age of Representation and the age of Man' (Amariglio, 1988: 595) is a correct reading of Foucault – which, however, doesn't render it meaningful.
48. 'On comprend comment entre ces positivités nouvellement formées – une anthropologie qui parle d'un homme rendu étranger à lui-même et une économie qui parle de mécanismes exterieurs à la conscience humaine – l'Idéologie ou l'Analyse des représentations se réduira à n'être plus, bientôt, qu'une psychologie, tandis que s'ouvre en face d'elle, et contre elle, et la dominant bientôt de toute sa hauteur la dimension d'une histoire possible' (Foucault, 1966a: 238). See also pp. 269 ff: 'Par le fait même, le besoin, le désir, se retirent du côté de la sphère subjective – dans cette région qui à la même époque est en train de devenir l'objet de la psychologie'.
49. The passage continues: 'C'est là, précisément, que dans la seconde moitié du XIXᵉ siècle, les marginalistes iront rechercher la notion d'utilité'.
50. See Foucault (1966b: 501 ff).
51. A more detailed sketch of such isomorphies is beyond the scope of this paper. I am currently engaged in a structural analysis of nineteenth-century capital theories, and I hope to render account of some of its results in a separate paper. Here, the examples given shall merely illustrate the direction and possible range of this type of research.
52. See Wicksteed ([1894] 1992: 86 and *passim*).
53. See Torrens (1821: 50).

REFERENCES

Amariglio, Jack L. (1988), 'The body, economic dicourse, and power: an economist's introduction to Foucault', *History of Political Economy*, 20(4): 583–613.

Cantillon, Richard (1755), *Essai sur la Nature du Commerce en Géneral*, translated by H. Hayek (1931) as *Abhandlung über die Natur des Handels im Allgemeinen*, Jena: Gustav Fischer.

Dobb, Maurice (1973): *Theories of Production and Distribution since Adam Smith: Ideology and Economic Theory*, Cambridge: Cambridge University Press.

Dosse, François (1991), *Histoire du Structuralisme*, Paris, 2 volumes; translated by S. Barmann (1996) as *Geschichte des Strukturalismus*, Hamburg: Junius.

Engels, Friedrich (1883), 'Das Begräbnis von Karl Marx', *Der Sozialdemokrat* (Zürich), Nr. 13 (22.3.1883), in Marx Engels Werksausgabe, Vol. 19, Berlin: Dietz: 335–9.

Engels, Friedrich (1925), *Dialektik der Natur*, Marx Engels Werksausgabe, Vol. 20, Berlin: Dietz.

Engels, Friedrich (1973), *Der Ursprung der Familie, des Privateigentums und des Staates* (1884), Marx Engels Werksausgabe, Vol. 21, Berlin: Dietz.

Foucault, Michel (1966a), *Les Mots et les Choses. Une Archéologie des Sciences Humaines*, Paris: Gallimard.

Foucault, Michel (1966b), 'Lets mots et les choses' (entretien avec R. Bellour, orig. in *Les Lettres Françaises*, No. 1125, 31 mars – 6 avril: 3–4), reprint in *Dits et Écrits I*, Paris: Gallimard: 498–504.

Foucault, Michel (1966c), 'Entretien avec Madeleine Chapsal' (orig. in *La Quinzaine Littéraire*, No. 5, 16 mai 1966: 14–15), reprint in *Dits et Écrits I*, Paris: Gallimard: 513–18.

Foucault, Michel (1966d), 'Une histoire restée muette' (orig. in *La Quinzaine Littéraire*, Nr. 8, 1–15 juillet 1966: 3–4), reprint in *Dits et Écrits I*, Paris: Gallimard: 545–9.

Foucault, Michel (1968), [Interview avec Michel Foucault] (entretien avec I. Lindung; orig. in *Bonniers Litteräre Magasin*, Stockholm, 37e année, No. 3, mars 1968: 203–11), reprint in *Dits et Écrits I*, Paris: Gallimard: 651–62.

Foucault, Michel (1969), *L'Archéologie du Savoir*, Paris: Gallimard; translated by A.M. Sheridan Smith (1993) as *The Archeology of Knowledge and the Discourse on Language*, New York: Barnes & Noble.

Freudenthal, Gideon (1997), 'Marx's critique of economic reason', *Science in Context*, 10(1): 171–98.

Jevons, William Stanley (1871), *The Theory of Political Economy*, reprint (1965) of the 5th edition, edited by H. St. Jevons, New York: Kelley.

Kant, Immanuel, *Kritik der Reinen Vernunft*, 1st ed. [A] (1781); 2 ed. [B] (1787).

Lévi-Strauss, Claude (1952), 'Social Structure' (paper given at the Wenner-Gren Foundation International Symposium on Anthropology, New York 1952, first published in A.L. Kroeber (ed.), *Anthropology To-Day*, Chicago 1953: 524–553), reprinted with some modifications as chapter XV of *Structural Anthropology* (*Anthropologie Structurale*, Paris 1958; London: Penguin Books, 1972: 277–323.

Lévi-Strauss, Claude (1960), 'The Scope of Anthropology' (Inaugural lecture at the *Collège de France*, 5. 1. 1960), reprinted as chapter 1 of *Structural Anthropology 2* (*Anthropologie Structurale Deux*, Paris 1973); translated from the French by Monique Layton, London: Penguin Books, 1976: 3–32.

Marx, Karl (1859), *Zur Kritik der politischen Ökonomie*, Marx Engels Werksausgabe, Vol. 13, Berlin: Dietz.

Marx, Karl (1864), *Das Kapital. Kritik der politischen Ökonomie*, Vol. 1, Marx Engels Werksausgabe, Vol. 23, Berlin: Dietz.

Marx, Karl und Friedrich Engels (1985), *Über 'Das Kapital'. Briefwechsel*, Berlin: Dietz.

Ricardo, David (1817 [1970]), *The Principles of Political Economy and Taxation*, in *The Works and Correspondence of David Ricardo*, edited by Piero Sraffa, Vol. 1, Cambridge: Cambridge University Press.

Roscher, Wilhelm (1854–94), *Grundlagen der Nationalökonomie. Ein Hand- und Lesebuch für Geschäftsmänner und Studierende*, 26th edition (1922), Stuttgart und Leipzig: Cotta.

Schulthess, Peter (1981), *Relation und Funktion. Eine systematische und theoretische Untersuchung zur theoretischen Philosophie Kants*, Berlin: Walter de Gruyter.

Smith, Adam (1776), *An Inquiry into the Nature and Causes of the Wealth of Nations*, edited (1976) by R.H. Campbell, A.S. Skinner and W.B. Todd, Oxford: Clarendon Press.

Torrens, Robert (1821), *An Essay on the Production of Wealth, with an Appendix, in which the Principles of Political Economy Are Applied to the Actual Circumstances of this Country*, London: Longman, Hurst, Rees, Orme, and Browne.

Turgot, Anne Robert Jacques (1766), *Réflexions sur la Formation et la Distribution des Richesses*; translated by V. Dorn (1903) as *Betrachtungen über die Bildung und die Verteilung des Reichtums*, with an introduction by Heinrich Waentig, Jena: Fischer.

Wahl, François (1968), 'Die Philosophie diesseits und jenseits des Strukturalismus, Teil I: Gibt es eine strukturalistische Episteme?', in François Wahl (ed.) (1968), *Einführung in den Strukturalismus (Qu'est-ce que le Structuralisme)*, translated (1981) by Eva Moldenhauer, Frankfurt/M.: Suhrkamp: 327–407.

Wicksteed, Philip Henry (1894), *The Co-ordination of the Laws of Distribution*, edited (1992) by Ian Steedman, London: Elgar.

4. A conservative approach to progress in economics

Jack Birner*

INTRODUCTION

The economics of today cannot be understood without knowledge of the developments – progress and stagnation – between 1930 and 1940. An important impulse to theoretical economics in the early 1930s was the introduction into the English-speaking world of the ideas of Knut Wicksell. This constituted a breakthrough in business cycle theory, which resulted in a clash between two competing theories: John Maynard Keynes's *Treatise on Money* (1930), and Friedrich Hayek's *Prices and Production* (1931a). Though a public confrontation remained restricted to Hayek's lengthy two-part review of Keynes's book, and Keynes's reply,[1] the controversy set the tone for the debates in business cycle and capital theory throughout the decade. Keynes developed his ideas into what became the *General Theory* (1936), and Hayek refined his theory of economic fluctuations in a series of publications culminating in *The Pure Theory of Capital* (1941). But never was the competition between the two theories clearer than just after the publication of *Prices and Production* in 1931.

Another important development in the early 1930s took place in the field of empirical economics. In 1931 the Econometric Society was founded. A year later, one of the first econometricians, Colin Clark, published *The National Income 1930–1932*. One of its purposes was to improve the quality of the descriptive statistical data[2] collected by the official sources in Britain, of which he is very critical (see his Introduction). But Clark wanted more. He needed reliable data for putting to the test the two most important and radically opposed economic theories of the day, Keynes's and Hayek's.

> I have used the notation and equations of Mr. Keynes's theory of money in this chapter because I find it possible to attach quantitative interpretations to them. I certainly do not wish to claim that my statistical work above 'proves' this theory as against the directly conflicting Theory of Money advanced by Dr. Hayek, although I hope that in the future it will be possible to devise a statistical *experimentum crucis*. But I trust that I have compiled sufficient information on the relative movements of the prices

... and the production ... of consumption goods and capital goods to be of service to the exponents of this theory, and I sincerely hope that they will be able to make use of the above data to express their theory in quantitative terms. (Clark, 1932: 138–9)

So, Clark's purpose is not to use statistical data for putting *a single theory* to the empirical test; the empirical test he has in mind is *to decide between two rival theories.* Clark is one of the first economists, if not the very first, to put the goal of *crucially testing rival theories* on his agenda.

Where did he get this idea? Before starting to work in economics, Clark had acquired a solid background in natural science. He had studied chemistry, obtaining second class honours in 1927. This was followed by a year's research in the radiochemistry of uranium and thorium. It was precisely in this field, radiation research, that in the previous decades a new theory of the structure of the atom had been proposed to replace classical mechanics: quantum mechanics. The revolution in physics had started with the so-called black-body radiation problem.[3] Classical mechanics was unable to explain this phenomenon. In his attempt to solve the problem, Max Planck introduced what was later to be called Planck's law of radiation, which contained Planck's constant, the measure of an elementary quantum of action. This marked the birth of quantum mechanics, which was to supersede classical mechanics. Two aspects of the developments in physics are of particular interest here. The first is that Niels Bohr proposed his so-called correspondence principle in order to characterize the relationship between the two theories. According to this principle, when certain parameters in the equations of quantum mechanics approach certain extreme values, classical mechanics can be derived from it as a special case. More will be said on the correspondence principle below.

The second important aspect of the revolution in physics was the unresolved problems that remained after quantum mechanics was developed. Two different theories explained radiation, and more in particular the propagation of light, equally well: one considered light as consisting of particles, the other as a wave-like phenomenon. Ever since, scientists have tried to design a way to decide between the two theories, but up till now no decisive test has been found. The idea that such a *crucial test* was needed was very much alive in the natural science of the first decades of this century.

CRUCIAL TESTS AND THE CORRESPONDENCE PRINCIPLE

The idea that it is possible to choose decisively between two rival theories on the basis of empirical evidence can already be found in the work of Francis

Bacon. Whenever there are two or more theories that purport to explain the same phenomena, a crucial experiment can establish for all time the truth of the true theory. This belief of Bacon's follows from his inductivism, and he would have had great difficulty accounting for a subsequent overthrowing of the 'winning' theory. A falsificationist conception of a crucial experiment that allows of a more dynamic picture of scientific progress is an experiment that falsifies at least one of a set of rival theories while corroborating one or more of the others. This is what we find in Karl Popper's description of the relation between Newton's mechanics and its predecessors:

> The cases (of scientific progress) I have in mind are cases in which there was no refutation. Neither Galileo's nor Kepler's theories were refuted before Newton: what Newton tried to do was to explain them from more general assumptions, and thus to unify two hitherto unrelated fields of inquiry. . . .
>
> It is in cases like these that *crucial experiments* become decisively important. We have no reason to regard the new theory as better than the old theory – to believe that it is nearer to the truth – until we have derived from the new theory *new predictions* which were unobtainable from the old theory, . . . and until we have found that these new predictions were successful. For it is only this success which shows that the new theory had true consequences (that is, a truth content) where the old theories had false consequences (that is, a falsity content).
>
> Had the new theory been refuted in any of these crucial experiments then we would have had no reason to abandon the old one in its favour – even if the old theory was not wholly satisfactory . . . In all these important cases [referred to by Popper] we need the new theory in order to find out where the old theory was deficient' (Popper, 1972: 246).

Popper uses the name 'correspondence principle' to refer to the relationship between a more general theory such as Newton's and special theories such as Kepler's or Galileo's: 'I suggest that whenever in the empirical sciences a new theory of a higher level of universality successfully explains some older theory *by correcting it*, then this is a sure sign that the new theory has penetrated deeper than the older one. The demand that a new theory should contain the old one approximately, for appropriate values of the parameters of the new theory, may be called (following Bohr) the "principle of correspondence" ' (Popper, 1972: 202).

This suggests that the deeper theory is closer to the truth (or has more verisimilitude) than the old one. But the notion of a crucial test is not dependent on verisimilitude: 'The same point – the importance of crucial tests – can be made without appealing to the aim of increasing the verisimilitude of a theory, by using [the] argument . . . [of] the need to make the tests of our explanations independent' (Popper, 1972: 246–7).[4] We will come back to the issues of the comparison of theories and the importance of independent tests later. I will first discuss an earlier link between physics and economics, the adoption of the scientific method by classical economists.

SCIENTIFIC ECONOMICS

Even though Clark's published work does not say anything about its source, it is very likely that he adopted the objective of constructing a crucial test between rival theories from physics. One and a half centuries earlier it was easier to trace the influence of natural science on economics. Classical political economists consciously tried to remodel their discipline according to what they thought was the method of physics: the deductive systematization of knowledge obtained by the construction and manipulation of idealized models of reality. The method was introduced in the hope of raising economics from the level of a collection of practical rules for public policy to the mathematical rigour of Euclidean geometry and Newtonian physics. According to Halévy, James Mill was the first to introduce the Euclidean metaphor in economics (in the *Edinburgh Review* of 1809).[5] Mill speaks of the deductive proof of consequences, like Euclidean theorems, from the laws of human nature. The French economist Jean-Baptiste Say had the similar purpose of improving upon the body of classical economics by systematizing it. In the Introduction to the *Traité d'Économie Politique* (first published in 1803) Say writes: 'The celebrated work of Dr. Adam Smith can only be considered as an immethodical assemblage of the soundest principles of political economy, supported by luminous illustrations' (Say, 1880: xix).[6] The Newtonian method, or what Say believed to be that method, was his shining example. He wanted to apply it with the purpose of bringing economic knowledge together in one system and of discovering new economic knowledge. The Newtonian influence is reflected by Say's terminology.

> Political economy, in the same manner as the exact sciences, is composed of a few fundamental principles, and of a great number of corollaries or conclusions, drawn from these principles. It is essential, therefore, for the advancement of this science that these principles should be strictly *deduced from observation* ... (Say, 1880: xxvi; emphasis added)[7]

In the Preface to his *Principles of Political Economy* of 1809 David Ricardo expresses his admiration for the method of Say's *Traité d'Économie Politique*, and it is mainly through Ricardo that the new method gained a permanent foothold in economics. Economists started looking for scientific laws: 'Thus political economy, which was for Adam Smith a branch of politics and legislation, has become for Ricardo the theory of the laws of the natural distribution of wealth' (Halévy, 1972: 267). Ricardo also underwent the influence of James Mill, who advocated the Newtonian principle of finding the smallest possible number of general laws to 'enable all the detail of phenomena to be explained by a synthetic and deductive method' (Halévy, 1972: 6). He took this over from Bentham, whose 'Utilitarianism, or Philosophical Radicalism, can be defined as nothing but an attempt to apply the principles of Newton to the affairs of politics and of morals' (Halévy, 1972: 6).

No doubt part of the attraction of the method of natural science lay in its sense of novelty. What the classical economists did not realize was that the Newtonian (and Galilean) method is part of a tradition that goes back much further. The method that characterizes this tradition is known as the method of analysis and synthesis (or resolution and composition). Hintikka and Remes (1974: 110) give the following description of the Newtonian method. It consists of

1. an analysis of a certain situation into its ingredients and factors;
2. an examination of the interdependencies between these factors;
3. a generalization of the relationships so discovered to all similar situations;
4. and the deductive applications of these general laws to explain and to predict other situations.

The aim of the method was to discover fundamental causes and to gain conceptual or theoretical control of the complex world. According to Zabarella, a predecessor of Galileo's,

> [t]he end of the demonstrative method is perfect science, which is knowledge of things through their causes; but the end of the resolutive method is discovery rather than science; since by resolution we seek causes from their effects so that we may afterwards know effects from their causes, not so that we may rest in a knowledge of the causes themselves. (Quoted in Randall, 1962, Book I: 294)

Zabarella did not impose the demand that the principles of natural science be mathematical. That was left to Galileo, who applied the method in a mathematical form. This had the enormous advantage that it allowed scientists to calculate the effects of the various factors.

> With this mathematical emphasis added to the logical methodology of Zabarella, there stands completed the 'new method' for which men had been so long seeking. By the mathematical analysis of a few simple instances we find the principle involved in them. From that principle we deduce further consequences, which we find illustrated and confirmed in experience. . . . This is the method called by Euclid and Archimedes a combination of 'analysis' and 'synthesis', and by the Paduans and Galileo, 'resolution' and 'composition'. (Randall, 1962, Book I: 307)

For 2000 years, the method of analysis and synthesis was not only a method of proof, it was also a method of discovery.[8] Newton, for instance, writes that, apart from giving rules for confirming already known hypotheses, the analytical procedure served as 'a rational method of finding these hypotheses and theories in the first place' (Hintikka and Remes, 1974: 110). It was not until the separation of context of discovery and context of justification, introduced by Reichenbach into modern philosophy of science, that the idea that proof and invention can be combined in one methodological framework seemed to have been abandoned.[9]

CORREPONDENCE AS A CONSERVATIVE LOGIC OF DISCOVERY

I write 'seemed', because the idea of a logic of discovery lived on and was taken further by Popper and some of his followers. The most general formulation of its central idea, or, as Popper would call it, its regulative principle, is that the development of science is cumulative; each and every new theory incorporates all reliable knowledge that previous theories have discovered. This is what progress consists of. Heinz Post baptized this regulative principle 'conservative induction' (Post, 1971). He and his former student Noretta Koertge present a number of case studies showing how this works (Koertge, 1969). They advance the challenging empirical claim that in the history of science *all* successful theories, or successful parts of theories, were preserved in later theories.[10] They, too, call this method the general correspondence principle. Post (1971: 218) describes it as follows:

(a) There is a rationale of scientific discovery, over and above mere trial and error. There is a series of restrictions . . . which render the activity of the scientist constructing new theories essentially different from that of a clueless rat trying one trapdoor after another (a remark probably also applying to any actual rat). 'In der Beschränkung zeigt sich der Meister.'

(b) These restrictions are 'theoretic', that is, based on internal analysis of available theory.

(c) The procedure is inductive, in the sense of leading from a weaker to a stronger theory ('weaker' at least in the sense that the succesful part S^* of the old theory is less precise or less general than the succesful part of the new theory L).

(d) It is also essentially inductive in retaining the old theory in a certain sense: it is conservative (as every good scientist is).

In this passage Post gives a detailed description of the correspondence principle that was proposed by Bohr and described by Popper.

The correspondence relation has also been analysed by Leszek Nowak (1980 and later work), Wladislaw Krajewski (1977) and John Watkins (1984). From their work the following characterization emerges.

Two theories, here called the new and the old theory (as the correspondence relation is usually studied as a relation of temporal succession), are said to correspond if:

1. The new theory is more general than the old one.
2. The new theory partly reconstructs the old one.
3. The new theory corrects the old one by replacing a parameter that was considered to be a constant by a variable.
4. The old theory is a limiting case of the new theory describing only what happens in a limited domain.
5. The new theory is logically incompatible with the old one.
6. The new theory explains why people holding the old theory thought their theory to be correct.
7. The new theory introduces a factor on which the value of the parameter that was considered a constant by the old theory depends.[11]

In slightly more formal terms we can characterize the notion of correspondence as follows (the old theory is designated by T_i and the new one by T_j). T_j corresponds to T_i if:

1. T_i contains a parameter F_1 which is a constant.
2. T_j contains F_1 as a variable.
3. F_1 is dependent on a variable F_2, which in T_i is not relevant for F_1.
4. If F_2 approaches a certain limit value, (for example, 0 or ∞), F_1 in T_j approaches the constant value of F_1 in T_i.

If all of the above conditions are fulfilled, we will say, following Krajewski (1977: 41–2), that the two theories are related by the *correspondence relation*; the old theory is called the *corresponded* theory, the new one the *corresponding* theory.

CORRESPONDENCE IN ECONOMICS

I started out by discussing Clark's intention to put the rival business cycle theories of Hayek and Keynes to the test. Clark realized that they could not be tested in the form they had; they had to be reformulated in order to *make* them comparable and amenable to a crucial test. He observes, for instance:

> From the point of view of the quantitative interpretation of Dr. Hayek's theory, it only remains to give data showing the extent to which there have been inflationary or deflationary departures from 'neutral money' during recent years. In the last essay in *Prices and Production* Dr. Hayek modifies the first simple concept of maintaining the supply of money (per head presumably) unchanged, introducing the idea that in order to obtain a 'neutral money' the quantity of money would have to move so as just to neutralise the effects of changes in velocity of circulation. But it is not clear (if I may be allowed to write somewhat elliptically) whether he is

referring to 'income velocity' or 'transaction velocity', and so I have worked out
figures on two separate assumptions. (Clark, 1932: 138–9)

Clark himself never carried out the task of making the rival theories fully
comparable. A very similar attempt to do so was undertaken by John Hicks in
1937. Hicks took Keynes's *General Theory* and the class of theories to which
Hayek's theory, perhaps in a later version than *Prices and Production*, and also
Pigou's theory belong, and which was dubbed 'classical theory' by Keynes.
But if Hicks can be said to have completed Clark's programme, he did so with
an important difference: 'Mr. Keynes and the "Classics" ' did not have an
empirical purpose. All the author wanted to do was to create a framework that
made it clear just what the differences were between Keynes's *General Theory*
and the theories that Keynes criticized.[12] Hicks says literally that there is no
such thing as a 'classical' theory of money (Pigou's theory runs in real terms)
so that he has first to *construct* one before being able to compare the classical
theory with Keynes's:

> If we can construct such a theory, and show that it does give results which have in
> fact been commonly taken for granted, but which do not agree with Mr. Keynes's
> conclusions, then we shall at last have a satisfactory basis for comparison. We may
> hope to be able to isolate Mr. Keynes's innovations, and so to discover what are the
> real issues in dispute. (Hicks, 1937: 148)

In the terminology introduced above, Hicks examined the relations between
the theories by constructing a corresponding theory. He goes about it as
follows. He presents the following theories:[13]

1. the classical theory: $M = kY$ $I = C(i)$ $I = S(i,Y)$
2. Keynes's 'special theory': $M = L(i)$ $I = C(i)$ $I = S(Y)$
3. Keynes's general theory: $M = L(Y,i)$ $I = C(i)$ $I = S(Y)$

where M is quantity of money, Y is total income, I is investment and, i is the
interest rate.

As I mentioned earlier, Hicks did not have any empirical goals in mind, let
alone a crucial test. Instead, he relied entirely on the formal structure of his
own reformulations, and on what we might call *a principle of symmetry*: 'In
order to elucidate the relation between Mr. Keynes and the "Classics", we
have invented a little apparatus. It does not appear that we have exhausted the
uses of that apparatus, so let us conclude to give it *a little run on its own*'
(Hicks, 1937: 156, emphasis added).

At this point Hicks introduces the unifying or corresponding theory. The
text continues:

With that apparatus at our disposal, we are no longer obliged to make certain simplifications which Mr. Keynes makes in his exposition. We can reinsert the missing i in the third equation, and allow for any possible effect of the rate of interest upon saving; and, what is much more important, we can call in question the sole dependence of investment upon the rate of interest, which looks rather suspicious in the second equation. Mathematical elegance would suggest that we ought to have Y and i in all three equations, if the theory is to be really General. (Hicks, 1937: 156; I has been replaced by Y)[14]

By this 'special-to-general' procedure he obtains

4.   the 'Generalized General Theory': $M = L(Y,i)$, $I = C(Y,i)$, $I = S(Y,i)$

The new theory unifies in one framework (or encompasses) the three previous theories. It has been arrived at by applying the procedure of correspondence. One of its special cases is Wicksell's theory: the interest elasticity of income equals zero, and the IS-curve is horizontal. By giving particular parameters of the generalized theory the value zero, we obtain the various special cases. A crucial test among the elements of any subset of special-case theories could now be carried out – at least in principle – by measuring the empirical values of the parameters of the generalized general theory. A modern econometrician would say: the estimation of the generalized general theory constitutes a test of the restrictions on the values of its parameters, and the restrictions tell us which of the special-case theories is data-admissible.

ECONOMETRICS AND THE TESTING OF ECONOMIC THEORIES

Clark considered testing economic theories, even the crucial testing of rival theories, as one of the goals of empirical economics. To what extent was this idea shared by others? In Ragnar Frisch's editorial of the first issue (1933) of *Econometrica*, the journal of the newly founded Econometric Society, testing is not entirely absent, but it is not considered to be among the main objectives of econometrics, at least not in the sense of testing to reject theories. Statistical data serve rather to improve theories. The testing of rival theories is not mentioned.[15]

This does not mean that it was not tried at all. The League of Nations wanted to have the many existent economic theories of the business cycle tested empirically. For that purpose, it initiated an ambitious and extensive research project, commissioning the work to Gottfried Haberler and Jan Tinbergen. Haberler's *Prosperity and Depression* (1937) presents a catalogue of the various business cycle theories and tries to synthesize them where possible into one coherent theory, as a preliminary to an empirical test of the various explanations.

> The choice between these [different possible solutions] can then be made only on the basis of empirical investigations. In many cases, theoretical reasoning supported only by such broad facts as one happens to know without special statistical or historical investigations can put intelligent questions, but cannot definitely answer them. (Haberler, 1937: 2)

Tinbergen was given the commission to test which of the many available theories of the business cycle was true (Tinbergen, 1939). According to Mary Morgan, Tinbergen was a pioneer: 'Other econometricians were beginning to get interested in testing models but few used many tests or understood what the problems were. Tinbergen clearly led econometrics in this field, but he still had to tackle the problem of the statistical testing of business cycle theories' (Morgan, 1990: 113–14). This was carried out in his second report to the League of Nations. For Tinbergen, much more so than for Frisch, one of the purposes of testing was to reject false theories. Apart from this *testing to reject*, Tinbergen, like Frisch (and Schumpeter in the first article of the first issue of *Econometrica* – Schumpeter, 1933), also mentions the measurement of the relative magnitudes of different effects as the purpose of testing.[16]

Another pioneer in econometrics was Tinbergen's fellow countryman Tjalling Koopmans. Like Tinbergen and Clark, he had a background in natural science, having trained as a physicist under Hendrik Kramers, the quantum theorist (Dresden, 1987). Koopmans, too, thought of econometrics as an instrument for falsifying economic theories.[17] Testing served both a positive and a negative purpose. Positive, in the sense of 'testing the relevance of . . . theories [of the cycle] with respect to country and period considered' (Koopmans, 1941: 158). What he means by 'negative' is explained in the following passage: 'It will be clear that the only unconditional inferences one may draw are negative. They state that this or that supposed causal connection is not in agreement with the facts reflected in the data' (Koopmans, 1941: 161). On the next page Koopmans is quite explicit on the role of testing in selecting a model:

> The drawing of such unconditional negative conclusions from the data represents the most direct type of statistical testing of business-cycle theories or of elements of such theories. It is, however, inconclusive. To make a further choice from the numerous explanations not so discarded requires the introduction, as the third logical element in the situation, of certain additional information. (Koopmans, 1941: 162)

So, the element of choice of models, if not a crucial test, is clearly present in Koopman's programme. But were empirical tests possible with the econometric instruments available in the 1930s?

PARAMETER INDUCTION INSTEAD OF CONSERVATIVE INDUCTION

The problem for macroeconomics is that laboratory tests are ruled out. Most economic 'experiments' are non-repeatable and non-controllable, and therefore the problem of errors of data measurements is compounded by the fact that observations are subject to probability distributions. Models should take this into account by being formulated in stochastic terms.

According to Morgan, this problem of non-experimental data is central to modern econometrics: '[E]conometrics developed as a substitute for the experimental method in economics, and ... the problems which arose were connected with the fact that most economic data had been generated in circumstances which were neither controlled nor repeatable' (Morgan, 1990: 73). Both Wesley Clair Mitchell, the statistical economist, and Tinbergen, the econometrician, held the methodologically sophisticated idea that statistical data may enable one to disprove a theory, not prove it.[18] But an important difference between statistical economists and econometricians was that in the early 1930s, '[i]n learning how to cope with the requirements of their statistical method, econometricians developed the important notion of an "econometric model" as the mid-way point between theory and data, to which both theory and data could be compared' (Morgan, 1990: 262). But they still lacked rules for 'experimental design'.

These were given by Trygve Haavelmo in 1944. His contribution made the separation between statistical economics and econometrics complete. Whereas statistical economists continued to think that they could infer regularities from data, '[e]conometricians, on the other hand, believed that data would deliver up their secrets only when faced with theory (in the form of a well-designed econometric model) and probability inference' (Morgan, 1990: 262–3). With Haavelmo's probability revolution it became possible to test theories.

> The more important practical result of Haavelmo's paper was that probability theory provided a framework for testing economic theories. The evaluation aspect was important: in early econometrics, data could be rejected but not theory. This was because applied results were judged according to a given theory; if results were thought suspect, it was usually interpreted as a problem of the data (because of the presence of errors, for example), rather than as something wrong with the theory. This problem became acute when researchers wanted to compare a number of different theories as there was no obvious way of proceeding. Tinbergen had experienced considerable difficulty in executing the League of Nations commission to test the available theories of business cycles and sort out which were correct . . . The first macroeconomic model to use the probability principles was built by L.R. Klein on behalf of the Cowles Commission . . . Haavelmo's work marks the shift from the traditional role of econometrics in measuring the parameters of a given theory to a concern with testing those theories. (Morgan, 1990: 256–7)

With the theoretical, a priori procedure for making theories comparable that was developed in Hicks's seminal article and the results of the probability revolution in econometrics, the elements for carrying out crucial econometric tests between rival theories were now available. It comes therefore as somewhat of a surprise that the objective of testing of theories, crucially or otherwise, disappeared from the econometricians' agenda. Instead of becoming the tool box for conducting empirical and comparative tests of economic theories, with the objective of making scientific progress according to the principle of *conservative induction*, econometrics came to be used almost exclusively for estimation purposes, that is, for determining the values of model parameters, a procedure for which Hans Albert has coined the appropriate term, of 'parameter induction'.[19]

WHY DID THE TESTING OF THEORIES MOVE TO THE BOTTOM OF THE AGENDA?

Morgan observes that despite the optimism of the Cowles group that they could deal with the problems of simultaneity bias and identification that marred Tinbergen's approach, their work between 1946 and 1952 was no better than Tinbergen's. Subsequent empirical work was not of very good quality, even though there were 'remarkable successes in discovering the formal statistical properties of simultaneous equations models. [But] the model selection problem is as pressing now as two generations ago but has tended to be suppressed in published reports of empirical investigations' (Morgan, 1990: 4). The emphasis on crucial tests and model selection gave way to other problems.

Technical Difficulties

One possible explanation for this change in the direction of econometrics is that, even though the statistical framework was now available, the problem of testing theories or models relatively to one another proved harder than may have been thought originally. According to Roy Epstein, the practice of structural estimation that became widespread was originally founded 'on the belief that Tinbergen's approach to empirical economics could be adapted to yield decisive tests of different economic theories and to design effective policies for changing an economic system' (Epstein, 1987: 223). Despite the fact that the appropriate statistical apparatus was developed, one of the problems that was not resolved was that of 'multiple hypotheses' or choice of models. This problem 'was primarily responsible for the first econometric theorists to abandon further work in the field. This problem tended to be neglected by the next generation of practitioners but urgently needs more careful attention for future modelling efforts' (Epstein, 1987: 224). Notice that choosing the correct model involves a relative test and is thus related to crucial testing.

The Paradox of Professionalization and the Phenomenon of Problem Drift

What happened is not unique to econometrics. In the course of its development a discipline typically generates its own technical and formal (mathematical) problems that have to be solved before further progress can be made. An appropriate technical apparatus has to be developed and refined. This sets in motion an internal dynamics that is to a large extent autonomous. This was also the case in econometrics.

> Between the 1920s and the 1940s, the tools of mathematics and statistics were indeed used in a productive and complementary union to forge the essential ideas of the econometric approach. But the changing nature of the econometric enterprise in the 1940s caused a return to the division of labour favoured in the late 19th century, with mathematical economists working on theory building and econometricians concerned with statistical work. By the 1950s the founding ideal of econometrics, the union of mathematical and statistical economics into a truly synthetic economics, had collapsed. (Morgan, 1990: 264)

We may call this the *paradox of professionalization*: in order to complete the original programme, it is almost inevitable that a newly founded discipline such as econometrics will lose sight of the original goals, because many technical problems have to be solved first and because the subject becomes professionalized: division of labour, specialization and the gaining in importance of the institutional, that is, organizational and social, framework. Without this the original problems are almost impossible to solve for technical and organizational reasons. With it the original problems may be forgotten and remain unsolved for that reason. As a discipline becomes more professionalized and specialized, the different specializations or areas of research may develop each at a different pace. In econometrics, these 'phase differentials' have been an important factor in the loss of interest in testing. Such phase differentials within a discipline[20] may lead to *problem drift*: the original, global problem recedes into the background and makes way for other problems. This is reinforced by the fact that attempts to solve local technical problems often generate further problems. This in turn may make the development of the various specializations of a discipline more uneven still.

For the period from 1930 to 1960, Duo Qin describes 'how the desire to test diverged into model evaluation in econometric theory on the one hand, and economic theory verification in practice on the other, as econometric testing theory took shape' (Qin, 1991: 2). However, the testing of economic theories was no longer at the top of the agenda. As far as testing was dealt with, it concerned statistical significance tests of parameters. From the 1940s onward the Cowles Commission concentrated on the development of estimation and identification methods rather than on hypothesis testing. This was because a 'strong view held then was that the adaptation of statistical tools for econometrics had much outpaced the data quality, the mathematization of economic theories, and the practice of empirical model building, as well as the computing capacity' (Qin, 1991: 21).

The State of Economic Theory

The need for crucial tests is most likely to be felt when rival theories are available. As far as economists were concerned, after 1936 there weren't any left. The Keynesian paradigm came to dominate economics. Later, with the reappearance of a serious rival to the Keynesian program – monetarism – the idea of a crucial test promptly reappeared, too, as we will see below. We may observe that the situation in the 1930s is very similar to contemporary macroeconomics: we have neither a solidly unified macroeconomic theory nor are there clearly identifiable alternative theories. This has probably contributed to the current relative decline of econometrics as an instrument for testing.

The Problems of the Day

When there are urgent practical problems to be solved, such as the reconstruction of the post-war economies, econometricians, just like other economists, come under pressure from politicians and may take short cuts in order to help solve these problems. Connected with the fact that Keynesian ideas dominated the scene for a long time is the fact that much of econometrics was geared towards application rather than theory development. It was adapted to being a support for economic policy rather than an instrument for theoretical progress. Econometric models were used for applied purposes and forecasting rather than theoretical analysis and trying to decide between rival explanations.

A CHANGING TIDE

Unintentionally, Hicks's IS–LM model became the cornerstone of modern macroeconomics. This simplifying device gave rise to a whole textbook industry. It also became the standard framework for macroeconomic empirical research, even though Hicks had never intended it for that use. The most straightforward empirical application the model could have been used for, namely to conduct a crucial empirical test, was conspicuous by its absence during the quarter-century that followed its publication. It was not until the controversy between the Keynesian orthodoxy (as it had become in the meantime) and the monetarists under Friedman, in the 1960s and 1970s, that the IS–LM model was used in attempts to settle the theoretical controversy by empirical means. This started with Friedman's reformulation of the old quantity theory of money into a theory of money demand (in Friedman, 1956). What he had to do further in order to challenge the dominant Keynesian theory on its own ground was to formulate a monetarist version of the theory of income determination. Though he did not complete this exercise, he succeeded in diverting the argument to the question of the stability of the money demand function.[21] Friedman shifted the controversy into the empirical domain by asserting that this function was empirically stable, and he 'also added that the persuasiveness of his argument depended crucially on the [money demand] function being represented parsimoniously, i.e. one needed only a small number of variables to specify an empirically stable relationship. This crucial step moved the macroeconomic argument into the empirical, statistical and econometric arena' (Desai, 1981: 62). Desai sees Friedman's work as giving an entirely new direction to econometrics: 'while early use of econometrics was to model business cycles or, later, to provide operationally usable models for fiscal policy makers, Friedman's innovation was to appeal to econometrics as a way of settling the choice between rival theories' (Desai, 1981: 62). And even though Friedman's move looks less of an innovation in the light of the early work of Clark, Haberler and Tinbergen, it was instrumental in breathing new life into the old programme of crucial testing (Birner, 1993b).

FURTHER DEVELOPMENTS

As a reaction to the structural-equation model approach, the monetarists, following Friedman, had revived the NBER single-equation approach, 'refurbishing it with new techniques associated with time series analysis' (Desai, 1981: 113). In its turn, this prompted an approach on the part of critics that relied once more on structural models in conducting a crucial test between the competing monetarist and Keynesian theories. Both traditions were largely an American affair. In the United Kingdom after the Second World War econometrics developed along lines that combined certain elements of both American traditions. It merged the structural approach advocated by the Cowles Commission with techniques of statistical time series analysis, and concentrated on the comparison of rival hypotheses accounting for the behaviour of time series.[22] From the 1960s, this British brand of time series econometrics became associated with the London School of Economics, where it underwent the influence of the ideas of Karl Popper and Imre Lakatos. It was in this intellectual climate that David Hendry, Jean-François Richard and Grayham Mizon developed the *encompassing principle* (or the encompassing approach), starting in about 1975. Encompassing is part of a method in econometrics that concentrates on the problem of model selection rather than parameter induction. It also rejects the procedure followed, for instance, by Friedman and Meiselman, of testing rival models by estimating their goodness of fit *separately*. Hendry mentions two disadvantages of this method (Hendry, 1988: 88). First, a wide range of models is associated with each particular theory. Second, test results can be (and typically are) used to revise the tested model rather than reject the theory, with the result that there is 'a proliferation of empirical results, each supporting conflicting rival theory models' (p. 88). This gives rise to a 'proliferation of non-nested models [which] is symptomatic of certain inappropriate aspects of present practice in econometrics' (Davidson et al., 1978: 662).

The encompassing principle is designed to avoid these problems. A proliferation of models can be prevented if one succeeds in ranking them according to some acceptability criterion. The two conditions necessary for such a ranking that are mentioned by Hendry are the ones we have encountered earlier: the models must be comparable and they must be tested relatively to one another. If a particular model is not a special case of another model (is not nested within another model), or if different models are not special cases of (nested in) the same more general model, they have to be *made* comparable.[23] This can be done by creating a common framework in which the rival models are nested. Once this has been accomplished, the restrictions of the general, nesting or encompassing model may be tested to decide which of the rival theories is most consistent with the empirical data.

An early explanation and application of the encompassing principle is Davidson et al. (1978). It compares three empirical studies of the consumption function in order to find out which is the best. The three econometric models are made comparable by being 'standardized': 'This allows us to nest the standardised contending theories as special cases of a general hypothesis and test to see which (if any) are acceptable on statistical grounds' (p. 663). The following principles are used in finding acceptable models:

[1]   we consider it an essential (if minimal) requirement that any new model should be related to existing 'explanations' in a constructive research strategy such that previous models are only supplanted if new proposals account (so far as possible) for previously understood results, and also explain some new phenomena.

[2]   to avoid directionless 'research' and uninterpretable measurements, a theoretical framework is also essential.

[3] to be empirically acceptable, an econometric model obviously must account for the properties of the data (e.g. the autocorrelation function in a time-series study). It is not valid to 'accomplish' this aim simply by not looking for counter-evidence.

[4] a further minimal requirement when modelling from a common data set is that the chosen model should explain both the *results* obtained by other researchers and *why* their research methods led to their published conclusions. (Davidson et al., 1978: 662)

This list (especially principles 1 and 4) is very similar to the correspondence principle as formulated by Popper,[24] and to Post's model of progress through conservative induction. Though the list of criteria for the acceptability of a model has been refined since,[25] correspondence has remained a central requirement.

Encompassing bears the traces of its ancestry in time series analysis[26] and Haavelmo's probability framework in its central concept of data-generating process (DGP). The DGP is the joint probability of the sample data on the endogenous and exogenous variables:

$$D(W_n{}^1|W_0,P),$$

where $W_n{}^1 = (w_1, w_2,\ldots, w_n)$ is the sample of n observations from the full set of relevant variables w, W_0 is the matrix of initial conditions, and P is a parameter vector. The set w is determined by the problem which is analysed, the competing theories which are to be compared, and the measurement equations (Mizon, 1984: 140). It is chosen so as to be uncontroversial, which yields such a general model that it is uninformative. 'Econometric modelling consists of judicious simplification of this DGP' (Gilbert, 1990: 281). This procedure is also known as the general-to-specific approach.

Its uninformativeness is the target of most of the criticisms levelled at the encompassing principle: the encompassing model constructed for making rival models comparable is ad hoc or uninterpretable in terms of an economic theory.[27] To this the advocates of encompassing replied that the role of the encompassing model is not primarily to provide an economic theory, but rather a statistical distributional framework. Without this common framework, the rival models cannot be compared in a straightforward manner.[28] It is only in the subsequent phase of searching for a model specification that economic theory plays a role. It serves as a guide for eliminating irrelevant variables (the DGP is marginalized with respect to these variables); for sorting out the endogenous and the exogenous variables (the endogenous variables are conditioned on the exogenous variables); and for finding simple representations of the conditioned and marginalized DGP. Econometrics is applied for estimating the values of the parameters in the representations that are found.

The distinction between the distributional framework, which has to satisfy particular *statistical* requirements in order to be acceptable, and the *theoretical* model, which is inspired by an economic theory, has been elaborated by Spanos (1990). He distinguishes between economic theory, the actual DGP, the observed data, the theoretical model, the estimable model and finally the empirical econometric model. Spanos presents a 'unifying methodological framework' that seems to be a further step in a trend which was revived by Friedman: to re-unite econometrics and statistics in a way that makes it possible to compare rival theories and find out by empirical means which is the best theory.[29]

In the encompassing approach the main emphasis does not lie on the correspondence between rival theories and a general encompassing model plus a crucial test, but on constructing a sequence of models each of which encompasses the previous one.[30] This is why advocates of the encompassing principle themselves speak of a progressive Lakatosian research programme. The most general encompassing model is the statistical common distributional framework, which is needed if the rival models are to be comparable. A crucial test, if we can still use that term, consists in determining whether a particular model encompasses a rival (and also fulfills a number of other requirements). If it does, it is also the best-fitting model (Hendry, 1988: 90).

On further analysis, the roots of encompassing are different, and much older. Popper's correspondence principle and Post's conservative induction rather than Lakatos's methodology of scientific research programmes seem to be the adequate philosophical framework. In fact, Hendry and his co-authors revive the idea that was central to the 2000-year-old tradition of analysis and synthesis: a logic of discovery that at the same time systematizes our knowledge according to the correspondence principle with the goal of making progress.[31] The data-generating process of Hendry is that most general empirical model of reality on which certain mathematical and statistical constraints have already been imposed. Structurally, this corresponds (in the colloquial sense of the word) exactly to the Polish model of idealization of Krajewski and Nowak.[32] In a dynamic perspective, the encompassing method is an instance of the conservative approach to progress in empirical economics.

MUST CRUCIAL TESTS BE EMPIRICAL?

Before concluding, I would like to return to the issue with which we started, crucial testing. In the spirit of Francis Bacon, Clark intended crucial tests to be empirical. Since Clark wrote his book, it has been discovered that empirical tests in economics, crucial or otherwise, are not easy. Economists do not seem to attach much value to empirically testing their theories anyway.

A procedure that is often followed instead to examine theories critically is a type of a priori, formal, or theoretical analysis in which empirical arguments play at most a very remote role.[33] Yet this does not seem to exclude the possibility of conducting crucial tests. Sraffa mentions crucial tests in the context of the debate on capital theory: 'This example [of price reversal] is a crucial test for the ideas of a quantity of capital and the period of production' (Sraffa, 1962: 478). In the capital theory debate not a single effort was made to put this idea into econometric and empirical practice. So what does Sraffa mean? Apparently that *if* in neoclassical models there is to be such a thing as a uniquely measurable quantity of capital, *then* price reversal should not be among the consequences of such a model. What Sraffa means by a crucial test is a mathematical counterexample.[34] This indicates the important fact that crucial tests may also be of a purely theoretical nature. Instead of being part of an empirical experiment, they are the core of a thought experiment. Demonstrating that a theory is internally inconsistent also constitutes scientific progress.

Scientific progress has two components which must be clearly distinguished: one theoretical, the other empirical. That is the crux of the correspondence relation. Correspondence may exist, and an explanatory relation between a new and an old theory may obtain, even if the new theory has not been tested empirically. There is nothing unusual about this. Explanation has to be distinguished from empirical testing. Explanatory power is one thing, corroboration another. Jevons' sun spot theory of the business cycle certainly has explanatory power, even though it turned out to be wrong.

SUMMARY AND SOME CONCLUSIONS

In the early days of econometrics, crucial tests of competing theories were high on the agenda of the discipline. The idea was introduced by economists who came from a background in the natural sciences: Clark, Tinbergen and Koopmans. The developments in natural science during the first decades of this century had linked the idea of a crucial test to the correspondence principle. This relies on a process in which rival theories are incorporated in one unifying theory. Clark lacked the appropriate unifying framework or corresponding model, the relevant statistical techniques and the data. One such unifying model was provided by Hicks. But he used it for purposes of theoretical comparison only, and had no intention of conducting a crucial empirical test between Keynes's theory and its 'classical' rival.

Tinbergen attempted to put the idea of crucially testing business cycle theories into practice, but his statistical apparatus was not up to the task. By the time Haavelmo had created the necessary probabilistic framework, interest in business cycles had waned, and other internal and external factors in econo-metrics had pushed (crucial) testing into the background. It was replaced by parameter induction.

Interest in crucial tests was revived with the re-appearance of two clearly identifiable rival theories in the monetarists-versus-Keynesians debate. Friedman and Meiselman set up a crucial test between two separate regression equations representing the rival theories. The criterion they proposed was the goodness of fit with the data. They were criticized by Ando and Modigliani (1965), who reintroduced the structural approach advocated earlier by the Cowles Commission. With the structural approach, they in fact reintroduced the correspondence principle; their procedure consisted of the construction of a model of which the two rival models were special cases when particular parameters had particular values. The test of the rival models consisted of esti-mating the general, corresponding model to see whether its parameter values favoured one or the other of the rival models.

In a separate development starting at the London School of Economics, the encompassing approach was developed. It was designed to compare rival models and theories and conduct a relative test among them. This approach was explicitly inspired by the concept of correspondence as formulated by Popper, but it was given a Lakatosian interpretation.

So, the idea of relatively or crucially testing rival models and theories in economics underwent some vicissitudes. The uneven treatment was due to the state and the development of econometrics itself, and was also influenced by external factors. I have already mentioned some, but before closing I want to draw attention to the fact that ideas from outside economics, in this case philosophy, have been instrumental in the re-emergence of comparative tests of theories in the encompassing approach, just as developments in natural science seem to have aroused interest in crucial tests in the economics of the 1930s. True progress is conservative on the level of theories, data, *and* methodology, and scientific discovery is to some extent *re*-discovery.

NOTES

*   This text integrates elements of two articles that have appeared previously in publications with a limited distribution (Birner, 1993, 1994).
1.   See Hayek (1931b, 1932); Keynes (1931).
2.   'After estimating the total of the National Income this book proceeds to an analysis of how it is produced, distributed and spent' (Clark, 1932: vi).
3.   The following sketch of the developments in physics follows Jammer (1966).
4.   The argument referred to is to be found in 'The Aim of Science' (Popper, 1973: Ch. 5).
5.   See Halévy (1972: 272).
6.   This is the American translation of the 4th edition of the *Traité*.
7.   Say uses the Newtonian expression 'deducing consequences from facts' frequently. For a very interesting discussion of what Newton means, see Worrall 2000.

8. For an excellent history of the method, see Randall (1961), and 1962, Vol. I, Book 2: II).
9. The method of analysis and synthesis allowed a vastly increased control of the world and a deductive systematization of knowledge, but the problem that was introduced with it was how idealized theories were related to reality, or perhaps, more correctly stated, how idealizing theories were related to models that are closer to reality. The application of the method went hand in hand with the realization of the Euclidean ideal of a strictly deductively organized body of knowledge in science. But this came at a cost: 'one had to pay for each step which increased rigour in deduction by the introduction of a new and fallible translation' (Lakatos, 1978: 90). This problem is discussed in Birner (1994, 2001), which also propose a solution. The terminology (method of analysis and synthesis) is reminiscent of the method of the Austrian School. In fact, Carl Menger is the first economist to give a clear formulation of this method for economics in a conscious attempt to become the Galileo of social science (see Birner, 1994). Unfortunately, his methodology founders on the failure to make the correct distinction between context of discovery and context of justification (see Birner, 1990).
10. 'Quite generally, the thesis may be put this way: no theory that ever "worked" adequately turned out to be a blind alley. Once a theory has proved itself useful in some respects, has shown its semantic simplicity or explanatory power, it will never be scrapped entirely. Even the phlogiston theory had features that were useful scientifically in its day, and those features translate smoothly into present theory' (Post, 1971: 237)
11. There may be special cases where a pair of theories do not exhibit all the characteristics mentioned while it may still make sense to speak of correspondence. For examples the reader is referred to Birner (2001).
12. Similar attempts are Reddaway (1936) and Lange (1938).
13. Notice that Hicks does not distinguish between definitional, behavioural and equilibrium equations, as is usual in more modern models. In his notation all three are conflated. Thus, the first equation in a modern model would be replaced by three separate ones, one specifying the demand for money, the second the money supply, and the third equating supply and demand. The second and third Hicksian equations would be replaced by several equations: the definitional $Y = C + I$, the behavioural $C = C(.)$ and $I = I(.)$, and the equilibrium equation $S = I$. If one keeps this in mind, Hicks's notation has the advantage of being succinct and concentrating on his aim, which is to bring out the differences among the various theories. Therefore I retain Hicks's original equations, except that I have replaced two of his symbols by their equivalents I and Y, which are currently better understood.
14. The mathematical elegance Hicks refers to points to the powerful heuristic role mathematics may play. For a discussion see, for instance, Birner (1993a).
15. See *Econometrica* (1933: 2), where observation is singled out as a source of inspiration for theory: 'fresh statistical and factual studies must be the healthy element of disturbance that constantly threatens and disquiets the theorist and prevents him from coming to rest on some inherited, obsolete set of assumptions'. In case this is read as suggesting testing to reject, I refer the reader to the passage in the editorial where Frisch emphasizes the use of quantitative study of the economy in order to measure the relative magnitudes of possibly opposite effects. See also the first article of the first issue, by Schumpeter, who supplements the editorial with 'comment and amplification'. Here, testing is conspicuous by its absence.
16. See Morgan (1990: 109); Tinbergen (1939, Vol. I: 12).
17. Epstein (1987: 53) discusses Koopmans (1941), a reaction to Keynes's negative comment on Tinbergen's work in econometrics. Epstein summarizes Koopmans' position as follows. The methodology of disproof was incapable of giving positive conclusions for the theories tested by Tinbergen. As Frisch had made clear, economic data will support quite different theories. Whereas in other sciences experimentation may narrow the range of feasible theories, in economics this is not possible. The only way of proceeding is to supplement the data with a priori information, mainly in the form of 'zero restrictions to yield a system of irreducible structural equations' (p. 54). The possibility that more than one theory may be supported by the data led Koopmans to advocate reporting all results in published work, and not merely the successful ones.

18. See Morgan (1990: 124–5). The same idea had been expressed by Hayek in 1929.
19. I must have heard Albert use this expression. I have been unable to locate it in his published work.
20. For another discussion of such phase differentials, see Basmann (1975), who concentrates on the discrepancy between theoretical economics and the means of testing theories and collecting data.
21. See Desai (1981: 60 ff).
22. For details of this development the reader is referred to Gilbert (1985).
23. For an extensive discussion by a philosopher of science of the problems related to the comparability of theories, see Watkins (1984). Watkins describes a way to make theories comparable by means of so-called counterpart consequences.
24. Although Hendry refers to Popper on several occasions, he does not mention the correspondence principle. Neither does Gilbert, but he quotes a standard case of correspondence when he says that the special theory of relativity encompasses Newtonian mechanics 'which could not explain the Michelson–Morley results' but is itself encompassed by general relativity theory 'as it cannot explain the visibility of the planet Mercury behind the Sun during a solar eclipse' (Gilbert, 1990: 289).
25. See Gilbert (1990: 285 ff).
26. More particularly Box–Jenkins analysis.
27. See Spanos (1990: 344), where other points of criticism are mentioned.
28. See Mizon (1984: 142–3; see also Gilbert (1990: 291).
29. Wen we compare the encompassing principle with the earlier work dealing with relative tests of rival theories and models, we see that with the exception of Friedman and Meiselman, correspondence is a central notion. But the correspondence principle is used in different ways. In Ando and Modigliani and in Stein the correspondence relation runs between the rival models on the one hand and the more general structural corresponding model on the other hand. The crucial test consists in testing the restrictions of the corresponding model. See Birner (1993a).
30. Mizon (1984) emphasizes the function of *comparing* models rather than choosing among them in the encompassing approach. See, for example, Mizon (1984: 170).
31. The method is perfectly described by the Polish idealization model, according to which the deductive relationship between abstract theory and empirical model is such that the empirical model is the most general set of premises. From the conjunction of these premises and additional constraints one derives the more abstract models or theories. For a discussion of this model of idealization, see Birner (1994 and 2001).
32. For a discussion of the relationship between general models that are closer to the empirical facts and more specific, idealized models, see the last chapter of Birner (2001).
33. See Birner (2001).
34. For the role of mathematical counter-examples in the development of economic theories, see Hands (1984) and Birner (1993a).

REFERENCES

Ando, A. and F. Modigliani (1965), 'Velocity and the investment multiplier', *American Economic Review*, September, pp. 693–728.

Basmann, R.L. (1975), 'Modern Logic and the Presuppositional Weakness of the Empirical Foundations of Economic Science', *Schweitzerische Zeitschrift für Volkswirtschaft und Statistik*, pp. 153–76.

Birner, J. (1990), 'A roundabout solution to a fundamental problem in Menger's methodology and beyond', in B. Caldwell (ed.), 'Carl Menger and his legacy in economics', *History of Political Economy*, annual supplement, pp. 241–61, Durham, NC: Duke University Press.

Birner, J. (1993a), 'Neoclassical economics as mathematical metaphysics', *History of Political Economy*, pp. 116–49.

Birner, J. (1993b), 'Testing economic theories empirically: the contribution of econometrics', in *Oekonomie und Gesellschaft*, in N. de Marchi (ed), *Non-Natural Social Science: Reflecting on the Enterprise of More Heat than Light*, History of Political Economy, annual supplement to Vol. 25, pp. 86–117.

Birner, J. (1994), 'Idealizations and theory development in economics: some history and logic of the logic of discovery', in B. Hamminga and N. de Marchi (eds), *Idealization IV: Idealization in Economics, Poznan Studies in the Philosophy of the Sciences and the Humanities*, pp. 277–301, Amsterdam: Rodopi.

Birner, J. (2001), *The Cambridge Controversies in Capital Theory; A Study in the Logic of Theory Development*, London: Routledge.

Clark, C. (1932), *The National Income 1930–1932*, London: Macmillan.

Davidson, J.E.H., D.F. Hendry, F. Sbra and J.S. Yeo (1978), 'Econometric modelling of the aggregate time-series relationship between consumer expenditure and income in the United Kingdom', *Economic Journal*, December, pp. 661–92.

Desai, M. (1981), *Testing Monetarism*, London: Pinter.

Dresden, M. (1987), *H.A. Kramers*, Berlin: Springer.

Epstein, R. (1987), *A History of Econometrics*, Amsterdam: North Holland.

Friedman, M. (1956), 'The quantity theory of money: a restatement', in M. Friedman (ed.), *Studies in the Quantity Theory of Money*, Chicago: Chicago University Press.

Friedman, M., and D. Meiselman (1963), 'The Relative Stability of Monetary Velocity and the Investment Multiplier in the United States, 1897–1958', in *Stabilisation Policies*, Commission on Money and Credit, New York: Prentice-Hall.

Gilbert, C.L. (1985) , 'The development of British econometrics', paper prepared for a joint session of the American Economic Association and the History of Economics Society, New York, December.

Gilbert, C.L. (1990), 'Professor Hendry's econometric methodology', in C. Granger (ed.), *Modelling Economic Series; Readings in Econometric Methodology*, pp. 279–303, Oxford: Oxford University Press.

Haavelmo, T. (1944), 'The probability approach in econometrics', Supplement to *Econometrica*, 12.

Haberler, G. (1937), *Prosperity and Depression*, Geneva: League of Nations.

Hands, D.W. (1984), 'The role of crucial counterexamples in the growth of economic knowledge: two case studies in the recent history of economic thought', *History of Political Economy*.

Hayek, F.A. (1929), *Geldtheorie und Konjunkturtheorie*, Wien: Julius Springer.

Hayek, F.A. (1931a), *Prices and Production*, London: Macmillan.

Hayek, F.A. (1931b), 'Reflections on the pure theory of money of Mr. J.M. Keynes I', and 'A rejoinder to Mr. Keynes', *Economica*, 11, pp. 270–95 and 398–403.

Hayek, F.A. (1932), 'Reflections on the pure theory of money of Mr. J.M. Keynes (continued)', *Economica*, 12, pp. 22–46.

Hayek, F.A. (1941), *The Pure Theory of Capital*, London: Routledge and Kegan Paul.

Hendry, D.F. (1988), 'Encompassing', *National Institute Economic Review*, 125, pp. 88–92.

Hicks, J.R. (1937), 'Mr. Keynes and the "Classics": a suggested interpretation', *Econometrica*, 5, pp. 147–59.

Hintikka, J., and U. Remes (1974), *The Method of Analysis*, Dordrecht: Reidel.

Jammer, M. (1966), *The Conceptual Development of Quantum Mechanics*, New York: McGraw-Hill.

Keynes, J.M. (1930), *Treatise on Money*, London: Macmillan.
Keynes, J.M. (1931), 'The pure theory of money: a reply to Dr. Hayek', *Economica*, 11, pp. 387–97.
Keynes, J.M. (1936), *The General Theory of Employment, Interest and Money*, London: Macmillan.
Koertge, N. (1969), '*A study of relations between scientific theories: a test of the general correspondence principle*', PhD thesis, University of London, London.
Koopmans, T.C. (1941), 'The logic of econometric business cycle research', *Journal of Political Economy*, 49, April, pp. 157–81.
Krajewski, W. (1977), *Correspondence Principle and the Growth of Science*, Dordrecht: Reidel.
Lakatos, I. (1978), in J. Worral and G. Currie (eds), *Mathematics, Science and Epistemology. Philosophical Papers Volume II*, Cambridge: Cambridge University Press.
Lange, O. (1938), 'The rate of interest and the optimum propensity to consume', *Economica*, 5, February.
Mizon, G. (1984), 'The encompassing approach in econometrics', in D.F. Hendry and K.F. Wallis (eds), *Econometrics and Quantitative Economics*, Oxford: Blackwell.
Morgan, M. (1990), *The History of Econometric Ideas*, Cambridge: Cambridge University Press.
Nowak, L. (1980), *The Structure of Idealization*, Dordrecht: Reidel.
Popper, K.R. (1972), *Conjectures and Refutations*, London: Routledge and Kegan Paul.
Popper, K.R. (1973), *Objective Knowledge*, Oxford: Clarendon Press.
Post, H.R. (1971), 'Correspondence, invariance and heuristics: in praise of conservative induction', *Studies in the History and the Philosophy of Science*, vol. 2, pp. 213–55.
Qin, D. (1991), 'Testing in econometrics during 1930–1960', paper presented at the conference on Testing in Econometrics, Tilburg, November.
Randall, J.H. (1961), *The School of Padua and the Emergence of Modern Science*, Padova: Antenore.
Randall, J.H. (1962), *The Career of Philosophy*, New York: Columbia University Press.
Reddaway, B. (1936), 'The general theory of employment, interest and money', *The Economic Record*, 12, June.
Say, J.B. (1980), *A Treatise on Political Economy*, Kelley reprint of the New America edition.
Schumpeter, J. (1933), 'The common sense of econometrics', *Econometrica I*, pp. 5–12.
Spanos, A. (1990), 'Towards a unifying methodological framework for econometric modelling', in C. Granger (ed.), *Modelling Economic Series; Readings in Econometric Methodology*, pp. 279–303, Oxford: Oxford University Press.
Sraffa, P. (1962), 'Production of commodities: A comment', *Economic Journal*, pp. 477–9.
Stein, J.L. (ed) (1976), *Montetarism*, Amsterdam: North Holland.
Tinbergen, J. (1939), *Statistical Testing of Business Cycle Theories*, Vol. I: *A Method and Its Application to Investment Activity*, Vol. II: *Business Cycles in the United States of America*, Geneva: League of Nations
Watkins, J.W.N. (1984), *Science and Scepticism*, London: Hutchinson.
Worrall, J. (2000), 'The Scope, Limits, and Distinctiveness of the Method of "Deduction from the Phenomena": Some Lessons from Newton's "Demonstrations" in Optics', *British Journal for the Philosophy of Science*, 51, pp. 45–80.

5. Metaphors in the *Wealth of Nations*

Sergio Cremaschi*

I intend to highlight the shaping of Adam Smith's discourse on the growth of wealth, the interactions between economic theory, moral theory and the theory of knowledge, and the ways in which theory and rhetoric safely coexist in his work.[1]

My main claim is that, either by chance or by insight, Adam Smith worked with a blissful combination of metaphors, a combination that helped in widening the scope of economic theory, imagining counterintuitive connections among separated fields, and shaping new hypotheses to be tested. Adam Smith's felicitous choice of his own bunch of metaphors depended on a number of factors: fashion, shared standards of taste, a received set of images and symbols, in a word, a 'scientific style'.[2]

SCIENCE AND ANALOGY IN THE *HISTORY OF ASTRONOMY*

Adam Smith left unpublished fragments of a 'philosophical history of the sciences and the arts'. Schumpeter once wrote that nobody 'can have an adequate idea of Smith's intellectual stature who does not know these essays',[3] but in fact he made hardly any use of them in his own reading of *The Wealth of Nations*. The editors of the Glasgow edition of Adam Smith's works have done a lot to redress the effects of Schumpeter's inadvertence, but some work is still waiting to be done.

Of these fragments, the most renowned one is *The History of Astronomy*, whose first three sections present Adam Smith's views on matters of methodology and epistemology, those views he apparently assumed to be of scarce interest to the reader of *The Wealth of Nations*. Adam Smith puts Hume's philosophy of mind to work as the basis of an historical reconstruction of the leading branch of natural science. As in Hume's epistemology, the Newtonian principle of 'analogy of nature' plays a main function. This is a key principle in the Newtonian methodological tradition stating that we may safely assume that nature is simple, and accordingly may be assumed to employ similar causes in order to bring about similar effects in different domains. The adoption of such a principle, combined with Hume's view of knowledge in terms of association of ideas, yields an original account of theory change. That is, the evolution of 'systems' (that is, theories) which account for the heavenly phenomena is governed by psychological laws. These laws prescribe that gaps in the familiar course of impressions to which our imagination has become accustomed be filled. In order to fill the gap, the mind may have recourse to imaginary ideas. Thus, the mind fills the gaps by means of 'invisible chains' or 'imaginary machines' made of ideas. A good imaginary machine in turn is one that would bring about the observed phenomena in a simple and familiar way.[4]

Every time we say that a new field of (previously disconnected) phenomena has been explained, or that a better explanation has been offered for the same field, this may imply that a new 'imaginary machine' has been built, that is, the gaps between disconnected phenomena have been filled by an 'invisible' chain of phenomena, taken from some more familiar field, that are imagined to lay behind the observable phenomena. In other words, an imaginary machine is built by taking another, more familiar, field as a 'model' for the explanandum, and mapping the chosen model over the explanandum. The chain of models thus gradually produced should eventually end up with some domain where the principles at work are 'visible', not just imagined or hidden behind the veil of phenomena. Technology is the best example of such a domain, since, in building tools and machines, knowing is doing.[5] This is why we see the various fields of natural phenomena *as if* they were machines.

If we assume that Adam Smith believed that this holds also for social phenomena, we may also account in a more convincing way for Adam Smith's intentions and for what he actually did in the field of the social sciences. He probably felt that his audience was interested primarily in the moral and political implications of his argument on the causes of the wealth and poverty of nations, and this is why in *The Wealth of Nations* he was careful to avoid such academic issues as methodology.

A remark may be added on analogy and metaphor. Analogy is believed by Adam Smith to be – along with simplicity and familiarity – one of the characteristics required by the human mind in order to accept new imaginary ideas as parts of the invisible chain between disconnected phenomena. Analogy is always a requirement, even if there may be an excess in its use.[6] Metaphor, on the contrary, is but one figure of speech, and it may be used with some positive aesthetic effect, if it is used with due respect to proportions. 'In every metaphor it is evident there must be an allusion betwixt one object and an other' (Smith, 1983, i.64: 29), but only if such an allusion consists in a resemblance is it a metaphor in a proper sense; if the allusion depends on a close connection, it is a kind of 'metonymie'. A metaphor is thus an 'alteration of the word . . . in its signification' (Smith, 1983, i.63: 28) and consists in giving the word a meaning 'to which it has some resemblance or analogy' (p. 28).

Adam Smith also believes, with the whole tradition of rhetoric stemming from Aristotle, that metaphor is one figure of speech that carries many dangers. He shares the suspicion widespread among modern philosophers (starting with Francis Bacon and the Royal Society) that only 'when the sentiment of the speaker is expressed in a neat, clear, plain and clever manner' (Smith, 1983, i.v.56: 29) is language used as a proper vehicle for ideas and that figures of speech 'have no intrinsic worth of their own'.[7] This concern with clarity and literality may make the actual use of metaphors by Adam Smith – not in poetry or novel, but in philosophical and economic writings – a tricky subject of study. It is true that Smith's texts – as Vivienne Brown notes – in spite of his own precepts in the *Lectures on Rhetoric*, are 'at times deeply metaphorical',[8] but I believe that the most important aspect of Adam Smith's metaphors are their below-the-waterline parts, that is, not the use Smith makes of metaphors but the effects he produces on received concepts and theories by making use of metaphoric transfer of meanings from one domain to another. In other words, not the illocutionary dimension (the effects the author produces by the utterance itself, be they intended or not),[9] but the perlocutionary dimension, that is, effects the author produces by the speech act as such, is the decisive part of the story I intend to tell; the latter effects are always beyond the control of the author, since the speech act is always in the framework of a conversation.[10]

PHYSICAL, BIOLOGICAL AND THEOLOGICAL METAPHORS IN *THE WEALTH OF NATIONS*

Unlike Malthus and, after him, other writers on economic subjects, Adam Smith did not prefix a methodological introduction to his main economic work. Indeed, a reader might look in vain for methodological comments of any kind throughout the five books of the work. Even worse, to our disappointment, speculations about first causes and original qualities lying at the root of 'principles' of economic behaviour, such as the propensity to truck and barter or the propensity to exchange, that occur in a number of passages of the *Lectures on Jurisprudence*, have been systematically deleted from the text of *The Wealth of Nations*. Smith more than once writes at these points: we do not need to ascertain whether the above principle is an original quality of human nature or may be reduced to some more basic quality; for our present concern we may take the above principle for granted.[11] And yet, Adam Smith was dramatically aware that even Newton's work, the most splendid achievement of human reason, amounted to nothing more than an ingenious creation of human imagination, which might be reduced to analogical transfer of ideas from one domain to another. How far is this dramatic awareness reflected in his work? That is, how far was he aware that any discovery of truths, not only in the field of nature but also in the parallel field of man and society, for example, the reconstruction of market mechanisms, amounted to a construction of imaginary machines?

Answers to this question range from the eighteenth-century view of Smith as a dogmatic social theorist, a proponent of the harmony-of-interests thesis and of an optimistic social theodicy,[12] to a post-modernist reading of Adam Smith as staging rhetorical devices with a view at producing persuasion in his own audience. I feel that full sense can be made of what Smith says only if we take a third way: my own answer, not surprisingly, lies somewhere in between. In order to substantiate it, I shall tell the eventful story of several families of metaphors crowding the pages of *The Wealth of Nations*. Let us start with a family enjoying the highest reputation in the eighteenth century: physical metaphors.

Mechanics

Apart from the occurrence of the idea of gravitation, which could hardly escape the reader's attention, the presence of several physical metaphors in *The Wealth of Nations* has generally gone unnoticed.[13] But the metaphors are there, and may be grouped easily according to their primary subjects. Two groups are based on mechanical subjects: the first is fall and rise, the second is circulation.

Concerning the subject of fall and rise, the first remark worth making is that economic magnitudes appear to be located in a two-dimensional space, with a vertical as well as a horizontal dimension. Accordingly, prices and profits may move downward or upward. Smith writes: 'the market price will <rise> more or less <above> the natural price' (Smith, [1776] 1976, I.vii.9: 73–4), 'The market price will <sink> more or less <below> the natural price' (I.vii.10: 74), and 'the <fall> of profit in them and the <rise> of it in all others immediately dispose them to alter this faulty distribution' (IV.vii.c.88: 630).[14]

These examples of ways of representing changes in economic magnitude by mapping these changes over a two-dimensional space carry the implication that change in the economy 'is' spatial movement. This implication opens the door to several questions, namely: if there are 'motions' of prices, profits and rents, what are the causes for such motions? Are they just efficient causes or also final causes? What kinds of laws, if any, govern these motions?

The primary subject of mechanical metaphors, besides upward or downward movements, is provided on a few occasions by circular movement. Smith writes that money is the 'great <wheel> of <circulation>' (Smith, [1776] 1976, II.ii.14: 289; II.ii.23: 291), that is, its function is that of smoothing the shift of other goods from one owner to another. In this passage, 'circulation' is a rotating movement of a wheel; in other passages it is rather the flow of a fluid, namely value, through the vessels of a living body. I will discuss these hydraulic or biological metaphors in what follows.

Dynamics

Other physical metaphors draw their primary subject from what is now another sub-discipline of physics, namely dynamics. Here not only spatial movements are at stake, but also their causes, that is, forces.

The occurrence of the idea of gravitation is familiar even to the reader of the bunch of standard quotations from *The Wealth of Nations* that used to appear in economics textbooks. Smith describes prices, natural rates of salaries, profits and rents as gravitating around some average or central point that may be called a natural price. 'Gravitating' means moving upwards and downwards, but with a tendency to come back towards some given point, as if this point was able to exert some kind of attraction. Smith here spells out the metaphor by an 'as if' clause. He writes that the natural price

> is, as it were, the <central> price, to which the prices of all commodities are contin-
> ually <gravitating>. Different accidents may sometimes keep them <suspended> a
> good deal <above> it, and sometimes force them down even somewhat <below> it.
> But whatever may be the obstacles which hinder them from settling in this centre of
> <repose> and continuance, they are constantly <tending> towards it. (Smith, [1776]
> 1976, I.vii.15: 75)

The most famous (and often misquoted) passage from *The Wealth of Nations* is a metaphor based on a dynamic subject. In more detail, it is based on the Newtonian way of equating a *vis a tergo* (that is, an impressed force, transmitted by direct contact between bodies) with a *vis attractiva* (that is, an attractive force by one body which carries out an 'action at a distance' on another body). In this notorious passage Smith writes:

> Every individual is continually exerting himself to find out the most advantageous
> employment for whatever capital he can command . . . and he is . . . <led> by an
> invisible hand to promote an end which was no part of his intention. (Smith, [1776]
> 1976, IV.ii.4–9: 456)

The passage is meant to illustrate how (in present-day jargon) market mech-anisms bring about the optimal allocation of capital. The passage has been quoted numberless times as an illustration of the harmony-of-interests thesis, or as proof of Smith's 'modernity' in forerunning the self-regulating mechanisms of post-marginalist microeconomics. In fact, what the passage tries to prove is that human actions can bring about the same effect, both in cases where the effect was intended and in cases where it was no part of the agent's intention.[15] In other words, Smith's claim is not the deterministic character of the cause–effect relationship but instead the equivalence of a final and an efficient cause or of a *vis a tergo* and a *vis attractiva*. No suggestion is made that the hand's invisibility implies its being the Hand of God, as was safely assumed by interpreters who used to read Adam Smith as the proponent of a dogmatically optimistic social theodicy centred on the harmony-of-interests thesis.

Hydraulics

At a number of places in *The Wealth of Nations*, circulation is the circular flow of a fluid rather than the rotating motion of a wheel. In fact in everyday language, at least in most modern languages, cash is 'liquid', which implies that money is 'a fluid'. This is an entrenched way of speaking of money on which Smith elaborates, spelling out the further implication that the laws of hydraulics that apply to fluids do apply to money as well. For example, while discussing one ruinous experiment in banking, he suggests that the

> coffers of the bank . . . resemble a water pond, from which, though a stream is continually running out, yet another is continually running in, fully equal to that which runs out; so that . . . the pond keeps always equally, or very near equally full. (Smith, [1776] 1976, II.ii. 59: 304)

Thus, the

> project of replenishing their coffers in this manner may be compared to that of a man who had a water-pond from which a stream was continually running out, and into which no stream was continually running, but who proposed to keep it always equally full by employing a number of people to go continually with buckets to a well at some miles distance in order to bring water to replenish it. (Smith, [1776] 1976, II.ii.76: 316)

A similar primary subject drawn from hydraulics provides the basis for another metaphor, invoked in order to account for the devastating effects of accumulation of gold and silver in Spain and Portugal after the conquest of South America. Smith writes:

> When you dam up a stream of water, as soon as the dam is full, as much water must run over the dam-head as if there was no dam at all . . . As the water, however, must always be deeper behind the dam-head than before it, so the quantity of gold and silver which these restraints detain in Spain and Portugal must, in proportion to the annual produce of their land and labour, be greater than what is to be found in other countries. (Smith, [1776] 1976, IV.v.a.19: 512)

Biology and Medicine

Almost inadvertently, as soon as blood is substituted for water, the primary subjects of metaphor shift from hydraulics to biology and medicine. Here it is

Harvey's discovery of the circulation of blood that provides the blueprint. Smith writes that the monopoly of the colony trade seems to have modified the 'natural balance' among different branches of the British economy and 'commerce, instead of running in a great number of <small channels>, has been taught to run principally in one <great channel>' (Smith, [1776] 1976, IV.vii.c.43: 604).

As a consequence, the 'whole system of her industry and commerce' has become less safe. This has made

> the whole state of her <body politick> less healthful, than it otherwise would have been . . . one of those unwholesome bodies in which some of the vital parts are over-grown . . . A small stop in that great blood-vessel, which has been artificially swelled beyond its natural dimensions, and through which an unnatural proportion of the industry and commerce of the country has been forced to circulate, is very likely to bring on the most dangerous disorders upon the whole body politick. (Smith, [1776] 1976, IV.vii.c.43: 604–5)

And he concludes that the blood,

> of which the circulation is stopt in some of the smaller vessels, easily disgorges itself into the greater, without occasioning any dangerous disorder; but, when it is stopt in any of the greater vessels, convulsion, apoplexy, or death, are the immediate and unavoidable consequences. (Smith, [1776] 1976, IV.vii.c.43: 605)

The latter quotation states that society is an organism, or a body. The quote embodies a mixed metaphor which maps the secondary subject over two primary subjects at once. In fact, at a certain level, commerce is the flow of a liquid; at a further level, this liquid is what nourishes a living organism. The idea of society as an organism is another entrenched image, lying at the root of the classical phrase, 'the body politick'. Some political theorizing has been done, starting with classical authors, by elaborating on this idea. In *The Wealth of Nations* the idea comes back more than once. For example, the effort of every man 'of bettering his own condition' is, for society as a whole, a 'principle' that keeps it healthy. We find here once more an explicit simile: 'This . . . effort of every man . . . [l]ike the unknown <principle of animal life> . . . frequently restores health . . . in spite, not only of the disease, but of the absurd prescriptions of the doctor' (Smith, [1776] 1976, I.iii.31: 343).

Smith elaborates further on this point while discussing the doctrines of the physiocrats. The focus of his criticism is the kind of artificialism that lies at the root of physiocracy. He notes that some 'speculative physician seems to have imagined that the health of the human body could be preserved only by a certain precise regimen of diet and exercise'. He seems to be alluding in fact to a famous Scottish physician of his time, Nicholas Cheyne, who was a proponent of a Christian Stoic view, recomending an ascetic regime (see Cheyne, 1725). Smith's remark is that experience, on the contrary, 'would seem to show that the human body frequently preserves, to all appearance at least, the most perfect state of health under a vast variety of different regimens' (Smith, [1776] 1976, IV.ix.28: 673), and that

> the healthful state of the human body . . . contains in itself some *unknown* principle of preservation, capable of preventing or correcting, in many respects, the bad effects even of a very faulty regimen. Mr. Quesnai, who was himself a physician . . . seems to have entertained a notion of the same kind concerning the <political body> . . . In the political body, however, the wisdom of nature has fortunately made ample provision for remedying many of the bad effects of the folly and injustice of man; in the same manner as it has done in the natural body. (Smith, [1776] 1976, IV.ix.28: 673–4; emphasis added)

The reader may note that the 'principle of preservation' lies at a level deeper than that of observable phenomena. It may be not unreasonable to think that it is the same non-observable level of 'invisible' chains, 'invisible hands' and 'imaginary' machines, and that the dual structure of observable phenomena and hidden connecting principles may be assumed to exist not only in nature, but also in society. In the latter case the hidden level includes behaviour of individuals in their private lives, that is, phenomena that are apparently unconnected to each other. Also in social phenomena, 'philosophy' proves to be able to bring about connectedness. In fact, 'the natural effort which every man is continuously making to better his own condition' (ibid.) plays in the body politick the same role as the 'unknown' principle of preservation plays in the biological body.[16]

Agriculture, or Energy

Another sustained metaphor, or an allegory, may be detected in Book II, where value is described as a substance, something like a force transformed into energy. Smith says that 'the labour of the manufacturer <fixes> and realizes itself in some particular subject or vendible commodity . . . It is, as it were, a certain quantity of labour stocked and stored up' (Smith, [1776] 1976, II.iii.1: 330). This quantity of labour stored in some portion of matter 'can afterwards . . . put into motion a quantity of labour equal to that which had originally produced it' (ibid.). What Smith seems to have in mind is a transformation of *labour* (active force) into *value* (energy) stored in *land* (matter).

It is this hidden fluid or substance that keeps the economy alive, and this 'abstract' entity survives in the transformation or consumption of material goods. In fact what is annually saved is as regularly consumed as what is annually spent . . . but it is consumed by a different kind of people . . . That portion which he annually saves, as. . . it is immediately employed as a capital, is consumed . . . by labourers . . . who reproduce with a profit the value of their annual consumption. (Smith, [1776] 1976, II.iii.18: 338)

Trying to sum up what is suggested by a review of the various families of metaphors, we could read some kind of allegory into *The Wealth of Nations*. This allegory represents the economy as a rotating wheel or a circulating fluid, following blueprints drawn from astronomy, biology and agriculture. Such a circular process is understood as a self-expanding process since, as soon as a new cycle begins, fresh portions of land and labour are 'attracted' into the economy's circular movement.

METAPHORS IN *THE THEORY OF MORAL SENTIMENTS* AND IN THE ESSAYS ON PHILOSOPHICAL SUBJECTS

The most famous passage from Smith, the invisible hand passage, actually occurs twice: the first time in *The Theory of Moral Sentiments* in connection with consumption and distribution, the second in *The Wealth of Nations*, with reference to investment. But other hands, more or less invisible, occur at other places in Smith's oeuvre.

An 'invisible hand' had already shown up in the *History of Astronomy*. After noting that the world-picture of ancient peoples used to ascribe to divine intervention only irregular events, not ordinary ones, he adds: 'Fire burns, and water refreshes; heavy bodies descend, and lighter substances fly upwards, by the necessity of their own nature; nor was the invisible Hand of Jupiter ever apprehended to be employed in those matters' (Smith, [1795a] 1980, III.2: 49).[17] *Of the External Senses* talks, instead of God's hand, of the hand of Nature. Smith writes that 'Alarm is always the fear of some uncertain evil beyond what is immediately felt, and from some unknown and external cause' (Smith, [1795b] 1980, 87: 168). It is an effect produced so quickly that it may seem 'an impression immediately struck by the Hand of Nature' (ibid.).

In *The Theory of Moral Sentiments* hands are mentioned twice. The first time, within the context of a discussion on the significance of wealth for human happiness, Smith suggests that the rich contribute, through an unintended effect, to the livelihood of their fellows. The rich

consume little more than the poor, and . . . by the gratification of their vain and insatiable desires, they divide with the poor the produce of all their improvements. They are <led by an invisible hand> to make nearly the same distribution of the necessaries of life, which would have been made, had the earth been divided into equal portions among all its inhabitants. (Smith, [1759] 1976, IV.1.10: 184)

The passage from *The Wealth of Nations* on the invisible hand and optimal allocation of capital has often been matched with this, but not with another passage in *The Theory of Moral Sentiments* where Smith mentions chessboards. Smith says that the 'man of system', that is, the doctrinaire political reformer

> seems to imagine that he can arrange the different members of a great society with as much ease as the hand arranges the different pieces upon a chessboard. He does not consider that the piece upon the chessboard has no other <principle of motion> of its own, altogether different from that which the legislature might choose to <impress> upon it. (Smith, [1759] 1976, VI.ii.2.17: 234)

The quoted passage (from the 1790 additions) is meant to stress the distinction between human intentions and unintended results. The implication is that individuals in society are like bodies provided with an original motion, previous to any 'artificial' intervention. One obvious consequence is that political artificialism is ineffective, since it ignores the 'dynamic' dimension of social life. A less obvious precondition of what Smith says is a picture of society that depicts it not as a machine but instead as a system that is never at rest. The source of this picture may be Hobbes's atomistic view of nature, consisting of parts endowed with an original principle of motion or, in the jargon of seventeenth-century natural philosophy, with a *conatus*. It may also be a closer source, namely the Newtonian view of the universe, where the planets are never at rest, and yet a state of equilibrium is produced by the principle of gravitation.

To sum up: metaphors are no less frequent in *The Wealth of Nations* than in other works by Smith with a more traditionally 'literary' character; indeed, the favoured primary subjects of metaphor appear to be the same in all of Smith's oeuvre. Only the theme of circulation is probably peculiar to *The Wealth of Nations*. When seen from this viewpoint, Adam Smith's discourse tends to sound much in the same voice in both *The Wealth of Nations* and *The Theory of Moral Sentiments*.[18]

SOURCES OF ADAM SMITH'S METAPHORS

Adam Smith's metaphors tend to be mixed, a kind of metaphor that never met with success among literary critics. And his way of building economic theories tends – pace the anti-baroque leanings of the 'Augustan Age' and his own stylistic precepts in the *Lectures on Rhetoric* – to yield allegories (that is, stories told by sustained use of a few metaphors). In fact, the sources from which he draws either primary subjects or metaphors to be developed further are at once previous economic doctrines, moral and political philosophy, natural philosophy, biology, medicine and agriculture. Several of these themes are mapped onto each other, or the implications of one metaphor are further developed by taking advantage of developments in the primary subject. Examples are Harvey's theory of sanguine circulation for the iatro-mechanical analogy or Newton's idea of gravitation for the pre-existing analogy of the social order and a state of equilibrium in a pair of scales. Thus the themes of society as an organism, money or value as fluids, labour as a force embodied into matter, circulation, passions as forces, individuals as atoms, society as a machine, gravitation and invisible hands coexist with each other and are occasionally blended together.

Let us look at several sources of the metaphors that have been reviewed above. One source is moral and political discourse. From this context derives the view of society as a kind of a cosmos. This view was widespread among Renaissance writers, combined with a Platonic assumption of a correspondence between microcosm and macrocosm. It won different implication as soon as the connotation of the primary subject (that is, the physical universe) underwent gradual modifications. The view of society as analogous to the Newtonian universe presented by English Platonic rationalists such as Ralph Cudworth and Samuel Clarke opened the way for a transfer of concepts of force and equilibrium from the physical to the social realm. Human passions were understood as forces causing social motion, and the rational order that is produced as a result of the combined effects of those passions – the non-rational behaviour of individuals notwithstanding – is equivalent to the equilibrium of the 'isolated system' of post-Galilean physics.

Another source is provided by previous economic theories, particularly those of economic pamphleteers of the seventeenth and eighteenth centuries. This provides a number of tentative analogies on which Smith elaborates. The economic pamphleteers of the seventeenth and eighteenth centuries repeated several times a few basic mechanical analogies. Hume, in 'Of the balance of trade' (1752b: 333), mentions the dam and the stream in order to stress the same point made by Smith in *The Wealth of Nations*. In 'Of money' he mentions wheels with reference to money but, curiously enough, he seems to think of trade not in terms of circulation, but of a machine run by wheels. In this connection he also talks of money in terms of oil which reduces friction. He writes: 'Money is not, properly speaking, one of the subjects of commerce . . . It is none of the wheels of trade: It is the oil which renders the motion of the wheels more smoooth and easy' (Hume, 1752b: 309).

Cantillon, in *Essai sur la Nature du Commerce en Général* (1755: I.x) talks of 'perpetual ebbs and flow' of market prices.[19]

Sources of Smith's circular view of the economy (besides the all-pervading stoic cyclical view of both history and nature) are the economic pamphleteers, such as Thomas Mun and Edward Misselden, and the physiocrats.[20]

One notorious source of Smith's views on value is Locke's theory of property, justified on the ground of the intercourse between man and land. Labour, according to Locke, '*makes the far greatest part of the value* of things, we enjoy in this world' (Locke, [1690] 1988, par. 42: 297). Since the labour of his body and the work of his hands are his property, what has been removed 'out of the State that Nature hath provided', he 'hath mixed his *Labour* with, and joyned to it something that is his own, and thereby makes it his *Property*' (Locke, [1690] 1988, 27: 287–8). Locke's labour is apparently a creative activity, while matter is a passive *res extensa*. Thus the former may be seen as a *force* which becomes *energy* when it is infused with matter. Such a vision may suggest one further implication that actually takes place in Smith, that is, the idea that value, as 'labour embodied', is a force or energy incorporated into material things.

Another notorious source of metaphors – and an occasion of heavy misunderstanding of Adam Smith's discourse – is post-Reformation theology. A contemporary example of use of the notion of the hand of God is in Priestley; he writes that the study of history 'strengthens the sentiments of virtue by the variety of views in which it exhibits the conduct of Divine Providence and points out the Hand of God in the affairs of men' (Priestley, [1788] 1972: 25).[21]

Biology, medicine and agriculture provide another family of sources. The most important theme from these sources is the idea of circular processes. Circulation started to be a fashionable idea since Harvey discovered the circulation of blood in the human body. Quesnay was himself a physician, and he looked at a familiar phenomenon, namely the 'circulation' of corn, from seed to crop, and back, through Harvey's lenses: thus corn became a fluid running though the body of society and bringing life to it; society itself was an organism, like a tree, and a fluid running through its trunk and branches used to bring nourishment, first produced by agriculture, to industry and commerce.[22]

Note that, once again, the older iatro-political simile was revived thanks to a re-description of the primary subject (that is, society is a body; but bodies live thanks to blood circulation; accordingly also societies have some 'circulation' of some kind of 'blood'). Thus, an already blurred source for one of Smith's mixed metaphors is the Physiocrats' view of the reproduction of wealth, understood in terms of agricultural cycles where seed is laid down into land, and comes back again, as crop, at the starting point of a new cycle. One implication of the physiocrats' circular view of the process of reproduction of wealth is the view of wealth as a 'substance'.[23] For the physiocrats, that substance was corn, which could be used as the *seed* for new wealth. In Smith, this same scheme is preserved, but substituting labour value for agricultural produce.

Let us come to the source of the main family of metaphors, namely physics.

From this source Smith draws his idea of 'equilibrium' (note that there is no such word in Smith). Smith's idea of 'equilibrium' is derived, through contamination, both from the gravitation of the Newtonian cosmos and from the scales, the body politic analogy typical of 'liberal' political thinking of the seventeenth and eighteenth centuries.[24]

Newtonian mass and Smithian value are twin concepts. An equivalent of the first definition of Newton's *Principia* can be traced in *The Wealth of Nations*, according to which quantity of matter, or mass, is in proportion to weight, resulting from density and bulk jointly. *The Wealth of Nations* may be assumed to give the following definition: goods are endowed with an intrinsic property, value. Value – given a stable monetary unit – is in proportion to monetary price; value per unit of commodity corresponds to the Newtonian density; product, measured in physical terms, corresponds to bulk.[25]

The idea of the invisible hand in *The Wealth of Nations* is one more item, together with gravitation, of the system of forces that keeps the economy as a whole in a state of balance, or spontaneously restores this state once it has been altered. In other words, the invisible hand belongs to the context of the physico-political analogy, not to that of the theologico-political analogy. A digression on the occurrence of the expression 'invisible hand' in the correspondence between Newton and his disciple and editor Cotes is in order here.

INVISIBLE HAND IN NEWTON

The notorious expression 'invisible hand' occurs, half a century before *The Wealth of Nations*, in a letter from Roger Cotes to Newton. The former raises an objection to Newton *à propos* gravitation; he argues that attraction of one planet by another, caused by a non-observable principle such as an attractive force, would look to the observer as the effect would look of an 'invisible' (that is, invisible to an observer under a given perspective) hand which would push a sphere laid on a table towards another sphere. In other words, the wording is used by Cotes to point to an example of a non-observable cause for an observable motion.

> Suppose two globes A & B [are] placed at a distance from each other upon a table, and that whilst A remains at rest B is moved towards it by an Invisible Hand. A by-stander who observes this motion but not the cause of it, will say that B does certainly tend to the centre of A, and thereupon he may call the force of the invisible Hand the centripetal force of B, or the attraction of A since ye effect appears the same as if it did truly proceed from a proper and real attraction of A. (Cotes, 1712: 392)

Cotes's invisible hand is not the hand of a God who impresses motion on planets or who intervenes in order to repair breakdowns in the great clock of the universe. Cotes's invisible hand is just a human hand pushing a globe placed upon a table while being hidden to an observer who is looking at the globe from a certain perspective. What is important for Cotes is the eventuality of an unobserved cause for an observed motion. He intends to stress the possibility of accounting for one phenomenon in two alternative ways.

Cotes's use of such an expression is important for us, even if it is unlikely that Smith may have been acquainted with his correspondence with Newton. There might have been some other shared source that I have been unable to detect, or there may have been some kind of oral tradition. In any event, in Cotes's letter the invisible hand simile was introduced in order to express the idea of alternative compatible causes for the same phenomenon. If one ranks Smith's invisible hand together with 'gravitation' and the 'animal principle', it turns out that multiple causality, or better, coexistence of observable causes and hidden causes, the former acting at a surface level and the latter at a deeper level, is constantly the focus of these different kinds of images.[26]

SMITHIAN ECONOMIC THEORY AND DEEP METAPHORS

Three comments are in order at this stage. The first concerns Adam Smith's description of the economy. The main elements are *labour* and *land*, inherited from Petty, Cantillon, Steuart and the physiocrats. According to Smith's scheme, production amounts to extracting commodities from land, and each commodity is equivalent to a portion of land into which some amount of labour has been infused. Another notion is drawn from the physiocrats, namely the idea of *renascent wealth*, or of wealth as something that may be the *seed* that will yield a crop, or more wealth. In Smith's construction, nothing is completely new: everything has been built using building blocks taken from the ruins of his predecessors' buildings; but the meanings of these building blocks are twisted and blended with each other in the course of the reconstruction process. The outcome is that, for example, productive labour is not only work spent in the production of agricultural produce, but also every kind of work spent in producing any kind of material good, or all work that 'fixes and realizes itself in some particular subject or vendible commodity, which lasts for some time at least after that labour is past' (Smith, [1776] 1976, II.iii.1: 330). In another language, labour-as-force is transformed into labour-as-energy, embodied into a portion of matter, and thus able to exert an attractive force on potential labour (or 'labour force'). Or again, it is the production of material goods that gives revenue, which one may later choose to consume or invest. If material goods are used as capital goods, more labour may be mobilized during the subsequent productive cycle. Mixed metaphors were usual in the baroque age and then went out of fashion. Adam Smith's mixed metaphors are used at a deeper level by a writer who is far from baroque in his style *qua* writer; the readers of *The Wealth of Nations* quite often misunderstood such metaphors, or the whole allegorical texture of the work, in that they tended to note just the simplest mechanistic analogies and to take them literally.

The second comment concerns differences and similarities between transfer of notions from previous phases of economic discourse and from other disciplines. It may be appropriate to note that the transfer of notions takes place either in a vertical dimension – within the history of the same kind of discourse – or in a horizontal dimension (crossing the border between different kinds of discourse, say, from natural science to social science). In both cases the freshly described mechanism or the 'imaginary machine' is not completely identical to the original one; it results from partial modification, always carrying some kind of extension. For example, when the physiocrats' cyclical view of the economy is transformed into Smith's cyclical view, it is labour value, not corn, that becomes the substance of self-renovating wealth; or also, when the Newtonian view of gravitation becomes Smith's view of gravitation of market prices, it is individuals as atoms (the etymology of both words is the same), not parts of matter, that are put into motion by forces leading them to mutual equilibrium.

The third comment is that in *The Wealth of Nations* a unified domain of the economic was constituted through a process of metaphorical redescription, carried out primarily by means of a device that has always been a literary critic's bogey, namely mixed metaphor. In my reading, the examples of metaphor-statements I have reviewed are clues to deeper metaphorical redescriptions. The national economy becomes for Adam Smith a whole, with its own 'laws' (that is, societal laws, different from 'laws' in a literal sense, that is, legal and moral laws), precisely in so far as it is described not in terms of individual human beings and physical goods, but in terms of the metamorphoses of a 'substance', exchange value. In this way a world emerges that is analogous to the Newtonian physical world, with its own forces, action at a distance, mass and energy. This world may be conceived of as an imaginary machine: the simple machine of 'gravitation' or the more complex machine of 'circulation'; but circulation is not only an analogon of the Copernican solar system: it is also, on a number of occasions, analogous to Harvey's human body, with blood circulation, and of the physiocrats' 'real' economy, with its circulation of corn (and here the mixed metaphor celebrates its own apotheosis). Finally, the 'imaginary machine' of wealth may somehow reflect an (unknowable) unified world order like that conceived by the stoics, with absolute causal necessity and a perennial cyclical movement. One may add that there is scarcely any room for the opposition of mechanicism and organicism, as it is commonly understood since Marshall's times. In fact, the life sciences went into a revolutionary phase in the second half of the eighteenth century. This accounts for the presence of biological analogy in the economics of both Quesnay and Smith. But the *raison d'être* of the biological scientific revolution was precisely the Newtonian legacy that inspired also the various projects of moral Newtonianism, where Smith's oeuvre belongs.[27] The key idea of the new approach to the life sciences was the assumption of a dual structure also for biological phenomena, following the blueprint of Newton's opposition of 'phenomena' and 'principles'.

To sum up, a basic physico-moral analogy provides the framework for Adam Smith's overall social theory, and not surprisingly for his theory of market mechanisms. Even the famous invisible hand passage depends on the basic physico-moral analogy and accordingly implies less than the received view believes: it is just meant to join a teleological with a causal explanation. Smith has recourse to other analogies, fitting them, as far as possible, to the basic machine analogy. For example, a blend of Locke's and the physiocrats' view yields a view of labour in terms of energy undergoing subsequent transformation. The circulation scheme expands the machine scheme, transforming it into some kind of self-expanding machine. A iatro-mechanical analogy is as pervasive as the physico-moral analogy in Adam Smith's thinking and provides the framework for his overall evolutionary theory of society and for those passages in *The Wealth of Nations* where he has recourse to a theory of the self-correcting power of society that helps amend market failures and mistaken policies.[28]

SMITHIAN METAPHORS AFTER ADAM SMITH

Let us ask one more question. If Adam Smith's metaphors are the mark of something deeper and more important than his literary style, did they leave any bequest to later economic thought? Let us see what happened to them when, at the turn of the century, *The Wealth of Nations* began to be quoted as the greatest authority in what was now believed to be the science of 'political economy'.

Let us start by reading the following passages from Ricardo's *Principles*: 'Gold and silver are no doubt subject to <fluctuations>' (Ricardo, [1819] 1951: 14); 'the correct language would be to say, that corn and labour have remained <stationary>, and all other things have <risen> in value' (p. 19); 'a <fall> in their value and not a <rise> in the value of the things with which they are compared' (p. 19); and 'labour, as being the <foundation>' (p. 20).

I suggest that the words marked in the above quotes embody frozen metaphors; they seem to imply the assumption of a spatial dimension in which the economy is placed, a universe of forces like that of Newtonian physics, and the idea of value as a physical object. If we follow the story told through Chapter 1 of the *Principles*, the value-as-a-substance mixed metaphor may be taken as a key to the chapter. The chapter's plot then becomes the following: value is a thing, a physical magnitude, consisting at once of Corn and of Labour, and this thing remains invariable through its transformations into various commodities.[29]

Let us consider now a few passages from Malthus's *Principles*: 'the <laws> which regulate the <movements> of human society' (Malthus, [1820] 1989: 11); 'Man . . . is the primary <source> of all demand' (p. 83); 'the separation of rents . . . is a <law> as invariable as the action of the <principle of gravity>' (p. 123, fn. 17); and 'the natural restrictions upon the importation of foreign corn during the war . . . may have directed the capital of the country into a <channel> more advantageous than that it would otherwise have <flowed>' (p. 328).

Here we have a set of statements embodying metaphors somewhat different from Ricardo's. Not unlike him, Malthus assumes the framework of Newtonian physics as a model, but, unlike him, the spatial/physical representation of the economy is subordinated to a higher-level representation based on a system of 'laws' or 'principles' that supervises the direction of the 'flows' and 'movements' through the 'channels' of the economy. These motives are combined with others, deriving from older strata of metaphorical redescription. One example is the following simile (applied to laissez faire): 'The ablest <physicians> are the most sparing in the use of <medicine>, and the most inclined to trust to the healing <power> of nature' (p. 15).

The simile is a variation on Adam Smith's application of the older iatro-political metaphor to the economy. Another simile is an elaboration of an earth-as-a-machine metaphor. Malthus writes: 'The earth has been sometimes compared to a <vast machine> . . . for the production of food and raw material; but, to make the resemblance more just . . . we should consider the soil as . . . a <great number of machines> . . . of very different original qualities and powers' (p. 135).

I suggest that for Malthus and Ricardo the description of the economy in *The Wealth of Nations* had already become a starting point, and Smith's metaphors were almost frozen metaphors. And yet, on the basis of such a shared vision, a number of differences emerge: there is a preference by each of them for certain nuances within this cluster of metaphors, or shifts in the barycentre of this cluster. Thus, the organic metaphor is constantly (albeit not exclusively) preferred by Malthus; one reason for this preference may be that it allowed for implications which responded to the need to take a multiplicity of factors (social, cultural, institutional) into account, which was in its turn prompted by his strategy and 'scientific style'.[30]

New metaphors (such as crises, growth, land as the outer limit to the expanding wheel of the economy), while apparently describing a Smithian world as if it was the world out there (or a 'natural kind'), may be understood as something more than rhetorical stratagems employed in order to depict the facts in some preferred way, and also something more than heuristic devices. They may be understood as shifts in the below-the-waterline part of their pre-comprehension of the subject matter and of the categories through which that subject matter might be organized or, in Foucault's words, in the shared *episteme*.

A shift introduced in a metaphor is a part of a more general strategy. For example, talk of economic laws may have different implications: laws may be expressions of an immanent physico-moral order of the world, as for the physiocrats, or they may be 'superimposed' on the original motion of such entities via the unintended-results principle, as for Adam Smith. In Malthus we find a preference for the expression 'cause' instead of law. Ricardo is fond of the expression 'law', albeit in his writings the term assumes a connotation opposite to that of the physiocrats: an economic law for Ricardo is more similar to a mathematical law than to natural law.

The introduction of new metaphors into an already shaped metaphorical (re)description of the world has the consequence of modifying it. A good example is the appearance of the idea of crisis in economic thought: the word 'crisis', in a political (and then economic) sense, comes into use at about the time of the French Revolution. 'Crisis' – etymologically, 'judgement' – comes from juridical, medical and theological jargon. The word started to be used in English in the last decade of the eighteenth century in order to describe the high risk of a sudden social change or a <revolution> (in its turn an astronomico-political metaphor). The first pamphlet by Malthus was entitled precisely *The Crisis*. In Malthus's political economy the permanent risk of under-consumption hints precisely at the risk of an economic crisis, in present-day jargon, or of the beginning of one of those 'intervals' of disturbances which used to show up between two 'permanent states' in the economy. We already met 'cycles' in Adam Smith, where they were a legacy of the stoical view of history. Yet, talk of 'crises', instead of 'cycles', conveys an image of historical trends as more precarious and unstable. This makes room for a prudent intervention by the politician, if not in the role of Adam Smith's 'man of System' trying to impart an artificial order to society, at least in that of a helmsman who avoids the opposite shoals of under-consumption and of too sudden rises in public expenditure.

A similar reconstruction might be made for other root metaphors used in economic discourse at Malthus's and Ricardo's time. One is that of 'growth' of food and population, central to Malthus's *Essay on the Principle of Population*; it brings into the picture one biological metaphor that was still absent in Smith, waiting to be explored by later evolutionary approaches in economics, from Marshall to social Darwinism. Another is the metaphor of Land as the Limit. At the time of the multiple discovery of the law of rent by Malthus and others, the Land, understood as a series of increasingly less efficient machines for the production of food, is yet another metaphor added to Adam Smith's vision. The new metaphor thus added modifies and expands one of the basic metaphors in his work, equilibrium.

Here, with the principle of population and rent theory, we face a feedback loop, where the addition of one more unit of population and/or food, or the tillage of one more unit of land, retroacts upon the whole system. Even if the kind of analogy is basically the same as in Smith's gravitation of prices, its role is quite different: in Smith the feedback acts within the economic system, whose development is basically governed by another logic; in Malthus the feedback governs the external boundaries of the economic system, and accordingly its chances of growth or stagnation.

DEEP METAPHORS

If metaphors are not just a marginal feature of Adam Smith's discourse, what use might we make of such metaphors? We may, with Braithwaite, Boyd and other philosophers of science from the 1950s and 1960s, look for their heuristic function, if any, and then go on with the more serious pursuit of studying how scientific terms have an empirical content, or refer, or <cut the world> at its proper <junctures>, or we may, with McCloskey, examine how metaphor works as one more way (besides 'story', 'logic' and 'fact') of introducing order, of unifying appearances and thereby, hopefully, of convincing an audience. But we may also try to single out deeper basic metaphors behind individual metaphorical statements. These deep metaphors mould ways of 'seeing' one domain (the economic) in terms of some other domain. And it is this Wittgensteinean process of 'seeing as' that lies at the root of any new conceptual mapping.[31]

For many economists, one of McCloskey's astonishing discoveries was that economists also use metaphors. And yet, despite their astonishment, the standard response has been: 'yes, thank you, and then?' In fact, this is the way that the 'orthodox' philosophy of science used to deal with the topic: metaphor-models are used by scientists as by anybody else, but they are useful at most in some preliminary phase – be it the context of discovery, as in Braithwaite, or the introduction of new scientific terms, as in Boyd – after which they are substituted by literal meanings. Metaphors may thus be present, and even ubiquitous, in science, but they have no permanent cognitive value. One reason for this defensive reaction is that metaphor is generally equated with vagueness, and science with precision.[32] McCloskey, on the contrary, insisted that metaphor is ubiquitous in economic discourse; that model building, the most mathematized part of the economist's job, which gives to economics the aura of a 'hard' science, is instead the point where it comes closer to poetry; that metaphor is always a 'way of doing things with words', and distinguishing its poetical and its scientific use means missing its specific function.[33]

McCloskey is right in giving metaphor as full citizenship in science as in poetry and in stressing the creative function of metaphor in science. What is wrong with such an account is, first, an equation of science with fiction as a different means of producing persuasion,[34] and second, a belief that the fact that economists make things with words pertains primarily to the perlocutionary aspect of language – and accordingly that the economist's use of metaphor is almost arbitrary, being one among other means for producing persuasion – and, as I will argue in the next paragraph, a fixation with the literary style of the economists' writings, overlooking what really matters, that is, their 'scientific style'.[35]

Things are even worse with Brown's (1994) discourse: if the reconstruction carried out in the present paper makes sense, the claim that metaphors are ubiquitous is fine; but this is not tantamount to saying that we may give any meaning we like to texts, reading metaphors freely. The success of Brown's attempt depends on the viability of the conclusion that 'if, following the meaning of vision metaphors in Adam Smith's *The Theory of Moral Sentiments*, vision refers to moral judgement, then the metaphor of the invisible hand signals that the invisible hand, being sightless and out of sight, is beyond the realm of moral discourse'.[36] But 'invisibility' of hands, chains, wheels, and hidden or imaginary machines of any sort depends on a distinction of a phenomenal and a deeper level of causal connections, not on the visibility of behaviour to a judge. And the ascription of the above meaning to Smith's 'invisibility' depends on the reconstruction of a context of received concepts and theories. *The Wealth of Nations* belongs to this context in force of objective reasons, not of any decision by the author of this paper. In other words, the reading of Adam Smith's metaphors need not be metaphorical, no less than theories on the chemical composition of sugar need be sweet.

To sum up: economists are not free to choose any metaphor they like, for they 'are subject to constitutive metaphors' and these 'are not picked up and discarded like heuristic metaphors or mere preferences'.[37] Mirowski's historical epistemology has granted metaphor a role much more basic than McCloskey's, looking beyond surface metaphorical expressions and identifying deep basic metaphors, such as the physico-moral parallel underlying the modern world-view which also moulded economic science. This overlaps fairly well with what I suggest here in so far as it means taking developments in post-empiricist philosophy of science on scientific metaphor seriously.[38]

Let me add some more words on these developments. The claim that science has recourse to anthropomorphic metaphors was first advanced by philosophers as different as Nietzsche and Peirce. The new rhetoricians, Richards and Burke, the aesthetician Stephen Pepper and, more recently, the linguist George Lakoff have reformulated the same claim. The Nietzsche–Peirce thesis contends that no genre of discourse is immune from tropes, scientific discourse included, and metaphor is the master trope of science, the basic tool for organizing and exploring the unknown, and thus – against Aristotle – it is more basic to science than to poetry. After the war waged by Galileo, the Royal Society and Newton against metaphor and rhetoric in the name of 'plain discourse' and 'facts', and after the Romantic rescue of metaphor in the name of a rebellion against the Enlightenment, metaphor was believed by both camps to be the mark of poetry, religion and myth, as opposed to the field of science where precision and literality rule. Still, a few decades ago, philosophers of science ranging from logical empiricists such as Hempel and Braithwaite to metaphysical realists such as Boyd, were prepared to condone models and analogies either as tools for a scientific heuristics or as means of introducing new scientific terminology. Mary Hesse, Donald Schön, Peter Achinstein, Marx Wartofsky, Thomas Kuhn and Gilles-Gaston Granger argued for the indispensable and non-provisional role of metaphor in scientific theory. A radicalized version of this view was formulated by George Lakoff, according to which metaphors are constitutive of languages and provide the conceptual underpinning of the 'life-world'. To study the role of metaphor in science, then, is tantamount to analysing the structure and interplay of mappings of different fields of phenomena onto each other.[39]

SCIENTIFIC 'STYLE'

What Adam Smith did in *The Wealth of Nations* was not a mere exercise in persuasion; neither was it the application of an analytic tool box to economic phenomena. His achievement was shaped by a handful of metaphors that produced fresh ways of *seeing as*. The partially sceptical epistemology he had learned from his friend David Hume helped in a way, namely in making his mind soft enough. He knew too well that the *economy* could not *really* be made of motions and attractions, dams and rivers, vessels and fluids; for he knew too well that even Newton, the intellectual hero of his century, had not lifted the veil which hides the concealed mechanism of nature. The legacy of Hume's moderate scepticism left him free of dogmas. But he did not limit himself to describing the phenomena. Indeed, he looked at the phenomena through his preferred metaphors and made his successors see them in a different way. As I have illustrated, the phenomena were no more the same for his successors Malthus and Ricardo. The reason for that is that the cognitive function of metaphors goes beyond the context of discovery; instead, metaphors did shape, or redescribe or carve off the very field of phenomena that was afterwards taken to be 'the' economy out there.

A role for metaphorical re-description in producing the very empirical basis of economic theory is no argument against truth and theoretical progress. Instead, it was a blissful choice of metaphors, different from his predecessors', that helped Adam Smith widen the scope of economic explanation, imagine counterintuitive connections among traditionally separated fields of phenomena and shape new hypotheses to be tested, while nothing in the 'observed' phenomena would have suggested such hypotheses. The combination was the result of a number of factors: historical contingencies, fashion, aesthetical standards and the scientific style of his age, as well as his own individual scientific style.

Let me add – in order to stress the difference between the approach that has been proposed here and those of McCloskey and Brown – that a scientific style is something else than the literary style of a scientist's writings; instead, it is 'style' in the same sense in which we talk of the baroque or neoclassical style for painting and architecture, that is, a complex of ways of expression bound together by elective affinities or family resemblance and yet able to confer some unity to artistic or literary products of one age or author and useful for decoding the 'language' of the same age or author. Applied to scientific theories, a style may be the complex set of factors that accounts for preference for certain ways of concept building and theorizing, that is, for something that comes virtually before writing. Understood in the latter sense, this category may prove useful for the history of economic thought, and it may help in exploring dimensions of the history of economic thought that go beyond pure methodology, if this is understood in a stricter sense, but that are also wider than the study of the literary style of economic texts.

NOTES

*   I wish to thank Marcelo Dascal for suggestions on metaphor and pragmatics, Gideon Freudenthal for suggestions on Newtonian science and Gianni Vaggi for his comments at the Graz Conference that forced me to dispel some of the mist hovering around my claims; what is left is my own.

1.   I develop a few suggestions on the role of metaphors in *The Wealth of Nations* presented in Cremaschi (1984: 147–8 and 187–9); basically the same suggestions were made in Fiori (1996); Mirowski independently reached similar conclusions (1989: 163–71).

2.   On the notion of 'scientific style' and its relevance to the history of economic thought, see Cremaschi and Dascal (1998).

3. See Schumpeter ([1954] 1994: 182).
4. See Smith ([1795a] 1980, II; 8–9: 42); for commentaries see Cremaschi (1981, 1984: Ch. 1, 1989: 85–87).
5. That is, technology is to Smith what geometry and politics were to Hobbes and history to Vico: see Cremaschi (1989: 85–7).
6. The role of analogy in Adam Smith's epistemology is discussed in some detail in Cremaschi (1981, and 1984: Ch. 1).
7. See the sensible comments in Brown (1994: 15–17); I disagree with the further implications drawn by Brown in the following.
8. See Brown (1994: 24).
9. See Brown (1994: 19 fn.) for the opposite view.
10. This is why scientific discourse, far from being monologic, is essentially dialogical or controversial. This is the reason why Brown's way of reviving *das Adam Smith Problem*, namely contrasting a dialogical character of *The Theory of Moral Sentiments* with a mono-logical character of *The Wealth of Nations*, is off the track from the very beginning.
11. This is one important mark of the Newtonian methodological legacy in Adam Smith's economic theory: see Cremaschi (1984: 138–51, 1992: 59–61).
12. 'Theodicy', after the title of a notorious work by Leibniz, indicates the solution of the prob-lem of the existence of evil in a world supposedly created by a benevolent God.
13. Exceptions are Foley (1976); Worland (1976); and Mirowski (1989). Foley is a useful source, but his overall interpretation of Adam Smith's system of ideas is quite old-fashioned.
14. Here and in the following quotations, I will mark words whose metaphorical valence I intend to point out.
15. For a similar point concerning the division of labour instead of the allocation of capital, see Smith ([1776] 1976, I.ii.1. 25.
16. Curiously enough, Quesnay had himself employed a biological metaphor (the national econ-omy is a tree; industry and commerce are the branches; agriculture is the land that feeds the tree) in order to make an anti-artificialist claim: 'il faut donc cultiver le pied de l'arbre, et ne pas borner nos soins à gouverner les branches; laissons-les s'arranger et s'étendre en liberté, mais ne negligeons pas la terre qui fournit les sucs nécessaires a leur végétation et à leur accroissement' (Quesnay 1758: 473).
17. For discussion of this passage, see Macfie (1971).
18. The claim of a coexistence of two different voices in Smith's economic work and in his moral work has been put forth in Brown (1994); for a criticism see Cremaschi (1997). The relevant point here is that the function of metaphors is both persuasive and cognitive in both works, and this may cast some doubts on the idea that the discourse is cast in one work in a 'dialogical' mould while in the other it is carried out within a 'didactical' framework.
19. See Brown (1984: Chs 2 and 3).
20. On the pamphleteers, see Brown (1984: Ch.1) on the physiocrats as well as on ancient sources, see Lowry (1974).
21. The image of the Hand of God has a long history before Priestley. It was a way of talking of God's action, derived from a way of representing God's action by painting a hand without a body, complying with the ban on images from the Bible. This way of representing God was usual in Jewish art and appeared occasionally also in Christian art. On the idea of the Hand of God, see also Macfie (1971).
22. See Quesnay (1758, 1757).
23. See Quesnay (1758); Mercier de la Rivière (1767: 206).
24. See Mayr (1986).
25. As suggested in Worland (1976); a discussion of Newtonian items in the theoretical struc-ture of *The Wealth of Nations* is in Cremaschi (1992: 61–4) see also Freudenthal (1982).
26. See Cremaschi (1984: 148–51); cf. Fiori (1996).
27. See Cremaschi (1992, 1981) and Freudenthal (1982).
28. See Jensen (1976); Cremaschi (1984: Ch. 4).
29. This is the suggestion made in Mirowski (1989: 163–71).
30. For more detailed discussion of this point see Cremaschi and Dascal (1998).
31. For more detailed discussion see Cremaschi (1987, 1988a, 1988b, 1997).

32. See Cremaschi (1988a, 1988b); Klamer and Leonard (1994: 20–21).
33. See McCloskey (1985, 1990, 1994); cf. Cremaschi (1996).
34. Instead, science and poetry or novels are not different in the use they make of metaphor, but they are nonetheless different in other respects, and these respects relate to practice, not to language.
35. Instead, economic metaphors are both cognitive and non-arbitrary, and their *illocutionary* aspect – as contrasted with the perlocutionary – is what matters.
36. Brown (1994: 26).
37. See Klamer and Leonard (1994: 43); see also Lakoff (1987); Henderson ([1982] 1993); Cremaschi (1988b).
38. See Mirowski (1989, 1994).
39. See Cremaschi (1987, 1988a, 1988b); cf. Gross (1990); Backhouse, Dudley-Evans and Henderson (1993).

REFERENCES

Backhouse, Roger E., Terence Dudley-Evans and William Henderson (1993), 'Exploring the language and rhetoric of economics', in W. Henderson et al. (eds), *Economics and Language*, London and New York: Routledge: 1–22.

Brown, Robert (1984), *The Nature of Social Laws: Machiavelli to Mill*, Cambridge and New York: Cambridge University Press.

Brown, Vivienne (1994), *Adam Smith's Discourse. Canonicity, Commerce and Conscience*, London and New York: Routledge.

Cantillon, Richard (1755), ed. by T. Tsuda (1979), *Essai sur la Nature du Commerce en Général*, Tokyo: Kinokuniya Book Store.

Cheyne, George (1725), *Essay on Health and Long Life*, fourth edition, London: Stahan.

Cotes, Roger (1712) 'Cotes to Newton' (Letter n. 985: 18 March 1712), in H.W. Turnbull and J.F. Scott (eds), *The Correspondence of Isaac Newton*, Vol. V, London: Cambridge University Press, 1959–1977, 11 vols.

Cremaschi, Sergio (1981), 'Adam Smith, Newtonianism and political economy', *Manuscrito*, 5(1): 117–34.

Cremaschi, Sergio (1984), *Il Sistema della Ricchezza: Economia Politica e Problema del Metodo in Adam Smith*, Milano: Angeli.

Cremaschi, Sergio (1987), 'Granger and science as network of models', *Manuscrito*, 11(2): 11–136.

Cremaschi, Sergio (1988a), 'Metafore, modelli, linguaggio scientifico: il dibattito postempirista', in V. Melchiorre (ed.), *Simbolo e Conoscenza*, Milano: Vita e Pensiero: 31–102.

Cremaschi, Sergio (1988b), 'Remarks on scientific metaphors', in M.L. Dalla Chiara and M.C. Galavotti (eds), *Temi e Prospettive della Logica e Filosofia della Scienza Contemporanee*, Vol. II, Bologna: CLUEB: 114–16.

Cremaschi, Sergio (1989), 'Adam Smith: sceptical Newtonianism, disenchanted republicanism, and the birth of social science', in M. Dascal and O. Gruengard (eds), *Knowledge and Politics: Case Studies on the Relationship between Epistemology and Political Philosophy*, Boulder, US and London: Westview Press: 83–110.

Cremaschi, Sergio (1992), 'L'illuminismo scozzese e il newtonianismo morale', in M. Geuna and M.L. Pesante (eds), Interessi, Passioni, Convenzioni. Discussioni Sette-centesche su Virtù e Civiltà, Milano: Angeli: 41–76.

Cremaschi, Sergio (1996), 'Review of D. McCloskey, knowledge and persuasion in economics', *Pragmatics and Cognition*, 4(2): 425–9.

Cremaschi, Sergio (1997), 'Review of V. Brown, Adam Smith's discourse', *Journal of Economic Methodology*, 3(1): 174–6.

Cremaschi, Sergio and Marcelo Dascal (1998), 'Malthus and Ricardo: two styles for economic theory', *Science in Context*, 11(2): 229–54.

Fiori, Stefano (1996), 'Order, metaphors, and equilibrium in Adam Smith's thought', *History of Economic Ideas*, 4(1–2): 175–204.

Foley, Vernon (1976), *The Social Physics of Adam Smith*, West Lafayette, US: Purdue University Press.

Freudenthal, Gideon (1982), *Atom und Individuum im Zeitalter Newtons. Zur Genese der mechanistischen Natur- und Sozialphilosophie*, Frankfurt a.M.: Suhrkamp; translated (1986) as *Atom and Individual in the Age of Newton*, Dordrecht: Reidel.

Gross, Alan G. (1990), *The Rhetoric of Science*, Cambridge, MA: Harvard University Press.

Henderson, William (1982), 'Metaphor and economics', in Backhouse (ed.), *New Directions in Economic Methodology*, London and New York: Routledge: 343–67.

Henderson, William, Terence Dudley-Evans, Roger Backhouse (eds) (1993), *Economics and Language*, London and New York: Routledge.

Hume, David (1752a), 'Of the balance of trade', reprinted in T.H. Green and T.H. Grose (eds) (1964), *Essays Moral, Political, and Literary*, Vol. I, Aalen: Scientia Verlag: 330–45.

Hume, David (1752b), 'Of money', reprinted in T.H. Green and T.H. Grose (eds) (1964), *Essays Moral, Political, and Literary*, Vol. I, Aalen: Scientia Verlag: 309–20.

Jensen, Hans E. (1976), 'Sources and contours of Adam Smith's conceptualized reality in the Wealth of Nations', *Review of Social Economy*, 34(3): 259–74.

Klamer, Arjo and Theodor C. Leonard (1994), 'So what's an economic metaphor?', in P. Mirowski (ed.), *Natural Images in Economic Thought*, Cambridge and New York: Cambridge University Press: 20–54.

Locke, John (1690), 'The second treatise of government', reprinted in P. Laslett (ed.) (1988), *Two Treatises of Government*, Cambridge and New York: Cambridge University Press.

Lowry, S. Todd (1974), 'The archaeology of the circulation concept in economic theory', *Journal of the History of Ideas*, 35(3): 429–44.

Lakoff, George (1987), *Women, Fire, and Dangerous Things: What Categories Reveal about the Mind*, Chicago: University of Chicago Press.

Macfie, Alec L. (1971), 'The invisible hand of Jupiter', *Journal of the History of Ideas*, 32(4): 595–9.

Malthus, Thomas Robert (1820, 1836), ed. by J. Pullen (1989), *Principles of Political Economy*, Cambridge: Cambridge University Press.

Mayr, Otto (1986), *Authority, Liberty and Automatic Machinery in Early Modern Europe*, Baltimore: John Hopkins University Press.

McCloskey, Donald N. ([1985] 1998), *The Rhetoric of Economics*, Madison, US and London, UK: University of Wisconsin Press.

McCloskey, Donald N. (1990), *If You're So Smart: The Narrative of Economic Expertise*, Chicago: University of Chicago Press.

McCloskey, Donald N. (1994), *Knowledge and Persuasion in Economics*, Cambridge and New York: Cambridge University Press.

Mercier de la Rivière, Pierre-Paul (1767), *L'ordre Naturel et Essentiel des Sociétés Politiques*, London.

Mirowski, Philip (1989), *More Heat than Light: Economics as Social Physics, Physics as Nature's Economics*, Cambridge and New York: Cambridge University Press.

Mirowski, Philip (ed.) (1994), *Natural Images in Economic Thought*, Cambridge and New York: Cambridge University Press.

Priestley, Joseph (1788), *Lectures on History and General Policy*, reprinted in J.T. Rutt (ed.) (1972), *Theological and Miscellaneous Works of Joseph Priestley*, Vol. XXIV, New York: Kraus Reprint.

Quesnay, François (1757), 'Grains', reprinted in (1958), *François Quesnay et la Physiocratie*, Vol. II, Paris: Institut National d'Études Démographiques: 459–510.

Quesnay, François (1758), *Tableau Economique*, reprinted in M. Kuczynski and R.L.

Meek (eds) (1972), *Quesnay's Tableau Économique*, London: Macmillan, and New York: Kelly.

Ricardo, David (1817), *On the Principles of Political Economy and Taxation*, reprinted in P. Sraffa (ed.) (1951), *The Works and Correspondence of David Ricardo,* Vol. I, Cambridge and New York: Cambridge University Press.

Schumpeter, Joseph A. ([1954] 1994), *History of Economic Analysis*, London: Routledge, and New York: Oxford University Press.

Smith, Adam (1759), *The Theory of Moral Sentiments*, reprinted in D.D. Raphael and A.L. Macfie (eds) (1976), *Glasgow Edition of the Works and Correspondence of Adam Smith*, Vol. I, Oxford: Oxford University Press.

Smith, Adam (1776), *An Inquiry into the Nature and Causes of the Wealth of Nations*, reprinted in R.H. Campbell, A.S. Skinner, and W.B. Todd (eds) (1976), *Glasgow Edition of the Works and Correspondence of Adam Smith*, Vol. II, Oxford: Oxford University Press.

Smith, Adam (1983), *Lectures on Rhetoric and Belles Lettres*, in J.C. Bryce (ed.), *Glasgow Edition of the Works and Correspondence of Adam Smith*, Vol. IV, Oxford: Oxford University Press.

Smith, Adam (1795a), *The Principles which Lead and Direct Philosophical Enquiries: Illustrated by the History of Astronomy*, reprinted in W.P.D. Wightman, J.C. Bryce and I.S. Ross (eds) (1980), *Glasgow Edition of the Works and Correspondence of Adam Smith*, Vol. III, Oxford: Oxford University Press.

Smith, Adam (1795b), *Of the External Senses*, reprinted in W.P.D. Wightman, J.C. Bryce and I.S. Ross (eds) (1980), *Glasgow Edition of the Works and Correspondence of Adam Smith*, Vol. III, Oxford: Oxford University Press.

Worland, Stephen T. (1976), 'Mechanistic analogy and Smith on exchange', *Review of Social Economy*, 34(3): 245–58.

PART III

Roundtable: Is There Progress in Economics?

6. On progress and the history of economic thought

Roger E. Backhouse

INTRODUCTION

As a community, historians of economic thought entertain very diverse attitudes towards the notion of progress in economics. Faced with this diversity,
many individuals find themselves torn in different directions. They want to
agree with both Mark Blaug (Chapter 2, this volume), who regards progress as
the most important question confronting the historian of economics, and
Donald Winch (Chapter 1, this volume), who is doubtful about whether it
really matters. The question I focus upon here is whether such an attitude is
coherent or reveals an element of schizophrenia.

The obvious way to reconcile the views of Blaug and Winch, of course, is
to argue that there are many questions the historian can try to answer. For some
of these progress will be important but for others it will not. In other words,
Blaug and Winch are interested in different things and the discipline should
embrace both perspectives. There is, however, more to be said. To see this,
consider a slightly different question: 'Does it make sense, in writing a history
of economic thought, to follow Winch on the transition that took place in political economy from Smith to Malthus, and then to follow Blaug when the story
gets to the twentieth century?' I hope to show that the answer is 'Yes'.

WHOSE CONCEPT OF PROGRESS?

The concept of progress is an inherently *normative* term – it is about things
becoming *better* in some sense. However, it is frequently used as if it were a
positive term. This is a recipe for confusion unless one of two conditions is
met. One is that the criterion for progress is made explicit every time it is used
and all discussions of progress are made relative to the criterion used. The
other is that there is a consensus on the criteria by which economics should be
judged.

As economists, it is right to speak of progress from our own point of view

– to judge it by what we, as economists, are trying to achieve. (As an aside it is worth noting that this may not be the same as the criterion used by politicians, businesses or other sources of funding.) There may well be reasons why we might wish to judge the past by the same criteria. We might, for example, wish to ask whether certain institutional structures were conducive to progress, or to compare our own generation's achievements with those of past generations. There is nothing wrong with doing this. However, unless we make it very clear that we are judging past economists by our own standards, and that these are not necessarily the standards of past generations, we are in danger of misreading the past. There is a sense in which such work is not history and should not be presented as such.

If we choose, instead, to engage in history – what, for the sake of brevity, I will call 'real' history – the idea of progress may have to fall into the background. Take the example of T.R. Malthus and the origins of what came to be termed 'classical political economy', recently analysed by Winch (1996). Our preconceptions about this are so strong, influenced by the interpretations constructed by generations of economists, that the only way to understand the period's writing may be deliberately to cut ourselves off from asking questions about progress – to work under a self-denying ordinance. Once we have done that, however, we can, if we are lucky, begin to see what Malthus and his contemporaries were trying to achieve. We may then be able to ask about what they would have considered to be progress and the extent to which they achieved this. We may, therefore, return to the question of progress, but it will be informed by history in a way that the economist's perspective will not.

Suppose we adopt this point of view and evaluate, so far as we are able, the contributions of past economists in terms of their own aspirations and beliefs. Can we then speak of progress in any grander sense? The answer may well be 'No', but it will not necessarily be 'No'. In so far as successive generations share the same goals, it makes sense to think of progress (or its absence) as part of a historical story. Lest this appear an archaic or, even worse, a 'positivist' notion, let me cite two authorities, neither of whom is usually considered a 'positivist'. Thomas Kuhn (1977: 321–2) suggested that, behind the historical relativity implied by shifts from one paradigm to another, scientists shared important values – accuracy, consistency, scope, simplicity and fruitfulness. Richard Rorty (1984: 65) goes further, writing that it may be possible to find common problems persisting over as much as a couple of centuries and, for example, write 'a story of the steps which led from Descartes to Kant'. If there are shared values (Kuhn) and common problems (Rorty) one can legitimately ask about progress in solving those problems. We may end up with a historically contingent account of progress, not a universal one, but that may be all that we want or need.

WHAT TYPE OF PROGRESS?

Even if we accept that progress is a normative term and we have decided to approach it from a specific point in history (our own or that of a previous generation), problems remain. Progress has more than one dimension. In *Truth and Progress in Economic Knowledge* (Backhouse, 1997: Ch. 8) I list five, radically different, ways in which we might think of scientific progress in general. Within each of these we can distinguish between theoretical and empirical progress, and I offer eight possible definitions of the former and four of the latter. It would probably be an exaggeration to say that this implies sixty possible definitions of progress (some of the combinations would not be interesting and others would not be very coherent) but it gives an idea of the scale of the problem. Progress is a very complex phenomenon.

Blaug takes up the idea of theoretical and empirical progress, arguing strongly that contemporary economics exhibits clear theoretical progress but a lack of empirical progress. Theories have been developed with greater precision and rigour, and they cover possibilities about which earlier generations did not even know how to theorize. On the other hand, the predictive power of economics has not increased. I do not wish to question any of these conclusions, with which I am in complete agreement. However, I wish to suggest other ways of viewing progress that might lead to a somewhat different picture.

To make my account concrete, I consider a specific example: a comparison of contemporary monetary economics with that offered in Henry Thornton's *Enquiry into the Paper Credit of Great Britain* (1802). Focusing on theoretical and empirical progress, we might point to increases in the scope and rigour of 'pure' monetary theory or improvements in the ability to forecast the consequences of policy changes or exogenous shocks. According to such criteria, contemporary economics exhibits enormous progress. However, these definitions are very narrow. Theoretical progress might, with equal justification, be interpreted as referring to our understanding of the structure of the financial system and how its various components interact. It is arguable that this requires simply a sound understanding of opportunity costs in relation to profit maximization, supply and demand in an environment where confidence and expectations were crucial. On such criteria, it would be possible to argue that Thornton had a theoretical understanding that, relative to the financial system of his day, was equal to that of contemporary economics. To defend the idea that there had been theoretical progress, one might have to argue that, because we know about succeeding centuries, we have theories about financial systems that did not exist in Thornton's day as well as theories about those with which he was familiar. Similarly, empirical progress might be used to refer to improvements in our knowledge of what is actually going on within the monetary system and of its effects on the economy. This includes financial statistics as well as index numbers of prices and the national accounts. On this score, there has surely been immense progress.

Once we take account of dimensions such as these, the notion that economics has exhibited theoretical but not empirical progress seems far less clear-cut. The case could be argued that, over 200 years, there has been little real theoretical progress but very real empirical progress – the opposite of the conclusion reached by Blaug (it is also the view of Hutchison, 1992). How can this be resolved? In part the explanation is that Blaug is concerned with the second half of the twentieth century, whereas I have chosen a much longer time period. The reason why this matters is that when one goes back before the 1930s, it becomes harder to apply distinctions that, because of our training, we view as fundamental to economics. One of these is the distinction between theoretical and applied economics. Given the structure of contemporary economics, this distinction is easy to draw, and with it comes a sharp distinction between theoretical and empirical progress. If we go further back, however, the distinction between theory and application becomes much more problematic (see Backhouse, 1998; Backhouse and Biddle, 2000). One consequence is that the distinction between theoretical and empirical progress becomes much harder to draw.

This reinforces the notion that progress has to be understood relative to a particular historical situation. Not only the criteria by which progress is judged, but economists' understanding of concepts that are basic to any discussion of progress (including theory, empirical work and even the concept of economics itself), are relative to specific historical situations. This reinforces the point, made earlier, that 'local' judgements about progress are much easier to make than 'global' ones. There is, however, an argument the other way. We might argue that, in general, it becomes easier to speak of progress the longer is the period over which we are looking. I suggest that the main reason for this is that, as the period over which we look becomes longer, the element of what might be called 'pure accumulation' becomes more and more important. We see progress simply because we see everything our predecessors saw, and more besides – in short, there is progress simply because we cannot go backwards. This, however, presumes that we do not forget. It is tempting to argue that the nature of contemporary economics is such that it is now easier for us to forget than it was when people were trained on the classics of generations earlier than their own.

RECONCILING HISTORY AND METHODOLOGY

I now return to the question with which I started: is it consistent to write a history that tries to integrate Winch's perspective on Malthus with Blaug's perspective on contemporary economics? The answer is 'Yes', for at least two reasons. The first (though arguably least important) reason is that Blaug is concerned only with the second half of the twentieth century and with academic economics. Comparison of recent econometric work with Tinbergen's early models, or even modern theories of industrial organization with Chamberlin's work, imposes far fewer problems than does, for example, comparing Debreu's theory of value with Adam Smith's. Historical investigation may be necessary to understand what Tinbergen and Chamberlin thought they were doing, and their purposes may not be what we expect given our training in modern economics. However, they are still relatively close to contemporary econometrics and industrial economics in a way in which Smith is not close to Debreu. Perhaps we are more likely to be deceived into thinking that twentieth-century economists are closer to their present-day counterparts than they are, but the potential errors, should we make such a mistake, are much smaller.

The second reason is perhaps the most important one. The inquiries into which Winch and Blaug are engaged are complementary to each other. Winch helps us to understand what Malthus and his contemporaries thought that they were doing and to understand, among other things, what they would have considered progress, or success, in the subject. He shows, for example, that Malthus had an agenda very different from that of contemporary economics (and even from his more secular followers in classical economics). There is no incompatibility between attaching importance to such ideas and also asking, with Blaug, whether and in what sense it is possible to speak of progress. Our answer to the historical question enables us to judge the significance of our answer to the normative question even though they remain separate questions. The history of economic thought should, therefore, have room for them both.

REFERENCES

Backhouse, Roger E. (1997), *Truth and Progress in Economic Knowledge*, Cheltenham: Edward Elgar.

Backhouse, Roger E. (1998), 'The transformation of U.S. economics, 1920–1960, viewed though a survey of journal articles', in Mary S. Morgan and Malcolm Rutherford (eds), *From Interwar Pluralism to Postwar Neoclassicism*, Annual supplement to *History of Political Economy*, 30, Durham, NC: Duke University Press.

Backhouse, Roger E. and Jeff Biddle (2000), 'The concept of applied economics: a history of ambiguity and multiple meanings', in Roger E. Backhouse and Jeff Biddle (eds), *The History of Applied Economics*, Annual supplement to *History of Applied Economics*, 32, Durham, NC: Duke University Press.

Hutchinson, T.W. (1992), *Changing Aims in Economics*, Oxford: Basil Blackwell.

Kuhn, Thomas S. (1977), *The Essential Tension*, Chicago, IL: University of Chicago Press.

Rorty, Richard (1984), 'The historiography of philosophy: four genres', in R. Rorty, J.B. Schneewind and Q. Skinner (eds), *Philosophy in History*, Cambridge and New York: Cambridge University Press.

Thornton, Henry (1802), *An Enquiry into the Nature and Effects of the Paper Credit of Great Britain*, reprinted 1939 with an introduction by F.A. Hayek, London: Allen and Unwin.

Winch, Donald N. (1996), *Riches and Poverty: An Intellectual History of Political Economy in Britain, 1750–1834*, Cambridge: Cambridge University Press.

7. Scientific progress: complexities of a contestable concept

Uskali Mäki

PROGRESS – NOW?

The official theme of this conference is progress in economics. The question we have been asked to consider in this panel is whether there has been progress in economics. My first gut reaction to this invitation was to wonder if there is an anachronism implied. Has the conference and the panel been organized by a bunch of uninformed reactionaries who haven't realized that there has been progress with regard to the notion of progress? Haven't most of us been persuaded that progress is a modernist enlightenment notion that has been dropped from the agenda of at least the more progressive forces in the intellectual arena? Haven't we learnt by now that it is to be taken as an indication of progress not to bother about progress any more?

As the formulations above suggest, the attempt to dispense with the notion of progress encounters difficulties that are similar to those faced by truth relativism: it is hard or impossible to deny the relevance or intelligibility of concepts such as progress or truth in a way that is not self-undermining. One cannot even use the concept of being reactionary without implying that of progress. I therefore feel safe and justified in gratefully joining the organizers in addressing the issue of progress in economics.

PROGRESS – WHAT?

My second gut reaction was that the issue of progress is immensely complex, blessed with deep ambiguities and a variety of rival and complementary perspectives. In the present era, the human mind has a propensity to ascribe progress – or the lack of it – to a variety of phenomena, including changes in the academic discipline called economics. These ascriptions are laden with multiple ambiguities and cannot be seriously assessed until sufficient disambiguations have been carried out. A limited selection of suggestions for such a project include the following.

1. 'Progress' is essentially a comparative term denoting a sequence in time. It implies comparison of states or properties across time. An entity X has property $P1$ at time $t1$ and has property $P2$ at time $t2$; or we may say property P of X has value $p1$ at time $t1$ and has value $p2$ at time $t2$. Depending on our further assessments, we may say that progress has or has not occurred through the passage from $t1$ to $t2$.

2. 'Progress' is essentially an evaluative term. It implies that (a) the sequence results in an outcome that is somehow better than the point where the sequence took off; or (b) the sequence has a good direction. If we say the sequence results in a better outcome, we mean that $P2$ is better than $P1$ or that $p2$ is better than $p1$. If we say the sequence has a good direction, we mean that $P2$ or $p2$ are steps in a longer sequence that is likely to lead to a better outcome, regardless of whether $P2$ is better than $P1$ or whether $p2$ is better than $p1$.

3. Progress can be attributed to changes that involve a variety of types of things – a variety of Xs. These types of things include data, concepts, theories, explanations, predictions, methods, questions, larger frameworks, academic institutions and so on. In each case, we may say that the concepts, predictions, questions, institutions and other aspects of economics make progress between $t1$ and $t2$. We refer to such sequences as conceptual, predictive, erotetic and institutional progress, respectively.

4. Given that progress is a matter of change of, or change in, properties, one has to look at the relevant properties Pi of the various Xs that participate in such changes. Each X has a natural range of properties, some of which are relevant for progress assessment. Thus, for data, the important properties may be taken to include 'comprehensiveness' and 'relevance' and 'accuracy of measurement'; for concepts, 'capacity to refer to real kinds' and 'harmony between reference and description'; for theories, 'truthlikeness' and 'explanatory power' and 'degree of confirmation'; for predictions, 'accuracy' and 'reliability'; for questions, 'capacity to lead to better explanations' and 'capacity to lead to an enlarged scope of theory'; for paradigms, 'problem-solving capacity'; and for academic institutions, 'capacity to promote better epistemic outcomes'. If there is change in such properties, it may be taken to constitute progress (cf. Kitcher, 1993; Backhouse, 1997).

5. Progress comes in different scales, from day-to-day, article-to-article progress on small-scale issues to long-term progress on larger theoretical formations or institutional structures. This constitutes a hierarchical continuum – or rather, continua – along which smaller-scale progressive changes take place within larger-scale theoretical frameworks and institutional structures that restrain and facilitate academic research. Changes that count as progress may thus include adding a new time series to the set

of data; a minor revision in an economic model; a major change in larger systems of research questions and theoretical concepts; a change in the organization and resourcing of a particular economics department; and a change in the publication conventions followed by the majority of leading economics journals with a concomitant change in research incentives.

6. Progress is being considered and assessed by two categories of people. First, those who potentially or actually make progress, namely practitioners of economic research, make observations about progress and may be driven by such observations. Second, spectators of economics, including historians and methodologists of economics, provide their own various perspectives on the assessment of progress in economics. Given that the resources, interests and perspectives of these groups – as well as the sub-groups therein – may differ in various respects and extents, the resulting observations may be more or less diverse. Practitioners typically – but not solely – pay attention to small-scale progress, while the spectators tend to have an inclination to emphasize large-scale progress.

7. Depending on one's philosophical outlook, one may feel comfortable with employing and applying the concept of progress to changes in economics (and elsewhere); or one may insist on discarding the concept altogether as inapplicable. Alternatively, one may be selective about the properties to which progress may be intelligibly or relevantly ascribed. For example, a Kuhnian may refer to improved problem-solving capacity as progress but refuse to talk about reaching higher degrees of truthlikeness.

Given the multiplicity of perspectives from which progress is being viewed, as well as the great variety of aspects of progress and of aspects of economics to which progress can or cannot be ascribed, it is unsurprising to conclude that the concept of progress is highly contestable. As an illustration, let us entertain ourselves by considering the controversial phenomenon called economics imperialism.

PROGRESS: ECONOMICS IMPERIALISM AS ILLUSTRATION

Economics has turned out to be an imperialistic discipline: it has expanded its domain by crossing disciplinary boundaries and is increasingly dealing with phenomena that used to fall within the purviews of fields such as sociology, political science, law, anthropology, ethics and epistemology. Among the exemplifications of this phenomenon, one may cite familiar books such as Gary Becker's *The Economics of Discrimination* (1957); Anthony Downs's *An Economic Theory of Democracy* (1957); James Buchanan's and Gordon Tullock's *The*

Calculus of Consent (1962); Mancur Olson's *The Logic of Collective Action* (1965); and Gary Becker's *The Economic Approach to Human Behavior* (1976).

Many economists celebrate this phenomenon (Stigler, 1984; Hirshleifer, 1985; Lazear, 1999). Given the contestability and complexity of the concept of progress, it should not come as a surprise if one were to claim that economics imperialism is potentially progressive in a number of different ways – and if others were to deny such a claim with passion. The next few paragraphs will sort out some of the kinds of potential progress that one might consider ascribing to economics imperialism. Naturally, a very detailed conceptual and empirical analysis will be needed to critically assess such ascriptions, including examining the conditions for turning potential progress into actual progress. Naturally, this cannot be done here.

A more detailed account of the epistemic aspect of the concept of economics imperialism is given elsewhere (Mäki, 2000a, 2000b), but the key ideas can be summarized as follows. Economics imperialism is an implementation of the highly respected ideal of explanatory unification. This ideal prescribes that scientists seek higher degrees of unification in their explanatory pursuits. Explanatory unification is a matter of explaining much by little, by invoking one and the same set of explanatory principles – allowing for some reinterpretations or modifications – in an attempt to explain a maximum number of different types of phenomena. Explanatory unification comes in different versions, depending on one's concept of explanation (Mäki, 2001).

Another notion has to be incorporated into that of unification: consilience. This is to be taken in its original Whewellian sense (Whewell, 1847) to bring in the right kind of dynamics. One starts with a situation in which a given theory T explains a class of phenomena $E1$. It later turns out that T also explains another class of phenomena $E2$. T was not originally designed to explain $E2$, thus it comes as a (pleasant) surprise that it does explain class $E2$. Expanding the domain of application of T in such a way may, and typically does, require modifications or reinterpretations of T, but these should not be so large as to alter the identity of T as T. This gives the rudiments of Whewellian consilience.

An account of the epistemic notion of economics imperialism now suggests itself in terms of explanatory unification and consilience. Economic theory – invoking explanatory principles such as those of rational choice, expected returns, market supply and demand – is first designed and taken to explain $E1$: economic phenomena as traditionally conceived. It later appears – after research efforts by people such as Anthony Downs and Gary Becker – that economic theory can also be used to explain $E2$ (and $E3$, $E4$, . . .): political and social phenomena traditionally conceived as non-economic and as belonging to the domain of explanation of other social sciences. A greater degree of explanatory unification has been achieved by crossing disciplinary boundaries. Even though Whewell's notion did not originally involve that of crossing disciplinary boundaries, this development can also be regarded as a matter of increased degree of consilience.

Now that we have a rough understanding of a concept of economics imperialism, we can consider the issue of progress. There are at least the following kinds of progress that may occur as the imperialists march on.

Improved Explanation of $E1$, $E2$, ...

According to this very basic idea, explanation is a matter of theoretical unification, thus attaining a higher degree of unification means that explanatory progress has occurred. A theory that explains more – or more efficiently – classes of explanandum phenomena than its predecessor or rival provides a better explanation of all those classes. In this simple sense, economics imperialism is potentially progressive.

Improved Explanation of $E2$, ...

A theory that unifies $E1$ and $\{E2, \ldots\}$ provides us with further explanatory information about $\{E2, \ldots \}$. More is learnt about $E2$ and other classes of phenomena $\{E3, \ldots\}$ that the theory was not originally designed to explain, namely that they are like $E1$ in explanatorily relevant respects. For example, phenomena pertaining to politics, marriage, crime and science are represented as outcomes of rational choice by individuals in interaction in market or market-like conditions. We thus learn new facts about them, suggesting that they are similar to classes of phenomena that were traditionally conceived as economic. Explanatory progress may occur.

Improved Confirmation

Increased explanatory unification is an achievement that broadens the evidential basis of the unifying theory. As new classes of phenomena are covered, evidence pertaining not only to $E1$ but also to $\{E2, E3, \ldots\}$ becomes available as new sources of confirmation. The theory becomes more testable and, if consistent with evidence, better confirmed. Economics imperialism may manifest empirical progress in this sense.

Improved Opportunity for Theory Modification

In applying a theory to explain new kinds of phenomena, the theory has to meet challenges that require potentially progressive modifications to it. These modifications may be based on perceived dissimilarities between $E1$ on the one hand, and $\{E2, E3, \ldots\}$ on the other: for example, when dealing with political and social phenomena, one has to add traditionally non-economic variables – such as trust and reciprocity – to the rational choice framework. Or those modifications may be inspired by newly discovered similarities between the various classes of explanandum phenomena: for example, economists may reconsider their notions of rationality and incentives also in their explanations of traditional economic phenomena. In both cases, learning and explanatory progress may occur thanks to economics imperialism.

Improved Standards

Supposing one holds the view that on average economics subscribes to higher – more 'rigorous' – standards of quality of research and argumentation than other social sciences, economics imperialism may help establish better standards in those neighbouring disciplines. Overall progress of standards may occur.

Improved Questions

Attempts to apply economic reasoning to traditionally non-economic domains may give rise to fruitful conflicts and an increased variety of viewpoints, and this may lead to novel questions and research agendas. Some of these novel questions may lead to better theories and explanations. Erotetic progress would have occurred.

PROGRESS: CONTESTATIONS

Using the same illustration, we can now try to throw some light on the contestability of the concept of progress. Having first specified the epistemic aspect of the concept of economics imperialism in terms of explanatory unification and consilience, I then listed some notions of progress that might be relevant as candidates for attribution to economics imperialism. My claim is that a few respectable and relatively uncontroversial candidates will offer themselves for attribution. This implies that if one wishes to resist economics imperialism as an allegedly progressive project, one has to (1) reject the idea of progress in general; or (2) reject one or more of those candidate concepts of progress; or (3) reject their attribution to imperialistic economics. The following lists a small selection of possibilities.

Improved Explanation of $E1$, $E2$, . . .

One may dispute – as I do – the idea that explanation amounts to unification. This implies that a higher degree of explanatory unification does not necessarily mean explanatory progress. Explaining a phenomenon is a matter of placing it theoretically in a picture of the way the world works, and unifying phenomena requires success in this primary explanatory task. Increased unification is at most a consequence of progress in explanatory power rather than its defining feature.

Improved Explanation of $E2$, . . .

The claim that we acquire new information about $\{E2, \ldots\}$ when unifying them with $E1$ requires that we are able to reliably substantiate a high degree of similarity between $E1$ on the one hand, and $\{E2, E3, \ldots\}$ on the other. Such attempted substantiations are often as easy to dispute as they are to provide. This relates to the next point.

Improved Confirmation

It is relatively uncontroversial that increased unification broadens the evidential basis of the unifying theory and thus increases its testability in principle. It is much more controversial, and easy to dispute, that the unifying theory has been reliably confirmed by the new classes of evidence. Much of the controversy around economics imperialism focuses on this issue.

Improved Opportunity for Theory Modification

It is relatively uncontroversial that the attempts to apply economic ideas to new domains has led to modifications and reinterpretations of some key principles in economic theory, and that this is potentially progressive. What one can more easily dispute is the direction and extent of these theoretical changes, say, by arguing that the changes unjustifiably remain within the boundaries of some unsound broad framework.

Improved Standards

One may dispute that the standards imported from economics to neighbouring disciplines are more rigorous in a genuine or appropriate manner. One may, for example, argue that those standards are inappropriate given the nature of the phenomena studied by social science disciplines other than economics.

Improved Questions

If one accepts that economics imperialism may initially give rise to fruitful conflicts, a larger variety of viewpoints and novel questions, the issue of whether progress will have occurred depends on the further consequences. The outcome may be a unified social science dominated by a relatively unchanged corpus of economic principles; a unified social science constituted by a set of principles where traditional rational choice and market interaction plays a relatively small role; or one or another fragmented and disintegrated collection of ideas and projects. Each such outcome may be assessed in a number of ways, depending on one's criteria of progress.

CONCLUDING WORD

The game of progress attributions will continue. Economists of various persuasions as well as non-economists will go on assessing parts and periods in economics in terms of progress. The foregoing exercise may serve as a modest reminder of the complexity and contestability of any given move in the game. Rather than letting these observations depress the contestants, awareness of them might help create an opportunity for making progress in the quality of conversations about progress.

REFERENCES

Backhouse, Roger (1997), *Truth and Progress in Economic Knowledge*. Cheltenham: Edward Elgar.
Hirshleifer, Jack (1985), 'The expanding domain of economics', *American Economic Review*, 75(6), December: 53–68.
Kitcher, Philip (1993), *The Advancement of Science*, Oxford: Oxford University Press.
Lazear, Edward P. (2000), 'Economic imperialism', *Quarterly Journal of Economics*, 115: 99–146.
Mäki, Uskali (2000a), 'Economics imperialism: concept and constraints', unpublished; (published in Portuguese translation as 'Imperialismo da Economia: conceitos e restricöes', *Economia*, 2, March 2000, 5–36).
Mäki, Uskali (2000b), 'Explanatory ecumenism and economics imperialism', forthcoming in *Economics and Philosophy*.
Mäki, Uskali (2001), 'Explanatory unification: double and doubtful', *Philosophy of the Social Sciences*, 31, 488–506.
Stigler, George (1984), 'Economics – the imperial science?', *Scandinavian Journal of Economics*, 86: 301–13.
Whewell, William (1847), *Philosophy of the Inductive Sciences*, London: John W. Parker.

B41

8. Progress in economics

Luigi Pasinetti

I have had the opportunity of facing this subject on at least two previous occasions (Pasinetti, 1985, 1986). Since my views on this subject have not substantially changed, I shall try to summarize them here.

The first of the two mentioned occasions was a conference in which the European Science Foundation asked scholars from different fields of learning (physics, mathematics, biology, medicine, sociology, linguistics, history, economics) to discuss the topic 'The Identification of progress in learning'. The economists in the group were Edmond Malinvaud (*rapporteur*) and myself (discussant). The challenge came to me from Malinvaud's statement that 'a commonly recognized process does not exist in economics by means of which scientific progress can be asserted' (Malinvaud, 1985: 167).

To me, the relevant question to face first of all appeared to be that of investigating the particular features of economic research as against other disciplines. The obvious area of comparison seemed to be physics, considered by many as 'the prototype of science'. I may list at least four features that seem to me as peculiar to economics:

1. First of all, unlike physics or astronomy or many other sciences, the object of economic studies is changing continually. When Ptolemy, 22 centuries ago, observed the planets and stars in the sky, he was looking at exactly the same universe which we explore today with the aid of the Hubble or of the radio telescopes. The observable universe has not changed (or has changed negligibly). We can simply probe into it in a better way. We are able to penetrate it further and deeper. This is not the case in economics. When Adam Smith, only slightly more than two centuries ago, was enquiring into the English society that was emerging from the Industrial Revolution, he was looking at something, not negligibly but quite profoundly, different from, let us say, Eurolandia today.

2. Second, economic research (again unlike physics) will tend sometimes to influence the events that are the object of study. The economist cannot simply stand back and observe, or explain, in a detached way. For example, when we try to understand the causes of unemployment or

of inflation, we obviously do so with the aim of devising means to overcome such undesirable phenomena.
3.   Third, economics deal with simple, down-to-earth, day-to-day problems
     that are everybody's immediate concern. It is enough to think of the deval-
     uation of a currency, or of the movements of wages and salaries, to real-
     ize how deeply these phenomena affect everybody's pocket.
4.   Fourth, many pronouncements on economic matters cannot avoid value
     judgements. Think of measures affecting the distribution of income and of
     wealth, or concerning the tax system, the price level, interest rates and so
     on. Value judgements can also be detected at the very basis of the 'vision
     of the world' which inevitably lies behind even abstract theorizing.

Yet, after listing these peculiarities of economic research, it must also be
stated that they do not cover the whole field. More specifically, not everything
that is studied by economics is continually changing. There are important
features of the economic system that may persist for quite long periods. Some
implications of the process of division and specialization of labour, for example, or some basic features of the pattern of evolution of customers' spending
(think of the so-called Engel curves) remain as relevant today as they were at
the time of Adam Smith. Again, not everything that the economists investigate
will, when understood, be used to influence events: far from it. Sometimes the
economists turn out to be powerless even when they think they should be able
to influence events. Again, not all subjects of economic analysis are of immediate concern to everyone. Some abstract elaborations in inter-temporal optimization theory, for example, are as far away from everyday life as the most
abstract philosophical speculations. And finally, not every statement the economists may make, not every conclusion they may reach, are conditional upon
value judgements. This extreme heterogeneity of the characteristics of
economic research, when compared with other disciplines, might itself be
listed as a fifth peculiarity.

It appears quite clear from these remarks that these peculiarities are bound
to create difficulties of communication, not only with the public at large, but
among economists themselves. How do economists themselves react to these
difficulties? How do they consider their theories? In a methodological essay in
1976, John Hicks made the following claim:

> In order that we should be able to say useful things about what is happening, before
> it is too late, we must select, even select quite violently. We must concentrate our
> attention . . . We must work . . . in some sort of blinkers. Our theories, regarded as
> tools of analysis, are blinkers in this sense. Or it may be politer to say that they are
> rays of light, which illuminate a part of the target, leaving the rest in the dark . . .
> But it is obvious that a theory which is to perform this function satisfactorily must
> be well chosen; otherwise it wil illuminate the wrong things. (Hicks, 1976: 208)

I tried to face the same problem in the other essay mentioned above (Pasinetti, 1986), but I did so in a different way. It seems to me that a more appropriate image to use is that of the theorizing process as a sort of telescope, which is used in both directions: to magnify, in one direction, those aspects on which the theorist has chosen to concentrate; and to shrink, in the opposite direction, or reduce to irrelevance, those aspects that are going to play a secondary role.

But who is going to choose the aspects that are to be magnified and those that are to be reduced? This is a worrying question. The answer that would seem obvious – 'the intuition of the theorist' – is in fact rather unsatisfactory. It has been pointed out, with specific reference to economics, that, at a pre-theoretical stage so to speak, one may identify the choice of a particular conception or 'vision of the world'. This, in the social sciences, may well be a device to achieve consistency among the types of simplifications that are made.

But it would be wrong to derive from this any conclusion about any necessary dependence of the theorizing process on pre-theoretical conceptions. It would also be wrong to argue for any supposed lower standard to be applied to the theorizing process in the social sciences, with respect to what happens in the physical sciences. Once the postulates have been stated, an economic theory acquires complete autonomy; as a theory it is entirely independent of the motivations that may have affected the choice of the postulates. And the standards of rigour and logical consistency of the analysis must obviously be the same as in any other field of investigation (including that of the physical sciences).

Yet it is undeniable that, quite apart from the logical consistency and rigour of any economic theory, the particular features of the simplifying process pose a problem at the stage of applicability and utilization; and this is relevant for society as a whole. How is society going to take heed of recommendations emanating from the prevailing theories, when alternative theories exist and are being proposed? And most importantly: to what extent should the development of alternative theories be encouraged or discouraged? These questions are not simply academic ones. A neutral attitude in this respect will not suffice: in a world like our own, today, the cost of so much research falls on the community as a whole. An answer to the questions just stated is therefore very important.

In the discussions on the nature of scientific progress that followed the publication of Kuhn's classic book (Kuhn, 1962), it has been taken for granted (but – it must be warned – with a view to physical sciences!) that the 'scientific revolutions', through which science is seen to proceed, leave space for one 'paradigm' at a time, and – in particular – that each paradigm, once discarded, is irretrievably obsolete.

A crucial question to ask is whether this is also the case for the social sciences. And it seems to me that there are too many reasons to be doubtful. In the history of economic thought, we do certainly identify quite different, and distinct, paradigms. But it is by no means clear that they should always succeed one another in a one-way direction. Or at least, a distinction should be made between the evolution of the analytical tools and the evolution of the ideas that are at the basis of any paradigm. Very often, in the physical sciences, the development of a new paradigm is indissolubly linked with the development of new analytical or even of new technological tools. This is not so in the social sciences. The development of new analytical tools may well lead to resuming and giving new vitality to an older paradigm, which had been discarded in the past and had fallen into oblivion because of unsolved difficulties which the new analytical tools were able to overcome. Therefore, if a certain one-way direction can be seen in the evolution and application of analytical tools, one cannot say the same of the succession of paradigms. This seems to indicate the importance and necessity, in economics (and in the social sciences in general), of a certain protection, so to speak, of the potentialities of the minority theories. Discussion on alternative lines to the prevailing ones should be promoted and encouraged, not suppressed (as the supporters of the prevailing theories have an inevitable tendency to do).

I shall conclude by mentioning that this pluralistic approach to the process of enhancing progress in learning is being proposed and supported not only by economists but also by scientists in other fields of research. To give a significant example, Professor Dik, who, at the European Science Foundation was reporting on progress in linguistics, concluded his report by stating:

> . . . my conclusions will be brief: the coexistence of different research traditions should be evaluated as a sign of vitality rather than of immaturity. Discussions across paradigm boundaries should be stimulated rather than shunted . . . Care should be taken that students get acquainted with the full intellectual wealth of the field. In research, possibilities for integrating the different disciplinary and interdisciplinary contributions should be actively pursued. And in research policy, one should avoid mistaking the ship for the fleet, even if one sail may temporarily eclipse most of the others. (Dik, 1985: 139)

How appropriately this seems to me to apply to economic research as well! And how clearly, in this light, can one appreciate the importance of the role to be played by the history of economic thought.

REFERENCES

Dik, S.C. (1985), 'Progress in linguistics' in T. Hägerstrand (ed.), *The Identification of Progress in Learning*, 115–39, Cambridge: Cambridge University Press.

Hicks, John R. (1976), ' "Revolutions" in economics', in Spiro J. Latsis (ed.), *Method and Appraisal in Economics*, 207–218, Cambridge: Cambridge University Press.

Kuhn, Thomas (1962), *The Structure of Scientific Revolutions*, 2nd edition, Chicago: University of Chicago Press.

Malinvaud, Edmond (1985), 'The identification of scientific advances in economics', in T. Hägerstrand (ed.), *The Identification of Progress in Learning*, 167–83, Cambridge: Cambridge University Press.

Pasinetti, Luigi L. (1985), 'Comment' on Edmond Malinvaud, 183–86.

Pasinetti, Luigi L. (1986), 'Theory of value – a source of alternative paradigms in economic analysis', in M. Baranzini and R. Scazzieri (eds), *Foundations of Economics: Structure of Inquiry and Economic Theory*, 409–31, Oxford: Basil Blackwell.

B41

9. Apparent progress due to forgetfulness or reinterpretation

Erich W. Streissler

OVERVIEW

Is there such a thing as progress in economics? As with most good questions in economics, the answer is, of course, *both 'yes' and 'no'*. Economics is the science in which commonly both A and non-A are true: at different points in time, under different circumstances, or even simultaneously in the behaviour of different economic agents.

There has been little which is new in *macroeconomics* since the early heyday of our science in the eighteenth century. Even there, though, there has been much that is new as far as *methods* are concerned, the analysis of empirical data and *measurement*. We moderns are confronted with a great wealth, if not a surfeit, of data. And yet – even here there might be exceptions: Gregory King, for example, may perhaps have provided his late seventeenth-century, not-yet-British, compatriots with more exact figures on the income distribution of their countrymen than we in Austria have at present as regards non-wage incomes.

Fritz Neumark propounded the idea that economic thought tends to be cyclical. There is much to be said for this idea. With a time-lag of about a quarter-century, one generation after the other rediscovers what had been well known to its forbears, though not infrequently under another name and, alas, not infrequently written in another language. There are well-documented waves of appreciation and deprecation of Adam Smith with a mean periodicity of about a century. What may be even more important is that basic economic circumstances tend to recur, to repeat themselves.

International financial markets and international private capital mobility was inhibited from 1914 to about 1980 or even 1990, for three-quarters of a century. Therefore, we are now relearning painfully what was common knowledge in the nineteenth and even in the eighteenth century. Austria – or was it then Germany? it is difficult to say – had its first international bond issues, denominated in a foreign currency, the pound sterling, in 1707, 1710, 1735 and 1737. The eighteenth century was already dominated to a high degree by capital market globalization and most authors knew it (for example, Richard Cantillon). And Böhm-Bawerk's treatment of the so-called 'twin deficit' problem (1914) – the fact that additional budget deficits might easily cause additional balance on current account deficits – in capital account terms, including his statement that the capital account tends to dominate the current account, might easily be superior to our treatment in national income account terms.

What is, however, more or less new is most of *microeconomics*. I do not think Hollander is correct in calling both Adam Smith and David Ricardo general equilibrium economists in the modern sense of neoclassical, or perhaps better, post-neoclassical, general equilibrium theory. They described an interconnected economic system, quantity flows in equilibrium and, of course (particularly in Ricardo) prices which, because of the constraints of an aggregate, were the mirror images of each other. But that was not general equilibrium as an *optimal pricing* system. The best proof of that is, perhaps, international comparative advantage in Ricardo, where Ricardo did not explicitly derive the optimal world price after specialization of each partner, but merely guessed at it by splitting the difference of the two cost prices. What the neoclassical or marginalist revolution brought about was thinking in terms of a *gamut of substitution possibilities*, a notion curiously unfamiliar to economists before the end of the nineteenth century, and deriving optimal prices in view of it.

This also entailed the possibility of analysing the *optimal pricing behaviour of firms*, which was simply not there before the twentieth century. It is safe to say that before the twentieth century, though monopoly is frequently mentioned, and a few people, such as Menger, even nibbled at monopoly theory, economists had no clear notion of so simple a problem as monopoly pricing. They stuck to the analysis of competition, which in a sense is a negation of intentional pricing behaviour.

Was there anything both new and likely to last in the economics of the second half of the twentieth century? Once more, not really in macroeconomics: For Keynes is just mercantilism somewhat improved, and there is little in Friedman that was not known to David Hume or, on the other hand, John Stuart Mill in his explanation that profitable speculation must be price stabilizing. Once more, the important advances were in microeconomics, both relative to the two 'classical' centuries, the eighteenth and the nineteenth, and relative to the first half of the twentieth century. The two ideas that have dominated the last three or four decades and which have changed economics fundamentally for ever are *risk preference* and *imperfect information*, especially asymmetric information.

Risk preference surfaced briefly with Mangoldt in the third quarter of the nineteenth century in Germany. But Mangoldt remained completely unappreciated, not least by the Austrians. Risk preference was, of course, pervasive in

Irving Fisher's theory of interest. But it did not really 'register' until the full assimilation of Neumann–Morgenstern utility: that is indicated by the fact that Schumpeter, up to the end, never understood it and Keynes thought nothing of Irving Fisher, whom, in contrast to Wicksell, he could read in English. That the manifold consequences of imperfect information for economic equilibria are wholly new ideas can perhaps best be seen in comparison with Menger. One of Menger's most consequential notions was that economic progress was progress in information content, but that, on the other hand, the time-consuming nature of the production process created uncertainty and, we might add, ever more uncertainty. These ideas were never fully worked out by Menger himself and were only taken up by Hayek as a very late successor. He worked them out fully in his 1945 article 'The Use of Knowledge in Society', which became, however, not the foundation of imperfect information theory but rather that of efficient financial markets.

In what follows, I shall briefly turn to a few macroeconomic points of, so to speak, non-progress, and to the difficulty of seeing that optimization over time might entail questions of risk preference. But to sum up this first preview, we might say that the concept of supply and demand was already fully understood in the mercantilist period and thereafter was not new; that the idea of scarcity or economic constraints was the main contribution of the classical period and was fully appreciated ever after; that substitution came in only with the neoclassical or marginalist revolution and was in this sense progress; and that, finally, the (closely related) issues of risk preference and imperfect information are the latest elements of genuine advance in economics from a present-day viewpoint. Notice that I have not included optimization or the marginal principle as steps on the road to progress in economics: Basically, they were there from the very start, only becoming somewhat better understood with time. The principle of opportunity cost, for example, can be found in Adam Smith's treatment of acquiring human capital qualifications.

THREE CASE STUDIES

As to non-progress in macroeconomics, it might, as a first case study, be a good idea to reread David Hume's 'Political Discourses' of 1752 and compare them with modern monetarism. Nearly all of Milton Friedman's positions are there, apart from the Fisher equation for the rate of interest (which is why I have called Friedman merely a pseudonym for Hume in the twentieth century): the long-run neutrality and the short-run non-neutrality of money, a kind of 'Phillips curve' and, above all, a purely real rate of interest are all there. However, in this original version, the logical difficulties of reconciling the postulates of short-run non-neutrality with long-run neutrality become much more visible than in the more modern versions, where they are just papered over. Hume himself explicitly points to the difficulty by confessing: 'This is not easily accounted for, if we consider only the influence, which a greater abundance of coin has on the kingdom itself' (p. 47). Hume argues for neutrality from the perspective of money as a (mere) unit of account. Then, of course, 'by itself' no change in the amount of money whatever can have any effect on prices. For short-run non-neutrality, Hume switches to a medium-of-exchange perspective and points out: 'some time is requir'd before the money circulate thro' the whole state, and make its effects be felt on all ranks of people. At first, no alteration is perceiv'd'. The uneven initial distribution of money is a persuasive argument for non-neutrality; but, having a stimulating effect on business activities, why should it completely lose this effect when spread evenly? One has to prove path-independence, which, in general, is impossible. The second argument of an increase in money at first not being fully 'perceiv'd' is a different one; it may have something, but need not have anything, to do with the uneven spread of initial stimulation. Finally, if we have a fully competitive world and no initial change in exchange rates, why should prices change when the amount of money changes? No single entrepreneur (assuming he is monopolistically competitive and does have some price-strategic scope) would dare to change his price for fear of being outcompeted. Would it not be more logical to assume, with Adam Smith (who, of course, had a theory of fixed natural prices determined by cost), that an additional amount of money not needed to circulate an additional quantity of product, would just flow out of the country to be invested elsewhere?

So, in a sense, the initial theory of the eighteenth century is superior to that of the present because now all the difficulties are merely plastered over with dogmatic stances. That 'neutrality of money' was not taken as seriously by the most informed specialists as it is quite often today, may be inferred from the fact that the term as such seems to have originated with the Austrians in the interwar period. But with them it explicitly designated a result of responsible monetary policy to be aimed at by the central bank, not an automatic consequence of whatever it does. And if the magisterial four-page survey by Hayek (1933) 'Über neutrales Geld' had not been unreadable in the USA in the 1970s because of the language, much of the debate about the implicit assumptions in Robert Lucas's (1972) famous piece on 'Expectations and the neutrality of money' would have become unnecessary; largely, it was a mere rediscovery.

A second case study is provided by the frequently stated remark that Ricardo's theorem of comparative advantage is a decisive step in the direction of 'progress' relative to Adam Smith, who had only known absolute advantage. A more acute analyst, however, such as Jürg Niehans (1990), would remark: 'The general idea of comparative cost did not originate with Ricardo. It had been clearly expressed by Adam Smith'. This is true; but remarks by

Smith that can be construed as propounding absolute advantage may also be found, though with some difficulty. Actually, it should be remembered that Smith's basic model of price determination was one with static (or fixed) factor prices, and then, with given wages, comparative advantage collapses into absolute advantage. But, even more important, Smith's basic model of foreign trade was a *two-factor* model with capital fixed and free labour, which can be employed the more, the more labour-intensive production is (cf. WN II. v. 34; IV. ix. 22 ff.). In this case foreign trade serves to increase total usable factor input, and thereby maximizes production: somewhat akin to the Heckscher–Ohlin model, capital-deficient countries will prefer to produce only labour-intensive commodities while capital-rich countries will produce and export capital-intensive commodities as well. Thus, Ricardo's and Smith's deductions on the advantages of foreign trade are simply *not comparable*, for they use different basic models. We may say that we consider Ricardo's model to be more generally applicable than that of Smith and that we therefore prefer it, but no more than that. 'Progress' cannot be clearly defined.

Finally, I offer a case study where we certainly can speak of progress because one author did not understand the full consequences of what he suggested. The Neumann–Morgenstern utility theorem, the idea of weighting utilities of states of nature with the probabilities of their occurrence, is extensively treated by Böhm-Bawerk in his habilitation thesis, 'Rechte und Verhaeltnisse vom Standpunkte der volkswirthschaftlichen Gueterlehre' (1881); and that book was well-known to Oskar Morgenstern. Böhm-Bawerk's analysis contains the famous 'lottery example' (that was about as far as he could do mathematics) and he explains certainty equivalents clearly. But he also considered it self-evident that the utilities would just be equal to the money payments, which still carries over to much of introductory-level game theory. In other words, he assumed risk-neutrality as a matter of course, in spite of the fact that in this case certainty equivalents become somewhat too easily definable to present any valuable information. In his own opinion Böhm solved just a little problem, and he did not even notice that he had solved it very restrictively. Neither he nor the judges of his thesis, Menger included, saw anything of importance in this attempt. It is particularly astonishing that the Austrians, who made so much of the concavity of the utility function in cases of static certainty, did not realize that its equivalent for intertemporal uncertainty would be risk aversion. Thus in spite of Böhm-Bawerk's very extensive treatment of the risk preference problem, much more extensive than the remarks of Ricardo on comparative advantage (which cover little more than a page), risk preference came to fruition only about three-quarters of a century later. But it was not a case of independent rediscovery, for Morgenstern knew Böhm-Bawerk's work intimately.

So 'progress' in economics may come about by the mere fact that someone else realizes only much later, what a monumental statement the original author had actually made.

REFERENCES

Böhm-Bawerk, Eugen von (1881), *Rechte und Verhältnisse vom Standpunkte der volks-wirthschaftlichen Güterlehre*, Innsbruck, Wagnersche Universitätsbuchhandlung.

Böhm-Bawerk, Eugen von (1914) 'Unsere passive Handelsbilanz', in: *Gesammelte Schriften*, F.X. Weiss (Hrg.), Vienna 1924, Hölder-Pichler-Tempski, 499–515.

Hayek, Friedrich A. von (1945), 'The Use of Knowledge in Society', *American Economic Review* 35, 519–530.

Hume, David (1752), *Political Discourses*, Edinburgh, Kincaid and Donaldson, Discourse III, 'Of Money', 41–59.

Lucas, Robert E., Jr. (1972), 'Expectations and the Neutrality of Money', *Journal of Economic Theory* 4(2), 103–124.

Niehans, Jürg (1990), *A History of Economic Thought – Classic Contributions, 1729–1980*; Baltimore and London, Johns Hopkins University Press.

Smith, Adam (1776), *An Inquiry Into The Nature And Causes Of The Wealth of Nations*, London, Strahan and Codell; *Glasgow Edition*, R.H. Campbell and A.S. Skinner (eds), Oxford University Press, 1976.

PART IV

Normative Economics

B41
D71

10. Is there progress in normative economics?

Philippe Mongin*

DIFFICULTIES SURROUNDING THE QUESTION, BUT WHY IT DOES ARISE

In this paper I take up the challenge of discussing progress in normative economics. The difficulties surrounding the enterprise are obvious. First of all, it is notoriously hard to say what exactly normative economics is about – welfare or choice, value judgements or the study of value judgements, economic policy or armchair evaluation. Economic methodologists or theorists have provided grand statements on how normative economics should be separated from positive economics and applied economics; see Keynes (1890), Robbins (1932), Samuelson (1947), Little (1950) and Archibald (1959), to name only a few. However, these accounts are hardly compatible with each other, and it is not always clear how they relate to the work actually done in economics. This paper will adopt the following non-commital view: the task of normative economics is to investigate methods and criteria for evaluating the relative desirability of economic states of affairs. This is a non-commital statement because it does not say whether normative economics itself endorses the evaluations (and thus *makes* value judgements) or just explores the way of making them (and thus only *relates to* value judgements). It does not decide either whether a more desirable state is one involving more welfare, or more choice, or more of anything else. Despite its generality the definition is not vacuous. It makes it clear that normative economics has a teleological rather than a deontological structure, to use the familiar ethical distinction. That is, normative economics draws conclusions about the rightness of actions (here, policy arrangements) from a prior investigation of the 'goodness' of economic states of affairs. The definition also encapsulates the claim that normative economics is primarily concerned with *evaluations*, and only derivatively with *recommendations*. For instance, there is room for assessing the functioning of markets, whether or not the resulting evaluations can be translated into relevant policies. This is a claim that I am going to take for granted here, even if some economists might disagree with it.

A second difficulty is that philosophers do not provide obvious guidance on the question I am tackling. Philosophers have nearly exclusively discussed progress in relation to science, while rarely contemplating the possibility that there is such a thing as *normative* science.[1] A further difficulty is that most of the available work on scientific progress deals with the empirical sciences; very little has been written on progress in logic and mathematics. Admittedly, even stated for empirical sciences like physics or biology, a suitable notion of *conceptual* progress could prove valuable for my purpose. Unfortunately, philosophy of science does not have so much to say about the more theoretical side of progress in the empirical sciences.[2]

Despite these bleak prospects, the question of this paper is a natural one to ask for anybody conversant with the field. Normative economics exhibits a relatively simple pattern of development, and to the specialist, this pattern is both *intelligible* and *oriented*. Many economists actually believe that it is a *progressive* pattern – although they cannot explain in detail what they mean. I am very much interested in making sense of this intriguing view and assessing it. I offer this as an excuse for embarking on an adventurous paper.

THE HISTORICAL PATTERN OF NORMATIVE ECONOMICS

The pattern is well known. The 'economics of welfare', as Pigou (1920) termed it, reformulated and extended some of the analyses of welfare and the efficiency of markets that could be found in Marshall and other early neo-classicals. Pigou's work is evidently more focused than his predecessors' piecemeal contributions. It is also more normative in the sense of my definition. Typically, it is clearer in distinguishing between the abstract conditions for increased welfare and the way they present themselves in the market or the way they can be implemented by the state. Pigou also made a step towards stating welfare conditions in terms of optimality conditions, although it is far from clear what his maximand was.[3] Whatever the exact meaning of his optimality conditions, he formulated them in such a way that they also bore on the distribution of income. Hence the easy and common reconstruction of Pigou's *Economics of Welfare* as being implicitly utilitarian – a reconstruction which I believe needs scrutinizing again. This old-style welfare economics is the first form of normative economics.[4]

The so-called *new welfare economics*, which crystallized in the 1930s, corresponds to the second form. It was much clearer than the old welfare economics about its premises – prominent among which was what we now call the Pareto principle – and it eventually reached a conceptually clear separation between the optimality conditions themselves and their application to markets.

The most famous applications obtained in these years were the so-called fundamental theorems of welfare economics – I am using again the modern terminology for simplicity. The first 'fundamental' theorem states that under relevant conditions, a competitive equilibrium satisfies the conditions for a Pareto optimum. The second 'fundamental' theorem says that under other relevant conditions, any Pareto optimum can be obtained as a competitive equilibrium after the agents' initial endowments have been modified by suitable lump-sum transfers.[5] Using different conceptual and technical means, the new welfare economics pursued a slimmer version of Pigou's programme. Officially, it put aside the evaluation of income distribution (left to the politician or the 'economist *qua* person'). The so-called compensation principle, on which I will expand later, was an attempt to go beyond the Pareto principle while stopping short of utilitarianism – and, allegedly, of any interpersonal comparisons of utility whatever.

The third stage corresponds roughly to two different forms of normative economics, that is, social choice theory on the one hand, and public economics on the other. Despite the obscurities in Pigou, the transition from the old to the new welfare economics seems to be relatively smooth and not too difficult to follow, while the transition to the third stage is neither. It is often said that Arrow's *Social Choice and Individual Values* in 1951 gave a fatal blow to the new welfare economics. However, this claim has been disputed violently by the welfare economists. Whatever its intended meaning, it cannot be that social choice theory superseded welfare economics in its traditional role of assessing the working of markets and proposing improvements in terms of corrective taxes and the like. The agenda of social choice theory is to investigate the various abstract methods of evaluating social states. Applications may or may not be market-related and anyhow enter social choice theory mostly by way of examples. From the 1970s onwards, it has been incumbent to the newly created discipline of public economics to discuss market optimality and policy corrections. According to an insider's suggestion,[6] public economics absorbed much of the content of the 'new welfare economics' that had survived social choice–theoretic criticism. Thus, there are two quite distinct forms of normative economics being currently practiced in parallel. There may be even more than two if one takes into account inequality theory and poverty theory, which have developed in a quasi-autonomous way from the 1970s and 1980s. Just by itself, the division process undergone by normative economics is enough to make the transition from the second to the third stage a complicated affair.

There is some evidence that normative economics might be undergoing a fourth change. The bulk of social choice theory up to the mid-1980s, and public economics throughout as far as I can judge, are *welfarist*. That is to say, they take the information provided by the individuals' utility functions to be necessary and sufficient data for the social choice or the public decision. This was the element of continuity between the third stage and the first two, as it were. From the broader point of view of social ethics, welfarism is a restrictive, and indeed conceptually problematic, principle to adopt. Internal criticism, especially Sen's later work, as well as the recent dialogue between philosophers and economists, have helped to bring this point home. Some economists have actually started to reorient social choice theory in a non-welfarist direction. Sometimes they dispense altogether with utility functions, as when analysing rights. More commonly, they supplement utility information with other sources, as when discussing talents and handicaps, opportunities and 'capabilities'. This theorizing is covered by labels such as 'economic theories of justice' or of 'equity', which suggest a philosophical potential that welfare economics never claimed for itself. But there are also numerous hints of economic applications, and even sometimes of how the new construals could be introduced into public economics. So arguably, normative economics is undergoing another metamorphosis. I hasten to add that not everybody in the field – even among those who actively contribute to reshaping it – would agree with this suggested diagnosis. Some of the theories also discussed under the 'economic justice' or 'equity' labels happen to be welfarist in the sense of this paragraph.[7] And it is a fact that public economists have hardly begun to catch up with the new developments. This said, nobody would deny that normative economics is on the move again, at least in its more theoretical parts, and that welfarism is one of the major issues currently under discussion.

We are now at a convenient historical distance to decide whether the third stage can be considered a progressive one. For this reason I will focus on this particular transition despite a corresponding drawback – that is, I will have to recast arguments that are well known to at least some of the readers. But I will give my own twist to the familiar story. Partly out of sheer incompetence, I concentrate my efforts on social choice theory, saying next to nothing about public economics. I do not think we are yet in a position to say anything definite about the last transition, but it turns out that my argument leads me to discuss it, however tentatively. I am going to argue that the transition to social choice theory was indeed progressive, but that the case against welfare economics was not properly sorted out until the fourth stage.

A PROVISIONAL DEFINITION OF PROGRESS

I start by contrasting intertheoretic with intratheoretic progress. It is perhaps not too difficult to recognize advances made within the confines of a given theory, especially when it is as clearly structured as are the new welfare economics and social choice theory. There is a story of successive clarifications of the two fundamental welfare theorems, and a story of successive refinements of Arrow's impossibility theorem. Both would exemplify a form of progress in normative economics, but this is not the form I am interested in diagnosing. Intertheoretic progress is what this paper is about.

When it comes to intertheoretic progress, controversy bursts out, and we can hardly do without an explicit definition. I will make a brave attempt at providing one. Let us then say that a shift from a theory T to a theory T' is progressive if: (1) T' provides a solution to at least one unresolved problem of T; (2) T' provides a solution to the main problems that T had already addressed and resolved in its own way; (3) T' raises new problems and manages to solve at least some of them.

This definition embodies the three ideas of (1) constructive criticism, (2) theoretical continuity, and (3) independence that are arguably the component parts of the common-sense notion of progress. Notice that if we take T and T' to refer to distinct variants of the same theory, we get a working definition of intratheoretic progress, supposing one is needed.[8] Importantly, the definition does not make particular reference to normative theories. The concept of problem-solving is broad – and vague – enough to apply to them as well as to theories in the empirical sciences and in mathematics. When problems are construed as either predictions to be confirmed or facts to be explained, we get a relevant case of the definition, and it then becomes close to that of a progressive shift in Lakatos (1970).

Actually, some of the experience gained in discussing Lakatos's methodology and related conceptions can be put to use here. As to (1), the analogy with the methodology of research programmes suggests that there are two possibilities to consider. Either the 'unresolved problem' is already recognized by T and is very much like a Lakatosian *anomaly* accompanying T. Or it is not only solved but also pointed out by T', in which case it is like a *novel fact*. We might expect both situations to occur with normative theories. It is arguable that standard ethical rules, such as utilitarianism, are accompanied by anomalies.[9] In normative economics, the many difficulties surrounding the compensation principle were treated, at least initially, like anomalies. I will expand at length on an example – Arrow's theorem – which illustrates the opposite analogy of a novel fact.

Something we learned from the discussions on the methodology of research programmes is that it is most delicate to construe theoretical continuity appropriately. Instead of (2) I might have required that T' solve *all* the significant problems already solved by T. This would be asking too much, exactly as Lakatos's (and Popper's)[10] famous requirement of non-decreasing content has proved to be exacting. To say that just *one* of the earlier problems needs to be solved would be too lax. Accordingly, I remain vague in my clause (2) even if this is not very satisfactory. Obviously, clause (3) plays the same role as the requirement of added content in Popper and Lakatos; it serves to exclude ad hoc modifications of T. Lakatos insisted against Popper that at least one of the independent predictions should be borne out by the facts. My suggestion for (3) parallels his own condition, and is presumably open to the charge of disguised inductivism that was levelled against it by the Popperians.[11]

Here is where the analogy breaks down. The classic requirements of increasing testable content in Lakatos and Popper imply that there are *logical* relations between successive theories. On the simplest construal, T and T' will share a subset of their logical consequences. If allowance is made for the obvious fact that theories need auxiliary statements in order to deliver predictions, this straightforward conclusion need not hold anymore. But it is still the case that T and T' will be logically related, although in terms of other statements and in a possibly non-transparent way. Nothing of the sort is implied by the above definition. T and T' might respond to the same problems using entirely different means. For instance, it can happen that the problems that T was resolving actively are shown not to *arise* in T'. I would regard this as an instantiation of clause (2). Generally, when the notion of a successful prediction gives way to that of successful problem-solving, much – perhaps too much – flexibility is introduced. The theories in a sequence declared to be progressive according to (1), (2) and (3) may well be loosely related to each other. Such a state of affairs would conflict with the intuition that progress is revolution-with-continuity, as it were. Having pointed out an a priori difficulty for my tentative definition, I can only hope that the narrative will suggest improvements.

THE SOCIAL CHOICE–THEORETIC CRITIQUE OF WELFARE ECONOMICS: HISTORICAL LANDMARKS

As I said, the new welfare economics clearly isolated and laid considerable emphasis on the problem of determining the conditions for maximum economic welfare (or the conditions for the general optimum, as they were also called). The problem was resolved while assuming nothing about the measurability and interpersonal comparability of utility – that is, in contemporary language, by invoking only the Pareto principle. For the purpose of this discussion I will restrict attention to the late restatements of this solution in Bergson (1938) and Lange (1942). These two papers were authoritative at the time. They exemplify the new welfare economics at its best, and are therefore suitable for a discussion of progress.

Bergson takes the step of discussing the economic welfare conditions in terms of a given function E – 'the Economic Welfare Function' (1938: 312) – that depends on all the individuals' consumptions of commodities and supplies of factors. Bergson just makes broad qualitative restrictions, that is, that E is increasing in consumption and decreasing in factor (that is, labour) supplied, and, at some point, that it satisfies the Pareto principle.[12] Bergson's contribution is to show that this thin set of assumptions is sufficient to obtain the already known conditions for maximum economic welfare, that is, that the marginal rates of substitution between commodities are equal from one individual to another, and similarly for the other relevant marginal substitution and transformation rates. As Bergson also explained, more special conditions that had also appeared in the past could be traced back to supplementary assumptions made on the shape of E – for instance, some of the conditions considered in the Cambridge tradition depended on assuming an additive form for E. Each time the relevant marginal conditions could be obtained as the first-order conditions of a constrained maximization programme, with the technical possibilities taken as the constraint.[13] Samuelson's *Foundations* (1947) followed Bergson's method of discussing the general optimum in terms of a welfare function; hence the expression used afterwards, 'the Bergson–Samuelson welfare function'.[14] For the purpose of the discussion to come, I mention that neither author was clear about the extent to which a 'Bergson–Samuelson welfare function' E requires interpersonal comparisons of utility. They knew that the Cambridge additive function does; but they had not sorted out whether E does *in general*.

The second part of Lange's paper contains a related and even clearer discussion of the general optimum than Bergson's, but the first part stands in sharp contrast with the latter's method of analysis. There, Lange introduced the (by now well-known) method of computing Pareto optima by maximizing one individual's utility function given that the technical possibilities are fixed *and* that the other individuals' utility functions are set at predetermined values. Thus, Lange also used the apparatus of constrained maximization but differently from Bergson. The importance of Lange's method is that it dispenses with the assumption of an underlying economic welfare function in order to reach welfare conclusions.[15]

Social choice theory has an immediate connection with Bergson's version of welfare economics, but not with Lange's. It is no coincidence that the latter is mentioned only in passing in Arrow's 1951 book, while the former is the target of an elaborate argument. Remarkably, after pointing out the wide generality of his notion of 'social choice' in Chapter 1, Arrow chose in Chapter 3 to specialize it to welfare economics. In this chapter he introduces his famous conditions,[16] not in full generality, but in terms of a 'social welfare function', and the latter is said to share important features with Bergson's own function. The argument started here about Bergson will extend throughout the book – it recurs in the next chapter on the compensation principle and culminates in chapter 6. At this juncture, Arrow goes beyond the initial claim that Bergson's function is *analogous* to one of his 'social welfare functions'. It is in effect *identical* to one of them, with the striking consequence that the impossibility theorem applies:

> Mathematically, the Bergson social welfare function has . . . the same form as the social welfare function we have already discussed . . . Hence, the Possibility Theorem . . . is applicable here; we cannot construct a Bergson social welfare function . . . that will satisfy Conditions 2–5 and that will lead to a true social ordering for every set of individual tastes. (Arrow, 1963: 72)

This is a crucial passage to understand the connections, both historical and logical, between the new welfare economics and social choice theory. On a few occasions in the book, Arrow even goes beyond the stage of rejecting Bergson's particular version of the new welfare economics. He also claims that his refutation of Bergson implies that the search for optimum conditions is meaningless.[17] But there cannot be a straighforward implication from one to the other. We have just seen that Lange's derivation of the marginal conditions does not depend on assuming a 'social welfare function'; hence it is immune to Arrow's critique. One interpretation of Arrow's claim is that he views the study of the general optimum as being *only a preliminary stage* in the construction of an economic welfare function. This is a view that I find hard to defend. If Arrow had really adhered to it, the work he did in the 1950s on the two fundamental welfare theorems would have been – it seems – pointless.[18] Clearly, the marginal conditions have an interest by themselves, even if they do not inform us about the difficult cases, such as those involving complicated externalities and those calling for distributional considerations. I am returning now to the critique of Bergson. At a later point I will come to the compensation principle, which provides another relevant link between welfare economics and social choice theory.

THE SOCIAL CHOICE – THEORETIC CRITIQUE OF WELFARE ECONOMICS: THE ARROW–BERGSON CONNECTION DISENTANGLED

Arrow's final rejection of Bergsonian welfare economics entirely depends on establishing that the economic welfare function is not only related to, but in effect identical with, a 'social welfare function' in his sense. This conclusion depends on three steps, the first and the second of which are unproblematic. The first step is purely semantic. Arrow's 'social welfare function' comes with a privileged interpretation of individual preference relations – they are meant to represent the individuals' evaluations of social states, as influenced by their 'values'. Bergson, and welfare economists generally, analyse social states in terms of individual consumptions and supplies of factors, and their notion of a utility function is meant to reflect the individual's ordinary, unelaborate preference – his 'tastes' as opposed to his 'values' in Arrovian terminology. As Arrow points out, this semantics can be accommodated by the 'social welfare function' viewed as a purely formal object. Where an objection could arise, however, is with the universal domain condition. If 'tastes' are construed according to standard microeconomics, that is, as preferences varying positively with consumption and negatively with labour expended, and depending on nothing else, there is a restriction on the set of available preference profiles. Hence a second, purely logical step, which consists in showing that the impossibility theorem holds for the accordingly restricted domain assumption ('Possibility Theorem for Individualistic Assumptions', 1963: 63).[19] In the sequel I will refer to this relevant domain assumption as 'modified universal domain'.

The ground is now cleared for the third and only really problematic step, that is, to defend each of the conditions – modified universal domain, independence of irrelevant alternatives, Pareto or related conditions, non-dictatorship and social ordering – in terms of the general objective and privileged interpretations of welfare economics. Arrow (1963: 73) is disappointingly brief when it comes to this fundamental discussion. Basically, he contents himself with pointing out again the general plausibility of his conditions.

Not surprisingly, the welfare economists plunged into the breach. While conceding that the theorem was perhaps applicable to politics,[20] they would claim that it was irrelevant to their field. 'We must conclude that Arrow's work has no relevance to the traditional theory of welfare economics, which culminates in the Bergson–Samuelson formulation', said Little (1952: 141). 'I agree with Little in barring Arrow's theorem from welfare economics', added Bergson (1954: 247). Two major points were made. I will take up each of them in turn.

The first point was that the very notion of a social welfare function, as defined on a *set* of many preference profiles, made no sense in welfare economics, and similarly for the conditions involving comparisons between two profiles. It was argued that welfare economics was restricted to *given* individual tastes, which meant, in Arrow's framework, a unique preference profile. According to the argument, welfare economics comparisons bear on changes in either the physical variables, such as individual consumptions, or the technological parameters, such as the firms' production functions. There is no sense in trying to extend these comparisons to cases of preference changes. When the Bergson function is decomposed in terms of the individual utility functions, it must be well understood that the latter are kept fixed. In other words, the economic welfare function is a function of functions only in the sense of a composed function, not of a functional.[21]

As it turned out from later discussions, this line of defence is a weak one to take. To *define* a 'social welfare function' on a set of many preference profiles would be immaterial if the conditions imposed on the function did not involve comparisons among several profiles at a time. This observation reduces the scope of the disagreement to the conditions themselves, and specifically to the subclass of those conditions which are involved in the making of 'interprofile' comparisons. The 1951 version had one too many of those problematic conditions; it disappeared from the neater 1963 version.[22] What remains open to the welfare economists' objection is independence of irrelevant alternatives as well as universal domain: the latter provides the stock of profiles between which the former allows one to make comparisons. But the work done by social choice theorists in the 1970s established that both independence and universal domain could be replaced by conditions stated for a *single* profile, leading to reproduction of the negative conclusion of Arrow's theorem in this less controversial framework.[23] I will denote these 'single profile' analogues of the initial conditions by universal domain* and independence*. Universal domain* is satisfied by welfare economics, given the standard assumptions of this theory. Independence* is more difficult to interpret. However, this difficulty should be reserved for a separate discussion; the initial condition of independence was also open to several interpretations or objections. Dealing with the welfare economists' first major point, I can record the following result: they made a big deal of an issue – 'single profile' versus 'multi-profile' social evaluation – which proved to be a merely technical one. If something goes wrong with the social choice–theoretic critique of welfare economics, it cannot have anything to do with that issue, but with the significance of the conditions in either framework.[24]

The second major point made by the welfare economists, notably Little (1952) and Bergson (1954), is that their economic welfare function should not to be interpreted as expressing the society's ordering but only an ordering relative to the society. But then, whose ordering is it? Arrow's opponents insist that it must be *a person's*. The welfare economist views himself primarily in the role of a consultant. He counsels officials who are to make large-scale decisions. He also counsels the ordinary citizens who are willing to employ him in order to decide, say, whether or not they will support a tax reform. Whichever is the case, the argument continues, welfare analysis relates to a person like you and me, not to a collective entity. The person will communicate his evaluative judgments to the welfare economist, who should be able to summarize them into a *coherent* criterion, that is, an ordering. The conclusion that the criterion is coherent is compelling, because we are here talking of a person, not of a collective entity, and the usual rationality considerations apply unproblematically at this level.

This forceful answer would seem to cut the ground from under Arrow's feet. I am not aware of an explicit rebuttal in the literature, which makes it worthwhile to offer one here. One version of the argument is easy to rebut because it involves a serious confusion about methodological individualism. The welfare economists claimed in effect that collective entities ('the community as such', Bergson, 1954: 243) did not *exist*. But it has been argued repeatedly and, I think, convincingly that methodological individualism is not the thesis that collectives do not exist. It is rather the (weaker) thesis that they cannot be automatically endowed with well-defined aims or objectives. Methodological individualism is a way of allocating the burden of proof. When it comes to firms or nations, the burden of proof is on whoever claims that there is such a thing as the firm's objective function, or the nation's long-term interests. From this cursory discussion I conclude that methodological individualism supports – if anything at all – the programme of investigating the conditions under which collective objectives can be defined, starting from the data of individual objectives. This is the programme of social choice theory broadly speaking.

Here is a further counter-argument. Even granting the welfare economists' premise that the welfare ordering is a person's ordering, there are difficulties for their position. It amounts to discarding all of Arrow's conditions but one, namely, the social ordering condition. A priori, the client might be of any ethical type. He might not even accept the Pareto principle and non-dictatorship. But if this is so, what is the role of welfare economics? It is reduced to the menial task of explaining how to maximize a function, whatever it is, under predetermined constraints. Surely, welfare economists have a higher opinion of their field. What led them astray is the implicit assumption that to form an ordering from the client's data is a trivial step. If one takes the 'economist as consultant' picture at all seriously, one must extend it to the *construction* of the ordering. This richer description eschews the charge of triviality. It is only at the construction stage that the traditional commitments of welfare economics – that is, the Pareto principle, and arguably non-dictatorship[25] – enter the picture. But then, social choice theory becomes relevant since it addresses the question of how to construct a welfare ordering for the client. Arrow's specific conditions, or rather the related single-profile conditions, are also relevant, at least prima facie. They might be dismissed at the end of the day, but there is sense in saying that they belong to theoretical welfare economics.[26]

The welfare economists' arguments relied not only on the two theoretical arguments which I have tried to dispose of, but also on invoking the tradition of their field. For instance, in the same passage I quoted from, Bergson wrote: 'I have thought here to make explicit that this follows simply from the very nature of the discipline' (1954: 247). From all I know, this remarkable pronouncement is unwarranted by the history of the subject. Admittedly, the notion of the economist as a 'counsellor' of individuals is a commonplace of pre-war economics. But I do not think that the welfare economists believed that the whole of their field should be reorganized around this single theme. It cannot accurately capture the objectives of normative economics, which is, to repeat, primarily an exercise in *evaluation*, and only derivately a system of *recommendations*. I do not think either that the welfare economists would really construe the theme as narrowly as it was construed in the previous argument.[27] To the contrary, there is evidence that: (a) more often than not, they intended the 'client' to be the collective entity, whatever that meant for them;[28] and (b) they were concerned with the construction of the economic welfare function, even though they would as a first approximation take it as given.[29]

To put it bluntly, the new welfare economics was groping after something like Arrow's aggregation problem, especially in the late pre-war formulations.[30] By denying this, the welfare economists have reformulated their enterprise in a bizarre way, which could not enhance its prestige among the general economists. I submit that their defensive move has decisively contributed to the decay of their field in the post-war years. Also, by denying this, the welfare economists have been distracted from offering a serious critique of Arrow's or related conditions. Even at a late stage, there was no fruitful discussion of those single-profile versions of the impossibility theorem which I have just shown are directedly related to the 'Bergson–Samuelson welfare function'.[31] This is too bad for welfare economics.

To return to the notion of progress, consider again requirement (1), namely that T' should provide a solution to at least one unresolved problem of T. In the previous discussion, the word 'problem' has come to mean two things. I suggested that the *general* problem of aggregating individual utility functions was nearly explicitly part of the conceptual background of the new welfare economics. The *specific* problem created by the impossibility theorem was of course invented by social choice theory, but given that the general problem was in the air, it must count as a problem also for welfare economics. I should state precisely what the specific problem was. I submit that the following version of the impossibility theorem is appropriate: 'a Bergson–Samuelson welfare function which is not based on interpersonal comparisons of utility is dictatorial'. This version is not Arrow's. It is single-profile, and based on universal domain* and independence*. Not only does it deflect the objection raised against Arrow's multi-profile framework, but – most importantly – its independence* condition can be interpreted as rendering the assumption that interpersonal comparisons are *not* made. Given this interpretation, all the conditions are acceptable to the welfare economists. They lead to the unpalatable conclusion of dictatorship – admittedly a less shocking conclusion in the single-profile than in the multi-profile context, but an unpalatable conclusion nonetheless. Now, how does social choice theory resolve the problem thus created? In one sense, the logical statement of impossibility by itself constitutes a 'solution'; in another sense, the 'solution' would be to make interpersonal comparisons in some specific way. I will return to this ambiguity after discussing the compensation principle.

A WORD ON THE COMPENSATION PRINCIPLE

The famous compensation principle of the new welfare economics provides a link with social choice theory which has perhaps attracted even more attention than the Arrow–Bergson debate. However, I view it as conceptually less significant than the latter, for reasons that need spelling out. In a nutshell, this is because the critique of the compensation principle does *not* have to rely on using the impossibility theorem – contrary to the critique of Bergsonian welfare economics, which absolutely needs it.

It is a familiar story to the economists. The compensation tests attempted to extend the range of welfare judgments permitted by the Pareto principle by taking into account the possibility of the gainers' compensating the losers. The Kaldor–Hicks test was inconsistent in the sense of leading to cycles, actually obvious cycles of order 2, but Scitovsky's more sophisticated 'double test' pretended to remedy this defect. Arrow argues that the Scitovsky test is also inconsistent.[32] The logical skeleton of his refutation is this. The binary relation implied by the Scitovsky test is incomplete; a natural way to make it complete is to declare two states x and y indifferent with each other if the test is conclusive neither for x against y, nor for y against x. However, indifference defined that way turns out to be intransitive, as a three-alternative example demonstrates (Arrow, 1963: 45). This fairly straightforward piece of reasoning stands by itself, regardless of the impossibility theorem.

Although Arrow does not do it explicitly, it is possible to base a refutation on his impossibility theorem. Take *any* binary relation R having the following two properties: first, it extends the partial ordering implied by the Pareto principle; second, it is complete. If R is obtained from a 'social welfare function', then assuming the Arrovian conditions other than social ordering, we conclude that R *must* be intransitive. This sounds like a powerful critique because it does not depend on the particular way of making the Scitovsky relation complete, in contradistinction with the previous argument. It does not even depend on selecting the Scitovsky relation in the first instance, and can thus be offered as a refutation of the compensation principle *in general*. However interesting it might be, the argument through the impossibility theorem seems unnatural because the Scitovsky test falls prey to a much simpler argument. This probably explains why Arrow chose to dismiss the Scitovsky test by means of a numerical example, and not in terms of the abstract argument just sketched.

Even if Arrow did not say it in so many words, there is a sense, both formal and conceptual, in which the impossibility theorem *explains* the failure of the compensation tests. Their motivation was to go beyond the Pareto criterion while still avoiding making interpersonal comparisons. Arrovian results teach us that this is an impossibility as soon as one insists on certain conditions, among which that of a complete ordering extension of the Pareto partial ordering.[33] This connection means good news for my thesis that the latter is progressive with respect to the new welfare economics. In the 1940s, the cyclicity of the compensation tests was construed somewhat as an *anomaly* accompanying an essentially sound theory. Given this construal as an anomaly, we have another successful application of requirement (1) in the definition of progress, and actually a neatly different one from the previous application to Bergsonian economics. Notice the particular notion of a 'resolution' involved here. It consists in showing that there cannot be a solution in the sense dreamt of by the welfare economists – a purely negative sense of the word 'resolution'.[34]

SOCIAL CHOICE THEORY AND THE CONDITIONS OF PROGRESS

Thus far, I have mostly been busy arguing that requirement (1) was met. Both to buttress this claim and reach a similar conclusion for conditions (2) and (3), I should pause and discuss the sense in which social choice theory can be said to *resolve* problems. Typical responses to Arrovian impossibilities involve either pursuing Arrow's main suggestion in 1951, that is, weakening the unrestricted domain assumption, or adopting Sen's (1970, 1982) and his many followers' method of introducing interpersonal comparisons. (In social choice theory, until recently, the Pareto principle has been regarded as unassailable.) Which road to choose depends on the intended interpretation. In terms of the welfare economics interpretation, the first road is a dead end. This much was already suggested by my discussion of universal domain*. The technically refined work which has consisted in exploring highly structured 'economic domains' by and large supports the claim that Arrow's theorem is robust to domain changes.[35] The welfare-oriented social choice theorists have usually explored the second road, and meanwhile formalized particular ethical criteria, some of which are completely standard (for example, utilitarianism), others not so (for example, Nash's product of utilities).[36]

The sense in which these exercises are problem resolutions is ambiguous for the following reason. Many social choice theorists are concerned mostly with exploring the compatibility or otherwise of given normative assumptions, without taking side strongly for or against them. They might point out that a condition is apparently acceptable, or open to criticism, but they would refrain from entering a proper normative debate. For instance, to solve the problem created by an impossibility result typically means for them to taxonomize and logically explore the ways of circumventing the impossibility, ideally by turning it into one or more positive characterizations. Their official notion of problem-solving is a *formal* one.[37] As an important application, it includes the case in which a previously raised problem is shown *not* to have any solution, as with the compensation principle. However, other theorists (like myself) believe that normative commitments are both unavoidable and desirable, and conclude that the ethical discussion is a very substantial part of the social choice exercise. For this group, solutions are given at the *substantial* level of normative decisions made for or against a condition, while taxonomies or conditional statements play the role of preliminary groundwork. It is important to realize that the two groups overlap massively in their ordinary work, even though they would disagree when asked to make their methodological positions clear. Some contributions are clearly purely formal, others are clearly substantial or at least offered as such. But a good deal of the puzzle-solving activity in the field falls in between.[38]

How does this sketch compare with what we know of the new welfare economists' attitude towards normative commitments? They were wary of certain 'value judgements' and willing to indulge in others. They took the Pareto principle to be both normatively commendable and indispensable, and they regarded judgements of interpersonal comparisons as being both normatively dubious and dispensable. These two *substantial* commitments defined a range of acceptable problems for which solutions could be sought. Within this range, solutions were mostly offered at the *formal* level, as is apparent, I think, in both Bergson's work and the original papers on the compensation principle. Comparisons of the new welfare economics with social choice theory may not be too difficult to implement if we are careful to limit them to problem-solving activities of the same type.

This warning helps to put into proper perspective requirements (1) and (2). For what it is worth, Bergson's economic welfare function is a formal device; so it is appropriate to compare the problem it raised with the following solution: 'either accept interpersonal comparisons of welfare, or give up the economic welfare function'. The solution is stated at the same level of generality as the function itself; there is no need to specify *which* interpersonal comparisons should be made. It is a truly informative resolution, and if it had been absorbed by the welfare economists, it would have reoriented their theorical work entirely. This completes the discussion of requirement (1). I think (2) can be fulfilled along similar lines, while taking into account the important fact that a good deal of the new welfare economics was diverted to public economics from the 1970s onwards. The formal analysis of the general optimum, and the way its conditions are realized by the markets or call for correctives – all this really belongs to public economics by now.

Both formal and substantial resolutions are welcome to count for the fulfilment of (3). This requirement is most easily satisfied by mentioning the wide range of problems in the 'theory of committees' that the social choice theorists both raise and solve, most often formally, but sometimes also substantially. These problems were clearly outside the initial range of the new welfare economics (and not only outside its ex post redefined range, once Arrow had come!). It is fair to recall at this juncture that modern social choice theory results not only from Arrow's pioneering book, but also from Black's *Theory of Committees and Elections* (1958) and earlier articles on the same topic. Alternatively, I could have stayed close to Arrow's initial contribution by mentioning the variant proved by Gibbard (1973), a justly famous result which opened up a whole new area of work – that is, the non-manipulability of social choice decisions.[39]

THE ASSUMPTIONS OF WELFARE ECONOMICS AND THE FOURTH STAGE OF NORMATIVE ECONOMICS

Although the main point has already been argued, that is, that the third stage was a progressive one, I would like to take a broader view of my topic and briefly re-examine the basic assumptions of welfare economics. As will become apparent, the point is to relate them to the *current* work, that is, what was tentatively called the fourth stage of normative economics. This will lead me to clarify, and actually qualify, the sense in which the third stage was progressive.

Welfare economics relies on conceptually loaded assumptions that have become better and better understood, and actually more and more heatedly criticized, with the passing of time. The following list is an attempt to capture them. I state them in terms of the ideal concept of normative economics that welfare economics is supposed to encapsulate.

I.   Normative economics is an exclusively teleological theory. That is to say, it will select a notion of the social good, and it will make all its evaluations and derived prescriptions dependent on this chosen notion.

II.   The chosen notion of social good is social welfare. Social welfare is initially an undefined term in normative economics. It will be explicated in terms of the next conditions.

III.   Social welfare in any circumstances is entirely determined by the data of individual welfare given these circumstances, and it increases when these data show an increase in individual welfare. Normative economics makes this claim precise in terms of the Pareto principle, as interpreted in welfare terms.

IV. Normative economics is concerned with a particular notion of a social state. Only economic variables enter the description of the states.[40] (In effect, the economic variables to be taken into account are the quantities of commodities consumed and of factors supplied by the individuals. The commodities may be either private or public goods.)

V. Individual welfare can be measured by an index of preference satisfaction.

VI. The index of preference satisfaction summarizes the individual's choice behaviour ('revealed preference theory').

VII. The index can be endowed with the standard properties of an ordinal utility function. For each individual, it varies in the obvious direction with this individual's quantities of goods and factors. The familiar nonsatiation and convexity conditions may be imposed. The assumptions will have to be suitably modified when it comes to risk and uncertainty, but again by borrowing standard microeconomic construals (such as the von Neumann–Morgenstern utility function).

VIII. The index is not comparable from one individual to another.

This is a rough picture, but it is sufficient for the conceptual discussion.[41] Welfare economists generally do not disentangle (V) from (VI) because they take 'revealed preference theory' for granted. Then, the statement corresponding to (V) and (VI) jointly goes like this in welfare economics:

> A person's welfare map is defined to be identical with his preference map – which indicates how he would choose between different situations, if he were given the opportunity for choice. To say that his welfare would be higher in A than in B is thus no more than to say that he would choose A rather than B, if he were allowed to make the choice. (de Graaff, 1957: 5).[42]

All of these assumptions can be, and indeed have been, called into question, either jointly or separately. Take (V) and (VI) together. For sure, welfare economists know that maximizing behaviour in the revealed preference sense does not have the same meaning as maximizing behaviour in the welfare sense. What they intend to say is only that the former can serve as a *measure* of the other for the purpose of the theory. Presumably, this is the reason why de Graaff employs the word 'defined' in the previous quote. Then, domain considerations should come to the forefront. The (purely extensional) coincidence of the two kinds of behaviour can only be justified by appealing to the particular notion of social states in welfare economics. This means that we should really consider (V) and (VI) jointly with (IV). But even with this charitable reading, the claim is more than dubious. Suppose that I have to choose between various baskets of apples and bananas, a matter relevant to the 'economic' notion of a social state. From the fact that x is my chosen basket, and y is not, the welfare economist still cannot infer that my welfare would be lower in y than it is in x. This is a *non-sequitur*. There may be all sorts of reasons why I choose x instead of y, not all of them to do with my welfare. Quite trivially, my tastes for apples and bananas might induce me to choose a basket with, say, too many bananas for my welfare. Some will perhaps be tempted to reply that non-welfare reasons show up as violations of the consistency of choices, but this would be a gratuitous assumption to make. A more standard reply is this. One cannot say that I am choosing too many bananas for my welfare if I really *choose* to have this basket. But this is tantamount to saying that, after all, welfare *is* the same thing as choice – a claim that was discarded at the outset as implausible. Notice that the familiar contention, 'people are the best judges of their own interest', is not sufficient to warrant the conclusion that choices provide a measure of welfare. The claim may be true without the people's good judgement surfacing in their choices.

One way or another, the critique just sketched has been made a number of times.[43] What I want to stress is the methodological point that this seemingly commonsensical critique has entered normative economics only recently. It is not well taken by social choice theory, which generally has little to contribute on *the interpretation* of the preference concept. For most social choice theorists, preferences are just preferences, whatever that means; and if they are pressed to provide an interpretation, they might very well follow the welfare economist into the trap of 'defining' welfare by choice.[44] It is really only in the work currently pursued about non-standard indexes of welfare, especially in connection with Sen's (1985) 'functionings' and 'capabilities', that the critique above has become broadly understood.

A different (and more sophisticated) critique of welfare economics results from focusing on (IV) and (V), while putting (VI) aside. To relate an economic notion of welfare to *any* concept of preference raises possible objections. Sen (for example, 1979, 1985) usually carries his critique by considering *actual* preferences – 'tastes' in Arrow's terminology. But it is possible to give a chance to the notion of *improved* preference in a sense that is not 'values' in the Arrovian sense, but rather preference for the individual's own good.[45]

These issues are often discussed in connection with the polysemic concept of *welfarism*. In Sen's and others' work, the notion usually refers to the claim that individual utility data are both necessary and sufficient to form an index of social welfare. A drawback of this definition is that it trades on an unspecified notion of 'utility', which leads to a case-by-case examination, with each relevant interpretation for 'utility' delivering a case. I find it clearer to define 'welfarism' as the claim that individual *welfare* data are both necessary and sufficient to form an index of social welfare. This position then becomes identical with assumption (III) in the list. The argument against sufficiency can be made in terms of socially undesirable aspirations, as in Hare's (1976) fanatic example or in Sen's (1970) Paretian Liberal paradox. The case against necessity is not so straightforward to argue, and might involve one considering the pitfalls of the Pareto principle in the uncertainty context, which would involve assumption (VII) in the discussion.[46] Actually, necessity is more commonly questioned in relation to still other implicit notions of 'welfarism'. One of them would go like this. 'Welfarism' is the claim that individual welfare data are both necessary and sufficient in order to form *a notion of the social objective* (rather than an index of social welfare). This sense of 'welfarism' is appropriate for those theorists who are willing to accept assumption (I) fully, but only a qualified version of (II).[47] The case against necessity is then expedited by taking note of highly desirable objective achievements such as good health, education, real freedom and so on. Consider finally the further variant resulting from replacing 'to form a notion of the social objective' by '*to evaluate social states*'. This definition is appropriate for those who do not even fully agree with (I), that is, those who do not believe that normative economics should be exclusively a teleological theory. The case against necessity is then made by insisting on rights, as in today's extensive literature following from another part of Sen's (for example, 1981) work – a literature which is permeated with deontological considerations.

This bird's-eye review was meant to support two methodological claims. First, as already emphasized, the argument against the new welfare economics had to wait far beyond the beginning stage of social choice theory in order to be properly sorted out. I mentioned Arrow's occasional anticipation of a far-reaching critique of the new welfare economics, that is, a critique which would hit not only the Bergsonian economic welfare function, but the Paretian core of welfare economics. Whatever Arrow's meaning was in 1951, I do not think that he fully had the conceptual means of pursuing this critique. The current discussions of 'welfarism' help to formulate it more appropriately. Second, there is a kind of reciprocal to the previous claim. The current discussions are best reorganized within the framework of a step-by-step refutation of the new welfare economics – even though the latter is old hat for today's readers. Precisely because they embody an intermediary stage of critical thinking, the Arrovian and post-Arrovian theories of the 1950s to 1970s are *not* a good polemical target to choose for 'post-welfarist' writers. It is better to shoot at a theory which is blunter about its conceptual commitments.

This brief excursion into the fourth stage teaches us something about the pace of progress in normative economics. It is both slow and irregular. We saw that it took about twenty years for social choice theory to produce the ('single-profile') technical variant of the impossibility theorem that would fill the gaps in Arrow's initial argument against the Bergson–Samuelson function. What we have seen in this section is that progress may be better appreciated by comparing a theory not with its immediate predecessor, but with an earlier theory. It is as if problems had a life of their own, some of them being quickly clarified, while the others drag on for years. But the time has now come to reconsider the definition of progress tentatively offered at the beginning of this paper.

CONCLUSIONS AND FURTHER ELABORATIONS

By way of conclusion, I return to each the three conditions and discuss possible qualifications or refinements. Consider requirement (1). The Arrow–Bergson connection probably illustrates how this condition is typically encountered in normative economics. Cases of recognized anomalies for T are sparser than cases of disturbing novel facts pointed out by T'. We should then expect the T theorists to deny what the T' theorists claim, that is, that there is a problem *for T*. To pass a judgment nonetheless, we need to complement requisit (1) with an *external decision procedure*. What I have done in effect is to consider the theoretical background of T, that is, its theoretical language and intended interpretations. If the problem could have been formulated in the theoretical language, and if once formulated, it would have fallen within the range of intended applications, the debate is settled for T'. I claimed that a suitable version of the impossibility theorem fitted this description. This claim involved me in some history of economic thought. Historical research is bound to play a role of arbitration since each camp will invoke 'the tradition of the field' against the other.

Consider now condition (2). It is disappointingly vague to mention only the *main* problems addressed and solved by T, but I see no way of improving on this part of the definition. Here is another feature that is worth stressing. The requirement that T' should continue to solve the main problems that T had solved is good enough to ensure continuity, but not to exclude that dubious resolutions will be perpetuated. In the empirical sciences the corresponding requisit – roughly, that T' recovers most of the corroborated content of T – ensures, at least in principle, that what is common to T and T' is also what is valuable. Of course, the contrast must not be overdone. Corroboration is arguably never definitive – and some problem resolutions can be. But there remains a substantial disanalogy, and it might indicate that only progress 'in the small' – not progress 'in the large' as in grand science – is really feasible for normative disciplines. Given the conceptual difficulties – actually, the mass of confusions – that social choice theory unconsciously borrowed from the new welfare economics, the progress from one to the other is more limited than my account of the brilliant Arrovian episode suggested. The sketch of the fourth stage has served to temper the initially enthralling picture.

Concerning (3), I will only mention that this condition does not insist on originality, at least in the following sense. It is sufficient if traditional conceptions are *made by T' to bear on the given problem*. The way in which social choice theory has again dragged the time-honoured rule of utilitarianism into welfare discussions is an example to the point.[48] There is a loose analogy between the claim made here about originality and a view that surfaced in the earlier philosophy-of-science discussion of novel facts. Against Lakatos's 'temporal' view of evidence, it was argued – successfully, I believe – that a new theory could be corroborated by evidence already known before it came into existence.[49]

Here is a last point, or rather a warning, I would like to make. Welfare economics died, or rather disintegrated progressively, for many different reasons, some of them unconnected with the emergence of a progressive alternative theory. The post-war years seem to have witnessed an increasing discontent with its policy conclusions. Thus, the 'theory of the second best' introduced after the war by Lipsey and Lancaster (1956) cast doubt on the relevance of the marginal conclusions as well as the analysis of the optimum more generally. The lasting achievements of the new welfare economics proved dubious after all, even to those who were *not* impressed by Arrow and his style of theorizing. This suggests that one should be clear about the following distinction. There is a difference between claiming that conditions (1), (2) and (3) apply with some dose of success to the historical development of normative economics, and claiming that these conditions provide the *causal factors* accounting for this development. The rational reconstruction of normative economics I have attempted here is itself evaluative, and does not by itself make causality claims. But hopefully, it suggests relevant conjectures to test. It is now for the historian of economics to enter stage.

NOTES

*   Thanks are due to Kenneth Arrow, Richard Bradley, Marc Fleurbaey, Wulf Gaertner, Nicolas Gravel, Daniel Hausman, Colin Howson, Alain Trannoy and John Worrall for very helpful discussions or comments on earlier drafts. The present version has also benefited from remarks made by the conference participants. The author has retained the copyright of this paper. The author is currently Lachmann Visiting Fellow at the London School of Economics, and wishes to thank the LSE and the Lachmann Foundation for support.
1. There is nonetheless a continental tradition of considering ethics as a normative science; see Kalinowski (1969) who traces it back to the Leipzig philosopher Wundt at the end of the nineteenth century. However, this tradition has had little influence even in France and Germany.
2. This has been emphasized by Laudan (1977: Ch. 2). His attempt to go beyond this negative diagnosis is meritorious but still sketchy.
3. As Arrow (1983: 18) wrote in a brief but acute commentary on Pigou.
4. I will put Pigou aside in the rest of this paper. There is a valuable chapter on Pigou in Myint's (1948) history of early welfare theories. But again, *The Economics of Welfare* calls for a detailed reappraisal.

5. Beginners sometimes believe that the two theorems taken together form an equivalence statement. This is not the case.
6. Hammond in his valuable survey of progress in public economics (1990).
7. Two prominent examples are the recent constructions based on the 'non-envy' and 'egalitarian-equivalent' concepts; see Fleurbaey and Maniquet (1999) for a survey. Fleurbaey (2000) has recently argued that the welfarism versus non-welfarism divide is perhaps not as crucial as the following question: does the given theory implicitly obey Arrow's independence condition, or does it not?
8. The three clauses together, and not just two of them, appear to be required even in the case of intratheoretic progress. Dan Hausman helped me to see this point.
9. Think for instance of the discussion (and eventual dismissal) of fanaticism in Hare's (1976) utilitarian theory. The notion of anomaly is by no means limited to the empirical sciences. Mathematical theories can be accompanied by anomalies, as Lakatos's (1963–64) classic polyhedron example shows.
10. See, for example, Popper (1963).
11. The issue of inductivism in the non-empirical sciences is touched on in Howson (1979). His paper also makes suggestions on how to apply Lakatos's methodology of scientific research programmes to non-empirical sciences like mathematics, and is thus an interesting exception to the state of the art described in the introduction.
12. Called the 'Fundamental Value Proposition of Individual Preference' by Bergson (1938: 318). The expression 'Pareto principle' became common only after the war (under Little's influence, it seems).
13. In keeping with the mathematical style of his time, Bergson used only intuitive arguments to conclude that the second-order conditions were satisfied.
14. I will be brief on Samuelson's welfare economics. Chipman (1982) discusses it in admirable detail.
15. There are further methodological differences between the two papers. Bergson is concerned with classifying the welfare conclusions in terms of various 'value judgements', while Lange tries to distinguish them in terms of their 'operational significance'.
16. Universal domain, positive association, independence of irrelevant alternatives, non-imposition, non-dictatorship, plus the social ordering assumption included in the very definition of a social welfare function. For simplicity, I will use the slightly different set of five conditions: universal domain, the (weak) Pareto principle, independence of irrelevant alternatives, non-dictatorship, social ordering. This set of conditions has emerged from the 1963 version and become standard afterwards. Sen's treatment (1970) follows this line.
17. 'We may go even further than Samuelson and doubt that any study of maximal alternatives will actually be useful in studying those aspects of social choice which are directly related to consumer's (and worker's) choice' (Arrow, 1963: 37). The same idea is put forward in (1963: 63–4) where, however, it is significantly qualified.
18. Interestingly, Arrow's major contributions to Paretian welfare theory take place roughly at the time of *Social Choice and Individual Values*. See his *Collected Papers*, Vol. 2, especially Chapter 2.
19. This variant result justifies the earlier cryptic comment in the book that 'the current analysis of maximal social states is applicable precisely when it cannot serve the function of a preliminary to a complete enumeration of the social ordering' (Arrow, 1963: 37).
20. The political interpretation is critically discussed in Little (1952), Bergson (1954) and Samuelson (1967). It is taken up in late textbooks on welfare economics as a kind of compromise between Arrow and the welfare theorists. An elaborate example is Feldman's (1980) text. It relates the Arrovian framework to the second welfare theorem as follows. The politically interpreted social welfare function decides *which* of the many Pareto optima should prevail; then the second welfare theorem is invoked to conclude that the selected Pareto optimum can be achieved as a competitive equilibrium.
21. Take Bergson's economic welfare function:

$$E = E\,(x_{11}, \ldots, x_{1m}, l_{11}, \ldots, l_{1m}, \ldots, x_{j1}, \ldots, x_{jm}, l_{j1}, \ldots, l_{jm},$$
$$\ldots, x_{n1}, \ldots, x_{nm}, l_{n1}, \ldots, l_{nm})$$

where $x_{j1}, \ldots, x_{jm}$ are the amounts of the m commodities consumed by individual j, and l_{j1}, $\ldots, l_{jm}$ are the amounts of labour expended by j in each of the m departments of production. Now applying the Pareto principle ('Individualism' in Bergson's terminology), we conclude that E can be written as:

$$W = W\,(U_1(x_{11}, \ldots, l_{11}, \ldots\,), \ldots, U_j(x_{11}, \ldots, l_{11}, \ldots\,), \ldots, U_n(x_{11}, \ldots, l_{11}, \ldots\,)\,).$$

The welfare economists' point is that only the variables of the U_j, not the U_j themselves, are allowed to vary.

22. Positive association, which is superseded by the familiar Pareto condition in the 1963 version and later texts. By targeting positive association, Little (1952: 141) shot in the wrong direction.

23. By order of historical precedence the relevant papers are those of Kemp and Ng (1976), Parks (1976) and Pollak (1979).

24. In retrospect this conclusion can be reinforced. A broad lesson that can be drawn is that few results (be they positive or negative) are lost when one moves from the multi- to the single-profile approach. It is just mathematically easier to work within the former, which explains why a number of social choice results first came in this form. For more on this see Roberts (1980).

25. As Alain Trannoy pointed out to me, the 'client' scenario seems to be compatible with accepting the possibility of dictatorship. Bergson (1954: 237) indeed claimed that non-dictatorship should be reserved for the political interpretation of Arrow's theorem. But this move would make vacuous the welfare economist's commitment to the Pareto principle. It leads back to the unsatisfactory view that the welfare economist helps his clients to maximize their utility functions, whatever these functions may be.

26. Compare the argument of this paragraph with Arrow's discussion of *individual* distributional ethics ('the ethics of Primus') in his *Collected Economic Papers*, Vol.1, Ch.3: 55–6.

27. Robbins (1932) might have. But he is not a welfare economist, and his positions were often regarded as extreme by the writers of the new welfare economics.

28. Evidence for this claim can be found in Lange (1942) and even more clearly in the debate over the second welfare theorem and the economic theory of socialism.

29. Clear evidence for this can be found in Bergson himself (1938: 323).

30. Arrow (1983: 26) puts it this way: 'Social choice theory was a child, if unwanted, of the Bergson–Samuelson social welfare function viewpoint'.

31. Samuelson's (1976) restatement in reply to Kemp and Ng (1976) unfortunately confuses the issues.

32. In point of scholarship, I do not know whether Arrow was preceded in his refutation of Scitovsky.

33. It seems fair to emphasize this restriction. Perhaps the inventors of the compensation principle did not have only *complete* extensions in mind; this would make their case a little more promising.

34. It is instructive to compare the Arrovian arguments discussed here with Chipman and Moore's (1978) refutation. These authors establish that each test, including Scitovsky's, is cyclical by constructing general equilibrium positions. Arrow's numerical example or the more roundabout argument through the impossibility theorem delivers the same conclusion without satisfying this economic constraint. The Arrovian refutation is in accord with the social choice framework, while Chipman and Moore's is more obviously *internal* to the new welfare economics.

35. See Le Breton and Weymark's (1996) survey of 'economic domains'.

36. See the surveys in d'Aspremont (1985), Sen (1986), Mongin and d'Aspremont (1998), and Bossert and Weymark (forthcoming).

37. For a good example of this methodological stance, see Fleurbaey (1996: Ch. 1).

38. More on this general discussion in Mongin (1999).

39. A methodological dispute is likely to take place in connection with this and related examples. Some writers in normative economics (for example, Fleurbaey, 1996) appear to believe that non-manipulability, and others implementation concepts, belong to an area different

from normative economics. As they construe it, the latter is concerned solely with norms and evaluations, not with the way in which they can be achieved in the economy. I see normative economics as being concerned also with implementation issues, even if I am emphasizing here the purely normative stage.

40. This can be formally explicated by assuming that non-economic variables are *separable* from economic variables within each individual welfare function. This is not a light assumption to make.
41. It has sometimes been said that welfare economics needed only to make assumptions about *variations* in individual and social welfare; see Little (1950). I discard this line of analysis partly for simplicity, partly because it does not seem very plausible to investigate variations in a quantity without saying what the quantity refers to.
42. Compare with related statements in Boadway and Bruce (1984: 8), Little (1950), Mishan (1969: 23–5), Winch (1971: 33–4).
43. I found out that it had already been made by the philosophers (not the economists!) participating in the conference, 'Human values and economic policy' (1967). Further occurrences are, among others, Broome (1978), Sen (1985), Mongin and d'Aspremont (1998).
44. I sadly noticed that this happened again at the latest meeting of the Society for Social Choice and Welfare in Vancouver, 1998.
45. This sense of preference is suggested by the important work of Griffin (1986) and Harsanyi (1977). Mongin and d'Aspremont (1998: 388–401) follow this line of thinking.
46. See Mongin (1997).
47. Presumably, the work on 'capabilities' follows this line of thinking.
48. Hammond (1982) and other contributors to the same volume emphasize that this rule is very much alive in public economics.
49. See Zahar (1983) and Worrall (1985).

REFERENCES

Archibald, G.C. (1959), 'Welfare economics, ethics, and essentialism', *Economica*, 26: 316–27.
Arrow, K.J. (1951), *Social Choice and Individual Values*, New Haven, Yale University Press; 2nd revised edition, 1963 (references are to the second edition).
Arrow, K.J. (1983), 'Contributions to welfare economics', in E. Cary Brown and R.M. Solow (eds), *Paul Samuelson and Modern Economic Theory*, New York: McGraw Hill: 15–29.
Arrow, K.J. (1983–84), *Collected Works. Vol.1: Social Choice and Justice, Vol.2: Social Choice and Justice*, Oxford, Blackwell.
d'Aspremont, C. (1985), 'Axioms for social welfare orderings,' in L. Hurwicz, D. Schmeidler and H. Sonnenschein (eds), *Social Goals and Organization*, Cambridge: Cambridge University Press, 19–76.
Bergson (Burk), A. (1938), 'A reformulation of certain aspects of welfare economics', *Quarterly Journal of Economics*, 52, 310–34.
Bergson, A. (1954), 'On the concept of social welfare,' *Quarterly Journal of Economics*, 68: 233–52.
Black, D. (1958), *The Theory of Committees and Elections*, Cambridge: Cambridge University Press.
Boadway, R.W. and N. Bruce (1984), *Welfare Economics*, Oxford: Blackwell.
Bossert, W. and J. Weymark (forthcoming), 'Utility in social choice', in S. Barberà, P. Hammond and C. Seidl (eds), *Handbook of Utility Theory*, 2. Dordrecht: Kluwer.
Broome, J. (1978), 'Choice and value in economics', *Oxford Economic Papers*, 30: 313–33.

Chipman, J. (1982), 'Samuelson and welfare economics', in G. Feiwell (ed.), *Samuelson and Neoclassical Economics*, Boston: Kluwer: 152–84.

Chipman, J.S. and J. Moore (1978), 'The new welfare economics 1939–1974', *International Economic Review*, 19: 547–84.

de Graaff, J. van (1957), *Theoretical Welfare Economics*, Cambridge: Cambridge University Press.

Feldman, A.M. (1980), *Welfare Economics and Social Choice Theory*, Boston: Kluwer.

Fleurbaey, M. (1996), *Théories Économiques de la Justice*, Paris: Economica.

Fleurbaey, M. (2000), 'The informational basis of social choice', THEMA, Université de Cergy-Pontoise, Cergy-Pontoise: mimeo.

Fleurbaey, M. and F. Maniquet (1999), 'Compensation and responsibility', forthcoming in K.J. Arrow, K. Suzumura and A.K. Sen (eds), *Handbook of Social Choice Theory*, Amsterdam: North Holland.

Gibbard, A.F. (1973), 'Manipulation of voting schemes: a general result', *Econometrica*, 41: 587–601.

Griffin, J. (1986), *Well-being*, Oxford: Clarendon Press.

Hammond, P.J. (1982), 'Utilitarianism, uncertainty and information', in A. Sen and B. Williams (eds), *Utilitarianism and Beyond*, Cambridge: Cambridge University Press: 85–102.

Hammond, P.J. (1990), 'Theoretical progress in public economics: a provocative assessment', *Oxford Economic Papers*, 42: 6–33.

Hare, R.M. (1976), 'Ethical theory and utilitarianism', in H.D. Lewis (ed.), *Contemporary British Philosophy*, 23–38.

Harsanyi, J.C. (1977), *Rational Behavior and Bargaining Equilibrium in Games and Social Situations*, Cambridge: Cambridge University Press.

Hook, S. (1967), *Human Values and Economic Policy*, New York: New York University Press.

Howson, C. (1979), 'Methodology in non-empirical disciplines', in G. Radnitzky and G. Andersson (eds), *The Structure and Development of Science*, Boston: Reidel: 257–66.

Kalinowski, G. (1969), *La Querelle de la Science Normative*, Paris: Librairie Générale de Droit et de Jurisprudence.

Kemp, M.C. and Y.N. Ng (1976), 'On the existence of social welfare functions, social orderings and social decision functions', *Economica*, 43: 159–66.

Keynes, J.N. (1890), *The Scope and Method of Political Economy*, (4th edition, 1917), New York: Kelley Reprints of Economic Classics, 1963.

Lakatos, I. (1963–64), 'Proofs and refutations', *British Journal for the Philosophy of Science*, 14: 1–25, 120–39, 221–45, 296–342.

Lakatos, I. (1970), 'Falsification and the methodology of scientific research programmes', in I. Lakatos and A. E. Musgrave (eds), *Criticism and the Growth of Knowledge*, Cambridge, Cambridge University Press: 91–196.

Lange, O. (1942), 'The foundations of welfare economics', *Econometrica*, 10: 215–28.

Laudan, L. (1977), *Progress and Its Problems*, Berkeley, CA: University of California Press.

Le Breton, M. and J.A. Weymark (1996), 'An introduction to Arrovian social welfare functions on economic and political domains', in N.J. Schofield (ed.), *Collective Decision-making: Social Choice and Political Economy*, Dordrecht: Kluwer: 25–61.

Lipsey, R.G. and K. Lancaster (1956), 'The general theory of the second best', *Review of Economic Studies*, 24: 11–32.

Little, I.M. (1950), *A Critique of Welfare Economics*, Oxford: Clarendon.
Little, I.M. (1952), 'Social choice and individual values,' *Journal of Political Economy*, 60: 422–32.
Mishan, E.J. (1969), *Welfare Economics: An Assessment*, Amsterdam: North Holland.
Mongin, P. (1997), 'Spurious unanimity and the Pareto principle', THEMA, CNRS and Université de Cergy-Pontoise, Cergy-Pontoise: mimeo.
Mongin, P. (1999), 'Normes et jugements de valeur en économie normative', *Information sur les Sciences Sociales/Social Science Information*, 38: 521–53.
Mongin, P. and C. d'Aspremont (1998), 'Utility theory and ethics', in S. Barberà, P. Hammond and C. Seidl (eds), *Handbook of Utility Theory*, 1. Dordrecht: Kluwer.
Myint, H. (1948), *Theories of Welfare Economics*, New York: Published for the London School of Economics by A.M. Kelley.
Parks, R.P. (1976), 'An impossibility theorem for fixed Preferences: a dictatorial Bergson–Samuelson welfare function', *Review of Economic Studies*, 43: 447–50.
Pigou, A.C. (1920), *The Economics of Welfare*, London: Macmillan (4th revised edition, 1932).
Pollak, R.A. (1979), 'Bergson–Samuelson social welfare functions and the theory of social choice', *Quarterly Journal of Economics*, 93: 73–90.
Popper, K.R. (1963), *Conjectures and Refutations*, London: Routledge.
Robbins, L. (1932), *An Essay on the Nature and Significance of Economics*, London: Macmillan (2nd revised edition, 1937).
Roberts, K.W.S. (1980), 'Social choice theory: the single and multi-profile approaches,' *Review of Economic Studies*, 47: 441–50.
Samuelson, P.A. (1947), *The Foundations of Economic Analysis*, Cambridge, MA: Harvard University Press.
Samuelson, P.A. (1967), 'Arrow's mathematical politics', in S. Hook (ed.), *Human Values and Economic Policy*, New York: New York University Press.
Samuelson, P.A. (1976), 'Reaffirming the existence of "reasonable" Bergson–Samuelson social welfare functions', *Economica*, 44: 81–8.
Sen, A.K. (1970), *Collective Choice and Social Welfare*, Amsterdam: North Holland.
Sen, A.K. (1979), 'Utilitarianism and welfarism', *Journal of Philosophy*, 76: 463–89.
Sen, A.K. (1981), 'Rights and agency', *Philosophy and Public Affairs*, 11: 3–39.
Sen, A.K. (1982), *Choice, Welfare and Measurement*, Oxford: Blackwell.
Sen, A.K. (1985), *Commodities and Capabilities*, Amsterdam: North Holland.
Sen, A.K. (1986), 'Social choice theory,' in K.J. Arrow and, M.D. Intrilligator (eds), *Handbook of Mathematical Economics*, III, Amsterdam: North Holland: 1073–1181.
Winch, D.M. (1971), *Analytical Welfare Economics*, Harmondsworth, Middlesex: Penguin Books.
Worrall, J. (1985), 'Scientific discovery and theory-confirmation', in J.C. Pitt (ed.), *Change and Progress in Modern Science*, Dordrecht, Reidel: 301–31.
Zahar, E. (1983), 'Logic of discovery or psychology of invention?', *British Journal for the Philosophy of Science*, 34: 243–61.

PART V

Monetary Economics

11. New lines of research in monetary economics

Augusto Graziani

FOREWORD

Fisher and Keynes, the two giants of monetary thought in the first half of the twentieth century, followed two different lines of thought in analysing the nature and role of money. Fisher concentrated his analysis on money as a means of payment, while Keynes emphasized the role of money as a stock of wealth.

Even before Keynes, the Cambridge tradition had pointed out the main function of money as that of being a stock of wealth: in fact, Marshall and Pigou had laid the ground for a similar interpretation (Marshall [1870] 1975, Vol. I: 165 ff.). When Keynes, in the *General Theory*, explicitly tied his analysis of unemployment to liquidity preference and the demand for money balances, the definition of money as a stock of wealth became generally accepted.[1] It does not seem that Fisher ever discussed the Keynesian theory of interest and money, clearly at odds with his own. The silent controversy ended with the complete victory of the Keynes–Hicks definition.[2]

It is clear that the two views differ only in their different emphasis, since no one ever denied that money is at the same time a means of payment and a stock of wealth. In fact the essential prerequisite for money to be kept as a privileged stock of wealth is that of being liquid, namely readily convertible into goods, and therefore of being a means of payment.[3]

THE ADVANTAGES OF THE KEYNESIAN DEFINITION

The Keynesian definition of money has several analytical advantages.

1. We have already mentioned (see note 2) the fact that the Keynesian definition makes it possible to define the utility of money as a direct utility, thus avoiding the circularity charge connected to the definition of the utility of money as an indirect utility.

2. A further advantage of defining money as a stock of wealth is to make it possible to explain demand failures in terms of fluctuations in liquidity preference, which makes the non-neutrality of money undebatable.

3. A final analytical advantage of the Keynesian definition is of making it possible to acquire a satisfactory definition of the equilibrium position. If defined as a stock of wealth, money is an observable variable also in a full equilibrium position, the existing money stock being the amount of money that agents consider it reasonable to detain. Instead, if money were just an intermediary of exchanges and nothing else, it would no longer be an observable magnitude. In fact, in a world free from uncertainty, in which money were just a means of exchange, money would be immediately spent as soon as available.[4] In the same world, agents would only ask for bank credit the very moment a payment were due and they would repay their debt as soon as possible.[5] In an equilibrium position money would simply disappear.[6] For money to be an observable magnitude, it must be kept by single agents for a finite period of time, no matter how short, thus taking the form of a cash balance. But since, as already mentioned, money is kept as a protection against uncertainty, this means that, for money to be an observable magnitude, the market must be operating under uncertainty. In a hypothetical market free from uncertainty, liquid balances would disappear and with them the possibility of observing and measuring the money stock in existence. As Benetti and Cartelier once remarked, if we abstract from uncertainty the very existence of money balances is ruled out, except when the economy is out of equilibrium (Benetti and Cartelier, 1990).[7]

It should therefore be reckoned that when Keynes, in the *General Theory*, defined money as a cash balance having the function of protecting the agents from uncertainty, he was choosing the only analytically satisfactory solution, in that he was adopting the only definition which makes of money an observable magnitude. It is no surprise that the Keynesian approach to money has been considered for over half a century the final conclusion of a long controversy.

Relevant as such advantages may be, it cannot be denied that the Keynesian conception of money does not go without considerable costs. The costs incurred in concentrating attention on money as a stock of wealth can be summarized as follows:

1. The Keynesian view of the money supply almost neglects any explanation of the process of money creation. Authors following the Keynesian tradition move between the two extremes of considering the money supply as an exogenously given magnitude and, at the other extreme, of considering

the money stock as an endogenous magnitude wholly determined by demand. In fact, the money stock in existence is the net result of two opposite processes of creation and destruction of money, each of which needs to be carefully analysed.

2. A further drawback of defining money as a stock of wealth is that it produces a tendency to consider the stock of money in existence in equilibrium as being the product only of government expenditure and taxation.[8]

3. A final weak point in the definition of money as a stock of wealth lies in the fact that it tends to neglect any connection between money and income distribution. The neoclassical approach emphasizes the neutrality of money, while the Keynesian approach stresses the connections between money and activity levels. Both approaches leave out the connections between money and the distribution of income. Only an analysis of the process of money creation, necessarily based on a sharp distinction between the banking and the firm sector, can let the mechanism ruling the distribution between wages and profits emerge.

REBIRTH OF THE FISHERINE APPROACH

In order to make clear the importance of defining money as a flow of payments, it is necessary to examine the whole process of creation and circulation of money. This is the task of the so-called 'circulation approach'. Such an approach does not reject the idea that money can be, and normally is, also a stock of wealth. It only supplements it with an analysis of the role performed by money as an intermediary of exchange.[9] The different phases of the monetary circuit can easily be described. The groups of agents considered are four: bank of issue, commercial banks, firms and wage earners.

1. The first step in the economic process is the decision taken by the banks to grant credit to firms, thus enabling them to start a process of production.[10] As already mentioned, circuit theorists usually assume that only firms are admitted to bank credit (Benetti and Cartelier, 1990; Cartelier, 1995).

   Since we consider firms as one integrated and consolidated sector, the only resource firms need to acquire in order to start production is labour and the only expenditure is the payment of the wage bill. All other exchanges can be neglected, being internal to the firm sector. Therefore the demand for bank credit coming from producers depends only on the wage rate and the level of employment (Moore, 1984, 1988; Graziani, 1989).[11]

Negotiations between banks and firms determine the amount of credit and the level of the interest rate.

2. The second phase of the economic process consists in the decisions concerning production and expenditure. A basic assumption of circuit theory is that firms enjoy total independence when deciding upon the real aspects of production, namely employment levels and the relative amounts of consumer goods and investment goods produced. Wage earners can only decide on how to distribute their money income among consumption expenditure, purchase of securities and addition to cash balances (bank deposits or notes). In the present simplified presentation, since we are neglecting the government sector, securities can only be issued by producers.[12]

3. In the third phase, commodities produced are put on sale. Consumer goods are sold to wage earners, while investment goods are exchanged inside the firm sector (firms having produced means of production sell them to other firms making use of them).

    The money that wage earners spend in the commodities market, as well as money spent in the financial market on the purchase of securities, flows back to the firms who can use it to repay their bank debt. To the extent that bank debts are repaid, an equal amount of money is destroyed. To the extent instead that wage earners use their money savings to increase their own cash balances, an equal amount of money remains in existence in the form of a debt of the firms and of a credit of wage earners towards the banks.[13]

4. Once the initial bank debt is repaid and money is destroyed, the monetary circuit is closed. New money will be created when the banks grant new credits for a new production cycle. This can take place almost automatically if firms, instead of repaying their bank debt, make use of the revenue coming from the sale of commodities and from the placement of securities to start a new production cycle. This doesn't mean that the firms have become financially independent: the very fact of making use, for a new production cycle, of liquidity granted by the banks for a preceding one, implies a renewal of credit on the part of the banks, which is tantamount to granting new finance.

If wage earners spend entirely the incomes received, whether in the commodity market or in the financial market, firms will get back the whole of their monetary advances and will be able to repay entirely their bank debt. In this case, as some would say, the circuit is closed 'without losses'. If instead wage earners decide to keep a portion of their savings in the form of liquid balances, firms are unable to repay their bank debt of the same amount. As a consequence, at the end of the production cycle the money initially created will not be entirely destroyed. If banks now intend to finance a new production cycle equal to the preceding one by granting the same finance, the total money stock will be increased. More precisely, it will be equal to the wage bill plus the new liquid balances set aside by wage earners at the end of the preceding cycle.

The conclusion to be drawn is that, in a closed economy, there is only one circumstance which can produce losses for firms as a whole and this is the decision of savers to hoard part of their savings in the form of cash balances. It might seem that in an open economy the decision of savers to place part of their savings in the foreign market might be an additional source of losses to national firms as whole. In fact, in an integrated financial market, national firms might issue securities not only in the national market but also in the financial markets of other countries, thus capturing the liquidity that the decisions of the savers might subtract from them.

Therefore, if we abstract from the case of an increase in liquidity preference, firms as a whole do not run any risk of global financial losses. On the other side, since it cannot be ruled out that single firms may incur losses, this means that, always abstracting from increases in liquidity preference, any loss incurred by a single firm must be balanced by an identical profit earned by some other firm. Mistakes in management made by one single firm, far from making the whole firm sector weaker, produce higher profits for other firms.

This conclusion leads to a careful revisitation of the idea that in a market economy profit can be taken to be an indicator of efficiency. To begin with, the fact that firms as a whole don't make losses is no proof of efficiency, since firms as a whole will always have balanced budgets, whatever their ability in reducing costs or in meeting consumers' preferences. On the other hand, if we consider single firms separately, the fact that one of them is making a profit is a signal not of absolute but only of relative good management, since profits earned by one firm may simply be the result of poor management and consequent losses incurred by other firms.

In addition to that, it is very doubtful whether the presence of some firms suffering losses, or even being on the verge of bankruptcy, will start a chain of bankruptcies and a general crisis. This may well happen. But the opposite solution is also possible: namely that profit-making firms acquire the unprofitable ones. If this is done, the reason would surely be to acquire a stronger market position, but the macroeconomic result would be to avoid individual losses spreading to the whole economy and generating a general crisis.[14]

From the preceding description, a number of features emerge which are considerably different from the typical assumptions of the neoclassical model.

In the model based on the monetary circuit, money is defined as a strictly endogenous magnitude.[15] The banking system grants credit to single agents, presumably firms, having to make a payment, for instance in order to pay wages. The moment the payment is made, the firms become the debtors and wage earners become the creditors of the bank. The result of the operation is the emergence of a stock of money equal in amount to the credit granted to firms. The money stock stays in existence as long as the debt of the firms is not repaid. Once the debt is repaid, the money circuit is concluded and the money initially created is also destroyed.

A point of convergence between circuit theory and the post-Keynesian school can be found in the analysis of income distribution. Here circuit theorists follow closely what was once named the Keynes–Kalecki formulation. First sketched by D.H. Robertson (1926) and by Keynes in his *Treatise on Money* (Keynes, 1930), this approach to income distribution was developed by Kalecki (1954), Kaldor (1956) and Robinson (1956). According to this approach, firms can decide the activity levels and the nature of production (consumption and investment goods), while wage earners, whatever the level of their money wage, can only buy real consumer goods in the amount made available by producers (Kregel, 1973: Ch. 10). Therefore the actual level of real wages is determined by producers and cannot be determined by regular market negotiations; at most, it can be the object of a political conflict. This point, which emphasizes the widely different market power of producers and wage earners, is sometimes expressed by saying that, in the labour market, wage earners can only negotiate money wages, not real wages. This doesn't depend on wage earners being irrational agents, or on their being subject to money illusion. In fact it is typical of a market economy that producers can decide the proportions of consumer goods and investment goods produced, while wage earners can only decide how their money wages will be spent. If wage earners had the actual possibility of negotiating the level of real wages, producers would correspondingly lose the possibility of determining the level and content of production. Assuming that producers can control the real side of production is tantamount to assuming that wage earners can only negotiate the money level of wages. As François Simiand once said, 'the level of money wages is a fact; the level of real wages is an opinion' (Simiand, 1932, Vol. I: 160).[16]

Once we consider the creation of money as the initial step in the economic process, a fundamental difference emerges between banks on one side and other financial intermediaries on the other.

Nowadays, it is common to consider banks on the same footing as other intermediaries. The special character of banks is sought after in directions other than the power of creating liquidity. A remarkable example is Stiglitz's analysis based on the fact that the market for bank credit lacks transparency and therefore in no case can be considered a perfectly competitive market. It seems however that, in his view, were it not for that fundamental circumstance, no real difference would exist between banks and other financial intermediaries (Stiglitz, 1999).

A second relevant example is the analysis provided by Tirole. While in his view banks should be carefully distinguished from non-financial companies, still a number of arguments concerning banks 'can be directly transposed to other financial intermediaries' (Tirole, 1994: 472).

Authors belonging to the circulation approach keep to a different view of banking activity, in that banks are considered creators of money, while other financial intermediaries are not. This is tantamount to saying that banks can alter the quantity of money while other intermediaries can only alter the velocity of circulation.

BANK CREDIT AND INVESTMENT

We now come to a more debatable point, namely the role of banks in financing investment. It is a common feature of present-day models of banking behaviour to assume that banks grant credit in order to finance investment.[17] This is in fact a traditional assumption going back to Wicksell's model. The point is, however, that Wicksell's model is so constructed that a precise correspondence exists between the categories of monetary savings and bank deposits on the one side, and investment and bank loans on the other. It can be shown however that Wicksell's unobjectionable result depends on his basic assumption of wages being paid in advance in real terms.[18] Now it so happens that followers of the neoclassical school, even when writing in Wicksell's wake, abandon the assumption of real wages being paid in advance in favour of the contrary assumption of wages being paid at the end of the production process. A consequence of this change in perspective is that investment is no longer defined as equal to the wage bill but as the amount of newly produced capital goods. In spite of that, followers of the neoclassical school think it legitimate to preserve Wicksell's conclusion as to the correspondence between bank loans and the finance used for investment.[19]

If we go back to the previous description of the single phases of money creation and destruction, it appears clear that a distinction has to be drawn between financing production and financing investment. The initial finance required by firms in order to start a production process is related to the whole costs of production. As already said, the initial requirement of bank credit can therefore be measured by the amount of the wage bill or by the value of inventories in possession of the firms. No specific connection exists between initial finance and investment.

Let us now go to the third phase of the circulation process, the phase in which firms try to get back the money they have spent. They can do that either by selling commodities or by placing securities on the financial market. The finance they get in either of these ways can be denominated final finance, and its function is to allow firms to repay their bank debt (the specific role of final finance was made clear long ago by Bresciani–Turroni, 1936: 21–22).

Let us now come to the way investments are financed. We can say that an investment has been financed once the new capital good has been sold to someone who wants to hold it as a form of wealth. The buyer can be a saver who invests liquidity in newly issued stock; or the buyer can be a firm having earned a profit. In both cases final finance is provided by savings, be it voluntary or forced. As previously said, this does not mean that saving corresponding to investment has to be made in advance. On the contrary, saving is formed at the same time as investment is performed, while liquidity used for producing the new capital good is destroyed with the final sale of the new capital good.

Of course the possibility cannot be ruled out that not all savings are used to purchase new capital goods (or securities representing them), and that a part of money savings is used to increase liquid balances. In that case, firms are unable to totally repay their bank debt. In this case, a number of questions might be raised concerning how investment has been financed, whether by saving or by bank credit, and by whose saving. Most authors would maintain that, in this case, investment is financed by bank credit. A more reasonable answer would run as follows. The firms have increased both their assets (newly acquired plants and equipment) and their liabilities (a higher bank debt, the amount of which corresponds to the increased liquid balances held by savers); this means that investment, as always, has found its counterpart in saving, the only difference being that savers have indirectly (namely through the firms of which they are the stockholders) increased their own bank debt in order to increase their money holdings.[20]

All this is of course typical macroeconomic reasoning, valid in so far as firms are considered as all being integrated and consolidated. In this case, an increase in the bank debt of firms can only arise from an increase in the demand for money balances. The case is different if we consider single isolated firms, since it may well happen that some firms are earning profits while others are incurring losses. On this, more later.

BANK CREDIT IN DEVELOPING ECONOMIES

What has already been said allows us to evaluate a widespread view, according to which the role of the banks in financing investment should vary according to the stages of economic development. In this view, the early stages of industrial development suffer from a typical lack of saving due to the low level of income. In this phase, the banking system should come in and supply finance by means of bank credit. In later stages of development, the support supplied by bank credit would no longer be required, being replaced by an adequate flow of households savings as well as by self-financing of firms (Chick, 1986; Chick and Dow, 1988; Dow and Dow, 1989; Studart, 1995; Arestis, 1996: 121).

In the light of what has been said above, this seems to be a most doubtful view. It is of course true that the initial production of new capital goods is financed by bank credit (this is true of any stage of development). When, however, firms try to fund their debt on the financial market, there will always be a flow of savings exactly equal to investment. Obstacles to funding bank credit can only arise in one of the following cases.

1. In a low-income country, savers may have a high liquidity preference and prefer to keep their financial wealth in the form of liquid balances. This can be especially true when financial markets are not well developed and do not offer attractive placements for savers.
2. Another possibility is that savers prefer to place their savings in government bonds instead of buying private securities.
3. Finally, savers may prefer to place their savings in foreign currencies.

In all such cases, the complete funding of bank credit is impossible and investors are unable to totally repay their bank debt. However, the root of the problem does not lie in a lack of saving due to the low level of income but in portfolio choices inducing investors to prefer forms of wealth other than private securities. Again, the role of bank credit is one of financing, not investment, but other forms of wealth, be it liquid balances held by households, government expenditure or capital flight abroad.

SOME RECENT MODELS OF THE BANKING SECTOR

A common feature of all macroeconomic models containing the banking sector is that loans granted by banks are defined as equal to the cost of investment performed by the firms. All such models make no distinction between initial finance (namely finance used to cover current costs of production) and final finance (namely finance needed in order to fund the initial bank debt). Since, however, in a macroeconomic model, bank credit should cover the cost of production of both consumer goods and capital goods, when reference is made to finance needed for investment purposes, it seems that what is being considered is final finance.

A first possible example is the Modigliani–Papademos model (the structure of the model is reproduced in the appendix).[21] It is clear that the structure of the model is such that the economy is observed in its equilibrium position.

Therefore the model does not define the liquidity needed for current exchanges; it only defines the liquid balances demanded by agents in the final equilibrium position. However, since in equilibrium the savings–investment equality holds and since, given the structure of the model, bank deposits are the only outlets for savings, the result is that bank credit appears to be the source of finance for all investment not covered by internal profits. In the final equilibrium position, the bank debt of the firms necessarily equals the increase in liquid balances demanded by agents and the monetary value of the fraction of investment which is not self-financed.

The very construction of the model raises considerable doubts.

1. To begin with, the fact of concentrating on the final equilibrium position brings about the consequence of neglecting the fundamental role of the banks, which is that of providing the amount of initial finance needed for current production and current exchanges.
2. A further peculiar consequence of the way the model is built is that the banks appear in the unusual role of providing finance for investment. At the same time, the liquid balances of households reflect current savings while the usual motives determining the demand for money (transactions, precautionary and speculative demand) disappear. This is only due to the fact that the model admits no financial market, so that bank deposits are the only possible outlet for savings.[22]
3. Finally, the fact that all current savings go into liquid balances, any other possible destination being ruled out, produces the consequence that, in the normal situation in which households save and firms invest, the stock of liquid balances is bound to grow without limits. It is usually understood that, in a growing economy, capital accumulation brings about an increase in the stock of securities, this being the financial counterpart of an increasing stock of real capital. An unlimited growth of the stock of bank deposits, connected not to current income but to capital accumulation, is a peculiarity of this model.

Other models including the banking sector are only partially different. A possible example is the Bernanke–Blinder (1988) model, the structure of which is also reproduced in the appendix. In this model, in contrast to the Modigliani–Papademos model, the financial market is present and the household's savings can be placed in securities (long-term securities can also be bought by the banks). Banks are held to keep reserves in legal tender (the origins of such reserves are not clear, in that they do not originate from a debt of the banks towards the central bank nor from a government deficit). Deposits are the only liability of the banks, while their assets are loans, bonds and reserves.

In this model, all investment not financed by internal finance of the firms or by placement of securities with savers is financed by bank credit.

The structure of this model also raises doubts. Let us neglect the problems raised by the determination of income distribution between wages and profits (this is why in the presentation of the model given in the appendix we neglect the role of the firms' savings). Since the model is built on the basis of accounting identities, the algebraic result is beyond discussion. The emerging problems are problems of interpretation. The firms' bank debt in existence in the final equilibrium position is equal to bank deposits and therefore to the liquid balances of households (legal tender is only used for the reserves of the banks). As a consequence, it is highly doubtful whether banks are financing a part of investment (as the authors would maintain) or the liquid balances demanded by households (as the Keynesian view would suggest).

CONCLUDING REMARKS

The present-day theory of the supply of money seems to be divided between two opposing tendencies, the one considering money as exogenous, the other viewing money as an endogenous magnitude. Beyond this divergence, the common feature of all models that include the money stock as one of the variables considered, is of observing the economy in the equilibrium position. It now happens that when money is the object of analysis, the fact of limiting the analysis to positions of full equilibrium is more limiting than in other cases. In fact, in the equilibrium position, the stock of money is by definition equal to the liquid balances required by the agents. Current additions to money balances are considered as originating from current savings and the existing money balances appear as the fraction of total wealth that the agents require to be held in liquid form. The inevitable result is that the flow of money used to finance current exchanges, a flow continuously produced and continuously destroyed, is totally neglected.

A similar approach has an immediate reflection on the interpretation of the role of banks. In some cases banks are totally neglected. This is the case with the standard IS–LM model, a model including the financial market but totally ignoring the money market and the problem of the creation of money. (It is not irrelevant that most handbooks of macroeconomics present a general model that ignores the banking sector, which is only introduced separately and at a much later stage of the presentation.)

A second, more recent approach leads to the inclusion of banks in the macroeconomic model. But, once more, the economy is analysed in its equilibrium position. The consequence is that, for savers, the role of the banks is viewed as one of offering deposits as a special form of saving; for firms, the role of the banks is one of providing the liquidity needed for investment. In no case are banks viewed as institutions creating means of payment for the circulation of commodities.

The circulation approach is an attempt to go in a different direction. More precisely, it is an attempt to start by recognizing the fact that money should be analysed in both its aspects: as money needed for current exchanges, and therefore continuously being created, circulated and destroyed, and also as money balances needed by agents in the position of final equilibrium.

The analytical consequences are clear. In the dominant approach, the money stock is viewed as being totally created by the government deficit and any demand failure can only originate from an increase in liquidity preference, namely in the pretence of the rentiers to get a higher interest rate (or in their refusal to accept a lower one). The circulation approach opens the much wider field of analysis concerning the mutual relationships between banks and firms, their negotiations, the very origins of the supply of money, and the possibility of demand failures originating from a lack of finance.

APPENDIX

The Modigliani–Papademos model can be synthesized by the following equations:

$$I(r_L) - S_{Imp}(Y) = dL(dZ) \tag{1}$$

$$r_s = f(r_{sc}) \tag{2}$$

$$I = I(r_L) \tag{3}$$

$$Y = 1/s(I) \tag{4}$$

$$S_W = I - S_P(Y) = D_{cc} + D_s = dL \tag{5}$$

$$I(r_L) - S_P(Y) = dL(dZ)$$

$$S = sW + sP \tag{6}$$

$$S_W = sW \tag{7}$$

$$S_P = sP \tag{8}$$

$$Y = W + P \tag{9}$$

$$W/P = O/(1 - O) \tag{10}$$

$$D_{cc}/D_s = f(r_s) \tag{11}$$

The model assumes that the only source of external finance is bank credit (the standard IS–LM model adopts an opposite assumption, since in that model banks are absent and the only source of finance is the financial market).

Equation (1) states that firms finance investment partly by means of internal savings, partly by having recourse to bank credit.[23] Equation (2) states that banks set the rate on time deposits as a function of the discount rate set by the central bank. Equation (3) defines investment as a function of the rate on bank loans. Equation (4) defines income according to the multiplier mechanism (the same propensity to save is assumed to hold for both households and firms); the same equation sets the equality between savings and investment. According to equation (5) household savings go entirely either in sight or in time deposits. Since no financial market is present, the only choice open to savers is between the two kinds of bank deposits. The equality between demand for loans (investment) coming from firms and motivated by investment decisions on one side, and credit creation (new deposits supplied) on the other, determines the rate on loans r_L.

Equations (6), (7) and (8) define saving of households, saving of firms and total savings. Equations (9) and (10) define total income and its distribution between households and firms according to a parameter that has to be taken as given. Finally, equation (11) defines the distribution of total deposits between sight and time deposits as a function of the interest rate on time deposits.

The model contains eleven endogenous and four exogenous variables: the discount rate, the two propensities to save, and the distribution of income between households and firms.

The Bernanke–Blinder model can be synthetically represented as follows. Deposits are the only liability of the banks, while their assets are loans (L), bonds (T) and reserves (Z):

$$D = L + T + Z$$

Therefore, loans offered are:

$$L^s = D - T - Z.$$

Since banks are held to keep a reserve equal to a fraction q of deposits, we can write:

$$L^s = 1/q \, Z - Z - B = (1/q - 1) \, Z - B.$$

The banks distribute their assets between loans and bonds according to the relative interest rates, r_L e r_B:

$$B = B(r_L, r_B),$$

$$L^s = L^s(r_L, r_B).$$

Investments are also a function of the two rates:

$$I = I(r_L, r_B)$$

and are financed through placement of securities, self-financing of firms and, for the residual, by means of bank credit, L^d.

If we neglect internal finance, we can write:

$$L^d = I(r_L, r_B) - B.$$

In the credit market, the equality between demand and supply determines the interest rate on bank loans. Since the demand for bank loans is given by:

$$L^d = I - T$$

and since the supply of loans is

$$L^s = D - T - Z,$$

the equilibrium condition is

$$I = L + T = D - Z.$$

In the money market, the supply of deposits is determined by the amount of reserves and the compulsory reserve ratio:

$$D^s = 1/q \, Z.$$

The demand for deposits is defined as a function of the rate of interest on bonds. The equilibrium condition:

$$D^d(r_B) = D^s$$

determines the rate of interest on securities. A similar formulation is very close to the Keynesian principle that the rate of interest on the financial market is jointly determined by liquidity preference and the quantity of money.

NOTES

1. It should be clearly stated that the *General Theory* is the only work in which Keynes lays the stress on money as a form of wealth. The articles published after the *General Theory* bring to the foreground the relevance of money as a means of payment (Keynes, 1937a, 1937b, 1939). This point is dealt with more extensively in Graziani (1989, 1991: 34 ff).

2. The demand for money defined as a demand for money balances and the utility of money defined as a protection against uncertainty produced a revision of the old interpretation of the historical origins of money. The traditional story as told by Menger (1892), Marshall (1923, Appendix A, 'A Note on the Evolution of Money') and Pantaleoni ([1894] 1957), was the story of a spontaneous selection of a medium of exchange, performed by the market among various commodities, starting from salt or cattle and ending up with gold and paper money. A similar interpretation is far from having been abandoned (Spinelli, 1999). The Keynesian interpretation of money, strictly connected as it was to uncertainty and protection against risk, has given rise to new interpretations of the origins of money. Heinsohn and Steiger (1996) connect the origins of money to the emergence of private property and individual risk. A third reconstruction, based on Knapp's state theory of money (Knapp, 1905), has been recently revived and adopted by Wray (1998).

3. This point is so clear that it hardly needs to be recalled. Ever since 1892, Menger had specified that 'the theory of money necessarily presupposes a theory of the saleableness of goods' (Menger, 1892: 243) and that: 'those commodities which . . . are most saleable have in every market become the wares which it is not only in the interest of every one to accept . . . but which are also those he actually does readily accept' (p. 248). However, Menger kept to the idea that the utility of money is an indirect utility, measured by the utility of the commodities that money can buy. Supporters of this view are exposed to the criticism that they are arguing in a circle (the amount of commodities that money can buy depends on the level of money prices; therefore the utility of money and consequently the demand for money also depend on its purchasing power; but at the same time, the value of money should depend on the demand for money). Definite progress was realized when Schlesinger (1914) and Hicks (1933) made clear that the utility of a money stock is a direct utility, consisting in the protection against uncertainty that liquid resources provide. In some sense, Irving Fisher anticipated Hicks when he wrote: 'in a world of chance and sudden changes, quick salability, or liquidity, is a great advantage. . . . The most salable of all property is, of course, money: and as Karl [*sic*] Menger pointed out, it is precisely this salability which makes it money. The *convenience* of surely being able, without any previous preparation, to dispose of it for any exchange, in other words its *liquidity*, is itself a sufficient return upon the capital which a man seems to keep idle in money form' (Fisher, 1930: 216; similar statements can be found in Fisher, 1911: Ch. II).

4. J.B. Say probably had something of the kind in his mind when he wrote: 'as soon as the production of a commodity is completed, the greatest desire of the producer is to sell it, lest the value of the product should decline while he keeps it in his own hands. But he is again in a hurry to get rid of the money obtained through the sale, lest the value of the money should also be reduced', thus ruling out the existence of a money balance in equilibrium (Say, 1826: 183).

5. Keynes clearly saw that, in an ideal competitive credit market, no one would go into debt if not the very moment a payment comes due (Keynes, 1936: 196; 1937a: 246 (C. W., XIV: 208); 1937b: 669 (C. W., XIV: 223).

6. In order to overcome this problem, some refined theorists imagine economic activity to take place not in continuous time but in segments of finite time (*morceaux de temps*) called 'quanta' (Schmitt, 1984: 54, 71 ff).

7. Ever since 1930, Erik Lindahl, who was working in the framework of a general equilibrium model, had remarked that money creation on the part of the banking system is only possible when the economy is out of equilibrium (Lindahl [1930] 1939, Part II; Ch. I). Similar statements can be found in later authors (Debreu, 1959; Arrow and Hahn, 1971: 338; Hahn, 1982). An indirect proof of this point is that Clower, in order to give a role to money in a

general equilibrium context, builds a model in which, in contrast to the typical structure of Walrasian models, exchanges are not synchronized and can only be started if at least some of the agents can finance their initial expenditures by means of a money balance in their possession. (Clower does not consider bank credit. In his model the origin of the initial money balances remains undefined; Clower, 1969: 202–11.)

8. If equilibrium is defined as a position in which in all markets, excess demands are zero and at the same time all agents have balanced budgets, the consequence is that, for equilibrium to prevail, all agents must have extinguished the whole of their debts, including any possible bank debt. If agents have no debts with the banking sector, no bank credit is being supplied and any money created by the banks disappears. The remaining money can only originate from a government deficit. Of course, if equilibrium were defined in a very strict way and the equilibrium conditions included a balanced government budget, not only bank money but any kind of money would disappear. In fact, as already mentioned, a rigorous definition of equilibrium tends to produce the conclusion that in equilibrium no money exists, money being a typical disequilibrium phenomenon. However, the most common definition of equilibrium is less rigorous and, while requiring all budgets of the private sector to be balanced, does not apply the same requirement to the government sector. The result is that a government deficit is not considered as being inconsistent with equilibrium, so that the increase in the money supply between two equilibrium positions can be defined as being equal to the government deficit not financed by means of newly issued government bonds ($dL = G - T - dB_G$), and the existing money stock as the cumulated increase in the money supply over time. For those who follow this line of thought, the only kind of money that can be in existence in equilibrium is government money.

9. A rich collection of essays on the circulation approach is contained in Deleplace and Nell (1996). A similar approach is developed in a flow-of-funds scheme by Godley (1999). For a synthetic description of the approach see Graziani (1989).

10. A description of the process of credit creation according to the circulation approach is contained in Rossi (1998).

11. Since the payment of the wage bill is followed by the production of some kind of finished or semi-finished product, there is a correspondence between the wage bill paid and the cost of produced commodities. The initial requirement of bank credit can therefore be measured both by the amount of the wage bill and by the value of inventories in possession of the firms. Some authors in fact prefer to say that the credit requirements of the firms are measured by the money cost of commodities being produced (this is the definition initially given by Hawtrey, 1923 and adopted by Godley, 1999). To some extent the two definitions are equivalent. If we refer to the bank debt of the firms in a single instant of time, it is correct to set it equal to the money value of commodities produced and not yet sold, namely semi-finished products plus inventories. If we refer to the initial credit requirement of the firms, and therefore to their demand for bank credit, it seems more correct to make credit requirements equal to the wage bill corresponding to the planned level of production. The last definition has the advantage of bringing to light the clear correspondence existing between the credit market and the labour market. Any increase in money wages or in employment gives rise to a higher credit requirement and to a consequent renegotiation of the agreements between banks and firms. This explains why firms, when negotiating with the unions for the determination of money wages, always try to figure out the possible reaction of the banking system. The attitude of the banking system will finally determine the possibility of paying a higher wage rate. In fact, as Keynes once said, 'the investment market can become congested through shortage of cash. It can never become congested through shortage of saving' (Keynes, 1937b: 669 [222]). The wage policy of the firms thus ultimately depends on the credit policy of the banks.

12. As already recalled, the assumption usually made in circuit theory of an economic mechanism in which firms decide upon the real magnitudes while wage earners can only determine their own monetary expenditures is borrowed from Keynes's *Treatise on Money* (Keynes, 1930, Chs X (i): 136, and XX: 315–17.

13. This point is clearly stated by Keynes: 'How much bank-credit they [the producers] have to borrow . . . depends . . . on the relative attractions of savings-deposits and of securities, respectively' (Keynes, 1930, Vol. I: 182). In addition to repaying the principal, firms have to

pay interest to the banks. Whether they pay interest in kind or in money terms is a debated question. Graziani (1989) shows that actual payment can only be made in kind. Wray (1996: 448–52) considers instead interest payments as a mere increase in bank debt; correspondingly, according to Wray, the consequent increase in loans is viewed by the banks as their monetary profit.

14. Stiglitz seems to neglect this possibility and to follow the opposite view, namely that the bankruptcy of a number of single firms can only be in the nature of a contagious disease (Stiglitz, 1999).

15. Godley's model is based on an explicit assumption of fully endogenous money (Godley, 1999). A story of the idea of endogenous money is given by Wray, (1990). In a subsequent book, Wray considers bank credit as endogenous and legal tender as exogenous (Wray, 1998: 111).

16. It is worth noting that the same mechanism indicated by Keynes and Kalecki for income distribution within the private sector is admitted by the neoclassical theory for the distribution of income between the private and government sectors. This is the mechanism of the so-called inflation tax, by which the government sector, without applying any explicit tax, gets hold of a portion of national product. There is however a difference in that, according to neoclassical theory, the possibility of getting hold of real goods by using purely monetary instruments is strictly limited to the government sector, and the mechanism making this possible is considered a wholly negative deviation from the ideal working of a market system. In the Keynes–Kalecki formulation, the same mechanism is considered instead as the normal working of a market economy.

17. A typical example is Rousseas (1996). Wray attributes this practice to the circulation approach in general, something which is far from being true (Wray, 1996: 457).

18. Wicksell's model implies the pre-existence of saving as a condition for realizing investment. Wicksell in fact adopts the classical framework in which, wages being paid in advance in real terms, a previous saving in kind has to be assumed as existing at the beginning of each period. The typical neoclassical formulation, by assuming that wages are paid at the end of the production process, rules out the presence of any previous saving. This point is developed in Graziani (1994).

19. It is in fact a common idea of all neoclassical authors that banks collect savings by accepting deposits and that, by granting loans, they finance investment. To that, the neoclassical school adds the policy prescription that banks should never grant loans exceeding the amount of deposits they have previously collected. The preceding propositions were defended with special emphasis by Cannan (1921) and Hayek (1933, Ch. IV, § 3). The same propositions met a severe criticism on the part of Schumpeter (1954, Part 4, Ch. 8, § 7). It is in fact easy to show that, if referring to the banking system as a whole, a similar prescription is untenable, since it is technically impossible for the banking system as a whole to collect deposits without having at the same time granted loans for the same amount. While in chronological terms the emergence of a deposit is simultaneous to the emergence of a loan, in logical terms, loans precede deposits. This mistake, concerning banking technique more than economic theory proper, invalidates the whole treatment of the savings–investment equilibrium to be found in the neoclassical model. This point is dealt with very clearly in J. Schmidt's paper on 'Finance and growth' (Schmidt, 1999).

20. This brings us close to a point raised by Hicks in his distinction between autonomous and overdraft sectors (Hicks, 1974). Autonomous sectors can rely on internal finance while overdraft sectors rely on bank credit. As shown in the text, if we adopt a Kaldorian theory of income distribution, the classification suggested by Hicks can only be made ex post. Autonomous sectors, namely sectors able to finance their own investments, can only be sectors earning profits, which means by definition that overdraft sectors are sectors making losses. Of course, all sectors might be autonomous for final finance (while in principle no sector can be autonomous for initial finance). It doesn't seem, however, that this is the kind of distinction Hicks had in mind.

21. See Modigliani and Papademos (1990). Only two models are considered here as typical examples. A careful and complete review of the subject is contained in Mazzoli (1998: Chs 2 and 3).

22. The same idea seems to be implicitly accepted by Stiglitz, when he speaks of the rationale for reserve requirements: 'Once we recognize that the bank need not limit its certification activities to the amounts it has on deposit, then there may be an imbalance between what individuals would like to save . . . and what other individuals or firms would like to invest' (Stiglitz, 1999: 72).
23. Since this is a macroeconomic model, the nature of such internal finance should be made clear. In fact it is difficult to conceive how firms as a whole can earn profits in money terms, in a model in which no money is created by government expenditure and the whole of money is created by bank credit which is a debt of the firms.

REFERENCES

Arestis, P.H. (1996), Post-Keynesian economics: towards coherence', *Cambridge Journal of Economics*, 20(1): 111–35.

Arrow, K.J. and F.H. Hahn (1971), *General Competitive Analysis*, Edinburgh: Oliver and Boyd.

Benetti, C. and J. Cartelier (1990), 'Monnaie et formation des grandeurs économiques', in J. Carteler (ed.), *La Formation des Grandeurs Économiques*, Paris: PUF: 323–53.

Bernanke, B.S. and A.S. Blinder (1988), 'Credit money and aggregate demand', *American Economic Review*, 78(2): 435–39.

Bresciani-Turroni, C. (1936), 'The theory of saving', *Economica*, 3,4: 1–23, 162–81.

Cannan, E. (1921), 'The meaning of bank deposits', *Economica*, 1: 28–36.

Cartelier, J. (1995), 'Payment systems and dynamics in a monetary economy', in G. Deleplace and E. Nell (eds), Money in Motion, New York: Macmillan: 200–38.

Chick, V. (1986), 'The evolution of the banking system and the theory of saving, investment, and interest', *Economie et Sociétés*, Série *Monnaie et Production*, 20(8–9): 111–26.

Chick, V. and S. Dow (1988), 'A post-Keynesian perspective on the relation between banking and regional development', in P.H. Arestis (ed.), *Post-Keynesian Monetary Economics*, Aldershot, UK: Edward Elgar: 219–50.

Clower, R. (1969), *Monetary Theory*, Baltimore: Penguin Books.

Debreu, G. (1959), *Theory of Value*, New York: Wiley.

Deleplace, G. and E. Nell (eds) (1996), *Money in Motion*, New York: Macmillan.

Dow, A.C. and S.C. Dow (1989), 'Endogenous money creation and idle balances', in J. Pheby (ed), *New Directions in Post-Keynesian Economics*, Aldershot, UK: Edward Elgar: 147–64.

Fisher, I. (1911), *The Purchasing Power of Money*, New York: Macmillan.

Fisher, I. (1930), *The Theory of Interest*, New York: Macmillan.

Godley, W. (1999), 'Money and credit in a Keynesian model of income determination', *Cambridge Journal of Economics*, 23(4): 393–411.

Graziani, A. (1989) *The Theory of the Monetary Circuit*, London: Thames Papers in Political Economy (also in C. Panico and M. Musella (eds) (1995), *The Money Supply in the Economic Process*, Aldershot UK and Brookfield US: Edward Elgar: 516–41).

Graziani, A. (1991), 'La théorie Keynésienne de la monnaie et le financement de l'économie', *Economie Appliquée*, 44(1): 25–41.

Graziani A. (1994), 'Real wages and the loans–deposits controversy', *Economie Appliquée*, 47(1): 31–46.

Hahn, F.H. (1982), *Money and Inflation*, Oxford: B. Blackwell.

Hawtrey, R.G. (1923), *Currency and Credit*, London: Longmans, Green, and Co.

Hayek F.A. ([1929] 1933), *Monetary Theory and the Trade Cycle*, London: Jonathan Cape.

Heinsohn, G. and O. Steiger (1996), *Eigentum, Zins und Geld. Üngelöste Rätsel der Wirtschaftsmissenschaft*, Reinbek: Rohwohlt.

Hicks, J.R. ([1933] 1982), 'Equilibrium and the cycle', in J. Hicks, *Money, Interest and Wages*, Oxford: Blackwell: 28–41.

Hicks, J.R. (1974), *The Crisis in Keynesian Economics*, Oxford: B. Blackwell.

Kaldor, N. (1956), 'Alternative theories of distribution', *Review of Economic Studies*, 23(2): 83–100.

Kalecki, M. (1954), *Theory of Economic Dynamics*, London: Allen & Uniwin.

Keynes J.M. (1930), *A Treatise on Money*, reprinted in D. Moggridge (ed.) (1971), *The Collected Writings of J.M. Keynes*, Vols. 5 and 6, London: Macmillan.

Keynes, J.M. (1936), *The General Theory of Employment, Interest and Money*, London: Macmillan, reprinted in D. Moggridge (ed.) (1973), *The Collected Writings of J.M. Keynes*, Vol. VII, London: Macmillan.

Keynes, J.M. (1937a) [1973]), 'Alternative theories of the rate of interest', *Economic Journal*, 47(2): 241–52, reprinted in D. Moggridge (ed.) (1973), *The Collected Writings of J.M. Keynes*, Vol. XIV, London: Macmillan: 201–15.

Keynes J.M. (1937b), 'The ex-ante theories of the rate of interest', *Economic Journal*, 47(4): 663–9, reprinted in D. Moggridge (ed.) (1973), *The Collected Writings of J.M. Keynes*, Vol. XIV, London: Macmillan: 215–23.

Keynes J.M. (1939 [1973]), 'The process of capital formation', *Economic Journal* 49(3), reprinted in D. Moggridge (ed.) (1973), *The Collected Writings of J.M. Keynes*, Vol. XIV, London: Macmillan: 569–74.

Knapp, G.F. ([1905] 1923), *Staatliche Theorie des Geldes*, München: Duncker & Humblot (English translation, *The State Theory of Money*, London: Macmillan, 1924).

Kregel, J.A. (1973), *The Reconstruction of Economics*, London: Macmillan.

Lindahl, E. ([1930] 1939), *Studies in the Theory of Money and Capital*, London: Allen & Unwin.

Marshall, A. (1923), *Money, Credit, and Commerce*, London: Macmillan.

Marshall, A. (1975), *The Early Economic Writings of Alfred Marshall*, ed. by J.K. Whitaker, London: Macmillan.

Mazzoli, M. (1998), *Credit, Investments and the Macroeconomy*, Cambridge: Cambridge University Press.

Menger, C. (1892) 'On the origin of money', *Economic Journal*, 2(2): 239–55.

Modigliani F. and L. Papademos (1990), 'The supply of money and the control of nominal income', in B.M. Friedman and F.H. Hahn (eds), *Handbook of Monetary Economics*, Vol. 1, Amsterdam: North-Holland Publishing Co.: 399–494.

Moore, B. (1984), 'Keynes and the endogeneity of the money stock', *Studi Economici*, 39(22): 23–70.

Moore, B. (1988), *Horizontalists and Verticalists: The Macroeconomics of Credit Money*, Cambridge: Cambridge University Press.

Pantaleoni, M. ([1894] 1957), *Pure Economics*, New York: Kelly and Millman.

Robertson, D.H. (1926), *Banking Policy and the Price Level*, London: P.S. King & Son.

Robinson, J. (1956), *The Accumulation of Capital*, London: Macmillan.

Rossi, S. (1998), 'Endogenous money and banking activity', *Studi Economici*, 66(3): 23–56.

Rousseas, S. (1996) 'The spheres of industrial and financial circulation revisited, and their implications for post Keynesian economic policy', in G. Deleplace and E. Nell (eds), *Money in Motion*, New York: Macmillan: 672–83.

Say, J.B. (1826), *Traité d'Économie Politique* (1st ed. 1803).

Schlesinger, K. (1914), *Theorie der Geld- und Kreditwirtschaft*, München: Duncker & Humblot.

Schmidt, J. (1999), 'Finance and growth: is Schumpeter really the founding father of modern theories of financial intermediation?', paper given at the ESHET Conference 2000 in Graz.

Schmitt, B. (1984) *Inflation, Chômage, et Malformations du Capital*, Paris: Economica.

Schumpeter, J.A. (1954), *History of Economic Analysis*, New York: Oxford University Press.

Simiand, F. (1932), *Le Salaire*, Paris: Alcan.

Spinelli, F. (1999), *La Moneta dall'Oro all'Euro*, Milan: Etas.

Stiglitz, J.E. (1999), *Towards a New Paradigm for Monetary Economics*, Milan, Mattioli Lectures, mimeo.

Studart, R. (1995) *Investment Finance in Economic Development*, London: Routledge.

Tirole, J. (1994) 'On banking and intermediation', *European Economic Review*, 38(3–4): 469–87.

Wray, L.R. (1990), *Money and Credit in Capitalist Economies. The Endogenous Money Approach*, Aldershot: Edward Elgar.

Wray, L.R. (1996), 'Money in the Circular Flow', in G. Deleplace and E. Nell (eds), *Money in Motion*, New York: Macmillan: 440–64.

Wray, L.R. (1998), *Understanding Modern Money*, Cheltenham, UK and Lyme, US: Edward Elgar.

E40
E50 B31 B15
G21

12. The credit theory of Carl Knies

Hans-Michael Trautwein*

INTRODUCTION

Because of his early treatise on the 'historical method' in political economy (1853), Carl Knies (1821–98) is nowadays ranked among the founding fathers of the (older) German historical school. His other opus magnum, a voluminous trilogy on money and credit (*Geld und Credit*, 1873–79), has received much less attention in the literature. The few references that one can find do not make the reading of the trilogy more attractive. One commentator stated that Knies, in his work on money and credit, did 'not succeed in applying the historical method to the analysis of concrete economic problems' (Schefold, 1987: 55).[1] According to Schumpeter (1954: 809), that was not a serious failure, since Knies's 'main performance was in the field of money and credit, where he made his mark as a theorist'. However, in the course of his *History of Economic Analysis*, Schumpeter keeps referring the reader to a later appraisal of that 'main contribution'. After having raised high expectations, he finally deals very briefly with Knies, asserting that *Geld und Credit* 'added but little to the topics covered by its title' (1954: 1081). Even more harshly, Wagner (1937: 55) accuses Knies of substituting classification for theory – a roundabout method of dodging the real issue.

Another reason for the neglect of Knies may be found in his staunch defence of metallism, a doctrine that soon after the publication of the trilogy appeared outdated in theory and practice. According to Knies, money is always and everywhere a material good – a commodity that must have intrinsic utility value quite apart from its monetary functions. The precious metals, notably gold and silver, were the natural candidates for playing the role of commodity money. Knies was neither the first nor the last to take that position. Roscher, the other founding father of the Historical School, had categorically stated that money is 'a commodity – no more and no less' (1854 [1878: 242]).[2] And there were numerous other economists who came to hold on to metallistic positions far into the twentieth century. But the writings of Knies seem to have left such a strong impression on German monetary economics that authors of surveys in the interwar period often picked him as the background antagonist of Knapp, whose *State Theory of Money* (1905) was no less classificatory than Knies's metallistic theory of credit, but apparently much closer to reality.[3] In recent years only the first part of Knies's trilogy, the volume on money, has attracted a few comments.[4] The two large volumes on credit seem to have fallen into oblivion.

A closer look at the works of Knies reveals nevertheless that he has influenced the development of monetary theory in subtle ways, for example through Böhm–Bawerk and Wicksell. Knies was a pioneer in the systematic exposition of the functions of money and credit. He was one of the first to apply the law of large numbers to the creation of loans and deposits in commercial banks, and to emphasize the importance of moral hazard and state verification problems, both for the evolution of financial systems and for the analysis of credit cycles. The following assessment of Knies's theory of credit provides a brief account of these contributions and relates them to the criticism mentioned above. Its focus is set on explaining how Knies's strong emphasis on the empirical and theoretical relevance of credit goes together with his rigorous metallism.[5] It shows that the autometallistic fallacies of Knies, in particular his 'real illusion' of the indispensability of commodity money, can be traced back to fundamental problems that all utility-based theories of value face in explaining the existence and interaction of money and credit.

THE NATURE OF CREDIT

The following account of Knies's theory of credit is based on his 'reflections on credit' (*Erörterungen über den Credit*) and two other articles that were published in *Zeitschrift für die gesammte Staatswissenschaft* between 1858 and 1860, and on *Geld und Credit*, his trilogy of 1873–79. In all these works Knies makes a point of carefully defining the subjects of analysis. The task is 'to find the general notion that comprises the specific, and to make it consistent' (1859: 565).[6] He rejects the functionalistic short-cuts to monetary theory that have come to dominate the textbooks of our time, usually defining their subject tautologically by the motto that 'money is what money does'.[7] Knies insists that 'the definition of money is not the definition of a function, but the definition of a good that fulfils specific functions' (1873: 163). Consequently he first discusses the essential properties of money, in order to deduce from them its functions (see the following section).

In the same manner Knies attempts to define the nature of credit. According to him credit transactions are to be understood as mutual transfers of goods across time (1876: 5–11). One party, the creditor, renders his or her service in the present, whereas the other party, the debtor, fulfils his or her obligations in the future. The intertemporal character of credit transactions distinguishes them from spot transactions, in which both transfers take place in the present,

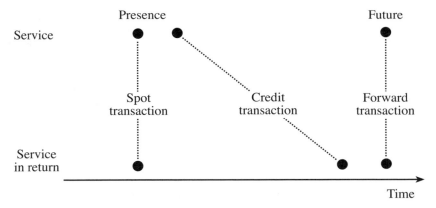

Figure 12.1   The temporal structure of market transactions

as well as from forward transactions, in which both transfers take place in the future (see Figure 12.1).

Money is explicitly included in Knies's definition of credit as a mutual transfer of goods. The possibility of making loans in kind is acknowledged, but described as a peripheral, backward phenomenon (1876: 100–102). Normally loans are made in terms of money, because credit is essentially an intertemporal exchange of *homogenous* goods. This distinguishes credit from all other transactions, which are based on the qualitative difference between the goods exchanged, directly or indirectly, through money. Money must be homogenous by certification. This makes it interchangeable – or 'fungible' in the terminology of Knies. The pieces of money that are used to repay the loan need not be exactly the same pieces that were borrowed. They should not even be that, since money must circulate in order to effect the transactions required to fulfil the loan contracts. Therefore credit naturally develops and gains in importance along with the evolution of monetary economies.

Even so, Knies (1876: 12) insists that credit is not simply an exchange of money now for money later. In the goods markets, it competes with spot trans-actions as a marketing device – in the sense of facilitating sales where cash is scarce. Moreover, it mediates the 'purchase and sale of uses of factor services' (*Nutzungen*). In his 'reflections on credit', Knies (1860: 169) goes as far as describing any exchange that involves the use of production factors as 'the exclusive domain of credit'. He explains that, since production requires time, factor services can only be paid for either before or after their appropriation.

This view was rather uncommon even in Knies's time. It suggests that it would be appropriate to distinguish between two spheres of credit in a market economy. In the sphere of production, the use of labour, land and capital (for example, machines on lease) implies credit relations to the extent that the factor services are rendered either before or after the payments of wage and rent. In the sphere of finance, firms borrow money from banks or wealth holders to pay for a large fraction of those factor services. Modern monetary theory deals almost exclusively with the second sphere, whereas Knies (1860) reflects only on the first sphere. He does not, at any rate, discuss the differences and interaction between the two spheres – for example, in terms of an interest rate mechanism. He admits nevertheless that, contrary to his definition, one cannot speak of a mutual transfer of homogenous goods in the case of wage payments for labour, as opposed to repayments of loans in terms of money.

In *Credit* (1876: Chs. I-IV), the use of labour in return for wages is no longer considered as a credit relation, whereas the close links between credit and capital are strongly emphasized. On the one hand, capital is the base of credit, 'because a person can only take the role of a creditor if and in so far as he owns capital' (1876: 120). On the other hand, credit is essential for promoting the use of capital in a decentralized economy (1876: 33). Knies characterizes capital as 'the fund of durable goods for future uses' (1873: 49, 61), rejecting its 'vulgar definition' as 'a sum of money given as a loan' (1873: 6). In his lengthy discussion of leases and loans, however, he confuses the two spheres of credit by treating leases of land or machines on the same level as loans in terms of money. The deeper reason behind this confusion may be found in Knies's definition of money as a good.

THE NATURE OF MONEY

A first look at Knies's volume on money (1873) seems to indicate that he followed a functionalistic approach, regardless of the criticism sketched above. The list of contents describes the sections of the 240-page-long chapter on money as a sequence of functions: money as the standard of value, the medium of exchange, the means of payment, the store of value, legal tender, and so on. Knies's analysis of these functions is systematic and precise. It was probably the best of its time and, as a look at modern textbooks quickly reveals, its basic layout has stood the test of time.[8]

However, following the ontological tradition of German political economy, Knies insists that money is not sufficiently defined by what it does. The question remains why it can do what it does. Here Knies distinguished carefully between the fungibility of money and the functionality that follows from it. In his words, money is 'the most fungible of all goods' (1873: 116). It is 'an intermediary good', whose use is 'neither the result of any particular convention nor the consequence of legal prescription ... but the natural outcome of exchange as such' (1873: 107 ff.). The fungibility of money is based on four essential properties, namely 'general demand' (*allgemeine Begehrtheit*), homogeneity, durability and complete divisibility.[9] For Knies it is self-evident that the precious metals gold and silver have all these properties and are therefore most functional in playing the role of money. Yet he stresses more generally, throughout the trilogy, that whatever functions as money must be an independently valued good:

> It is a law of nature that, for measuring or stating the specific quantitative relations in and of a quantitatively definable object, only such objects can be used as standards for measurement which themselves possess the quality that is to be quantified ... Whatever may be found out in other respects, *money* in the sense of a standard of economic value, *must itself be an object of value.* (1873: 113 ff. – italics in the original)

This proposition raises two questions: what determines the value of money, and can money be replaced by credit?

WHAT DETERMINES THE VALUE OF MONEY?

Are the functions of money inseparable from the physical presence of specific commodities (such as precious metals) that, independent of their monetary functions, are equivalent to the goods measured and exchanged?

Knies (1873: 115–23) sets about answering question (1) by reviewing the first chapters of *Das Kapital* by Karl Marx (1867). He rejects the latter's reduction of the exchange value of goods and money to the 'socially necessary' input of labour. Knies generally defines the exchange value of goods as their 'generic' or 'fungible use value' (*Gebrauchswerth*). Both terms refer to the 'social taxation' of 'summary total demand' and 'existing total supply' of the good in question. According to Knies (1873: 123 ff.), the exchange of goods is induced by differences between their social taxation and the individual estimates of their specific use values. Here his language is opaque. The argument seems to amount to nothing more than saying that the value of a good rises with its 'fungibility' (in the sense of marketability), without making clear what those two notions exactly mean in terms of supply and demand. In particular, Knies does not discuss any feedbacks of differences between the individual and the social valuation of goods, nor does he take account of elasticities of substitution or other relevant factors. Thus he has next to nothing to say about the formation of relative prices and money prices.

When it comes to money, Knies (1873: 135–43) emphasizes that the general medium of exchange represents fungibility as such. He insists nevertheless that money is a good that differs from other goods only by being more fungible – a matter of degree rather than a substantial difference. The general acceptance of money is based on its high degree of acceptance as a commodity. Knies's definition of the value of money is complex and, as we will see, somewhat ambiguous. On the one hand he contends that money has a specific use value as the general medium of exchange. On the other hand he insists that the value of money must be 'independently assessed' in other uses. That other use value co-determines the exchange value of money – here some arbitrage argument suggests itself, but Knies fails to give an exact explanation of the process by which the value of money is determined. He asserts that gold and silver are the ideal materials to fulfil monetary functions because, apart from being fungible, they have high value for other uses, such as jewelry. In the view of Knies, the functionality of money is thus indispensably based on its metal content.

CAN MONEY BE REPLACED BY CREDIT?

What is the answer of Knies to question (2)? Despite his belief in the indispensability of commodity money, Knies acknowledges the great potential of credit (including clearing mechanisms) to economize on the use of commodity money. He discusses at great length the widespread opinion that bills of exchange, bank notes, transfers of deposit and 'paper credit' are components of the volume of money, in addition to specie. He rejects any such wider definition of money, on the grounds that all those forms of credit are claims to money which arise in the course of transactions. Hence they cannot be money as such. Knies includes the claims in the set of non-monetary goods, because they are based on transactions of the latter (even though they are claims to money), and because they too are frequently exchanged for cash. He then formulates an early version of the Clower constraint: 'Simply being valuable does not make a good a claim to another good of specific value. No other good can be money simply because it can itself be acquired with money!' (1873: 165)

An exception is made for the bank note. Knies admits that it is 'a hybrid, a bastard', sprung from the combination of the properties of an instrument to circulate claims and a means of payment (1873: 206). He pleads for a state monopoly of note issue, because bank notes are essentially non-interest-bearing loans to the emitting banks. Free issue of notes carries the risk of over-emission. Profit-maximizing banks will not maximize the social returns to economizing on specie. They tend to abuse their free access to capital by emitting an excessive amount of claims to money: 'It is a dangerous illusion to believe that the cost-free 'creation' of claims to money in the shape of bank notes can be regulated by the standards that apply to the production of goods with inputs of capital' (1873: 313).

If, however, the note issue is to be turned into a social monopoly, is it not then in the power of the state to replace specie by other kinds of money? Knies does his best to wriggle out of this conflict with his definition of money. First he attacks the belief that the state 'can create money and money value out of nothing' (1873: 187). In his view, this is an ancient fallacy, just as absurd as the idea that the government could declare 'a mountain to be twice as high as it is in reality, or two pounds to be six pounds' (1873: 189). It is the duty of good government to regulate the monetary system, but the regulations must take account of the determination of value through the market process. In its regulation of coinage and the note issue the government must therefore refer to 'real money' as the standard of value and general means of payment. Knies points out that the indispensability of the commodity base is testified by the names of the currencies, which are in general borrowed from the weight units of precious metals. It is not in the power of the state to choose arbitrary standards of value:

> A truly new inscription, such as ten Sasa or a hundred Hoho would pose an unsolvable conundrum for everyone. It would have to be stated that they are equivalent with the name of a real object of value, such as ten grams of gold or a hundred *Loth* of silver.[10] (1873: 188)

What would Knies have said about the truly new inscription '100 Euro'? He would certainly have had a hard time explaining that the equivalent 195.58 deutschmarks or 655.96 French francs were 'real objects of value'.

It is only fair to see Knies as a child of his times, in which almost everyone believed in the indispensability of a gold (or silver) backing of the currency. That should not prevent us from spotting the inconsistency in his argument. According to Knies, the exchange value of money is determined *both* by the 'fungible use value' of the precious metals in their alternative uses (such as jewelry) *and* by their use value as general media of exchange and definite means of payment (1873: 135–43). As pointed out above, he does not discuss any arbitrage process or other market process that would let both uses co-determinate the value of money; nor does he show that anything that is presented as money without having any other use value must lose its monetary functions in the market process. For Knies, the 'fungible' utility of the monetary commodity in both uses is the one and only determinant of its value. In that case, however, the acceptance of a certain kind of money as a general means of payment must be included in the determination of its value. Even at the times when Knies was writing his *Money and Credit* it was conceivable that – due to the positive network externalities of a common medium of exchange – the state could achieve the general acceptance of certain means of payment that embodied the standard of value without having any alternative use value (for example, inconvertible bank notes). It follows from the logic of

Knies's argument that such means of payment have value and that they therefore must be considered as money.

Knies himself tacitly accepts this conclusion in a later section (1873:
257–313), where he discusses the role of fiat money and the transition to a
state monopoly of note issue. Now he acknowledges that legal tender in the
form of bank notes or other paper has all the characteristics of a means of
payment. He insists nevertheless that it is wrong to describe inconvertible
paper currency as paper money or even credit money:

> Any use of paper as legal tender inevitably presupposes that gold or silver function
> as legal standards of value and prices, even when and where the use of any other
> means of payment [apart from the paper currency] is forbidden. 'Paper money' and
> 'credit money' are names that have been carried over from an isolated function; by
> the strict standards of science they make just as much sense as 'wooden iron' or
> 'trust based on distrust'. (1873: 269)

Finally the long discussion about money substitutes boils down to the argument that what is defined as money must fulfil all the functions of money and
– most importantly – the role of the standard of value (1873: 112ff.). Whatever
may be said in favour of this definition, Knies's belief that the standard of
value must be a commodity with alternative use value is a non sequitur. But
two interesting conclusions emerge from the section on currency (1873: Ch.
III.7), indicating a delicate balance in the conduct of monetary policy.

On the one hand, inconvertible paper currency or fiat money is no credit.
According to Knies it should rather be seen as 'the medium of circulating an
authorization of payment that replaces money' (1873: 266). Fiat money is at
best a claim to a different composition of its own kind (for example, a ten-
pound note to be exchanged into ten one-pound notes), but it is not a claim to
money of a different kind. Consequently the issuing authority is not a debtor
and the holder of the paper is not a creditor. Defining those pieces of paper as
legal tender, the state can appropriate goods from their recipients, because the
paper is accepted for tax payments and therefore finds general acceptance in
market transactions (1873: 277–90). Knies stresses that the self-authorization
to pay with intrinsically useless paper carries a great risk of fiscal abuse of the
monetary system. This can easily turn into a large depreciation of the currency,
'one of the worst plagues that can beset a modern economy' (1873: 281).

On the other hand, Knies points out that the free issue of notes by commercial banks leads to market failures. Since banks can make profits with the
issuance of notes, there is a tendency of competition to produce claims to
money in excess of reserves. Such systemic disproportions are bound to result
in periodical liquidity crises (1873: 201ff.). Here Knies defines a positive role
for the state: to monopolize the note issue, in order to avoid market failures,
by way of timely restrictions of the credit supply.

THE DETERMINANTS OF INTEREST

In a work on money and credit of altogether 1200 pages, one might expect to find a theory about the level and structure of interest rates in a prominent place. The first two volumes of Knies's trilogy are certainly full of critical remarks about usury laws, interest regulations and earlier theories of interest, but they do not give a positive explanation of interest. This is developed only in the last volume (1879: Ch. VIII). There Knies defines the 'gross rate of interest' that is charged in loan contracts as the sum of 'pure interest' and the 'accessory rewards' (1879: 1). Knies begins his analysis with the latter.

There are two categories of accessory rewards. In lease contracts and other transfers of the use of real capital, they constitute insurance premia that serve to protect the claims of the creditors by a consolidation of risks. In the case of money loans, the surcharge on pure interest must be considered as risk premia, since – according to Knies – the loss of financial capital cannot be insured (1879: 20–28). Creditors demand a premium, an additional income that compensates them for their risk-taking. Knies is critical of this practice, because it creates a moral hazard problem that tends to reinforce itself. The relevant passages are worth quoting at some length:

> The risk premium is paid only by those debtors who did not incur the loss for which provision was made, and in whose case the considered risk actually turned out to be zero, whereas it is not paid by those debtors in whose case the risk turned out to be 'infinitely large' and the actual outcome was a loss. The creditor *A* can gain the premium once the creditor *B* has incurred the loss of assets that signals the risk. Since only the good debtors pay the premium whose charge is justified with reference to the losses incurred by the bad debtors, no increase in the risk premium can reduce the frequency of bad debt. It tends, on the contrary, to increase that frequency, because good debtors face a greater burden of repayment. And there are many people who will take an attitude of indifference vis-à-vis their obligations as soon as they realize the impossibility of fulfilling them! All increases of bad debts will in turn lead to rises in the risk premia that the good debtors have to pay. (1879: 21)

The risk of moral hazard is rather high because it is frequently impossible to say what the fair risk premium should be. Knies draws attention to a state verification problem, both ex ante and ex post:

> Even though the risk premium is fixed beforehand in each case, it can never be the result of a proper 'calculation' of the risk. The real outcome is never the confirmation, it is in any case a falsification of the calculation that underlies the premium. This is exactly why it cannot be used to prove for any third party that the creditor has made an error in his estimation of the size of the imminent risk – a very important fact for finance and law! . . . In particular the behaviour of a great many creditors in the course of a 'trade crisis' . . . shows that, under certain conditions, the 'preconceived' opinion of creditors disregards any proper examination of the risk in each single case. (1879: 21)

The first part of this passage might be read as if Knies disputed the practicability of probability calculus on the trivial grounds that actual values tend to deviate stochastically from expected values. The second part shows, however, that he discusses a real problem. Expressed in modern terms, the problem is to form correct expectations about the transitions from independent specific risks (a given distribution of probable outcomes) to systemic risks, to true uncertainty (in the sense of Knight, 1921) or to market uncertainty in speculative bubbles.

Even though Knies's distinction between real and financial capital in terms of insurable and uninsurable risk is not entirely correct,[11] it is useful as it draws attention to the fact that loans in terms of money have some potential to create macroeconomic coordination problems. As Knies was to emphasize in a different context, they contribute to periodical excesses in the expansion of production and consumption. In this way they generate systemic risks of default and amplify cyclical fluctuations of real activity (see the following section).

After having dealt with the accessory rewards, Knies proceeds to discuss 'pure interest'. He goes to great lengths to show that the pure rate of interest is neither an immoral product of usury nor a natural price. It is the market price for the use of temporarily transferred goods (1879: 30–131). More essentially, Knies considers the rate of interest to be a variable share of the rate of return to the use of capital goods. Within certain limits the interest level is determined by the competition for loans among borrowers in industry and commerce who seek to maximize their net profits (1879: 85–108). The upper limit is normally set by the 'productivity of capital', which in the words of Knies is the 'use value of capital as the means to earn business income'. This upper limit can be reached or even exceeded when many entrepreneurs need to borrow money to secure the continued existence of their firms, even at the cost of negative profit incomes.

The lower limit of interest is normally set by the wealth owners' claims to an income from the use of their capital by way of credit. However, Knies (1879: 35ff.) rejects all interpretations of interest as a premium on 'the labour of saving' or 'abstinence from the present consumption of goods' – an approach that had gained some prominence in the tradition of Nassau Senior (1836).[12] Abstinence from consumption is not a sufficient explanation for the existence of credit and interest, because savers cannot make use of a great portion of the goods that they possess – so they do not have to abstain. Moreover, they could just as well sell those goods instead of lending them (or their financial equivalent).

In a later passage, however, time preference for consumption creeps back in as a determinant of the lower limit of the pure interest rate. There Knies (1879: 98) writes that '[t]he stimulus of receiving interest must be greater than the stimulus of consumption now instead of consumption later; it must counter any aversion to the postponement'. But time preference is not a sufficient condition for determining the interest minimum. Knies (1879: Ch. IX) identifies several countervailing factors, most prominently the aversion or inability of wealth owners to make productive use of their own capital – arguments that could be expressed in terms of a time preference for leisure. Knies even goes to the extreme of making out a wealth owner's motive for being content with a zero rate of interest. This is the case where 'capital owners are simply interested in the maintenance of capital for a certain time' or where they even 'value a later return of their capital higher than keeping it in their possession' (1879: 165). Thus the rate of time preference for consumption is not necessarily positive.

Finally it is worth mentioning that Knies had a clear notion of the influence of changes in the price level on the nominal rate of interest:

> Whenever there has been a general change in the value of money during the term of the loan, the repayment by the debtor would not be equivalent . . . to the quantity of value defined [in the contract], but to the quantity of value augmented or diminished by the effective difference in the value of money. If that change is to be taken into account and if there is no doubt about the expected direction of change, a specific element in the determination of the rate of interest will be brought into force by the expectations of both parties. If the value of money is likely to fall, for example, the creditor will demand a risk premium. (1879: 106)

This adjustment goes nowadays under the name of the Fisher effect.[13]

THE FUNCTIONS OF BANKS AND THE EFFECTS OF CREDIT

There are many passages in the trilogy where Knies discusses the effects of credit on prices and production at some length. Yet it is hardly possible to summarize his views on the matter, as they remain dispersed and vague, if not contradictory. A telling example of the ambiguity in Knies's judgement in this respect is his discussion of the effects of credit on the total supply of goods. In Chapter VI (1876) he praises the eminent importance of credit 'for the whole cultural life of mankind', only to qualify the praise by asserting that credit can accomplish a redistribution of existing goods only, but not a change in their total supply (1876: 241). In Chapter IX (1879) he states, on the other hand, that credit can help to increase total production by transforming small savings into big loans to large enterprises which make more efficient use of the resources (1879: 135–42, 186–201). The corresponding economies of scale and scope in industrial production are only mentioned in passing. Instead

Knies emphasizes that the evolution of the social division of labour creates economies of scale and scope in the extension of credit. The outcome of this process is a concentration of credit in specific institutions – the banks (1879: Ch. X).

As in the case of money, Knies's analysis of the functions of banks is very systematic and quite advanced by the standards of its time, especially with regard to loan size and loan term transformation. Knies shows that banks increase the social efficiency of credit transactions not only by their interme-diation between lenders and borrowers; simple gains from the specialization of the intermediaries could, after all, be realized by lending short and borrow-ing long – the normal asymmetry of terms for risk-averse actors in financial markets. What is more specific and interesting about banks is their reversal of the asymmetry of terms: their core business is to borrow short and lend long. Referring to the law of large numbers, and including a numerical example, Knies demonstrates that there is always a certain share of demand deposits that remains untouched, even after interbank clearing. The banks can use these 'inactive deposits' as reserves for the extension of long-term loans, making profits from the spreads between deposit rates and lending rates (1879: 241–54). In a later chapter he remarks that commercial banks with the privi-lege of note issue can profit from the circulation of their bank notes in exactly the same manner as from the 'non-circulation of their inactive deposits' – both are liabilities that the banks can use as assets (1879: Ch. XIV). All they have to do is to make provision for the case that unexpected reserve drains occur, lest they develop into ruinous bank runs. Knies (1879: 417–23) points out that many banks do not even hold reserves for this case, but deposit or borrow money at big banks. As a consequence all the metallic liquidity reserves of the economy are concentrated in 'central institutions', conferring the highest degree of acceptance on the bank notes issued by those institutions.

The macroeconomic potential for credit expansion that arises from the progress of banking makes Knies think about 'the natural limits of credit' (1879: 210–14). In the chapters on banking (1879: Chs X–XIV) he does not, however, give any direct answer to this question. The more relevant passages can be found in his earlier reflections on the interaction of credit and prices (1876: Ch. VI), which may well be regarded as a monetary theory of the busi-ness cycle.

A SYNTHESIS OF CURRENCY AND BANKING POSITIONS

In his discussion of the effects of credit on the general price level, Knies takes a position on the controversy between the currency and banking schools in

England (1876: Ch. VI). He concludes that 'neither the "banking theory" nor the 'currency theory' can be endorsed', because both schools are wrong with regard to the role of bank notes (1876: 286). Yet he constructs a synthesis of both theories that preserves the quantity-theoretical framework of the currency school, while making room for reverse causation from prices to the monetary aggregate, as postulated by the banking school.[14]

The trick of the synthesis is to define the volume of bank notes as a determinant of the velocity of money (1876: 261–70). According to the currency principle, bank notes should be considered as money – not so according to Knies. In his view they are claims to money that function as substitutes in circulation only. If the volume of money proper (specie) is constant, an increase in the volume of circulating bank notes is equivalent to an increase in the velocity of circulation of the monetary base. The subtleties of Knies's distinction between money proper and the velocity effects of bank note circulation, and the differencies between his position and the position of the currency school, are easily understood if the argument is put in terms of the Fisherian equation of exchange in its growth-rate version:

$$p = (m + v) - t$$

where p denotes the rate of inflation, v is the change in the velocity of circulation, and m and t are the growth rates of the volumes of money and transactions respectively. What both views have in common is the positive effect of an increase in the volume of bank notes on the price level: all else equal, it is positive ($p > 0$). But the two views differ on the causes. According to the currency principle, the rise in the price level must be caused by an increase in the volume of money ($m > 0$). According to Knies, it is caused by a rise in velocity ($v > 0$). Anticipating the objection 'that the value of money has not been diminished by the enormous expansion of modern finance', Knies points out that this was due to the integration of many new regions into global trade, to the increasing share of production for markets (as opposed to subsistence production), and to great progress in the division of labour (1876: 295). The globalization of markets in the times of Knies could accordingly be written in short hand as: $v = t > 0$.

The banking-theoretical argument of reverse causation (from prices to money) is found in the passages where Knies discusses conflicts between money and credit that tend to produce liquidity crises in a regular fashion. In his view one of the main effects of the evolution of credit is to facilitate large speculative transactions that involve assets owned by other people.[15] Thus the interdependence of various enterprises may be much stronger than indicated by the degree of 'real division of labour' (1876: 302–15, 1879: 139–42). If people speculate that prices will rise, and if they can borrow 'money', total demand will increase, eventually inflating the price level. Self-fulfilling expectations of rising prices are, according to Knies, frequently the main stimulus of 'extraordinary enlargements of industrial plants'. Here, however, the price mechanism sets a 'natural limit to credit':

> As production reacts to the rise in market demand by increasing supplies – and the greater the rise in the prices of goods, the greater will be the efforts made – it generates itself the force that brings the movement to a halt and then reverses it. By and by, current demand will be satiated and then, eventually, oversaturated. The same crucial effect that a new abundant crop tends to have on trade speculation in commodities, such as coffee, shows up as the consequence of excessive industrial production. The rest of the story – the constraints on consumption, the effects of maturities of repayments, the forced sales at lower prices by some, with many others following suit, the rapid fall of prices to the level of 'dumping prices', and so on – is by and large the same [in both cases]. (1876: 306)

In barter economies as well as in cash economies such crises will normally be confined to a few sectors. In credit economies, partial crises tend to evolve into general crises by way of debt deflation and by the generalization of the pessimistic mood in stock exchanges and the banking system (1879: 136–41, 1879: 139–42).

In his review of Tooke, Knies argues that the circulation of bank notes makes crises worse because 'a subsequent depreciation of the notes can spread the disaster to groups of people who had stayed away from the addictions of passionate speculation' (1876: 315). Yet he agrees with Tooke on the adverse consequences of prudent banking. In the course of a crisis cautionary discretion of banks leads to strong contractions of lending and note issues. In this way the decline of the price level produces a corresponding downward adjustment of the monetary aggregate – clearly a case of reverse causation. The feedback of prices to credit is intensified by the abrupt change in the real rate of interest that results from concomitant increases in the risk premium and the fall of sales prices. The decrease in the loan supply is thus followed by a decrease in loan demand. The volume and share of distress borrowing rises, on the other hand, without any consideration of the rate of interest. In his passages on this phenomenon Knies comes close to modern discussions of adverse selection in finance. But the Fisher effect is not relevant in this context, because deflation is not anticipated by (any of) the parties when they conclude the loan contracts. In the view of Knies, the core problem is the determination of note issues by private profit interests. Since the underlying credit relations play a significant role in 'the causation of modern crises', he pleads for a state monopoly on note issue that should be used to stabilize the monetary system both before and during crises (1873: Ch. III.7, 1879: Ch. XIV). The tune of his message is very similar to the thrust of the argument in another book that came out in the same year: Walter Bagehot's *Lombard Street* (1873).

THE ROLE OF METALLISM

This long summary of Knies's positions on money, credit and interest has exposed two core propositions that the modern reader might find incompatible with each other. On the one hand, Knies emphasizes the eminent importance of credit (including bank notes) for trade and development. On the other hand, he insists that only full-blooded coins are and can be money (even though the monetary aggregate – or, in the terminology of Knies, the 'quantity of means of payment' – may include bank notes). How do these two propositions go together?

There are three possible interpretations. The propositions may be read as a general warning. Or they are taken to reflect the *Zeitgeist*, if not the state of the art in the 1870s. Or they are understood as an attempt to make the value theory of Knies consistent.

Following the first interpretation, Knies's trilogy should be read as a general warning of the systemic risks of credit – and consequently as a call for financial regulations according to the principles of solidity. That interpretation may be favoured by the friends of the gold standard, but it does not find support in the works of Knies. He certainly demanded political restrictions on credit and warned of its abuse by way of seignorage. But the passages about moral hazard and the speculative amplification of business cycles are not normative comments; they are part of the positive analysis. Moreover, they are well balanced by long discourses about the social advantages of credit. It should be noted that Knies, unlike many of his contemporaries, did not demand any quantitative restriction of the credit supply to gold (or silver) reserves. He was an autometallist in the sense of believing in natural limits of credit that are enforced by the demand for gold and silver in other uses. The state should certainly take control of the note issue in order to prevent excesses which would have to be corrected by painful crises. But Knies was highly critical of interest regulations and other restrictions on banking. He was just as much in favour of establishing 'a sufficient degree of elasticity of credit' as he was concerned with the 'solidity of credit'.

As for the *Zeitgeist* interpretation, it may be argued that it was completely out of the question for Knies and his contemporaries that the international monetary system could work without any commodity base. Even this interpretation is easily refuted by the evidence of the works in question. Knies developed his metallist position in critique of other authors who had put forward visions of pure credit economies. It seems that Knies's exceptional preoccupation with the phenomenon of credit had been stimulated by the three-stage theory of his teacher and friend Bruno Hildebrand, who postulated that societies naturally evolve first from barter economies into money economies and then into credit economies – a blessed state in which wasteful competition is superseded by mutual trust (Hildebrand, 1848: 276–9). In his critique of Hildebrand and similar visions of Henry Dunning Macleod, Knies asserted again and again that 'in its functions as a medium of exchange, our metallic money . . . may, to some extent, be replaced by "substitutes" and various manipulations of transactions, but not in the least in its function of a general standard of value' – because as such it 'must itself be an object of value' (1860: 154 f, 1873: 113 f, 1876: 63–95, 1879: 205 f).

This insistence on the intrinsic value of the standard of value can be read as support for the third interpretation, according to which Knies developed his metallism from his utility theory of value. Following this interpretation, he tried to avoid the circular reasoning of marginal utility theory that Wicksell (1903) came to denounce as 'the blind spot of monetary theory': namely to propose that the exchange value of money is determined by its utility (just as the value of any other good), with its utility depending on its purchasing power – and hence on its exchange value. Knies attempted to preserve the unity of monetary theory and value or price theory by defining money as a valuable good. Even though he had an early notion of the Clower constraint, which draws a strict dividing line between money (as the general medium of exchange) and goods,[16] he insisted that money must have intrinsic value derived from alternative uses of its physical properties.

Historical progress in money and banking has falsified this hypothesis. In the words of Knies, gold has been replaced by 'wooden iron' – or, to put it differently, autometallism has been knocked out by fiat money. It is with some irony of history that Knies's other metaphor – his phrase about 'trust based on distrust', which was coined to demonstrate the absurdity of the notion of 'credit money' – helps to understand why fiat money has come to rule the roost. Fiat money does not normally come into existence independently. It is created in reaction to the banks' extension of loans and deposits, which induces some demand for cash. Fiat money is in this way based on 'trust', on the expectation that the loan-financed projects will pay off. On the other hand, fiat money is not a claim to anything else – as Knies himself had pointed out (see above). Its use as a definite means of payment in the settlement of debts shows that, at the same time, 'trust' (in terms of loans) is based on 'distrust' (in claims to cash).

Why could fiat money take over the role of the standard of value? Because it is (at least hypothetically) more stable than commodity money. As Knies noted, money in its function as a standard of value differs from other standards by being variable (1858: 272–8, 1873: 130–34). Yet he overlooked that the variability of a standard may impair its functionality. In the case of a standard of value, variations in value produce specific costs of information and bargaining that may reduce its acceptance. This is why, not long after the publication of Knies's trilogy, monetary theory began to move towards inflation targeting.[17]

If monetary policy is oriented towards minimizing changes in the general price level (measured by some composite index), it cannot be restricted to tracking the variations in the supply and demand for a specific good such as gold. Since money is now completely freed from any ties to a commodity base, its acceptance must be guaranteed by keeping the purchasing power of nominal incomes and wealth more or less constant. In other words, since money is no longer 'scarce by nature', its functional 'scarcity' must be contrived by monetary policy. The interaction between such policy and the acceptance of the respective currency by wealth owners and other agents reveals externalities in the use of a standard of value that have made any alternative uses of money obsolete.

Equating the value of money with its purchasing power is no longer only a theoretical shortcut. It is a matter of fact. Yet it would be anachronistic to blame Knies for having overlooked the forces that have helped that tautology to come true. In his time, price indexation was in its infancy. The pioneering works of Tooke, Newmarch, Soetbeer and others had not yet been translated into guidelines for monetary policy. Moreover, a quick look at the inflation record of the twentieth century shows that it would be naïve to describe the evolution of monetary policy as the fulfilment of dreams about a constant standard of value. Even in our day Knies would be able to collect plenty of evidence for his observation that many crises result from conflicts between demand for an elastic supply of credit and the contrived scarcity of means of payment that appears necessary to ensure the payment's acceptance. Whether the costs of stabilizing the monetary system have been lowered by freeing it from its commodity base remains an open question.

With the benefit of hindsight we may state that Knies's metallism is outdated. Yet the obsolescence of his theory of the exchange value of money is not just a matter of history. The theory was inconsistent right from its conception. As Knies started by declaring the fungibility of money – in modern terms, its acceptance – a determinant of its exchange value, he should have gone through with this reasoning in virtuous circles, acknowledging that the existence of positive externalities in the use of intrinsically useless means of payment, which are created as a by-product of credit, may be a sufficient explanation of the value of money. This argument would at least have been consistent with his utility-based approach to the theory of value. Knies preferred instead to stick to his 'real illusion' of a monetary good, which relegated him to the ranks of the neglected thinkers in the history of economic ideas.

CONCLUDING REMARKS

In his attempts to integrate money and credit into the framework of value theory, Knies has apparently chosen the wrong track. Yet his approach is instructive in so far as it helps to expose fundamental difficulties in modern attempts to integrate intrinsically useless money into the framework of a general equilibrium theory that is based on the concept of marginal utility. Knies would hardly have approved of the modern approaches to modelling money that are, for example, presented in the canonical *Handbook of Monetary Economics* (1990). The models that are based on overlapping generations, cash-in-advance constraints or other frictions set their focus on this or that function of money, presenting it as a solution looking for the adequate problem. The most popular modelling strategy is to find some friction that provides a tractable (and mostly just a minimal) deviation from the core model of perfect markets. Along this route, modern approaches produce shortcuts that were sharply criticized by Knies:

> Money gains acceptance as such by way of its functions. But it is quite inadmissible to form a scientific judgement simply by selecting one or the other of the widely recognized functions of money ... On the contrary, the essential properties of money must extend far beyond the diversity of its particular functions, such that money can fulfill them all. (1873: 112 f)

If Knies himself failed to provide a general explanation of the essential properties of money, what was his positive contribution to monetary theory? There is no straightforward answer to this question. His systematic exposition of the functions of money and banking is now the standard fare of textbooks to the extent that nobody seems (or needs) to care where those patterns came from and how much they were influenced by Knies, Walker or other writers of their time.

What Knies wrote about expectations under uncertainty and information asymmetries in terms of moral hazard and problems of state verification, looks very modern. Unfortunately the clairvoyance of the old masters itself is – at least for some time 'ex post' – a state verification problem. It is recognized only once the corresponding (re)discoveries have been made in modern theory. And then it is rarely possible to ascribe the discovery to any specific influence of some old master.

Yet there are a few cases in which the influence of Knies on other old masters is (more or less) well documented. Eugen von Böhm-Bawerk, John Bates Clark, Edwin R.A. Seligman, Max Weber and Friedrich Wieser were all students in the seminar of Knies at the University of Heidelberg.[18] Böhm-Bawerk, Clark and Seligman contributed to the *Festschrift* for Knies, which is still well known for Böhm-Bawerk's critique of the Marxian system (Böhm-Bawerk, 1896). Weber was a successor of Knies as professor of political economy, both at Freiburg and at Heidelberg. Even though Böhm-Bawerk, who quoted Knies extensively in his works on capital and interest, and Weber, who wrote a long essay on the methodology of Knies, were highly critical of their teacher, it is quite evident that their thinking was strongly influenced by him.[19]

In the context of credit theory, perhaps the strongest connection between Knies and modern monetary theory was established by Wicksell in his *Interest and Prices* (1898). In the section on Knies's synthesis of currency and banking concepts, it was shown that his strict separation of money and credit made Knies define the means of payment that are created by way of bank lending as factors that affect the velocity of circulation of money. The same trick was used by Wicksell in his attempt to prove the general validity of the quantity theory. Defining the cashless transfers between bank accounts as a factor of velocity, Wicksell was able to extend his quantity-theoretical explanation of the value of money to the hypothetical extreme of a pure credit economy, which helped to bring out the interaction of interest and prices.

Developing this vision of a cashless world, Wicksell (1898 [1936: 66]) explicitly referred to another idea of Knies: to the law of large numbers as the base of the mechanism by which the banks can create loans and deposits in addition to the deposits they have received through payments. Wicksell is nowadays ranked among the fathers of monetary macroeconomics and inflation targeting. He was, at any rate, one of the earliest economists to demand that 'the regulation of prices' be freed from 'the caprices of the production and consumption of gold' (1898 [1936: 194]). It is an irony of fate that his use of Kniesian ideas helped to discredit the metallism of Knies and his contemporaries.

NOTES

* I wish to thank Bob Dimand, Riccardo Faucci, Harald Hagemann and the participants of the conference of the *Dogmenhistorischer Ausschuß des Vereins für Socialpolitik* at Ulm, 1999, and of the session at the ESHET meetings at Graz, 2000, for helpful comments and references. It goes without saying that I am supposed to take the blame for all remaining errors.
1. See also Wagner (1937: 54f) and Salin (1951: 141).
2. Barkai (1989: 184, 197) gives clear priority to Roscher for having developed his monetary theory a generation (about 20 years) before Knies who is said to have 'adamantly' followed 'Roscher in his vision of nature of money and the theory of the determinants of its value'. This could be read as support for Schumpeter's verdict of non-originality.
3. For surveys see, for example, Diehl and Mombert (1923) and Wieser (1927). For critical assessments of Knapp (1905) see Ellis (1934) and Trautwein (1998).
4. In the companion volume to the (1996) reprint of *Das Geld*, Häuser (1996) sets the focus on Knies's analysis of the functions of money, and Yagi (1996) examines Knies's critique of Marx (1867).
5. See Trautwein (1999) for a more detailed discussion of Knies's monetary writings, in particular with regard to capital theory and to Knies's use of the historical method.
6. In the following, all references and quotations that carry dates refer only to works of Knies; translations from the German original are all mine.
7. Following Schumpeter (1954: 1086) and Häuser (1996: 37 n.9), this functionalistic motto was not – as is nowadays often assumed – coined by John Hicks, but by Francis A. Walker, a contemporary of Knies.

8. See also Häuser (1996: 39ff.), who emphasizes the pioneering role of Knies in this respect.
9. Knies (1873: 115ff.) originally defines the fungibility of money as its interchangeability: '[O]ne quantity of it can function as the equivalent of a second or third quantity of the same size'. In the further course of his treatise on money, he shifts the emphasis from homogeneity to marketability in the sense of general acceptance.
10. A *Lot* or (in Knies's old spelling) a *Loth* is an ancient measure varying between 15.5 and 16.6 g.
11. Even in leases of real capital, some risks cannot be insured against and must be borne by the creditor (such as the effects of certain catastrophes, wars and so on). It is, on the other hand, possible to pool and insure against risks in certain categories of monetary loans. In another chapter of the same volume, Knies himself mentions 'insurance premia' in the interest rate on bank loans (1879: 260).
12. For a critical comment on Senior's theory of capital and interest, see Trautwein (2000).
13. However, this is not to suggest any (direct) influence of Knies on Irving Fisher. Even though Fisher visited Germany in 1893–94, when Knies was still professor in Heidelberg, he did not get acquainted with the latter – unlike other American economists of the time, such as John Bates Clark. Fisher (1906: 54–60) refers to Knies only in the context of capital theory.
14. Barkai (1989: 197) argues that Knies's 'theory of the value of money is Roscher par excellence. It goes without saying that he is in full accord with him on the rejection of the quantity theory, which at best both would view as a Ricardian aberration from his own teachings on value, and at worst an inexplicable English vice. It was this message of [Roscher's] *Grundlagen* – the irrelevance of the quantity of money and of interest rate for the determination of the price level – which became the hallmark of German economics through the earlier 1920s'. Even though Knies made some critical remarks about the quantity theory, they are not to be found in the passages quoted by Barkai (who refers to Knies 1879: 156 f). In particular, as will be seen below, it is not correct to infer that Knies discarded the quantity theory altogether – at any rate not as radically as Roscher. For a more detailed account of Knies's reception of the currency–banking controversy see Holtfrerich (1988).
15. Knies does not condemn speculation, but he discusses various aspects of moral hazard in business loans. According to Knies, the fundamental problem is that borrowers reap all the profits, if they are successful, whereas they let the lenders take their share, if they fail.
16. See the passage in Knies (1873: 296) which has been quoted above. Mises (1980: 96 f) actually praised Knies for his distinction between consumer goods, producer goods and exchange goods.
17. See Laidler (1991) and Boianovsky and Trautwein (2001).
18. See Eisermann (1996) and Schefold (1996: 6).
19. See Böhm-Bawerk (1884, 1888), and Weber (1982). On the complicated relation between the capital theories of Knies and Böhm-Bawerk, see Trautwein (1999: fn 27). On the influence of Knies on Weber, see Hennis (1988: 54–77).

REFERENCES

Bagehot, Walter (1873), *Lombard Street. A Description of the Money Market*, London: Kegan Paul.
Barkai, Haim (1989), 'The old historical school: Roscher on money and monetary issues', *History of Political Economy*, 21: 179–200.
Böhm-Bawerk, Eugen von (1884), *Geschichte und Kritik der Kapitalzins-Theorieen*, Innsbruck: Wagner'sche Universitätsbuchhandlung.
Böhm-Bawerk, Eugen von (1896), 'Zum Abschluß des Marxschen Systems', in Otto von Boenigk (ed.), *Staatswissenschaftliche Arbeiten: Festgabe für Karl Knies*, Berlin: Haering: 87–205.

Böhm-Bawerk, Eugen von (1888), *Positive Theorie des Kapitals*, Vol. 1, Jena: Gustav Fischer.

Boianovsky, Mauro, and Hans-Michael Trautwein (2001), 'The Bank Rate of Interest as the Regulator of Prices – an Early Draft by Knaut Wicksell', *History of Political Economy* 33, pp. 485–513.

Diehl, Karl and Paul Mombert (eds) (1923), *Ausgewählte Lesestücke zum Studium der Politischen Ökonomie. Erster Band: Zur Lehre vom Geld*, 4th edition, Jena: Gustav Fischer.

Eisermann, Gottfried (1996), 'Carl Knies in seiner Zeit', in the companion volume to the facsimile reprint of *Das Geld* by Carl Knies, Düsseldorf: Wirtschaft und Finanzen: 53–97.

Ellis, Howard (1934), *German Monetary Theory, 1905–33*, Cambridge, MA: Harvard University Press.

Fisher, Irving (1906), *The Nature of Capital and Income*, New York: Macmillan.

Häuser, Karl (1996), 'Knies als Geldtheoretiker', in the companion volume to the facsimile reprint of *Das Geld* by Carl Knies, Düsseldorf: Wirtschaft und Finanzen: 31–52.

Handbook of Monetary Economics (1990), ed. by Benjamin Friedman und Frank Hahn, Amsterdam, New York: North Holland.

Hennis, Wilhelm (1988), 'Eine "Wissenschaft vom Menschen". Max Weber und die deutsche Nationalökonomie der Historischen Schule', in Wolfgang Mommsen und Wolfgang Schwentker (eds), *Max Weber und seine Zeitgenossen*, Göttingen: Vandenhoeck & Ruprecht: 41–83.

Hildebrand, Bruno (1848), *Die Nationalökonomie der Gegenwart und Zukunft*, Frankfurt: Rütten.

Holtfrerich, Carl-Ludwig (1988), 'Zur Rezeption der Bullion- und der Banking-Currency-School- Kontroverse in Deutschland', in Harald Scherf (ed.), *Studien zur Entwicklung der ökonomischen Theorie VI*, Berlin: Duncker & Humblot: 9–27.

Knapp, Georg Friedrich (1905), *Staatliche Theorie des Geldes*, Leipzig: Duncker & Humblot.

Knies, Carl (1853), *Die politische Oekonomie vom Standpunkte der geschichtlichen Methode*, Braunschweig: Schwetschke; 2nd revised edition: *Die politische Oekonomie vom geschichtlichen Standpuncte*, Braunschweig: Schwetschke (1883).

Knies, Carl (1858), 'Ueber die Geldentwerthung und die mit ihr in Verbindung gebrachten Erscheinungen', *Zeitschrift für die gesammte Staatswissenschaft*, 14: 260–92.

Knies, Carl (1859, 1860), 'Erörterungen über den Credit', *Zeitschrift für die gesammte Staatswissenschaft*, 15: 561–90 (Part I) and 16: 150–208 (Part II).

Knies, Carl (1873), *Das Geld. Darlegung der Grundlehren von dem Gelde (Geld und Credit, Erste Abtheilung)*, Berlin: Weidmann.

Knies, Carl (1876), *Der Credit. Erste Hälfte (Geld und Credit, Zweite Abtheilung)*, Berlin: Weidmann.

Knies, Carl (1879), *Der Credit. Zweite Hälfte (Geld und Kredit, Zweite Abtheilung)*, Berlin: Weidmann.

Knight, Frank (1921), *Risk, Uncertainty and Profit*, New York: Macmillan.

Laidler, David (1991), *The Golden Age of the Quantity Theory*, Hemel Hempstead: Philip Allan.

Marx, Karl (1867), *Das Kapital. Kritik der politischen Oekonomie*, Vol. 1, Hamburg.

Mises, Ludwig von (1980), *The Theory of Money and Credit*, reprint of the 2nd English edition of *Theorie des Geldes und der Umlaufsmittel* (1912), Indianapolis: Free Press.

Roscher, Wilhelm (1854), *Die Grundlagen der Nationalökonomie. Ein Hand- und Lesebuch für Geschäftsmänner und Studierende*, Stuttgart: Cotta, translated by John J. Lalor as *Principles of Political Economy*, Chicago: Callaghan & Co.

Salin, Edgar (1951), *Geschichte der Volkswirtschaftslehre*, 4th edition, Bern, Tübingen: Haupt.

Schefold, Bertram (1987), 'Karl Knies', in *The New Palgrave*, Vol. 3, London, Basingstoke: Macmillan: 55.

Schefold, Bertram (1996), 'Zum Geleit', introduction to the companion volume of the facsimile reprint of *Das Geld* by Carl Knies (1873), Düsseldorf: Wirtschaft und Finanzen: 5–12.

Schumpeter, Joseph Alois (1954), *History of Economic Analysis*, London: Allen & Unwin.

Senior, Nassau W. (1836), *An Outline of the Science of Political Economy*, London: W. Clowes & Sons.

Trautwein, Hans-Michael (1998), 'G.F. Knapp – an economist with institutional complexion', forthcoming in Warren Samuels (ed.), *European Economists of the Early 20th Century – Studies of Neglected Continental Thinkers*, Vol. II, Aldershot: Edward Elgar.

Trautwein, Hans-Michael (1999), 'Knies' Erörterungen über den Kredit', forthcoming in Christian Scheer (ed.), *Studien zur Entwicklung der ökonomischen Theorie XX: Roscher und die Ältere Historische Schule*, Berlin: Duncker & Humblot.

Trautwein, Hans Michael (2000), 'Seniors Beitrag zur Kapital- und Zinstheorie', in Nassau William Senior, *An Outline of the Science of Political Economy – Vademecum zu einem Klassiker der Verteilungstheorie* (companion volume of the facsimile reprint of Senior (1836), Düsseldorf: Wirtschaft und Finanzen, pp. 53–77.

Wagner, Valentin Fritz (1937), *Geschichte der Kredittheorien*, Wien: Julius Springer.

Weber, Max (1982), 'Knies und das Irrationalitätsproblem', in Johannes Winckelmann (ed.), *Max Weber: Gesammelte Aufsätze zur Wissenschaftslehre*, 5th edition, Tübingen: Mohr: 41–145.

Wicksell, Knut (1898), *Geldzins und Güterpreise. Eine Studie über die den Tauschwert des Geldes bestimmenden Ursachen*, Jena: Gustav Fischer, translated as *Interest and Prices. A Study of the Causes Regulating the Value of Money*, London: Macmillan (1936).

Wicksell, Knut (1903), 'Den dunkla punkten i penningteorin', *Ekonomisk Tidskrift*, 5: 485–507.

Wieser, Friedrich (1927), 'Theorie des Geldes. Allgemeine Lehre vom Gelde', in *Handwörterbuch der Staatswissenschaften* (4th ed.), Vol. 4, Jena: Gustav Fischer: 681–717.

Yagi, Kiichiro (1996), 'Carl Knies und die Wertformenanalyse bei Marx', in the companion volume to the facsimile reprint of *Das Geld* by Carl Knies (1873), Düsseldorf: Wirtschaft und Finanzen: 99–115.

PART VI

Trade and Location

13. On the new economic geography and the progress of geographical economics

Stephen J. Meardon

The 'new economic geography' is an offspring of international trade theory whose birth was heralded by Paul Krugman, its initiator and most prominent advocate, as a way to 'incorporate the insights of the long but informal tradition in [economic geography] into formal models' (1991: 484). Krugman's methodological view of the role of formal models in economics – 'as a practical matter formalism is crucial to progress in economic thought' (1998b: 1829) – buttresses his advancement of the new economic geography as an exemplar of progress in economics. My purpose in this chapter is to think about the sense in which Krugman's advancement is valid, and the sense in which it is problematic.

KRUGMAN'S HISTORICAL NARRATIVE AND APPRAISAL

Krugman's view of the progress made between the older literature and the new economic geography is repeated in numerous articles and books, among them Krugman (1991, 1993, 1995, 1998a, 1999) and Fujita, Krugman and Venables (1999). His narrative runs basically as follows: many of the fundamental ideas of the new economic geography were expressed much earlier by authors of international trade theory, spatial economics and development economics, among them Bertil Ohlin, August Lösch and Gunnar Myrdal. However, these theorists were not able to reconcile satisfactorily a perfectly competitive market structure, which they were accustomed to modelling, with increasing returns to scale, which they knew was necessary to engender 'circular causation' and the resulting spatial agglomeration of production. In the face of this obstacle theorists like Ohlin and Myrdal (if not Lösch) resorted to purely textual and intuitive explanations. Indeed they made a principled stance of leaving the math aside and explaining with text alone.

Yet in the end it was a vain stance. Economic theory is essentially a collection of models. Broad insights that are not expressed in model form may temporarily attract attention and even win converts, but they do not endure unless codified in a repro-ducible – and teachable – form. You may not like this tendency; certainly econo-mists tend to be too quick to dismiss what has not been formalized (although I believe that the focus on models is basically right). Like it or not, however, the influence of ideas that have not been embalmed in models soon decays. And this was the fate of [Myrdal and others'] high development theory. (Krugman 1995: 27)

Likewise the influence of spatial economics decayed, as did all of Ohlin's insights that were not captured neatly by the 2 × 2 × 2 Heckscher–Ohlin–Samuelson model. Generations later, though, general equilibrium models of imperfect competition were produced that did reconcile satisfactorily the explicit modelling of market structure with increasing returns. Krugman applied one such model, that of Dixit and Stiglitz (1977), first in international trade theory and later in the long-neglected (by mainstream economists) field of economic geography. The modelling framework he introduced allowed an explanation of spatial agglomeration with some fresh insights, in addition to the heretofore unformalized ones of Ohlin, Lösch and Myrdal: the centrality of increasing returns, the regular patterns of market areas and the circular logic of agglomeration. The new economic geography was born.[1]

So runs Krugman's narrative, and my purpose is not to argue that it is wrong. Nor will I trumpet the irony of his metaphor of modelling as taxidermy and argue against his prescriptions of method (with which I generally agree); nor will I argue against the elegance and desirability of the models themselves (by which I have already been seduced).[2]

Instead, the questions I want to address are as follows. In Krugman's appraisal of the progress of the new economic geography, what is the conse-quence of his wearing at once three hats: those of theorist, methodologist and historian of thought? How seriously can his appraisal, which is partly a self-appraisal, be taken? Does the new economic geography indeed represent 'progress' in economics?

'Progress' will have to be defined, and I will do it in the following way: progress is made only when an author meets the criteria for progress estab-lished by earlier authors, whatever those criteria might be. The definition may seem too permissive, but I will argue to the contrary that it is strict. Like Krug-man's notion of progress, but for an entirely different reason, it rules out nega-tive appraisals by critics external to the research program (for example, Martin, 1999). In addition and more importantly, it rules out positive appraisals that are either self-appraisals (for example, Krugman's) or method-ological appraisals (for example, Krugman's) ostensibly from a privileged position outside the research program. That is to say, the new economic geog-raphy cannot be judged to be progress beyond Ohlin, Myrdal or Lösch just because a new economic geographer says it is so, or just because methodology suggests it is so – but only because Ohlin, or Myrdal, or Lösch have laid out criteria that indicate it is so.

Let us see how the new economic geography fares by this standard. To do so, before discussing the new economic geography, we must review each of the three earlier authors.

OHLIN AND THE INFLUENCES OF HECKSCHER AND CASSEL

The theory of international trade of the nineteenth and early twentieth centuries, encapsulated in works ranging from David Ricardo's *On the Principles of Political Economy and Taxation* ([1821] 1951) to Frank W. Taussig's *International Trade* (1927), did not prohibit discussion of agglomeration, but neither did it encourage such discussion. The theory explained the pattern of trade and gains from trade by means of comparative costs of production. International differences in costs implied, and were implied by, international wage differentials. It was expected that such differentials would exist and persist, because factors that were mobile within countries were fairly immobile between them:

> Thus England would give the produce of the labour of 100 men, for the produce of the labour of 80. Such an exchange could not take place between the individuals of the same country. The labour of 100 Englishmen cannot be given for that of 80 Englishmen, but the produce of the labour of 100 Englishmen may be given for the produce of the labour of 80 Portuguese, 60 Russians, or 120 East Indians. The difference in this respect, between a single country and many, is easily accounted for, by considering the difficulty with which capital moves from one country to another, to seek a more profitable employment, and the activity with which it invariably passes from one province to another in the same country. (Ricardo, [1821] 1951: 135–6)

The theory appeared satisfactory in so far as it was consistent with casual empirical observations: wages *were* observed to differ, and factors *were* rather immobile. Since the evidence corroborated the theory, there was no particular puzzle regarding factor migration, and so no particular reason to wonder about factor agglomeration.

In a roundabout way, the introduction of an alternative explanation of trade based on differences in factor proportions spurred thought about agglomeration. Eli Heckscher ([1919; 1942] 1991) assumed proportions of productive factors to vary both across countries and in the production of different commodities. International differences of factor returns in autarky reflected differences in the relative scarcity of factors, and trade constituted the implicit exchange of the services of a country's relatively abundant factor for the services of its relatively scarce factor. 'Thus trade must continue to expand', he wrote, 'until an *equalization of the relative scarcity of the factors of production has occurred*' (p. 54). In other words, even if factors were immobile between countries, international trade might be expected to equalize wages between countries. The observation that factors were *not* immobile – or at the very least were less immobile in the early twentieth century than they were at the height of Ricardo's career – suggested even more strongly that factor prices ought to be equalized. Yet, Heckscher further observed, factor prices were *not* equalized internationally. His theoretical innovation led him to find a puzzle in evidence that earlier theorists saw as corroboration of their work.

Heckscher considered some obstacles that might prevent factor price equalization. Transportation costs were one such obstacle, and extreme disparities in factor proportions were another (p. 58). As these obstacles prevented factor price equalization, they created the incentives for the migration of factors that clearly took place in reality. Thus, by way of a model that pointed towards factor price equalization even in the presence of factor *immobility*, Heckscher was led to enquire further into factor *mobility*.

Bertil Ohlin, Heckscher's student at the Stockholm Handelshögskolan from 1917 to 1919, followed the direction of his mentor. Ohlin was also influenced, however, by the tutelage of Gustav Cassel, who became his advisor after he enrolled for graduate studies at the Stockholm Högskola in 1920. Cassel had just published in 1918 his *Theoretische Sozialökonomie* (translated into English in 1932 as *The Theory of Social Economy*), founded upon a mathematically specified general equilibrium system of price determination. The circumstances were exactly right for Ohlin, by all accounts a precocious and brilliant student, to meld Heckscher's trade model with Cassel's formal general equilibrium model.[3] To that hybrid Ohlin added innovations of his own and conceived a relationship between trade theory and another field, location theory. He sought a unification of the two fields – attempting to explain, in addition to the pattern of trade, the migration of factors, and with migration the agglomeration of industry.

Cassel's influence upon Ohlin's work lay largely in the modelling tools he taught his student to apply. Cassel wrote that '[i]n order to illustrate clearly the mechanism of pricing, it is necessary to present the relation between the various factors in the price-fixing process in mathematical form' (Cassel, 1932: 137). His model involved a system of simultaneous equations with equal numbers of equations and unknowns, similar to that of Walras. For Cassel, the system of equations was not just an alternative method of illustrating the notion of general equilibrium, which some might prefer to express or read in plain text. Rather, the equations were the only means of understanding general equilibrium deeply:

> In order to illustrate clearly the mechanism of pricing, it is necessary to present the relation between the various factors in the price-fixing process in mathematical form. . . . The work is, however, so arranged that these paragraphs may be omitted without interrupting the general connection. The reader, in that case, will simply have to put aside any thought of a deeper study of the problems just mentioned. (Cassell, 1932: 137)

Cassel broke the Marshallian habit of confining the maths to the appendices. The maths now took centre stage, albeit a very small part of it. Mathematical exposition would gradually come to occupy more space; illustration of the interdependence of variables by means of a system of simultaneous equations would become the standard for models to be considered both relevant and persuasive. Ohlin adhered to that standard, both in his 1924 PhD thesis, *Handelns Teori* (*Trade Theory*), and in his expansion of it in the 1933 classic *Interregional and International Trade*.

The 'mathematical illustration' in Ohlin's *Handelns Teori* follows Cassel's style and notation, but extends his analysis to two trading regions. Each region, as in Cassel's model, produces multiple goods with multiple factors; but unlike Cassel's model the production coefficients are variable, depending on factor prices. As Heckscher had done with his verbal model, Ohlin used his algebraic model to study the assumptions required for equalization of factor prices across regions to occur. And like Heckscher, having worked with the assumptions, he hastened to relax them and move in the direction of greater realism.

The foremost barrier he considered to equalization of factor prices was interregional transportation costs (Ohlin, [1924] 1991: 103). Transportation costs would drive a wedge between the price paid for a commodity in the region that exports it and the price paid in the region that imports it – and if commodity prices were not equal across regions, neither would factor prices be equal. Furthermore, if factor prices were unequal between regions then there would be an incentive for migration between regions.

Trade theory as Ohlin endeavoured to refashion it concerned commerce among various geographical units; between the geographical units there existed transportation costs for trade in commodities and partial but incomplete mobility of productive factors. That much he had in common with Heckscher. But with no apparent antecedent in the work of either Heckscher or Cassel, Ohlin seized upon an idea: there was no reason to assume the geographical units were countries. If international trade theory allowed varying degrees of transportation costs and factor mobility, then the differences between international trade, interregional trade or 'interlocal trade' were *just* a matter of degree. All ought to be subsumed by the same theory.

Ohlin further developed this idea of 'a general localization theory', as he put it (1933: 243), in *Interregional and International Trade*. He wrote that location theorist Alfred Weber's work had 'profoundly influenced the material' he presented in at least one chapter, and he discussed the concentration of industry in terms of the opposition of agglomerating and deglomerating forces. It is clear that when he wrote in 1933 that '[i]nternational trade theory cannot be understood except in relation to and as a part of the general localization theory' (p. 142), he meant not only, as in his 1924 PhD thesis, that the same theory should apply to international, interregional and interlocal trade. He meant that the theory should subsume, in addition to trade theory, the existing field of location theory that in 1924 was not familiar to him. The general theory would be one of *trade and agglomeration*.

Ultimately, though, Ohlin was unable to build the theory he envisioned with the tools he had committed himself to using. In so far as he brought trade theory closer to becoming a special case of location theory, he did it by abandoning the common assumptions of factor immobility and frictionless trade. Having done that, he could only take the analysis so far while remaining anchored to the Casselian general equilibrium framework. A main feature of the real-world space economy that Ohlin thought the 'general localization theory' ought to explain was the persistent inequality of factor prices across space; yet even *partial* factor mobility, meaning mobility hindered by some friction, would ultimately equalize factor prices if factor movement continued until an equilibrium was reached. Ohlin concluded that '[a] study of interregional trade on the basis of partial mobility of some of the productive factors obviously cannot involve the investigation of equilibria . . . Instead, an analysis of different shocks and their effects must be a description of a process' (Ohlin, [1924] 1991: 103).

'Process' was outside the boundaries of the static Casselian model, but a description of it could at least be grounded on the model. There was another problem, though. In reality factor prices tended to be unequal spatially, not just during an 'adjustment process', but persistently: such was the case between cities and the surrounding countryside. How then did agglomerations of productive factors in cities, and the consequent persistent differences in factor prices between cities and the countryside, arise? Again the Casselian framework failed Ohlin. He tried to discuss the problem, mentioning the role of 'indivisibilities' (as in fixed costs, which would give rise to increasing returns to scale) in agglomeration – but the more he did so the farther he strayed from his guiding model.

In the end the model could not address adequately a basic question of the general localization theory. In 1979, a few months before he died, in an essay entitled 'Some insufficiencies in the theories of international economic relations', Ohlin wrote,

I made an attempt to use the location and regional approach to the analysis of international commodity and factor movements in the book I published in 1933 and am happy that some prominent economists have made much further progress. ... However, no one has yet made a serious attempt to build a general location theory and introduce national borders and their effects as modifications in order to illuminate international economic relations and their development by a method other than conventional trade theory. (Ohlin, 1979: 6)

To Ohlin, progress meant:

1. Constructing a 'general localization theory' whose models are imbued with the spirit of Casselian general equilibrium.
2. Using the models to explain at once the pattern of international trade, the movement of productive factors between and within nations, and the spatial agglomeration of factors.

LÖSCH

The magnum opus of August Lösch (1906–45), *The Economics of Location*, is very wide-ranging but remembered mostly for the mathematical model at its core. The model represents a large part of what eluded early twentieth-century location theorists Alfred Weber (1929), Andreas Predöhl (1925, 1928), Hans Weigmann (1926) and Tord Palander (1935): a mathematical general equilibrium model that was explicitly spatial, and that furthermore met Weigmann and Palander's requirement of imperfectly competitive markets.

More than any previous location theorist, and more than any author whatsoever since Ohlin, Lösch strove to unify trade theory and location theory. He sought a theory of location, production and trade in continuous space that made no prior assumptions about the relevant geographic units. Ohlin's broadening of the discourse in trade theory to include 'interlocal trade' and 'interregional trade' as well as international trade had been propitious: it made the point that there is something arbitrary and inappropriate about selecting the 'nation' as the relevant unit. Lösch argued, however, that it was just as arbitrary and inappropriate to assume that the Heckscher–Ohlin model was comprised of regions or localities (however those were defined) as of nations. Instead of beginning the analysis with assumptions about the size and nature of economic regions, the unified trade and location theory should let the region itself be endogenous. Lösch proposed a model that would allow him to 'discover whether and how, under rational assumptions, an economic boundary can be expected to arise' (Lösch, 1954: 104). What had to be developed was a theory of 'market areas'.

Lösch began by assuming a flat and featureless plane upon which raw materials, consumers and farmers with aspirations to manufacture goods are distributed evenly. Consumers are identical in their demands for goods, and manufacturers are monopolists in the production of their goods within their market areas. Each manufacturer's good has to be transported from his location in two-dimensional space to all the consumers in his market area. Transportation costs are proportional to distance. For any given mill price a spatial 'demand cone' can be drawn, as in Figure 13.1, with quantity demanded on the vertical axis and spatial coordinates in relation to the manufacturer (who resides at the origin, *P*) on the horizontal plane. Consumers located exactly at the manufacturing site will pay the mill price and demand quantity *PQ*. Consumers located farther away will pay the mill price plus transportation costs, so they will demand a lesser quantity. Beyond a certain distance, represented in Figure 13.1 as *PF*, the manufacturer will not be able to sell his good. The total quantity demanded for any given price is simply the area under the demand cone.

Such is the basic model for individual producers in isolation of each other; it might be considered the 'partial equilibrium' model. How does a network of identical producers behave, though?

Lösch showed diagrammatically that if two-dimensional geographic space were filled as completely as possible with the circular bases of non-overlapping demand cones, then no matter how large or small the circles might be, there would be some consumers not inside any of them. But that would imply the presence of unexploited profit opportunities. The ideal market area thus

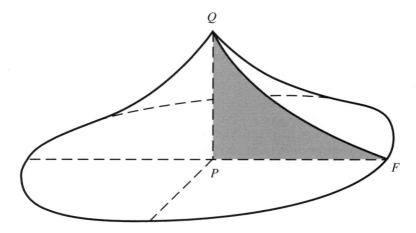

Source: Lösch, 1954: 106.

Figure 13.1   Lösch's spatial demand cone

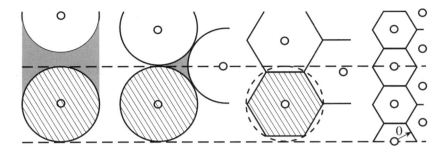

Source: Lösch, 1954: 110.

Figure 13.2 Development of a network of hexagonal market areas, in four stages from left to right

cannot be a circle. It must be a shape that can form a network exhausting all two-dimensional space: specifically, a hexagon. Lösch's thinking is illustrated by Figure 13.2.

Having determined the general shape of market areas, it was possible to specify the general equilibrium problem. Given that the space economy was composed of a network of hexagonal market areas, the variables to be determined simultaneously were the number of hexagons, their common size, the precise coordinates of their centres and the price paid for the goods at the centres.

This model informed all of Lösch's book, established his reputation in location theory and represented very nearly the unification of location theory and trade theory that Ohlin, and also Weigmann and Palander, had sought. The problems the latter three encountered were in modelling space explicitly, modelling explicitly the interdependence of productive units, incorporating imperfectly competitive markets, formalizing the model as a system of simultaneous equations (thus meeting the Casselian standard), explaining spatial variations in equilibrium prices endogenously and drawing from the model a convincing explanation of agglomeration. Lösch accomplished all but the last of these objectives.

He did try to address agglomeration using the model, but the result, while graphically elegant, seems intuitively unsatisfying. Lösch imagined several networks of hexagons superimposed upon one another, each representing market areas for a different good with different transportation costs. Each network consisted of hexagons of a different size, so the centres of its hexagons had different spatial coordinates from those of hexagons in the several other superimposed networks. If one were to look at a map of all the market centres from all networks, there would inevitably be clusters of centers, as shown in Figure 13.3. The clusters represented agglomerations of production.

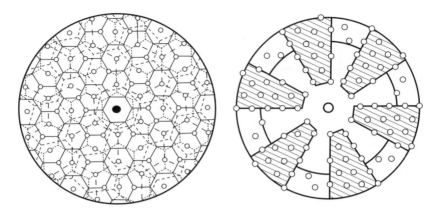

Notes:
Left: superimposed networks of hexagonal market areas.
Right: market area centres in superimposed networks, with hexagonal borders hidden.
Shaded areas are relatively agglomerated.

Source: Lösch, 1954: 125.

Figure 13.3   Löschian agglomeration

This sort of agglomeration is agglomeration by chance – perhaps not an entirely compelling explanation. There might arise a greater objection, though, of which Lösch was well aware: one might say it all makes up a beautiful structure which does not explain much. We do not observe hexagonal market areas, and to the extent that we observe clustering of economic activities, we have no reason to believe it is due to the overlapping of hexagonal market areas. Nor does the model suggest any means of testing whether it is or is not. Lösch's answer to this objection is revealing. He likens the modeller to an architect who, in succumbing to demands for testing, would be submitting his blueprints for comparison to the real world.

> But a comparison with existing structures will not show whether his blueprints are accurate; in our case, that is, whether the theoretical structure has been properly erected. For the existing structure may be as faulty as the projected one. Whoever tries nevertheless to do so, whoever anxiously submits the results of his thinking to the judgment of the existent, that is, to tradition, shows little confidence in his own reason.
>   No! Comparison now has to be drawn no longer to test the theory, but to test reality! Now it must be determined whether reality is rational. (1954: 363)

To Lösch, progress meant:

1. Building an abstract mathematical model in which the boundaries of regions, that is, market areas, are defined endogenously rather than arbitrarily.
2. Examining patterns of market areas that arise from the model in order to determine the ideal.
3. Comparing ideal patterns of market areas with reality – not to test the model, but to test the optimality of reality.

MYRDAL

Near the end of his life Gunnar Myrdal admitted to a 'conservatism' of thought that led him to retain and repeat more or less unchanged views throughout his career (1984: 159). His primary concern was the persistence of underdevelopment in poor regions, and his prescription emphasized internationally coordinated aid and planning. To make his case he developed the 'principle of cumulative causation' and applied it to analyse numerous variations of the underdevelopment problem: poverty among black Americans in *An American Dilemma* (1944), international inequalities in *Economic Theory and Underdeveloped Regions* (1957) and inequalities of wealth within countries in *Asian Drama* (1968). The principle is central to his entire oeuvre, and appears again in his Nobel lecture ([1974] 1989: 13).

The principle of cumulative causation opposes the notion of stable equilibrium at the core of neoclassical general equilibrium theory. Contrary to that notion,

> there is no such tendency toward automatic self-stabilization in the social system. The system is by itself not moving toward any sort of balance between forces but is constantly on the move away from such a situation. In the normal case a change does not call forth countervailing changes but, instead, supporting changes, which move the system in the same direction as the first changes but much further. Because of such circular causation a social process tends to become cumulative and often to gather speed at an accelerating rate. (Myrdal, 1957: 13)

Applied to regional disparities, the principle of cumulative causation implies that migration, capital movement and trade have 'backwash' effects whereby any minor initial advantages possessed by one region will tend to increase until regional inequalities are dramatic. Regions expand in economic size by attracting labour and capital, but rather than a decrease in factor prices in the expanding region and a rise in factor prices in the contracting region, which would eliminate incentives for further factor movements and restore 'equilibrium', the result is exactly the opposite. Investment attracts yet more investment, and migration more migration. The world is characterized, in other words, by increasing returns. A rising volume of trade between regions, by broadening the market for the output of growing regions, reinforces the rationale by which minute initial advantages become decisively established and then widen. Ultimately some regions will be rich and others poor, for no reason other than that some are rich and others poor.

> [W]ithin broad limits the power of attraction of a [commercial] center today has its origin mainly in the historical accident that something was once started there and not in a number of other places where it could equally well or better have been started, and that the start met with success. Thereafter the ever-increasing internal and external economies – interpreted in the widest sense of the word to include, for instance, a working population trained in various crafts, easy communication, the feeling of growth and elbow room, and the spirit of new enterprise – fortified and sustained their continuous growth at the expense of other localities and regions where, instead, relative stagnation or regression became the pattern. (Myrdal, 1957: 27)

To the extent that neoclassical general equilibrium economics did not allow expression of the principle of cumulative causation, Myrdal argued that it ought to be set aside. In one of his stronger statements he called for young economists in developing countries 'to have the courage to throw away large structures of meaningless, irrelevant and sometimes blatantly inadequate doctrines and theoretical approaches' (1957: 104). One might take this as a repudiation of mathematical modelling, but that would be a misreading of Myrdal. To him the problem was not modelling *per se* but the misapplication of the particular models associated with 'neoclassical general equilibrium theory' – by which Myrdal, as an economist trained in the interwar period and above all as a Swede, meant Cassel's system and its progeny, Heckscher–Ohlin–Samuelson.

The equilibrium concept in Cassel's system led economists to complacency in addressing problems of underdevelopment, for numerous reasons. It conjured up the illusion of a harmony of interests, when in fact interests were commonly in opposition; it suggested that disparities were self-correcting, and thus led to an anti-state bias, when in fact state intervention was necessary to prevent disparities from becoming cumulatively wider; it led to a presumption of the optimality of free trade, when in fact free trade, at least in developing countries, was a 'logically untenable and, indeed, fallacious doctrine' (Myrdal, 1957: 98). But while Cassel's system led inexorably to untenable results, modelling in general need not. Whereas the neoclassical equilibrium metaphor was one of a ball settling at the bottom of a bowl, other models and other metaphors were conceivable: for example a cylinder rolling on a plane, coming to rest in 'equilibrium' anywhere on the plane; or a pencil balanced precariously on its tip until pushed only slightly, and then falling at an accelerating rate (Myrdal, 1957: 145). These alternative metaphors could correspond to alternative mathematical structures:

Marshall's theory of external economies and, indeed, much earlier analysis of increasing returns had reached outside the field dominated by the notion of stable equilibrium. . . . The present lively discussion on the economic development of underdeveloped countries, including the building of dynamic models, also often moves outside the theoretical framework of the stable equilibrium approach. (Myrdal, 1957: 146)

Not only was such a modelling effort conceivable, it was desirable. Indeed it was necessary for – in Myrdal's own words – 'progress'. Specifically, the 'coefficients of circular causation of all the factors in the system' would have to be studied in order to make 'real progress in national planning' (1957: 88); in addition the model would have to be synthesized with trade theory in order to make progress in understanding the real world:

> If ever we come nearer to the formulation of a general theory of economic underde-velopment and development, it would remain a difficult but necessary task to inte-grate it into our general economic theory and, in particular, to make it and the theory of international trade consistent with each other. For, to hold logically unconnected and, in fact, mutually inconsistent theories is hardly a satisfactory state of affairs.
>
> To accomplish this integration would most certainly, on the one hand, imply considerable adjustments and changes in general economic theory. The changes would then reflect the progress in our perception of the world economy attributable to the intensified studies of the long-term problems related to the facts of economic inequalities and the dynamic processes of underdevelopment and development. (Myrdal, 1957: 161)

Contrary to Krugman's narrative, then, Myrdal did not take a principled stand for textual analysis against mathematically specified theory. Rather, he took a principled stand for abandoning theory that was inapplicable to prob-lems of underdevelopment, whether the theory was mathematized or not – and supplanting the theory with one that was applicable, mathematized or not. Having taken that stand he laid out the criteria for further progress. To Myrdal, progress entailed:

1. Developing mathematically specified models illustrating the principle of cumulative causation, allowing departures from equilibrium that were not necessarily self-correcting.
2. Taking the model to the data to estimate the 'coefficients' of circular causation.
3. Synthesizing the model with international trade theory.

KRUGMAN AND THE NEW ECONOMIC GEOGRAPHY

It is common for papers in the new economic geography genre to begin by articulating what is known as the 'folk theorem of spatial economics'. The reader is first asked to imagine a world in which productive factors are spread evenly across space – to abstract from obvious geographical determinants of industry location like mountains and rivers, and allow the author to explain how concentrations of productive factors might otherwise arise. The folk theorem states that if productive factors are spread evenly over space, and transporting goods across space is costly, then increasing returns of some kind must be central to an explanation of why we see spatial agglomerations of economic activity. If instead there were diminishing or constant returns, then in the face of transportation costs for inputs and outputs it would be advantageous to produce all goods in very small quantities where factors of production were already located – that is, everywhere. Every agent would be a firm in himself, and there would be no agglomeration.

In order to explain spatial agglomeration without relying on 'geography' in the traditional sense (mountains, rivers and so on), the new economic geography must therefore allow some role for increasing returns. The next question is how to represent the increasing returns: for whom will they be internal economies, and for whom will they be external? The answer depends on what sort of spatial agglomeration one is interested in explaining and the modelling tools one uses. By commonly employing the Dixit and Stiglitz model of monopolistic competition, the new economic geography features increasing returns at the firm level that in turn produce pecuniary externalities transmitted through markets.

The link between increasing returns internal to the firm and pecuniary externalities functions as follows: if one firm increases production, this increases demand for its inputs, which are produced in part by a second firm. The second firm witnesses the higher price for its product and takes this as a signal to increase production. In doing so, because of firm-level increasing returns, the second firm's average cost decreases. Thus the production decision of the first firm has the external effect, transmitted through the price mechanism, of decreasing the second firm's costs; and thus a modelling tool that allows firm-level increasing returns also allows the representation in general equilibrium of economy-wide externalities. This makes the modelling tool best suited for studying the largest and broadest spatial agglomerations.

'Agglomeration' in new economic geography models means that more monopolistically competitive firms are located in one region than in another. The discussion of the determinants of agglomeration and dispersion is framed in terms of the opposing forces favouring each.

Acting in favour of dispersion is the interaction of transport costs and possibly – this may vary among models – either a dispersed output market (when transport costs are high) or factor market competition (when transport costs are low). To illustrate, assume that some share of the output market is fixed geographically in each of two points, representing two regions in geographic space. If transport costs are high enough there is almost autarky between the two regions, so industry must be dispersed across regions.

The same result may be obtained, however, if transport costs are low enough. Agglomeration bids up factor prices in the more agglomerated region. If factor prices were higher in that region, however, and transport costs low, there would be profit opportunities for firms to enter the less agglomerated region and ship a large portion of their output to the more agglomerated region. The presumed agglomeration would not be sustainable, so again industry will be dispersed across regions.

Acting in favour of agglomeration, on the other hand, are transport costs and the pecuniary externalities arising from firm-level increasing returns to scale. If transport costs are neither too high nor too low, then relative agglomeration in one region may provide its own rationale for further agglomeration in that region. Suppose, for example, a profit opportunity in one region induces entry there of an additional firm and hence production of an additional variety. That region now becomes more agglomerated relative to the other region. The price index decreases in the agglomerated region relative to the other region, because consumers in the more agglomerated region do not have to pay transport costs for the majority of the varieties they consume. Furthermore, nominal wages increase in the more agglomerated region because, as a result of the additional firm's entry, there is greater aggregate production and thus greater demand for labour. Higher nominal wages eliminate the profit opportunity that the firm entered to exploit, but meanwhile something has changed: with a lower price index and higher nominal wages, real wages are now higher in the more agglomerated region than in the less agglomerated region. This induces labour to migrate to the more agglomerated region, which depresses nominal wages. At given prices, however, lower nominal wages imply additional profit opportunities. So there is entry of additional firms; and entry of additional firms sets the same process in motion once again.

It may not be immediately clear where increasing returns and pecuniary externalities enter the story. Pecuniary externalities are realized when one firm's entry results ultimately in positive profits for all firms, by means of the effect of real wages on migration and the effect of migration on nominal wages. Without increasing returns there would be no incentive for migration, because the price index would never be lower in the more agglomerated region than in the less agglomerated region. Why should it be, if all the varieties produced in the more agglomerated region (or as many substitutes for them as desired) could just as well be produced on a smaller scale in the less agglomerated region?

Not all new economic geography models work in exactly the fashion of the preceding few paragraphs, which were written bearing in mind particularly the model of Krugman (1991). Details may vary: the dispersing force may include diseconomies of city size, as in Krugman and Livas (1996); monopolistically competitive firms may use the output of other such firms as intermediate inputs, creating explicit input–output linkages as in Venables (1996); there may be any number of regions or any number of monopolistically competitive industries, as in Puga and Venables (1996); there may be studies of agglomeration in regions with varying sizes and shapes, as in Stelder (1998). The punch-line of most variations, however, is the same. Because firms are linked by pecuniary externalities, the rationale of agglomeration is circular; because the rationale is circular, reinforcing itself, there may be a multiplicity of equilibria. If there is to be agglomeration, its location is typically indeterminate, depending not on the model's parameterization but rather on the initial conditions from which the circular rationale begins. If chance (or arbitrary choice of the modeller, or 'history') gives a small advantage to one location, it will build upon itself and that will be the agglomeration site.

In short, one could fairly characterize the new economic geography as consisting of a set of mathematically specified models, based largely on the Dixit–Stiglitz model of monopolistically competitive market structure, in which:

1. Increasing returns internal to firms imply, in general equilibrium, the existence of pecuniary externalities transmitted among firms through markets.
2. Markets are separated spatially and transport costs must be incurred to ship goods between regions.
3. Pecuniary externalities take the following form: firm entry in one region may create additional profit opportunities for providers of inputs and outputs in that region, inducing further entry rather than abating it.
4. Consequently there is a circular logic to regional agglomeration, as well as the sudden unravelling of agglomeration that may come about after sustained changes in exogenous variables or parameters.
5. If agglomeration arises, it could arise in any one of multiple regions.
6. Agglomeration, then, is explained ultimately in terms of initial conditions, historical accident, and arbitrary policy choice.

PROGRESS?

If Popper is right about the myth of induction, those who want to 'tell it as it is' will find themselves driven to 'tell it as it should be': by telling the story of past developments one way rather than another, they will necessarily be revealing their implicit view of the nature of scientific explanation. (Blaug, 1980: 33)

To Blaug's statement one could add that some story-tellers reveal their implicit methodological views more than others do – and some even reveal them explicitly. Such is the case with Krugman, who is at once theoretician, prescriptive methodologist and historian of the theory he produces. Because his roles are entangled, his appraisal of the new economic geography as an exemplar of progress is weakened. His narrative is at once compelling and suspicious: compelling in that he probes admirably numerous intellectual antecedents of the new economic geography, and does so to clarify precisely how the mechanics of the new models produce their insights; suspicious in that the thread of progress that is woven into the narrative is taken directly from his methodologist hat – a hat of that particular style appreciated by those who read and write the literature he advances as progress. Krugman's methodological prescription requires building mathematical models, because 'to help economics as a discipline progress', he argues, 'it is important that your colleagues (and your students) understand how you arrived at your conclusions, partly so that they can look for weak points, partly so that they may find other uses for the technical tricks you used to think an issue through' (1998b: 1835). Not surprisingly, then, his appraisal of the progress made between the works he identifies as antecedents and the new economic geography is based on the extent to which the works are formulated mathematically. Specifically:

1. Regarding Ohlin, Krugman writes that his 'vision seems to have gotten a bit blurry when it came to the ideas that make up the new economic geography', in large part because he tended to 'fuzz over the distinction between internal economies of scale and external increasing returns'. Ohlin's fuzziness is in contradistinction to later theorists who 'finally managed to "tame" [that is, model] imperfect competition and hence to feel comfortable talking about internal scale economies' (1999: 6, 7).
2. Regarding spatial theorists, including Lösch, Krugman absolves them 'for their failure to develop full maximization and equilibrium models' because they did not have the necessary technical tricks at their disposal. He adds, however, that 'one can perhaps complain about their failure to understand how far short of that ideal they were falling' (1995: 87).
3. Regarding development economists, including Myrdal, Krugman writes that the new economic geography is the redeemer of their '[g]ood ideas . . . left to gather dust in the economics attic for more than a generation' because they were not modelled mathematically. The new models thus offer vindication of the 'great minds [who] retreated to the intellectual periphery' (1995: 84).

The whiff of Whiggishness above is unmistakable, which is regrettable because there *is* a case to be made for progress – a case Krugman unwittingly undermines. He slams shut the door that might let in external appraisal with so much force that it swings open the other way. Consider: given that Krugman's appraisal of progress comes from methodology, how might he answer the critique of someone like geographer Ron Martin, who is far removed from the new economic geography research program? Martin (1999: 77) identifies what he considers a 'serious flaw in the "new geographical economics", namely its neglect of *real* places', which is the inevitable result of mathematical modelling. In his own discipline, mathematical models were cast aside

> not because the mathematics of maximisation-and-equilibrium had (temporarily) reached their limits, nor because geographers were unable intellectually to elaborate those mathematical tools, but precisely because of the realisation that formal mathematical models impose severe limits on our understanding. (Martin, 1999: 81)

By this view the progress Krugman claims for the new economic geography is illusory. Progress in geographical economics consists of improving our understanding of real geographic places. Progress cannot be made by pushing mathematical modelling any further, because mathematically modelled places do not adequately resemble real places. The new economic geography therefore does not constitute progress.

Because Krugman's appraisal of progress comes from methodology, his answer to the critique might be: 'Our different appraisals are traceable to our different methodological prescriptions. We have different notions about how science progresses. I think my notion is better than yours, and we will have to leave it at that. To me your critique doesn't matter'.

To which Martin could reply: 'Fine, but your methodological prescription is self-referential. Your prescription is to do what you do, and if one does so then one makes progress. Given that, the statement that your research program constitutes progress is tautological – so *it* doesn't matter'.

And it is difficult to argue with the latter argument, except by saying, 'Well, the same goes for you!'

By founding his appraisal of progress on methodology, Krugman leads himself into a dispute that cannot be adjudicated.[4] By effectively ruling out appraisals from sources external to his research programme, he lends those appraisals just as much validity as his own. But a different approach is possible. One can try to let the earlier theorists, beyond whom 'progress' is either claimed or denied, define the term themselves. That has been the approach of sections 2 through 4 of this paper. We may now compare the characteristics of the new economic geography detailed in the previous section with the criteria of progress distilled from the works of Ohlin, Lösch and Myrdal, and see how the new literature fares.

Progress beyond Ohlin?

For the most part the new economic geography measures up favourably to Ohlin's criteria. It is undeniably an integrated framework for studying spatial agglomeration and the pattern of trade, and the models are framed in mathematical and general equilibrium terms.

Whether the models are in the 'Casselian spirit' is less certain. Models of the new economic geography typically involve large numbers of simultaneous equations that are non-linear in both the parameters and the endogenous variables, so analytical solutions for the endogenous variables are impossible. Most of the insights of the models must therefore be presented in diagrams generated by numerical methods, not in terms of the models' algebra.

Progress beyond Lösch?

Comparison of the new economic geography to Lösch's criteria appears less favourable, or favourable with more qualifications. Most of the literature's models are not suited for carrying out Lösch's inquiry into the boundaries of economic regions. The models' 'regions' are represented by two or more points in space – where space, for tractability, is usually limited to one dimension, or perhaps the periphery of a circle. Stelder (1998) pushes space a bit further and considers agglomeration on a two-dimensional plane, but the plane is composed of a grid of a finite number of possible agglomeration sites. Fujita, Krugman and Venables (1999: Ch. 17) allow firms to locate anywhere on a continuum on the periphery of a circle, but nowhere off the periphery of the circle. Neither model is built in a space that is both continuous and fully two-dimensional, as Lösch had in mind. To date, then, the new economic geography cannot determine the borders of economic regions endogenously as Lösch sought to do. There may be multiple equilibrium agglomeration sites, but their locations in two-dimensional space always have an element of arbitrariness imposed by the modeller. Moreover, in the new economic geography there is really no discernable end to 'market areas': firms at each location must sell to firms or consumers in all other locations, because otherwise the marginal product or utility of the firms' goods at those locations would be infinite.

Krugman (1995: 63) writes that some new economic geography models (for example, Fujita, Krugman and Venables, 1999: Ch. 17) can depict an economy that 'spontaneously organizes itself into a pattern of central places with roughly equal-sized market areas', and the pattern is 'like the regular spacing of centers imagined by Christaller and Lösch'. But he is suggesting more similarity between the models than there really is. 'Market areas' are not defined in new economic geography models, and if they were their limits would be determined arbitrarily to some degree by the modeller. Lösch and Krugman are addressing different questions. The new economic geography does offer abstract mathematical models, as did Lösch, but they are not models in which the boundaries of regions are determined endogenously. The new economic geography does not (yet?) meet the first of Lösch's criteria for progress.

On the other hand, the new economic geography is very well suited to address Lösch's question of whether 'reality is rational' – perhaps even better suited than Lösch's model. Two insights of the new economic geography are the dependence of patterns of agglomeration on initial conditions and historical accident, and the persistence of those patterns once they are set in place. Moreover the models are founded upon maximizing agents whose utility functions are specified. It is easy to simulate different equilibrium patterns of agglomeration and compare measures of welfare among the equilibria.

Progress beyond Myrdal?

There is no question that the new economic geography meets two of Myrdal's criteria of progress: the models do illustrate the principle of cumulative causation, allowing departures from equilibrium that are not self-correcting; and the models are fully synthesized with trade theory. Indeed the basic modelling framework, albeit without factor migration, was applied first in international trade theory as a means of explaining intra-industry trade before Krugman adapted it to think about spatial agglomeration. In these respects the new economic geography meets remarkably well Myrdal's criteria. Reading Myrdal today, one could quite easily interpret several passages as part of a manifesto for the new economic geography.

Myrdal, however, was not as fond of a priori theory as was Lösch, so he had the additional criterion of 'taking the model to the data to estimate the "coefficients" of circular causation'. The new economic geography fails by that criterion. Davis and Weinstein (1997) have extracted testable propositions from the models that differ from those of factor endowments trade models, and have then asked of various data sets, 'Which general class of models better explains the data: Heckscher–Ohlin or the new economic geography?' Their question may be interesting, but it takes us no closer to comparing the relative validity of different new economic geography models, or calibrating the models to explain observed patterns of agglomeration and predict future changes. With this in mind Krugman has admitted that 'the new economic geography has been more successful at raising questions than answering them' (1998a: 173). Raising good questions without also doing estimation and prediction was not enough for Myrdal, though – so to that extent the new economic geography cannot be said to represent progress.

In sum, by letting the earlier authors define progress, the new economic geography fares reasonably well. Appraising the literature by the criteria of Ohlin, Lösch and Myrdal, it appears to represent qualified progress. Moreover, because the criteria are not self-referential, as Krugman's are, the appraisal may be more convincing.

Yet one might wonder, 'So what?' Krugman's criteria for progress, while flawed for the purpose of appraisal, at least provide theorists with an agenda for future research. Letting the earlier authors define the criteria of progress would appear to do the opposite: appraisal becomes less problematic, but there is no obvious reason to follow a research agenda set by dead men.

I would like to think that the approach taken in this chapter is useful for a number of reasons. It forces one to think about what progress means, and to acknowledge the different criteria of progress in theoretical work, past and present. It makes one take more care with historical narrative, and be more self-conscious about the (perhaps inevitable) practice of 'telling it like it should be' according to one's own notions of progress. And it might even allow one to see virtues and flaws in the new literature that would otherwise be hidden by blind spots.

NOTES

1. W. Brian Arthur (1990) offered similar intuition for the influence of increasing returns in spatial agglomeration, albeit through different methods (Arthur, 1989). Some readers will find his absence from the story that follows conspicuous. However, because Arthur's methods and exposition are not basically in the Casselian general equilibrium tradition, his work falls outside the new economic geography genre as I define it. Krugman's narrative of the history of the genre makes very little mention of Arthur. In one short article in *Slate* (Krugman, 1998c) he explains why. The question of whether this part of Krugman's narrative, too, is problematic (as well as the question of whether I have accepted it implicitly, and perhaps unquestioningly), may be of interest to some – but I will not answer the question here.
2. My PhD dissertation (Meardon, 1999) is centred on a new economic geography model, and in developing it I benefited from a conversation with Krugman.
3. Notwithstanding Weintraub's (1998) account of how the meaning of 'formalism' has varied over the twentieth century, I will use the term interchangeably with 'mathematical general equilibrium modelling'. For the purpose of this paper the usage should be acceptable provided that neither Ohlin nor Lösch nor Myrdal defines progress explicitly in terms of 'formalism' but means something else by the word – which none does.
4. One way (to which I allude) of stating the crux of the problem is that 'methodology doesn't matter', as in Weintraub (1989).

REFERENCES

Arthur, W. Brian (1989), 'Competing technologies, increasing returns, and lock-in by historical events', *Economic Journal*, 99: 116–31.
Arthur, W. Brian (1990), 'Positive feedbacks in the economy', *Scientific American*, February: 92–9.

Blaug, Mark (1980), *The Methodology of Economics*, Cambridge, UK: Cambridge University Press.

Cassel, Gustav (1932), *The Theory of Social Economy*, 2nd edition (translated from the fifth German edition by S.L. Barron), New York: Harcourt Brace.

Davis, Donald and David Weinstein (1997), 'Economic geography and regional production structure: an empirical investigation', Paper presented at the CEPR/NBER Joint International Seminar in International Trade, Royaumont, France.

Dixit, Avinash and Joseph E. Stiglitz (1977), 'Monopolistic competition and optimum product diversity', *American Economic Review*, 67: 297–308.

Fujita, Masahisa, Paul Krugman and Anthony Venables (1999), *The Spatial Economy*, Cambridge, MA: MIT Press.

Heckscher, Eli ([1919; 1942] 1991), 'The effect of foreign trade on the distribution of income' (translation of 'Utrikshandelns Verkan på Inkomstfördelningen'), *Ekonomist Tidskrift*, 21 (1919): 1–32. In H.S. Ellis and L.A. Metzler (eds), (1949), *Readings in the Theory of International Trade*, Philadelphia: Blakiston Co. Reprinted in Harry Flam and M. June Flanders (eds), *Heckscher–Ohlin Trade Theory*, Cambridge, MA: MIT Press.

Krugman, Paul (1991), 'Increasing returns and economic geography', *Journal of Political Economy*, 99: 483–99.

Krugman, Paul (1993), 'On the relationship between trade theory and location theory', *Review of International Economics*, 1: 110–22.

Krugman, Paul (1995), *Development, Geography, and Economic Theory*, Cambridge, MA: MIT Press.

Krugman, Paul (1998a), 'Space: the final frontier', *Journal of Economic Perspectives*, 12: 161–74.

Krugman, Paul (1998b), 'Two cheers for formalism', *Economic Journal*, 108: 1829–36.

Krugman, Paul (1998c), 'The legend of Arthur: a tale of gullibility at *The New Yorker*', *Slate* online magazine, 14 January. Accessible at Paul Krugman's web page, http://web.mit.edu/krugman/www/legend.html.

Krugman, Paul (1999), 'Was it all in Ohlin?' Paper presented for the centennial celebration of Bertil Ohlin, Stockholm. Accessible at Paul Krugman's web page, http://web.mit.edu/krugman/www/ohlin.html.

Krugman, Paul and Raul Livas (1996), 'Trade policy and the third world metropolis', *Journal of Development Economics*, 49: 137–50.

Lösch, August (1954), *The Economics of Location* (translation by William H. Woglom and Wolfgang F. Stolper of *Die räumliche Ordnung der Wirtschaft*, 2nd revised edition, 1944), New Haven: Yale University Press.

Martin, Ron (1999), 'The new "Geographical turn" in economics: some critical reflections', *Cambridge Journal of Economics*, 23: 65–91.

Meardon, Stephen J. (1999), 'Trade liberalization and the geographic distribution of industry in the United States and Mexico', PhD dissertation, Duke University, Durham, NC.

Myrdal, Gunnar (1944), *An American Dilemma*, New York: Harper.

Myrdal, Gunnar (1957), *Economic Theory and Underdeveloped Regions*, London: G. Duckworth.

Myrdal, Gunnar (1968), *Asian Drama*, New York: Pantheon.

Myrdal, Gunnar (1984), 'International inequality and foreign aid in retrospect', in Gerald M. Meier and Dudley Seers (eds), *Pioneers in Development*, Oxford: Oxford University Press.

Myrdal, Gunnar ([1974] 1989), 'The equality issue in world development', Nobel lecture, reprinted in *American Economic Review*, 79(6): 8–17.

Ohlin, Bertil (1933), *Interregional and International Trade*, Cambridge, MA: Harvard University Press.

Ohlin, Bertil (1979), 'Some insufficiencies in the theories of international economic relations', *Essays in International Finance*, 134, Princeton: Princeton University Department of Economics, International Finance Section.

Ohlin, Bertil ([1924] 1991), *The Theory of Trade* (translation of Ohlin's PhD thesis, *Handelns Teori*, Stockholms Högskola, 1924), in Harry Flam and M. June Flanders (eds), *Heckscher–Ohlin Trade Theory*, Cambridge, MA: MIT Press.

Palander, Tord (1935), *Beiträge zur Standortstheorie*, Uppsala: Almqvist & Wiksells boktryckeri a.b.

Predöhl, Andreas (1925), 'Das Standortsproblem en der Wirtschaftstheorie', *Weltwirtschaftliches Archiv*, 21: 294–331.

Predöhl, Andreas (1928), 'The theory of location and its relation to general economics', *Journal of Political Economy*, 36: 371–90.

Puga, Diego and Anthony Venables (1996), 'The spread of industry: spatial agglomeration in economic development', *Journal of the Japanese and International Economies*, 10: 440–64.

Ricardo, David ([1821] 1951), *On the Principles of Political Economy and Taxation*, 3rd edition, Pierro Sraffa (ed.), Cambridge, UK: Cambridge University Press.

Stelder, Dirk (1998), 'Central places in the real world: some 2D geographic experiments for Europe with a Krugman agglomeration model', Paper presented at the 45th Regional Science Association International meetings, Santa Fe, New Mexico.

Taussig, Frank W. (1927), *International Trade,* New York: Macmillan.

Venables, Anthony (1996), 'Equilibrium locations of vertically linked industries', *International Economic Review*, 37: 341–59.

Weber, Alfred (1929), *Alfred Weber's Theory of the Location of Industries* (translation by Carl Joachim Friedrich of Alfred Weber, *Über den Standort der Industrien*, 1909), Chicago: University of Chicago Press.

Weigmann, Hans (1926), *Kritischer Beitrag zur Theorie des internationalen Handels*, Jena: G. Fisher.

Weintraub, E. Roy (1989), 'Methodology doesn't matter, but the history of thought might', *Scandinavian Journal of Economics*, 91: 477–93.

Weintraub, E. Roy (1998), 'Controversy: Axiomatisches Mißverständnis', *Economic Journal*, 108: 1837–47.

14. How new is the 'new trade theory' of the past two decades?

Andrea Maneschi

This paper takes up the theme of whether there is progress in economics by examining a paradigm known as the 'new trade theory' that was developed by international trade theorists over the past two decades. Authors contributing to it include James Brander, Avinash Dixit, Wilfred Ethier, Gene Grossman, Elhanan Helpman, Paul Krugman, Kelvin Lancaster and Barbara Spencer. Mainstream trade theory based on the Heckscher–Ohlin model posits not only internationally identical production functions, but assumptions such as constant returns to scale and the associated market structure of perfect competition, which some of the new trade theorists have rejected in favour of increasing returns to scale and imperfectly competitive or oligopolistic market structures. They claim that their models mirror more accurately the markets in which most industrial commodities are exchanged, and explain phenomena such as intraindustry trade that the Heckscher–Ohlin theory could not account for.

First, I explore in greater depth the reasons for the birth of this new paradigm. Compared with its mainstream alternative, the new trade theory offers fresh insights into the nature of the gains from trade, and new rationales for trade that often dispense altogether with the notion of comparative advantage. Second, its antecedents in the history of economic thought, which hark back to Adam Smith, are examined. Of special relevance are Smith's productivity theory of trade, according to which productivity rises with specialization induced by the expansion of the market, and the infant industry argument for protection popularized by J.S. Mill. Third, the extent to which 'progress' was achieved by the new trade theorists with respect to the mainstream theory of trade is assessed. Fourth, in so far as the new theory was inspired by its antecedents in the history of economic thought, its progress is evaluated with respect to these classical antecedents, and to Bertil Ohlin's advocacy of economies of scale as a rationale for trade that complements that based on factor endowment differentials. The extent to which the theoretical advances that mark the new trade theory constitute a net advance over the classical and neoclassical theories that preceded it is assessed in the concluding section of this chapter.

THE BIRTH OF THE NEW TRADE THEORY

The new trade theory arose from dissatisfaction with the mainstream Heckscher–Ohlin–Samuelson (H–O–S) trade theory, which gathered strength after the Leontief paradox raised the first doubts concerning its validity. When the USA was considered the world's most capital-abundant country at the end of World War II, Leontief (1953) discovered instead that it exported labour-intensive and imported capital-intensive commodities. His finding produced a flurry of articles designed to explain it or to reformulate the underlying H–O–S theory. The further tests that followed extended this theory to a greater number of factors than the two (capital and labour) considered by Leontief, used later data or were applied to countries other than the USA. In the case of the USA, the Leontief paradox was sometimes reversed (especially with more recent data), at other times reaffirmed. Neo-Ricardian economists argued instead that the Leontief paradox is not a paradox at all because of the way that capital is measured in empirical work, as an aggregation of heterogeneous capital goods.

The doubts cast on the validity of mainstream trade theory that were sown by the Leontief paradox were reinforced by mounting evidence that a considerable proportion of world trade was occurring between industrialized countries rather than (as would have been predicted by the H–O–S theory) between more complementary economies such as those of developed and developing countries. The industrialized countries instead had fairly similar factor endowments, and much of the trade between them was of an intraindustry nature. This called for a different explanation in which economies of scale play an important role in addition to factor endowments. The increasing importance of multinational corporations as important global trading entities pointed in the same direction.

The new trade theory was preceded by earlier contributions that eluded the straitjacket of the Heckscher–Ohlin theory in order to explain particular types of trade. Posner (1961), Vernon (1966) and Hufbauer (1966) deserve special mention as marking the first departures from the Heckscher–Ohlin assumption that technology and tastes are identical everywhere. Products were instead assumed to go through a life cycle that begins in the country where they are first invented and manufactured, before being adopted by consumers in foreign countries and eventually imitated by foreign firms. The assumption that technology differs across countries, at least for a certain length of time conditioned by the expiration of patents and other property rights, and by the degree to which technologies can be successfully imitated abroad, made such models closer in spirit to Ricardo than to Heckscher–Ohlin. However, they were somewhat ad hoc in nature, and did not offer an overarching paradigm that could be regarded as a valid alternative to the traditional one.

A first group of articles on the new trade theory appeared about two decades ago, and was inspired by the theory of industrial organization deriving from the work of Edward Chamberlin (1933) on monopolistic competition.[1] Following on articles by Spence (1976), Dixit and Stiglitz (1977) and Lancaster (1979), models of trade in differentiated goods produced under increasing returns to scale were developed by Krugman (1979a, 1979b), Lancaster (1980) and Dixit and Norman (1980). The assumptions of perfect competition and constant returns were abandoned in favour of imperfect competition and increasing returns at the firm level. At about the same time, Ethier (1979, 1982) presented trade models based on increasing returns due to Marshallian external economies, carrying further Frank Graham's argument for protection. Such increasing returns, being external to the firm, are compatible with perfect competition. Whether the models of the new trade theory featured Marshallian external economies, or economies of scale in industries marked by product differentiation, they presented rationales for trade that were alternative (or additional) to comparative advantage based on differential factor endowments.

A third type of innovation introduced by Brander and Spencer (Spencer and Brander, 1983; Brander and Spencer, 1985) derived from the theory of oligopoly, and had historical antecedents in the work of A.A. Cournot and J. Bertrand. Given the richness and variety of the literature based on these three strands of the new trade theory, I will omit consideration of oligopoly models so as to examine more closely the issue of the recent progress in trade theory as represented by the first two types of trade models featuring increasing returns.[2]

ANTECEDENTS OF THE NEW TRADE THEORY

Historians of economic thought search for precedents of theoretical innovations such as the new trade theory. No lesser a figure than the putative founder of classical political economy, Adam Smith, has been invoked as its progenitor. Thus Krugman argued that

> The long dominance of Ricardo over Smith – of comparative advantage over increasing returns – was largely due to the belief that the alternative was necessarily a mess. In effect, the theory of international trade followed the perceived line of least mathematical resistance. Once it was clear that papers on noncomparative-advantage trade could be just as tight and clean as papers in the traditional mold, the field was ripe for rapid transformation. (Krugman, 1990: 4)

Krugman's models are in fact based on increasing returns and dynamic phenomena such as learning by doing that suggest the benefits from specialization resulting from the division of labour, a concept made famous in

Smith's *Wealth of Nations*. Even before the birth of the new trade theory, economists began to re-examine Smith's ideas on the causes and benefits of international trade. These ideas were displaced by David Ricardo's principle of comparative advantage, which illustrated in numerical terms the advantages of trade in wine and cloth between England and Portugal. It was this principle, and not any insight that Smith advanced in the *Wealth of Nations* in favour of free trade, that established the theory of international trade as the oldest subfield of economics. This principle remained the mainstay of trade theory for over a century, and was generalized to many commodities and countries. Its primacy was first challenged by Bertil Ohlin (1933) who, inspired by his teacher Eli Heckscher (1949), developed an alternative model of trade based on factor endowments. The question is whether Ricardo as well as Heckscher–Ohlin should now be dethroned in favour of the restoration of the dynamic trade theory suggested by Smith.

The features of Smith's trade theory were ably expounded by Myint (1958, 1977), Hollander (1973) and Bloomfield (1975). Myint identified two separate theories of trade in the *Wealth of Nations*, which he called the 'productivity' theory and the 'vent-for-surplus' theory. According to the former, the advantage of foreign trade is that

> the narrowness of the home market does not hinder the division of labour in any particular branch of art or manufacture from being carried to the highest perfection. By opening a more extensive market for whatever part of the produce of their labour may exceed the home consumption, it encourages [the trading country] to improve its productive powers, and to augment its annual produce to the utmost, and thereby to increase the real revenue and wealth of the society. (Smith, [1776] 1976: 447)

Smith had devoted a whole chapter of Book I of the *Wealth of Nations* to elaborating the fact that the division of labour is limited by the extent of the market. By expanding the size of the market, foreign trade allows a greater division of labour and its attendant increase in productivity.[3] By lowering the costs of commodities, higher productivity in turn induces a greater volume of trade. Trade thus holds out the prospect of an irreversible feedback process whereby a nation's productivity, which initially gave rise to trade, is itself modified by the very trade which it stimulates. Several models of the new trade theory are also based on a feedback process of this type, and can thus claim Smith as progenitor.

A second important antecedent of the new trade theory is the infant industry argument for protection, first suggested with reference to the developing American economy by Alexander Hamilton ([1791] 1966), and elaborated in much greater detail by John Rae (1834). Thanks to Rae's advocacy, it was adopted by John Stuart Mill in his *Principles of Political Economy* ([1848] 1920), whereupon it became an integral part of British political economy.

Friedrich List, in his advocacy of protection for developmental purposes, was also inspired by Hamilton's arguments in favour of an 'American system', and transformed them into a full-blown rationale for a 'national system of political economy' (List [1841] 1885). An important strand of the new trade theory, epitomized in the titles of two of Krugman's articles (1984, 1987a), 'Import protection as export promotion: international competition in the presence of oligopoly and economies of scale' and 'Is free trade passé?', has re-examined the advantages of economic protection.[4] Krugman's answer to the question of whether free trade is passé is a complex one, that neither supports nor rejects free trade: 'New trade theory suggests that [free trade] is unlikely to be the best of all conceivable rules. It is very difficult to come up with any simple set of rules of the game that would be better, however' (1987a: 142). To the infant industry and terms of trade arguments for protection, the new trade theory has thus added another intellectually respectable argument, though one fraught with troublesome political implications, suggesting that in most cases free trade, like honesty, remains the best policy.

More recent antecedents of the new trade theory include articles by Graham (1923), Young (1928) and Williams (1929), which expressed unease with the neoclassical theory of trade for its inability to incorporate the pervasive phenomenon of increasing returns. Their contributions presented a cogent critique of mainstream theory, and may have inspired the paradigm proposed by the new trade theorists.

PROGRESS OF THE NEW TRADE THEORY WITH RESPECT TO MAINSTREAM TRADE THEORY

We now examine the extent to which the new trade theory can be regarded as marking progress with respect to the mainstream H–O–S theory, before evaluating in the next section its progress with respect to its classical and neoclassical antecedents. The founders of the new theory did not design it to replace the H–O–S theory as the sole explanation of trade flows. Factor endowments are still recognized as the chief explanation of trade in primary and natural-resource-intensive commodities. The new paradigm is primarily meant to explain trade in manufactures subject to increasing returns. Some of its models combine intraindustry trade in manufactures with interindustry trade based on factor endowments, so that comparative advantage remains a subsidiary but essential explanation of trade flows.

A second reason that the new theory cannot assume the mantle of authority earlier worn by the H–O–S theory is that it consists of a set of heterogeneous models, each of which is based on particular assumptions regarding technology, market structure (including the number of firms in an industry), consumer tastes and other features. There is a corresponding heterogeneity of rationales for trade, types of gains from trade and scopes for public policies, including strategic trade policy. The H–O–S theory is instead based on 'canonical' assumptions that are well understood and agreed on by its practitioners.

Within its limited purview, the new trade theory can be regarded as marking a clear milestone on the road to a more realistic theory of trade, shorn (in many though not all cases) of the assumptions of perfect competition and constant returns to scale that had become increasingly hard to maintain for world trade in manufactures. Indeed, its ascendancy can be regarded as a case study of successful paradigm change, of the type that satisfies the conditions laid down by Kuhn (1962) for a scientific revolution.[5] It is a delayed response to the unease that the emergence of the Leontief paradox produced in many trade economists. This unease, however, did not deter them from continuing to work within the confines of the H–O–S tradition for want of a more satisfactory alternative paradigm.[6] On the other hand, neo-Ricardian economists welcomed the Leontief 'paradox' believing that it was not a paradox at all. It confirmed instead their view that 'capital' as measured by Leontief does not behave like a homogeneous aggregate since it is a sum of values of heterogeneous items. These cannot be added up into a substance ('jelly capital') that behaves like a homogeneous factor of the type featured in the Heckscher–Ohlin theory.[7]

The new trade theory could successfully account for anomalies that the Heckscher–Ohlin paradigm was powerless to explain, such as the phenomenon of intraindustry trade, and the related fact that most of the increase in world trade in the post-war period occurred among the industrialized countries. Its models could throw light on the fact that trade tends to be more intense, the more similar countries are in their factor endowments. A key to the success of the new trade theory was the formulation of mathematical models of imperfectly competitive industries marked by economies of scale, where the gains from trade include not only increased consumption of the goods consumed before trade, but a greater variety of commodities available at cheaper prices due to longer production runs in the exporting countries.

PROGRESS OF THE NEW TRADE THEORY WITH RESPECT TO ITS HISTORICAL ANTECEDENTS

While the new trade theory offers incontrovertible advantages *vis-à-vis* the mainstream H–O–S theory, though circumscribed to the manufacturing sector of the economy, can it likewise be said to mark progress with respect to its historical antecedents? These include Smith's productivity theory of trade in the *Wealth of Nations*, the infant industry argument for protection, Frank

Graham's advocacy of protection for increasing-returns industries, and Bertil Ohlin's championing of economies of scale as an important complementary reason for trade.

Smith's productivity theory of trade contains profound insights on the nature of the cumulative technological improvements associated with the division of labour, which lead to changes in a country's comparative advantage. The latter is thus shaped by the experience acquired through past production, or learning by doing. Instead of being exogenously given, comparative advantage is determined by an evolutionary or feedback process, and thus contrasts not only with Ricardian trade theory, where it is based on given technologies in the two trading countries, but with the Heckscher–Ohlin theory based on factor endowments and internationally identical production functions. Smith's perception that the division of labour is limited by the extent of the market, which includes the world market as well as the domestic one, inspired the construction of models that are lineal descendants of his productivity theory, where history and initial conditions determine an economy's evolutionary pattern.

A rich and mathematically sophisticated literature by the new trade theorists is now available.[8] It occasionally acknowledges or pays lip service to Adam Smith or later precursors, but in the main proceeds under its own steam to establish its credentials using the modelling methodology that is standard among present-day economists. The degree of mathematical rigour with which assumptions are expressed and deductions reached from them undeniably marks progress with respect to the way in which the precursors of the new theory expressed themselves. It is hard to imagine any other way in which the new theory could have gained adherents among trade economists and established itself as a valid alternative to the H–O–S theory. Some of its models contain new insights into the creation of comparative advantage. An example based on Arrow's (1962) learning-by-doing model is Krugman (1987b), whose model features learning curves where cumulative past output determines current productivity. If international spillovers of external economies are partial rather than complete, labour productivity rises faster in the country that first produces a traded good. Moreover,

> [l]ike a river that digs its own bed deeper, a pattern of specialization, once established, will induce relative productivity changes that strengthen the forces preserving that pattern. Clearly, history matters here even for the long run . . . Comparative advantage is 'created' over time by the dynamics of learning, rather than arising from underlying national characteristics. (Krugman, 1987b: 47)

Comparative advantage is endogenous rather than exogenous, and is created by the same forces that lead to productivity increases thanks to an expanded division of labour. Krugman's model, as he himself recognizes, does not explain how a given pattern of specialization originally began: 'the model here is clearly too stark in its assumption that dynamic scale economies are the only source of specialization and trade. Allowing for other sources – particularly differences in factor endowments – would surely soften the results' (p. 54). His model blends insights from Smith and Ricardo. The complementarity of these insights and their resulting synthesis show that Ricardo has not been dethroned by Smith as the founder of the theory of international trade. Comparative advantage, suitably reinterpreted, retains a vital role in the new trade theory. However some of its models do feature what Krugman (1990: 4) labels 'noncomparative-advantage' trade, since even economies that in autarky are identical in every respect can find it profitable to trade.[9]

The infant industry argument for protection dates from mercantilist times, and was subsequently articulated by Hamilton, Rae, List, Mill, Marshall and Taussig, among others. Although it has come under attack from some economists (Baldwin, 1969; Irwin, 1996), certain forms of the argument are accepted by the new trade theorists. In fact, much of the new trade theory can be regarded as providing sophisticated arguments for some forms of protection to provide favourable initial conditions, such as subsidies for research and development activities. As Grossman and Helpman (1991) argue,

> Once the push from policy has enabled an initially lagging country to catch up, the policy can be removed without reversing the process that has been set in motion. This presents a clear case of policy *hysteresis*; a temporary policy can have permanent effects. . . Evidently government policy can turn a stagnant economy into a growing one, and an importer of high-technology products into an exporter of these goods. (Grossman and Helpman, 1991: 207, 231)

While Grossman and Helpman do not label this an infant industry argument, the models of created comparative advantage that they present can be said to mark 'progress' in relation to the traditional arguments for infant industry protection, and have helped to restore its validity among present-day economists.

Ethier (1982) took up the rationale for the protection of increasing-returns industries first formulated by Graham (1923). By means of an elegant two-sector model of an economy consisting of a constant-cost industry and a decreasing-cost one, he was able to shed light on the policy implications for increasing-returns industries that Graham arrived at by means of laborious numerical examples. Ethier showed that protection can indeed be superior to free trade for one of the countries, as claimed by Graham, but only if they are fairly equally sized. Ethier's model does not yield an infant industry argument since protection, once instituted, cannot be revoked. Though intellectually indebted to Graham, his paper marks 'progress' by arriving at results that Graham had been unable to reach.

Another important antecedent of the new trade theory is what Bertil Ohlin described in the title of Chapter 3 of *Interregional and International Trade* (1933, 1967) as 'Another condition of interregional trade'. He argued there that a powerful secondary reason for trade is economies of scale, due to the indivisibility of certain factors of production and the consequent need to concentrate activities geographically. Moreover, 'this conclusion that interregional trade reduces the disadvantages of indivisibility corresponds to the previous conclusion that trade mitigates the disadvantages of an unequal geographical distribution of productive agents' (1967: 40). This cause of trade and specialization, and source of gains from trade, is additional to differential factor endowments. Ohlin's anticipation of the new trade theory is rather remarkable for its details as well as its general thrust. Thanks to economies of scale, even regions with identical factor endowments can gain from trade, and the particular industries in which each region specializes are a matter of chance:

> Assume that a number of regions are isolated from each other, and that their factor endowments and their demand are so balanced that the relative prices of factors and commodities are everywhere the same. Under the assumptions of Chapter I, no trade is then possible. As a matter of fact, insofar as the market for some articles within each region is not large enough to permit the most efficient scale of production, division of labour and trade will be profitable. Each region will specialize on some of these articles and exchange them for the rest. *The character of this trade will be entirely a matter of chance if factor equipment is everywhere the same, for it doesn't matter whether a certain region specializes in one commodity or another*, just as uniformly endowed individuals can with equal advantage specialize in any kind of work. (Ohlin, 1967: 38; emphasis added)

Ohlin thus fully anticipated the 'noncomparative-advantage trade' developed by Krugman (1990: 4). He even blended the two prime reasons for trade that he identified in his 1933 book. Since some industries subject to economies of scale are labour-intensive, while others are capital-intensive, 'the different growth of these industries in different regions causes a shift in the demand for factors of production and makes their relative scarcity unequal. . . . This makes further division of labour profitable' (Ohlin, 1967: 38). Hence trade can result from either differences in endowments or economies of scale.[10]

Ohlin remarked on the importance of history and accident in moulding a country's specialization in trade, a feature also stressed by Krugman (1991). Authors such as Grossman and Helpman (1991) refer to this as *hysteresis*, a term employed in the passage quoted above, and use this concept to show (inter alia) that research activity can become concentrated in the country that acquires a technological lead in an industry. Ohlin's view was that

> The location of an industry in one region and not in another might simply be due to chance, the industry having gained strength in that particular region and having

reached an efficient scale. Since it cannot profitably be carried on in every region because the total demand is too small, it tends to remain where it was first located. *. . . If the actual location of production is not that which the available factors would seem to indicate, the usual explanation is that this location was natural in earlier times, and when certain industries have once been established in a place, there is a tendency for them to remain there. Friction of various kinds here is responsible.* (Ohlin, 1967: 39; emphasis added)

Though he qualified his statement by observing that its effects can continue for only a limited length of time, Ohlin offered several examples of cases where 'friction' (the present-day hysteresis) dominates the location of industry.

Some models of the new trade theory have used mathematical analysis and the new findings of the theory of industrial organization to express Ohlin's insights with precision and elegance. While they thereby display a measure of technical sophistication with respect to what preceded them, one cannot but be struck by the degree to which Ohlin was able to anticipate many of their results on the basis of intuition alone.

DOES THE NEW TRADE THEORY CONSTITUTE PROGRESS?

The new paradigm and its antecedents raise intriguing questions about the nature of 'progress' in economics, and of paradigm shifts that allow a return to previously abandoned paradigms such as trade due to increasing returns. The 'endogenous' comparative advantage associated with the new trade theory can be contrasted with the exogenous one found in models of the Ricardian or Heckscher–Ohlin type. Its endogeneity can be traced to the insights that Adam Smith presented to the world 224 years ago. Is 'progress' then nothing but the reappearance in new dress of essentially old ideas? Are we tasting new wine in rather old bottles? And is it really different from the old wine they contained before?

Historians of economic thought have answered such questions many times before. In comparing older economic theory with that of the more recent past, they have tried to measure the degree of 'progress' that has been achieved, and what such progress consists of. Some economists regard the latest theories as having effectively supplanted the older theories of the same type, first by eradicating any errors that lurk in them, then by going well beyond them. If this were true, there would hardly be any need to pay attention to the history of economic thought, which becomes a repository for the wrong opinions of dead men. I believe that such a view is incorrect, since the older theories have often provided insights that inspired their descendants, and may contain other insights that have been temporarily lost from sight.[11] While the latest theories score well in clarity and overall rigour, these advantages may have been purchased at the expense of properties that are not expressible in quantitative terms but are nonetheless important, as illustrated below.

It would be equally incorrect to take the 'scriptural' view (as Boulding, 1971, calls it) that there has been no progress at all in economic analysis since the time of Adam Smith, and that the new trade theory lacks any originality beyond dressing itself in the technical vocabulary and mathematical language that are nowadays *de rigueur*. One of the strengths of the new theory is indeed that it can establish with precision results that were formerly intuited, but whose plausibility could not be confirmed, or previously unsuspected results. Beyond that, the tools of modern economic theory allow trade economists to create models that portray the functioning of economies of present-day complexity, rather than the simpler economies that existed one or two centuries ago.

As Boulding argues, it is best to view the modern writers as complementing rather than substituting for the older writers. Walker (1999) notes that 'the constant interplay between past and present economic studies becomes evident. Past ideas come to be used in the formulation of current theory and the understanding of past ideas requires the application of present economics to achieve a clear expression and satisfactory evaluation of them' (p. 17).[12] Boulding provides evidence for this complementarity by citing the title of Merton's (1965) book, *On the Shoulders of Giants*, and noting that the modern writers are capable of greater achievements precisely because (like Newton, who used that expression) they have been able to stand on the shoulders of the giants that preceded them. The older writers are part of the 'extended present' (another of Boulding's apt concepts to describe the period of time which intellectual interaction embraces), and 'whether economists . . . need to pay any attention to the classical economists or to any writers of the past depends on one's estimate of the extent to which the evolutionary potential of these past authors has been realized or exhausted' (Boulding, 1971: 230).

I believe that this evolutionary potential is far from exhausted. An example of this relates to models of the new trade theory based on the assumption of monopolistic competition, which yield interesting insights into the nature of trade and the gains from trade by reconciling increasing returns with a degree of interfirm competition. Referring to the monopolistically competitive model underlying Chamberlin's 1933 book, rather than to the models of the new trade theory based on it, Richardson (1975) noted that while it 'corresponds much more closely to Smith's vision than does the perfectly competitive model . . . it retains a static character foreign to Smith; preferences and production possibilities are given and the equilibrium appropriate to them represents a configuration of production that will remain the same so long as they do not change'

(p. 355). Richardson argued that Smith postulates instead 'a disequilibrium theory in the sense that he views the economy as in a state of constant and internally generated change' (p. 351). This view is inconsistent with models yielding the economic analog of a mechanical state of equilibrium, whether a static or a dynamic steady-state equilibrium.

Richardson's critique recalls earlier critiques of the concept of equilibrium in economics. In his classic paper on 'Increasing returns and economic progress', Allyn Young stated:

> No analysis of the forces making for economic equilibrium, forces which we might say are tangential at any moment of time, will serve to illumine this field [of new products appearing, firms assuming new tasks and so on], for movements away from equilibrium, departures from previous trends, are characteristic of it . . . [T]he counter forces which are continually defeating the forces which make for economic equilibrium are more pervasive and more deeply rooted in the constitution of the modern economic system than we commonly realise. (Young, 1928: 528, 533)

His views were echoed by Nicholas Kaldor (1972) in an article significantly titled 'The irrelevance of equilibrium economics', in which he argued that increasing returns are incompatible with any notion of equilibrium. Since many of the new trade models yield a long-run steady state equilibrium, and the latter is not a faithful representation of reality, further work is needed to take full advantage of Smith's insights by formulating a theory of trade based on disequilibrium rather than equilibrium. This is only one example of the ways in which the writings of past authors can be sifted for useful hints that can inspire the work agenda of modern theorists.

Has there been progress in international trade theory over the past two decades? My answer is a qualified 'yes', qualified by my admiration for the remarkable intuition of economists such as Ohlin, which led them to anticipate many of the findings of the new trade theory even though they were unacquainted with its impressive technical machinery.

NOTES

1. The new trade theory was referred to by James Brander as the 'industrial organization (I-O) approach to trade theory' (Baldwin, 1992: 804).
2. The new trade theory models of the type discussed above, based on increasing returns as an explanation of trade, are ably surveyed in Krugman (1987c).
3. Smith provided the example of the discovery of America, which expanded the market for European commodities and allowed 'new divisions of labour and improvements of art, which, in the narrow circle of the ancient commerce, could never have taken place for want of a market to take off the greater part of their produce' ([1776] 1976: 448).
4. On the policy implications of the new trade theory, see also Baldwin (1992), Bhagwati (1989, 1994), Krugman (1986).
5. See Bensel and Elmslie (1992).

6. The Leontief paradox was analysed by de Marchi (1976) as a fascinating case study of the varied reactions of the economics profession when confronted with a significant anomaly in a prevailing scientific research program. He identified four types of reaction, the most significant being that of 'the third group, led by Samuelson though over a fifteen year period embracing a succession of prominent theorists, who chose to all but ignore the Leontief paradox' (p. 115). The reaction of de Marchi's fourth group was to seek an alternative to the factor endowments model, a search which eventually matured into the new trade theory. On the profession's response to the Leontief paradox, see also Blaug (1992: Ch. 11).

7. Like the new trade theory, the neo-Ricardian approach to trade theory presents itself as a paradigm alternative to the Heckscher–Ohlin one. The neo-Ricardian trade contributions include Mainwaring ([1974] 1979), Metcalfe and Steedman ([1973] 1979), Parrinello (1979), Steedman and Metcalfe ([1973] 1979), and other articles in Steedman (1979). A neo-Ricardian critique of the Leontief paradox is presented in Metcalfe and Steedman ([1973] 1979).

8. See, for example, the articles collected in Kierkowski (1984), Krugman (1990) and Grossman (1992). The new trade theory has been surveyed in many articles and books, including Helpman (1984, 1990), Helpman and Krugman (1985), Krugman (1989), Bhagwati (1989) and Baldwin (1992). The last two are by mainstream trade theorists who cast a sceptical look at parts of the new trade theory.

9. On the continuing validity of the concept of comparative advantage in the new trade theory, and the richer connotations this concept has acquired, see Maneschi (1998).

10. This is also the implication of the model of Helpman (1981), who subtitled his paper 'A Chamberlin–Heckscher–Ohlin approach'.

11. This anti-historical view is also rejected by authors such as Boulding (1971), Blaug (1996) and Walker (1999).

12. This view is echoed by Cesarano (1983), who claims that 'the study of past authors may disclose constructs, and links between constructs, which, though forgotten, may be important for current research' (p. 77).

REFERENCES

Arrow, K.J. (1962), 'The economic implications of learning by doing', *Review of Economic Studies*, 29(3): 155–73.

Baldwin, R.E. (1969), 'The case against infant industry protection', *Journal of Political Economy*, 77(3): 295–305.

Baldwin, R.E. (1992), 'Are economists' traditional trade policy views still valid?', *Journal of Economic Literature*, 30 (June), 804–29.

Bensel, T. and B. Elmslie (1992), 'Rethinking international trade theory: a methodological appraisal', *Weltwirtschaftliches Archiv*, 128(2): 249–65.

Bhagwati, J. (1989), 'Is free trade passé after all?', *Weltwirtschaftliches Archiv*, 125(1): 17–44.

Bhagwati, J. (1994), 'Free trade: old and new challenges', *Economic Journal*, 104 (March): 231–46.

Blaug, M. (1992), *The Methodology of Economics: Or How Economists Explain*, 2nd edition, Cambridge: Cambridge University Press.

Blaug, M. (1996), *Economic Theory in Retrospect*, 5th edition, Cambridge: Cambridge University Press.

Bloomfield, A.I. (1975), 'Adam Smith and the theory of international trade', in A.S. Skinner and T. Wilson (eds), *Essays on Adam Smith*, Oxford: Clarendon Press: 455–81.

Boulding, K.E. (1971), 'After Samuelson, who needs Adam Smith?', *History of Political Economy*, 3: 225–34.

Brander, J. and B. Spencer (1985), 'Export subsidies and international market share rivalry', *Journal of International Economics*, 18(1/2): 83–100.

Cesarano, F. (1983), 'On the role of the history of economic analysis', *History of Political Economy*, 15(1): 63–82.

Chamberlin, E.H. (1933), *The Theory of Monopolistic Competition*, Cambridge, MA: Harvard University Press.

de Marchi, N. (1976), 'Anomaly and the development of economics: the case of the Leontief paradox', in S.J. Latsis (ed.), *Method and Appraisal in Economics*, Cambridge: Cambridge University Press: 109–27.

Dixit, A.K. and V. Norman (1980), *Theory of International Trade*, Digswell Place: Cambridge University Press.

Dixit, A.K. and J.E. Stiglitz (1977), 'Monopolistic competition and optimum product diversity', *American Economic Review*, 67: 297–308.

Ethier, W.J. (1979), 'Internationally decreasing costs and world trade', *Journal of International Economics*, 9 (February), 1–24.

Ethier, W.J. (1982), 'Decreasing costs in international trade and Frank Graham's argument for protection', *Econometrica*, 50(5): 1243–68.

Graham, F.D. (1923), 'The theory of international values re-examined', *Quarterly Journal of Economics*, 38 (November): 54–86.

Grossman, G.M. (ed.) (1992), *Imperfect Competition and International Trade*, Cambridge, MA: MIT Press.

Grossman, G.M. and E. Helpman (1991), *Innovation and Growth in the Global Economy*, Cambridge, MA: MIT Press.

Hamilton, A. ([1791] 1966), 'Report on the subject of manufactures', in H.C. Syrett et al. (1966), *The Papers of Alexander Hamilton*, Vol. X, New York: Columbia University Press.

Heckscher, E.F. (1949), 'The effect of foreign trade on the distribution of income', in H.S. Ellis and L.A. Metzler (eds), *Readings in the Theory of International Trade*, Homewood, IL: Irwin: 272–300. First published in Swedish in 1919.

Helpman, E. (1981), 'International trade in the presence of product differentiation, economies of scale, and monopolistic competition: a Chamberlinian–Heckscher–Ohlin approach', *Journal of International Economics*, 11(3): 305–40.

Helpman, E. (1984), 'Increasing returns, imperfect markets, and trade theory', in R.W. Jones and P.B. Kenen (eds), *Handbook of International Economics*, Vol. I, Amsterdam: North-Holland: 325–65.

Helpman, E. (1990), 'Monopolistic competition in trade theory', *Special Papers in International Economics*, No. 16, Princeton: International Finance Section, Princeton University.

Helpman, E. and P.R. Krugman (1985), *Market Structure and Foreign Trade: Increasing Returns, Imperfect Competition, and the International Economy*, Cambridge, MA: MIT Press.

Hollander, S. (1973), *The Economics of Adam Smith*, Toronto and Buffalo: University of Toronto Press.

Hufbauer, G.C. (1966), *Synthetic Materials and the Theory of International Trade*, Cambridge: Harvard University Press.

Irwin, D.A. (1996), *Against the Tide: An Intellectual History of Free Trade*, Princeton: Princeton University Press.

Kaldor, N. (1972), 'The irrelevance of equilibrium economics', *Economic Journal*, 82(328): 1237–55.

Kierzkowski, H. (ed.) (1984), *Monopolistic Competition and International Trade*, Oxford: Clarendon Press.

Krugman, P.R. (1979a), 'Increasing returns, monopolistic competition, and international trade', reprinted in P.R. Krugman (1990), *Rethinking International Trade*, Cambridge, MA: MIT Press: 11–21.

Krugman, P.R. (1979b), 'A model of innovation, technology transfer, and the world distribution of income', reprinted in P.R. Krugman (1990), *Rethinking International Trade*, Cambridge, MA: MIT Press: 139–51.

Krugman, P.R. (1984), 'Import protection as export promotion: international competition in the presence of oligopoly and economies of scale', reprinted in P.R. Krugman (1990), *Rethinking International Trade*, Cambridge, MA: MIT Press: 185–98.

Krugman, P.R. (ed.) (1986), *Strategic Trade Policy and the New International Economics*, Cambridge, MA: MIT Press.

Krugman, P.R. (1987a), 'Is free trade passé?', *Journal of Economic Perspectives*, 1(2): 131–44.

Krugman, P.R. (1987b), 'The narrow moving band, the Dutch disease, and the competitive consequences of Mrs. Thatcher: notes on trade in the presence of dynamic scale economies', reprinted in P.R. Krugman (1990), *Rethinking International Trade*, Cambridge, MA: MIT Press: 106–20.

Krugman, P.R. (1987c), 'Increasing returns and the theory of international trade', reprinted in P.R. Krugman (1990), *Rethinking International Trade*, Cambridge, MA: MIT Press: 63–89.

Krugman, P.R. (1989), 'Industrial organization and international trade', in R. Schmalensee and R.D. Willig (eds), *Handbook of Industrial Organization*, Vol. II, Amsterdam: North-Holland.

Krugman, P.R. (1990), *Rethinking International Trade*, Cambridge, MA: MIT Press.

Krugman, P.R. (1991), 'History versus expectations', *Quarterly Journal of Economics*, 106(2): 651–67.

Kuhn, T.S. (1962), *The Structure of Scientific Revolutions*, Chicago: University of Chicago Press.

Lancaster, K. (1979), *Variety, Equity and Efficiency*, New York: Columbia University Press.

Lancaster, K. (1980), 'Intra-industry trade under perfect monopolistic competition', *Journal of International Economics*, 10(2): 151–75.

Leontief, W.W. (1953), 'Domestic production and foreign trade: the American capital position re-examined', *Proceedings of the American Philosophical Society*, 97 (September): 331–49.

List, F. ([1841] 1885), *The National System of Political Economy*, translated by S.S. Lloyd, London: Longmans, Green, and Co. First published in German in 1841.

Mainwaring, L. ([1974] 1979), 'A neo-Ricardian analysis of international trade', reprinted in I. Steedman (ed.) (1979), *Fundamental Issues in Trade Theory*, New York: St. Martin's Press.

Maneschi, A. (1998), *Comparative Advantage in International Trade: A Historical Perspective*, Cheltenham, UK: Edward Elgar.

Merton, R.K. (1965), *On the Shoulders of Giants*, New York: Harcourt, Brace & World.

Metcalfe, J.S. and I. Steedman ([1973] 1979), 'Heterogeneous capital and the Heckscher–Ohlin–Samuelson theory of trade', reprinted in I. Steedman (ed.) (1979), *Fundamental Issues in Trade Theory*, New York: St. Martin's Press.

Mill, John Stuart ([1848] 1920), *Principles of Political Economy*, 7th edition, ed. by W.J. Ashley, London: Longman, Green and Co.

Myint, H. (1958), 'The "classical theory" of international trade and the underdeveloped countries', *Economic Journal*, 68(270): 317–37.

Myint, H. (1977), 'Adam Smith's theory of international trade in the perspective of economic development', *Economica*, 44(175): 231–48.

Ohlin, B. (1933, 1967), *Interregional and International Trade*, Cambridge, MA: Harvard University Press.

Parrinello, S. (1979), 'Distribution, growth and international trade', in I. Steedman (ed.) (1979), *Fundamental Issues in Trade Theory*, New York: St. Martin's Press.

Posner, M.V. (1961), 'Technical change and international trade', *Oxford Economic Papers*, 13(3): 323–41.

Rae, J. (1834), *Statement of Some New Principles on the Subject of Political Economy, Exposing the Fallacies of the System of Free Trade, and of Some Other Doctrines Maintained in the 'Wealth of Nations'*, Boston: Hilliard, Gray, and Co.

Richardson, G.B. (1975), 'Adam Smith on competition and increasing returns', in A S. Skinner and T. Wilson (eds), *Essays on Adam Smith*, Oxford: Clarendon Press: 350–60.

Robinson, J. (1933), *The Economics of Imperfect Competition*, London: Macmillan.

Smith, A. ([1776] 1976), *An Inquiry into the Nature and Causes of the Wealth of Nations*, Oxford: Clarendon Press.

Spence, A.M. (1976), 'Product selection, fixed costs, and monopolistic competition', *Review of Economic Studies*, 43: 217–35.

Spencer, B. and J. Brander (1983), 'International R&D rivalry and industrial strategy', *Review of Economic Studies*, 50: 707–22.

Steedman, I. (ed.) (1979), *Fundamental Issues in Trade Theory*, New York: St. Martin's Press.

Steedman, I. and Metcalfe, J.S. ([1973] 1979), 'Reswitching, primary inputs and the Heckscher–Ohlin–Samuelson theory of trade', reprinted in I. Steedman (ed.) (1979), *Fundamental Issues in Trade Theory*, New York: St. Martin's Press.

Vernon, R. (1966), 'International investment and international trade in the product cycle', *Quarterly Journal of Economics*, 80(2): 190–207.

Walker, D.A. (1999), 'The relevance for present economic theory of economic theory written in the past', *Journal of the History of Economic Thought*, 21(1): 7–26.

Williams, J.H. (1929), 'The theory of international trade reconsidered', *Economic Journal*, 39(2): 195–209.

Young, A.A. (1928), 'Increasing returns and economic progress', *Economic Journal*, 38(152): 527–42.

15. The 'institutional factor' in the theory of international trade: new vs. old trade theories*

Sergio Parrinello

INTRODUCTION

In the development of the pure theory of international trade, from the late 1960s up to the present day, the following directions of theoretical work appear prominent. Until the late 1970s we find:

1. The dimensional issue:
   a. beyond the dimensions of the $2 \times 2 \times 2$ model.[1]
   b. reappraisal and criticism of the Heckscher–Ohlin, Samuelson, Rybcyznsky theorems from the point of view of capital theory.[2]
2. Theories with exogenous limits imposed on distributive variables and equilibrium unemployment:
   a. neo-Marxian and neo-Ricardian models.[3]
   b. neoclassical models in which rigidities in distributive variables are subsumed under the theory of 'market distortions'.[4]

After the 1970s other main directions emerged and can be grouped under the following headings:

3. Trade theory with external economies, increasing returns, imperfect competition, location-agglomeration theory.[5]
4. Trade theory in which the 'institutional factor' is assumed to be endogenous.[6]

A terminological clarification is necessary. In this chapter (3) and (4) are called the 'new trade theory', although in the current literature this expression is used to denote mainly (3). 'Old trade theories' include both Ricardo's classical approach and Heckscher–Ohlin's neoclassical trade theory. Furthermore the term 'institutional factor' will be used as a catch-all term to encompass concepts such as institutions, social norms, laws, rules, standards, conventions, customs *and* political agencies.

The new trade theory represents novel perspectives compared with the old trade theories and at the same time constitutes a resumption of Adam Smith's and Ohlin's ideas. Increasing returns and different institutional arrangements or different causes of such arrangements explain international specialization and trade flows even between countries which are identical in terms of factor endowments, technology and preferences for private goods. In this context the pattern of trade – even in the weak sense of a chain of exportable/importable goods cut somewhere by reciprocal demand – cannot be determined by a comparison of two isolated countries. Comparative advantage can be affected by historical accidents and become a solution to a general political-economic equilibrium system. As a consequence, the institutional factor appears as a crucial element in a non-purely-verbal distinction between theories of interregional trade and theories of international trade. This distinction is acknowledged in the non-analytical discourse of the old trade theories, but it is seldom revealed in the formal models by which such theories are formulated. The new trade theory has the merit of dealing with this hidden factor explicitly.

This paper presents: (1) a reappraisal of some ideas of Smith, Ricardo and Ohlin which anticipate the role assigned to the institutional factor in the new theory; (2) a critical assessment of how this factor is modelled in the trade theory in which the 'institutional factor' is assumed to be endogenous (see (4) above); (3) a general evaluation of the progress brought about by the new trade theory; and (4) an indication of how the same factor can be treated according to (2a) above and in the light of the old trade theories.

THE INSTITUTIONAL FACTOR IN THE OLD TRADE THEORIES: SMITH, RICARDO AND OHLIN REVISITED

Kindleberger (1978) has emphasized the concept of *magistracy* that is found in Adam Smith with regard to the theory of international trade. In Smith, magistracy means three distinct functions performed by the government: (1) protection of society from violence and injustice by other societies, (2) protection of each member of society from similar hostile behaviour by other members of the same society, and (3) the supply of public works. According to Kindleberger the main point inspired by the Smithian concept of magistracy is that:

> *there is no necessary connection between free trade and laissez-faire* . . . Law and order are complements to foreign trade . . . To permit the competition and free trade . . . some institutions may be necessary to protect a country from the most untoward effects of competition from abroad . . . At a more fundamental level, the difference between interregional and international trade explored by Ohlin lies in the existence within a nation of a government that tempers the wind to the shorn lamb through

various redistribution devises, while in international trade such mechanisms (for example, foreign aid) are rudimentary, if they do in fact exist . . . One intangible public good or institution is the state itself. (Kindleberger, 1978: 3, 5 emphasis added).

I agree with this view. I agree less with the criticism that Kindleberger addresses to Smith: 'It was perhaps the fallacy of misplaced concreteness that led Adam Smith to separate out "roads, bridges, canals and harbours" from public or collective goods such as law, order, justice, weights and measures, and stable money' (Kindleberger, 1978: 7; see also Kindleberger (1983)). Of course, the distinction between tangible and intangible public goods does not justify as such a separate treatment of public works and what I call the institutional factor. Both categories are public goods according to the standard characterization centred on the lack of rivalry and of excludability. The important difference between the two lies in their different responses to a changing environment. The extent to which public works adapt to external changes is not different from that which pertains to private fixed capital and mainly reflects technical conditions. By contrast, social norms and laws are subjected to special inertia because of coordination and enforcement problems.

With regard to Ricardo I wish to reiterate a position already presented by Negishi (1985) and Parrinello (1988a), according to which the textbook Ricardian model is a misinterpretation of Ricardo's trade theory. In fact, the Ricardian model is constructed as a special case of a neoclassical model of international trade: only one immobile factor, labour, and fixed labour coefficients whose differences across the trading countries are interpreted as differences in technologies. By contrast Ricardo's own theory of comparative advantage can be founded on differences in the production sets which depend on different institutions and in principle are consistent with the assumption of a uniform technology. Furthermore that theory does not rule out international movements of capital and labour. We read in Ricardo, as (passage already quoted in Negishi, 1985):

> Experience, however, shows that the fancied or real insecurity of capital, when not under the immediate control of its owner, together with the natural disinclination which every man has to quit the country of his birth and connections, and intrust himself, with all his habits fixed, to a strange government and new laws, check the emigration of capital. These feelings, which I should be sorry to see weakened, induce most men of property to be satisfied with a low rate of profits in their own country, rather than seek a more advantageous employment for their wealth in foreign nations. (Ricardo, 1951: 136–7).

Therefore, capital and labour movements can be limited, but not prevented, by differences in the internal institutional factors and this limitation resolves itself into differences in the rate of profit. In Ricardo this feature adds to the role of that factor in explaining the differences in subsistence real wages in trading countries. Hence, the important feature of Ricardo's theory of international trade is that the institutional factor is a source of intercountry differences in the distributive variables which can explain the existence of comparative advantage even in the presence of uniform tastes and uniform technical knowledge across countries.

As to Ohlin's contribution, many passages of the new appendix[7] found in the revised 1968 edition of his 1933 book and in his 1979 article show that, contrary to the vulgar interpretation, his preferred approach, the Walras–Cassel general equilibrium ('mutual interdependence' in his words) theory, includes among the givens not only the traditional factor endowments, technology and preferences, but also the institutional factor. It also appears that Ohlin's scientific program in the field of trade theory is not confined to the explanation of the pattern of trade in terms of the $2 \times 2 \times 2$ factor proportions model, but that he aims to apply the general equilibrium approach to that theory and to enrich the latter by giving it an institutional content. In fact, he recommends us to go beyond the simple H–O model and to take into account, besides tariffs and quotas, also the *internal* institutional factor in order to explain international trade. We read (Ohlin, 1968: 309, italics added):

> Besides the costs for the use of certain quantities of the factors of production – quantities needed for production and transportation – the costs of production also include *taxes and social welfare fees*, many of which bear an important relation to international trade and yet are not included in general systems. It has long been a mystery to me why existing accounts of international trade pay so little attention to these problems. So many books and articles discuss the impact of a certain type of taxation, viz., tariffs levied at the border when goods are imported, yet they devote no space to the question of *how other kinds of taxation* can affect trade.

Despite this wide focus, Ohlin stretched too far the notion of factor proportions as the unique determinant of the pattern of foreign trade. In particular, he seems to claim that intercountry differences in the institutional factor (and differences in technology as well) can be *resolved* into differences in factor proportions. In Ohlin's (1979) article we read:

> The character of legislation and regulations about social rules of behaviour, for example, hours of work per week, *exercises an influence on factor proportions.* Highly important also are the systems of taxation and subsidies – their features and levels – as well as the system of social-insurance payments. *More work is needed to illuminate the development of the supply of factors of production in each country*, not only their movement between countries . . . *One should perhaps count British political administration as one of the important 'factors of production' exported to the colonies – an export that provided relatively favourable conditions for economic development. We economists have perhaps used an unduly narrow definition of the factors of production* and failed to distinguish between the different qualities of

labour that are required for economic development . . . In one way or another, the behaviour of institutions like trade unions may exercise an important influence on costs and trade. (Ohlin, 1979: 5–11, emphasis added)

It is clear from the above passages that Ohlin's perspective is much wider than the narrow scope of the H–O model with which his name is usually associated. However, it is not clear whether Ohlin is suggesting that institutions should be included in trade theory as a special additional factor of production, besides and on the same grounds as the typical neoclassical factors (labour and capital with or without land), or instead he is saying that the endowments of such traditional factors, measured so to speak in efficiency units, should be assumed to depend on the institutional factor. In any case a certain tension is encountered in the choice of the hypotheses if we pursue such an extension of the H–O model. We should take into account that the 'feasibility' of technical processes reflects not only the technical knowledge but also the 'institutional factor' of the country: social norms, standards, laws, rules and conventions determine, jointly with technical knowledge, which processes are feasible and which are not (Parrinello, 1988b). Even if, following the H–O model, technical knowledge is assumed to be evenly diffused across the two countries, the set of feasible processes can be different because the institutional factor and the endowment of other public goods can be different. If the government, which is assumed to be their provider, is a *representative* government, the assumption of differences in institutional factors across countries can hardly be disjointed from the assumption of different preferences in the two countries, related to different cultures and lifestyles. Of course, we might choose the assumption that preferences for private goods are the same and independent of the amounts of public goods available, whereas preferences for public goods are different, and then, if public goods are assumed to be exogenous in the model, we might go on to assume uniform preferences across countries. But this asymmetric procedure appears to be a purely ad hoc device.

Hence the assumption of specific institutional factors in the trading countries is at odds with the assumption of a uniform technology and uniform preferences that characterizes the Heckscher–Ohlin–Samuelson approach.

THE ' INSTITUTIONAL FACTOR' IN THE NEW TRADE THEORY

The new trade theory seems to be a theoretical body which is more unified in the field of increasing returns and imperfect competition than in its institutional extension. In fact, the contributions of Grossman and Helpman (1991), Helpman and Krugman (1986) and Krugman (1990, 1991) appear to be complementary to the neoclassical tradition. By contrast, the focus of the new trade theory on the 'institutional factor' appears rather eclectic and it is difficult to find a unifying feature in this field of analysis beyond the treatment of this factor as a public or collective good.

I will first illustrate by means of a simple adaptation of Jones's (1971) model the distinction between the notion of an exogenous and an endogenous institutional factor in the neoclassical theory of international trade. Admittedly, this formulation is a sort of straw man whose role here is simply to point out some weaknesses of the neo-institutional approach of the type advocated by Posner (1972) and North and Thomas (1973), when applied to the theory of international trade.[8]

Assume a closed economy in which the quantities X_1, X_2 of two goods are produced only by labour. Let a_1, a_2 be the amounts of labour per unit of output in the two industries. The institutional factor is represented by a public good which enhances the productivity of labour in the two private industries. The quantity of this good is measured by the amount of labour, L_p, used to produce the good itself. Let

$$a_1 = a_1(L_p), \ a_2 = a_2(L_p) \tag{1}$$

be the labour coefficient functions, both decreasing with L_p. A uniform nominal wage rate w rules in the economy and a uniform tax rate per unit of employment, t, is raised in each industry. Assuming zero profits, we can write the following general equilibrium model, composed of the price equations under perfect competition,

$$p_1 = (w + t)a_1$$
$$p_2 = (w + t)a_2 \tag{2}$$

the budget equation of the private sector,

$$p_1 X_1 + p_2 X_2 = (w + t)(L - L_p) \tag{3}$$

where L is the given total labour supply, and the budget equation of the public sector,

$$t(a_1 X_1 + a_2 X_2) = w L_p \tag{4}$$

The preferences of the representative consumer are described by the utility function

$$U = U(X_1/L, X_2/L).$$

For simplicity the public good is supposed not to enter into the utility function.

Assuming that in equilibrium both goods are consumed, the optimal consumption condition is:

$$\frac{U_1}{U_2} = \frac{p_1}{p_2} \tag{5}$$

where U_i is the marginal utility of good i.

A case of an exogenous institutional factor is represented by a given amount of the public good L_p. For example, L_p can measure the degree of security, or an industrial standard, or a law which imposes a certain weekly working time. Under suitable conditions of concavity imposed on function (1) and on the utility function U, equations (1)–(5) can determine the equilibrium values of relative prices p_i/w, labour productivities $1/a_i$, quantities X_i, $i = 1,2$, the allocation of the labour force between the amount L_p and the amounts employed in the private industries, and the tax rate t.

By contrast, a simple example of an endogenous institutional factor consists in assuming that the amount of the public good, L_p, is provided by the government as a public choice. In the ideal case in which the objective function of the government coincides with the utility function of the representative consumer, a 'political economy' equilibrium is found by the value of L_p that solves the problem

MAX $U(X_1/L, X_2/L)$.
Lp
s.t. (1),(2),(3),(4),(5).

In this maximization problem L_p does not appear in the objective function, but only in the constraints (1), (3), (4). The interpretation of the solution is straightforward. Since equilibrium is associated with full employment, there is a trade-off between the amount of labour (employed in the private sector), which directly affects utility through the production of consumption goods, and the amount of labour (employed in the public sector), which affects consumer utility only indirectly, by increasing the productivity of labour in the two industries. It is important for the theory of international trade whether or not the two functions $a_1 = a_1(L_p)$, $a_2 = a_2(L_p)$ possess the same elasticity at each amount L_p. In general they will not. Then the equilibrium of two closed economies with different amounts of the public good L_p can be accompanied with different equilibrium relative prices, p_1/p_2, although the labour coefficient functions (1) are the same in the two countries.

Suppose now that the economy is a small economy and that it opens to foreign trade of private goods at a fixed world price, $P = P_1/P_2$. Without special assumptions we cannot predict the good in which the country will specialize from the comparison between the autarky price p_1/p_2 and the world price P. The government intervention might subvert the comparative advantage at the autarky level of L_p by changing the amount of the public input in order to achieve the highest utility of the representative consumer. We can say that the endogenous institutional factor brings about *endogenous* comparative advantages.

This case of an endogenous institutional factor has been chosen to illustrate some difficulties rather than to suggest an appealing direction for further research. The choice of the objective function of the government, the amount of information attributed to it and the measure of the public good (if the institutional factor is a law, what could be meant by *the amount* of law, measured by a continuous variable such as L_p?) are preliminary problems for this approach. I shall by-pass such problems. Furthermore I shall neglect the strategy problem that we encounter if we assume a two-country model where each country is not 'small'. In this case we meet a strategy problem which involves the two governments (see Krugman, (1986) and game theory would be the common tool of analysis.[9]

Still assuming that the above difficulties can be circumvented, a basic problem remains and derives from a too bold application of the method of equilibrium for explaining institutions and institutional change. What is the notion of such economic-political equilibrium? Some questionable features of such equilibrium have been indicated by Field (1981) and Basu, Jones and Schlicht (1987) in their critical assessment of the neo-institutionalism advocated by North and Thomas (1973). They convincingly argue that we should reject the extreme approach, according to which the causal variables of the changes in the institutional factor can be reduced only to changes in economic parameters: endowments, technologies and preferences via price changes, with the exclusion of non-economic variables. The criticism points out that some basic rules cannot be explained in this way and must be taken as exogenous with respect to the economic process. The weakness of the approach should not be attributed to the (legitimate) aspiration of explaining institutions and policy, but to the kind of economic explanation based exclusively on the principle of rational choice and competitive selection.

Yet, even without taking such a narrow economic position, the new trade theory with endogenous institutions is questionable, because it deals with the institutional factor as if all features of this factor could be subsumed under the familiar notion of public good, of which national defence, lighthouses and technical knowledge are typical examples. This simplistic reduction neglects the fact that institutions, rules, customs and so on, besides being non-rival and non-excludable to a certain extent, possess special features which bring about an asymmetry between the explanation of their emergence and the explanation of their persistence. Economic theory can offer plausible explanations of why an already established institutional setting persists in the face of a change in the environment and why this setting can become suboptimal even if it was initially optimal; but it does not offer a satisfactory explanation of why that setting emerged rather than others. Historical, instead of structural, explanation, and inertia, hysteresis and path dependency are prevailing in this area of enquiry (see Akerlof, 1976). Pervasive indeterminacy of equilibrium, conceived as a terminal point of a dynamic process, would be combined with pervasive multiple equilibria in a Walrasian sense.

SOME CONCLUSIONS ON PROGRESS

In Krugman's words:

> The 'new' trade, growth, and business cycle theories of the past decade have suggested to us a world view of economics that is very different from that of most pre-1980 theory. Pervasive increasing returns and imperfect competition; multiple equilibria everywhere; and often decisive role for history, accident, and perhaps sheer self-fulfilling prophecy: these are the kind of ideas that are now becoming popular. (Krugman, 1991: 8–9)

This statement of the specific analytical features of the new theory seems to announce progress in the theory of international trade and to apply to the comprehensive field that includes both streams (3) and (4) as mentioned in the introduction. Can we share this view? Let us first dismiss some criticism pertaining to certain easy claims of theoretical novelty and then let us focus on a specific criterion of progress.

First, let us leave aside the criticism that tends to downgrade the contribution of the new theory because its main ideas can already be found in the old economists. The argument that Smith, Ricardo, Ohlin and others[10] anticipated the role of increasing returns, of history and of the institutional factor in trade theory is not a conclusive criticism as such. Second, we should be tolerant of terminology that exaggerates the novelty of the theory itself. For instance, some representatives of the theory state, as a novel feature, that comparative advantages are *endogenous* in the new trade theory, without reminding us that these advantages are also endogenous in the old H–O–S model, albeit for different reasons.[11] Third, we do not insist on the fact that multiple equilibria and dynamic indeterminacy of equilibrium had already been recognized as non-exceptional features of general equilibrium theories before the 1980 theory.

Instead, let us turn our attention to a more substantial problem concerning the progress of the new trade theory. If the pure theory of international trade means a theory that explains why *some trade exists*, then progress exists because that theory adds some further 'causes' of trade to the old kit of inter-country differences in factor proportions, technology and preferences. However, the pure theory of international trade aims *to explain* not just the existence of *some* trade, *but the pattern of international trade*. Is there any progress in the theory of the pattern of trade? The answer depends on which notion of explanation the theory is supposed to serve.

If explanation means prediction, then one main feature of the new theory is the lack of a general theorem that allows one to predict the pattern of trade on the basis of the structural givens of the trading countries. A similar limitation was already clear before the emergence of the new models of trade. In partic-ular, the debate on the dimensional issue related to the theory of capital has shown that the pattern of trade in the multi-commodity case cannot be causally determined, on the basis of factor proportions, in the absence of special assumptions. At least the meaning of the traditional theorems has to be changed and the change weakens the predictive role of their original versions. Instead of *causal relations* between exogenous features of the economies and the pattern of trade, the new interpretation can establish only *correlations* between the latter and other endogenous variables (see Metcalfe and Steed-man, 1981).

We conclude that the new theory enriches the theory of international trade because it analyses the role of additional causes of trade, but at the cost of increasing the number of factors responsible for the indeterminacy of the pattern of trade. From this perspective the assessment of progress in the new trade theory cannot be separated from the assessment of Ohlin's research programme that recommends extending the theory of international trade along the Walras–Cassel guidelines and including also the institutional factor; and in turn the assessment of the Ohlin–Samuelson research programme, as Blaug (1992) has already pointed out, cannot be separated from the assessment of the modern general equilibrium programme. Then, if explanation of trade means prediction of the pattern of trade, progress by the new trade theory is very limited indeed. The new theory shares the lack of predictive content of the general equilibrium theory for an integrated economy, in which the existence of multiple equilibria and path dependency becomes the rule, in so far as it imposes no testable restrictions on the pattern of exchange and specialization among many agents. 'Almost anything might happen as regards the pattern of international trade' is the motto that can be written at the end of the above quotation from Krugman.

This negative evaluation of the new theory must be suspended if we aban-don the instrumentalist position centred on the equation that explanation equals prediction, and we want instead to use the theory to understand histor-ical patterns of international trade. In this different perspective, which is close to the hermeneutic tradition,[12] the new trade theory might cast some light. We must wait and see whether simulations, ex post predictions and understanding of international economic history can be usefully carried out on the basis of the new theory and whether the formal models of the new theory are more useful for this purpose than the non-formalized ideas found in predecessors like Smith, Ricardo and Ohlin. The paucity so far of this kind of investigation makes premature the assessment of progress according to this different criterion.

My argument suggests that trade theorists should retreat to the safer ground in which the theory of international trade takes into account the existence of different *exogenous* institutional factors in the trading countries, on which the comparative advantages depend. The explanation of such differences should be left to the historical narrative instead of being a rational choice of public goods.[13] In the next section I will argue that the institutional factor can usefully be modelled as an *exogenous* source of comparative advantage and that a non-Walrasian theory of international trade is better apt to embed such a factor, compared with the Heckscher–Ohlin–Samuelson tradition.

THE EXOGENOUS INSTITUTIONAL FACTOR IN A NON-WALRASIAN APPROACH

A basic non-Walrasian trade approach (called the NW approach from now on) has already been adopted in some models of international trade (see Emmanuel, 1969; Parrinello, 1970; Steedman, 1979; Negishi, 1985). Assume a two-country world economy in which many goods are produced with the aid of the same goods and labour. In the simplest case, given sets of linear processes with no joint production are available in the two countries. The processes may be different across countries and constant returns to scale prevail everywhere. The apostrophe denotes the symbol attached to one of the two countries. The typical closure of the NW model consists in assuming the real wages, w and w', as given in the two countries; and imposing a given relation between the corresponding rates of profits, r and r'. In the simple case a fixed proportion $r = cr'$ (see also Negishi, 1985) is assumed with c a positive parameter reflecting a *compensating profit rate differential* related to different risks of investment and obstacles to capital movements across the two countries. In this model capital is mobile across countries, subject to the limitation of this differential. Furthermore, since in principle each commodity is produced and can be used as a means of production in combination with labour, the NW approach inherently represents a theory in which the number of inputs is greater than the number of products. The international long-period equilibrium is ultimately determined on the basis of the same logic underlying the choice of techniques within an integrated economy. Equilibrium is associated with a uniform wage rate and a uniform profit rate in each country, but these rates can differ across countries. It is also compatible with involuntary unemployment and with capital and labour movements across the two countries within the limits of balanced trade and the differentials in the distributive variables. With regard to capital movements, we can envisage a 'multinational' class of capitalists who can freely invest in both countries. The model should be slightly revised and reinterpreted if we adopt Ricardo's idea that each country has its own capitalists who are more reluctant to move their capital abroad than at home. In this case the two classes of capitalists may have different propensities to invest abroad because of different idiosyncrasies about foreign institutions, cultures and languages existing abroad.[14]

How can a model of the type described above be extended to deal with the exogenous 'institutional factor' and how will such extensions perform in comparison with the extension of the Walrasian model within the same field ? A *natural* feature of the NW approach which includes the ' institutional factor' is that the set of production processes and individual tastes can be assumed to be different across countries. We say 'natural' because such a model is not constructed for the sake of demonstration of theorems which relate the pattern of trade to the economic structure of the isolated countries. In addition, to the extent that the institutional factor is *produced*, its production process should be represented by means of a time-phased analysis. Of course, an important difference exists between such a process and the processes in the private sector. The former absorbs private inputs and perhaps benefits from other public inputs, but no price equation with a uniform profit rate should be associated with this process. This special 'production' process should be assumed to be activated *exogenously* in so far as it is not governed by competition and profit-seeking behaviour. Then different private production processes can be assumed to correspond to different quantities of public goods *in each country*. Such representation implies that differences in the institutional factor across countries bring about differences in comparative advantages and affect the pattern of trade specialization in so far as they do not equally affect productivity across industries.

A certain caution is required in making assumptions for extending the NW approach through the inclusion of the institutional factor. I will suggest two warnings. First, *equilibrium* in the NW approach is compatible with unemployment and with labour mobility across countries. In particular, unemployed workers from one country can move to the other country even under the prospect of remaining unemployed, if the social norms, for example, unemployment benefits, are more favourable in one country than in the other. In general, labour movements can occur not just because they are induced by capital movements, but because people can *vote also with their feet*. If the institutional factor should be related to the action of a representative government, a certain indeterminism in the equilibrium solution would be unavoidable in the absence of further assumptions which put a limit on the changes in the composition of the population of each country and in the corresponding political consensus for different institutional factors. This kind of indeterminism adds to that encountered in the absence of public goods in a one-country model. In fact equilibrium unemployment with given wages can be associated with the presence of a labour force which is homogeneous in terms of efficiency but heterogeneous in terms of tastes: in this case it is indifferent for a firm to hire certain workers instead of others, but the composition of the social product depends on the composition of aggregate demand, the latter being affected by which workers are actually employed and which remain unemployed.

The second warning is more fundamental because it concerns the limitations of the comparative statics that is usually performed to examine the gains and the losses from trade. Such comparative analysis must imply a *comparative institutional analysis*. In particular, we must avoid what Södersten (1980) called 'the flaw in Ricardo's argument', but which indeed reflects Ricardo's implicit value judgment without flaw. The point is well known: in the absence of a redistribution policy there is no guarantee that moving from autarky to free trade will not harm some group of consumers. In Södersten's words:

> the doctrine of free trade was one of the cornerstones of economic liberalism. We have now arrived at the slightly paradoxical situation that this doctrine can be saved only if a policy of intervention is pursued concomitantly with it. Hence it follows that economic liberalism in the sense of letting market conditions determine production and consumption, can be justified on welfare grounds without reservation, only if redistribution goes with it. (Södersten, 1970: 22)

This argument can be used in the current debate about increasing globalization. It suggests that the comparative statics analysis used to prove the welfare properties of international trade must be constrained in a certain sense. We should assume not only a given assortment of techniques (whose choice is endogenous), but also a given assortment of institutional settings which limits the number of states of the economy which the trade theorist can compare in his comparative statics. The exogenous institutional factor associated with such states must belong to the given institutional feasible set. This set should be chosen on the basis of historical investigation and separate analyses offered by other social sciences. From this point of view, the usual comparative analysis of a closed versus an open economy can lead to arbitrary conclusions, either because free trade might not bring about gains in a non-ambiguous sense or because such comparison would not be allowed because one or even both terms of reference (for example, the closed versus the open economy) might not belong to the feasible institutional set. For example, the complete absence of tariffs with no other compensating public intervention might not be feasible. In particular, with regard to marginal analysis, the partial derivative of the equilibrium value of a certain endogenous variable (for example, the real wage rate), relative to a certain institutional variable (for example, the amount of a tariff), becomes undefined, if the change in the latter, under the *ceteris paribus* clause, is infeasible. Marginal changes in individual institutional variables might not be allowed. Only a cluster of changes in institutional variables might be possible.

NOTES

*   The author wishes to thank Ian Steedman for his linguistic revision of this draft and comments, under the usual exemption from responsibility.
1. See Jones and Scheinkman (1977), Deardorff (1980), Ethier (1984).
2. See Steedman (1979), Smith (1984).
3. See Emmanuel (1969), Parrinello (1970, 1988a), Steedman and Metcalfe (1972), Negishi (1985, 1989).
4. See Brecher (1974) and others.
5. See Lovasy (1941), Lancaster (1980), Helpman and Krugman (1986), Krugman (1990, 1995), Grossman and Helpman (1991).
6. See Lindbeck (1976), Casella and Feinstein (1990), Clarida and Findlay (1991), Bhagwati and Hudec (1996).
7. In this appendix Ohlin anticipates one of the main results of the new trade theory under item (3) above: 'Even in a case where the endowment of factors is the same in various countries, trade is possible between them – as well as between regions within each country – because specialization and large-scale operations entail advantages' (Ohlin, 1933, 1968: 309].
8. Recent developments of that approach can be found in the works of Casella and Feinstein (1990), Clarida and Findlay (1991) and Casella (1996), and the following model does not do justice to some interesting insights of the latter contributions.
9. In this regard, recent contributions apply the theory of clubs in order to answer the following interesting question related to the current perspective of globalization and harmonization of norms across the trading countries:

    Without setting preconditions for free trade, without formal treaties between governments, would trade itself lead individuals to establish similar standards? . . . If some convergence occurs, does it need to be inefficient, as in many 'race to the bottom' arguments, or can it be the appropriate response to the changed allocations caused by trade flows? (Casella, 1996: 120).

10. In Chapter 13, Meardon has rightly emphasized the anticipatory role played by Myrdal (1957) through his idea of cumulative causation. We can add also the name of Kaldor for his path-breaking role in respect to the new trade theory.
11. A different issue is that in the new trade theory the comparative advantages of two countries cannot be determined by comparing the equilibrium states of the two isolated economies.
12. Elsewhere (Parrinello, 1999) I have dealt with the distinct roles that can be assigned to economic theories on the basis of the two notions of explanation, that is, prediction and understanding.
13. Schumpeter (1961: 4–5) writes: 'when we succeed in finding a definite causal relation between two phenomena, our problem is solved if the one which plays the 'causal' role is non-economic. We have then accomplished what we, as economists, are capable of in the

case in question and we must give place to other disciplines. If, on the other hand, the causal factor is itself economic in nature, we must continue our explanatory efforts until we ground upon a non-economic bottom.'

The supporters of the recent neo-institutionalist models of trade with endogenous government might agree with Schumpeter's position either because their 'political economy' is supposed to be a discipline different from economics or because they believe that explaining government behaviour *à la* North has not yet trespassed on the borders of economic explanation and therefore is a legitimate extension. Whatever position they take in this respect, there remains the criticism of the dubious notion of 'equilibrium institutions' underlying the neo-institutional approach.

14. In this case we should take into account that the compensating profit rate differentials can be different between the two classes of capitalists. Then, a specific fixed c coefficient is assumed to apply to each class, and international investments will be ruled by the class with the lowest c.

REFERENCES

Akerlof, G. (1976), 'The economics of caste and the rat race and other woeful tales', *Quarterly Journal of Economics*, 90: 599–617.

Basu, K., E. Jones and E. Schlicht (1987), 'The growth and decay of custom: the role of the new institutional economics in economic history', *Explorations in Economic History*, 24: 1–21.

Bhagwati, Jagdish and Robert E. Hudec (eds) (1996), *Fair Trade and Harmonization, Prerequisites for Free Trade*, Vol. I, Cambridge, MA: The MIT Press.

Blaug, Mark (1992), *The Methodology of Economics: or How Economists Explain*, Cambridge: Cambridge University Press,.

Brecher, R. (1974), 'Minimum wage rates and the pure theory of international trade', *Quarterly Journal of Economics*, 88(1): 98–116.

Casella, Alessandra (1996), 'Free trade and evolving standards' in Jagdish Bhagwati and Robert E. Hudec (eds), *Fair Trade and Harmonization, Prerequisites for Free Trade*, Vol. I, Cambridge, MA: The MIT Press.

Casella, Alessandra and Jonathan S. Feinstein (1990), *Public Goods in Trade: On the Formation of Markets and Political Jurisdictions*, NBER Working Paper No. 3554 Cambridge, MA: National Bureau of Economic Research.

Clarida, Richard H. and Ronald Findlay (1991), *Endogenous Comparative Advantage, Government, and the Pattern of Trade*, NBER Working Paper No. 3813 Cambridge, MA: National Bureau of Economic Research.

Deardorff, A. (1980),'The general validity of the law of comparative advantage', *Journal of Political Economy*, 88(5): 941–57.

Emmanuel, A. (1969), *L'Echange Inégal*, Paris: Librairie François Maspero; English edition (1972), *Unequal Exchange*, B. Pearce, Monthly Review Press.

Ethier, Wilfred (1984), 'Higher dimensional issues in trade theory', in Ronald Jones and Peter Kenen (eds), *Handbook of International Economics,* Vol. I , Amsterdam: Elsevier Science.

Field, A.J. (1981), 'The problem with neoclassical institutional economics: a critique with special reference to the North/Thomas model of pre-1500 Europe', *Explorations in Economic History*, 18: 174–98.

Grossman, Gene and Elhanan Helpman (1991), *Innovation and Growth in the Global Economy*, Cambridge, MA: The MIT Press.

Helpman, Elhanan and Paul R. Krugman (1986), *Market Structure and Foreign Trade (Increasing Returns, Imperfect Competition, and the International Economy)*, Cambridge, MA: The MIT Press.

Jones, Ronald (1971) 'A three factor model in theory, trade and history' in J. Bhagwati et al. (eds), *Trade, Balance of Payments, and Growth: Essays in Honor of Charles Kindleberger*, Amsterdam: North Holland.

Jones, R.W. and J. Scheinkman (1977), 'The relevance of the two-sector production model in trade theory', *Journal of Political Economy*, 85(5): 909–35.

Kindleberger, Charles P. (1978), 'Government and international trade', *Essays in International Finance*, No. 129, July.

Kindleberger, Charles P. (1983), 'Standards as public, collective and private goods', *Kyklos*, 36(3): 377–96.

Krugman, Paul R. (ed.) (1986), *Strategic Trade Policy and the New International Economics*, Cambridge, MA: The MIT Press.

Krugman, Paul R. (1990), *Rethinking International Trade*, Cambridge, MA: The MIT Press.

Krugman, Paul R. (1991), *Geography and Trade*, Leuven, Belgium and Cambridge, MA: Leuven University Press and The MIT Press.

Krugman, Paul R. (1995), 'Increasing returns, imperfect competition and the positive theory of international trade' in Gene M. Grossman and Kenneth Rogoff (eds), *Handbook of International Economics,* Vol. III, Amsterdam: Elsevier Science.

Lancaster, K. (1980), 'Intra-industry trade under perfect monopolistic competition', *Journal of International Economics*, 10(2): 151–75.

Lindbeck, A. (1976), 'Stabilization policy in open economies with endogenous politicians', *American Economic Review,* 66, May: 1–19.

Lovasy, G. (1941),'International trade under imperfect competition', *Quarterly Journal of Economics*, 55, August: 346–56.

Metcalfe, Stan and Ian Steedman (1981), 'On the transformation of theorems', *Journal of International Economics*, 11: 267–71.

Myrdal, Gunnar (1957), *Economic Theory and Underdeveloped Regions*, London: Duckworth.

Negishi, Takashi (1985), *Economic Theories in a Non-Walrasian Tradition*, Cambridge: Cambridge University Press.

Negishi, Takashi (1989), *History of Economic Theory*, Amsterdam: North Holland.

North, Douglas (1979), 'A framework for analysing the state in economic history', *Explorations in Economic History*, 16: 249–59.

North, Douglas and R.O. Thomas (1973), *The Rise of the Western World*, Cambridge: Cambridge University Press.

Ohlin, Bertil ([1933] 1968), *Interregional and International Trade*, Cambridge, MA: Harvard; revised edition (1968), Harvard University.

Ohlin, B. (1979), 'Some insufficiencies in the theories of international economic relations', *Essays in International Finance,* No. 134, Princeton: Princeton University, Department of Economics.

Parrinello, S. (1970), 'Introduzione ad una teoria neoricardiana del comercio internazionale', *Studi Economici*, 267–321.

Parrinello, S. (1988a), ' "On foreign trade" and the Ricardian model of trade', *Journal of Post Keynesian Economics*, 10(4): 585–601.

Parrinello, S. (1988b), 'Costi comparati e norme sociali', Società Italiana degli Economisti, Rome, 28 October, mimeo.

Parrinello, S. (1999), 'Explaining and understanding economic events by contrasting alternatives', *Metroeconomica*, 50: 325–50.

Posner, R.A. (1972), *Economic Analysis of Law*, Boston: Little, Brown.

Schumpeter, J. (1961), *Theory of Economic Development*, Oxford.

Smith, Alasdair (1984), 'Capital theory and trade theory', in Ronald Jones and Peter Kenen (eds), *Handbook of International Economics,* Vol. I, Amsterdam: Elsevier Science.

Södersten, Bo (1980), *International Economics*, second edition, London: Macmillan.

Steedman, Ian (ed.) (1979), *Fundamental Issues in Trade Theory,* London: Macmillan.

Steedman I. and J.S. Metcalfe (1972), 'Reswitching and primary input use', *Economic Journal*, 82: 140–57.

16. Location theory and mathematical programming: progress or rediscovery?

Manuel Fernández López*

> In economics it is difficult to prove originality; for the germ of every new idea will surely be found over and over again in earlier writers. Irving Fisher (1930)

The background and ways of scientific progress in economics are commonly explored and furthered either through *finer treatments* of known materials or by adding *new independent instances*. This paper intends to contribute to the latter type of research, by making known to scientists two main and yet substantially unexplored contributions.

The discovery and initial development of *spatial economics* and *linear programming* is currently associated with the contributions of Johann von Thünen and George Dantzig, dated 1826 and 1947 respectively.[1] But as will be shown in this paper, they were anticipated in great detail by the contributions of two Spanish scientists (both born in Galicia, Spain), namely the engineer Pedro Antonio Cerviño (1757–1816) and the professor José Barral-Souto (1903–76). Both performed higher teaching and scientific research in Argentina. The elucidation of these two new cases will, I hope, expand and enrich our current knowledge on those subject matters.

I dare to assume that both cases are not familiar to European scientists, and so in the first two sections brief sketches of their fields of research are offered.[2] Then I proceed to approach them as multiple discoveries. The life sketches of both scientists are included as addenda.

LOCATION THEORY

The work by Pedro A. Cerviño, *Nuevo Aspecto del Comercio del Rio de la Plata* (*New Aspect of the Rio de la Plata Trade*)[3] is dated April 1801. By 'new aspect' the work meant a *new model of economic development*, which he proposed to base upon agricultural exportation, through Argentine ships and a network of river wharves. In Cerviño's paper (1801) the spatial viewpoint was pervasive. The work exhibits plenty of spatial categories, such as homogeneous surface, distance, centre or port, and circular shape,[4] by means of which he built a system of circular agricultural surfaces:

> The first circle of a league from the city, they devoted to town, and to gardens to supply vegetables, dried vegetables, and fruits . . . The next league, a larger circle . . . they devoted to farms to sow wheat and other seeds of general consumption . . . [T]he three remaining leagues, or the largest circle . . . they devoted to shepherds and cattle-breeding'. (pp. 180–81)

Other traits of the *New Aspect* are the following.

1. Availability of more efficient means of transportation: roads with negligible slope, navigable rivers ('channels'): '[America] has inward countries, and coasts: channels open to communication' (p. 110); 'Transport facility, through good roads . . . the channels that cheapen transportation' (p. 121); 'a wonderful ramification of navigable channels' (p. 166); 'so many and so large navigable rivers' (p. 167); 'the location of Buenos Aires at the mouth of the Uruguay and the Parana rivers, in which there flow the other navigable rivers of the province . . . the evenness of roads and the great channels that converge to it' (pp. 161–2); 'the lands communicated to this Capital, either through navigable channels or through even roads' (p. 167).

2. River banks apt to serve as wharves: 'it comes to our notice that we had so good wharves' (p. 147); 'the 70 ships that are assumed within this port, which in itself is a natural dock' (p. 150); 'the Parana bank, up to [the city of] Santa Fe, made all their available wharves so many other nocturnal wharves' (p. 127); 'all along the southern bank of our river is a wharf' (p. 141).

3. The building of a number of small wharves to fill the lack of a sole large port: 'a great number of ships wants a large port. The Río de la Plata hasn't any, and for the same reason must fill its lack with a great number of small wharves (p. 131); 'we have in mind to authorise all their small wharves' (p. 132).

4. Each wharf promotes the development of a circular agricultural surface: 'The development coming from this circle to encourage the workers of the nation' (p. 120); 'The multiplicity of wharves will multiply the Trade centres, and the latter the development circles' (p. 131); 'through the multiplicity of wharves, will be multiplied the development of agriculture and industry' (p. 133).

5. The interweaving of the agricultural surfaces served by the various wharves stretches the original agricultural surface along the river banks: 'it is possible to enlarge this circle, by means of good Roads . . . the navigable channels stretch it' (extract, p. 59); 'The easiness of transportation

through good roads, shall produce some enlargement to the development circle; the channels that cheapen transportation, will stretch it' (p. 121); 'it will expand more surface to tilling' (p. 136);'The circle of its development does not find anything that hinders its enlargement. The evenness of the roads and the great channels that cross it stretch [the circle of development] to an immense distance' (pp. 161–2); 'is a circle . . . stretched along the river banks' (p. 180); 'The wharf-multiplicity will multiply the Trade centres, and the latter will multiply the circles of development, that mutually interweaving will depict a plane of larger surface' (p. 131).

A *mathematical demonstration* of Cervino's proposal of transport mixing is offered presently. The above statements may be formalized as follows. Let $p = c + tr$ be the price of an agricultural good, as determined in the 'market' or 'centre'; where c is the cost of agricultural inputs ('value of the wares and implements'), including a normal profit, tr the land freight, at the rate t per unit of distance, and r the distance from the farm to the centre. The soil is a homogeneous non-sloping plane, and as r may be taken from the centre in every direction, it becomes the radius of the open circle $x^2 + y^2 < r^2$, $r = K/t$, where K is the total transport cost. The centre, market or city is crossed by a rectilinear means of transportation (a river, channel or railway) whose transport rate per unit of distance is $f < t$ at some distance x' from the centre. On the 'river' a wharf or trans-shipping point is assumed to exist. The new budget balance is $K = tr' + fx'$, where r' is the maximum land distance attainable at the rate t after spending fx' in 'river' transport. This adds, to the first circle of radius r, a smaller circle of radius r' that enlarges the agricultural surface, whose boundary is $(x - x')^2 + y^2 = r'^2 = (r - fx'/t)^2$. If all along the 'river' there are such wharves, then x' becomes a real variable, and the latter formula is that of a family of circles. The new agricultural surface is bounded by the envelope of the infinite circles of radius r'. By deriving with respect to r', the parametric equations follow:

$$x = x' + k^{-1} (r - x' k^{-1})^2, \quad y = \pm (1 - k^{-1})^{-\frac{1}{2}} - (r - x' k^{-1}), \quad k \equiv t/f$$

Eliminating x' the straight lines of the envelope follow:

$$y = \pm (1 - k^{-2})^{-\frac{1}{2}} - (r - x k^{-1})$$

The envelope is tangent to the first circle in $x = r k^{-1}$, $y = rk^{-1} \sqrt{k^{-2} - 1}$. In the arc $-x < rk^{-1} < x$, this is an economically meaningful boundary.

Therefore, the boundary of the agricultural surface is

$$(r - x k^{-1})^2 - (1 - k^{-2})y^2 = 0, \quad r k^{-1} < |x| < K/f$$
$$x^2 + y^2 = r^2 \quad 0 < |x| < r k^{-1}$$

and the normals (through the origin) are $y = \pm (k^2 - 1)^{\frac{1}{2}} x$, which generate families of parallel lines: $y = \pm (k^2 - 1)^{\frac{1}{2}} (x - x')$. Solving for x' gives us $x' = x \pm (k^2 - 1)^{\frac{1}{2}} y$. This value of x' is the optimum wharf for each point on the normal line, either on the envelope or interior to it. It follows by deriving K with respect to x' and equating to zero (minimum transport cost). The optimum land route is always parallel to the envelope's normal; and the latter is dependent only on the parameters K and k.

Although written 25 years earlier, Cerviño's scheme of spatial configuration is comparable to von Thünen's. It anticipated his pattern of concentric circles around a market of port; and the land use coincided with Thunen's. As the work aimed to found a development strategy fitted to the country's peculiarities, its case study was more complex than Thünen's. It considered not a sole centre, but several: 'This circle was to be tangent to that of the next town, and so the whole terrain would be filled' (p. 181). Also, it considered not a state in isolation, but one open to the rest of the world. The 'homogeneous plane' was not a simplifying assumption, but a stylizing of the pampa. Besides, it worked out the reshaping of land rings as long as land transportation might be combined with transportation through water: therefore, when both land and water transport were available, the largest circle of cultivation became enlarged along the river crossing the city (a result shown geometrically by von Thünen).

MATHEMATICAL PROGRAMMING

Jevons (1871) wrote: 'it is clear that economics, if it is to be a science at all, must be a mathematical science'. In 1871 his was the voice of one crying in the wilderness. Today it is the dominant viewpoint in science. The same trend was followed by Argentine economists: by the end of the nineteenth century the mathematical method began to be used, first by Professor A. Schneidewind (the Argentine Launhardt) and, since the 1920s, by engineer T. Sánchez de Bustamante and Professors Luis Roque Gondra and Hugo Broggi. But it was merely an adherence to an approach, without questioning or introducing fresh proposals, with the exception of Sánchez de Bustamante's discovery of the marginal revenue curve (de Bustamante, 1918) and Hugo Broggi's critique (Broggi, 1923) of Walras's procedure of proving the existence of general equilibrium by simply counting equations and unknowns, but without developing a general proof such as Wald's.

Mathematical programming is based on inequalities, convex sets and non-negativity conditions. The works of Kantorovich (1939), Hitchcock (1941), Cornfield (1941) and Stigler (1945) are usually quoted as the first steps in that direction. A forerunner of this approach was José Barral-Souto, Professor of the University of Buenos Aires. In 1939 he began to elaborate the theory of comparative advantage; according to his own account: 'In 1939 I set out to clear up the common confusion originating in the fundamental axiom of international exchange'.[4] He would soon find that a rigorous statement needed to take into account, besides productivities, the constraints imposed by the production capacity and consumption needs. During 1939–40 he developed a new approach through linear inequalities. He also worked on the notions of *optimum* and *efficiency*, that would be worked out ten years later by Koopmans. His work was published in 1941.

Leontief ranked it as an anticipation of the essence of the linear programming approach in economic theory. Recall that the simplex algorithm was published by Dantzig six years later, and its application to the theory of international trade was achieved in 1949 by Samuelson. Kantorovich, Stigler, Koopmans, Leontief and Samuelson were awarded the Nobel Prize in Economics, a fact that highlights the worth of Barral-Souto's contribution.

In 1939 Barral-Souto taught two lessons on economics in place of Professor L.R. Gondra. Those lectures may be the key to the story. Every teacher knows the strain that is experienced at the time of preparing a lecture and teaching it, all the more in the case of a 'special lecture' to be taught at a course which is not one's own. Let us recall the process of mind adaptation to problem-solving, after intense and lengthy concentration, pointed out by Nobel prize winner Ramón y Cajal. The need to teach Ricardo's theorem could have stimulated Barral-Souto to detect flaws in current proofs. His unpublished report on his research life (dated c.1967) seems to confirm that the search for a new proof of the Ricardian theory of comparative advantage was preceded by scrutiny of and reflection on the issue, either during his brief experience as professor of economics, or while translating Nogueira de Paula's book. Barral-Souto, since 1934, had published a number of papers on inequalities, and that had formed a fertile ground for a new approach. Perhaps the crucial decision was taken after the reading of 'Linear inequalities systems and their applications to the study of convex solids' by La Menza,[5] published in 1937 in the *Annals of the Argentine Scientific Society*. Until then the notion of comparative advantage was discussed[6] in terms of formulae such as $a1/a2 > b1/b2$, where the a's and b's stood for labour costs in two countries, 1 and 2, in the production of a unit of commodities A and B, respectively. Those formulae meant an order of magnitude between two quantities, not constraints to economic processes. 'A rigorous statement . . . required to take into account, besides productivities . . . [the] limitations given the maximum capacity of total production and the wants of consumption goods' (Barral-Souto 1968: 1). Taking the latter into account led Barral-Souto to the realm of convex polyhedra and to employ a kind of mathematics unusual to the economist of the 1930s, except for the small group around Karl Menger in Vienna. Between 1939 and 1940 Barral-Souto restated the traditional approach, and reached a new solution in terms of linear inequalities. His paper was published in the books of the Institute of Biometry, as No. 10 in *Revista de Ciencias Económicas* (1941), in *Revista Brasileira de Estadistica* (*Brazilian Journal of Statistics*) (1942), and much later, in *International Economic Papers* (1967). The latter was Wassily Leontief's suggestion; in a letter dated 19 June 1961, he wrote to the dean of the Faculty of Economic Science (University of Buenos Aires), Dr William Leslie Chapman, '[there is] a very interesting article published in 1941 in which Professor José Barral-Souto has in essence anticipated the linear programming approach to economic theory'.

Traits of Barral-Souto's approach are as follows.

1. The classical optimization model does not demand a priori non-negativity of solutions. This requirement alone turns the problem into one of *mathematical programming*. Barral-Souto's work specifically constrained the feasible set to *positive* values (not to *non-negative* ones, as would be usual later on): 'the nature of the problem requires the values represented by these symbols [quantities of goods, time employed and total time available] all to be positive' (Barral-Souto 1967: 3)

2. A remarkable feature is the decomposition of the total quantity of each production between two elements: the unit level of production (which he calls 'productivity') and the operative scale of each activity. In contrast to Leontief, he does not normalize quantities in terms of the respective production volume, but like von Neumann, defines productive activities over some time period. The operative scale is a given time extent, not a scale of production. Therefore, for two distinct goods 1 and 2, Samuelson's and Barral-Souto's notations are x_1, x_2 and a_1t_1, a_2t_2, respectively, where Barral-Souto's t_i's are formally identical to von Neumann's 'intensities of production', and the dimension of the a_i's: $a_i = [AT^{-1}]$.

3. The notion of 'efficiency' is linked to the production possibility frontier, defined as the set of 'efficient' points. In Barral-Souto's words: 'The position is one of maximum efficiency in the sense that although a different position may result in a greater output of one of the two goods, this would necessarily be at the expense of a reduction in the output of the other, or of an increase in working time. In other words, if any other position offers advantages, this is at the cost of some sacrifices' (Barral-Souto, [1941] 1967: 43, n.5). Besides solving the problem of comparative costs, Barral-Souto anticipated by ten years Koopmans' notion of 'efficiency' (Koopmans 1951, 1977).

Barral-Souto's paper on comparative advantage (1941) introduced innovating concepts in economic analysis: linear inequalities, convex sets and boundedness of resources. His contribution is comparable to those of von Neumann (1937), Samuelson (1949) and Koopmans (1951). Leontief considered that Barral-Souto's paper 'has in essence anticipated the linear programming approach to economic theory'.

The 'New Aspect' and the 'Fundamental Principles': Multiple Discoveries?

Discoveries
It may be argued whether a given past writing is a worthy contribution to economic science, especially when the alleged contribution was not continued by the scientific community. But in connection with spatial economics or linear programming, there seems to exist no doubts about their scientific status. Both are chapters of economic analysis. They are not mere opinions, nor empirical findings, nor policy suggestions.

Sameness
Did Cerviño discover Thünen's location theory? Did Barral-Souto discover linear programming? It may be argued whether Cerviño's or Barral-Souto's contributions are exactly the same subject matter as we know it at present. The quite different circumstances that surrounded their work must be taken into account.

a. Cerviño wrote in a colony traversing the beginning of an agricultural stage, while von Thünen did so in a kingdom with a long agricultural history. Notwithstanding, Cerviño's rings are like Thünen's. This is attributable to the fact that their spatial schemes both stem from a rational deduction from an assumption of maximum. They differ, however, in that Thünen took into account just one centre and Cerviño several centres. Pushing his case forward, Cerviño came to take into account the tangency of the largest rings of any centre in relation to the next one, anticipating in some measure Lösch's approach (1940).
b. Barral-Souto and Samuelson (1949) reached comparable results. Both approached the same problem with similar tools, applied to the same past writing, namely, Ricardo's chapter on foreign trade. Samuelson (1962: 8) suggested that the very idea of programming was already in Ricardo's mind. In this case, as is obvious, the necessary tools were available only in the second half of the 1930s.

With regard to Barral-Souto's contribution the issue may arise whether it is linear programming proper, as in Kantorovich or Dantzig, a successful *case study*, as in Stigler or Hitchcock, or simply a linear formalization of Ricardo's problem, as in Samuelson (1949). Leontief pointed to the first alternative: 'Barral-Souto has in essence anticipated the linear programming approach to economic theory which was "discovered" in the United States four years later'.[7] That is to say, it was not *still* linear programming as a general algorithm of solving, but it was indeed a *valid foreshadowing* of the linear programming approach, of no less importance than other anticipations, such as Hitchcock's (1941), Koopmans' (1942) or Stigler's (1945). I suggest that Barral-Souto's contribution should be considered on an equal footing.

Independence

The quality of independence allows us historians of economics to detach mere adaptation from true creation, and therefore to focus on the mechanisms and conditions involved in scientific progress. Independence guarantees that we are dealing with really new cases. To examine *independence*, let us recall first that 1826 is the standard date of von Thünen's statement of location theory, and 1947 is the date of Dantzig's statement of the simplex method. Both contributions under study here are dated significantly *before* the indicated dates. This fact proves anticipation of discovery, and implies independence.

a.   Von Thünen published his results in 1826; and in testimonies or biographies not the least trace can be found of Cerviño or the Argentinian pampas (as appears, for example, the *Wealth of Nations*). Besides, Cerviño's paper did not reach the press until 1955.

b.   Barral-Souto published his results in 1941, while Kantorovich did so in 1939. The only thing to prove is Barral-Souto's independence in relation to Kantorovich. Economics was not the main career of either. Barral-Souto was an actuarial mathematician and statistician. He had such command of advanced mathematics that it would had availed him to understand Kantorovich's writings, but he had no command of the Russian language. Furthermore, Kantorovich's paper was not published in other European languages until 1960, when it was translated into English by *Scientific Management*. The world outside Russia remained wholly unaware of Kantorovich's contributions, as accounted for by Koopmans.

Imperfect Communication

The decision to start and continue some research, and ocasionally the finding of a new result, implies ignorance of others' works, if any. Argentina's remoteness from the main scientific centres has been a constant challenge for its economists to devise their own solutions to urgent economic issues, disregarding possible solutions already existent but perhaps not relevant to that environment.

Publication lags and non-publication

a. Hardly had Cerviño finished the *New Aspect* when a subscription was opened to collect funds in order to print it. Manuel Belgrano acted as trustee of the fund. A long list of contributors was formed, headed by Belgrano. However the paper was never printed, and it was passed to posterity as a manuscript. In due course, after 154 years, *New Aspect* was published by the modern press. By that time, its efficacy in advancing general science had wholly vanished. In fact it was not published as a scientific work, but as a historical rarity – as a resource for historians, whether economical, cultural or political. To economic science proper, the publication lag was virtually infinite, equivalent to non-publication.

b. Did Barral-Souto's paper have a similar fate? Seemingly not. Were it not for Kantorovich's work, which remained unknown up to the 1960s, Barral-Souto's contribution could be deemed as the very pioneer of modern linear economics. However, the *Revista de Ciencias Económicas* was an economic journal still less well known than the *Ekonomisk Tidskrift*, and the 'Principios fundamentales de la división del trabajo' meant for the scientific community as much (or as little) as Ohlin's 'Till frågan om penningteoriens uppläggning' (1933). Barral-Souto's work contained the germ of linear programming, as Ohlin's contained the germ of Keynes's propensity to consume, liquidity preference and multiplier. Both were published in journals not accessible to the greater part of the scientific community, having so little practical effect as to be non-publication. As is well known, ignorance of the Swedish school caused great harm to policy-making in other countries. That is why the *Ekonomisk Tidskrift* began to be published in English. Barral-Souto undoubtedly intended to reach a circle of readers larger than allowed by the modest *Revista de Ciencias Económicas*, and sent the paper to *Revista Brasileira de Estadística* wherein it was published in 1942. But the practical effect was not improved.

Ignorance of literature
A natural ground for repeating a discovery is ignorance that the discovery had already been made. In the cases under study, ignorance if any should be allocated to von Thünen (1826) in relation to Cerviño (1801), and to Samuelson (1949) in relation to Barral-Souto (1941).

a. Thünen did not hesitate to quote Smith, Ricardo and Say as authorities,[8] nor Smith and Thaer as his masters.[9] Anybody would feel honoured to be their disciple or follower. But what if the forerunner was an obscure surveyor and professor of mathematics at Buenos Aires? It is likely that Thünen's scientific probity would still have led him to acknowledge such a forerunner if he had been aware of his work. Simply he had no such chance.

b. Neither Kantorovich (1939) nor Barral-Souto in 1939[10] nor Samuelson (1949) knew about the others' works. This fact is highly significant: beyond the quite different socio-political status of each of them, and working independently of one another, they reached a result that was fundamentally alike.

Language

The Argentine Generation of 1837 – the Argentine intellectuals Alberdi, Echeverría, Gutiérrez, Sastre – rejected the Spanish language as a rude tool of expression, and recommended the higher qualities of the French language. That position was deemed wrong by later Argentine intellectuals. However, it was not far from the truth as far as scientific communication was concerned. As Latin had unified European culture in the Middle Ages, and so allowed people to overcome political scattering, economics found two languages of communication: it was born as a French–English science, and the languages of scientific interchange were French and English in the nineteenth century, just as it was English in the twentieth century. Both contributions introduced here were originally produced in Spanish, and so were bound to be neglected by the international scientific community.

Mathematics

Mathematics is a language: it serves those who command it, and precludes from communication those who ignore it. Its efficacy was relative to where and with whom it was used. In the nineteenth century economics was taught in Germany at law schools where mathematical approaches had no room at all. There was, however, one exception: the speciality of transportation was taught at engineering schools, where mathematics was the means of communication. In both cases under study, the authors were professors of mathematics and mastered higher mathematics beyond the level used by the economics of the time.

a. Cerviño chose not to employ formal mathematics, in his paper, but did not give up the technical language. His paper advocated, in essence, the building of a port on the western bank of the Rio de la Plata, and aimed to persuade authorities and sway public opinion.

b. Barral-Souto chose formalization, or rather a new formalization. His paper did not offer a solution to a practical problem, but only economic analysis, which lent itself to a formal language. He was professor of a mathematical speciality. Besides, by 1941 two decades had already elapsed since Professor Gondra's fight against non-mathematical economics, which ended with the (reluctant, in some cases) acceptance of mathematics in the teaching of economics. That did not guarantee, however, that a paper such as Barral-Souto's was readable by those who studied economics at the University of Buenos Aires. Perhaps it was accessible only to a few scholars, in particular those with whom Barral was in contact, such as Professors Elías A. De Cesare, Carlos E. Dieulefait or Fausto I. Toranzos. To them, however, linear inequalities and convex sets did not signify anything new, and their applications were not their concern.

Exposition

a. It seems unnatural to evaluate the diffusion of a work that was not even printed, such as the *New Aspect*. Its internal division, however, was no better than Gossen's book. Let us recall that the latter was but a long monograph, with chapters separated by hyphens, that did not appeal to prospective readers. The *New Aspect* had no headings that concisely conveyed the contents: the contents had to be discovered through the reading itself. The first part evokes a historical monograph. The following pages seem to be a study on navigation in the Rio de la Plata. After 1801, the next readers were the members of the First Committee of government (1810), who looked in it for a study to ground the building of a port. The spatial approach is not particularly emphasized in the text, and it is introduced accidentally (just as labour division and specialization arise in Plato's *Republic*). Cerviño's style of writing, and the relative neglect of location theory in mainstream economics, did not help to highlight Cerviño's contribution to spatial economics.

From an ideal viewpoint, it would be desirable the author himself were to emphasize his new contributions, to attract the particular attention of the reader. But authors themselves are not necessarily aware of their place in science. As we all know, Walras thought that his main contribution to science was the concept of *rareté*, not general equilibrium analysis.

b. The opposite is true for Barral-Souto's paper. This scientist, in the 1930s, published a number of papers in the *Mathematical Bulletin*, for which reason he was used to expressing himself in rigorous formal terms. It could be alleged that his style was tedious – as were his lectures, which I had the privilege to attend – but not devoid of consistency. The problem was otherwise. Gondra's two decades of fighting for 'pure economics' had succeeded, at most, in making neoclassical economics accepted, but much less the mathematics that tooled that knowledge. For Barral-Souto it was a useless victory: his own approach had nothing to do with Pareto's mathematics. Inequalities and convex sets were not employed by economists, and only professional mathematicians had some familiarity with them. Those who began to employ those tools in economics, such as Menger's group in Vienna, could hardly be called economists. And a contribution which was ahead of his time, as Niehans (1995: 10) has pointed out, may be more difficult to explain than one which is 'blowing in the wind'.

The Influence of the Environment

The earliest challenge of the last two hundred years of Argentine economic history has been to put a huge endowment of fertile, unused land at the service of profitable exchange with the rest of the world. Land use patterns and comparative advantage thus became the main concern of some of the country's best minds, to the point of discovering valuable scientific truths, independently of the current trend of science in Europe.

Political conditions

The *New Aspect* did not come about independently of political events. In the bosom of the Spanish colonial régime, Manuel Belgrano's efforts opened the door to reforms that eventually led to the breaking of ties with Spain. Belgrano founded a School of Navigation – later suppressed by the Spanish crown. Cerviño offered an inaugural lecture in 1799, in which he promised that northern ports could be reached with Argentine-made ships. Thus he challenged the monopolist interests then taking over the consulate. One of its members, Alzaga, demanded that Cerviño be denied permission to speak in public unless previous censorship of his writings had been effected. Shortly after, discussion on ports began between Buenos Aires and Montevideo. Cerviño contributed to Buenos Aires' interests by writing the *New Aspect*, under the pseudonym of 'An able and striving patriot'.

Ideologies

Between Cerviño and Thünen a striking parallel may be found in relation to political attitudes. Both had to traverse revolutions, and each in his time did not evade supporting representative government. Cerviño, who already in 1810 was an urban colonel (as a result of his participation during the English invasions), participated in the town hall open meeting of 22 May 1810, where he voted in favour of entrusting the government to a committee of neighbours. Thünen, on other hand, had to live through the 1848 revolution, when he was elected representative to the National German Assembly at Frankfurt, an appointment he could not fulfil for reasons of health. Both took land use as their object of study, and their writings both show a certain inclination towards planning. But there was a difference. In Thünen's world rural activity was already existent, and his aim was to find a rational foundation for it. In Cerviño's world rural activity was something to create and develop, with the aim of modernizing a rude economy and making fuller use of a productive potential that was almost unexploited, largely because of the lack of a transportation system.

Economic conditions

a. In contrast to discoveries motivated by circumstantial events, such as quantity theory as stated by Bodin, Cerviño's spatial approach was tightly linked to the structural and invariant traits of the Argentine pampa, which allowed him to produce without violence to facts the stylized concept of *homogeneous plane*. To that must be added the consideration of the Parana River as an alternative means of transport. Both circumstances – homogeneous plane and means of transport – contributed to produce some spatial model. It would have taken a great stretch of the imagination for Cerviño to have conceived his spatial model under different geographical conditions.

b. In Barral-Souto's work – as in Samuelson's (1949) – is elaborated a case of high abstraction and simplification, as compared with concrete economic conditions. But the binary relation '≤' has been often used in economic theory with the meaning of incomplete or less than full employment use of a resource. This possibility has existed from time immemorial. However, the first half of the 1930s was characterized by overall unemployment of resources, material as well as human. The first models with inequalities date back, precisely, to 1933 onwards (Wald, Schlesinger, von Neumann).

The Influence of the State of the Art

Common problems

A driving force in the opening of new frontiers to knowledge is the acknowledgement of flaws in received knowledge.

a. Cerviño's work was motivated by a discussion between interest groups from Montevideo and Buenos Aires about the opening of an alternative port on the western bank of the Rio de la Plata. To the obvious reference to the natural fitness of both ports (an aspect which favoured Montevideo), Pedro Cerviño added, as a trait favourable to Buenos Aires, the analysis of the productive potential of the agricultural hinterland of Buenos Aires, which led him to study distance and transport costs to the port, as determinants of land use and the grouping of production in land rings.

b.   Barral-Souto also started from a rather fuzzy version of the theory of international trade, and perceived the lack of an explicit consideration of 'the constraints imposed by the finiteness of total production capacity' (Barral-Souto 1968: 1).

Common tools

a.   Neither Cerviño nor Thünen were true economists. The first was a surveyor of engineering; the second, an agricultural producer with university studies. They did not shine for their proficiency in economics, although Thünen had read the main economists and Cerviño had a better background in mathematics. Cerviño was naturally led to a geometric vision of the pampa: 'Geometry in its early stages is surveying'.[11] Cerviño–Thünen's rings are but an exercise in two-dimensional analytic geometry; and the celebrated enlargement of the largest circle towards the river banks results from deriving parametric equations. Thünen's axioms, and their equivalent in Cerviño's work, may be understood as a case of the axiomatic approach, but also as a stylized view of real complexities, or a reduction of reality to the simple canonical cases of geometry.

b.   What Koopmans called the 'interaction of problems and tools' is apparent as in no other case, the statement of comparative advantage by means of the techniques of mathematical programming, and with it their constraints and non-negativity conditions. Barral-Souto in 1939, as well as Kantorovich (1939) and Samuelson (1949), linked programming with comparative advantage.

Common paradigms

The outer boundaries of Thünen's rings are maximum stretches of expansion: beyond them a given production cannot be increased without incurring some loss. In Ricardo's foreign trade theory, countries maximize their income, and by doing so the world's income is maximized. In both cases the economic agents devise plans to maximize either profits or welfare, and individual plans as a whole maximize the outcome for society. The roots of this paradigm go back to Quesnay, Genovesi and Smith. Was it a paradigm shared by Cerviño and Barral-Souto?

a.   The *New Aspect* considered each producer to operate following a calculus of profitability. Beyond a certain distance, for example, a producer desists from some productions because they 'are not profitable'. The task of the statesman is to make feasible profitable private production by allotting to farmers land whose surface is in direct proportion to the distance to the centre, and also to supply them with an infrastructure favourable to exportation.

b. Barral-Souto's concerns – specialization, labour division and exchange – are some of the oldest issues in economic science. They were dealt with by Plato in *Republic*. In such cases the word 'economy' was most frequently used in the sense of a more efficient use of a scarce resource. 'Economics, wrote Samuelson, is suggestive of economizing or maximizing'.[12]

Summary

1. Beyond difficulties of identification, multiple discoveries seem to be rather extended phenomena.
2. Imperfect communication turns out to be a major source of multiple discoveries.
3. Political, ideological or economic frameworks seem to have exerted a weak influence.
4. The command of similar tools – either mathematical or economic – favoured the discovery of similar models when researchers were confronted with similar real problems.

ADDENDA

Cerviño's Life Sketch

Pedro A. Cerviño was born in Pontevedra, Galicia, Spain in 1757 and died in Buenos Aires, Argentina on 30 May 1816. Engineer of the army and 'surveyor of the boundary line', he arrived at the Rio de la Plata in 1782 in the capacity of member of the commission of boundaries between Spain and Portugal. As the commission broke down in 1783, he was incorporated in the third Crew, as assistant to Azara. With Azara, Cerviño made several trips: in 1783 he took part in a scientific journey to the Chaco region; in 1784 he travelled to Paraguay; in 1796 he accompanied Azara on an inspection of the guards and forts along the frontier of Buenos Aires, and wrote a travel diary. In 1798 Cerviño drew for the Consulate of Buenos Aires a cartographic chart of the port of Ensenada de Barragán and a 'spheric chart of the Rio de la Plata'. In 1799 he was appointed Director of the Nautical School, which he inaugurated on 25 November 1799 with his reading of a paper titled 'Neptune's trident, the world's sceptre'. Counsellor Alzaga, on 3 January 1800, urged that Cerviño's writings and speeches be examined before being published, for which reason the *New Aspect of the Rio de la Plata Trade* was written under the pseudonym

'A striving and skillful patriot', being later on (erroneously) attributed to the poet Manuel José de Lavardén.

Barral-Souto's Life Sketch

J. Barral-Souto was born in Oleiros, La Coruña, Spain on 23 October 1903 and died in Buenos Aires in 1976. On 9 March 1921 he was admitted to the sole course in economic sciences given at the University of Buenos Aires, then called 'Doctorate in economic sciences (although it meant an undergraduate course). On 19 May 1925 he obtained the degree of public accountant. On 5 April 1929 he entered the course of actuary. His final examinations were on industrial or labour law (30 March 1931) and finance (16 July 1931). During 1926–30 Barral-Souto took the first two years of a doctorate in physico-mathematical sciences at the Faculty of Physico-mathematical Sciences of the University of La Plata. This included courses on mathematical analysis (trigonometry and algebra, mathematical analysis I and II) and two courses on geometry (metric and projective geometry, and descriptive geometry). In 1927 Barral-Souto entered the Institute of Banking Policy, directed by Professor Baiocco, to whom he was attached for several decades. There he directed students' researches, later included in *Statistical Analysis of some Banking and Related Series* (1929). On 23 July 1928 he became an Argentine citizen. In 1929 he published his first paper: 'Calculation of the effective rate of a bond' in *Revista de Ciencias Económicas*, the faculty's economic journal. In the same year he began to study biometrics under Professor José González Galé. On 10 and 30 December, respectively, he passed with a grade of A+ examinations in actuarial mathematics and biometrics. In 1930 the Institute of Biometrics was created as a complement to the course in actuary. Barral-Souto entered there on 24 September 1930 as a tutor in practical exercises. In 1933 he enrolled in a contest to fill the post of assistant professor of statistics. To that end he wrote a monograph on 'Bernoulli's scheme and masculinity-rates in the City of Buenos Aires (1900–1931)' (70 pp., unpublished). On 6 November 1933 he was appointed assistant professor of statistics, a post he held until 27 January 1942. He had to give eight lectures on that subject in several academic years. He fulfilled that requisite in 1934, 1935 and 1939. On 2 April 1934 he submitted a doctoral dissertation on 'Expression of a lifelong annuity by an integer power series of the rate of interest variation' (jury: Professors José González Galé, Argentino V. Acerboni, Teodoro Sánchez de Bustamante, Benjamín Arriague, and the faculty's Dean Enrique César Urien), graded 'outstanding' on 18 July 1934. In *Boletín Matemático* he published: 'The calculating machine in the calculation of roots' (July 1934), 'On Steffensen's inequality' (September 1934), 'A proof of Tchebicheff's inequality' and 'A finite inequality' (October 1934), 'Five interesting values of an overall average' (November 1934), 'On Jensen's inequality' (June 1935), 'A study of the derivative of an overall average' (July 1935) and 'Around the sign of a derivative' (October 1935). In 1936 he shared in the foundation of the UMA (Argentine Mathematical Union), where he acted as member of the council in 1943–44 and in 1944–45. On 9 October 1937, after four years as assistant professor of statistics, he produced the paper, 'The mode and other averages, special cases of the same mathematical expression', published as No. 3 of *Cuadernos de Trabajo (Working Papers)* of the Institute of Biometrics. Other working papers of his authorship were: No. 4: 'Life insurance with variable capital' (1938); No. 6: 'A rational theory of economic systems', by Nogueira de Paula (1939; Spanish translation by J. Barral-Souto); No. 7: 'Interpolation and fitting of the generalized logistic curve' (1938); and No. 10: 'The fundamental principles of labour division' (1941). On 12–26 September 1936 he replaced Professor L.R. Gondra for two weeks, taking six lectures, a task that invited him to a perusal of Gondra's treatise *Elements of Political Economy* (1933). He again acted as a substitute taking six lectures from 18 August to 1 September 1937. Scientific institutions to which he adhered were Argentine Scientific Society (1937); Mathematical Association of America (1937–61); Institute of Mathematical Statistics (1937); American Mathematical Society (1938–54); Econometric Society (1938); American Association for the Advancement of Science (elected fellow 'in recognition of your standing as scientist', 27 December 1940); American Statistical Institute (regular member, 31 January 1941, First Vice-President, 1957–65; Honorary President, 16 October 1965); Argentine Notarial Institute (1949); American Statistical Association (1953); International Institute for the Scientific Study of Population (1953); and Argentine Academy of Economic Science (1966, seat no. 19).

NOTES

*   Inspiration for the present paper was drawn from Niehans's paper (1995). The pattern of analysis is his, but the data and also possible mistakes are mine.
1. The precise date is July 1947, when George Dantzig proposed the linear programming model (Dantzig 1963: 15).
2. The author is not aware of other communications on both cases here dealt with, except his own previous papers published in Spanish. For this reason it may be useful to intersperse several extensive quotations. For P.A. Cerviño's contributions I refer to Fernández López (1980, 1982a, 1982b, 1982c, 1982d, 1989b, 1989c, 1995), and for Barral-Souto's, to Fernández López (1989a, 1992, 1995).
3. Cerviño's (1801) manuscript is in the Congress of the Nation, Buenos Aires, Argentina. It was published in 1955 by Raigal, with modern spelling and a preliminary study and notes by Enrique Wedovoy.
4. Consider, for example, the following phrases: 'This capital [has] in its surroundings not less than ten thousand square leagues of arable land, in which there is not the least stone of an inch that might hinder cultivation' (p. 186), 'a plane of larger amplitude' (p. 131) and 'The

circle of its development does not find anything that hinders its enlargement' (pp. 161–2). The category distance: 'the efforts of cultivation, diminish in inverse proportion as the distance to the port' (p. 180), 'it progresses inversely as to the distance' (p. 120) and 'in geometric proportion as the distance to the centre'. Centre or port: 'A merchant port is a centre of trade, where surplus ware and manufactures are gathered to transport them where there is want of them' (p. 120), 'the centre of our trade must be located at the most advantageous place', 'Buenos Aires is therefore the best chosen centre on this river' (p. 161) and 'D. Pedro de Mendoza . . . chose Ensenada . . . as the centre of the emporium he was trying to found' (p. 168). Circular shape: 'Then all these points equidistant from the port, depict a bounded circle' (p. 121) Barral-Souto (1968: 1).

5. Francisco La Menza (1892–1977): Argentine mathematician, Italian born.
6. For example, in Haberler's *International Trade* (1933).
7. Letter to the Dean of the Faculty of Economic Sciences, University of Buenos Aires, 19 June 1961.
8. Der Isolierte Staat, I, §5 a.
9. Der Isolierte Staat, II, § i.
10. Cf Barral-Souto (1968) for this date.
11. Samuelson, (1970: 2; 62).
12. Samuelson, (1970: 2; 62).

REFERENCES

Barral-Souto, José ([1941] 1967), 'The fundamental principles of the division of labour', *International Economic Papers*, 12, translations prepared for the International Economic Association, London: Macmillan and Co. and New York: St Martin's Press: 31–62.

Barral-Souto, J. (1968), 'Personal judgement about three works'. [An account of three of his scientific contributions in order to be appointed Professor Emeritus]. Unpublished M.S., University of Buenos Aires: Archive of the Faculty of Economic Science.

Broggi. U. (1923), 'Vilfredo Pareto y la teoría del equilibrio económico', *Revista de Ciencias Económicas*, Series II, 11(27): 141–53, October. Ital. trans. 'Sull'economia paretiana', *Giornale degli Economisti*, June 1924, 331–3.

Cerviño, Pedro A. ([1801] 1955), *Nuevo Aspecto del Comercio del Río de la Plata* (manuscript kept at the Congress of the Nation, Buenos Aires, Argentina. Published in 1955 by Raigal Press, mistakenly attributing the authorship to Manuel José de Lavardén).

Dantzig, G.B. (1963), *Linear Programming and Extensions*, Princeton, NJ: Princeton University Press.

Fernández López, M. (1980), 'La pampa y el análisis espacial: algunos predecesores de Von Thünen', *Económica*, La Plata, Argentina, XXVI(3): 137–63.

Fernández López, M. (1982a), 'Matemática y economía en el Virreinato del Río de la Plata', *Annals, Meeting on the History of Argentine Scientific Thought*, Buenos Aires, Vol. I, 83–90.

Fernández López, M. (1982b), 'Primitivos escritos sobre organización del espacio argentino', *XLIV National Geographical Week*, La Rioja, Argentina. Published in Abstracts by GÆA- Argentine Society of Geographical Studies, Buenos Aires: 9.

Fernández López, M. (1982c), 'Espacio y Economía: el *Nuevo Aspecto del Comercio del Río de la Plata*, cuna del pensamiento espacial argentino', *Annals, Argentine*

Political Economy Association, XVII Annual Meeting, La Plata, Argentina, Vol. I: 391–422.

Fernández López, M. (1982d), 'Agricultura, transportes y comercio exterior en el siglo XIX. Pedro A. Cerviño y el elprojecto agrario argentino', IVas Jornadas de Historia Económica Argentina, Faculty of Economic Science, University of Rio Cuarto and Argentine Economic History Association, Rio Cuarto, Argentina: 617–31.

Fernández López, M. (1989a), 'José Barral-Souto y los orígenes de la programacion lineal', *Annals, Meeting on the History of Argentine Scientific Thought*, Buenos Aires, Vol. IV: 83ff.

Fernández López, M. (1989b), 'Superficies agrarias y modos de transporte', in Luis Eugenio Di Marco (ed.), *Finanzas Públicas y Desarrollo Regional (Ensayos en honor de Horacio Núñez Miñana)*, Córdoba: National University of Córdoba, Argentina: 98–110.

Fernández López, M. (1989c), 'Thünen-Palander envelopes and agricultural frontiers', *Annals, Argentine Political Economy Association*, XXIV Annual Meeting, Rosario, Argentina, Vol. II: 249–62.

Fernández López, M. (1992), 'La larga marcha hacia la programacion lineal', *Annals, Argentine Political Economy Association*, XXVII Annual Meeting, Punta Chica, Buenos Aires, Vol. I: 797–808.

Fernández López, M. (1995), 'Diez ideas-fuerza de economistas argentinos, *Foro económico*, I:(1), Buenos Aires, November: 23–55.

Haberler, G. (1933), *Der internationale Handel*, Berlin: J. Springer.

Hicks, J.R. (1960), 'Linear Theory', *The Economic Journal*, 70, 671–709. Also in American Economic Association and Royal Economic Society, *Surveys of Economic Theory*, III, Resource Allocation, New York: St Martin's Press, 1967, 75–113.

[DOSSO] Dorfman, R., P.A. Samuelson, and R.M. Solow (1958), *Linear Programming and Economic Analysis*, New York: McGraw-Hill Book Company.

Cornfield, J. (1941), Unpublished Memorandum. [First statement of the diet problem. Quoted by DOSSO (1958: 9), Hicks (1960: 94), and others].

Dantzig, G.B. (1951), 'Maximization of a Linear Function of Variables Subject to Linear Inequalities'. In Koopmans (1951: 339–47).

Hitchcock, F.L. (1941), 'The Distribution of a Product from Several Sources to Numerous Localities, *Journal of Mathematics and Physics*, April, 20, 224–30.

Jevons, W.S. (1871), *The Theory of Political Economy*, Pelican Classics edn, R.D. Collison Black (ed.), Harmondsworth: Penguin Books, 1970.

Kantorovich, L.V. (1939), *Mathematischeskiye Metody Organizatsiyi i Planirovanya Proizvodstva*, University of Leningrad, 67 p. Eng. trans., 'Mathematical Methods in the Organization and Planning of Production', *Management Science*, July 1960, 6: 366–422, with an *Introduction* by T.C. Koopmans, 363–5.

Koopmans, T.C. (1942), 'Exchange Ratios between Cargoes on Various Routes', memo, dated 1941, in *Scientific Papers of Tjalling C. Koopmans*, Berlin, 1970.

Koopmans, T.C. (1951), *Activity Analysis of Production and Allocation. Proceedings of a Conference*, New York and London: Wiley.

Koopmans, T.C. (1977), 'Concepts of Optimality and Their Uses', *American Economic Review*, June, 67(3), 261–74.

La Menza, F. (1937), *Los sistemas de inecuaciones lineales y sus aplicaciones al estudio de los cuerpos convexos*, Buenos Aires: Est. Gráfico 'Tomás Palumbo', also in *Annals of the Argentine Scientific Society*, Buenos Aires, 1937.

Leontief, W.W. (1961), 'A note by Prof. Leontief' [Letter to the Dean of the Faculty of Economic Sciences, University of Buenos Aires, 19 June 1961], *Revista de Ciencias Economicas*, July–December 1963, 210.

Lösch, A. (1944), *Die räumliche Ordnung der Wirtschaft*, 2nd ed. Jena: Gustav Fischer, Eng. trans. *The Economics of Location*, New Haven and London: Yale University Press, 1954.

Morton, J.E. (1944), Principios Fundamentales de la Division del Trabajo, by Jose Barral-Souto, review, *American Mathematical Monthly*, 51(1).

Neumann, J. von (1937), 'Über ein ökonomisches Gleichungssystem und eine Verallgemeinerung des Brouwerschen Fixpunktsatzes', *Ergebnisse eines mathematischen Kolloquiums*, *8*, 73–83.

Niehans, J. (1995), 'Multiple discoveries in economic theory', *European Journal of the History of Economic Thought*, 2(1): 1–28.

Ohlin, B. (1933), 'Till frågan om penningteoriens uppläggning', *Ekonomisk Tidskrift* 35(2): 45–81, Eng. trans. 'On the formulation of monetary theory', *History of Political Economy*, 10(3), Fall 1978, 353–88.

Samuelson, P.A. (1949), *Market Mechanisms and Maximization* (RAND Corporation, Part I, 'The Theory of Comparative Advantage', March 28, 1949), in J.E. Stiglitz (ed.) *The Collected Scientific Papers of Paul A. Samuelson*, Cambridge, MA, and London, England: The MIT Press, 1966, Vol. I, 426–38.

Samuelson, P.A. (1962), 'Economists and the history of ideas', *American Economic Review*, March: 1–18.

Samuelson, P.A. (1970), 'Maximum Principles in Analytical Economics', Nobel Memorial Lecture, December 11, 1970, in R.C. Merton (ed.) *The Collected Scientific Papers of Paul A. Samuelson*, Cambridge, MA, and London, England: The MIT Press, 1972, Vol. III, 2–17, also in A. Lindbeck (ed.) *Nobel Lectures. Economic Sciences 1969–1980*. Singapore: World Scientific Publishing Co., 1992, 62–77.

Sanchez de Bustamante, T. (1919), *Investigaciones de Economía Matemática*, Buenos Aires.

Stigler, G.J. (1945), 'The Cost of Subsistence', *Journal of Farm Economics*, *27*, May, 303–14.

Thünen, J.H. von (1826), Der Isolierte Staat in Beziehung auf Landwirtshaft und Nationalökonomie, Hamburg: Perthes.

PART VII

Currents of Thought

17. Contemporary responses to the *Tableau Économique*

Richard van den Berg*

Calculations are to the economic science what bones are to the human body. Without them it will always be a vague and confused science, at the mercy of error and
prejudice. (François Quesnay)[1]

More than 240 years after François Quesnay's *Tableau Économique* was
published, the fascination of economists with this first formal depiction of the
circular flow of goods and money in the economy continues. Indeed, in recent
decades Quesnay's attempt to outline a quantitative 'skeleton' of the economy
has received the most unanimously positive press since it was first exposed to
the world. As is quite well known, the earlier reception of the *Tableau* was far
less favourable.

Many of the books and articles about Quesnay's model note the mixed
reception it received in the past by starting with a short enumeration of the
opinions of famous earlier students of the *Tableau*. However, a preoccupation
with the alleged similarities between Quesnay's analysis and current economic
theories often prevents a more than cursory look at the opinions of earlier
commentators.[2] In particular, little seems to have been written about the reception of the *Tableau Économique* by Quesnay's contemporaries.

In this paper an attempt is made to fill what is felt to be a lacuna in the literature about the *Tableau Économique*, by means of a re-examination of the
earliest responses to this novel analytical tool. There are two reasons for this
exercise, which both related to the general theme, 'Is there progress in
economics'? First, if the *Tableau* was the seminal contribution to economic
theory that it is nowadays recognized to be, then it is interesting to see what
kinds of reactions first greeted this innovation. The earliest reception may tell
us something about the way orthodox or other opinion copes with a major
theoretical innovation, and thus about how the discipline progresses. Second,
do any of the early responses to the *Tableau* shed light on the continuing
debate about the precise meaning and purposes of Quesnay's invention? Or
has our understanding of the *Tableau* progressed much further than that of the
first generation of commentators?

THE DISSEMINATION OF THE *TABLEAUX*

Before discussing the responses to the *Tableau Économique* during the Ancien Régime, it is worth briefly considering the publishing history of Quesnay's construction. There is no need to go over this history in any great detail, since it has been well documented (see Weulersse, 1910, I: 61–71; Meek, 1962: 265–72; Kuczynski and Meek, 1972). For the purposes of this paper the main question to consider is which versions of the *Tableau* were most likely to have been known to contemporary readers.

The original version of the *Tableau*, the zigzag construction, occurred in a number of publications. It is likely that only Quesnay and Mirabeau knew the earliest two 'editions' of the zigzag (probably dating from the end of 1758 and early 1759 respectively). Possibly even Dupont and Baudeau, who became devoted adherents to Quesnay's teachings a few years later, did not know of the existence of these two *Tableaux*.[3] The first version that is likely to have been known to a somewhat larger public is the so-called 'third edition' of 1759. However, this work, which Baudeau refers to as a 'magnificent edition', had a very limited print run and was soon unavailable. Although this publication was known at the time as the famous first edition of the *Tableau*, it is not the work from which most readers would have known Quesnay's construction.[4]

However, from the start it was Quesnay's intention to give his zigzag the widest possible exposure. As Weulersse (1910, I: 69) points out, initially he wanted to have it published in the *Mercure de France*, but this idea was soon abandoned. Instead the chosen vehicle became Mirabeau's serial publication, *l'Ami des Hommes*. In 1761, in the second part of the sixth volume of this popular work, the *Tableau Économique avec ses Explications* was for the first time made available to a large public. Two years later several more zigzags appeared in *La Philosophie Rurale* (first edition, November 1763). According to Graslin (1767: 158 n.a) it was especially this last work which made the *Tableau* known to *tout le monde*, by which he probably meant most educated French men and women with an interest in political economy. Although the *Rural Philosophy* also contained a new kind of *Tableau*, known as the '*Précis*', I have not been able to find any contemporary references to this version. The final version of the *Tableau* was published in the *Journal de l'Agriculture, du Commerce et des Finances*, in June 1766. The next year it was reprinted in *Physiocratie*, Dupont's collection of texts of the *economistes*.[5]

In short, Quesnay's contemporaries could have learned about the *Tableau* from a number of sources, and even though it is not always possible to do so, as we will see, in a few cases it is important to establish which precise version they referred to.

MYSTERIOUS MATHEMATICS

It is perhaps a little surprising that for the majority of Quesnay's critics in the late 1760s and the 1770s the *Tableau Économique* was not a primary target. That is to say, there were few writers who bothered to criticize the precise assumptions, figures and calculations of the *Tableaux* in any detail. There seem to have been two general reasons for this paucity of detailed discussion. First, scepticism of Quesnay's method, and the physiocrats' claims for it, disinclined many learned contemporaries to study the *Tableaux* closely. Second, the mechanisms and arithmetic of the *Tableaux* were simply found too difficult.

With respect to the very general objections that were raised against the deductive style of reasoning of Quesnay and his followers, these are chiefly important for understanding their failure to convince more educated men of the value of their attempt at quantitative economic analysis. In this context, Voltaire's criticism of the physiocrats is sometimes seen as significant (see Groenewegen, 1983: xix; Vaggi, 1987: 871). In his pamphlet '*l'Homme aux quarante écus*' (1768), Voltaire poked some fun at a 'geometrician', who can readily apply his political arithmetic to all kinds of social and economic questions.[6] A more direct and more substantial expression of a similar scepticism was given in the same year by Mably in his *Doutes Proposée aux Philosophes Économistes*. Mably's main point against the pretensions of Quesnay and his followers is that in the social sciences one cannot draw conclusions that have the same status as mathematical truth.[7] While his objections are a criticism of the spirit of physiocratic reasoning in general and are not specifically directed at the analysis of the *Tableau Économique*, this geometric construction is surely implicated. It should not be forgotten that Quesnay and Mirabeau themselves claimed that the *Tableau* was an almost infallible tool for the discernment of the ideal moral order of society. For instance, in *L'Ami des Hommes* (1761:103) Mirabeau argued that one only had to study the *Tableau* superficially to understand the value of any human law and ordinance.[8] The scepticism with which influential *philosophes* like Voltaire and Mably greeted such inflated claims indicates that the physiocrats' attempt at formal theorizing fell foul of the more subtle thinkers of the Enlightenment.

In addition to the general feeling that the *Tableaux* were symptomatic of an inappropriate use of deductive reasoning, it was all too easy for the critics of the physiocrats to dismiss the calculations as nonsensical. The scheme was scoffed at as a collection of 'hieroglyphs' (Graslin, 1767a: 158), an 'incomprehensible writing' (Mably, quoted by Hecht, 1958: 274), or even 'a monument of imbecility' (Linguet, 1771). Precisely because we know that the *Tableaux* were in fact much more than arithmetical mystifications, it is easy to underestimate the difficulties that even sympathetic readers experienced in understanding the *Tableau*. For example, there is evidence that some of Quesnay's closest followers struggled to comprehend the scheme,[9] and it is remarkable that so few of them succeeded in providing an account in their own words of the working of the model.[10] Only a couple of competent explanations of the *Tableau* were published by younger physiocrats. The best known of these is Baudeau's '*Explication du Tableau Économique à Madame de ***'*, which first appeared in the *Ephémérides du Citoyen* in 1767 and 1768. This exposition was of the type that would nowadays probably bear the title *The Tableau Economique for Dummies* (it exhibits the same slightly condescending tone common to manuals of this type). Another, little-known, account is given by Le Trosne (1777: 320–24). Both contributions are devoted to the explanation of the 'Formula' version of the *Tableau*, which seems to have been considered by them as the definitive version. While demonstrating that these physiocrats understood this *Tableau* rather well, there are few new departures in these accounts. It seems that even if Quesnay's followers emancipated themselves on individual points from their master, they found it too hard to introduce their original ideas to the formal apparatus of the *Tableau*.[11] This is even true for an original thinker of the stature of Turgot.[12]

The fact that an understanding of the *Tableau* required a special effort, added to the general mistrust, noted above, of the application of 'deductive reasoning' to the moral sciences, accounts for a situation in which a sceptical attitude towards Quesnay's model soon became widespread. It can be said that this general opinion even influenced writers who sympathized with most of the economic convictions of the *économistes*. A good illustration of this is a reaction of the Abbé André Morellet in his polemic with Linguet. In 1775, the latter accused Morellet of being a disciple of Quesnay and of worshipping the *Tableau Économique*.[13] To this Morellet replied that he did indeed generally agree with the views of the *économistes*, that they were 'honest citizens, whose intentions are always right and whose zeal is as pure as it is active, and who have taught many useful truths for the first time, or have made them familiar' (Morellet, 1775: 32). However, he continued, he could not be called an *économiste* because 'it has to be said, [I] have never understood the *Tableau Économique*, nor pretended to explain it to anybody' (p. 33). Morellet thus almost took pride in his inability to understand the *Tableau*. Given the general unpopularity of the construction by the mid-1770s, this was not much of an admission. Adam Smith too struck a fashionable note when he somewhat derisively reported that Mirabeau had compared the invention of the 'Œconomical Table' with the inventions of writing and of money (Smith, 1776, IV: ix; cf. Mirabeau, 1763: 19).

DETAILED CRITICISM

Due to the enormous success of the *Wealth of Nations*, later generations of readers with an interest in political economy were most likely to hear for the first time about the *Tableau Économique* in Smith's book. Perhaps it can be said that the tone of mild irony with which Quesnay's model was referred to there did not invite a subsequent first-hand study. Even though the passage in the *Wealth of Nations* at least prevented the model from being entirely forgotten, the classical economists of the nineteenth century appear to have shown precious little interest in its function and working (see Pressman, 1994: 2).[14]

Considering the general and often somewhat superficial criticism discussed in the previous section, it may be asked if the *Tableau* had *ever* been seriously studied outside the circle of Quesnay's devotees. The answer to this question is affirmative. For a short period, in 1767 and 1768, the content of the *Tableau* was the subject of a more substantial polemic in a small number of books and periodical articles. Hereafter interest in Quesnay's model seems largely to have waned. The next section will focus on three writers who published some detailed comments on various versions of the *Tableau*. These writers are Forbonnais and Graslin, who both criticized the zigzags in books published in 1767, and Isnard who, somewhat belatedly, discussed the model in 1781.

As will be seen, the character of the critiques of these three writers is very divergent. The *Tableau* was clearly open to criticism from many different sides. To allow some comparison, it is useful to examine for each of the commentators the following three issues. First, what, if any, were the methodological objections against Quesnay's novel quantitative approach? Second, did these writers understand and agree with the 'mechanics' of the *Tableau*? Third, did they agree or disagree with the way the *Tableau* purported to analyse economic relationships such as the effects of luxurious consumption, and the hoarding of money?

Forbonnais

The first substantial criticism directed at the *Tableau* was provided by François Véron de Forbonnais in the book *Principes et Observations Économiques*, published at the beginning of 1767.[15] Not only was Forbonnais the first critic who, as Baudeau expressed it, 'wrote *ex professo* against the *Tableau*' (Baudeau, 1767b: 196), his attack was all the more significant because it came from one of the most famous economists in France at the time. Opponents of the physiocrats saw Forbonnais' attack as the moment that an old master could no longer tolerate the new-fashioned posing of the *économistes* (see, for example, *Journal Encyclopédique*, 1767: 60).

Many of Forbonnais' objections against the model are of a methodological nature. They concern, first, the manner in which Quesnay and Mirabeau use empirical data to establish the general quantitative assumptions of their model, and second, the way they use calculations to confirm their economic principles.

The criticism of Quesnay's tendency to use broad generalizations is a theme that recurs again and again in the *Observations*. The effect of this practice, Forbonnais warns, is that 'the local truth is sacrificed to speculative calculations' (Forbonnais, 1767: 208).[16] The reluctance he expresses about the sacrifice of variations within empirical data, signals an interesting disagreement about the use of generalizations in economic theory. Quesnay can be said to purposefully abstract from many aspects of economic reality in order to discover its basic structures. It is an approach that has been praised by modern commentators who argue that many of Quesnay's generalizations were in fact fortunate 'stylizations' that approximated real traits of the French economy of the *ancien régime* (see, for example, Meek, 1962: 295–6; Eltis, 1984: 7).

In contrast, Forbonnais is far less generous in his appraisal of Quesnay's use of 'stylized facts'.[17] He emphasizes the point that political economy is an art, rather than a science, which aims to provide a flexible structure within which all empirical data can be accommodated.

> [People with truly useful economic knowledge] employ their natural sagacity to observe the facts, the framework which relates them to several principles at the same time, and the essential and true relations between them. The result will give them modifications that accommodate every kind and every circumstance. They are like painters who distinguish characteristic forms where others only see [indistinguishable] masses, they draw with a free hand and true to nature the proper trait that differentiates each object from all others of its kind. (Forbonnais, 1767: 314, cf. 312)

Forbonnais is far from being a naïve 'pure' empiricist who objects to any theorizing. However, he believes that general economic assumptions should only serve a limited purpose. Instead of being used as the starting point for abstract quantitative reasoning, economic principles should provide guidance in empirical investigations and practical decision making (Forbonnais, 1767: 313). The alternative approach can only lead to conclusions that are radically divorced from economic reality: '[Mirabeau and Quesnay] do not know the facts, and being continuously unaware of the real object, they only talk all the time of what they imagine. They consistently talk of it and end up by saying that they have demonstrated it' (p. 311). This type of reasoning is, if not dangerous, at least thoroughly useless for informing practical policy, since '[m]ethodical and theoretical books have up to now perhaps served more to mask insolent ignorance with scientific jargon, than to forming men of practise' (p. 313).[18]

A second kind of criticism, which is much closer to that of modern students, is attempted by Forbonnais when he considers what he calls 'the mechanical construction of the tableau' (p. 172). His general position with regards to the operation of the *Tableau Économique* is that it is an unwieldy instrument to demonstrate economic ideas.[19] While he points out that he actually agrees with most of the opinions of the physiocrats, the calculations that the model yields often exaggerate and sometimes even contradict the real truth of the convictions of Quesnay and Mirabeau (p. 285).

It should be noted that the comments Forbonnais devotes to the 'mechanics' of the *Tableaux* all refer to those in the sixth part of *l'Ami des Hommes*.[20] He therefore does not acknowledge the changes made to the *Tableau* in the *précis* version and the 'formula', something which, as we will see, Baudeau did not fail to point out.[21]

Forbonnais criticizes in particular the depiction of the activities of the manufacturing class in the *Tableau*. In the first place, he notes that in the zigzag the figures in the column representing this class suggest that it is not 'sterile' at all. It is assumed that 300 million of annual advances are made, '[y]et the column of expenditures that are called sterile add up to 600 million, from which one could infer that manufacture, like agriculture, can produce one hundred percent over the capital that is employed in it' (p. 173). This means that Quesnay and Mirabeau 'have established the contrary of what they wanted to teach' (p. 173), that is, that manufacture is productive instead of sterile. Somewhat surprisingly, Forbonnais does not conclude from this that the doctrine of the sterility of industry is wrong, but that the calculations of the zigzag are mistaken.[22] He argues that the manufacturing class can surely never be as productive as agriculture (pp. 173–4).

A second point Forbonnais raises concerns the assumption in the *Tableau* that each class spends half of its income on agricultural products and half on manufactures. This is especially wrong with regard to the expenditures of artisans, according to Forbonnais. They do not spend half, but always *all* of their income on the purchase of agricultural products, that is, subsistence goods and raw materials (p. 181). The reason why Forbonnais stresses this point becomes clear later in his work when he discusses the presumed harmful effects to reproduction of 'disproportionate' luxurious consumption (pp. 224–45). He points out that according to the calculations of the 'dynamic' *Tableau* in *Ami des Hommes* agriculture will suffer if spending on manufactured products is one-twelfth greater than spending on agricultural products and will benefit if it is the other way around (p. 230).[23]

According to Forbonnais, the problem with the calculations that are used to demonstrate the decline in reproduction that will follow the increase in spending on luxury products, is that they assume that the manufacturing class spends less than its whole income on agricultural products. Only because this is assumed will an increased spending on luxury manufactures be detrimental to agricultural production. However, if it is recognized only that any increase in the manufacturing class's income is wholly spent on agricultural products, then it is clear that no harm will be done to agriculture: 'industry necessarily returns all it receives from the proprietors to the land. Therefore whether the proprietors spend a quarter, or a third, or half, or three-quarters of their revenue on industry, this expenditure does always necessarily return to the earth' (p. 225).

Thus if more is spent on luxury manufactures by proprietors, artisans will spend more on food and raw materials.[24]

It can be said that there is some merit in Forbonnais' criticisms of this aspect of the 'dynamic' *Tableau*. He clearly has understood the arithmetical trick Quesnay employed to show how agricultural production declines: his calculations rely on the assumption that not only proprietors change their consumption pattern, but members of the 'sterile' class do too. In a sense Forbonnais anticipates modern critics by pointing out that if, instead, the industrial class spends all its income on purchases from agriculture, the latter sector will not decline even if the spending pattern of the proprietors shifts towards luxury consumption.[25] The reason for Forbonnais to insist on this point is that if there is no danger to the prosperity of the state, then there is no justification to dictate to consumers on what kind of goods they should spend their money.[26]

Forbonnais also criticizes Quesnay's analysis of the role of money in the *Tableau* (pp. 211–19 and 287–300). His main point is that the physiocrats recognize only one function of money, namely its function as a means of payment.[27] The idea that too large a money stock in the economy is useless is wrong. What Quesnay seems to deny, according to Forbonnais, is that money also has a function as *immeuble*: it is a means of saving capable of earning its owner interest (p. 212). Not only is the existence of savings in an economy useful to individuals, it is also beneficial to the state as a whole. Offering a rather mercantilist reflection, Forbonnais argues that savings are also a *moïen de puissance* for the state, because they allow it to wage war since such events always necessitate large loans. While it is interesting that Forbonnais objects to Quesnay that money also has a function as a store of value, he does not really address the latter's fears that this use may endanger circulation. Forbonnais' analysis of the role of saving is rudimentary with compared with that of Turgot. In particular, he has little to say about the role of savings in the process of capital formation, an analysis Turgot develops rather brilliantly.

The impact of *Principes et Observations* can be gauged from the heated exchanges that ensued in the French periodicals throughout 1767 and into 1768.[28] The *Gazette du Commerce* wrote that the *Tableau* had been 'shown to be wrong in it calculations and its principles' (1 August 1767, 61: 600 n.). Such a conclusion demanded a reply from Quesnay's camp. Baudeau provided the most substantial one in the *Ephémérides du Citoyen* (1767b, VIII: 153–200). Little is said in this reply about the methodological points of Forbonnais. Instead Baudeau concentrates on the refutation of the criticisms of the calculations of the *Tableau*.

Curiously, he seeks to demonstrate that Forbonnais has not understood the model by referring extensively to the figures used in Quesnay's article 'Analyse'. Thus he tries to disprove Forbonnais' criticism of the original zigzag version of the *Tableau*, by using the 'Formula' version. Accordingly, Baudeau argues that in the *Tableau* the farmers do *not* spend half, but a third of their incomes on manufactures.[29] The manufacturing class for its part does not spend half but all its income on purchases from the agricultural class. At the beginning of the year it has one milliard of advances, which it spends on the purchase of raw materials, and during the year it receives one milliard from the proprietors which is spend on the purchase of food. Thus in total the sterile class spends two milliards, which is equal to the value of its annual product (pp. 189–90). What Baudeau implies by this demonstration is that if Forbonnais cannot even understand these basic facts, one cannot take his criticism seriously. But in effect Baudeau sidesteps some thorny questions by not referring back to the original version of the *Tableau*. At best Baudeau's disingenuous response implies that in his opinion Forbonnais' objections had already been addressed in the final version of the *Tableau*. At worst, he did not understand the differences between the mechanisms of the two kinds of *Tableaux*.

Graslin

A second detailed critique of the *Tableau* appeared towards the end of 1767 in the remarkable *Essai Analytique* of Graslin (1767a). This work was bound to attract much less attention than Forbonnais' publication. Not only did the author not have any reputation as an economic writer, the often abstract nature of his theory will also have made the book unattractive reading. In the *Essai*, which is better known for its novel 'psychological' theory of value, Graslin devotes Chapters IX to XI (pp. 159–225) to a critical examination of the *Tableau*.

With regard to methodology, Graslin's critique of Quesnay is quite different from that of Forbonnais. While the latter argues for an approach that is more empirical, Graslin asserts that he introduces the scientific method of Descartes to economics.[30] By this he means an approach to economics whereby one reasons from first principles that are largely derived from introspection. Without such foundations any attempt to apply mathematics to economics is doomed to be an empty exercise. Referring to the works of 'our political calculators', the *économistes*, he asserts:

In order to give weight to modern opinions they have thought it sufficient to support them with calculations. This is a mistake. Calculations are nothing but reasoning that is expressed by means of signs upon which operations can be carried out. However, since the most precise reasoning cannot conclude anything unless it is based on evident principles, the most accurate calculations only prove anything insofar they are consequences of some truth that is already known. (Graslin, 1767a, I: 6–7).

Unlike many other critics Graslin is not offended by the view of Quesnay and his followers that economic theory should be founded on 'evident principles'. Instead he maintains that the physiocrats have not arrived at the *right* evident principles due to their ignorance of the proper Cartesian method.[31] The 'first principles' Graslin claimed to have discovered comprise a theory of value, which is elaborated at the beginning of his *Essai*. He uses this theory to criticize what may perhaps be called the physiocratic 'theory of value'.

Quesnay repeatedly states that it is not simply the abundant surplus production of agricultural goods *in physical terms*, which is beneficial to the economy as a whole. Instead it is the great *monetary value* of the agricultural net product, because it is this magnitude that is paid to the class of landowners and which gives rise to its beneficial spending. In Quesnay's opinion only the combination of (physical) *abondance* and (monetary) *cherté* of the agricultural produce will guarantee the *opulence* of the nation.

According to Graslin this position is untenable. In his theory the exchange value of goods is based on the combined factors of 'need' (*besoin*) and 'scarcity' (*rareté*) (Graslin, 1767a: 24; see note 32). Whenever goods of a certain class are supplied in more abundant quantities, the market value of individual units of that good must *fall* relative to other classes of goods. This fall in price of agricultural goods may 'excite the reproduction of other objects of wealth, because these have more value relative to the products of the land. But the opposite has to be concluded when the products of the land have a *higher* value' (p. 182; emphasis added). Graslin thus argues that a good can only rise in value when there is a relative lack of supply, and whenever this happens the relative value of other goods will fall correspondingly. On the other hand, an increase of agricultural production will result in a fall of agricultural prices and a corresponding increase in the prices of manufactures.

Graslin is highly critical of the beneficial role that is attributed in the *Tableau* to the spending of the class of landowners. In Quesnay's scheme the spending of the landowner class strikes a right balance when its income is divided equally between agricultural products and manufactures. In contrast, it is Graslin's conviction that the spending of the idle class of landowners typically distorts the 'normal' proportions in production within the economy. By this normal order Graslin means something quite specific: it is the one that ensures that the needs of the labouring population are satisfied in their proper 'order of intensity'.[32] The landowners upset this order by spending income they did not earn by their labour, to satisfy frivolous needs.

This position informs his discussion of the physiocratic question of whether the decision of proprietors to save is detrimental for circulation and reproduction (pp. 197–201). In contrast to Quesnay, Graslin maintains that such a decision can only have positive effects.[33] When landlords decide not to spend part of their income, it is likely that they will forgo objects that would have satisfied their least urgent needs (*derniers besoins*). When they suppress their urge to buy such luxury products, the value of these products will fall (p. 199). The result of this, Graslin argues, is that more 'useful' objects will be produced (p. 199). These ideas, which ultimately appear to be based on a political sentiment against the existence of an idle class of landowners, lead Graslin to a position that is more disapproving of the spending of landowners on luxury products than that of the physiocrats.[34]

A final point, which Graslin raises several times, is that according to him monetary flows and real flows are confused in the *Tableau* (see especially pp. 160–67 and 220–24). In order to understand the real exchanges that take place in the economy, Graslin argues, one should be able to abstract from the existence of money and 'revert to the state of direct exchange of one thing for another' (p. 163). If this is done, however, it becomes clear that the *Tableau* is flawed.

> it should be possible to do away with money, without changing anything to the basis of the system. Yet, it is easy to see that when money is done away with, the system, which one has tried to portray in the *Tableau Economique*, loses its basis and support. Therefore, the *Tableau Economique* does not represent anything real and is, if I am permitted this expression, nothing but a *tableau de fantaisie*. (Graslin, 1767a: 224)

It has to be said that Graslin does not really clearly demonstrate this view. Nevertheless the observation that if one would abstract from money and only consider physical exchanges, some flaws in the *Tableau* would be exposed, is an important one. The reason for this is that, as we will see, Isnard does exactly that fourteen years later.

Despite some interesting isolated points, Graslin's critique of the *Tableau Économique* is on the whole somewhat disappointing. It did not evoke a refutation from any of the physiocrats. In his review of the *Essai*, Dupont confined himself to the remark that Graslin had criticised their system without having taken the trouble to try to understand it (Dupont, 1768, II: 169).[35] Also, in polemic between Graslin and Baudeau, the former's criticism of the *Tableau* does not figure.

Isnard

The most interesting contemporary critique of the *Tableau Économique* can be found in the *Traité des Richesses* of Achilles Nicolas Isnard. This book was published in 1781, by which time the influence of physiocratic theory had been on the wane for over a decade. This is probably one of the reasons why Isnard's comments aroused little interest at the time.[36]

Direct observations about the *Tableau Économique* occur in a number of places in the *Traité* and it takes some effort to piece these comments together. As part of his critique of Quesnay, Isnard puts forward an alternative formalization of the process of economic reproduction. As will be seen, this alternative model is in fact a substantially amended version of the *Tableau*.

Before looking at Isnard's construction, it is important to note that, in contrast to Forbonnais and Graslin, this critic does by and large agree both with the physiocrats' views on the proper method for economic research and with their basic perception of the economic system. Having been trained as an engineer, Isnard fully endorses Quesnay's quantitative approach to the social sciences. The task of the social scientist consists primarily of measuring economic quantities and finding fundamental arithmetical relationships between variables.[37] It has to be said that Isnard also shares with Quesnay the rather inflated expectations about the kind of knowledge this approach will yield. Their science is trusted to lead to nothing less than objective and precise knowledge of the best organization of society that conforms to human nature. Economic science is the applied science of the natural laws of society.

With regard to Quesnay's seminal conception of the economy as a single reproductive system, this view is fully endorsed by Isnard. Central to Isnard's quantitative analysis is the notion that the economy is capable of producing a 'disposable product', or surplus, in excess of the goods that are required as 'means of production' (see especially Isnard, 1781, I: xi, 60, 92–3).[38]

Isnard's alternative model of economic reproduction, which he refers to as a *systeme de richesse*, is presented as an instrument to disprove a number of aspects of the physiocratic doctrine. The fundamental affinity between this model and the *Tableau Économique* is somewhat obscured by the fact that he uses a novel way of expressing economic relations. Instead of using Quesnay's pictorial approach, Isnard uses an algebraic expression to indicate the relations between inputs and outputs and between sectors. While this formal change is certainly an advance, in order to facilitate the comparison between the two models it is useful to rewrite one of Isnard's numerical examples in the form of the *Tableau*. This gives the picture shown in Figure 17.1.[39]

The above figure can be used to illustrate some of what Isnard calls the 'mistakes regarding the principles of the general circulation of wealth' in the *Tableau Économique* (Isnard, 1781, II: 9). Perhaps the most crucial difference

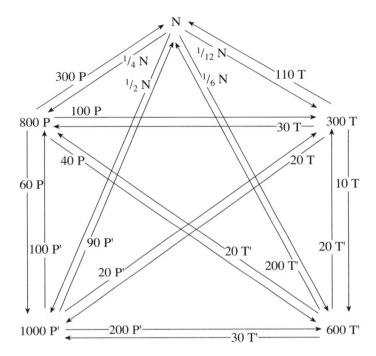

Source: Isnard (1781, 1: 40–41).

Figure 17.1   Tableau based on Isnard

between Isnard's model and the *Tableaux* is that in the former the exchanges of products between the industries are expressed in terms of physical quantities. Unlike the *Tableaux*, where all quantities are expressed in monetary values, the letters P, P′, T, T′ and N in Isnard's example denote physical units of five different kinds of products. As a consequence it is very easy to establish which physical inputs enter in each process of production. Moreover, it is also very easy to determine the size of the physical surplus produced in each sector. In each case it is simply obtained by deducting from the total produce of a sector the quantities used for production in the other sectors.[40] In this example the surplus has a physical composition of 300 P, 590 P′, 130 T, and 300 T′.[41]

Clearly, in Isnard's opinion not just one sector is 'productive'. One of the main purposes of his work is to establish precisely this point. It is important to note that in doing this he introduces a more precise definition of the notion of productivity. Being 'productive' in a physical sense merely means producing quantities in excess of the reproductive requirements for that good of all producing sectors.

Since Isnard's example only shows physical exchanges, it is not possible to say anything about *costs* of production, and about the distribution of the surplus. Additional assumptions have to be made concerning relative prices. Isnard is fully aware of this.[42] By assuming a set of relative prices for physical units of the five products in the above example, he demonstrates that the distribution of the physical surplus depends on the prices of inputs and outputs.[43] It is this point which forms Isnard's most significant critique of Quesnay. The latter's theory of distribution is criticized at some length in the following passage:

> One could reproach [the physiocrats] for having represented the landowners as being seated on a throne and distributing to both sides the salaries of the two classes according to how they value their advances, their talents, their activity, etc . . . . [However] there is exchange everywhere, it is in exchange that values are determined, [and] it is through the values that each proprietor of labour, of products and of capital attract a part of the disposable wealth.
>
> The *Economists* have said that *industry is not productive* and that *the class of those who work up the products of the land is a sterile class*. . . . Those authors [also] have not at all regarded the interest on wealth as a disposable product. They have regarded the product of the sale of the things produced by capital as a repayment of those costs; . . . they have said that in the general distribution of wealth, labour and capital only receive the salaries due to that labour and to that capital (Isnard, 1781: 40 n; emphases in the original).

In this passage Isnard makes two important points against Quesnay's theory of distribution. First, it is not necessarily true that the whole surplus produced in the economy is allotted to the class of landowners. Other classes may well be able to appropriate some of the 'disposable wealth'. Second, the distributive outcome depends on the relative prices pertaining in the economy. This second point is particularly interesting. Perhaps it can be said that Isnard implicitly accuses Quesnay of laying down a desired distribution ('the whole surplus is appropriated by the landowners') that requires the assumption of a specific set of relative prices. This is exactly the conclusion reached by some modern commentators (see Gilibert, 1989).

In contrast to Quesnay, Isnard's own views with respect to the distribution of the 'disposable wealth' produced in the economy are much more flexible. According to him, 'an infinite number' (Isnard, 1781, I: 41) of sets of relative prices is possible. That is to say, as long as relative prices remain within the range in which the reproduction of the various commodities is assured, the precise distribution of the surplus is an open question. All that can be said definitely is that 'the real mass of disposable wealth will always be divided among those [producers] for whom the value of their products exceeds the value of the costs' (p. 42).[44]

One important reason why Isnard criticizes Quesnay's idea that the whole surplus is received by the class of landowners is that this does not allow for the existence of profit. This type of income is clearly seen by Isnard as a return over and above the capital advanced, which is part of the 'disposable product' of the economy. In this respect his theory resembles those of Smith and Turgot. Even though Isnard does not incorporate the notion of profit as a surplus income into his model in a very satisfactory manner, his attempt is significant nevertheless.[45] It shows that Isnard tried to remedy what later generations of commentators saw as one of the main deficiencies of the *Tableau* as a depiction of a capitalist economy. It lacked an income category for the crucial class of the owners of produced means of production. Not until Marx would a similar attempt be undertaken to amend Quesnay's *Tableau Économique*.

CONCLUSION

The earliest responses to the *Tableau Économique* were rather mixed. By the late 1760s the most common attitude of Quesnay's critics was one of scepticism about his generalizing quantitative approach. A widespread opinion seems to have existed that economic life could not be adequately analysed by means of calculations that were based on a few simple principles and grand abstractions.

This popular view was substantiated most fully by the detailed critique of the *Tableau* that was provided by Forbonnais. His objections were largely of a methodological nature. They concerned the empirical reliability of the figures used by Quesnay and the validity of the conclusions drawn with the aid of his calculations. The methodological objections of Graslin were quite different. Instead of objecting to a quantitative approach per se, he maintained that Quesnay's theory lacked what one might call the right 'micro' foundations. It seems fair to say that ideas of both Forbonnais and Graslin about the proper economic method differed too radically from those of Quesnay to occasion any constructive criticism of the *Tableau*. While they made the effort to raise points about specific flaws of the *Tableau*, one gets the impression that they did not really find the construction worth preserving at all.

Indeed very few of Quesnay's contemporaries acknowledged that he had introduced a valuable tool to economics that may not yet have been flawless, but at least initiated a new type of quantitative analysis that was worth pursuing further. Quesnay's closest followers did on the whole not exhibit such a constructive but critical attitude. They were more inclined to consider the *Tableau* as a faultless masterpiece not amenable to improvements. Perhaps they also lacked the mathematical ability pursue this task.

The only eighteenth-century critic of Quesnay who succeeded in developing his formal model in a novel way was Isnard. Neither part of the close circle of the *économistes* nor a prominent *philosophe* or administrator, this engineer independently carried Quesnay's promising line of quantitative analysis further. His contribution was not very significant in terms of the influence on the subsequent development of economic thought. However, in terms of analytical progress his work is highly relevant.

By carefully distinguishing between real and monetary aspects of production and exchange, Isnard extricates a number of ideas that were mixed in Quesnay. Maintaining the latter's basic idea of the economy as a reproductive system capable of producing 'disposable wealth', he arrives at a clearer definition of the surplus in purely physical terms. Having done this, he criticizes the *Tableau* for not making the relationship between distribution and relative prices explicit.

Isnard's critique of the *Tableau* would seem to be a clear case of early analytical progress within a strand of quantitative economics that in our time comprises input–output analysis and Sraffian economics. However, the fact that it took several generations of economists before further refinements of and new departures from the *Tableau Économique* were forthcoming illustrates that progress in economics is at times very indirect and slow.

NOTES

*   This is a substantially shortened version of the paper presented at the ESHET conference in Graz.
1. Quesnay makes this remark in a letter to Mirabeau (Archives Nationales, Ms. 779, 4 bis, p. 2 note; quoted by Weulersse, 1910, II: 124). It was adopted with minor changes in the preface of *Philosophie Rurale* (1763: xix–xx).
2. An exception is the reception of the *Tableau* by Marx, which has been studied several times. For the relation between Quesnay's model and Marx's schemes of reproduction see, for example, Buffandeau (1967), Nagels (1970) and Gehrke and Kurz (1995).
3. Meek (1962: 272 n.2) argues that since Dupont did not know the first two editions, he took the third edition to have been the first one and its publication date as December 1758. Baudeau makes the same mistake (see *Ephémérides du Citoyen*, 1767a, I: 23 n.).
4. Not only Baudeau (see his note in the *Ephémérides*, 1767, I: 48) and Dupont (1769, VI: 40–41) referred to this edition; so did Forbonnais (1767, I: 161) and Graslin (1767a: 158 n.a). However, they do not pretend to have actually read this work.
5. Quesnay used this version in two more articles, both entitled '*Problème Économique*', the first of which was also first published in the *Journal de l'Agriculture* (August 1766) and the second in *Physiocratie*.
6. However, since this geometrician is clearly not Quesnay, but De Parcieux, it should be said that Voltaire's criticism is not exclusively aimed at the physiocrats.
7. He argues: 'moral and political truths are not the same as geometrical truths ... No dispute is possible about the propositions of Euclid, while in moral and political matters there is nothing about which the best trained and most enlightened men are not divided' (Mably, 1768: 56). The reason for this difference, according to Mably, is that political language is never value free or disinterested. While mathematicians talk about simple objects, morality and politics is always about more complicated things. 'Therefrom arises

the difficulty to make oneself understood, because different people do not attach the same meaning to the same words. Add to those obstacles obstructing the discovery of the truth, one hundred prejudices and one hundred particular interests, which mislead us without us noticing it' (p. 57).

8. The pretension that the *Tableau* would allow an understanding of objective rules of justice is also mocked by Forbonnais (1767: 302): 'It is not surprising the *Philosophie Rurale* calls [the *Tableau*] the tree of life. Undoubtedly, allusion is made to the story of the tempter demon, who aroused the pride of our first father by promising that the fruits of the tree would make him equal to God, by giving him perfect knowledge of good and evil'.

9. Fox-Genovese (1976: 268 n.38) notes that Dupont left unfinished a manuscript in which an explanation of the 'Formula' version is attempted. She takes this as evidence that Dupont could not explain the *Tableau* to his own satisfaction (also see Weulersse, 1910, I: 71). Earlier Mirabeau had struggled to understand the zigzag (see Meek, 1962:115).

10. According to one modern commentator this was so because 'no physiocrat other than Quesnay himself appears to have understood the mechanism' (Fox-Genovese, 1976: 268). As the contributions of Baudeau and Le Trosne show, this is surely an exaggeration.

11. For example, Le Trosne (1777: 939) clearly states that, like agriculture, the manufacturing sector uses fixed capital (*avances primitives*). But he does not allow for this kind of capital in his account of the *Tableau*.

12. In his correspondence with Dupont, Turgot indicates that he conceived his famous *Reflections on the formation and the distribution of wealth* (1766) as a development of the analysis of the *Tableau*. However, he admits that he abandoned the idea to give any mathematical formalizations to his opinions. He writes: '[The *Reflections* are] a type of outline of the analysis of the working of society and the distribution of wealth. I did not want to include any algebra in it, and there is only the metaphysical part of the *Tableau économique*' . . . (letter to Dupont dated 9 December 1766 in Schelle, 1913–23, II: 519; translation in Groenewegen, 1977: xvii–xviii; cf. Schelle 1913–23, III: 378).

13. See Linguet (1775: 32–3). Linguet was particularly dismissive of attempts to apply arithmetic and geometry to politics. In 1768 he wrote about the ascendancy of Quesnay's theory: 'A frantic love for mathematics seized all minds. Arithmetic and geometry seemed to have become the national language . . . From that general enthusiasm arose a new science, the *economic science*, which in its turn produced a mad passion to penetrate the mysteries of government and to appraise the revenues of the sovereign' (*Pierre Philosophale*, p. 3; translated from Weulersse, 1910, II: 129 n.1).

14. One of the few exceptions was Joseph Lang (1811).

15. The long second part of this work, which has the title 'Observations sur le Tableau Œconomique' and runs over 155 pages, is especially devoted to a critique of the *Tableau*.

16. Examples of physiocratic generalizations noted by Forbonnais are the assumption that wherever *la grande culture* is practised the net revenue is equal to the annual advances (Forbonnais argues that this proportion varies widely due to differences in the quality of lands; Forbonnais, 1767: 193–4); the implicit assumption that income per head is the same throughout the working classes of the economy (he points out that regional differences exist; pp. 197–8); that the more abundant agricultural capital becomes, the fewer men are employed in this sector of the economy and that the more productive agriculture is, the greater the need to export part of the surplus (both assumptions are too general according to Forbonnais, pp. 200, 201).

17. In addition to arguing that such generalizations are always at the expense of 'local truths', he accuses Quesnay and Mirabeau of simply being wilfully ignorant of many 'facts'. See for example the section in which he contests the physiocratic estimates of the decline in agriculture and population since the late sixteenth century. Forbonnais bases himself here mainly on Bodin and accuses Quesnay of relying too much on the estimates of Boisguilbert (Forbonnais, 1767: 255–86).

18. It is interesting to note that the reproach that Quesnay's ideas are too abstract and that they could or should not have been used to support economic policies, that is, that doing so is committing the 'Ricardian vice', is repeated by some historians of economic thought in our day (see Hutchison, 1988).

19. 'As far as our intelligence has permitted us to understand those works, we recognise truths everywhere, with the exception of a small number of propositions, but the manner in which those truths are expressed and applied does not always seem correct' (p. 164).

20. He justifies this limitation with the remark that according to him a reading of this work, together with the article 'Grains', 'suffices to understand the bases of [Quesnay's] system, its course and its results' (Forbonnais, 1767, I: 165).

21. Occasional references to the *Philosophie Rurale* show that Forbonnais did know this work. However the *précis* version of the *Tableau* is not mentioned. Neither does he discuss the 'Formula' version, which was published in the year before Forbonnais' observations.

22. Modern commentators also make the point that the figures in the zigzags seem to contradict Quesnay's views on the sterility of industry. See, for example, Pressman (1994: 24).

23. On page 224 of Forbonnais' work is a copy of the *Tableau* of page 66 of *l'Ami des Hommes*, in which a proprietor's income of 1050 is divided into 437.10s and 612.10s for expenditures on agricultural and industrial products respectively. That is, five-twelfths is spent on agricultural goods and seven-twelfths on manufactured goods.

24. The most one can say is that the spending on agricultural products is more indirect, and therefore reduces 'the certainty of a prompt return of money to the farmers' (Forbonnais, 1767: 232). However, the authors of the *Tableau* have confused this phenomenon with a decline in spending on agricultural products and fall in the farmers' incomes, 'two things that are very different' (p. 234).

25. See Gehrke (2000) for an overview of the recent controversy between writers who maintain that the *Tableau* cannot really demonstrate that a shift in consumption patterns towards luxury consumption will lead to economic decline and those who argue that it can. The former view is based on reformulations of Quesnay's construction as in input–output models with fixed coefficients, while the latter calls such restatements into question.

26. 'Of course everything is susceptible to excess, but the combination of the right of property and the real needs of the public is the only measure to be consulted' (p. 243). The proviso that the state should not be harmed is important in one case, the 'consumption of useless foreign products in exchange for our money' (p. 245).

27. In Quesnay's opinion there has to be a definite proportion between the stock of money in the economy and the annual product. He usually assumes that the money stock has to be equal to the net product, a view that is presumably based on the idea that rents are paid annually and that the money stock has to be sufficient to allow this payment.

28. The most important anti-physiocratic contributions appeared in the *Journal de l'Agriculture*, which from the beginning of 1767 had a new editor, the Abbé Claude Yvon, who replaced Dupont (see Sgard, 1991, II: 588). This journal printed several extracts from Forbonnais' book (in April, May, June, July, October and November 1767). Other contributions defended Forbonnais against the attacks of the physiocrats (for example, September 1767). In the next year Forbonnais himself joined the debate once more with a critical review of Abeille's *Principes sur la Liberté du Commerce des Grains* (August 1768). Other periodicals that placed contributions that were predominantly against the physiocrats were the *Gazette du Commerce* (1767a, 1767b, 1767c, 1767d) and the *Journal Encyclopédique* (1767).

29. This is so because 'annual expenditure of the productive class is three milliards: two milliards of [agricultural] products which it retains for its own consumption, and one milliard of manufactures which it buys from the sterile class' (Baudeau, 1767b: 188).

30. 'I have applied to economic matters the method of the Restorer of Philosophy, by only allowing any principle after having submitted it to the proof of doubt and experience' (Graslin, 1767: 4; cf. 3).

31. This is not the place to discuss the question whether Graslin's method can in fact be called truly Cartesian. However, the fact that one of the fiercest critics of the physiocrats claims to oppose them by using the method of Descartes is interesting in the light of the view of some modern commentators who have claimed that Quesnay's economics can be called 'Cartesian economics' (see, for example, Pribram 1983). Some of the most outspoken critics of Quesnay's approach, besides Graslin one can think of Condillac, presented theories that claimed to be deduced more rigorously from first principles.

32. These views are underpinned by an idiosyncratic theory of value, which cannot be discussed here at any length. Very briefly, according to Graslin each class of goods, or 'object', has an 'absolute' value, which depends on the place of the corresponding human need within an invariable order of psychological intensity. The ratio of 'absolute value' between two classes of goods, say grain and wine, is always the same. However, market prices (or 'relative' values) of individual units of goods within a class do vary relative to those in other classes due to 'scarcity'. Whenever the production of some goods is 'disproportionate', say in response to the improper spending patterns of an idle class, then relative values of individual units of goods differ from the absolute value proportions between the 'objects'.

33. Apart from the real effect of a shift in the composition of outputs discussed above in the main text, Graslin argues that the withdrawal of a part of the money stock from circulation can only have nominal effects. This is because a reduction in the money stock will result in a fall in the money prices of products (or appreciation of the value of precious metals): 'Money only represents wealth. The mass of money in circulation represents the mass of things to be exchanged. It follows, first, that when the proprietor hoards the money originating from his revenue, there would be no other effect than that all pieces of money that are in circulation would acquire a greater representative value, without any change in real wealth' (p. 198).

34. It does not escape his attention that Forbonnais has, on the contrary, criticized Quesnay for believing that luxurious consumption has harmful effects. He notes that: 'the Author of the *Principes & Observations Economiques* . . . distances himself too much from [the physiocratic doctrine] in his discussion of the *luxe de décoration*. I have proven that luxury is destructive of wealth and principally of the objects of basic needs, not because, as the Author of the *Philosophie Rurale* pretends, it gives too wide a circulation to the revenue of the soil, but because it adds new values to the mass, at the expense of the old ones, and because it augments the number of needs, etc.' (p. 215).

35. This review of Graslin's work is in the form of a letter to Saint Peravy, whom Dupont encourages to attempt a more complete refutation. The result of this request is a review of the *Essai*, which was published in Volume 10 of the *Ephémérides* of 1768 (pp. 165–206). This text is remarkable for the short outline of the theory of (extensive) differential rent that it contains (see Van den Berg, 2000), but does not discuss Graslin's comments on the *Tableau*.

36. This is in contrast to the response of more recent commentators like Schumpeter (1954) and Jaffé (1969) who have drawn attention to the fact that some ideas in the *Traité des Richesses* anticipate Léon Walras's general equilibrium theory. Klotz (1994) provides a recent re-examination of Jaffé's claim that Walras was actually influenced by Isnard.

37. 'Knowing nature, perceiving matters and their co-ordination, observing their qualities, their actions, their forces, calculating or measuring their quantities or their magnitudes, and the quantities of forces, of movements and of actions in order to discover their relations, *voilà* the procedure of the philosopher. It is in this manner that one will arrive at the *science*, and this will be the *science* of man, when the observation, the discoveries and the perceived and found relations will be useful to man' (Isnard, 1781, I: vii).

38. Nevertheless, there seem be two interesting differences between the intended meaning of the calculations in the work of Isnard and Quesnay. Isnard seems to use his calculations primarily as numerical examples to clarify a number of analytical points. The pretence in Quesnay's work that the figures used in the *Tableau* are based on some empirical estimates of the optimal development of French agriculture is missing in Isnard's work. A second difference, related to this, is that the particular preoccupation of Quesnay with the optimal proportions between economic variables (advances to net product, propensities to consume agricultural and industrial products) receives much less attention from Isnard. Nevertheless, in a more general sense Isnard's analysis has a similar focus on the questions of reproduction and the distribution of the surplus.

39. Two more numerical examples appear in the *Traité*, on page 36 of Volume I and pages 4 and 5 of Volume II. The former is a system with two products/industries; the latter has eight.

40. Note that consumption of own production is not considered in this example. This in contrast with the simpler example on page 36 of Volume I.

41. The question why the 'social surplus' has this composition is not addressed explicitly by Isnard. But it may be argued that, as in the *Tableau*, this composition is a response to a given pattern of 'final demand'. The difference, however, is that this is not only the 'final demand' of the landowners, but of all those classes that receive part of the value surplus.

42. He makes the point that inputs and outputs can only be compared in terms of (exchange) value most clearly in a pamphlet that was published some years after the *Traité*: 'Since commodities or products of different kinds enter into the costs of production, a relation of homogeneity has to be given to those products, which allows them to be compared to one another [.] [T]his relation is obtained from the *values* that those commodities or products obtain in exchange, or from the comparison made between all commodities or products to one commodity which serves as a common measure [. . .]' (Isnard 1789: 7–8; emphasis added).

43. He assumes a *numéraire* A and the relative prices $T = A$, $T' = 2A$, $P = A$, $P' = 3A$, and $N = 1200\,A$ (Isnard, 1781, I: 41). Now the costs of production can be added up: '. . . the costs of 300 T will be 300 A, the costs of 600 T' will be 850 A, the costs of 800 P will be 670 A, the costs of 1000 P' will be 740 A, [and] the costs of upkeep, repair and replacement of N will be 1080 A' (pp. 41–2). Since the value of the outputs can also be found using this set of relative prices, one can calculate how the surplus is distributed over the five sectors: 'The disposable revenue of the owners of T will be zero [300 A – 300 A]; that of the owners of T' will be 350 A [1200 A – 850 A], that of the owners of P will be 130 A [800 A – 670 A], that of the owners of P' will be 2260 A [3000 A – 740 A], [and] that of the owners of N will be 120 A [1200 A – 1080 A]' (p. 41).

44. This aspect of Isnard's theory of distribution is discussed at greater length in Steenge and van den Berg (2001).

45. In short, Isnard imagines 'interest on wealth', or profit, to exist only in the class of *propriétaires des richesses foncieres* (represented by N in the example in the main text). Thus, with regard to this example, he states that the 'interest rate is 10%' (p. 42), a figure which is based on the ratio between the value of the disposable wealth allotted to the owners of durable capital N, 120 A, and the value of the produce of that class, 1200 A. In contrast, Isnard does not see the disposable products in the agricultural and industrial sectors as rate of return over capital advanced.

REFERENCES

Baudeau, Nicolas (1767a), 'Avertissement de l'auteur', *Ephémérides du Citoyen*, I: 1–24.

Baudeau, Nicolas (1767b), 'L'ordre naturel et essentiel des sociétés politiques', *Ephémérides du Citoyen*, VIII: 153–200.

Baudeau, Nicolas (1767–70), 'Explication du Tableau Économique à Madame ***', *Ephémérides du Citoyen*, 1767 Vols XI and XII, 1768 Vol. III, and 1770 Vol. II. Béardé de l'Abbaye, . . .,

Baudeau, Nicolas (1770), *Recherches sur les Moyens de Supprimer les Impôts, Précédées de l'Examen de la Nouvelle Science*, Amsterdam: Marc Michel Rey.

Buffandeau, P. (1967), 'Le "Tableau économique" dans l'histoire de la pensée économique', *Revue d'Histoire Économique et Sociale*, 45: 381–401.

Du Pont, Pierre Samuel (1768), 'Lettre de M. du Pont, [. . .] à M. de Saint Peravy', *Ephémérides du Citoyen*, II: 165–88.

Du Pont, Pierre Samuel (1769), 'Notice abrégée des différents écrits modernes qui ont concouru à former la science de l'économie politique', *Ephémérides du Citoyen*, VI.

Eltis, W. (1984), *The Classical Theory of Economic Growth*, London: Macmillan.

Forbonnais, François Véron de (1767), *Principes et Observations Œconomiques*. Amsterdam: Marc Michel Rey.

Fox-Genovese, E. (1976), *The Origins of Physiocracy: Economic Revolution and Social Order in Eighteenth Century France*, Ithaca, NY: Cornell University Press.

Gazette du Commerce de l'Agriculture et des Finances, (1767a), Lettre à MM. les auteurs de la Gazette du Commerce', 55, 11 July: 540–41.

Gazette du Commerce de l'Agriculture et des Finances, (1976b), 'Annonce de livre', 61, 1 August: 600–601.

Gazette du Commerce de l'Agriculture et des Finances, (1767c), 'Observations des auteurs de la Gazette . . .', 70, 1 September: 691–3.

Gazette du Commerce de l'Agriculture et des Finances, (1967d), 'Réponse à l'auteur anonyme', 104, 29 December, Supplement: 1–3.

Gehrke, C. (2000), 'The analysis of *"dérangements"* in the *Tableau Économique*', paper presented at the International Conference on Input–Output Techniques, 21–25 August, Macerata, Italy.

Gehrke, C, and H.D. Kurz (1995), 'Karl Marx on Physiocracy', *European Journal of the History of Economic Thought*, 2(1): 53–90.

Gilibert, G. (1989), 'Review of *The Economics of François Quesnay* by G. Vaggi', *Contributions to Political Economy*, 8: 91–6.

Graslin, Jean-Joseph-Louis (1767a), *Essai Analytique sur la Richesse et sur l'Impôt*, London.

Graslin, Jean-Joseph-Louis (1767b), 'Lettre aux auteurs de la Gazette du Commerce', *Gazette du Commerce de l'Agriculture et des Finances*, 67: 665–6.

Groenewegen, P.D. (1977), The Economics of A.R.J. Turgot, The Hague: Martinus Nijhoff.

Groenewegen, P.D. (1983), *Quesnay. Farmers 1756 and Turgot. Sur la Grande et la Petite Culture*, Reprints of Economic Classics, Sydney: University of Sydney.

Hecht, J. (1958), 'La vie de François Quesnay', in *François Quesnay et la Physiocratie*, Paris: Institut National d'Etudes Demographies, Vol. I: 211–94.

Hutchison, T. (1988), *Before Adam Smith*, Oxford: Basil Blackwell.

Isnard, Achilles Nicolas (1781), *Traité des Richesses*, London (Lausanne): François Grasset.

Isnard, Achilles Nicolas (1789), *Réponses aux Principales Objections à Faire Contre l'Impôt Unique*, publisher unknown.

Jaffé, W. (1969), 'A.N. Isnard, progenitor of the Walrasian general equilibrium model', *History of Political Economy*, 1(1): 19–43.

Journal Encyclopédique (1767), 'Principes et observations économiques', June, IV(ii): 59–68.

Klotz, G. (1994), 'Achylle Nicolas Isnard, précurseur de Léon Walras?', *Economies et Sociétés*, 20–21 (10–11), 29–52.

Kuczynski, M., and R.L. Meek (1972), *Quesnay's Tableau Économique*, Royal Economic Society, London and Basingstoke: Macmillan.

Lang, Joseph (1811), *Grundlinien der politischen Arithmetik*, edited by Götz Uebe (1988), Bern: Peter Lang.

Le Trosne, Guillaume-François (1777), *De l'Ordre Social*, Paris: Debure.

Linguet, Simon-Nicolas-Henri (1771), *Réponse aux Docteurs Modernes*, London.

Linguet, Simon-Nicolas-Henri (1775), *Théorie du Libelle,* Amsterdam.

Mably, Gabriel Bonnot (1768), *Doutes Proposée aux Philosophes Économistes sur l'Ordre Naturel et Essentiel des Sociétés Politiques*, The Hague (Paris): veuve Durant.

Meek, R.L. (1962), *The Economics of Physiocracy. Essays and Translations*, reprinted in 1993, Fairfield NJ: A.M. Kelley.

Mirabeau, Victor Riqueti de (1761), *L'Ami des Hommes*, Volume 6, Part 2: *Tableau Économique avec ses Explications*, Avignon.
Mirabeau, Victor Riqueti de (1763), *Philosophie Rurale ou Économie Générale et Politique de l'Agriculture, Réduite à l'Ordre Immuable des Loix Politiques & Morales, qui Assurent la Prospérité des Empires*, Amsterdam: Les Libraires Associés.
Morellet, André (1775), *Réponse Sérieuse à M. L[inguet]*, Amsterdam.
Nagels, J. (1970), *Genèse, Contenu et Prolongements de la Notion de Reproduction du Capital Selon Karl Marx, Boisguillebert, Quesnay, Leontiev*, Brussels: Editions de l'Institut de Sociologie de l'Université Libre de Brussels.
Pressman, S. (1994), *Quesnay's Tableau Économique: A Critique and Reassessment*, Fairfield: A.M. Kelley.
Pribram, K. (1983), *A History of Economic Reasoning*, Baltimore: Johns Hopkins University Press.
Schelle, G. (1913–23), *Oevres de Turgot et Documents le Concernant*, Paris: Félix Alcan.
Schumpeter, J.A. (1954), *History of Economic Analysis*, reprinted in 1994, London: Routledge.
Sgard, J. (1991), *Dictionnaire des Journaux 1600–1789*, Paris: Universitas.
Smith, Adam (1776), *An Inquiry into the Nature and Causes of the Wealth of Nations*, K. Sutherland (1993), Oxford: Oxford University Press.
Steenge, A.E. and R. Van den Berg, (2001), 'Generalising the *Tableau Économique*; Isnard's *Systeme des Richesses*' (forthcoming).
Vaggi, G. (1987), 'Physiocrats', in J. Eatwell, M. Milgate, N. Newman (eds), *The New Palgrave: A Dictionary of Economics*, Vol. 3: 869–76.
Van den Berg, R. (2000), 'Differential rent in the 1760s: two neglected French contributions', *European Journal for the History of Economic Thought*, 7(2): 181–207.
Voltaire, François Marie Arouet de (1768), *The Man of Forty Crowns*, translation of *L'Homme aux Quarante Écus'*, London: Becket and D'Hondt.
Weulersse, G. (1910), *Le Mouvement Physiocratique en France*, Paris: Felix Alcan.

18. Progress in Austrian economics from Menger to Lachmann

Sandye Gloria-Palermo

INTRODUCTION

No doubt progress in economics is not a linear process. The establishing of the Austrian tradition offers one of the most striking instances of this peculiarity. The principles expressed by Menger were not taken up again from the outset by his followers. The first two generations of Austrian authors somehow deviated from the Mengerian originality and it was not until the 1940s that the Mengerian tenets were rediscovered by Mises and Hayek and, later on, in the 1970s, reorganized into a coherent framework.

The aim of this paper is to appraise how much road has been covered between Menger's embryonic statements and modern formulations of Austrian economics. The question is, apart from deviations and culs-de-sac, how much has been added to Menger's original contribution?

In order to answer this question it is first necessary to identify what constitutes the core of the Mengerian originality. Dynamic subjectivism, the causal-genetic way of thinking and non-determinacy, it will be argued, represent the bases of the Austrian school as Menger founded it. We will then examine to what extent his followers have been improving on each of these principles. The perspective of the paper is thus rather general, mainly dealing with methodological and conceptual considerations, the objective not being to provide a detailed account of the evolution of particular theories such as business cycle theories or market process theories.

THE MENGERIAN ORIGINALITY

In Menger's view, economics belongs to the group of theoretical sciences, which means that it automatically receives the status of an exact science. This concept of economics as an exact science clashes directly with the position of the German historical school, which favours a historical approach with the intention of highlighting empirical regularities. For Menger, on the contrary, the status of exact science stems from the fact that it is possible to develop precise and universal theoretical laws explaining economic phenomena. More precisely, the scientific approach defended by Menger is purely analytical and consists in breaking down complex economic phenomena into their most simple elements, a logical decomposition in terms of relations of causality. On a methodological level, his objective is:

> to reduce the complex phenomena of human economic activity to the simplest elements that can still be subjected to accurate observation, to apply to these elements the measure corresponding to their nature, and constantly adhering to this measure, to investigate the manner in which more complex phenomena evolve from their elements according to definite principles. (Menger, [1871] 1950: 46–7)

Now, what are these simplest elements that Menger has in mind and which constitute the essential causes of complex economic phenomena? At the simplest level of individual choices, the primary cause explaining behaviour reflects the human need to have certain goods at one's disposal in order to live, this translating into the search to satisfy one's needs. Throughout his work, Menger emphasizes the individual as a starting point for causal explanation of all economic phenomena. The author considers human behaviour which seeks to satisfy needs as the most simple premise upon which everything may be built, thereby defining economics according to a strict subjectivist base. This is defined as the principle of 'economizing'.[1]

In his 1883 work, Menger continues and goes deeper into the methodological foundations which, in his opinion, should underlie any theoretical science and economics in particular. Essentialism and universalism, the two principles at the core of Menger's methodology which were already introduced in the *Grundsätze*, are here confirmed and justified. The scientific approach, whose ultimate aim is to acquire general knowledge on phenomena, consists in systematically researching ultimate causes which are the very essence of these phenomena, by establishing general laws having a universal character, that is, knowing no exceptions:

> The goal of scholarly research is not only the *cognition*, but also the *understanding* of phenomena. We have *gained cognition* of a phenomenon when we have attained a mental image of it. We understand it when we have recognized the reason for its existence and for its characteristic quality (the reason for its *being* and for its *being like it is*). (Menger, [1883] 1963: 43)

Understanding an economic phenomenon means identifying the causal process which brings it into being, starting from its most elementary cause – economizing – to the most complex manifestation of the phenomenon under analysis.

The Focus on Economic Process

Clearly, Menger's conception of economics clashes with marginalism. The opposition was first made explicit by Hans Mayer. Mayer ([1932] 1994: 57) distinguishes between two types of theoretical approach to the question of how economic prices are formed: *causal-genetic theories* which, 'by explaining the formation of prices, aim to provide an understanding of price correlations via knowledge of the laws of their genesis', and *functional theories* which, 'by precisely determining the conditions of equilibrium, aim to describe the relation of correspondence between already existing prices in the equilibrium situation'.

Through this interpretative framework, Mayer examines the cognitive value of the major functional theories on price formation.[2] The capacity of these theories to explain reality and to widen the theorist's knowledge is restricted, according to Mayer, to describing quantitative relations between prices which, in turn, describe the situation of equilibrium, the central reference. According to Mayer, these theories do not increase the understanding of the economic system since formal relationships depict a particular situation – a state of equilibrium – in which the price formation process has already taken place implicitly. Mayer criticizes what is fast becoming the major approach in economics, namely, the formalist approach:

> Equilibrium equations . . . are obtained from previously established definitions and identity statements drawn explicitly or implicitly from one another. These are then used to derive, through purely logical inference, a nexus of substitution relations which can evidently give no more knowledge of reality than was already contained in the premises. This is real 'derivation' in the sense of 'proofs' in pure logic and mathematics, and not the acquisition of new knowledge about correlations in the real world. (Mayer, [1932] 1994: 148)

Menger's scientific approach well illustrates the causal-genetic way of thinking as defined by Mayer.[3] The price theory developed in the *Grundsätze* is not a theory of equilibrium prices but a theory of the *process of price formation*. It will be remembered that, within the Mengerian logic, the real level of exchange prices could a priori not be calculated in an unequivocal manner by the theory. The real level depends on the way in which a particular trading process takes place and the theory can merely fix the limits of a price interval. Menger's theory of price determination is particular in that it gives no explanation of the equilibrium level of prices. Indeed, in line with the methodological approach guiding his developments as a whole, the author goes into the determination of the *essential causes* at the origin of the mechanism of price determination. In this context, the essence of the explanation of monetary exchange lies in the economizing behaviour of man.

A NON-DETERMINIST VIEW OF ECONOMICS

Menger's methodological position is at the origin of deeper divergences with marginalism on analytical grounds: causality in itself involves the idea of time, whereas the marginalist analogy with mechanics provides economics with a static analytical framework centred on the study of equilibrium positions.[4] The simple assertion that economic action takes place in real time allows the introduction of two fundamental factors into the analysis: uncertainty and knowledge. These two factors, in turn, form the basis of the non-determinacy of economic phenomena. Let us consider the consequences of the introduction of real time within Menger's logic.

In this respect, the privileged area of analysis concerns production: as we know, Menger characterizes production as a causal process which connects goods of different orders. This process is sequential and definitely refers to a temporal perspective: 'The idea of causality, however, is inseparable from the idea of time. . . . However short the time periods lying between the various phases of this process may often appear, . . . their complete disappearance is nevertheless inconceivable' (Menger, [1871] 1950: 67–8). There is a fixed time lapse between the moment when goods of higher order are gathered and obtaining the good from the corresponding first order. At the outset of the process, there is uncertainty as to the quantity and quality of the good that will finally be available to satisfy the needs in question. This type of uncertainty is, in Menger's opinion ([1871] 1950: 71), 'one of the most important factors in the economic uncertainty of men'. The fact that production is described as a temporal process also leads to an emphasis on the role of producers' expectations. To be precise, economic activity for the agents consists in providing goods which are directly or indirectly necessary to satisfy needs: 'the concern of men for the satisfaction of their needs thus becomes an attempt to *provide in advance* for meeting their requirements in the future . . .' (Menger, [1871] 1950: 79). Agents must anticipate future needs before beginning the production process. Taken in this light, the production process forces the Mengerian economic agent to gather a certain quantity of information before being able to go ahead with planning economic activity. More exactly, the individual must have at his disposal not only the information relative to the quantity of goods of the first and higher orders necessary to meet his future needs, but also the information relative to the quantity of goods actually at his disposal. Uncertainty comes again into play. A priori, the quantity of first order goods is a direct function of the intensity of the individual's needs. This, again, may vary between the moment the agent carries out his forecasts and the moment when the causal production process comes to an end. Moreover, the factor of uncertainty arises in the quantity and quality of goods of the first order that will actually be produced.

The fact that economic activity occurs over time also leads us to look at the question of the information and knowledge of agents from a dynamic point of view. Indeed, within a Bergsonian conception, the passage of time does not take on the neutrality of a Newtonian concept. It is more a question of time turned, in a causal manner, towards the efficiency of decision-making. The passing of time, indeed, does not leave the state of agents' knowledge unchanged. From this point, Menger's conception of time turns out to be heterogeneous and subjective. The passage of time enhances the individual in an unforeseeable and continuous manner. It is in itself a source of change and novelty which alters the information the economic actors take into account when drawing up their expectations and making their economic decisions.

> If it is generally correct that clarity about the objective of their endeavors is an essential factor in the success of every activity of men, it is also certain that knowledge of requirements for goods in future time periods is the first prerequisite for the planning of all human activity directed to the satisfaction of needs. . . . The second factor that determines the success of human activity is the knowledge gained by men of the means available to them for the attainment of the desired ends. Wherever, therefore, men may be observed in activities directed to the satisfaction of their needs, they are seen to be seriously concerned to obtain as exact a knowledge as possible of the quantities of goods available to them for this purpose. (Menger, [1871] 1950: 89–90)

Menger's *homo oeconomicus* has little in common with the calculator–maximizer of Walras. It does not refer to an actor with perfect information. The Mengerian *homo oeconomicus* makes his decisions on the basis of his perception of the economic world around him and constantly reviews his expectations as his knowledge changes with time and as he realizes the mistakes he may have made in the past.

Dynamic Subjectivism

As we have just argued, the adoption of a Bergsonian concept of time is at the root of the deep rift between Menger and marginalists. The Austrian tradition concentrates on analysing the evolutionary processes of economic phenomena whose indeterminate nature is in no doubt. Marginalists, on the contrary, concentrate their interest around the static positions of equilibrium of economic systems. Moreover, Menger's conception of time gives rise to a second fundamental difference with marginalists. This concerns the form and nature of subjectivism in the analysis.

Static subjectivism, present in the marginalist tradition, should be distinguished from the *dynamic subjectivism* of Menger's approach.[5] The subjectivist dimension of marginalist analysis is restricted to the introduction of subjective factors on the demand side, the aim being to counterbalance the importance of objective factors passed down from the classical theory on the supply side.[6] Moreover, given his preferences, decision-making by a marginalist *homo oeconomicus* is completely mechanical and predetermined. From an analytical point of view, the agent is totally defined by his preferences. Austrian subjectivism, as Menger introduces it, is much more radical than the marginalist conception: it is not limited to preferences but is rather enlarged to expectations, costs, the conception of time (Bergsonian) and knowledge perception. According to O'Driscoll and Rizzo (1985: 22), dynamic subjectivism 'views the mind as an active, creative entity in which decision-making bears no determinate relationship to what went before', whereas static subjectivism is characterized by the fact that 'the mind is viewed as a passive filter through which data of decision-making are perceived. To the extent that the filter can be understood, the whole process of decision-making is perfectly determinate'.

The Mengerian conception of subjectivism is, from many aspects, of dynamic nature: the means–ends framework is at the core of Menger's definition of economizing; agents are engaged in a process of acquisition of knowledge in order to modify and improve their plans of action; knowledge depends on the information agents could acquire about causal connection between their desires and economic goods; Mengerian agents live in a world of uncertainty where the occurrence of errors is indeed possible; decisions should be based upon expectations agents make about an unknown future, leaving room for their creative abilities. Jaffé describes the Mengerian *homo oeconomicus* as follows:

> Man, as Menger saw him, far from being a 'lightning calculator', is a bumbling, erring, ill-informed creature, plagued with uncertainty, forever hovering between alluring hopes and haunting fears, and congenitally incapable of making finely calibrated decisions in pursuit of satisfactions. Hence Menger's scales of the declining importance of satisfactions are represented by discrete integers. In Menger's scheme of thought, positive first derivates and negative second derivates of utility with respect to quality had no place; nothing is differentiable. (Jaffé, 1976: 521)

To sum up, Austrians have inherited from Menger a particular conception of economics: economics, considered as a social theoretical science, requires an approach which is radically distinct from that used in natural science and in particular distinct from formalism; as a social science, its aim is to understand the process of emergence of economic phenomena such as value, prices, money, firms and so on, as the result of the interaction between individual plans; the Austrian approach thus develops theories of a causal-genetic nature in contrast to functional theories; this approach falls into the framework of the subjectivist paradigm to the extent that the essence of socio-economic phenomena is restricted to achieving individual plans (principle of economizing), these plans being built upon agents' subjective knowledge and perceptions of their environment.

MODERN IMPROVEMENTS

The next question is: how much has been done since Menger with respect to the traits constituting the Austrian originality? What improvements have been made as regards subjectivism, the causal-genetic way of thinking and the rejection of the omnipotence of the equilibrium diktat? I propose here to put aside the numerous mistakes and deviations that have punctuated the process of constitution of the Austrian tradition and to concentrate upon progress proper.

Causal-genetic Thinking, Mathematical Tools and the Reference to Equilibrium

The adoption of a causal-genetic way of thinking in economics has a direct consequence as regards the use of mathematical tools; contrary to a widespread idea, Austrians are not against any incursion of mathematics into economics, but reject the use of certain kinds of mathematical tools such as functional mathematics.[7] Indeed, according to Mayer (1932), Menger does not dogmatically reject any recourse to mathematics in economics, but he rejects mathematics in the only form that was available at the end of the nineteenth century, that is, functional mathematics, which is not adapted to economics as Menger defines it. The Austrian position against formalism is the result of an ontological investigation, of an investigation of the nature of economic phenomena and economic understanding. Menger's position in this respect is straightforward:

> My opinion is that the method that should be adopted within pure economics cannot simply be called 'mathematical' or 'rational.' We should investigate not only relations between magnitudes but also the *essence* of economic phenomena. But how can we know this essence – the essence of value, entrepreneurial profit, labour distribution, bimetallism and so on – in a mathematical way? Even if the mathematical method was purely and simply justified, in any case, it would not fit with the solution of the part of the economic problem mentioned above.
>
> However, I cannot accept the mathematical method at all, even for the determination of the laws of economic phenomena.
>
> The problem which many consider to be the most important is the formation of the *laws* according to which goods are exchanged for goods. Among goods, we German people include means of production as well as products, more precisely all the things that contribute directly or indirectly to the satisfaction of human needs.

Are the quantities of goods which we exchange in trading (quantities that change according to time and place!) arbitrary or are they ruled by fixed *laws*? This is the question.

Now, it is at the same time clear that the purpose of our investigations will never be reached through the mathematical method. It is necessary rather that we come back to the simplest elements of phenomena which are generally very complex – therefore that we determine *analytically* the last constitutive factors of phenomena.

Let us consider the theory of prices. If we want to have access to knowledge of the laws which rule goods exchange, it is first necessary to come back to the motives which lead men to act within exchanges, to the facts which do not depend on the will of traders, which have a causal relation with goods exchange.

We should come back to the needs of men, to the importance they give to the satisfaction of needs, to the quantities of different goods which different economic agents own, to the subjective importance (subjective value) that different economic agents confer on given quantities of goods and so on (translated from Antonelli, 1953: 279–81).

As soon as the aim of the theorist is to understand the process of emergence of a phenomenon through causal decomposition into its primary elements, formalization in the form of a system of simultaneous equations is inappropriate since it turns a blind eye to the sequence leading to the formation of the phenomenon, focusing exclusively upon the ultimate outcome of the process. Rejection of mathematical formalism by Austrians is thus justified because a direct correspondence exists between formalist tools (mainly functional relationships, derivatives and systems of simultaneous equations) and the functional approach defined by Mayer. Menger's refusal of functional mathematics should thus be analysed as an ontological awareness of the specificity of the economic explanation rather than as evidence of the formal weakness of the Austrian leader; in that sense it represents decisive progress. The next step would consist in acknowledging the symmetrical correspondence that exists between constructivist mathematics and causal-genetic theories; such recognition would open the door to the introduction of a particular type of mathematical tool in the modern Austrian framework. However, modern Austrians have been reluctant to commit themselves in that direction, justifying to some extent the criticism of dogmatism addressed towards them.[8] Don Lavoie (1994) has warned Austrians about their chilly attitude towards the use of mathematical tools. Such an attitude is nowadays hardly justifiable to the extent that theorists have at their disposal a wide array of techniques, no longer confined to the formal tools of equilibrium analysis. We are referring to computational simulations, genetic algorithms and evolutionary games and models and more generally to the whole set of techniques of a constructivist nature that might allow us to formalize the Austrian analysis of the market process and offer new avenues fully compatible with the causal-genetic way of thinking. Contrary to neoclassical models, the objective is not to appeal to formalization in order to find a solution to a given problem, such as the optimal vector prices associated with a specific economic configuration, but rather to bring about simulations of the economic process under analysis, with, first of all, a heuristic intention.

Contrary to Weintraub (1985: ix) who, after having distinguished between functional and causal explanations, affirms, without any doubt, that economics leans on the first category of relationships, modern Austrians pick up again the Mengerian agenda, thereby relying on a causal-genetic approach to phenomena. Understanding an economic occurrence thus means identifying the (essential) causes at the origin of the process the outcome of which is the phenomenon under analysis. The analysis of the market process soon imposes itself as the main theme of investigation. Menger investigated the causes of economic progress and more generally the dynamic elements of change. The forces of change in his analysis flow from the principle of economizing and from his analysis of the role of knowledge. Progress and change depend on the way in which agents acquire new knowledge about the relationships between goods of different orders and between goods and individual satisfaction. The analysis of the market as a process was deepened later on by Hayek (1978b), who defined the market as a process of discovery and diffusion of knowledge. Kirzner (1973) then developed the well-known theory of entrepreneurship in order to try to justify analytically the convergence of the competitive process towards a situation of general equilibrium. Finally, Lachmann provided a non-deterministic view of the market process as the result of the conjunction of both equilibrating and disequilibrating forces. Despite their own specificities, these authors all belong, explicitly or not, to the causal-genetic tradition. At this point, let us note for instance the formal similarity of the approaches of Lachmann and Kirzner. The point of departure for Kirzner is the criticism regarding the over-preoccupation of the standard theory with the concept of equilibrium. Kirzner's aim is thus to complete this approach with a theory of the *market process* leading to the equilibrium analysed by neoclassical authors. If the reference to Mayer is obvious, the similarity is however only formal, with Lachmann and Kirzner developing two different interpretations of the causal-genetic approach. Indeed, Lachmann (1982) states that the question is that of explaining the process of formation of market prices which are not necessarily equilibrium prices, whereas the theory of entrepreneurship explains how the economic system converges towards the full compatibility of individual plans, that is, ultimately towards equilibrium prices.

This rapid confrontation witnesses the absence of consensus among modern authors on the question of the place and status of the concept of equilibrium in Austrian theories. The opposition emerges even more explicitly when examining the issue of subjectivism.

The Subjectivist Paradigm

The subjectivist paradigm can be defined as a research programme whose aim is to explain social phenomena in terms of their inherent meaning, that is, in terms of what they represent for the participating actors.[9] Taken in that sense, subjectivism is often depicted as being the basic and unifying feature peculiar to the Austrian tradition and also the locus for progress in economics (Hayek, 1952: 31).[10] Indeed, following Lachmann, the evolution of the Austrian tradition can partly be described as a three-step story in which the subjectivist dimension has continuously been intensified.

The first stage is related to Menger, of course, and with what it appears legitimate to call the Viennese subjectivist revolution. As already stressed above, Menger develops from many aspects a dynamic kind of subjectivism. However, there is no doubt that the conception he proposes remains to some extent incomplete and stuttering. Remember in particular how Menger describes in the *Grundsätze* the consumption structure of an economy through a sort of social hierarchy of individual needs and wants, or how he distinguishes between imaginary and real wants, thereby confronting the subjective opinion of agents with an objective reality. It has been the task of the successive generation of Austrian authors to get rid of these contradictions and to explicitly define Austrian economics according to a dynamic subjectivist base.

The post-planning-debate analyses of Mises and Hayek may be interpreted as the second stage of the evolution of the subjectivist paradigm. By means of the notion of the individual plan, the subjective dimension extends the concept of needs towards the means–ends framework guiding the economic actions of agents. An individual plan is drawn up by the agent on the basis of his own subjective knowledge. The agent's knowledge stems from his personal interpretation of the information at his disposal. Therefore, the dynamics of the market process arises from the way in which knowledge is spread, modified and subjectively acquired over time. Knowledge is the foundation upon which agents formulate and alter their plans.

The subjective nature of knowledge is at the origin of the difficulties of functional approaches in dealing with the analysis of the market process. A priori, orthodox theories can take only the concept of objectively quantifiable information into account but not that of knowledge, which, in a Mengerian perspective, may be defined as the subjective interpretation of available information at any given moment. In the same way, by definition, human action takes place within time, time being the dimension in which all changes in agents' knowledge take place: 'as soon as we permit time to elapse, we must permit knowledge to change and knowledge cannot be regarded as a function of anything else' (Lachmann, 1976a: 127–8).

The third stage in the process of development of the subjectivist paradigm concerns the extension of subjectivism to individual expectations; this has been stepped over by Lachmann, who finds sufficient premises in the works of Mises and Hayek witnessing the reappearance of the Mengerian originality. The first chapters of Mises' *Human Action* provide a first important insight for Lachmann to take the subjective nature of expectations into account. In Chapter 5 in particular, where the necessarily temporal dimension of all human action is examined, Mises develops a Bergsonian conception of time whose direct consequence is to associate a certain degree of uncertainty to the result of action. 'Every action refers to an unknown future. It is in this sense always a risky speculation' (Mises, 1949: 106).

Lachmann interprets the speculative dimension inherent in all human action as the result of the subjectivism of individual expectations directed towards an unknown but imaginable future. However, Mises never mentions expectations and never goes into the consequences of the speculative dimension inherent in all human action. Lachmann develops the idea of Mises by drawing his inspiration from Shackle's conception of a kaleidic society characterized by the occurrence of unexpected changes that disrupt pre-existing decision-making patterns.

Hayek's analysis of knowledge deals with expectations, but only in a static perspective, removing any appeal to imagination and individual speculation during the formation of plans. Knowledge, defined as the interpretation of past experience, is the element in which subjectivism of economic actors manifests itself. The concept of individual plan nevertheless enables an extension to expectations in the sense that a plan is the result of two distinct types of knowledge: knowledge originating from subjective interpretation of past experience *and knowledge directed towards the future*, this, according to Mises, being the speculative part inherent in all human action. Concerning this second element, however, Lachmann notices that in Mises and Hayek 'expectations were, on the whole, treated as a mode of foresight, a rather unfortunate but inevitable consequence of imperfect knowledge' (Lachmann, 1976b: 58).

Accepting the full implications of dynamic subjectivism means getting rid of any reference to equilibrium, the market process being described as a continuous indeterminist process. Indeed, inconsistency of plans is the direct consequence of the introduction of subjective expectations. Plans are divergent because subjective expectations are based on the image that agents form about an 'unknown though not unimaginable' future (Lachmann, 1976a: 59). Competition may lead to diffusion of new knowledge, but appropriate expectations cannot be diffused in any way, for once they have revealed themselves relevant they are already obsolete and need to be revised; no *ex ante* criterion of success exists. Inconsistency of plans challenges the traditional view of a tendency towards equilibrium. Market is an undetermined process governed by the interaction of balancing *and* disturbing forces. The economic configuration emerging from the interaction of individual plans is definitely one of disequilibrium. In that perspective, there is no more reason to emphasize the equilibrating function of the market. Divergence of plans is the consequence of the extension of subjectivism to expectations and represents, within the Lachmannian view, the propeller of change. This seems to be the logical outcome of the consistent application of subjectivism.

Progress in Austrian economics thus leads to a serious limit: taking account of the full implications of subjectivism leads economists to question any reference to the traditional concept of equilibrium, taking the risk of being criticized, as Lachmann and radical subjectivists are, of theoretical nihilism.

The Equilibrium Reference

It follows from the above analysis that finding an alternative concept to the equilibrium reference is the most challenging issue Austrians have faced since Menger's dissent from marginalist determinacy. Such a concept should allow us both to reject a determinist view of economic phenomena and to avoid the pitfalls of theoretical nihilism. From this perspective, progress in Austrian economics may be described as the continuous deepening and clarification of the concept of economic order: Menger first gives the orientation through his investigation of the nature of organic phenomena; from 1937 onwards, Hayek replaces the reference to equilibrium with the notion, albeit somewhat still vague, of order; in the 1970s, Lachmann reaffirms the Mengerian legacy with his analysis of institutions as orientation schemes; O'Driscoll and Rizzo define the concept of pattern coordination as a fruitful synthesis of Hayek's spontaneous order and Lachmann's orientation scheme.

In his 1883 book, Menger begins an analysis of socio-economic (organic) institutions, opening the door to the Hayekian concept of spontaneous order. More generally, the concept of economic order represents a relevant alternative to general equilibrium and constitutes one of the bases of the modern Mengerian approach. An order is a state of affairs in which a multiplicity of elements of different nature are connected in such a way that knowing some of the spatial or temporal components allows us to form acceptable prognostics about the rest (Hayek, 1973: 42). Economics should be limited to predicting general characteristics of interacting structures between economic agents; that is, it should be restricted to determining the nature of the order which is susceptible of emerging from a specific institutional setting, whereas the prediction of particular facts goes beyond the competence of economists (Hayek, 1978a: 181).

In Lachmann's analysis (1970), institutions are defined as the set of rules of conduct and behavioural norms guiding agents in a world of radical uncertainty. Institutions provide *orientation schemes* in which human action takes place. In a kaleidic society, human action is not determined but neither is it arbitrary, the individual's free will fully expressing itself only in the context of specific limits provided by the institutional environment. From an analytical viewpoint, the theory of institutions developed by Lachmann aims at reducing the indeterminacy emanating from the extension of subjectivism to expectations in a context of radical uncertainty. Taking institutions into account enables the process of formation of individual plans to be specified more accurately. Institutions are recurrent patterns of conduct which limit the volatility of actions, henceforth providing a kind of fixed reference point within the kaleidic society in which individuals interact (Lachmann, 1970: 49–50).

O'Driscoll and Rizzo (1985) develop an approach which, despite having a stronger link with the concept of equilibrium, follows the perspective of Lachmann. Their work is interesting for two reasons: it seeks to provide an answer to the criticism of nihilism whilst at the same time indicating a possible way out for the development of Menger's subjectivist tradition towards a theory of institutions.

The Economics of Time and Ignorance fits into the extension of the subjectivist paradigm, dynamic subjectivism being, according to O'Driscoll and Rizzo, the essence of the Austrian tradition. Although the authors do not use the term 'radical subjectivism', they nevertheless stick to a similar idea: the fact that human action takes place within time and that individuals act in a world of ignorance (in the sense of Shackle, not in that of Kirzner) implies the explicit introduction of the dimensions of uncertainty and speculation into the analysis. Within this context, the aim of the authors is to demonstrate that the fact of taking account of real time does not necessarily lead to chaos and pure indeterminacy. O'Driscoll and Rizzo propose in that perspective the concept of *pattern coordination* as an alternative concept of equilibrium. This concept is based upon the distinction Hayek draws between the typical and unique characteristics of events. 'The plans of individuals are in a pattern equilibrium if they are coordinated with respect to their typical features, even if the unique aspects fail to mesh' (O'Driscoll and Rizzo, 1985: 85).

This alternative concept of economic order is based upon the coordinating role assumed by the set of rules and institutions of the system at hand. Social rules and institutions are able to reduce the level of uncertainty faced by agents, without necessarily being able to eradicate it entirely. Institutions offer general and stable rules of conduct, which are the typical characteristics of the system and influence agents when forming their expectations. Institutions thus constitute a limit regarding differences in interpretations; they are guiding points in a world of ignorance which agents may use to find their way.

Lachmann's (1970: 37) statement that 'human action is not determinate but neither is it arbitrary' finds concrete development in the concept of pattern coordination. The work of O'Driscoll and Rizzo does indeed contribute to deepening the orientation principle anticipated by Lachmann, providing, in this way, a further step in the attempt to reconcile the kaleidic view of Shackle with the idea of the existence of a market order.

CONCLUSION

The above analysis highlights how the role of institutions takes paramount importance within the Austrian tradition, giving consistency to the view of the market process as a non-determined but non-chaotic phenomenon. The Austrian tradition revives in that way an old conception of economics, perceived as a social science whose essential purpose, as Menger ([1883] 1963: 147) put it more than a century ago, is closely connected with the question of theoretically understanding the origin and change of organically created social structures.

NOTES

1. The term used by Menger ([1871] 1950: 116) is *Bedürfnisbefriedigung*, literally the satisfaction of needs and desires.
2. In particular, Mayer analyses the theories of price formation developed by Cournot, Jevons, Walras, Pareto and Cassel in detail.
3. For a more general analysis of the causal-genetic way of thinking in economics, see Cowan and Rizzo (1996).
4. This does not mean that the temporal dimension is absent in the Walrasian logic; but Walras's conception differs from that of Menger and refers to a logical view of time whereas a real approach of temporality is developed in the *Grundsätze*. O'Driscoll and Rizzo (1985), more precisely, place *the Newtonian conception of time*, which was adopted by marginalists following the logic inherent in the analogy with mechanics, in opposition to the *Bergsonian conception* which highlights the subjective and discontinuous nature of time for economic agents in the Mengerian framework.
5. Cf O'Driscoll and Rizzo (1985: Ch. II).
6. Objective production costs still determine the supply curve in the analysis of Jevons and Marshall, the latter rejecting the theory of opportunity costs offered by Wicksteed (1910) and Davenport (1908).
7. More generally, what is questioned is the use of formalist mathematics as it was instituted by Hilbert in the 1920s.
8. Some of the few engaged in that direction are Langlois (1992) and Koppl (1994), who have tried to pull the Austrian tradition towards a neo-institutional logic and use to that purpose the framework of iterative games to explain the emergence and evolution of institutions; and Witt (1989, 1992), who has tried to pull the Austrian analysis towards the evolutionary framework.
9. Lachmann (1990) borrows this definition from Shackle (1972).
10. In this respect, White (1977: 4) defines the Austrian tradition in the following words: 'What unifies this school of thought – what might be called its theme – is the methodological outlook of its members: subjectivism'.

REFERENCES

Antonelli, E. (1953), 'Le souvenir de Léon Walras: Léon Walras et Carl Menger à travers leur correspondance', *Economie Appliquée*, 6.

Cowan, R. and M. Rizzo, (1996), 'The genetic-causal tradition and modern economic theory', *Kyklos*, 49: 273–317.

Davenport, H. (1908), *Value and Distribution*, Chicago: University of Chicago Press.

Hayek, F. von (1952), *The Counter-Revolution of Science: Studies on the Abuse of Reason*, Indianapolis: Liberty Press.

Hayek, F. von (1973), *Law, Legislation and Liberty: A New Statement of the Liberal Principles of Justice and Political Economy*, 1: *Rules and Order*, London: Routledge and Kegan Paul.

Hayek, F. von (ed.) (1978a), *New Studies in Philosophy, Politics, Economics and the History of Ideas*, London: Routledge and Kegan Paul.

Hayek, F. von (1978b), 'Competition as a discovery procedure', in F. von Hayek (ed.) (1978a), Ch. 12.

Jaffé, W. (1976), 'Menger, Jevons and Walras de-homogenized', *Economic Inquiry*, 14.

Kirzner, I.M. (1973), *Competition and Entrepreneurship*, Chicago: University of Chicago Press.

Kirzner, I.M. (ed.) (1994), *Classics in Austrian Economics*, Vols 1–3, London: W. Pickering.

Koppl, R. (1994), 'Invisible hand explanations', in P. Boettke (ed.), *The Elgar Companion to Austrian Economics*, pp. 192–6, Aldershot: Edward Elgar.

Lachmann, L. (1970), *The Legacy of Max Weber*, London: Heinemann.

Lachmann, L. (1976a), 'On the central concept of Austrian economics: market process', in E. Dolan (ed.), *The Foundations of Modern Austrian Economics*, pp. 126–32, Kansas City, MO: Sheed & Ward.

Lachmann, L. (1976b), 'From Mises to Shackle: an essay on Austrian economics and the kaleidic society', *Journal of Economic Literature*, 14, pp. 54–62.

Lachmann, L. (1982), 'The salvage of ideas: problems of the revival of Austrian economic thought', *Journal of Institutional and Theoretical Economics*, 138(4) pp. 629–45.

Lachmann, L. (1990), 'G.L.S. Shackle's place in the history of subjectivist thought', in D. Lavoie (ed.) (1994), *Expectations and the Meaning of Institutions. Essays in Economics by Ludwig Lachmann*, London: Routledge.

Langlois, R. (1992), 'Orders and organizations: towards an Austrian theory of social institutions', in S. Boehm and B. Caldwell (eds), *Austrian Economics: Tensions and New Directions*, pp. 165–83, Boston: Kluwer Academic Publishers.

Lavoie, D. (ed.) (1994), *Expectations and the Meaning of Institutions. Essays in Economics by Ludwig Lachmann*, London: Routledge.

Mayer, H. (1932), 'Der Erkenntniswert der Funktionellen Priestheorien', English translation: 'The cognitive value of functional theories of price', in I.M. Kirzner (ed.) (1994), *Classics in Austrian Economics*, Vol. 2.

Menger, C. (1871), *Grundsätze der Volkswirtschaftslehre*, English translation (1950), *Principles of Economics*, Glencoe: The Free Press.

Menger, C. (1883), *Untersuchungen über die Methode der Socialwissenschaften und der Politischen Oekonomie insbesondere*, English translation (1963), *Problems of Economics and Sociology*, Urbana: University of Illinois Press.

Mises, L. von (1949), *Human Action. A Treatise on Economics*, London: William Hodge and Company Limited.

O'Driscoll, G. and M. Rizzo (1985), *The Economics of Time and Ignorance*, Oxford: Basil Blackwell.

Shackle, G.L.S. (1972), *Epistemics and Economics. A Critique of Economic Doctrines*, Cambridge: Cambridge University Press.

Weintraub, E.R. (1985), *General Equilibrium Analysis. Studies in Appraisal*, Cambridge: Cambridge University Press.

White, L. (1977), 'Methodology of the Austrian school', Occasional Paper, Center for Libertarian Studies, reprinted in S. Littlechild (ed.) (1990), *Austrian Economics*, Vols 1–3, Series: Schools of Thought in Economics, 10, pp. 371–408, Aldershot: Edward Elgar.

Wicksteed, P. (1910), *The Common Sense of Political Economy*, London: Macmillan.

Witt, U. (1989), 'The evolution of economic institutions as a propagation process', *Public Choice*, 62 pp. 155–72.

Witt, U. (1992), 'Turning Austrian economics towards an evolutionary theory', in S. Boehm and B. Caldwell (eds), *Austrian Economics: Tensions and New Directions*, pp. 215–36, Boston: Kluwer Academic Publishers.

E12
E13

19. Walras' law and the IS–LM model: a tale of progress and regress

Hansjörg Klausinger*

INTRODUCTION

The integration of macroeconomics into the framework of general equilibrium analysis marked a vital step from the 'economics of Keynes's to the neoclassical synthesis version of 'Keynesian economics'. Two crucial elements in this process were the translation of the *General Theory* into the terms of the IS–LM model and the application of Walras' law. It is not merely by accident that Hicks – whose approach towards the *General Theory* was shaped by *Value and Capital* – was the most influential protagonist in the early development of both these ideas. Thereby the neoclassical synthesis provided the unifying framework for analysing and discussing Keynesian topics, as for example the controversy between the liquidity preference and the loanable funds approach to the determination of the rate of interest. However, in the course of this development a host of subtle analytical problems emerged – for example with respect to the time structure of period analysis and the proper handling of stocks and flows. Starting with the early attempts by Hicks and Patinkin and culminating in the final accomplishment of a consistent stock–flow version of IS–LM by Foley and Buiter, most of these problems could be resolved within the general equilibrium framework. In this sense one may consider the steady refinement of the analytical tools used in IS–LM analysis as an example of 'theoretical progress'.[1] Yet curiously enough, side by side with this increasing analytical sophistication, simplified and superficial treatments have persisted up to the present, not only in many textbooks but also in more 'high-brow' contributions.[2] Thus it seems that many adherents (and foes alike) to the neoclassical synthesis have neglected these lessons from the debates on the integration of Walras' law into macroeconomic theory.

It is this theme of regress after progress on which the following contribution will concentrate. It consists of five sections. The next (second) section gives a brief historical overview on the progress towards a consistent version of IS–LM. The third section sketches as a point of reference the two alternative period equilibrium versions of IS–LM. Then the fourth section provides three examples of regress in examining (i) the meaning of the flow equilibrium condition of the market for bonds, (ii) the derivation of the liquidity trap and (iii) the validity of Poole's rule (introducing a kind of Walras' law for shocks).

PROGRESS IN MODELLING IS–LM AND WALRAS' LAW

In the following we will give a short overview on the progress in developing a consistent general equilibrium framework for stock–flow analysis with references to the IS–LM model.

As is well known, from the beginning the attempt to interpret Keynes's theory in terms of general equilibrium introduced Walras' law into the debate. The crucial conflict in this regard referred to the determination of the rate of interest by the money versus the bond market, or what turned out as the controversy between liquidity preference and loanable funds theory. Already in his first review of the *General Theory* Hicks (1936: 92) pointed out: 'If . . . the demand for every commodity and factor equals the supply, and if the demand for money equals the supply of money, it follows by mere arithmetic that the demand for loans must equal the supply of loans . . .', where 'mere arithmetic' is a reference to Walras' law as the aggregation of budget restrictions. Therefore he claims: 'The choice between them [the method of eliminating the loan market or the money market] is purely a question of convenience' (p. 93).[3]

Leaving the liquidity preference–loanable funds controversy aside[4] and concentrating on the development of IS–LM, the next vital step towards the integration of Walras' law was taken by Patinkin. In the first and second edition of *Money, Interest and Prices* (Patinkin, 1956, 1965), he supplements the usual equilibrium loci of the goods and of the money market by another explicit one for the bond market. First, this is applied to the full employment case (Patinkin 1965: 253ff.) and then to the case of involuntary unemployment (328ff.), where the goods market equilibrium is carefully reinterpreted as the condition of equality between income and expenditure. Thereby Patinkin assumes, for the sake of simplicity, that changes in income have an identical effect on bond demand and bond supply, so that the bond market equilibrium (BB) curve is horizontal (281ff.). Obviously general equilibrium is where the three curves (IS, LM and BB) intersect and from that it follows that the equilibrium interest rate cannot be said to be determined by a single market. Furthermore Patinkin is well aware that the ways in which, for example, additional investment demand is financed will determine which of these curves are jointly shifted and that consequently any shock that shifts one curve must at least shift one of the other two curves, too. Consequently Walras' law also implies a restriction on the derivatives of the relevant excess demand functions, a point later elaborated by Tobin and Brainard (1968) with regard to asset markets.[5] Patinkin is also quite explicit in stating 'that the savings = investment condition is *not* an alternative statement of the equilibrium condition in the bond market' (Patinkin, 1965: 272). In this regard Patinkin's construction can be said to have anticipated vital elements of the consistent integration of Walras' law; however, what is missing is a clear period structure of the model when it refers to stocks and flows.

A related debate that came to a provisional solution by Patinkin's device was that about the dynamics of the rate of interest. Following Samuelson's statement of the law of demand and supply by the formula $\dot{p} = H[D(p) - S(p)]$, $H(0) = 0$, $H' > 0$ (Samuelson, 1946: 263), the obvious question was which market (that is, the excess demand of the money or the bond market) would then govern the movements of the rate of interest. In this context liquidity preference theory (as favoured by Klein, 1950) would thus make the movements of the interest rate depend on the (stock) excess demand in the money market, and loanable funds theory (as favoured by Fellner and Somers, 1950) on the (flow) excess demand of bonds. As Brunner (1950) pointed out, by invoking Walras' law both formulations imply non-intuitive reactions with respect to the market eliminated from the analysis. For example, the liquidity preference formulation implies that the rate of interest might change although there is no excess demand in the bond market (250ff.). Eventually Patinkin (1958) supplied a unifying framework in which to discuss the different dynamic specifications by interpreting the IS–LM–BB curves as the isokines of the corresponding phase diagram. Thereby he confirmed the different and non-intuitive results of the two competing specifications and he agreed with most participants of the debate that ultimately the question could only be settled on empirical grounds.[6]

Another issue that figured prominently in the debate was that of stock versus flow analysis. In a partial equilibrium framework the liquidity preference approach was identified with stock equilibrium, whereas the loanable funds approach apparently dealt with flow equilibrium (see again the contributions by Klein and Fellner and Somers). Brunner (1950: 249) was able to reconcile these divergent views by demonstrating that stock and flow equilibrium led to the same results for a given period provided that there had been stock equilibrium in the preceding period, so that stock equilibrium turned out as the more natural specification. Patinkin (1965), in his general equilibrium formulation, resorted to stock equilibrium for money and bonds combined with flow equilibrium for goods; obviously (but without an explicit justification) equilibrium in his account refers to the end of the period considered. Another step at disentangling stock and flow dynamics was made by taking account of the government budget constraint (see, for example, Christ, 1968;

Blinder and Solow, 1973). This constraint linked flows (for example budget deficits) with changes in asset supply (for example money or bonds); obviously a similar constraint applied to the private sector as well.

However, a kind of breakthrough was only achieved by Foley's distinction between two consistent formulations of stock and flow equilibrium in discrete time, namely beginning and end-of-period equilibrium (Foley, 1975). These two specifications as applied to the IS–LM–BB model will be replicated below. According to which specification is used, we will arrive at different versions of Walras' law and, as Foley (p. 320) demonstrated, the determination of the rate of interest conforms to the liquidity preference or the loanable funds approach, respectively, when the beginning or the end-of-period formulation is used. A series of contributions followed, dealing for example with the relationship between the specification in discrete and in continuous time and with the conditions for equivalence between different specifications, culminating in Buiter (1979, 1980). Furthermore the consistency of this approach was authoritatively proved (for Keynesian balance-of-payments models) in the interchange between Kuska (1978) and Buiter and Eaton (1981).

Finally in the discussion of the period version of Patinkin's model, May (1970) and Woglom (1980) noticed the crucial connection between the parameters of the model and the length of the period considered. When there are parameters that denote a stock–flow relationship, as for example the so-called 'Cambridge k', then their (absolute) value will vary with the length of the period. Therefore by making the period sufficiently long one can force the BB curve to become downward-sloping. Similarly, if the period length goes to zero, so that time becomes a continuous variable, k will increase without bound and the LM and the BB curve will coincide (as in the beginning-of-period equilibrium version of the period model).[7]

A CONSISTENT PERIOD VERSION OF IS–LM

The IS–LM model consists of a condition for flow equilibrium, income equals expenditure or, equivalently, $I = S$ (investment = saving), and two conditions for stock equilibrium, an explicit one for the money market, $M = L$ (money supply = money demand), and one for the bond market, $B = B^d$ (bond supply = bond demand), usually left implicit. Because of the co-existence of flows and stocks, the time dimension of the variables must be carefully specified: the model refers to a period of time [0, 1], that starts at $t = 0$ and ends with $t = 1$. This time period is the one relevant for the specification of the flow variables, whereas the relevant point of time for the specification of the stock variables is either 0 or 1 and is indicated by a subscript. During the time period wealth can be accumulated or decumulated, as per definition: $\Delta W \equiv W_1 - W_0 = S$ (the change in wealth = saving). Correspondingly, changes in stocks are denoted by $\Delta B^d \equiv B_1^d - B_0^d$ and $\Delta B \equiv B_1 - B_0$ and so on.

The following models are simplified versions in the spirit of Foley (1975) and Buiter (1980).[8] Accordingly there are two ways for consistently specifying IS–LM, namely end-of-period and beginning-of-period equilibrium. These will be examined in turn.

End-of-period Equilibrium

In the end-of-period specification the equilibrium of investment and saving refers to the flows within the period [0, 1], the equilibrium of the money and the bond market to the stocks at the end of the period ($t = 1$). Therefore the existing stocks at the end of the period, after taking account of the changes (accumulation or decumulation) within the period, must equal stock demand. We formulate the model with the three equilibrium conditions, (1) to (3), and with the usual parameter restrictions:[10]

$$I(i, u) = S(Y, W_1); I_i < 0, I_u = 1, S_Y > 0, S_W < 0, \tag{1}$$

$$L_1(Y, i, W_1, v) = M_1 \equiv M_0 + \Delta M; L_Y > 0, L_i < 0, 0 \le L_W \le 1, L_v = 1, \tag{2}$$

$$B_1^d = B_1 \equiv B_0 + \Delta B. \tag{3}$$

Here and in the following Y denotes income, i the rate of interest and u and v are shift variables in investment and money demand. Notice that the stocks at the beginning of the period, M_0 and B_0, and therefore also wealth $W_0 \equiv M_0 + B_0$, are exogenously given, and that $W_1 = W_0 + S$.[9] The shape of the functions of bond demand and supply is left open, as it will be shown that it cannot be determined independently of (1) and (2).

We start by deriving the effects of Y, i and W_0 on the respective excess demands, that is, the slopes and shifts of the IS, LM and BB curves. As these excess demands depend on end-of-period wealth, we must distinguish between the direct effects (as determined by the above parameter restrictions) and the indirect effects operating on saving and thereby on wealth. For example differentiating S leads to:

$$dS = S_Y dY + S_W(dW_0 + dS) = \frac{1}{1 - S_W}(S_Y dY + S_W dW_0),$$

where S_Y is the direct effect of income and $S_Y/(1 - S_W)$ is the total effect.

By similar calculations we obtain from differentiating (1), (2) and (3):

$$d(I - S) = -\frac{S_Y}{1 - S_W}dY + I_i di - \frac{S_W}{1 - S_W}dW_0 + du = 0, \tag{4}$$

$$d(L_1 - M_1) = \left(L_Y + L_W \frac{S_Y}{1 - S_W}\right)dY + L_i di + \left(\frac{L_W}{1 - S_W} - M_{0W}\right)dW_0$$
$$+ \; dv - d\Delta M = 0, \tag{5}$$

$$d(B_1^d - B_1) = \left(B_Y^d + B_W^d \frac{S_Y}{1 - S_W}\right)dY + B_i^d di$$
$$+ \left(\frac{B_W^d}{1 - S_W} - B_{0W}\right)dW_0 - d\Delta B = 0, \tag{6}$$

where

$$M_{0W} \equiv \frac{dM_0}{dW_0}, B_{0W} \equiv \frac{dB_0}{dW_0}, M_{0W} + B_{0W} = 1.$$

In the above equations we must be careful to distinguish between dM_0 and $d\Delta M$, the former referring to a change in the stock at the beginning of the period, the latter to a change during the period. As usual with the given parameter restrictions the IS curve is downward-sloping and the LM curve is upward-sloping in $Y - i$ space.

Now we introduce Walras' law, which states the following restriction:

$$B_1^d - B_0 - \Delta B + L_1 - M_0 - \Delta M + I - S = 0. \tag{7}$$

Therefore excess demand in the bond market is determined by the excess demands of the two other markets, so that the equilibrium conditions (1) and (2) imply (3)

$$B_1^d - B_0 - \Delta B = M_0 + \Delta M - L_1 + S - I. \tag{8}$$

Taking account of the definition of wealth, (8) can be expressed equivalently as

$$L_1 + B_1^d - \Delta B - \Delta M + I = M_0 + B_0 + S \equiv W_1. \tag{9}$$

By differentiating (9) in turn with respect to W_0, Y, i, v and u, we arrive at the following set of parameter restrictions:

$$\frac{L_W}{1 - S_W} + \frac{B_W^d}{1 - S_W} = 1 + \frac{S_W}{1 - S_W} \Rightarrow L_W + B_W^d = 1; \tag{10}$$

$$L_Y + L_W \frac{S_Y}{1 - S_W} + B_Y^d + B_W^d \frac{S_Y}{1 - S_W} = \frac{S_Y}{1 - S_W} \Rightarrow L_Y + B_Y^d = 0; \tag{11}$$

$$L_i + B_i^d - \Delta B_i - \Delta M_i + I_i = 0; \tag{12}$$

$$1 + B_v^d - \Delta B_v - \Delta M_v = 0; \tag{13}$$

$$1 + B_u^d - \Delta B_u - \Delta M_u = 0. \tag{14}$$

For the sake of simplicity we assume that there are no endogenous changes to the money supply during the period, that investment demand is financed by supplying bonds and that autonomous changes to money demand mean a switch to or from bond demand. That is:

$$\Delta M = 0; \, \Delta M_i = \Delta M_u = \Delta M_v = 0; \tag{A1}$$

$$\Delta B = I + u; \, \Delta B_i = I_i, \, \Delta B_u = 1, \, \Delta B_v = 0; \tag{A2}$$

$$B_v^d = -1. \tag{A3}$$

As can be seen from (12) to (14), these assumptions are mutually consistent. From these assumptions (12) simplifies to:

$$L_i + B_i^d = 0. \tag{12'}$$

Inserting these restrictions into (6) gives:

$$d(B_1^d - B_1) = \left[-L_Y + (1 - L_W) \frac{S_Y}{1 - S_W} \right] dY - (L_i + I_i) di + \left(\frac{1 - L_W}{1 - S_W} - \frac{dB_0}{dW_0} \right) dW_0 - du - dv = 0, \tag{15}$$

so that:

$$\left. \frac{\partial Y}{\partial i} \right|_{BB} = \frac{L_i + I_i}{(1 - L_W) \dfrac{S_Y}{1 - S_W} - L_Y} = ? \tag{16}$$

Because of the indeterminate sign of (16) both upward and downward-sloping BB curves are consistent with restriction (9).[11] However, it is easily proved that the slope of the BB curve cannot be steeper than that of LM nor flatter than that of IS. Furthermore shifts in IS and LM, respectively, cause compensating shifts in BB.

Beginning-of-period Equilibrium

In this specification the equilibrium of investment and saving refers again to the flows within the period [0, 1], but the equilibrium of the money and the bond market to the stocks at the beginning of the period ($t = 0$). The three equilibrium conditions, (1*) to (3*), are then:

$$I(i, u) = S(Y, W_0), \tag{1*}$$

$$L_0(Y, i, W_0, v) = M_0, \tag{2*}$$

$$B_0^d = B_0. \tag{3*}$$

The total differentials of the excess demands are:

$$d(I - S) = -S_Y dY + I_i di - S_W dW_0 + du = 0, \tag{4*}$$

$$d(L_0 - M_0) = L_Y dY + L_i di + (L_W - M_{0W}) dW_0 + dv = 0, \tag{5*}$$

$$d(B_0^d - B_0) = B_Y^d dY + B_i^d di + (B_W^d - B_{0W}) dW_0 + B_v^d dv = 0. \tag{6*}$$

Qualitatively similar to the end-of-period case, we obtain again a downward-sloping IS curve and an upward-sloping LM curve.

As equilibrium in the two markets for stocks is realized before the flow market for the period is activated, Walras' law is split up into a wealth restriction (7*) on the one hand and a budget restriction for the flow variables (14*) on the other hand. The wealth restriction is given by:

$$L_0 + B_0^d = M_0 + B_0 \equiv W_0. \tag{7*}$$

Therefore the excess demand in the bond market is identical to the excess supply in the money market, so that the equilibrium conditions are identical, too:

$$B_0^d - B_0 = M_0 - L_0. \tag{8*}$$

By differentiating (7*) we again get a set of parameter restrictions, that is:

$$L_i + B_i^d = 0, \tag{9*}$$

$$L_Y + B_Y^d = 0, \tag{10*}$$

$$L_W + B_W^d = 1, \tag{11*}$$

$$1 + B_v^d = 0. \tag{12*}$$

Inserting these results into (6*) gives:

$$d(B_0^d - B_0) = -L_Y dY - L_i di - \left(L_W - \frac{dM_0}{dW_0}\right) dW_0 - dv, \tag{13*}$$

so that, of course, the LM curve and the BB curve coincide in the case of beginning-of-period equilibrium.

The remaining flows within the period, that is I and S as well as ΔB and ΔB^d, ΔM and ΔL, must fulfil a budget restriction. Thereby an excess of expenditure over income is mirrored by a respective excess of the sum of the flows of money and bond supply over the sum of the flows of money and bond demand:

$$I - S = \Delta B + \Delta M - \Delta B^d - \Delta L. \tag{14*}$$

We may stipulate the assumptions equivalent to the end-of-period version:

$$\Delta M = 0; \tag{A1*}$$

$$\Delta B = I. \tag{A2*}$$

Furthermore we see that what had to be assumed in the end-of-period version as (A3) now follows from the restriction (12*).

Inserting (A1*) and (A2*) into (14*) we arrive at

$$S = \Delta B^d + \Delta L, \tag{15*}$$

which just means that the whole of planned saving is split up between increasing the demand for bonds or that for money. Note, however, that in this model there is no equilibrium condition involving these asset flows.

SOME EXAMPLES OF REGRESS

In the following we will provide three examples where analysis within the IS–LM framework did lack the consistency achieved in the contributions surveyed above.

Equilibrium of the 'Flow Capital Market'

There is a long and time-honoured tradition of identifying the flow demand and supply of the bond market with investment and saving. This identification (or one might say, confusion) of demand and supply of the flow capital market with investment and saving, respectively, was ascribed by Keynes (1936: Ch. 14) to the 'classical approach' (which he rejected). It is, however, not part of the 'loanable funds approach' as formulated by Robertson (1940: 2ff.) and Ohlin (1937), which takes into account such monetary factors as hoarding and money creation as components of the flow demand or supply of the capital market. Yet recently the classical approach has been revived, now in the guise of an interpretation of the IS curve of Keynesian macroeconomics, by Felderer and Homburg (1986, 1994: 128ff.).[12] A similar argument can be found in the textbook of Mankiw (1997: 62ff.) where the demand and supply of loanable funds are equated, in the model of long-run equilibrium, with investment and saving.

Specifically, Felderer and Homburg (1986: 458) proposed to distinguish within the IS–LM model between two types of the bond market: a market for the existing stocks (the bond market in the usual sense) on the one hand and a market for flows (sometimes termed 'capital market'), with ΔB^d and ΔB as demand and supply, on the other hand. Furthermore they identified the condition $I = S$ with the equilibrium condition for the 'capital market'. This proposition will now be examined within the period equilibrium framework as established above.

For the specification of end-of-period equilibrium the distinction between a stock and a flow market for bonds makes no sense: there are not two different markets or equilibrium conditions, but only the single equilibrium condition for the single bond market at the end of the period, which refers to the sum of the bonds existing at the beginning of the period and of the flow of newly supplied bonds (and similarly so for bond demand). Consequently, if the bond market was in equilibrium at the end of the preceding period (that is, the beginning of the current period), then obviously end-of-period equilibrium of stocks implies also equilibrium of the flows during the current period. Moreover it was shown above that the conditions for investment–saving and bond market equilibrium (the IS and the BB curve) differ in this model.

Therefore as noticed by Felderer and Homburg (1986: 465ff.), the equilibrium condition of the 'capital market' is only meaningful for the specification of beginning-of-period equilibrium. The relation between investment–saving equilibrium and the flow demand and supply of bonds, ΔB^d and ΔB, and of money, ΔL and ΔM, is then determined by the restriction (14*).

From (14*) and from assumption (A1*) follows $\Delta B^d - \Delta B = S - I - \Delta L = 0$ as the equilibrium condition for the flow capital market. Taking total differentials in the neighbourhood of equilibrium, where $\Delta \tilde{L} = 0$, and for simplicity disregarding the shift variables, we obtain

$$d(\Delta B^d - \Delta B) = dS - dI - dL = (S_Y - L_Y)dY - (I_i + L_i)d_i + (S_W - L_W)dW_0 = 0,$$
(1.1)

which is definitely not identical with the condition for $I = S$. For example, the slope in $Y - i$ space of the curve (let's call it FF) for equilibrium in the flow capital market is

$$\left.\frac{\partial Y}{\partial i}\right|_{FF} = \frac{I_i + L_i}{S_Y - L_Y} = ?$$
(1.2)

which is not necessarily downward-sloping as for IS.

Furthermore we can look at the model when in beginning-of-period equilibrium for period [0,1], so that the values for Y and i are determined by the equilibrium conditions. Then from (14*) and (A1*) and because of $I = S$ in equilibrium, the condition for flow equilibrium in the capital market $\Delta B^d - \Delta B$ implies $\Delta L = 0$. However as $\Delta L = L_Y \Delta Y + L_i \Delta i + L_W \Delta W = L_W \Delta W$ and $\Delta W = S > 0$, $\Delta L = 0$ implies $L_W = 0$ or consequently $B_W = 1$. Only under this condition will beginning-of-period equilibrium of the model also imply flow equilibrium in the capital market. Or, expressed differently, the FF curve is not only different from the IS curve, the IS, LM and FF curves will also not intersect at a common point except under this special condition.

Therefore it must be concluded that in the case of end-of-period equilibrium the stock equilibrium condition for the bond market implies the flow equilibrium condition, yet it is different from the condition for investment–saving equilibrium. And in the case of beginning-of-period equilibrium the equilibrium condition for the 'capital market' is neither part of the model, nor in general identical with the condition for investment–saving equilibrium, nor is it necessarily implied by beginning-of-period equilibrium conditions.

The Liquidity Trap

Within the Keynesian macro-model of the neoclassical synthesis, the liquidity trap constitutes a special case that challenges the existence (and stability) of full employment equilibrium. The trap is usually identified with a horizontal LM curve at a positive rate of interest. However more often than not the characterization of the trap – in textbooks and even in more scientific contributions – is rather superficial: it is said that in the liquidity trap money demand will not only become infinitely interest-elastic but money demand itself infinite; or the trap is described verbally as a situation of 'absolute liquidity preference' where all asset owners prefer to hold money instead of bonds. Examples of such statements abound in the literature.

With regard to the early literature, it should be noted that Hicks was more cautious than later popularizers of the liquidity trap in stating that the LM curve 'will probably tend to be *nearly* horizontal on the left. . .we can think of the curve as approaching these limits asymptotically' (Hicks, [1937] 1982: 109) and that 'if the supply of money is increased, the curve LL moves to the right . . ., but the horizontal parts of the curve are *almost* the same.' (p. 111; emphasis added in both quotations). It was again Patinkin (1965: 223 and 349ff.) who criticized careless representations of the trap by invoking Walras' law. For example, he noticed that an infinite demand for money in the trap would imply an infinite supply of bonds.

Nevertheless, careless treatments of the liquidity trap are still common. Examples of the kind of reasoning criticized above are provided by Branson (1989: 154ff. and 181), Gordon (1993: 176f.), Dornbusch and Fischer (1998: 243 and 249), as well as by Felderer and Homburg (1994: 121ff., 144ff.), Klatt (1995: 61ff.) and Jarchow (1998: 76 and 196).

Outside the textbooks, too, despite its longevity, controversy on the liquidity trap has not subsided since Patinkin, as is demonstrated by a host of new contributions. One strand of the literature has reopened the debate on the consistent integration of the bond market into the IS–LM model and thereby questioned the existence or stability of the liquidity trap; see, for example, Größl-Gschwendtner (1991: 171, 1993: 174f.), Barens and Caspari (1992: 343f., 1995), Ernst (1992: 337), Ernst and Walpuski (1993a, 1993b: 583ff., 1996: 249f.) and Klausinger (1995: 232ff.). Another strand dealt with the different versions of the trap to be found in the *General Theory*. However, in their careful study Beranek and Timberlake (1987) committed a vital error by confusing the horizontal part of the money demand function (as implied when money and bonds become perfect substitutes) with a discontinuity of the money demand function. Obviously the latter interpretation would endanger the existence of asset equilibrium in the trap at all. The erroneous nature of this interpretation was pointed out by Cushman (1990) (see also Beranek and Timberlake, 1990); it will also be neatly demonstrated by the derivation below.

In the following we formulate a consistent derivation of the liquidity trap by means of the Keynes–Tobin version of the speculative demand for money. As we shall also examine the relation between the liquidity trap and the Pigou effect, it is most convenient to use the end-of-period equilibrium framework. (However, all results can easily be translated into the version of beginning-of-period equilibrium.)

Taking the equilibrium conditions (1) to (3) as the point of departure, we give now a more concrete specification of the money demand function as:

$$L_1(Y, i, W_1) = kY + L_s(Y, i, W_1), \tag{2.1}$$

where L_s refers to speculative demand and end-of-period wealth is given by (9).

The speculative component of money demand is derived from the individual decisions of the asset owners. The asset owner j decides how to allocate disposable wealth, $W_{s,j}$, between money and bonds, according to whether the actual rate of interest i exceeds the expected rate of interest i^* or not, so that:

$$L_{s,j} = \left\{ \begin{matrix} 0 \\ [0, W_{s,j}] \\ W_{s,j} \end{matrix} \right\}, \; \text{if } i \left\{ \begin{matrix} > \\ = \\ < \end{matrix} \right\} i_j^*, \quad W_{s,j} \equiv W_j - kY_j. \tag{2.2}$$

Obviously for $i = i^*$ the asset owner is indifferent between money and bond holdings.[13]

The individual interest rate expectations (weighted by the respective disposable wealth) are assumed to be distributed according to a probability density function $f(i)$ such that:

$$f(i) = \left\{ \begin{matrix} = \\ > \\ = \end{matrix} \right\} 0, \; \text{if} \left\{ \begin{matrix} i > i_+ \\ i_+ \geq i \geq i_- \\ i_- > i \end{matrix} \right\}, \tag{2.3}$$

where $f(i)$ is the share of wealth of asset owners with $i = i^*$. It is assumed that there is an upper and a lower bound to the expected interest rate, $i_+ \geq i_- > 0$.

The corresponding probability distribution function is:

$$F(i) = \int_{-\infty}^{i} f(i)di \quad \text{with} \quad \int_{-\infty}^{+\infty} f(i)di = \int_{i-}^{i+} f(i)di = 1. \tag{2.4}$$

Consequently the share $l(i)$ of aggregate disposable wealth that is held in cash is $1 - F(i)$ and the effect of i on l, $l_i = -f$.

The aggregate speculative demand for money and the corresponding demand for bonds are therefore given by

$$L_s = l(i)W_s, \quad l(i) \equiv \begin{Bmatrix} 0 \\ 0 \leq 1 - F(i) \leq 1 \\ 1 \end{Bmatrix}, \text{ if } \begin{Bmatrix} i > i_+ \\ i_+ \geq i \geq i_- \\ i_- > i \end{Bmatrix}. \tag{2.5}$$

$$B^d = [1 - l(i)]W_s. \tag{2.6}$$

The distinct values of the rate of interest in (2.5) may be identified as belonging to the 'classical', 'normal' and 'Keynesian' region.

Then $i = i_-$ represents a situation of 'absolute liquidity preference'. However, none of the usual statements on the liquidity trap is true for this case. Neither is money demand infinite at $i = i_-$ nor is the interest elasticity:

$$L(i_-) = kY + W_s = W, \tag{2.7}$$

$$\varepsilon(i_-) \equiv L_i(i_-)\frac{i_-}{L(i_-)} = -i_- \frac{f(W - kY)}{W} = 0 \tag{2.8}$$

because of $f = 0$. As can be seen money demand equals (but cannot exceed) total wealth, which is finite, and the interest rate elasticity (evaluated at the left-hand-side derivative) is therefore zero.

Furthermore, and more importantly, the state of absolute liquidity preference at $i = i_-$ does not correspond to a point on the LM curve. This can easily be verified by deriving the LM curve. The total differential of the money market equilibrium condition, $M_0 = L_1$, renders:

$$dM_0 = 0 = (1 - l)kdY - fW_s. \tag{2.9}$$

Therefore the slope of the LM curve is given by:

$$\left.\frac{\partial Y}{\partial i}\right|_{LM} = \frac{fW_s}{(1-l)k} \begin{Bmatrix} = \\ > \end{Bmatrix} 0 \text{ if } \begin{Bmatrix} i > i_+ \\ i_+ \geq i \geq i_{\min} \end{Bmatrix} \tag{2.10}$$

which is finite throughout (the curve is not horizontal). Here $i_{\min}$ is the value of i (on the LM curve), calculated at $Y = 0$. Again substituting into the equilibrium condition for $Y = 0$ we see:

$$M_0 = L_1 = l(i_{\min})W_1 = l(i_{\min})(M_0 + B_0 + S), \text{ or} \tag{2.11}$$

$$l(i_{\min}) = \frac{M_0}{M_0 + B_0 + S} < 1 \Rightarrow i_{\min} > i_-.$$

Therefore the only possibility for establishing a 'true' liquidity trap within this model is to assume identical interest rate expectations, so that from the asset owners' point of view money and bonds become perfect substitutes.[14] Then aggregate money demand is:

$$L = kY + l(i)W_s, \quad l(i) = \begin{cases} 0 \\ [0,1] \\ 1 \end{cases} \text{if } i \begin{cases} > \\ = \\ < \end{cases} i^*. \tag{2.12}$$

This implies a horizontal LM curve at $i = i^*$ for $Y \le M_1/k$.[15]

As the next step, we calculate the partial derivatives of the (excess) demand functions in the trap region. The relevant results are:

$$L_i \to -\infty, \, B_i^d \to +\infty; \tag{2.13}$$

$$L_Y = (1 - l)k, \, B_Y^d = -(1 - l)k; \tag{2.14}$$

$$L_W = l, \, B_W^d = 1 - l \tag{2.15}$$

Upon substitution it turns out that the consistency restrictions (10) to (12') are fulfilled as required.

This brings us to the question of the Pigou effect, $S_W < 0$. Rabin and Keilany (1986) have argued that in the liquidity trap any increase in wealth (or of real balances) would be fully absorbed by money demand so that there cannot be a Pigou effect. The way out of the liquidity trap would thus be blocked, as an increase in real balances could not spill over to consumption (and decrease saving).[16]

Obviously this argument is invalid for the beginning-of-period specification: As can be seen from (8*), an excess demand for money is just compensated by an excess supply of bonds of the same magnitude, with no effect on expenditure. Yet also for the end-of-period specification, the consistency restrictions (10) to (12), as satisfied in the liquidity trap by (2.13) to (2.15), are compatible with any value of S_W, in particular with $S_W < 0$. This means, of course, that Walras' law does not rule out the existence of the Pigou effect in the liquidity trap (if consistently specified).

The formal results are straightforward. We model the Pigou effect by an equiproportionate increase in the real value of money and bonds, assuming both to be fixed in nominal terms, so that:

$$\frac{dW_0}{W_0} = \frac{dM_0}{M_0} = \frac{dB_0}{B_0} \equiv \pi \Rightarrow M_{0W} = \frac{M_0}{W_0}, B_{0W} = \frac{B_0}{W_0}. \tag{2.16}$$

As the interest rate is fixed in the trap at $i = i^*$, the effect on income can be calculated from the IS curve:

$$\frac{di}{d\pi} = 0; \frac{dY}{d\pi} = -\frac{S_W}{S_Y} W_0 > 0. \tag{2.17}$$

Finally, money demand passively adapts to the increase in the real money supply:

$$\frac{dL_1}{d\pi} = M_0. \tag{2.18}$$

We may thus conclude that the assertion of the logical impossibility of a Pigou effect in the liquidity trap is plainly wrong.

The Optimal Monetary Instrument: Poole's Rule

The third example concerns the analysis of the optimal monetary instrument. In a seminal paper Poole (1970) examined this question within an IS–LM framework and derived 'Poole's rule', according to which the relative efficiency of the money supply as a monetary instrument, as compared with the rate of interest, depends positively on the ratio of the variance of real relative to monetary shocks. The underlying assumptions are that the central bank knows the deterministic components of the IS and LM equations and that it can control the expected value of output by the suitable choice of its instruments. However the actual value of output may deviate from its expected value because of (unanticipated) random shocks to commodity and money demand. As these deviations differ according to the monetary instrument chosen, the optimal monetary instrument can be determined by minimizing the variance of output (around its expected value). Despite the numerous 'revolutions' in macroeconomic theory, Poole's is still considered a 'useful model', even by high-brow monetary theorists (cf. Blanchard and Fischer, 1989: 575ff.).

We start by recapitulating Poole's model. The equations (3.1) and (3.2) are to be interpreted as linear approximations in the neighbourhood of equilibrium to the IS and LM curve (1) and (2) with $S_W, L_W = 0$. To economize on notation we introduce the following abbreviations: $S_Y \equiv s$, $I_i \equiv -g$, $L_Y \equiv k$, $L_i \equiv -h$, so that all parameters are positive. Equations (3.3a) and (3.3b) define monetary policy with a money supply and an interest rate target, respectively.

$$sY = a - gi + u, \tag{3.1}$$

$$M = kY - hi + v, \tag{3.2}$$

$$M = \overline{M} \equiv \frac{(kg + sh)\overline{Y} - ah}{g}, \tag{3.3a}$$

$$i = \overline{i} \equiv \frac{a - s\overline{Y}}{g}. \tag{3.3b}$$

The symbols are the same as used above, $\overline{Y}$ denotes the target value of output, $\overline{M}$ and $\overline{i}$ the corresponding values of the monetary instruments; u and v are random components in commodity and money demand, respectively, the so-called 'real' and 'monetary' shocks, with $u, v \equiv N(0, \sigma_j^2), j = u, v$.

The model can be solved for the variance of output in each of the two regimes. For the money supply regime (denoted by M) we arrive at:

$$\sigma_Y^2(M) = \frac{1}{m^2}(h^2\sigma_u^2 - 2hg\sigma_{uv} + g^2\sigma_v^2), \quad m \equiv sh + kg > 0, \tag{3.4}$$

whereas for the interest rate regime (denoted by i):

$$\sigma_Y^2(i) = \frac{1}{s^2}\sigma_u^2. \tag{3.5}$$

Although Poole (1970: 206f.) noted the possibility of a non-zero covariance between real and monetary shocks, usually the analysis proceeds from the assumption that $\sigma_{uv} = 0$. This results in the following condition for the superiority of the money supply regime:

$$\frac{\sigma_v^2}{\sigma_u^2} < \frac{m^2 - s^2h^2}{s^2g^2} = \frac{kg(kg + 2sh)}{s^2g^2} \equiv \lambda > 0. \tag{3.6}$$

The relative performance of the money supply regime is the better the smaller the ratio of the variance of monetary to real shocks and it becomes definitely superior to the interest rate regime if this ratio falls below λ, which is determined by the parameters of the model – Poole's rule.

At this stage of the argument we again introduce Walras' law and apply it to the end-of-period equilibrium version of the model. At first we rewrite Walras' law (7) as:

$$(I - S) + (L - M) + (B^d - B) = 0, \tag{3.7}$$

where all the variables include the relevant stochastic shocks.[17] We define the respective deterministic components of demand as $\hat{I}, \hat{L}$ and $\hat{B}^d$, so that $I - \hat{I} =$

u, $L - \hat{L} = v$ and $B^d - \hat{B}^d = w$, where w is another random variable, a 'financial' shock. Then we examine the deterministic part of the model where all random shocks are set to zero. Obviously Walras' law applies also to this version and it renders:

$$(\hat{I} - S) + (\hat{L} - M) + (\hat{B}^d - B) = 0. \qquad (3.8)$$

At last, subtracting (3.8) from (3.7), we see that Walras' law implies a restriction on the stochastic shocks, namely:

$$u + v + w = 0 \qquad (3.9)$$

From equation (3.9) we can derive the following three symmetrical restrictions on the variances and covariances of the shock variables:

$$\sigma_u^2 + 2\sigma_{uv} + \sigma_v^2 = \sigma_w^2, \qquad (3.10a)$$

$$\sigma_u^2 + 2\sigma_{uw} + \sigma_w^2 = \sigma_v^2, \qquad (3.10b)$$

$$\sigma_v^2 + 2\sigma_{vw} + \sigma_w^2 = \sigma_u^2. \qquad (3.10c)$$

The stochastic structure of the three shocks, u, v and w, is represented by their variances and covariances, that is, in sum by six parameters. Taking account of the restrictions (3.10a–c), all feasible structures can be fully described by the three parameters σ_u^2, σ_v^2 and σ_{uv}. (For example, σ_u^2, $\sigma_v^2 > 0$; $\sigma_{uv} = 0$ implies $\sigma_w^2 = \sigma_u^2 + \sigma_v^2$, $\sigma_{uw} = -\sigma_u^2$, $\sigma_{vw} = -\sigma_v^2$.) Thus Equation (3.4) specifies the variance of output under the money supply regime for any such structure. However, the usual assumption $\sigma_{uv} = 0$ is only one among infinitely many that are all feasible.

The crucial question then is if Poole's rule remains valid for other feasible stochastic structures. We shall demonstrate in the following by way of a counter-example that this need not be the case.

A characteristic feature of the usual assumption, $\sigma_{uv} = 0$, is that the origins of shocks are located exclusively in the commodity and money market. The financial shock in the bond market just mirrors the real and monetary shocks, but there are no autonomous shocks in the bond market. This implies that, for example, an increase in commodity demand due to a positive real shock, $u > 0$, is financed by a simultaneous decrease in the demand for bonds, $w < 0$, that is, by 'selling bonds'. However, this assumption that it is the demand for bonds that acts as a kind of buffer stock is not necessarily the most plausible one. To the contrary, with money balances as buffer stocks – a notion propagated, for example, by Laidler (1984) and Bain and McGregor (1985) – real shocks would be absorbed by deviations of money demand from its target level, $u > 0$ implying $v < 0$. In this case real and financial shocks would be autonomous and the monetary shock just their mirror image. It is this counter-example that we examine in the following.

Now suppose σ_u^2 and $\sigma_w^2 > 0$ are given and $\sigma_{uw} = 0$. From the restrictions (3.10a–c) follows:

$$\sigma_v^2 = \sigma_u^2 + \sigma_w^2 \tag{3.11}$$

and

$$\sigma_{uv} = -\sigma_u^2. \tag{3.12}$$

Inserting (3.11) and (3.12) into (3.4) renders the variance of output under a money supply regime:

$$\sigma_Y^2(M) = \frac{1}{m^2}[(h+g)^2 \sigma_u^2 + g^2 \sigma_w^2], \tag{3.13}$$

whereas the results of the interest rate regime are still given by (3.5). By comparing (3.13) and (3.5) we obtain the condition for the superiority of the money supply regime:

$$\frac{\sigma_w^2}{\sigma_u^2} < \frac{m^2 - s^2(h+g)^2}{g^2} \equiv \mu. \tag{3.14}$$

Obviously the left-hand side of (3.14) will be positive, so that the condition can only be fulfilled if $\mu > 0$. This is, however, not guaranteed by the parameter restrictions:

$$\mu = [m - s(g + h)] \, [m + s(g + h)] = (k - s)g[2sh + g(k + s)], \tag{3.15}$$

so that

$$\mu > 0 \Leftrightarrow k - s > 0. \tag{3.16}$$

Looking at Equation (14), it turns out the sign of $k - s$ cannot be determined a priori, so that $k - s < 0$, and therefore $\mu < 0$, is at least logically possible. (In fact it corresponds to the case of a downward-sloping BB curve.) Yet in this case the interest rate regime is always superior to a money supply regime, irrespective of the variances of the shocks.

This can easily be seen by transforming (3.16) so that Poole's rule can be applied directly:

$$\frac{\sigma_v^2}{\sigma_u^2} = \frac{\sigma_w^2}{\sigma_u^2} + 1 < \mu + 1. \tag{3.17}$$

Decreasing the variance of monetary relative to real shocks still improves the performance of the money supply regime. However, as the ratio of these variances cannot fall below one, the money supply regime will never dominate as long as $\mu < 0$.

Therefore taking account of the restrictions imposed by Walras' law focuses attention on the diversity of feasible stochastic structures and on the crucial dependence of Poole's rule on the specific structure assumed. As the assumption of the statistical independence of monetary and real shocks has persisted more or less unquestioned in the models of the new classical macroeconomics (see, for example, Sargent and Wallace, 1975 and Parkin, 1978) as well as in the more recent literature on monetary targeting (cf. Svensson 1999), there seem still to be some lessons to be learnt from the not-so-recent literature on Walras' law.

NOTES

*   Section 2 of this paper owes much to a stimulating correspondence with Ingo Barens and Volker Caspari. Section 3.3 of this paper was already discussed in the staff seminar of the Department of Economics (Vienna University of Economics and Business Administration) and in the private seminar of Helmut Frisch (Technical University Vienna). Critical comments by all the participants, in particular by Ingo Barens, Helmut Frisch, Franz Hof, Alfred Stiassny, Erich Streissler and Michel De Vroey, are thankfully acknowledged. A most valuable technical improvement of the paper is due to a hint by Fabio Rumler. Of course, remaining errors and omissions are my own.

1.   For the notion of 'theoretical progress' (in distinction to 'empirical progress') cf. Blaug (Chapter 2, this volume).

2.   Although traditional Keynesian macroeconomics experienced a dramatic loss of reputation in the last decades, the works referred to above remain relevant as the reduction of macroeconomics to the interaction of the goods and the money market (as in IS–LM) still permeates many contributions.

3.   For a similar formulation see also Hicks (1939: 158). It should be noted that in the 1937 version of Hicks's IS–LM-model income is in nominal and not in real terms. On the consistency of this formulation (as contrary to the usual one) see Barens (2000).

4.   See, for a more thorough investigation, Klausinger (1992).

5.   In a careful if somewhat eclectic analysis of the IS–LM–BB model, McCaleb and Sellon (1980: 403ff.) examined the restrictions on the slopes of these curves implied by Walras' law.

6.   For an attempt at such an empirical investigation see, for example, Ferguson and Hart (1980).

7.   However, as Hellwig (1975) pointed out, the compatibility of models in continuous time, which imply continuous transactions, with the foundations of the transactions demand for money is dubious.

8.   The basic simplification consists in neglecting the distinction between current and expected variables and between the different points in time when expectations are formed.

9.   For simplicity, here and in the following capital gains and losses from holding bonds are disregarded, that is, bond supply is specified as B_0 instead of B_0/i.

10. Subscripts indicate partial derivatives.
11. Note that the parameter L_Y refers to a stock–flow relation whereas S_Y refers to a relation between two flows. Therefore the value of L_Y will depend on the length of the period (decrease with increasing period length), but S_Y will not. Consequently, the slope of the BB curve will depend on the length of the period, too. For example, for very short periods BB must be upwards sloping.
12. For early critiques see Maussner (1988) and Barens and Caspari (1995).
13. This formulation follows Keynes (1936: 166ff.) and Tobin (1958). For sake of simplicity we concentrate on expected capital gains and losses and disregard the interest income from bonds. See Chick (1983: 200ff. and 219ff.), who similarly uses Keynes's normal rate instead of Tobin's critical rate of interest in deriving the speculative demand for money.
14. For simplicity we neglect the possibility that f is monotonically but not strictly monotonically decreasing so that $L(i)$ could become a kind of step-function. This would allow the possibility that LM would be horizontal in the neighbourhood of equilibrium but not throughout. This (not very interesting) possibility is analysed by Beranek and Timberlake (1987: 391ff.) as the so-called 'strong version'.
15. Obviously, the LM curve is continuous, in particular it does not contain 'holes' in its horizontal part, as suggested erroneously by Beranek and Timberlake (1987: 394).
16. For the ensuing debate, see Rabin and Keilany (1987, 1988), Coulombe (1987) and Mayer (1988).
17. Note that all excess demands are measured in nominal units.

REFERENCES

Bain, A.D. and P.G. McGregor (1985), 'Buffer-stock monetarism and the theory of financial buffers', *Manchester School*, 53: 385–403.

Barens, I. (2000), 'Born under a Bad Sign: The Origin and Early History of AS–AD', Paper presented at the 2000 ESHET Annual Conference, Graz, mimeo.

Barens, I. and V. Caspari (1992), 'Ist die Liquiditätsfalle instabil? Ein Kommentar zur Interpretation des IS–LM-Systems durch Größl-Gschwendtner', *Jahrbücher für Nationalökonomie und Statistik*, 210: 339–45.

Barens, I. and V. Caspari (1995), 'Was stellt die IS-Kurve dar: Gütermarkt oder Kapitalmarkt? Versuch einer Klärung', mimeo Technische Universität Darmstadt.

Beranek, W. and R.H. Timberlake (1987), 'The liquidity trap theory: a critique', *Southern Economic Journal*, 54: 387–96.

Beranek, W. and R.H. Timberlake (1990), 'The liquidity trap theory: reply', *Southern Economic Journal*, 56: 812–14.

Blanchard, O.J. and S. Fischer (1989), *Lectures on Macroeconomics*, Cambridge and London: MIT Press.

Blinder, A.S. and R.M. Solow (1973), 'Does fiscal policy matter?' *Journal of Public Economics*, 2: 319–37.

Buiter, W.H. (1979), *Temporary Equilibrium and Long-run Equilibrium*, New York and London: Garland.

Buiter, W.H. (1980), 'Walras' Law and all that: budget constraints and balance sheet constraints in period models and continuous time models', *International Economic Review*, 21: 1–16.

Buiter, W.H. and J. Eaton (1981), 'Keynesian balance of payments models: comment', *American Economic Review*, 71: 784–95.

Chick, V. (1983), *Macroeconomics after Keynes*, Deddington: Phillip Allan.

Christ, C. (1968), 'A simple macroeconomic model with a government budget constraint', *Journal of Political Economy*, 76: 434–43.

Coulombe, S. (1987), 'A note on the Pigou effect and the liquidity trap', *Journal of Post-Keynesian Economics*, 10: 163–5.

Cushman, D.O. (1990), 'The liquidity trap theory: comment', *Southern Economic Journal*, 56: 807–11.

Dornbusch, R. and S. Fischer (1998), *Macroeconomics*, 7th edition, New York: McGraw-Hill.

Ernst, M. (1992), 'Die Stabilität der Liquiditätsfalle und des klassischen Bereichs im IS–LM-System', *Jahrbücher für Nationalökonomie und Statistik*, 210: 336–8.

Ernst, M. and D. Walpuski (1993a), 'Integration von Wertpapiermarkt und Geldmarkt im Keynesschen Makromodell', *Jahrbücher für Nationalökonomie und Statistik*, 212: 463–79.

Ernst, M. and D. Walpuski (1993b), 'Stabilitätsanalyse der Extrembereiche der LM-Funktion', *Wirtschaftswissenschaftliches Studium*, 11: 583–5.

Ernst, M. and D. Walpuski (1996), 'Integration von Geld- und Wertpapiermarkt im Keynesschen Makromodell. Eine Replik', *Jahrbücher für Nationalökonomie und Statistik*, 215: 244–51.

Felderer, B. and S. Homburg (1986), 'Eine Fehlinterpretation des Keynesianischen Modells', *Jahrbücher für Nationalökonomie und Statistik*, 201: 457–68.

Felderer, B. and S. Homburg (1994), *Makroökonomik und neue Makroökonomik*, 6th edition, Berlin: Springer.

Fellner, W. and H.M. Somers (1950), 'Stock and flow analysis: comment', *Economica*, 18: 242–5.

Ferguson, J.D. and W.R. Hart (1980), 'Liquidity preference and loanable funds: interest determination in market disequilibrium', *Oxford Economic Papers*, 32: 57–70.

Foley, D.K. (1975), 'On two specifications of asset equilibrium in macroeconomic models', *Journal of Political Economy*, 83: 303–24.

Gordon, R.J. (1993), *Macroeconomics*, 6th edition, New York: Harper and Collins.

Größl-Gschwendtner, I. (1991), 'Die Stabilität der Liquiditätsfalle und des klassischen Bereichs im IS–LM-System', *Jahrbücher für Nationalökonomie und Statistik*, 208: 166–71.

Größl-Gschwendtner, I. (1993), 'Replik zur Gegendarstellung von Barens, Caspari: "Ist die Liquiditätsfalle stabil?" ', *Jahrbücher für Nationalökonomie und Statistik*, 211: 173–6.

Hellwig, M. (1975), 'The demand for money and bonds in continuous-time models', *Journal of Economic Theory*, 11: 462–4.

Hicks, J.R. (1936), 'Mr. Keynes's theory of employment', *Economic Journal*, 46: 238–53.

Hicks, J.R. (1937), 'Mr. Keynes and the classics', reprinted in J. Hicks (1982), *Money, Interest and Wages. Collected Essays on Economic Theory*, Vol. II, Oxford: Basil Blackwell: 100–15.

Hicks, J.R. (1939), *Value and Capital*, Oxford: Clarendon Press (2nd ed. 1946).

Jarchow, H.J. (1998), *Theorie und Politik des Geldes I*, 10th edition, Göttingen: Vandenhoeck und Ruprecht.

Keynes, J.M. (1936), *The General Theory of Employment, Interest and Money* (= *The Collected Writings of John Maynard Keynes*, Vol. VII, London: Macmillan, 1973).

Klatt, S. (1989), *Einführung in die Makroökonomie*, 2nd edition, München-Wien: Oldenbourg.

Klausinger, H. (1992), 'Keynes on saving, hoarding and finance', in S.T. Lowry (ed.), *Perspectives on the History of Economic Thought*, Vol. VIII, Aldershot and Brookfield: Edward Elgar: 232–50.

Klausinger, H. (1995), 'Der Wertpapiermarkt im Keynesschen Modell: Einige kritische Anmerkungen', *Jahrbücher für Nationalökonomie und Statistik*, 214: 226–37.

Klein, L.R. (1950), 'Stock and flow analysis in economics', *Economica*, 18: 236–41.

Kuska E.A. (1978), 'On the almost total inadequacy of Keynesian balance-of-payments theory', *American Economic Review*, 68: 659–70.

Laidler, D. (1984), 'The "buffer stock" notion in monetary economics', *Economic Journal*, 94, supplement: 17–34.

Mankiw, N.G. (1997), *Macroeconomics*, 3rd edition, New York: Worth.

Maussner, A. (1988), 'Strom- und Bestandsrestriktionen in makroökonomischen Modellen', *Jahrbücher für Nationalökonomie und Statistik,* 205: 316–31.

May, J. (1970), 'Period analysis and continuous analysis in Patinkin's macroeconomic model', *Journal of Economic Theory*, 2: 1–9.

Mayer, Th. (1988), 'Absolute liquidity preference and the Pigou effect: a comment', *Journal of Post-Keynesian Economics*, 10: 653–4.

McCaleb, Th.S. and G.H. Sellon (1980), 'On the consistent specification of asset markets in macroeconomic models', *Journal of Monetary Economics*, 6: 401–17.

Ohlin, B. (1937), 'Some notes on the Stockholm theory of saving and investment', *Economic Journal*, 47: 53–69, 221–40.

Parkin, M. (1978), 'A comparison of alternative techniques of monetary control under rational expectations', *Manchester School*, 46: 252–87.

Patinkin, D. (1956), *Money, Interest and Prices*, 1st edition, Evanston: Row, Peterson and Co.

Patinkin, D. (1958), 'Liquidity preference and loanable funds: stock and flow analysis', *Economica*, 25: 300–18.

Patinkin, D. (1965), *Money, Interest and Prices*, 2nd edition, New York: Harper and Row.

Poole, W. (1970), 'Optimal choice of monetary policy in a simple stochastic macro model', *Quarterly Journal of Economics,* 84: 197–216.

Rabin, A. and Z. Keilany (1986), 'A note on the incompatibility of the Pigou effect and a liquidity trap', *Journal of Post-Keynesian Economics*, 9: 291–6.

Rabin, A. and Z. Keilany (1987), 'A note on the Pigou effect and the liquidity trap: reply', *Journal of Post-Keynesian Economics*, 10: 166–7.

Rabin, A. and Z. Keilany (1988), 'Absolute liquidity preference and the Pigou effect: a reply', *Journal of Post-Keynesian Economics*, 10: 655–7.

Robertson, D.H. (1940), *Essays in Monetary Theory*, London: King.

Samuelson, P.A. (1946), *Foundations of Economic Analysis*, Cambridge: Harvard University Press.

Sargent, T.J. and N. Wallace (1975), ' "Rational expectations", the optimal monetary instrument, and the optimal money supply rule', *Journal of Political Economy*, 85: 215–28.

Svensson, L.E.O. (1999), 'Inflation targeting as a monetary policy rule', *Journal of Monetary Economics*, 43: 607–54.

Tobin, J. (1958), 'Liquidity preference as behavior towards risk', *Review of Economic Studies*, 25: 65–86.

Tobin, J. and W.C. Brainard (1968), 'Pitfalls in financial model building', *American Economic Review*, 58 (P. & Proc.): 99–122.

Woglom, G. (1980), 'Are period models well defined?', *Journal of Macroeconomics*, 2: 333–50.

20. Information costs, deliberation costs and transaction costs: a parallel treatment[*]

Maurice Lagueux

It seems reasonable to say that everything which is valuable has a cost. Accordingly, one may conclude that useful information, rational deliberation and advantageous transactions are three services which should have a cost just like any other services. However, it is well known that, in contrast to more standard services, these have enduringly been perceived by most economists, at least until the mid-twentieth century, as zero-cost commodities. Buyers and sellers were assumed to get information, to deliberate and to negotiate about various kinds of transactions, but no specific cost was associated with such activities. Economic agents being assumed to choose what they consider the most advantageous to them, it would have been inconceivable in this context that these agents would drop the allegedly free benefits drawn from more information, more deliberation and more transactions. And, since searching for information, deliberating and negotiating can take a great deal of time (not to mention various other correlative expenses) and since it is well known, at least since Benjamin Franklin, that 'time is money', assuming zero cost for these desired benefits was tantamount to assuming that the activities that provide them were accomplished instantaneously. But to dispose instantaneously – without devoting any time or other kinds of resources to the acquisition of such a commodity – of all the information which might be economically relevant implies that all possible knowledge is already available or, put otherwise, it implies omniscience to start with. Similarly, to arrive instantaneously – without devoting any time or other kinds of resources to improving any aspect of the process – at the decision which, on any conceivable occasion, would have resulted from a deliberation about the respective advantages of all possible alternatives implies perfect and unbounded rationality. Finally, to be in a position to buy any conceivable kind of commodity at its correct price instantaneously – without devoting any time or other kinds of resources to negotiation – implies that everything is marketable to start with or, if one prefers, that what I will call 'omnimarketability' prevails. Accordingly, most traditional economic models have been designed in such a way that they describe omniscient and perfectly rational agents who are trading an indefinite amount of goods which are all readily available for exchange.

Each of these three features of traditional economic models is very well known. Rather than discussing further any one of them in particular, what I would like to do is to show that there exists a parallel between the three phenomena involved and to explore to what extent they raise similar types of problems for economic analysis. In addition, I wish to inquire whether the conclusions drawn from the analysis of any one of these phenomena is applicable to the others. This parallel treatment will shed some light on the fact that the concept of cost has increasingly been overextended by economists during the second half of the twentieth century. I will conclude by showing that, while it has made a better understanding of the workings of the market possible, the progressive extension of this concept, when taken beyond certain limits, tends paradoxically to destroy the very meaning of a market economy.

VARIOUS KINDS OF PROHIBITIVE COSTS

In fact, it was only when concerns were raised about the blatantly unrealistic character of each one of all-embracing attributes like omniscience, perfect rationality and omnimarketability that economists turned their attention to the specific costs associated with information, deliberation and transaction. For an economist, indeed, if a commodity which is desired and considered important is bought in a far too limited quantity to satisfy the corresponding need, it is natural to conclude that potential buyers are restrained by a prohibitive cost. Thus, when it was pointed out that the prevalence of ignorance makes omniscience an extravagant and even preposterous postulate, some economists were inclined to conclude that if knowledge and information were severely limited, it was due to the *prohibitive cost of information*. It is true that it is possible to acquire more information by taking appropriate means, but such an acquisition imposes costs in money and time which can become so high that one can reasonably prefer to live with a limited amount of information than to acquire still more of it.[1] Similarly, when it was pointed out through evidence accumulated through empirical inquiries that people frequently behave in a way clearly at odds with what is expected from rational behaviour, some economists were led to explore the idea that such apparently irrational behaviour was largely due to the *prohibitive cost of supplementary deliberation*. It is true that it is possible by taking appropriate means to improve the quality of the deliberation which precedes important decisions, but such an improvement imposes costs in money and time which can become so high that one can reasonably prefer to shorten deliberation and be satisfied by the situation reached with the help of a 'bounded' rationality.[2] These first two cases are closely related: information and deliberation have complementary functions in the process of arriving at the most advantageous situations. They are, however, conceptually quite different since information might be complete but not used given limitations affecting the required deliberation; conversely, deliberation might be perfect given the limited amount of information available. The third case to be considered here seems to be quite different, but it is also closely related to the first two. When it was pointed out that externalities were pervasive and that there were many things which cannot be bought and sold as marketable commodities, some economists concluded that such a resistance to marketability was due to the *prohibitive cost of transactions*. After all, it is possible, by engaging in costly negotiations (like those required by the trade of pollution rights), to transform into marketable goods various situations which used to be associated with externalities.[3] The parallel can be illustrated by Table 20.1.

In these three cases, the economists' strategy was the same because the problems faced were similar. The core of this strategy was the claim that if real-world markets do not work as they should according to the ideal model of the market, this must be due to the fact that reaching the optimal point determined by the ideal model is costly and that anything which has a cost should not continue to be bought in cases where the benefit of an extra unit of it is overwhelmed by the cost incurred in obtaining it. By drawing attention to these costs, economists managed to explain the presence of ignorance, of irrationality and of externalities in such a way as to render these phenomena no longer a challenge to economic theory. Even if economic agents desire to get as much information as they can, the cost of information can be such that it might be preferable to choose to remain ignorant to some degree. Even if economic agents tend to arrive at the best decision through a deliberation which bears on any relevant aspect of a question, the cost of deliberation can

Table 20.1   A parallel presentation of the three cases

	Knowledge	Rationality	Market
Zero-cost model	Omniscience	Unbounded rationality	Omnimarketability
Empirically observed	Ignorance	Irrationality	Externalities
Relevant costs	Information cost	Deliberation cost	Transaction cost
Prohibitive cost	Limited information	Bounded rationality	Limited marketability

be such that it might be just wise to be happy with what a bounded rationality suggests (and consequently to take decisions which look irrational from a certain point of view). Even if economic agents tend to rely on economic transactions to buy any kind of benefits (like protection from pollution), the cost of organizing this kind of transaction can be so high that it might be advantageous to decide not to buy such extremely costly commodities, leaving the market in a situation that old-fashioned economists (wrongly) used to present as 'external' to the market.

By proceeding this way, economists integrate into an all-embracing potential market all these features of the real world (ignorance, irrationality, externalities) which made most neoclassical models of the market so unrealistic. To some extent, this strategy seems justified. After all, it is true that there exist various kinds of costs. At the beginning of the nineteenth century, most economists were inclined to consider only production costs, but this was clearly revealed to be nonsense. How could one not count transportation costs? The cost of a commodity available at a given place cannot be the same as the cost of the same commodity available at its point of production in a distant country. But if it is so, why exclude distribution costs? The cost of a commodity available in small units at any place and at any time cannot be the same as the cost of the same commodity available as a part of a large lot only at the factory on the day of its production. And what about advertising costs? As Stigler claimed (1961: 220ff.), they should be seen as the price (frequently embodied in the market price of the commodity) of an efficient and economic transmission of useful information about commodities currently on sale.

THE FURTHER EXPANSION OF THE NOTION OF COST

However, in order to ensure the smooth functioning of a market which would realistically make room for the cumbersome features which are kept out of its ideal model, should we expand the notion of cost further to include anything which must be paid (be it money, time, psychological stress or other resources)? If one accepts this perspective, one can even be inclined to include in costs what must be spent in money, time and otherwise for physically and juridically *organizing a market* for a given commodity. Accordingly, one will consider that the goods from which we can possibly get benefits but which are not presently in sale in an actual market – like most rights to pollute or to be protected from pollution – are just commodities for which a proper market has not yet been organized, apparently because the organizing costs were prohibitive up to now. When Ronald Coase said that, in a world with zero transaction costs, farmers could buy protection against the sparking from trains passing their fields or, depending on the legal situation, railway companies could buy the right to damage farmers' crops with their sparking, he suggested that *in the real world* the transaction costs for organizing such markets were prohibitive to such a degree that these commodities *look* as if they were external to the market. For someone who thinks in such a way, anything – and especially any potential agreement – which can provide a benefit or avoid a nuisance can be considered as a potential commodity to eventually be sold on a potential market.

Among the costs incurred by the smooth workings of the market, one has to make room for information costs. It is true that by paying more and more it is possible to increase the information available. And, with more information, not only more goods could be made available but better decisions could be made about them. Buyers and sellers may engage in more or less costly searches for information concerning identity of potential sellers and buyers or prices of commodities.[4] Entrepreneurs can pay either an expert in a relevant domain or somebody who will retrieve useful information from libraries or other documentation centres. However, to increase information does not mean just getting the information which is already available in books or archives. When a company pays to get more information, it pays also for research. Such research tends naturally to include the discovery of new relevant knowledge which is usually just more difficult (and normally more costly) to obtain than the knowledge which is currently available. When the detection of the 'available' knowledge requires sophisticated searching techniques and when the discovery of new knowledge supposes the gathering of various pieces of available knowledge, the distinction between search and research becomes difficult to make. In this context, one can consider that all the possible knowledge which is to be discovered in future time is just made up of commodities which can be acquired by incurring information costs which, of course, quickly become clearly prohibitive. When President Kennedy decided to put a man on the moon within ten years, he decided that the USA would incur the almost prohibitive cost of discovering the new knowledge required to realize such an ambitious project.

Be that as it may, even a fully informed economic agent has to take decisions based on computation and deliberation. The more important the amount of information available is, the more lengthy are the computations and deliberations required to take the best decision. But computation and deliberation have a cost. The costs to pay include money and time but also what Gary Becker once called a 'psychic' cost (Becker, 1976: 7) since the stress caused by a long deliberation can easily exceed the money expenses involved. In any case, it is reasonable to think that by accepting to pay more and more in money, time and psychological stress, it is possible to increase the chance to reach a point which is closer and closer to an optimum given the constraints of the situation. For example, hiring a team of counsellors is probably an efficient way to take good decisions and this is one of the means adopted by those who can incur the cost involved, but this would be an excessive and inaccessible cost for most people, who would be content instead simply to weigh the pros and cons of a decision.

Thus, with these successive extensions of the notion of cost, virtually everything which happens in the world is integrated into an all-embracing market, but paradoxically enough the implications of this economic view of the world might be catastrophic for economic theory. Let me, from this point of view, consider successively transaction costs, deliberation costs and information costs.

NULLIFYING THE NOTION OF THE MARKET?

Inspired by Coase's paper on social cost, many economists proposed extending the scope of transaction costs to let them include any possible cost which would be caused by the eventual transformation of any source of benefit into a marketable commodity. It is true that some pollution rights have even been implemented to deal with various situations and it is possible to negotiate them on a highly artificial market, but can we conclude from this that any benefit or any nuisance is marketable in principle with the help of similar devices? No doubt that Coase theorem is a splendid piece of theory, but, as constantly emphasized by its author, it works so well precisely because it postulates zero transaction costs. Paradoxically, the theorem was the target of a considerable number of objections from those who overlook the fact that it claims to be valid only in a zero transaction cost world which, incidentally, is the 'world of modern economic theory' that Coase 'was hoping to persuade economists to leave'.[5] My own reservation in relation to Coase – or more precisely to some interpretations of Coase's analyses – goes precisely in the opposite direction. For Coasians, the temptation was great to assign an economic cost to every kind of potential transaction, and especially to transactions which would be required to build up a market where there was no market to begin with. However, the concept of 'cost' only has an economic meaning within the framework of the market; therefore, it cannot be used (except metaphorically) outside this framework. And building up a market is an activity which is typically performed outside a pre-existing market.

For example, would it be sensible to say that the right to pollute with sparking or anything else, or the right to be protected from pollution, is just a commodity whose price in the real world includes transaction costs whose prohibitive character is responsible for the fact that such commodities are not actually exchanged on a market? Such was the view held by Carl Dahlman (1979), a disciple of Ronald Coase. Once transaction costs have been placed on the same footing as the more familiar production and transportation costs, it seems normal to raise the same question which is raised concerning these kinds of costs. Why incur these costs if they are themselves larger than the benefits to be derived from an eventual transaction? After all, you might dream of owning a Ferrari, but if you consider that its price (made up essentially of production costs) is so high than the benefits expected from owning such a car would be overwhelmed by the inconveniences of paying such a cost, you could decide not to realize this dream without concluding for this reason that this absence of transaction corresponds to a situation which is not optimal. Dahlman's central idea was to apply such a consideration to transaction costs. If you suffer from pollution, you might be ready to pay a substantial amount for being delivered from this nuisance, but since there is no pre-existing market which offers you this possibility, you cannot realize this desire unless you accept that you will incur the extremely high costs (in campaigning, organizing, monitoring and so on) which are required to *organize* such a market. If, in this situation, you choose not to engage in such a costly enterprise because the required costs exceed your potential gains, there is no reason, according to Dahlman, not to conclude that the situation is optimal as it is.

An odd consequence of this way of thinking is that, once all transactions costs have been taken into account, *almost any static situation will look optimal*. If no transaction goes on to improve a situation, it is tempting to conclude that this is because the *costs* of an eventual transaction (for example, the cost of organizing and monitoring would-be transactors) added to the payment involved in those eventual transactions make it unprofitable. If, for example, the railway company persists in polluting the crops even when the nuisance to farmers is greater than the benefit obtained by the company from doing so, it is, in one sense, because the 'transaction' costs (the cost of organizing a substantial number of farmers, forcing them to reveal their true preferences and collecting the amount required to convince the railway company to reduce its operations or to adopt a less polluting technique) would be so great that, added to the amount of the bribe payable to the company, it *would* exceed the potential benefit to the farmers. Any situation whatsoever is optimal since any improvement would be implemented were its costs – including transaction costs and costs of any other type – low enough to make it socially profitable. It was just such a conclusion that Mishan anticipated with apprehension when he wrote in 1971 a rather ironic paper entitled 'Pangloss on pollution' (Mishan, 1971). The reference to Dr Pangloss, the pleasant champion of 'the best of all possible worlds' in Voltaire's *Candide*, was meant to suggest how the inclusion of transaction costs can dramatically change the analysis of pollution and transform into an optimal situation what was until then considered to be one of the most serious challenges to economists' confidence in the virtues of the market.

It might even be possible to push the matter still further by claiming that such an argument could make optimal any political situation whatsoever. Any dictatorial government, even one particularly inimical to free market, could be justified by an extension of this argument apparently based on the functioning of the market. Dictatorial governments' activities interfere significantly with the consumption functions of their citizens by restricting their individual liberty. However, if the inconvenience suffered by these citizens was really that important, they could collectively bribe the government to reduce its liberty-limiting activities to an optimal amount. If they do not attempt to bribe the government, it is clearly because such transactions would involve costs (information costs, organization costs, decision-making costs and monitoring costs) which would be much higher than the benefits expected. Thus, paradoxically enough, it would make sense, according to this market view of the world, to characterize the situation in this dictatorial country as optimal as it is![6] Naturally, one might object to such an application of the transaction cost approach to a political (as opposed to an economic) situation. However, the *actual* relation between a railway company and the polluted farmers is not a typical economic relation and, consequently, it is not clear that alleged economic and political situations are really as different as they seem to be at first thought. As is well known, many prisoners do manage to bribe their jailers! And, after all, the application of economic analysis to political situations is, as is also well known, one of the major contributions of economic theory in recent decades. In any case, the goal of this comparison was not to dramatically suggest that political and economic situations are equivalent, but rather to illustrate that, if pushed to the limit, the overextension of the concept of cost destroys the very meaning of the concept of a market. If any kind of human interaction can be considered an optimal market situation, a market is no longer a particularly interesting structure.

Let us now consider the case of deliberation costs, which naturally include computation costs and other associated costs. If these costs were extended to include any cost potentially incurred by someone managing to improve the quality of a decision, any decision whatsoever might be considered rational and even optimal since any apparently irrational move could be presented as the best decision given the marginal cost of extra deliberation. Naturally, one could object that a decision which turns out to have disastrous consequences could have been avoided with not such a costly extra amount of deliberation, but, even in this case, if the extra deliberation were not engaged in, it would normally be due to the quite rational (if not well-informed) assessment according to which the estimated cost (mostly psychological in this case) of such extra deliberation was estimated to be larger than the *expected* disutility of the adopted course of action. Frank Knight had already presented such a conclusion as self-evident as early as 1921: 'It is evident that the rational thing to do is to be irrational, where deliberation and estimation cost more than they are worth'.[7] Many people (including very probably Frank Knight) may find that such a conclusion is not particularly catastrophic for economics, but it implies that optimization itself turns out to be an almost contradictory notion since, in many situations which are far from being atypical, optimizing implies refraining from optimizing. Through an overextension of the notion of cost, the notion of optimization (when all alleged costs are taken into account) loses its very meaning since, here again, any situation whatsoever might be presented as optimal, just because the cost required for arriving at a different and objectively more optimal situation was judged too high and, for this reason, sufficient to make the economically 'optimal' situation less optimal than the adopted one.

What about information costs?[8] Since optimization, and especially long-term optimization, may require not only vast knowledge of the present situation but also some knowledge of the future, including some knowledge of the state of science and technology in the future, it is difficult to draw the line between the cost of information about the present and about the future state of the world. Pushed to its limits, the idea of extending this kind of cost to include any expenses related to the acquisition (including the discovery) of any kind of useful information would virtually reduce technical progress to a simple choice between techniques since the discovery of new techniques would be considered just a matter of cost which might of course quickly be judged prohibitive. In such an extreme situation, it would be the notion of long-term optimization which would tend to lose its meaning since any situation whatsoever would be considered optimal in some sense, even in the long term, once one takes into account the prohibitive cost of the investments in further research and investigations which would allow one to reach more immediately the long-term optimal position of economic models. More precisely, it is the notion of knowledge and the notion of time which would lose their meaning for economics since, by this overextension of the notion of cost, the difference between the known and the unknown, and the difference between the respective knowledge of different periods, would tend to vanish. As far as I know, no economist has ever adopted such an extravagant position. As a general rule, the frontier between the known and the still unknown, present knowledge and future knowledge, has been respected. Instead of being absurdly extended to include the cost of acquiring all possible knowledge, the notion of information cost has remained limited to the already quite extreme cost of (eventually) acquiring all the presently available (relevant) knowledge.

TWO NOTIONS OF COST

I would like to argue that a frontier of this kind should be established in the two other cases discussed above. Instead of including the costs of all possible deliberations which could be done in order to optimize the result of a decision, only the cost eventually incurred by an optimizer who chooses to pay for means to improve the quality of a decision which are offered for sale – such as the eventual hiring of the services of counsellors available on the market – should be included in what counts as a cost when it comes to discussing the optimality of a decision. The estimated psychological cost of the extra deliberation which *might* have been made to reach a theoretical optimal point should not be considered when establishing this economically optimal point.[9] By proceeding in this way, the notion of economic optimization will find new life because it will no longer be true that any adopted position will be said to be optimal thanks to the accounting of these avoided psychological costs. Naturally, it would still be possible to say that it is *preferable* for any reason to adopt a position which is *not optimal* from the point of view of economic costs, but this sounds much more sensible than the view according to which any situation whatsoever could be said to be optimal.

It seems still more important to apply the same idea to transaction costs. Only actual transactions or actual negotiations to obtain a commodity which is *available* on some market should be considered as transaction costs. The cost of convincing a dictatorial government to change its mind is not an economic cost, not because we are dealing with political matters but because there is no such thing as an available market for ways of governing. In political contexts, where power is held by the mafia and where the price to pay for obtaining such and such decisions or such and such rights is fixed and well known, it would be quite correct to present as an economic cost the bribe or the 'tax' needing to be paid to obtain something. The problem with Dahlman's interpretation of Coase's views is not that it is applied to a domain which does not concern economics but that it refers to the creation of commodities which do not exist on an actual market. The problem is also that it suggests that buying such commodities is just a matter of negotiations similar to those which (at least implicitly) go on in any transaction. We must refrain from overextending the notion of the cost of transaction; not everything is a commodity, not every human relation is a market relation and not every situation where people refrain from searching for new transactions is an optimal situation. While it may be true that 'there is no such thing as a free lunch', it is not true that every kind of lunch is available and for sale on the market.

To conclude, I would like to observe that the psychological (and moral) notion of a sacrifice should be distinguished from the economic notion of a cost; the same goes for the notion of harm. Any human activity requires sacrificing something and is thus harmful from some point of view, but it is not true that anything which is sacrificed in such a context can be exchanged on a market. It sounds more fruitful to say that there is no economics without some form of *actual* – and not only metaphorical – market. Once they are separated from the context of a market – a place where real commodities are *really* exchanged – economic concepts, and especially the concept of cost, tend to lose their very meaning and to become self-contradictory.

NOTES

*   The author would like to thank Bruce Maxwell, Philippe Mongin and Richard Sturn for their very useful comments. Financial assistance from the SSHRC (Ottawa) and the Fonds FCAR (Quebec) was also greatly appreciated.
1.   The idea that information has a cost which explains that people can rationally decide to stop their search for information was clearly discussed by Stigler (1961).
2.   As is well known, Herbert Simon developed the idea of a bounded rationality through most of his works; for a survey with an accent on the concept of deliberation cost, see Conlisk (1996), for example, pp. 671ff.
3.   The literature on transaction costs and on internalization of externalities through negotiations has been extremely abundant since the publication by Ronald Coase of his seminal paper (Coase, 1960). For a useful critical survey, see Medema and Zerbe (2000).
4.   See Stigler (1961). For an interesting discussion of the relations between Stigler's analysis and Simon's views on bounded rationality and costs related to deliberation, see Mongin (1986).
5.   See Coase (1988: 174); quoted by Medema (1995: 1043) who frequently emphasizes and documents this crucial fact.
6.   I have discussed such an example in relation to Coase's theorem and Dahlman's paper in 'Learning from the debate on externalities' in Backhouse et al. (1998: 120–47).
7.   Knight, *Risk, Uncertainty and Profit* (1921), quoted by Conlisk (1996: 686).
8.   In some sense, information costs raise a problem similar to the one raised by deliberation costs, since one can argue that any situation is optimal given that the marginal cost of information is too high to justify further inquiry, but this effect is subordinated to the limitation of deliberation (which requires information). So I will consider here only the effect of overextending the notion of information costs per se (that is, concerning the cost of information over all possible knowledge).
9.   Jon Elster made a point which is akin to this when he denied that bounded rationality can be reduced to maximization once the information costs (or more properly the deliberation costs) are taken into account. See Elster, 1979: 136.

REFERENCES

Backhouse, Roger, Daniel Hausman, Uskali Mäki and Andrea Salanti (eds) (1998), *Economics and Methodology: Crossing Boundaries*, London: Macmillan and New York: St. Martin's Press.

Becker, Gary (1976), *The Economic Approach to Human Behavior*, Chicago: University of Chicago Press.

Coase, Ronald H. (1960), 'The problem of social cost', *Journal of Law and Economics*, 3: 1–44.

Coase, Ronald H. (1988), *The Firm, the Market and the Law*, Chicago: University of Chicago Press.

Conlisk, John (1996), 'Why bounded rationality?', *Journal of Economic Literature*, 34: 669–700.

Dahlman, C.J. (1979), 'The Problem of Externality', *Journal of Law and Economics*, 22: 141–62.

Elster, Jon (1979), *Ulysses and the Sirens*, Paris: Maison des sciences de l'homme, and Cambridge: Cambridge University Press.

Medema, Steven G. (1995), 'Through a glass darkly or just wearing dark glasses? Posin, Coase, and the Coase theorem', *Tennessee Law Review*, 62: 1041–56.

Medema, Steven G. and Richard O. Zerbe Jr. (2000), 'The Coase theorem', *Encyclopedia of Law and Economics*, Cheltenham: Edward Elgar.

Mishan, E.J. (1971), 'Pangloss on pollution', *Swedish Journal of Economics*, 73: 113–20.

Mongin, Philippe (1986), 'Simon, Stigler et les théories de la rationalité limitée', *Rationality and Society, Rationalité et Société*, London: SAGE, 25: 555–606.

Stigler, George (1961), 'The Economics of Information', *Journal of Political Economy*, 69: 213–25.

PART VIII

Reflections on the Classical Long-period Method

21. Produced quantities and returns in Sraffa's theory of normal prices: textual evidence and analytical issues

Fabio Ravagnani*

In *Production of Commodities* Sraffa (1960) provides a rigorous formulation of the classical theory o~~_____ In accordance~~ with his reconstruction of the basic feat_____ fa, 1951), he takes as independent variable ~~Piero Sraffa~~ nodities, (ii) the methods available for pro_____ tributive variable, and demonstrates that wi_____ os of commodities, as well as the residual _____ ined univocally and in an economically sigr_____ work, no distinction is made between the _____ roduction cycle as an input and the price o_____ an output at the end of the process. To use a concise expression, we may say that the theoretical prices are assumed to be 'constant' over the production period.

Let us now consider the position of the economy defined by the independent variables (i)–(iii) together with the relative prices and values of the distributive variables resulting from the equations of production. How should this position be interpreted? One widely accepted view is based on the passages of *Production of Commodities* where Sraffa relates his analysis to the theories of the old classical economists (p. v) and identifies his theoretical prices with their 'natural prices' or 'prices of production' (§ 7). It is accordingly argued that the prices obtained from Sraffa's equations are to be interpreted in the same way as those determined by Smith, Ricardo or Marx, that is, as the exchange ratios that would tend to prevail, in conditions of free competition, when the produced quantities of the different commodities conform to the respective 'effectual demands'. This in turn implies that the whole theoretical position is to be regarded as a *normal* position, aimed at defining a centre of gravitation for the prices and quantities of the actual economy (cf. for example Garegnani, 1990a: 132; Mainwaring, 1984: 12–13; Caravale, 1985: 185, and 1988: 1337–8; Mongiovi, 1991: 719, n. 3; Kurz and Salvadori, 1995: 4–5, 416–17).

It must be said, however, that not even the scholars who advocate the above interpretation are unanimous in their assessment of Sraffa's contribution. In particular, different opinions appear to be held as to whether the notion of normal position defined in *Production of Commodities* – characterized as it is by 'constant' prices – should be confined to situations where the produced quantities or the methods in use are strictly invariant in time, or instead constitutes an appropriate tool for a general analysis of value and distribution. We shall seek to stimulate further discussion on this point by examining Sraffa's own views and the analytical issues arising from them. The first section thus provides textual evidence showing that Sraffa considered the classical normal position to be compatible with a tendency of the produced quantities to change in time, although he did not dwell on the question of how the previously mentioned 'constancy' of the theoretical prices could be reconciled with that tendency in the absence of any restriction on returns. The second section identifies two alternative attitudes that can be adopted with respect to the evidence reported and the related analytical issue. The first is to take that evidence fully into account and try to clarify the foundations of Sraffa's views. The other is the attitude prevailing in the current renditions of the classical theory of value, which appear more or less implicitly to question those views, and in some cases decidedly advocate a 'dynamic extension' of the analysis. Both are discussed in this paper. It is argued that while there seems to be no obvious reason for denying the applicability of Sraffa's theory of normal prices to non-stationary economies with 'variable returns', the third section, it is doubtful that a satisfactory dynamic analysis can be developed in a classical context (the fourth section). Reference will be made throughout the paper to the simplified case of single production and overabundant resources examined in the first chapters of Sraffa's book, thus ensuring that the controversial problems arising under more complex conditions do not interfere with the basic issue under consideration.

SRAFFA ON THE APPLICABILITY OF THE CLASSICAL NOTION OF 'NORMAL POSITION'

We shall begin our discussion by examining the relevant features of the economic systems analysed in Part 1 of *Production of Commodities*. First of all, it can be noted that the assumption on the production conditions of the economy introduced in §11 – the hypothesis of 'self-replacing state' – is entirely compatible with the presence of strictly positive net outputs of capital goods. This fact deserves to be stressed, since, under the above-mentioned interpretation asserting the coincidence of produced quantities and effectual demands, we are forced to presume that the surpluses of means of production appearing in the theoretical position will be demanded by one or more industries in order to increase production in the future.

Moreover, in the footnote appended to §3 the author qualifies the argument put forward in the first two chapters of the book by making it clear that the analysis extends to all kinds of 'viable' economies. And since viability allows for the presence of *negative* net outputs of capital goods, the reader may legitimately conjecture that the theory also applies to situations in which some industries are not fully replacing their stocks of means of production, and will accordingly tend to *contract* their production levels. This conjecture is indeed confirmed by Sraffa himself in a comment on Harrod's review of *Production of Commodities* (Sraffa, 1962). We may recall here that Harrod focused on the introductory example of a subsistence economy with two industries, producing wheat and iron respectively,[1] and concluded that the exchange ratio of those commodities would ultimately be determined through a sort of reproduction principle. The repetition of the production processes on an unchanged scale, he noted, requires in fact that the quantity of wheat exceeding that necessary for rebuilding the wheat industry's stocks be exchanged for the analogous excess of iron (Harrod, 1961: 783). In the first part of the comment, however, Sraffa rejects this conclusion and states that in his theory the relative prices are determined by the equations of production, and not by Harrod's principle. To substantiate this assertion, he proposes that the introductory example of *Production of Commodities* be modified by arbitrarily altering the proportion in which wheat and iron are produced, so that the resulting system of production will necessarily display a surplus of a commodity and *a deficit* of the other. He then points out that with the new system of production thus obtained, which is obviously incompatible with an exact repetition of both production processes, the equations of production continue to determine the relative price (and a profit rate equal to zero) precisely as in the original case. Here Sraffa definitely refers to a theoretical position of the economy that cannot be associated with a stationary state.[2]

A careful reading of the assumptions formulated in *Production of Commodities* and the comment published in 1962 thus makes it clear that Sraffa did not intend to confine the classical notions of normal position and normal prices to the particular cases where the physical surplus is wholly allocated to households for consumption purposes, but extended those notions to the more general situations in which positive net outputs (deficits) of means of production are present, and the production level accordingly tends to rise (to fall) in one or more sectors. Sraffa's theory of normal prices thus appears to be quite open as regards the direction in which the individual sectoral outputs may tend to evolve. Furthermore, this feature of the theory cannot derive from an assumption of strict invariance of production methods with respect to activity levels ('constant returns to scale'), as Sraffa states from the outset that his analysis never depends on that assumption.

Sraffa's views on the applicability of the classical concepts of normal position and normal prices can, however, give rise to the question of how reference can be made to 'given' quantities and 'constant' prices in positions of the economy where constant returns are not postulated and the presence of surpluses (deficits) of capital goods entails a tendency of outputs to change in time. Should it not be admitted that under those circumstances the technical coefficients would tend to change and the relative prices would vary accordingly?

In the rest of the paper we shall discuss different answers to this question. Before moving on to that, however, it is worth stressing that the point at issue arises within the strict domain of Sraffa's price theory and therefore has nothing to do with other important economic problems that are not examined in *Production of Commodities*. In particular, it has nothing to do with the study of the determinants of produced quantities (effectual demands) or with the analysis of the causes determining the evolution of those quantities over time.

THE VIEW CONVEYED BY CURRENT RENDITIONS OF SRAFFA'S THEORY

Returning now to our specific topic, two alternative attitudes can be adopted with respect to the evidence reported and the related analytical issue. The first and most natural approach is to acknowledge that evidence and seek to clarify the foundations of Sraffa's views. The attitude that appears to have prevailed in the literature is, however, quite different, and can be illustrated here through reference to Hicks's (1990) assessment of Sraffa's contribution. Hicks offers no discussion of Sraffa's views, but takes it for granted that the theoretical positions defined in *Production of Commodities* can only be regarded as abstract representations of *stationary* economies (p. 100). Starting from this premise, he then argues that in order to emancipate the analysis from the hypothesis of stationarity, the theorist should necessarily resort to a dynamic framework, that is, he should consider the simultaneous evolution of the relative prices and produced quantities over a succession of interrelated time periods. Finally, as a first step towards a general dynamic theory, he suggests that the study of economies operating in conditions of constant returns and balanced growth would provide a suitable starting point for analysis. In this setting, Sraffa's equations would still have a useful role to play (p. 100).

Hicks's assertions about the limitations of the classical normal position as an analytical tool should come as no surprise in view of the fact that in *Value and Capital* (1939) he had already criticized the traditional equilibrium notion of marginal theory on the same grounds.[3] It must be admitted, however, that a similar view is conveyed – at least implicitly – by many current renditions of Sraffa's theory, which in fact confine the analysis to economies that are either stationary or in balanced growth (cf. for example Pasinetti, 1977: Ch. 5; Main-waring, 1984; Bidard, 1991; Kurz and Salvadori, 1995). For the purposes of the present discussion, it is particularly interesting to single out, from this group of contributions, the opinion of the authors who directly address the issue mentioned in the previous section. For example, Kurz and Salvadori explain the restrictions introduced in their treatment of the classical theory of value and distribution as follows:

> The analysis presented so far has been exclusively concerned with . . . long-period positions of the economic system characterized by 'stationary prices', with the price of a commodity obtained as an output at the end of the production period being the same as the price of that commodity used as an input at the beginning of that period. It has been indicated repeatedly, though, . . . that in order to exhibit this property, an economic system has to fulfill certain requirements. For example, . . . *in the presence of nonconstant returns to scale the system must be stationary. Otherwise, relative prices would have to change.*[4]

The authors thus seem to believe that the classical normal positions as defined by Sraffa are inherently inconsistent unless they relate to stationary economies or postulate constant returns to scale.[5] They accordingly conclude that, beyond those special cases, a proper analysis should not be limited to a single period of time, but should instead consider '*the whole time path* of prices and produced quantities' (Kurz and Salvadori, 1995: 298, emphasis added).

From what has been said so far, it should be clear that careful evaluation of Sraffa's views on the applicability of the classical concepts of normal position and normal prices has significant implications as regards the direction in which current research in the field of classical economics should be oriented. It is therefore in a constructive spirit that we shall now submit some considerations concerning the alternative routes identified in this section. Given the complexity of the questions involved, we do not claim to offer more than a framework of reference for further discussion.

RECONSTRUCTING THE FOUNDATIONS OF SRAFFA'S VIEWS

Let us begin by exploring the first route, that is, by seeking to reconstruct the foundations of Sraffa's views. To this end, it will be useful to recall that, in the traditional conception of both the old classical authors and the founders of marginal theory, the abstract notion of normal position has a sufficiently definite empirical counterpart. This theoretical position is in fact conceived as a guide to the average levels of the prices and quantities of the actual economy, taken over a time interval long enough to allow the competition of capitals to manifest its effects, and furthermore to allow, through the repetition of transactions, for compensation of the accidental factors that may influence the actual prices. This general conception has in turn some implications for the interpretation of the independent variables of the classical approach. In particular, the outputs appearing in a classical normal position will broadly correspond to the quantities of the various commodities demanded on average in the time interval that delimits the analysis. Moreover, the normal position will consider the production of those 'average' quantities through the technique regarded as dominant in the same time span, and will therefore include a theoretical system of production to be taken as representative of the conditions which tend to prevail in the actual economy. On this interpretation, the net outputs of capital goods in the 'representative system of production' will basically reflect the average growth of the industries employing those commodities in the time interval under consideration. In the same way, deficits of means of production will be a reflection of the *decline* of the sectors employing those commodities.[6]

Having thus specified the nature of the relevant independent variables, we can go on to a closer examination of the requirements that a theoretical position defined along Sraffa's lines must fulfill in order to qualify as a normal position (centre of gravitation). In this connection it can be argued that a consistent definition of a centre of gravitation is indeed compatible with some implicit tendency of the independent variables to change, provided that this tendency can be considered sufficiently slow *in relation to* the forces that are supposed to engender the gravitation of the actual magnitudes towards their theoretical levels. Thus, in the context of classical theory, an appropriate definition of the normal position and normal prices does not require either the strict constancy of outputs or 'constant returns to scale' in all industries. It only requires that the change in sectoral outputs inherent in the representative system of production be not so intense as to jeopardize, through an induced variation in the technical coefficients, the 'persistence' of the independent variables in the time interval to which the theoretical position refers. Here it would seem that Sraffa tacitly *assumed* this requirement of persistence to be fulfilled also in the presence of surpluses (deficits) of capital goods.

Now, two distinct but complementary observations can be put forward with regard to the assumption that we are attributing to Sraffa.

First of all, on purely logical grounds it must be pointed out that the classical notion of normal position contains no feature contradicting the assumption in question, that is, no feature forcing us to conclude that the change in sectoral outputs that may be implicit in the representative system of production, and any related tendency of the technical coefficients to vary, will be appreciable in the time interval delimiting the analysis. Note in particular that once the persistence of the outputs and methods has been assumed, the determination of the dependent variables cannot lead to results in conflict with that hypothesis. This absence of logical reasons for questioning the persistence of the 'data' in the classical theory of value deserves to be emphasized, as it marks an important element of difference with respect to the version of marginal theory that has recently become most popular, that is, the version derived from Walras.[7]

Second, there seems to be no evident reason for presuming that the assumption of persistent independent variables will prove untenable when the theory is applied to the study of real economic systems. To illustrate this point, let us return to the above-mentioned correspondence between theoretical and actual magnitudes. We have seen that the surpluses (deficits) of capital goods in the representative system of production will be essentially a reflection of the growth (decline) of the different industries in the actual economy. This implies that, when the theoretical position refers to a time interval in which the growth (decline) of the various sectors remains comparatively limited, it could legitimately be assumed that the tendency of outputs to vary implicit in the representative system will itself be quite moderate. Moreover, under those conditions it could reasonably be postulated that this implicit tendency will bring about no substantial modifications in the technical coefficients. For instance, it could safely be maintained that moderate increases in production levels will be insufficient to provide significant stimulation either for the processes of division of labour identified by the classical authors as the mainspring of 'increasing returns' or – in the case of less pervasive phenomena – for the 'increasing returns to scale' due to the three-dimensional nature of space stressed by Kaldor (1972) in his critique of general equilibrium theory.

It therefore appears that, in applying the theory, the economist would be justified in assuming the persistence of the independent variables – and, more generally, in presuming that the theoretical position he has constructed qualifies as centre of gravitation – whenever that position relates to a time interval compatible with both (1) a limited growth (decline) in the various sectors of the actual economy, and (2) a sufficient mobility of capital and repetition of transactions. On the other hand, a determination of the normal position complying with these conditions could prove viable in a wider range of situations than one might think. Indeed, many would probably concede that an appropriate determination will be feasible when the investigation concerns phases of the actual economy characterized by low growth rates in the different industries, or by sectoral growth rates fluctuating around low central values. The underlying idea is that slow growth would plausibly allow for the consideration of a time interval fulfilling requirement (1) and being, at the same time, long enough to support the hypothesis of sufficient mobility of capital. It should be noted, however, that a proper determination of the normal position could in principle be feasible also in the opposite case, that is, when the investigation focuses on a phase of intense and protracted growth. The reason for this lies in the fact that when growth accelerates, the flow of investment in *additional* capital goods will necessarily be larger, in proportion to the existing stock, than in times of slow growth. And in so far as that larger flow will tend to be directed primarily towards the most profitable branches of industry, it is conceivable that profit differentials across sectors could be corrected more quickly. A shorter time interval may accordingly suffice to justify the hypothesis of adequate mobility of capital, and by referring the theoretical position to that shorter interval it may be possible to reconcile condition (2) on capital mobility with the requirement (1) of limited sectoral growth.

ON A PROPOSED 'DYNAMIC EXTENSION' OF CLASSICAL THEORY

In the light of the foregoing considerations, it does not appear at all obvious that a dynamic extension of the classical theory of value is really *necessary* in order to deal with non-stationary economies with 'variable returns'. On the other hand, there are reasons for doubting whether the proposed extension can be implemented without sacrificing distinctive aspects of classical analysis, and indeed whether it can provide an adequate tool for studying the economic systems of the real world. Some of the problems arising in a hypothetical dynamic framework have in fact already been identified in the literature, mainly in connection with the foundations of the theory of demand that would then be required (Garegnani, 1990a: 131), or with the need to include the agents' subjective expectations among the determinants of prices (Kurz and Salvadori, 1995: 341). In what follows we shall instead focus on two additional sources of difficulties that are less frequently discussed.

Let us first wonder on which data an intertemporal reformulation of the theory should be based. In this connection it is important to note that the circumstances taken as 'given' in the classical approach are subject to a considerable degree of mutual dependence. This feature of the approach has recently been stressed by Garegnani, who has also suggested how that interdependence could appropriately be taken into account in analyses of economic change founded on the traditional method of comparing normal positions (Garegnani, 1987: 564–5; 1990a: 130). By contrast, the capacity of a dynamic model to deal satisfactorily with the interactions among produced quantities, distribution and methods appears doubtful. Some idea of the difficulties that arise can be given by brief reference to von Neumann's model, which is often regarded as a fundamental starting point for the dynamic extension of classical theory. As is well known, this model assumes that the real wage is fixed at a subsistence level that does not change from period to period, and that the set of available production methods is invariant with respect to activity levels and over time. Now, the first assumption could be justified provisionally through a hypothesis of unlimited availability of labour, both in the present and over the whole future, coupled with the classical conception of competition in the labour market (high and protracted unemployment does not cause an indefinite fall in wages, but tends to keep them at the minimum level compatible with workers' survival). It is clear, however, that as soon as the awkward hypothesis on labour availability is dropped, it must be admitted that the expansion of economic activity is bound to affect the workers' bargaining position, and the assumption of a wage fixed at a constant subsistence level will accordingly become untenable. It would thus become necessary to introduce some principle linking the wage rate to the evolution of produced quantities, but since the classical approach provides no foundation for a quantitative specification of such a principle, there is a risk of having to resort to an arbitrary formalization.

The same problem arises when von Neumann's second assumption is abandoned and it becomes necessary to analyse the evolution of production methods. Consider for instance the basic insight of the old classical authors that the evolution of methods is influenced by the extent of the market. Formally this influence could be incorporated into a dynamic model by assuming that the set of methods 'expands' as demand and production increase, in the sense that additional, superior methods are made available. The model should accordingly include among its data a distinct specification of the available techniques for any hypothetical output vector, but again it is difficult to see on which basis this could plausibly be accomplished. After all, even engineers' assessments of the possibility of modifying current methods in order to achieve higher production levels have proved unreliable on many occasions, and have sometimes been clearly disproved by the direct experience of entrepreneurs inclined to take risks.[8]

Finally it must be said that the relevance of the proposed extension remains doubtful independently of these difficulties, as it is not easy to imagine what correspondence could be established between the prices resulting from the analysis and those we observe day by day on current markets. In general terms, it would appear hard to deny that the theory of value cannot account for the prices observable at any particular moment, since these may be affected by a whole range of accidental factors, but can only provide guidance to the average levels of the actual prices as emerging from a repeated activity of production and exchange. The dynamic extension faces a problem with regard to the latter task, however, because it is not easy to relate the *dated* prices of an intertemporal model to averages of actual prices taken over a sequence of activities. Consider for instance the different exchange ratios attributed by the model to the same commodity seen as an input at the beginning of the production period (time t) and as an output at its end (time $t + 1$). It is unclear how a pair of distinct 'average prices' providing an empirical counterpart for those ratios could meaningfully be drawn from the series of transactions associated with a repeated production cycle. On the other hand, lack of clarity as to how the dating of prices might be reconciled with a repetition of activities can only prompt an alternative interpretation of the theoretical prices as exchange ratios ruling at separate *instants* in time, which in turn would prevent any significant correspondence with the observable prices. In this situation one could repeat for the intertemporal reformulation of classical analysis the same warning included in a recent, authoritative assessment of the perspectives of general equilibrium theory: 'the risk . . . seriously exists that the discipline . . . loses touch with real problems [and] develops on its own into a scholastic' (Malinvaud, 1991: 66).

NOTES

*   These notes build on the content of a communication presented at the conference on 'Sraffa and Modern Economics' held in Rome in October 1998. The author wishes to thank – without, however, implicating – the many friends and colleagues who provided stimulating comments on earlier drafts, and in particular V. Bikov, A. Campus, R. Ciccone, I. Eliseeva, P. Garegnani, M. Piccioni, N. Salvadori, A. Trezzini and F. Vianello. Financial support from MURST (the Italian Ministry of Higher Education and Technological and Scientific Research) is gratefully acknowledged.
1.   Sraffa (1960, § 1).
2.   For a broader discussion of this part of Sraffa's comment, cf. Ravagnani (2001).
3.   Although close examination of the argument in *Value and Capital* indicates that a fundamental reason for the rejection of the traditional equilibrium concept can be traced back to Hicks's perception of the theoretical difficulties surrounding the notion of capital – difficulties, that is, which pertain exclusively to the marginalist approach to value and distribution (cf. Garegnani, 1976: 30–39).
4.   Kurz and Salvadori (1995: 339, emphasis added). For a correct interpretation of the above quotation, it should be noted that when the authors list the requirements that the 'economic system has to fulfill', they are not referring to the *actual* system, but to the idealized representation of the economy provided by the theory (Kurz and Salvadori, 1995: 1). It is also clear from the context in which the passage is framed that the authors' critical remarks do apply to the simplified case of single production and non-scarce natural resources examined in this paper.
5.   The same objection is raised by Bidard (1990: 127–8): 'Consider two consecutive periods 0 and 1 with three dates 0, 1 and 2 [and let A_t, l_t, B_t respectively denote the input matrix, the labour input vector and the output matrix for period t ($t = 0, 1$)]. The production conditions within period 0, as represented by (A_0, l_0, B_0) lead to the determination of the price vector p_0 solution to [Sraffa's equations] for these data . . . The price vector p_1 within period 1 is similarly determined by the new data (A_1, l_1, B_1). But [Sraffa's system of price equations] presumes that the price vectors at the beginning and at the end of the period are identical and, in a circular process of production, two different prices cannot be ascribed to the same good at date $t = 1$, as it is considered an output in period 0 or an input in period 1. *If the physical data (A_0, l_0, B_0) and (A_1, l_1, B_1) differ, the uniqueness of the price vector at $t = 1$ requires*

that their rows be proportional, which is a constant returns assumption' (emphasis added). Cf. also Bidard (1991: 19–21, 30–31).

6. Consider, for example, a hypothetical normal position including the following system of production, obtained by modifying the introductory example of *Production of Commodities* as indicated in Sraffa (1962):

$$224 \text{ qr. wheat} + 9.6 \text{ t. iron} \rightarrow 320 \text{ qr. wheat}$$
$$90 \text{ qr. wheat} + 6 \text{ t. iron} \rightarrow 15 \text{ t. iron}$$

314	15.6

According to the interpretation suggested in the text, this theoretical system could be taken as representative of the production conditions prevailing in the 'actual' economy in a time interval characterized by a decline in the social demand for wheat, accompanied by an induced contraction in the production of the other commodity required for cultivation, that is, iron. The presence of a surplus of wheat and a deficit of iron in the representative system would then indicate that, in the interval under consideration, the quantity of wheat produced still tends to exceed that advanced throughout the economy (the excess being directed to the satisfaction of the capitalists' consumption demand) while the produced amount of iron, cycle after cycle, tends to be adjusted to the decreasing demand coming from the agricultural sector.

7. As is well known, when Walras' equilibrium equations are modified by introducing the inequalities which ensure their consistency (cf. for example Morishima, 1964: 83–92), the determination of the quantities of capital goods currently produced will typically contradict any hypothesis of persistence of the data (Garegnani, 1976: 36–7; 1990b: 21–2, 49–51).

8. The Japanese steel industry during the 1950s and 1960s provides an instructive example. Gold (1974, 1981) reports that under the pressure of rapidly increasing demand for steel, and without any careful experimentation, Japanese managers decided to operate blast furnaces of much greater size than that recommended by US engineers, the world's leading experts. This gamble against the prevailing technical view proved successful and was later justified by the managers on the grounds that '[i]f the demand is great enough, it is worth taking the risks of increasing scale' (Gold, 1974: 11). The case reported by Gold, with the fundamental role played by the subjective attitude of entrepreneurs in the specific situation, not only documents the difficulty of quantitatively assessing the prospective impact of substantial demand increases on the availability of methods, but also reveals how ill-founded it would be to suppose that the methods suitable for production levels much higher than current ones, though partly unknown in the present, could still be regarded as 'given' in the sense that they objectively exist in nature and will automatically be discovered when higher levels of production are planned.

REFERENCES

Bidard, C. (1990), 'From Arrow–Debreu to Sraffa', *Political Economy: Studies in the Surplus Approach*, 6: 125–38.

Bidard, C. (1991), *Prix, Reproduction, Rareté*, Paris: Dunod.

Caravale, G. (1985), 'Diminishing returns and accumulation in Ricardo', in G. Caravale (ed.), *The Legacy of Ricardo*, Oxford and New York: Basil Blackwell: 127–88.

Caravale, G. (1988), 'Condizioni di domanda ed equilibrio naturale nelle teorie classiche e di tipo classico', *Rivista di Politica Economica*, 12: 1303–51.

Garegnani, P. (1976), 'On a change in the notion of equilibrium in recent work on value and distribution', in M. Brown, K. Sato and P. Zarembka (eds), *Essays in Modern Capital Theory*, Amsterdam: North Holland: 25–45.

Garegnani, P. (1987), 'Surplus approach to value and distribution', in J. Eatwell, M. Milgate and P. Newman (eds), *The New Palgrave: A Dictionary of Economics*, Vol. 4, London: Macmillan: 560–74.

Garegnani, P. (1990a), 'Sraffa: classical versus marginalist analysis', in K. Bharadwaj and B. Schefold (eds), *Essays on Piero Sraffa: Critical Perspectives on the Revival of Classical Theory*, London: Unwin Hyman: 112–41.

Garegnani, P. (1990b), 'Quantity of capital', in J. Eatwell, M. Milgate and P. Newman (eds), *The New Palgrave Series: Capital Theory*, London: Macmillan: 1–78.

Gold, B. (1974), 'Evaluating scale economies: the case of Japanese blast furnaces', *Journal of Industrial Economics*, 23: 1–18.

Gold, B. (1981), 'Changing perspectives on size, scale and returns: an interpretive survey', *Journal of Economic Literature*, 19: 5–23.

Harrod, R. (1961), 'Review of *Production of Commodities*', *Economic Journal*, 71: 783–7.

Hicks, J.R. (1939), *Value and Capital*, Oxford: Clarendon Press.

Hicks, J.R. (1990), 'Ricardo and Sraffa', in K. Bharadwaj and B. Schefold (eds), Essays on P. Sraffa: Critical Perspectives on the Revival of Classical Theory, London; Unwin Hyman: 99–102.

Kaldor, N. (1972), 'The irrelevance of equilibrium economics', *Economic Journal*, 82: 1237–55.

Kurz, H. and N. Salvadori (1995), *Theory of Production: A Long-period Analysis*, Cambridge: Cambridge University Press.

Mainwaring, L. (1984), *Value and Distribution in Capitalist Economies: An Introduction to Sraffian Economics*, Cambridge: Cambridge University Press.

Malinvaud, E. (1991), 'The next fifty years', *Economic Journal*, 101: 64–8.

Mongiovi, G. (1991), 'The Ricardo debates: a comment', *Canadian Journal of Economics*, 24: 717–23.

Morishima, M. (1964). *Equilibrium, Stability and Growth: A Multi-sectoral Analysis*, Oxford: Clarendon Press.

Pasinetti, L.L. (1977). *Lectures on the Theory of Production*, London: Macmillan.

Ravagnani, F. (2001). 'Notes on a mischaracterization of the classical theory of value', *Review of Political Economy*, 13, pp. 355–63.

Sraffa, P. (1951), 'Introduction', in P. Sraffa (ed.), *The Works and Correspondence of David Ricardo*, Cambridge: Cambridge University Press: xiii–lxiii.

Sraffa, P. (1960), *Production of Commodities by Means of Commodities*. Cambridge: Cambridge University Press.

Sraffa, P. (1962), 'The Production of Commodities: A Comment', *Economic Journal*, 72: 477–9.

22. On the long-period method: a comment on Ravagnani

Heinz D. Kurz and Neri Salvadori*

The previous chapter by Ravagnani is divided into four sections. In the first section Ravagnani shows, quite convincingly, that in Sraffa's view the system of prices analysed in *Production of Commodities by Means of Commodities* applies to an economy which need not be stationary or quasi-stationary, that is, expanding at a rate of growth that is uniform across all industries. In the second section Ravagnani, starting from Hicks (1990), attributes to a number of interpreters of Sraffa's analysis, including ourselves (Kurz and Salvadori, 1995), the view that 'the theoretical positions defined in *Production of Commodities* can only be regarded as abstract representations of stationary economies'. In the third section, which is the most relevant one, he argues that Sraffa's theoretical position

> is in fact conceived as a guide to the average levels of the prices and quantities of the actual economy, taken over a time interval long enough to allow the competition of capitals to manifest its effects, and furthermore to allow, through the repetition of transactions, for a compensation of the accidental factors that may influence the actual prices.

He continues:

> [A] consistent definition of a centre of gravitation is indeed compatible with some implicit tendency of the independent variables to change, provided that this tendency can be considered sufficiently slow *in relation to* the forces that are supposed to engender the gravitation of the actual magnitudes towards their theoretical levels. Thus, in the context of classical theory, an appropriate definition of the normal position and normal prices does not require either the strict constancy of outputs or 'constant returns to scale' in all industries. It only requires that the change in sectoral outputs inherent in the representative system of production be not so intense as to jeopardize, through an induced variation in the technical coefficients, the 'persistence' of the independent variables in the time interval to which the theoretical position refers. Here it would seem that Sraffa tacitly *assumed* this requirement of persistence to be fulfilled also in the presence of surpluses (deficits) of capital goods.

Finally, Ravagnani drives home his point by raising, in the fourth section, a number of difficulties concerning the conceptualization of the set of 'data' on which 'an intertemporal reformulation of the theory should be based'.

The argument developed in the third section shows clearly, we believe, that there is no unbridgeable gulf separating the views advocated by Ravagnani, on the one hand, and us, on the other. First, we share his interpretation that Sraffa did not take his price equations to apply only to the singularly special (and thus uninteresting) case of a stationary or a quasi-stationary economy (in conditions of free competition). In fact, what is explicitly referred to in Sraffa's analysis is a uniform rate of profits, not a uniform rate of growth equal to or larger than zero. Much of Ravagnani's reasoning revolves around the conditions to be met in order for the solutions of Sraffa's price equations to qualify as useful theoretical *approximations* of observable magnitudes, and we do not dispute his concern with specifying these conditions and the corresponding concept of 'theoretical approximation'.[1]

Secondly, Ravagnani's argument at the same time makes it abundantly clear that the prices ascertained in terms of a 'classical' system of equations of production as developed by Sraffa apply *rigorously* or strictly only in cases in which either returns to scale are constant or the economy is stationary. In note 6 of his paper Ravagnani refers to the way in which Sraffa countered Harrod's interpretation of the price equations as applying to a stationary economy. Sraffa stressed that what matters is the solution of the price equations. He modified the first example of his book (see Sraffa, 1960: 3) in such a way that the system was no longer in a 'self-replacing state'. Comparing the two systems, the reader will easily see that the re-proportioning of the original system was carried out by Sraffa as if returns to scale with regard to both industries were constant. It is indeed on this assumption that the new system of production gives the same price solution as the original system.

Put in a nutshell, then, Ravagnani's argument amounts to the observation that the solution of Sraffa's price equations approximates theoretically the corresponding observable magnitudes in an economy which is changing slowly enough or, we might add, in which returns are not 'too variable'. We have no qualms with this view.

While the conditions just alluded to may be said to cover an important class of phenomena, it hardly needs to be stressed that they do not cover all cases the economist might want to study. Two examples must suffice: the first concerns exhaustible resources, the second obsolete machines (see also Kurz and Salvadori, 1995: Ch. 12). It is not immediately clear how exhaustible resources could be subsumed under the long-period method. In this case the prices of the resources, and other prices as well, typically can be expected to change over time because in conditions of free competition the rate of profit obtained by conserving the resource tends to equal the rate of profit obtained in production (see Kurz and Salvadori, 2001). Interestingly, Sraffa was clear at an early stage of his work, which was to lead to his 1960 book, that the assumption of self-replacement of an economic system does not always mimic reality. In a note dated 25 March 1946 from his hitherto unpublished papers, he pointed out with regard to exhaustible resources:

> But how are we going to replace these natural things? There are 3 cases: a) they can be reproduced by labour (land properties, with manures and so on); b) they can be substituted by labour (coal by hydroelectric plant: or by spending in research and discovery of new sources and new methods of economising) c) they cannot be either reproduced nor substituted[2] – and in this case they cannot find a place in a theory of *continuous* production and consumption: they are *dynamical facts*, that is a stock that is being gradually exhausted and cannot be renewed, and must ultimately lead to destruction of the society. But this case does not satisfy our conditions of a society that just manages to keep continuously alive. (Sraffa's papers, D3/12/42: 33; second emphasis added)[3]

The note from his unpublished papers[4] cited above indicates that to Sraffa exhaustible resources constitute 'dynamical facts' which cannot be studied rigorously in a framework in which prices do not change. Hence, a dynamic theory would be needed. Ravagnani puts forward a number of considerations which stress the difficulty, if not impossibility, of such an analysis. Interestingly, in yet another unpublished document Sraffa also reminded us of the intrinsic difficulties of elaborating such a theory. One of his notes reads:

> It is 'a fatal mistake' of some economists that they believe that by introducing complicated dynamic assumptions, they get nearer to the true reality; in fact they get further removed for two reasons: a) that the system is much more statical than we believe, and its 'short periods' are very long, b) that the assumptions being too complicated it becomes impossible for the mind to grasp and dominate them – and thus it fails to realize the absurdity of the conclusions. (Sraffa: D3/12/11 (33))

This warning has to be taken seriously. At the same time, to be aware that a journey one might want to embark on is full of dangers is not a sufficient reason not to undertake it. We understood our own excursions into partly uncharted territory always as just probing steps and expressed warnings as to the explanatory power of the models elaborated (see, for example, Kurz and Salvadori, 1995: 359). However, looking back at our own efforts in this regard we feel that we learned something about the problem under consideration and also about the pitfalls the theorist ought to avoid.

The second example we should like to mention is obsolete machines. Ravagnani also touches upon this example in his paper. Sraffa subsumes obsolete machines under the theory of differential rent:

> Machines of an obsolete type which are still in use are similar to land in so far as they are employed as means of production, although not currently produced. The quasi-rent (if we may apply Marshall's term in a more restricted sense than he gave it) which is received for those fixed capital items which, having been in active use

in the past, have now been superseded but are worth employing for what they can get, *is determined precisely in the same way as the rent of land*. (Sraffa, 1960: 78; emphasis added)[5]

Sraffa's proposition can immediately be utilized when obsolete machines are in short supply so that the prices are determined by the conditions of production of the processes in which obsolete machines are not used. Then the prices of obsolete machines turn out to be determined as residuals. However, if obsolete machines are not in short supply and therefore some non-obsolete machines will not be produced for a while, then the obsolete machines behave exactly as exhaustible resources do. In section 2 of Chapter 12 of our book (Kurz and Salvadori, 1995) we clarified both points (also with the help of some exercises kindly provided to us by Giuseppe Freni). It is quite natural to conjecture that Sraffa considered the latter case as not very important.

Coming back to the principle relating quantities, prices and quasi-rents in Sraffa's book, it suffices to draw the reader's attention to §88, in which the cases of 'extensive' and 'intensive' diminishing returns are dealt with. Sraffa concludes with regard to both: 'In this way the output may increase continuously, although the methods of production are changed spasmodically' (1960: 76). It is clear that here Sraffa is not referring to a system in motion or a dynamical analysis, but to a comparative static analysis of stationary economies with different output levels. However, we learn from his argument that when we analyse changes in outputs over time of a given economy, then these changes by themselves need not affect prices and income distribution as long as there are no changes in the methods of production. Yet we learn at the same time that even small or 'slow' changes in outputs may entail 'spasmodic' changes in the methods of production employed, and therefore in prices. In such conditions the 'approximation' to which Ravagnani wants to limit the analysis may be not considered satisfactory any longer. At any rate, in the case discussed the prices at the time in which inputs are bought are different from the prices at the time in which outputs are sold.

We conclude that there are aspects of reality which are a part of the domain investigated by economists and which cannot fully and satisfactorily be analysed using the procedure suggested by Ravagnani. Following him in this regard would involve neglecting problems which cannot sensibly be neglected. In the context of his criticism of Marshall's partial equilibrium analysis, Sraffa (1925) stressed that some approximations are useful and appropriate, but some others are not:

Our argument is not concerned with the greater or lesser approximation of the assumption that the prices and quantities of the other commodities which use a factor in common with the commodity under consideration, remain unchanged. Our argument is that that assumption is absurd, and contradicts the preceding hypothesis, for the increase in production of a commodity leads to an increase in cost that has equal importance for that commodity and for the others of the group; so that *it cannot be taken into consideration for one and ignored for the others.* (Sraffa, 1998: 361; emphasis added)

Applied to our present problem, we cannot follow Ravagnani when what we want to study is exactly returns that are not constant or a system of prices that needs to change over time as a consequence of the assumptions made. In other words, we cannot at the same time neglect something and yet consider it as relevant. If that something cannot fully and satisfactorily be dealt with in terms of some method or approach, then a somewhat different method or approach or a less partial analysis should at least be tried out to see how far we can get with it.[6]

NOTES

*   We should like to thank Christian Gehrke and Rodolfo Signorino for useful comments.
1. It is in this spirit that we wrote in the introduction to Chapter 12, 'On limits to the long-period method', of our 1995 book: 'the long-period method employed throughout the preceding chapters of this book could be defended on the grounds that it is applicable, as a first approximation, to cases in which these changes [in the factors affecting relative prices and income distribution] are indeed sufficiently slow and gradual. Moreover, given the unsatisfactory state of economic theorizing in cases in which this premise is not met, the long-period method appears to be the only acceptable one available at present' (Kurz and Salvadori, 1995: 341).
2. This is Sraffa's formulation, which we left as it is.
3. The papers are kept at Trinity College Library, Cambridge. The references follow the catalogue prepared by Jonathan Smith, archivist. We are grateful to Pierangelo Garegnani, Sraffa's literary executor, for permission to quote from the hitherto unpublished material.
4. In his book Sraffa mentions exhaustible resources only in passing and on a par with land: 'Natural resources which are used in production, such as land and mineral deposits . . .' (1960: 74). He thus follows Ricardo's lead who, in Chapter III of the *Principles*, subsumed the case of exhaustible resources under that of land, which is considered a renewable resource. We may thus conjecture that Sraffa intended to provide only a first approximation to the problem of exhaustible resources in terms of the theory of differential rent.
5. As is well known, Knut Wicksell in this context spoke of 'rent goods'.
6. This last point involves some subtle methodological questions (see Signorino, 2001).

REFERENCES

Hicks, J.R. (1990), 'Ricardo and Sraffa', in K. Bharadwaj and B. Schefold (eds), *Essays on Piero Sraffa: Critical Perspectives on the Revival of Classical Theory*, London: Unwin Hyman: 99–102.
Kurz H.D. and N. Salvadori (1995), *Theory of Production: A Long-period Analysis*, Cambridge: Cambridge University Press.
Kurz, H.D. and N. Salvadori (2001), 'Classical economics and the problem of exhaustible resources', *Metroeconomica*, 52: 282–96.

Signorino, R. (2001), 'On the limits to the long period method: a note', *Review of Political Economy*, 13: 245–51.

Sraffa, P. (1925), 'Sulle relazioni fra costo e quantità prodotta', *Annali di Economia*, 2: 277–328. English translation by John Eatwell and Alessandro Roncaglia in L.L. Pasinetti (ed.) (1998), *Italian Economic Papers*, Vol. III, Bologna: Il Mulino, and Oxford: Oxford University Press: 323–63.

Sraffa, P. (1960), *Production of Commodities by Means of Commodities: Prelude to a Critique of Economic Theory*, Cambridge: Cambridge University Press.

23. Sraffa's price equations: a stationary economy or 'normal positions'?

Pierangelo Garegnani

SEVEN POINTS FOR DISCUSSION

1. It is often argued that Sraffa's (1960) analysis relates to a stationary or steady growth economy (for example, Hicks, 1990: 100, 1985, *passim*; Samuelson, 2000, 136): even authors sympathetic to Sraffa's classical approach appear sometimes to view that assumption as being entailed by his equations, where the prices of the commodity inputs at the beginning of the production cycle are the same as those of the outputs at the end of it. Although I have not had the opportunity to give close consideration to some recent literature on the matter, certain points raised in this session induce me to submit for discussion a few reflections on the subject, one with which I have been concerned in the past (Garegnani, 1976).

I shall here argue for two theses. The first is that, in the context of classical theory in which Sraffa (1960) must be placed, the forces that are seen to govern the economy do not admit of a formalized dynamic *theory* based on dated prices as distinct from admitting of dynamic *models*, which can of course always be built, if relevant, in order to deal with particular questions or explore the logical implications of assumptions admitted to be special. The second thesis is that, in contemporary literature, consideration of price changes[1] within the equations determining prices has *not* been the result of an attempt at a closer approximation to reality, but rather a purely doctrinal development intended to remedy logical deficiencies internal to the dominant theory of prices. As I have contended elsewhere and shall recall below, the consideration of price changes in the equations determining prices makes it more difficult and not more easy to relate theory and observable phenomena.[2]

I will proceed by listing, in the rest of this section, seven points summarizing my position, and I will then comment on the matter in the three sections that follow. Thus, in section II, I will focus on some lack of clarity in the claims I am discussing as to whether the prices whose changes should be considered are, in classical terms, 'market prices' or 'production prices'. We shall contend that such prices cannot but be production prices, and hence can correspond to actual prices only when the latter are averaged over a period of time allowing for a sufficient repetition of transactions. This directly contradicts any 'dating' of such prices. In section III, the argument of section II will be used to review the meaning and importance of the traditional 'normal position'. Finally, in section IV, we shall see why, even apart from the preceding general considerations, a formalized general 'dynamic' theory appears to conflict with the premises of classical theory.

2. The seven points by which I would summarize my position are as follows:

i.   The thesis according to which the prices appearing in Sraffa's equations relate to a stationary or 'steady-state' economy seems to rest on a misapprehension of the analysis based on 'normal positions' which Sraffa revives – and to which both classical and neoclassical theorists constantly referred until recent decades.[3] The constancy of prices assumed in defining the normal position of the economy is an abstraction founded on the *persistence* (paras. 5–6 below) and not the *constancy* of the determining forces and is therefore compatible with ongoing changes in the economy, the study of which is in fact the main purpose of the theory.

ii.   The misapprehension results from accepting the apparent argument which since Hicks's *Value and Capital* (1939) has generally been provided within the dominant theory for the shift away from the traditional notion of equilibrium and towards the 'temporary' or 'intertemporal' equilibria which that book was influential in introducing. As is well known, the argument runs in terms of a need to consider, in the definition of the equilibrium itself, the changes which prices undergo or are expected to undergo in any non-stationary economy.[4] The traditional 'normal position' of the economy, defined independently of any such price changes, had accordingly to be reinterpreted as relating to a stationary or steady-state economy where normal prices would not change over time.

iii.   The misapprehension is thus due to overlooking what a closer reading of Hicks (1939) is sufficient to reveal as being the real argument for the change – namely the impossibility which by then had begun to emerge of dealing with capital as a 'factor of production' within the framework of the 'normal position', contrary to what the founders of the theory had originally postulated. The misapprehension is due, that is, to overlooking that what caused introducing price changes in the definition of an equilibrium was not a preoccupation to go beyond what a logically consistent 'normal position' could reveal about reality: it was, on the contrary, the impossibility of a consistent treatment of that position. What prompted the introduction of those changes was essentially the failure of the attempt carried out over a century to reconcile the concept of capital as a 'factor of production', characteristic of the modern demand and supply theory of distribution, with the notion of a normal position of the economy always and unanimously used to ensure a sufficient correspondence between theory and observation in economics. As shown by the inconsistency of Walras' original general equilibrium system, the normal position and its basic condition of a uniform rate of return on the supply prices of the capital goods required conceiving capital as a single magnitude – which is what by the time of *Value and Capital* (1939), after his *Theory of Wages* ([1932] 1964), where the single magnitude was postulated, Hicks had to admit is impossible.[5] Capital could only be conceived of as a vector of heterogeneous 'factors', making it impossible to satisfy the condition of a uniform rate of return on the supply prices of the several capital goods, and therefore to refer to normal prices *persistent enough to be determined independently of their changes.*

iv. Despite its apparent plausibility, little or no foundation seems thus attributable to an alleged need to introduce price changes and dated quantities into an analysis like Sraffa's which revives the approach to relative prices and distribution of the 'old classical economists' (Sraffa, 1960: v). This is an approach that suffers from no logical difficulty in dealing with capital as a set of distinct capital goods (Garegnani, 1960: vii–viii) and is quite consistent with the 'normal position' method. Indeed, one aim of its revival is just to do away with the neoclassical presuppositions concerning a determining role of the 'capital endowment', and the corresponding need to abandon the conception of the normal position.

v. The above misapprehension has on the other hand been made easier by the fact that, as I noted in 1976 (pp. 42–44), a criticism of the traditional normal position, parallel to that by Hicks and the subsequent neoclassical literature, has come from the Keynesian side, from Joan Robinson in particular. The motivation was different, and even opposite, in that it was designed to supersede rather than preserve the traditional demand and supply framework. It can however be argued that the criticism rested on an incorrect identification of the 'normal position' with its neoclassical representation in terms of an 'equilibrium' between demand and supply of 'productive factors', and hence with full employment of labour. It therefore overlooked the basic deficiencies of the neoclassical notion indicated above under (iii): when those deficiencies are overcome, as happens within a classical framework, we can deal with labour unemployment without in any way abandoning the notion of the normal position (as Ricardo's chapter 'On machinery' in the *Principles* or Marx's conception of the 'reserve army' of unemployed labour had made clear in their time).[6]

vi.   If the doctrinal difficulties of neoclassical theory causing the abandonment of the traditional normal position are absent in classical theory, equally absent are the *endogenous* price changes on which neoclassical pure theory has come to rely in its contemporary reformulations. This is so, because the engine of those endogenous changes – the capital endowment – loses the determining role for prices it has in neoclassical equilibria.[7]

vii.   In classical theory, changes in the economy and in its normal positions are instead seen to originate from circumstances analysed *outside* that 'core' of the theory which is alone susceptible of a systematically formalized treatment – outside, that is, what Sraffa defines as the 'system of production' (for example, Sraffa, 1960: 33) represented in his price equations. Thus, for example, changes in wages may originate from broader socio-institutional and demographic elements affecting the bargaining position of workers and, unlike in a labour demand and supply setting, they cannot usefully be expressed by means of equations forming a single system with the price equations. More inductive methods taking into account historical factors are required. More generally, neither the evolution of the wage, nor that of the technical conditions or the outputs – the 'intermediate data' of the classical 'core' – can be viewed as susceptible of being expressed in terms of mathematical relations general and definite enough to provide the conceivable basis of a systematic formalized theory (as distinct from a 'model': cf. para. 1 above) running in terms of dated quantities and prices.

WHICH PRICE CHANGES?

3. Let us now clear the ground for a more detailed discussion of the issue by noting the apparent dependence of the claimed need to introduce changing prices on the assumption of production occurring by yearly cycles (para. 1 above): if agriculture has production cycles, industrial production is generally continuous. Though it would help us obtain a better grasp of the claim to see how it can translate in terms of continuous production, when outputs can be ascribed to inputs of the same date,[8] we shall now simply *assume* that all production occurs in yearly cycles.

Let us then proceed to ask which are the classical prices whose changes we should consider in passing from inputs to outputs: 'market prices' or 'normal prices'? The *prima facie* plausibility of the need to admit price changes between when the inputs are bought and when the outputs are sold seems to rest on referring to the prices *actually* paid for the inputs, and *actually* received for the outputs, that is, to the classical 'market prices' at the respective instants.

Then, however, the price equations would drastically change the meaning they have in Sraffa, which is that the equalization there represented uniformity between prices of commodities and normal expenses of production, that is, the revenues of producers calculated at their normal levels, would now refer to the 'market' rates of profits, wages and rents resulting from the 'market' prices of the commodity. And even assuming, as is generally done, that only a single market price exists for a commodity at each instant of time (and the same applies to the services of labour, capital goods and land used in each industry), such actual relative prices and distributive variables are essentially unknowable in classical theory except for the *sign* of their deviation from their natural or normal relative levels relevant in turn for the *sign* of the direction of their change as outputs change accordingly.[9] Any attempt to determine those prices further would require special assumptions, thus again moving away from the domain of *theory* and into that of *models* (para. 1 above). We should stress that we would here be on a quite different ground from neoclassical theories, where 'temporary' equilibrium prices could be imagined to be (approximately) determined by 'temporary' demand and supply functions, which would find no basis in a context of classical 'market prices'.

It might, however, be argued that 'expected', rather than realized, 'market' prices should be considered. But even leaving aside the problems caused by the indefiniteness of expectations, it appears that expected prices cannot be used in that role in a classical context. Their use would imply a sequence, like that of Hicks's (1939) 'weeks', and therefore also the consideration of *realized* prices besides expected prices, and we would then meet the difficulty of determining market prices we have just mentioned.

4. That should clarify that, contrary to what one may naïvely think, the price changes we are told we should consider in a non-stationary economy cannot have anything to do with the prices which producers *actually* pay for the inputs and receive, or expect to receive, for the outputs. Indeed there would be no reason why, even in a stationary economy as generally understood, *i.e.* with constant *normal* prices, such day-to-day *market* prices should ever be constant.

Thus, it seems, the relative prices whose changes it is alleged we should consider would have to be the normal prices themselves, redefined by the corresponding price equations as what we may then call 'intertemporal normal prices' or 'intertemporal production prices'[10] – and their changes would be those associated with the changes in outputs, wages or technical knowledge,[11] the 'intermediate data' of the 'core' where classical prices are determined.

However, as soon as we try to deal with such changes in normal prices we meet, I believe, an intrinsic contradiction. The normal prices appearing in the price equations, whether for the commodity inputs or the outputs, could only correspond to *average prices* obtained through a sufficient repetition of transactions over time. But this repetition is precisely what is excluded by the dating of the prices, which would force us to conceive of the intertemporal price as realized at the appropriate instant of time.[12]

No reason in fact exists for prices at the specified instant *t* to be at their correct intertemporal level rather than at any accidental market level. In particular, there is no reason why the correct intertemporal production prices for the *t, t + 1, t + 2* and so on outputs, should have been expected when their production cycles were started at *(t − 1), t, t + 1*,[13] or earlier, as would be necessary (though not sufficient) for those prices to be realized. Changes in intertemporal normal prices could be perceived by, and govern the behaviour of, individual agents only as changes of *average* prices, and therefore through a *repetition* of the transactions.

WHY THE 'NORMAL POSITION'?

5. The above should suffice to explain why, before the progressive emergence of the doctrinal difficulties we saw under points (iii) and (v) of para. 2, all theorists shunned consideration of price changes in the general determination of prices.[14] The way they came to do so was by distinguishing two kinds of prices complementing each other. Those of the first kind were the normal prices, on which the theory could usefully focus because their changes could be ignored in determining them. The second was that of the 'actual' prices, whose changes were considered, but only as deviations from normal prices which could reasonably be held to cancel each other out, letting the corresponding normal price emerge over time as an average of the actual ones. Thus, with respect to the second kind of price, the theory's concerns were fundamentally confined to arguing the mutual compensation of their changes.

At the basis of that procedure there ultimately lay what we may describe as a 'Basic observation' about the economy: it is that prices, while differing from time to time and even from transaction to transaction, are remarkably 'persistent' in their long-run averages since their variations are *either* slow relative to the time required for a sufficient compensation of the deviations, or are 'one-off' changes, such that after a limited period of transition graduality of changes re-establishes itself.

6. That Basic observation is, it appears, what has suggested, and allowed for, an equally basic distinction between two kinds of *forces* acting on prices and, in particular, on relative prices. On the one hand, there are the forces which, in Marshall's words, consist of 'passing events, and . . . causes whose action is fitful and short lived' and which 'influence actual value at any time, the market value as it is often called'. On the other hand,

we have the 'persistent causes' which in the long run 'dominate value completely'(Marshall, 1920: 349–50).

Now, the distinction between the two species of *prices* that we traced in para. 5 above follows naturally from this distinction between the two kinds of *forces*. In the first place the persistence of the causes of the normal price allows us to abstract from the gradual changes which the normal price might be undergoing over time.[15] This as we saw has nothing to do with denying the possibility of sharp 'one-off' changes in those determinants (for example, an important invention), or with overlooking the long-term effects of the gradual changes we are ignoring in determining the normal price (for example, the net investment in a neoclassical context, or the extension of cultivation in Ricardo); indeed, as we recalled in para. 1, the method of the normal positions has the precise purpose of studying the effects of such changes by comparisons of the position before and after the change.

In the second place, the same persistence allows the inevitable day-to-day changes of the actual prices to be represented as deviations from the normal prices compensating each other over time: this it does by permitting a repetition of transactions occurring on the basis of nearly unchanged data. The inclusion in the determination of normal price of all the factors whose action is seen to be persistent warrants the compensation.[16]

The persistence of the normal price is thus a necessary condition of the two-prices method of para. 5 for avoiding the introduction of price changes into its determination. A second condition necessary for it is of course the tendency of the actual prices to their normal levels, whichever accidental level they might be in at any given moment. Without this tendency, there is evidently no reason why the repetition of transactions allowed by the persistence of the price should permit it to emerge as a guide to an average of the actual positions. Now, if the difficulties about capital we saw in para. 2 at point (iii) have undercut the persistence of the determinants, making the introduction of price changes inevitable, the difficulties concerning the stability of the neoclassical equilibria have also favoured the abandonment of the normal position by throwing into question its second necessary condition. It is in fact beginning to emerge that this second kind of difficulty, in the most decisive part, is altogether independent of the long-known income effects, with which neoclassical theory has managed to coexist: rather, they are a second effect, besides the non-persistent character of the new equations, of the deficiencies of the neoclassical notion of capital.[17]

ON THE CLASSICAL ANALYSIS OF CHANGES

7. It is to the basic observation rather than to any deficiencies of the mathematical tools available at the time that I believe we should turn for explaining the traditional unanimous reliance upon normal prices determined independently of

their changes over time. The mathematical tools for an economic dynamics had in fact been ready since Newton's time, and Marshall, who came to economics from mathematics, just as Wicksell or Pareto did, was quite explicit on the substance of the matter in a passage I have often quoted:

> Thus, then, dynamical solutions in the physical sense of economic problem are unattainable. And if we are to adhere to physical analogies at all, we must say that statical solutions afford starting points for such rude and imperfect approaches to dynamical solutions as we may be able to attain to. (Marshall, 1898: 387–9)[18]

To my knowledge the reasons prompting Marshall's statement have never been countered by Hicks or in the literature which followed in the wake of *Value and Capital*. The fact is of course that the doctrinal difficulties which those authors had to face at the time left them little choice but to change the notion of equilibrium, with the entailed introduction of dated prices in the determination of the system. A theoretical discontinuity as would have been involved in abandoning, with the notion of capital as a single quantity the determining role of the 'capital endowment', and hence the demand and supply approach to distribution and relative prices, was inconceivable at the time, when that was taken to be economic theory *tout court*. Even Keynes had apparently found its abandonment inconceivable enough to place himself in the contradictions I have tried to examine elsewhere (1978–79). However, the alternative provided by Sraffa's rediscovery of the classical approach exists now, and it would be paradoxical to introduce into his system a procedure based on intertemporal prices, which is one of the most striking sequels of the deficiencies he criticizes in neoclassical theory.

8. Let me conclude by quickly turning to points (vi) and (vii) on my initial list of para. 2. The endogenous price changes which had to be introduced in the equilibria of contemporary theory are, we said, those originating from the changes in the capital endowment resulting from savings and investment (point vi para. 2). But in classical theory the capital endowment constitutes no part of the determinants of prices in the formalized 'core' of the theory, and no similar 'dynamic' analysis can accordingly be conducted there.

More generally the causes of price changes in classical theory, though they act *through* the 'intermediate data' consisting of the real wage, the outputs and the technical knowledge, will normally originate from outside the 'core', and the analysis of their effects will also normally require going beyond it. This means that their action will not be of a kind which can be expressed in terms of formal quantitative relations general and definite enough to be significant for a theory, as distinct from a model concerned with special assumptions or particular questions (para. 1 above). And this is true independently of the difficulties we saw as besetting the *meaning* of dated prices, and of the irrelevance in a classical context of the doctrinal difficulties they are meant to remedy.

APPENDIX

What we recalled in para. 8 about the separation between the determination of relative prices, on the one hand, and that of outputs or wages on the other might perhaps be interpreted in terms of what has been described as 'piece-meal theorizing' in the sense of a methodological position for which

> No special set of causal factors is predominantly responsible for all major economic phenomena. In each given problem situation, the economist must isolate the major causal factors by empirical investigation and theoretical ingenuity'.[19]

It appears, however, that the above separation in classical theory has to be interpreted as the characteristic feature of an analysis, which constitutes no less of a unitary *system* because of it. The separation, that is, should be envisaged as a natural adaptation of the method of analysis to a reality in which two broadly different but strictly interacting kinds of objective forces are seen to operate in the economy. First, there are forces of competition which, by tending to realize uniform rates of profits, wages and rents, establish the purely quantitative relations of the 'core' between such rates and the prices. These forces are, however, seen to operate within a setting of institutional and historical forces forming, together with those of competition, a coherent system. The theory has then to reflect this system of objective forces. Outputs, wages and technical conditions are 'intermediate data' in the 'core' not because of any choice of isolating the determinants of relative prices and the non-wage variables, a choice which could then apply to different variables as the problem investigated changes. They are 'intermediate data' because the nature of the dependencies, their complexity and variability, relative to the comparatively simple and constant character of the forces of competition analysed in the 'core', is seen to require two different methods of analysis: a mainly deductive method for the purely quantitative relations of the 'core' which have sufficiently definite general properties, and more inductive and historical methods for the determination of wages, outputs or the technical conditions of production, in which the relations of the 'core' are, so to speak, immersed.

NOTES

1. The introduction of price changes referred to here should of course not be confused with the consideration of changes in prices by means of the *comparison* of two different positions of the economy.
2. See, for example, Marshall's passage quoted in para. 7 below about a 'dynamics in the physical sense' being impossible in economics.
3. See Garegnani (1976: 269); see also by the same author 1960 (Appendix E).

4. 'The current supply of commodities depends not so much upon what the current price is as upon what the entrepreneurs have expected it to be in the past' (Hicks, 1939: 116–7): hence the claimed need to abandon what Hicks there calls 'static theory'.

5. The argument is presented in Garegnani (1976: 34–5, 31–2), where Hicks's statements concerning the fact that 'people . . . would often introduce in their static theory a "factor of production", capital, ... supposing that [it] could be treated like the static factors' (1939: 116) are also reported and discussed. For the inconsistency of Walras' original general equilibrium system, see Garegnani (1960: Part I, Chs. II-III and Appendix G).

6. Cf. Garegnani (1978–79; also 1989: 359). It seems to be argued sometimes as if the 'normal position' by itself entailed acceptance of Say's law (see, for example, Roncaglia, 2000: 174). In fact what is here meant by a 'normal position' of classical theory is simply the equality between 'effectual demand' and 'quantity brought to market' (Smith, ([1776] 1950), Ch. VI), which concerns the *relative* outputs corresponding to a *given* long-period level of activity, irrespective of whether that level is or is not influenced by aggregate demand (cf., for example, Garegnani, 1997: 141–2; cf. also for the compatibility between the classical analysis of distribution and prices and deficiencies of aggregate demand, Garegnani, 1978–79; Roncaglia's more general position is discussed in Garegnani, 1990: 150–58).

7. At the level of theory (as distinct from that of models: para. 1 above), Hicksian dated prices appear mainly to have been confined to the endogenous changes resulting from variations in the capital endowment. This limitation of the neoclassical 'dynamics' seems significant in revealing that its motivation lies in the difficulties which capital raises for normal prices rather than in a need to consider price changes as such, in which case demographic or technological changes would certainly be of no less importance than the changes caused by savings. (For an analogous, surprising limitation to outputs of the dynamics at times envisaged for classical theory, see note 11 below).

8. See Garegnani (1960: 25–30).

9. See Garegnani (1997: 160–61).

10. They would be determined by production equations characterized by dated prices and by a uniform effective rate of interest (profits) expressed as the own rate of interest of the numeraire (see, for example, Garegnani, 2000b: 397, 434; for the notion of the 'effective rate of interest' see pp. 392 n., 434 n.).

11. Constant returns to scale are at times mentioned as an assumption sufficient to replace that of stationarity in order to avoid introducing dated prices in the equations of production. It is difficult, however, to see why the changes of a non-stationary economy should come from changes of outputs only and not also from changes in technical conditions or in distribution, when, of course, constant returns would be of little avail. (The fact that the outputs of a given period limit the possible outputs of subsequent periods may perhaps tempt a modern economist to envisage some dynamic analysis based on endogenous changes in outputs, with corresponding changes in relative prices because of variable returns to scale. However, even if we could leave aside the generality of capital destruction, obviously no unique functional relation could be generally established such that the output of t determines that of $t + 1$. More importantly, we shall argue in para. 8 of the text that at the level of generality of the theory as distinct from that of models, changes in outputs, when relevant, can only be dealt with outside the 'core' and by the correspondingly more inductive methods.)

12. It might perhaps be thought that we could interpret the 'date' of a production cycle as covering a number of such cycles, so as to have the dated price correspond to an average of actual or market prices. However, the same market prices would then enter the price average for the commodity as input, as for the commodity as output, except for the accidental market prices of the commodity of its earliest use (as input) and of its latest appearance (as output) in this period, depriving of significance the distinction between the two (average) prices. Nor could we replace the tendency to the normal price by the tendency to the sequence of dated prices: the accumulation of errors over time would make 'early' deviations count for more than 'later' deviations, and prevent their compensation. It has sometimes been argued that persistence is indeed a condition for approximating the actual prices of a non-stationary economy – a better approximation being then seemingly provided by a dynamic analysis with 'dated' prices. However, that thesis seems to overlook the essence of the question,

which is that the dated prices have no observable correspondent (para. 4 in the text) and, more basically, that no formalized dynamic analysis appears to be possible at the level of even theory (pars. 1 and 8 in the text).

13. The tendency to realize those prices will be the tendency to a uniform effective rate of profits (see note 11) which, with no repetition possible, would essentially have to refer to the expected prices.

14. In neoclassical theory in particular, even if we could leave aside the question of the observable content of dated prices which arises there too, there are the well-known difficulties connected with the indefiniteness of the horizon and of the meaning of a perfect foresight about future agents with their tastes and technology.

15. The basic observation should clear the doubts at times expressed about whether the speed of the adjustment to the normal price is sufficiently high relative to that of the changes in the latter to warrant the assumption of its constancy (see, for example, Caminati, 2000: 208). It is indeed hard to think that, as is sometimes suggested, contemporary technical change has altered those relative speeds and undermined the validity of the basic observation. It would e.g. be a curious coincidence that such a striking change in economic reality should have occurred at about the time when Hicks had to admit the logical impossibility of introducing into the analysis 'a factor of production, capital, and its price interest' (note 5, above).

We may also note that another objection frequently raised against the normal positions, their possible 'path dependence' (see, for example, Caminati, 2000), does not in fact apply to the *classical* normal position as distinct from the *neoclassical* one. The fact that the analysis of changes can be conducted outside the 'core' of the theory (par. 8 below) allows for any possible 'path dependence' of the normal position. Path dependence is a problem for the *neoclassical* normal positions, which rest on data whose changes are mostly thought not to be analysable in economic theory and are correspondingly treated as independent of the changes they cause in the system. Path dependence is indeed strictly associated with the irreversibility of economic changes, which flies in the face of a demand and supply analysis as of any analysis conducted in the mathematical terms of reversible functions.

We may here wonder whether something similar to the Basic observation about prices, applies also to outputs. A distinction may here be relevant between the two theories. Neoclassical distribution entails a strict interrelation between prices and outputs, so the persistence of prices is thus one with persistence of the output levels. The same is not true in classical theory where the persistence of prices only excludes changes of outputs large enough to trigger appreciable decreasing returns from natural resources or appreciable increasing returns from division of labour.

16. In 1848, J.S. Mill ([1848] 1909) referred to 'the centre value towards which . . . the market value of a thing is constantly gravitating, and any deviation from which . . . sets forces in motion tending to correct it . . . On an average of years sufficient to enable the oscillations on one side of the central line to be compensated by those on the other, the market value agrees with the natural value' (Mill, 1909: 453). For similar passages see, for example, Ricardo, (1951: 91–2; Walras, 1954: 380; Pareto, 1896–7: 25–6; Clark, 1907: 85–6; cf. also the passage by Marshall quoted in the text.

17. See Garegnani (2000b), in particular p. 443.

18. An argument brought at times in defence of dated prices is the need to deal with exhaustible resources, where decisions as to the conservation of the resource by its owner would be based on such prices. The scarcity made visible by the coexistence of processes using the resource with different intensities clearly depends on the policy of conservation of the resource for future use by its owners. Now, according to the argument, owners would aim to maximize the value of the resource over time, given the interest rates expected for the future. Observation and theory alike throw doubts on that argument. Such a paramount case of exhaustible resource as oil seems to suggest that the royalty for the resource will generally respond more to 'the relative strength' of users and owners *who compete in sharing the value of the advantage which the resource gives in production*, than to an intertemporal pricing which would generally be founded on circumstances too distant in time and too uncertain and complex in their occurrence to provide the owners with more than a reservation price

founded on a reasonable certainty of some future use, the royalty for which can however be only a matter of speculation.

19. The passage is from Hausman (1981: 183–4), who wrote it in a different context. It is quoted with reference to the present context in Signorino (2001: 6). For what appears to be a similar position, see Roncaglia (2000: 162).

REFERENCES

Clarke, J.B. (1907), *Essentials of Economic Theory*, New York.

Caminati M. (2000), 'Concorrenza, lungo periodo e cambiamenti economico', in M. Pivetti (ed.), Piero Sraffa, pp. 203–25, Naples: Carocci.

Garegnani P. (1960), *Il capitale nelle teorie della distribuzione,* Milan: Giuffré.

Garegnani P. (1976), 'On a change in the notion of equilibrium in recent work on value: a comment on Samuelson', in M. Brown, K. Sato and P. Zarembka (eds), *Essays in Modern Capital Theory*, Amsterdam: North Holland.

Garegnani P. (1978–79), 'Notes on consumption, investment, and effective demand', I and II, *Cambridge Journal of Economics*, 2(4): 335–53 and 3(March): 63–82.

Garegnani P., (1989), 'Some notes on capital, expectations and the analysis of changes', in G.R. Feiwel (ed.), *Joan Robinson and Modern Economic Theory*, London: Macmillan.

Garegnani P. (1990), 'Sraffa's production of commodities: classical versus marginalist analysis' and 'Reply' (to discussants), in K. Bharadway and B. Schefold (eds), *Essays on Piero Sraffa*, London: Unwin Hyman.

Garegnani P. (1997), 'On some supposed obstacles to the tendency of market prices towards natural prices', in G. Caravale (ed.), *Equilibrium and Economic Theory*, London: Routledge.

Garegnani P. (2000b), 'Savings, investment and the quantity of capital in general intertemporal equilibrium', in H. Kurz (ed.), *Critical Essays on Piero Sraffa's Legacy in Economics*, Cambridge: Cambridge University Press.

Hausman, D.M. (1981), *Capital Profits and Prices. An Essay in the Philosophy of Economics*, New York: Columbia University Press.

Hicks, J.R. ([1932] 1964), *The Theory of Wages*, 2nd edition, New York: St. Martin's Press.

Hicks J.R. ([1939] 1946), *Value and Capital*, Oxford: Clarendon Press.

Hicks J.R. (1985), 'Sraffa and Ricardo: a critical view', in G.A. Caravale (ed), *The Legacy of Ricardo,* Oxford: Blackwell.

Hicks J.R. (1990), 'Ricardo and Sraffa', in K. Bharadwaj and B. Schefold (eds), *Essays on Piero Sraffa*, London: Unwin Hyman.

Marshall A. (1898), 'Distribution and exchange', *Economic Journal.*

Marshall A. ([1920] 1962), *Principles of Economics*, 8th edition, London: Macmillan.

Mill, J.St. ([1849] 1909), *Principles of Political Economy with Some of Their Applications to Social Philosophy*, London: Longmans Green.

Pareto V. ([1896–7] 1961), *Cours d'Économie Politique*, 2 vols; Italian translation, Turin: Boringhieri.

Ricardo D. (1951), *Principles of Political Economy*, Vol. 1, *Works*, edited by P. Sraffa, Cambridge: Cambridge University Press.

Roncaglia A. (2000), 'Produzione di merci a mezzo di merci: critica dell'approccio marginalista e ricostruzione dell'approccio classico' in M. Pivetti (ed.), *Piero Sraffa*, Naples: Carocci.

Signorino, R. (2001), 'On the limits to the long-period method in classical economics. A note', *Review of Political Economy*, 13: 245–51.

Smith, A. ([1776] 1950), An Inquiry into the Nature and Causes of the Wealth of Nations, two vols., London: Dent and Son.

Sraffa P. (1960), *Production of Commodities by Means of Commodities. Prelude to a Critique of Economic Theory,* Cambridge: Cambridge University Press.

Walras, L. (1954), *Elements of Pure Economics*, edited by W. Jaffé, London: Allen & Unwin.

Index